Fodor's

ESSENTIAL
NEW ZEALAND

Welcome to New Zealand

From the Bay of Islands' pristine beaches in the north to the soaring pinnacles of Milford Sound in the south, New Zealand is a stunner. Glaciated mountains, steaming volcanoes, and lush forests give adventurers a vast array of ecological playgrounds to explore. While hikers retreat to 14 national parks, bird-watchers find their bliss on peaceful Stewart Island. But it's not all parks and rec. Māori enclaves display deep native heritage, idyllic vineyards produce world-class wines, and vibrant dining and arts scenes thrive in cities like Auckland and Wellington. As you plan your upcoming travels to New Zealand, please confirm that places are still open and let us know when we need to make updates by writing to us at this address: editors@fodors.com.

TOP REASONS TO GO

★ **Superb Wine:** Hawkes Bay's Bordeaux blends, Marlborough's sauvignon blancs, and more.

★ **Hobbits:** Lord of the Rings tours in Glenorchy and Matamata take fans to Middle-earth.

★ **Water Sports:** Incredible sailing, surfing, rafting, kayaking, and diving.

★ **Māori Culture:** Native traditions are shared in craft workshops and ceremonial feasts.

★ **The Great Walks:** Ten famous trails, including the Milford Track, entice hikers.

Contents

Fodor's Features

Contents

MAPS

Chapter 1

EXPERIENCE NEW ZEALAND

25 ULTIMATE EXPERIENCES

New Zealand offers terrific experiences that should be on every traveler's list. Here are Fodor's top picks for a memorable trip.

1 | Abel Tasman National Park

As New Zealand's smallest and most-visited park, Abel Tasman offers visitors golden beaches, limestone caves, and awesome rock formations, all easily accessible via hiking or kayaking. (Ch. 9)

2 Wineries

From Marlborough to Hawke's Bay to Wairapa, New Zealand's world-famous fine white wines and rich reds are thanks to its cool winters and mild summers. (Chs. 6–10)

3 Filming Locations

The filming location for the Lord of the Rings movies, New Zealand has become synonymous with Middle-earth. Tours go from Hobbiton to Mt. Doom. (Chs. 6, 8)

4 Wellington

New Zealand's capital city is filled with fascinating museums, a blossoming art scene, and some of the country's best culinary offerings. (Ch. 8)

5 Christchurch

After a series of earthquakes, this small city has reinvented itself as an artsy mecca, thanks to projects like its Cardboard Cathedral and the stunning Center of Contemporary Art. (Ch. 10)

6 Stewart Island

On this small remote island, explore Rakiura, the country's newest national park, glimpse kiwi birds in their natural habitats, and spot the stunning southern lights. (Ch. 12)

7 The Coromandel Peninsula

A remote getaway of white-sand beaches, native forest, and quirky cafés, this low-key part of the country is filled with opportunities to fish, cycle, and relax with the locals. (Ch. 5)

8 Glacier-trekking

The country's Southern Alps serve as a wonderland of glacier-filled landscapes, with plenty of opportunities to trek and explore these icy behemoths up-close. (Chs. 9, 11)

9 Rugby

Rugby union is serious business here, and the most famous team is the All Blacks. You can attend a match in person at a stadium or just watch in a pub. (Chs. 3, 8)

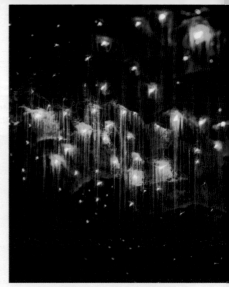

10 Whanganui National Park

New Zealand's longest navigable river serves as the centerpiece of this park, and you can explore the Whanganui via canoe, kayak, or raft. (Ch. 7)

11 Waitomo Glowworm Caves

This massive system of underground limestone caves is filled with electric blue inhabitants that give off an otherworldly glow. (Ch. 7)

12 Aoraki/Mount Cook National Park

Rising 12,316 feet, Aoraki is New Zealand's largest mountain. Its national park also offers turquoise glacial lakes and high alpine tundra hikes. (Ch. 11)

13 Rotorua

Sitting on top of the most active segment of the Taupo Volcanic Zone, Rotoura offers a multitude of volcanic springs and thermal pools that serve as nature's hot tubs. (Ch. 6)

14 Milford Sound

Within glacier-carved Fiordland National Park, you'll find sublime Milford Sound and its dramatic waterfalls, glacial lakes, and awe-inspiring mountain peaks. (Ch. 11)

15 The Bay of Islands

A collection of 144 islands, the Bay of Islands is a stronghold of both New Zealand and Māori history, along with chances for scenic kayaking and fishing. (Ch. 4)

16 The Great Walks

Scattered over New Zealand's national parks are 10 Great Walks, ranging from day hikes to multiday tracks (trails) that explore the country's diverse and spectacular scenery. (Chs. 3–12)

17 Bird-watching

From kiwis on Stewart Island to royal albatrosses in Otago to penguins in Fiordland, you don't have to be a bird nerd to appreciate New Zealand's diverse feathered population. (Ch. 12)

18 Beaches

New Zealand has over 9,300 miles of coastline, which ripples and zigzags to create bays, coves, fjords, and countless beaches perfect for surfing, sunbathing, and swimming. (Chs. 3–7)

19 Tongariro National Park

If you've ever wanted to hike a volcano, New Zealand's oldest national park is home to three, including the one that stood in for Mt. Doom in the Lord of the Ring movies. (Ch. 6)

20 Auckland

New Zealand's biggest city, the entry point of most visitors, welcomes travelers with its vibrant restaurants, gorgeous beaches, and active harbor. (Ch. 2)

21 Whale-watching in Kaikoura

The Pacific coastline of Kaikoura is the country's best spot for whale-watching and one of the only places in the world where you have the chance to spot a sperm whale. (Ch. 9)

22 Queenstown

Long known as the Adventure Capital of the World, this small and lively city is a jumble of ski slopes, rivers, and alpine areas that make it a haven for everything adrenaline-pumping. (Ch. 11)

23 Māori Culture

Learn about the vibrant culture of the Māori, the indigenous people of New Zealand, by visiting the Te Papa Museum or participating in a traditional *hāngi* meal. (Chs. 6, 8)

24 Skiing

With all its mountains, New Zealand is a skier's paradise, from volcanic cones like Mt. Ruapehu on the North Island to the massive Southern Alps on the South Island. (Chs. 6, 11)

25 Extreme Sports

If you've ever wanted to skydive, cliff dive, or bungy jump, New Zealand has the best variety of adventure activities, in unbelievably gorgeous settings. (Ch. 11)

WHAT'S WHERE

1 Auckland. The City of Sails is New Zealand's biggest city, its economic capital, and its most diverse city, home to Polynesians, Asians, and other immigrants. Dynamic, driven, and gorgeous, it's the perfect introduction to New Zealand.

2 Northland and the Bay of Islands. Northland has a large population of Māori, ancient kauri forests, salty harbors, and ocean inlets. The Bay of Islands is known for diving, sailing, and sunning on the isolated beaches of 100-plus islands.

3 The Coromandel and the Bay of Plenty. Close to Auckland, the region has white-sand beaches, blue seas, native birds, and steep hills carpeted with forest. The Coromandel has a café-and-board-shorts culture, while the Bay of Plenty is a Māori cultural hub.

4 East Coast and the Volcanic Zone. Taupo, a vibrant city next to New Zealand's largest lake, is bordered by volcanoes in Tongariro National Park; nearby Turangi claims to be the trout-fishing capital of the world. Te Urewera's wilderness contrasts with a mix of artsy café towns like Napier, wineries, and beach towns like Tolaga Bay, where Māori community life is still present.

5 North Island's West Coast. Mt. Taranaki broods over Egmont National Park and the rural industrial area affectionately known as the 'Naki. A thin highway loops through surf towns, tropical coastline, black-sand beaches, and the lower West Coast farmland. Outside of Wellington, State Highway 1 is bordered by Kapiti Coast beach towns, farmland, and the Tararua Ranges. Kapiti Island is a protected reserve where endangered birdlife thrives.

6 Wellington and the Wairarapa. Cafés, art galleries, and cinemas overflow in the vibrant capital city. It's bordered by steep hillsides studded with Victorian homes and an expansive harbor and crowned by Te Papa, New Zealand's largest museum. Lyall and Houghton bays attract surfers, while the Miramar Peninsula is home to Peter Jackson's film empire. The Wairarapa, northeast of Wellington, is one of the country's best wine regions, famous for its windswept coasts.

WHAT'S WHERE

7 Upper South Island and the West Coast. Across the Cook Strait is the Marlborough Sounds, known for seafood, sunshine, sauvignon blanc, sailing, and the Queen Charlotte Track. To the southeast, the wineries of Blenheim rise up into snowcapped mountains plunging to the Kaikoura coastline. To the west, the artistic town of Nelson gives way to Abel Tasman National Park. The West Coast is rugged with sights like the Punakaiki Pancake Rocks and the twin glaciers, Franz Josef and Fox.

8 Christchurch and Canterbury. Easy-going Christchurch is experiencing a post-earthquake rebuild, with its British-style gardens and meandering Avon River. To the north is the thermal resort town,

Hanmer Springs. To the east is the Banks Peninsula, another volcanic remnant of green hills and hidden ocean inlets, as well as the French-flavored town of Akaroa. To the west, the flat, vast Canterbury Plains extend to remote Arthur's Pass and the Southern Alps and Aoraki/Mt. Cook, New Zealand's tallest peak.

9 The Southern Alps and Fiordland. The Southern Alps is populated by alpine towns. Queenstown is known as the Adventure Capital of the World and offers up any extreme sport you can think of. Wanaka is quieter, though no less scenic, while artsy Arrowtown displays the area's gold-rush history. Remote Glenorchy is the gateway to spectacular hiking tracks. Best known for the Milford Sound and track, Fiordland is a raw, brooding forest.

10 Otago, Invercargill, and Stewart Island. The southern part of the South Island has two main towns: Invercargill and Dunedin. Dunedin is the livelier of the two, due in part to its university. The towns are bordered by the Otago Peninsula, rich in albatrosses, seals, and penguin colonies, and the Catlins, known for its bird-rich forests. To the very south lies Stewart Island, with its colonies of kiwi birds and Rakiura National Park.

New Zealand Today

Kia ora, or welcome, to the "Youngest Country on Earth." New Zealand's moniker may specifically reference its place as the last landmass to be discovered, but it also speaks to the constant geological, social, and political shifts the country has undergone as it has tried to find its national identity. Tectonic hotbeds include its three active volcanoes and the still-growing Southern Alps on the South Island. In a nation of farmers with frontier ancestors, Georgina Beyer, a transgender former sex worker, won a rural seat against a conservative opponent in 1999, while Prime Minister Jacinda Ardern is the world's youngest female head of government, and only the second elected head of government to give birth while in office. New Zealand's Ernest Rutherford was the first person to split the atom, but the country remains passionately anti–nuclear. The national rugby team, the All Blacks, continues to dominate the field as one of the best rugby teams in the world, though many Kiwis still consider themselves to be underdogs in sport.

A TALE OF TWO ISLANDS

Together, the North and South Islands make up the majority of Aotearoa—Land of the Long White Cloud. New Zealand is roughly the size of Colorado (with a slightly smaller population), but you are never more than 150 miles from the sea. New Zealand's two main islands are more than 1,000 miles long and together encompass nearly every environment on the planet: glaciers, white-sand beaches, fjords, rain forests, alpine forest and lakes, agricultural plains, and volcanic craters and cones.

The South Island is the stunner: the colorful beaches, inlets, and sunny vineyards of the north give way to the Southern Alps, a mountain range that can only be crossed in three places (Arthur's Pass, Lewis Pass, and Haast Pass). Aoraki/Mount Cook National Park contains New Zealand's tallest mountain (Aoraki/Mt. Cook, 12,316 feet) and another 19 peaks that are more than 10,000 feet. Forty percent of the park is covered by glaciers. On the West Coast, dense native forest, wild weather, and a sparse population provide a frontier feel. At the southern end of the West Coast is primeval Fiordland National Park, more than 3 million acres of raw wilderness. Together, Fiordland, Aoraki/Mount Cook, Westland Tai Poutini, and Mount Aspiring national parks form Te Wāhiponamu, a UNESCO World Heritage Site encompassing 6.4 million acres, nearly 10% of New Zealand's total landmass.

On the East Coast of the South Island, sea life ranges from the giant 65-foot male sperm whale to the 5-foot Hector's dolphin. On land, ideas of preserving the wildlife are different from what you'd expect. Saving birds and trees entails ridding the area of possums and cats—mammals that are not native to New Zealand.

Fourteen miles separate the North and South Islands over the rough Cook Strait, but the two islands are worlds apart. Due to its volcanic origins, the North Island has fertile farmlands and rejuvenated native forest. More than three-quarters of New Zealand's 4.2 million people live on the North Island, which tends to have milder weather and a more forgiving landscape. Long beaches sweep up both coasts past small communities (many still predominantly Māori). Te Urewera National Park and two out of three of New Zealand's longest rivers (Waikato and Whanganui) are found near the Central Plateau. Here you'll also discover New Zealand's largest lake (Taupo).

A TALE OF TWO CULTURES

New Zealand is 900 miles from the nearest landmass. Its relative isolation and geographical diversity have affected its population. On a whole, New Zealanders are genial, reserved, and friendly, but they don't suffer fools or braggarts lightly. An isolated past, when things were either unavailable or expensive, led to a nation of inventors: Kiwis invented the jet boat, bungy jumping, and the electric fence, to name a few. They were the first to climb Mt. Everest, and the first to give women the vote.

New Zealand is a bicultural nation. New Zealanders of European descent (Pākehā) make up 80% of the population, while Māori make up 15% (the rest is largely Pacific Islanders and Asian), and the future is still unclear. There are two camps: most New Zealanders want to move forward as "one New Zealand," but a significant portion still sees Māoridom as a culture set apart. Although some New Zealanders consider the reconciliation process to be labored and an impediment to forward progress, Māori is an oral culture, and others feel that continuing to discuss the past is a way of making certain it isn't lost in the present.

KIWI QUALITY OF LIFE

New Zealand is consistently rated as one of the best places to live and is one of the most active nations: Kiwis seem to be born with a love of the outdoors, and families tramp, caravan, sail, and play rugby, cricket, and netball together. Most New Zealanders are well educated. They value travel highly, with one-quarter of the population traveling overseas every year, often for their post-school O.E. (overseas experience). Kiwis don't tend to be religious, though most identify with one of the four main Christian religions (Catholic, Methodist, Presbyterian, and Anglican). New Zealand isn't a wealthy nation, either: most Kiwis prefer a good work–life balance to an overflowing bank account.

A GREEN FUTURE

The Department of Conservation is taking a more active role on environmental issues, reflecting the national love of the outdoors and the importance of the landscape to the country's burgeoning tourism industry. Although New Zealand is making great strides in sustainability, the country aims for a "100% Pure" lifestyle and is still introducing initiatives (including heavy fines for littering) as part of a "Keep New Zealand Beautiful" campaign. There is a push to have more people driving electric cars. New Zealand is also facing a challenge in rising obesity in 25% of adults, a binge-drinking problem, youth gang culture and violent crime, and an increase in poverty. Basically, it's facing many of the same problems as the Western world—just on a smaller scale.

IMPACT OF COVID-19

Despite their quality of life, many New Zealanders express concern for the country's future, and the specter of COVID-19 in its many variant forms is affecting the way people live. The government has adopted a cautious approach to opening borders though with that comes tight requirements. The country has become very used to lockdowns or restricted movement when cases are found in the community, and social distancing is accepted when there are flare-ups. Every space has a scannable QR code to enable contact tracing if the virus surfaces in any way. These days, many Kiwis always travel with a face mask and hand sanitizer. Wearing a face mask is a legal requirement on all forms of public transport. The most important thing is to retain an open mind and be prepared for change since some of these restrictions may remain well into 2022 and beyond.

What to Eat and Drink

PAVLOVA
The country's most beloved dessert is this meringue-based concoction with a soft inside and a crispy outside, served with whipped cream and fruit. It's typically made at home during the holidays, but many bakeries sell it year-round, too.

WINE
Wine is huge here, with a variety of areas all over the country producing high-quality whites and reds. Popular regions include Marlborough, Hawke's Bay, Gisborne, and Central Otago. Sauvignon blancs and pinot noirs are particularly well-regarded here.

LAMB
No matter where you go in New Zealand, lamb is bound to be on the menu. Sheep farms are everywhere, and lambs raised on Kiwi farms are grass-fed and have a more pronounced flavor with a more tender cut. You'll find lamb in the form of chops, steaks, and racks, and it tends to be much cheaper than in the United States.

L&P
Lemon & Paeroa, otherwise known as L&P, is New Zealand's most famous soft drink. It's a carbonated lemon-flavored drink (even sweeter than Sprite), and it's what you'll get if you ever order a lemonade here.

FISH-AND-CHIPS
Originally an export from the British colony days, fish-and-chips has remained popular thanks to the country's reliance on the fishing industry. Just like in England, expect lightly battered fish (typically snapper, hoki, or terakihi) served alongside crispy fries.

KŪMARA FRIES
One of the most well-known New Zealand vegetables, a *kūmara* is like a sweet potato or yam. Seasoned in various ways, kūmara fries are a common choice for a side to a fast food or pub meal.

HOKEY POKEY ICE CREAM
Fresh dairy is delicious here, and one of the most popular ice cream flavors is called Hokey Pokey. It consists of vanilla ice cream mixed with golden honeycomb toffee, and it is a mainstay at most ice cream shops in the country.

GREENSHELL MUSSELS
Native to New Zealand, Greenshell mussels are found in the area of the Marlborough Sounds; the town of Havelock is known as the Greenshell mussel capital of the world. They have a green hue to their edges, and are usually larger than other mussels. Also called green-lipped mussels, enjoy them doused in a butter-garlic sauce.

CRAYFISH
Not to be confused with the smaller shrimp-like species common in the American south, New Zealand crayfish are hard-shelled lobsters ranging in colors from speckled orange to purple, with eight small legs instead of two large front claws. Their flavor is a bit different than lobster, but the meat's consistency is the same.

SPEIGHT'S BEER
One of New Zealand's most beloved brands of beer, Speight's is available at just

A New Zealand winery

about every store and bar in the whole country. The most common is a draught-style lager, and variations include Speight's Summit, with all-natural ingredients, and Speight's Traverse, a low-carb option.

HĀNGI
A Māori *hāngi* is a culinary experience and a classic Māori cultural tradition. The preparation involves steaming meat, seafood, and vegetables for several hours in a large underground pit. It's often paired with a concert (similar to a Hawaiian luau).

BLUFF OYSTERS
If you're used to garnishing your oysters with lemon juice and cocktail sauce to mask the flavor, think again. The Bluff oyster, in season, is one of the largest and tastiest you'll ever try, and it's considered by many to be the most delicious oyster species

in the world. Found in the Foveaux Strait, between the South Island and Stewart Island, they are served all over the country, but are most common in the south. Other names include dredge oysters, mud oysters, and flat oysters.

MUTTONBIRD
For those who appreciate delicacies, muttonbird (also known as sooty shearwater) is a species of seabird that is served saturated in bull kelp, giving it a briny taste. The more south you travel, the fresher it gets, because muttonbirds are mostly found on Australia's Muttonbird Island, located off the coast of Stewart Island. It's very rarely even talked about outside of Australia and New Zealand, so this is certainly one flavor you can't get elsewhere.

VEGEMITE
A condiment as common as peanut butter and jelly are in the States, New Zealanders put vegemite on their toast in the morning or snack on it any time of the day. (You might also hear about its close cousin, Marmite, which is the same flavor, but with a different name). This thick black spread is made from leftover brewers' yeast extract with various spices added in and often has a bitter saltiness. This means it's an acquired taste: don't just go for a straight spoonful out of the jar; rather, add it to your toast with some eggs and bacon, and it just might inspire your taste buds.

What to Buy

ABALONE

You'll find the iridescent blue-gray abalone (or *paua*) shell inlaid on wooden homewares or silver jewelry. The shells come from a species of sea snail found throughout New Zealand's coasts, and you can even comb beaches to find slivers in the sand that wash ashore all over the country.

KETE BAGS

Woven out of New Zealand flax leaves and traditionally made by the Māori, kete products usually come in the form of backpacks, handbags, or wallets. The weaving process, called *raranga*, is the same process used to weave floor mats and belts.

WILD FERN'S BEE VENOM

The skincare industry is thriving in New Zealand, with companies like Wild Fern using ethical and sustainable local sources for their products. One of the most popular is their bee venom, which you'll find used in eye creams, face masks, moisturizers, and lip plumpers.

CARVED WOOD

The art of wood-carving, also called *whakairo rakau*, is considered an ancient and respected Māori skill. You'll see beautifully Māori-carved wood products for sale throughout the country, everywhere from boutique shops to airports.

POUNAMU

Also known as greenstone or jade, this is the national gem of New Zealand. Local lore says buying it for yourself is bad luck, so have a travel companion officially purchase it for you. The stone is mostly made into ornamental pieces or jewelry, but it's often carved into different symbols, which all have specific meanings and stories.

MERINO WOOL

New Zealand is the world's second-largest wool producer (after Australia), and high-country merino wool is the most sought after. Merino wool clothing and products are sold nearly everywhere (just make sure the label confirms it was actually made here). Wool sweaters, leggings, hats, scarves, and gloves all make for great (and warm) souvenirs.

WHITTAKER'S CHOCOLATE

A native New Zealand brand, Whittaker's is the second-leading chocolate company in the country after Cadbury. The family has been making chocolate at their main factory in Porirua for more than 120 years. Buy some to take home for a sweet souvenir.

Pounamu, or jade carving

OLIVE OIL
More than 20 varieties of olive trees are available in New Zealand, where olives are grown from Northland to Central Otago, but New Zealand's nascent olive oil industry varies widely in quality. The best olive oils have a smooth, non-cloying texture and nutty, peppery flavors. Two of the best brands are Simunovich (produced south of Auckland) and Frog's End Estate (outside Nelson), both of which have earned accolades for their extra-virgin varieties.

MANUKA HONEY
Produced by bees that pollinate the manuka bush, manuka honey is used in all sorts of medicines, beauty products, and herbal remedies. It's also a delicious natural sweetener that makes a great souvenir you can purchase from a health food store or local farm.

PUKEKO
The pukeko, or swamp hen, is a ubiquitous native bird, but it took artist Kevin Kilsby to turn the bright blue and red creature into an icon. His whimsical, decorative clay creations—with big red beaks, impossibly long, skinny legs, and gumboot-clad feet—come in several sizes and designs. You can find the statuettes in souvenir shops all over the country.

RUGBY GEAR
As the world's leading rugby union team, the New Zealand All Blacks have quite the fan following here. So do your best to fit in by purchasing a jersey, scarf, or hat and show your support for the All Blacks, whether you make it to a game or just cheer them on from a bar.

Best National Park Adventures

KAYAKING IN NELSON LAKES

This national park is focused around two gorgeous glacier-formed lakes: Rotoiti and Rotoroa, both of which are excellent places to kayak. Pull up to a quiet stretch of pebble beach to observe the park's rocky peaks and intense greenery, where all you will hear are the birds and the breeze.

SWIMMING IN ABEL TASMAN

Abel Tasman offers gorgeous scenery in the form of beaches, golden sand, and limestone caves, and one of the most unique ways to see it all is by taking it in via a skydive.

HIKING IN MOUNT ASPIRING

There are no roads here, but luckily this breathtaking, unspoiled landscape is made for hiking, and invites you to explore its river valleys, deep wilderness, and unusual Red Hills. Check with the Department of Conservation on weather conditions before you head out.

BOAT CRUISING IN FIORDLAND

The country's biggest park offers scores of boat trips that take you through its two main sounds: Milford and Doubtful, and get you close to waterfalls, penguins, and dolphins.

CAVING IN KAHURANGI

Within New Zealand's second-largest park, you'll find some of the country's most interesting rock formations as well as a spectacular network of underground caves. Local guides can take you on cave tours and cave-dives in the Pearce and Riwaka rivers.

VOLCANO HIKING IN TONGARIRO

Home to three spectacular volcanoes (Tongariro, Ruepehu, and Ngauruhue, which doubles as Mt. Doom), the famed Tongariro Alpine Crossing has been described as the best one-day hike in the world, taking you over red craters, green and blue lakes, and wild open countryside.

BIRD-WATCHING IN RAKIURA

Taking up 85% of Stewart Island, this park and its impenetrable wilderness are home to a striking variety of birds. Water taxi companies can drop you off at bird sanctuary Ulva Island, or take off on a hike on your own and spot a few of the island's 20,000 kiwi birds.

FLIGHTSEEING IN AORAKI/MOUNT COOK

In the heart of the Southern Alps lies New Zealand's largest mountain, Aoraki/Mt. Cook. The best way to get close is via a flightseeing tour; certain tours can also take you to land and trek on the famed Tasman Glacier.

CANOEING IN WHANGANUI

New Zealand's most canoed river is the heart of this national park and was granted the status of a person through a government law. It offers a gentle gradient and calm rapids. Paddle through the lush wilderness to Pipiriki, or head out to the lower reaches to explore historic Māori riverside settlements.

SCENIC DRIVING IN EGMONT

Within New Zealand's second-oldest park, Mt. Taranaki rises 8,261 feet, dominating the landscape. Actually climbing the volcano is for serious mountaineers only, but you can drive up three access roads that lead you to the forest-lined lower slopes, offering stunning views.

Best Wineries

MT. DIFFICULTY, OTAGO

The Central Otago wine region is filled with vineyards hemmed in by staggering white-capped mountain ranges, producing earthy rich reds. Mt. Difficulty Wines is known for its sustainable and organic wines, which you can taste in its gorgeous setting.

ALLEN SCOTT FAMILY WINEMAKERS, MARLBOROUGH

New Zealand's largest, most well-known wine region is Marlborough, which produces 70% of the national crop and some world-class sauvignon blancs. One highlight of the area is Allen Scott Family Winemakers, a family operation that produces excellent chardonnay, pinot noir, and riesling.

FROMM WINERY, MARLBOROUGH

Also in the Marlborough region, Fromm is a Swiss-based company with both Kiwi and European roots. Having planted their first vines over 25 years ago,

they have the oldest malbec vineyard in the country and continue to produce an especially delicious pinot noir.

HUNTER'S WINES, MARLBOROUGH

One of the best-known women in the New Zealand wine business, Jane Hunter is a pioneer of wine-making in Marlborough. Within the rustic farm house that doubles as a wine cellar, you can taste sauvignon blancs, pinot noirs, and Māori-inspired bubbly. The garden showcases a collection of rare native plants, and the rotating artists-in-residence regularly contribute to the decor.

WAIRAU RIVER WINES, MARLBOROUGH

Established in 1978, this family-owned winery in Blenheim was one of the first official grape growers in the region. Today, they have multiple vineyards producing excellent sauvignon blanc, along with an on-site restaurant specializing in wine parings.

KAHURANGI ESTATE, NELSON

Located close to Kahurangi National Park, this winery specializes in aromatic grapes that produce sweeter than usual wines. It also has one of the oldest riesling vines on the South Island, and it's one of the most scenic places to enjoy a glass or two, thanks to Mt. Arthur in the background.

NEUDORF VINEYARD, NELSON

For an example of how impressive a small winery can be, head to Neudorf Vineyard, which has been producing wine in the Moutere Valley since 1978. Thanks to a worldwide reputation for excellent pinot noirs and chardonnays, the owners are able to pack a one-two punch of delicious wine amid an intimate, friendly setting.

BLACK ESTATE, WAIPARA VALLEY

A local landmark, Black Estate is home to two vineyards and an award-winning restaurant. Some of their most popular wines include cabernet franc, chenin blanc, pinot noir, and chardonnay.

Allan Scott Family Winemakers

PEGASUS BAY, WAIPARA VALLEY

Entirely family-owned and run, Pegasus Bay is open for tastings, education, and, of course, for purchasing delicious wine. Pinot gris, chardonnay, and pinot noir are highlights, as is the winery's natural amphitheater that regularly hosts classical concerts and operas.

MARTINBOROUGH VINEYARD, THE WAIRARAPA

This region is known for small wineries like Martinborough Vineyard, which produces some of New Zealand's best pinot noirs. Their chardonnay is also excellent.

MISSION ESTATE WINERY, HAWKE'S BAY

The country's second-largest wine region, Hawke's Bay is famous for chardonnays, cabernet sauvignons, syrahs, and merlots. You'll find them all here, at the oldest winery in New Zealand (it dates back to 1851).

CRAGGY RANGE WINERY, HAWKE'S BAY

For Hawke's Bay's most picturesque winery, visit Craggy Range, which offers breathtaking views of Te Mata Peak. Sample the excellent chardonnays, merlots, and syrahs, and be sure to spend some time at the excellent, French-inspired, on-site restaurant.

GIBBSTON VALLEY WINES, OTAGO

As the best-known winery in Central Otago, Gibbston Valley also has the honor of being home to the first vines planted in the region. Today, it offers premium wines in a beautiful setting along with an impressive cheese plate and sandwich menu. For an intimate wine tasting, be sure to visit the wine cellar/cave for a tour.

GOLDIE VINEYARD, AUCKLAND

This winery was the first to plant grapes on Waiheke Island, part of the Hauraki Gulf Islands in Auckland. There's an on-site wine research institute for those who are truly interested in the wine-making process; casual fans can just enjoy a personalized tour or, possibly, the specacular nine-course degustation menu that is served just four times a year.

Best Beaches

WHARARIKI BEACH
South Island beaches are captivating, particularly in Abel Tasman National Park and neighboring Golden Bay. The sands are indeed golden, and the water is jade green; Wharariki Beach has one of the most breathtaking coastlines in the whole country.

90 MILE BEACH
Actually stretching just 89 miles, this beach spans the length of the Aupouri Peninsula from Kaiaia to Cape Regina. Part of the Te Araroa Trail (one of the world's longest walking trails), it's perfect for surfing, swimming, and fishing.

RAGLAN
A world-renowned surfing paradise, Raglan is a town in the Waikato region ripe with opportunities for water adventures, including kayaking and paddleboarding. The best beaches for surfing are Manu Bay and Ngarunui Beach, with plenty of classes for newbies too.

COROMANDEL-WAIHI BEACH
Located at the bottom of Coromandel Peninsula, Waihi is a town on the western coast of the Bay of Plenty, which has one of the most beautiful coastlines in New Zealand. With a 9 km (5½ mile) shore, it's perfect for safe surfing, swimming, and long walks.

ŌHOPE BEACH
On the eastern side of the Bay of Plenty, Ōhope stretches for 11 km (7 miles), surrounded by forest trails that can take you into the foot of Te Urewera National Park. The gentle waves and warm water means this is a great place to learn how to surf.

FITZROY BEACH
Located in New Plymouth, Fitzroy runs alongside the Coastal Walkway and is a popular destination for swimming and surfing. It's especially suitable for families.

ST. CLAIR BEACH
In Otago, St. Clair lies on the outskirts of Dunedin, an excellent break from the bustling city center. It has consistent surf breaks, easy swimming, and the only heated saltwater pool in the country.

WAIHEKE ISLAND
Part of the Hauraki Gulf Islands outside Auckland, Waiheke is a former hippie hideaway turned upscale vacation retreat with vineyards and local cafés. Luckily, it still has charming beaches like Oneroa, Palm, and Onetangi.

Fitzroy Bea...

KAITERITERI BEACH

With access to Abel Tasman, Kaiteriteri is one of the region's prettiest beaches, thanks to its golden sand, rocky islets, and deep clear water. You can even cycle here from Nelson via the Great Taste Trail.

CATHEDRAL COVE

One of Coromandel's most distinctive features is this slice of beach by the town of Hahei. The stunning rock arch makes for a gorgeous setting to swim and snorkel in the cove's calm waters. It can be reached via hiking, kayaking, or a water taxi.

TAYLOR'S MISTAKE

This beach just outside of Christchurch has the best surfing waves in the area but is still calm enough for swimmers to enjoy. Hikers and bikers also enjoy coming here for the excellent clifftop views. Be on the lookout for dolphins playing in the waters.

KAREKARE BEACH

Known for its black volcanic sand, Karakare is a 50-minute drive from downtown Auckland and offers surfing, walking, and picnicking in a setting filled with waterfalls and rain forest landscapes.

New Zealand History

AOTEAROA

According to Māori legend, the demigod Maui sailed from Hawaiki (believed to be one of the French Polynesian islands) in his canoe, and he caught a huge fish, which he dragged to the surface. The fish is the North Island; Maui's canoe is the South Island.

This legend describes New Zealand's history, which is one of hardship, fortitude, and discovery. This brave, isolated, and young country is still creating its history, day by day.

Māori oral traditions say it began with the moa hunters, believed to have arrived in the 9th century, possibly from east Polynesia, which could make them related to present-day Māori. In AD 925, Kupe sailed from Hawaiki and discovered New Zealand. He returned to Hawaiki, named it Aotearoa (Land of the Long White Cloud), and passed on the sailing coordinates. In AD 1350, eight war canoes landed in New Zealand, marking the beginning of Māori culture on the landmass. Their existence was a battle of brutality and beauty. Warriors were trained at a young age, and tribal warfare and sheer survival led to a low life expectancy. At the same time, Māori became accomplished tattoo, carving, and weaving artists.

EUROPEANS ARRIVE

In 1642, the Dutch captain Abel Tasman sighted the South Island, near Punakaiki, and officially put New Zealand on the map. Captain Tasman never actually set foot in New Zealand, though—he left after his boat was attacked by Māori in Golden Bay.

In 1767, Captain James Cook visited "Nieuw Zeeland" (as it had been named) in the *Endeavour,* and he is responsible for accurately charting the coastline. The

whalers and sealers arrived in the 1790s, nearly obliterating sea-life populations in a matter of decades. Māori also suffered from the introduction of European diseases and firearms, which they used on each other in their brutal land wars.

THE TREATY OF WAITANGI

One of the most important dates in New Zealand history is February 6, 1840, when Māori signed the Treaty of Waitangi with the British. The Treaty guaranteed Māori rights to their land, but it gave the British sovereignty. The hope of this treaty was that it would end land wars, tame lawlessness, and put New Zealand beyond the reach of French settlement. The New Zealand capital was moved from Russell in the Bay of Islands to Auckland, where it remained for 25 years.

But Māori continued to lose their land to both the government and local settlers. When Pākehā (Europeans) outnumbered Māori for the first time in 1858, Māori tribes banded together, declaring Waikato's Te Wherowhero the first Māori king. This only galvanized the British further, and violent land wars continued well into the 1860s.

BOOM YEARS AND SOCIAL CHANGES

Meanwhile, on the South Island, gold was discovered, leading to a booming period of growth in the areas around Queenstown, Arrowtown, and Otago, including the establishment of New Zealand's first university in 1869 in Dunedin. The nation's capital was also moved to Wellington (1865), and Māori were given representation in parliament two years later. By 1880, the government had established free public schooling, and railroads and roads were beginning to crisscross the country. New Zealand also became the first country to legalize unions in 1878, and it was the first country to give women the vote in 1893.

Although well versed in land wars, New Zealand got its first taste of international war in 1899, when it backed the British in the Boer War. New Zealand's allegiance to the Crown made for a bloody 50 years. In World War I, New Zealanders were part of the epic battle at Gallipoli in Turkey; 10% of the population joined the Australian and New Zealand Army Corps (ANZAC), which helped to form the strange and unique bond with Australia, but nearly 17,000 New Zealanders died in the conflict. New Zealand also entered the fray in World War II, once again sustaining heavy casualties that rocked the tiny country's population.

THE POST-WWII YEARS

The 1950s through the 1980s were a time of huge economic growth, then bust, populated with local tragedies. In 1952, the country's population soared to more than 2 million, and, in 1953, local boy Edmund Hillary with Sherpa Tenzing Norgay became the first to summit Mt. Everest. Postwar, the economy was at an all-time high. Within the next few decades, however, disaster struck again and again, including the 1953 Mt. Ruapehu eruption that killed 151 people when a lahar derailed a train, the sinking of the ferry *Wahine* off Wellington's coast in 1968, and the plane crash in Antarctica in 1979 that killed all 257 passengers. The economy went into a slump, and maddash government efforts only seemed to make things worse.

The 1980s were defined by stands that started to give New Zealand her own identity. In 1981 much of the population was in an uproar about the South African rugby team touring New Zealand. Apartheid protesters flocked to the

streets and clashed with Kiwis who felt that politics had no place in rugby. In 1984, the Labour government put a ban on nuclear-powered or-armed ships, despite pressure from the United States because of its anti-nuke stand. In 1985, the Greenpeace ship *Rainbow Warrior* was blown up in Auckland by the French. In 1987, New Zealand won the inaugural Rugby World Cup—a feat it repeated in 2011 and 2015.

IN THE NEW MILLENNIUM

Māori culture has experienced a resurgence and greater integration, but, in 2003 a new debate flared as Māori requested a legal inquiry into their precolonial customary ownership of the seabed and shore. Thousands of protesters marched on Parliament in support of Māori claims. New Zealand ratified the Kyoto Treaty in late 2002, and it bound itself to new environmental regulations. On February 22, 2011, a magnitude 6.3 earthquake caused massive destruction in Christchurch and killed 181 people. In the past decade, New Zealand has seen its tourism numbers grow, thanks largely to its fame as the setting of Peter Jackson's Lord of the Rings trilogy. More recently, an attack on the Al Noor mosque in Christchurch, where 51 people were killed and 40 injured, has driven the government to focus its energy on establishing a better understanding of diversity in its many forms.

Best Tours in New Zealand

You can always travel without a guide, but in unfamiliar territory you'll learn more with a knowledgeable local by your side. If you're interested in a multiday excursion book it at least several weeks in advance. The companies listed here cover large regions of one or both islands.

With most adventure-tour companies, the guides' knowledge of the environment is matched by a level of competence that ensures your safety even in dangerous situations. The safety record of adventure operators is extremely good. Be aware, however, that most adventure-tour operators require you to sign waivers absolving the company of responsibility in the event of an accident. Courts normally uphold such waivers except in cases of significant negligence.

Biking

Season: October–March.

Best Locations: Countrywide.

Cost: Multiday tours start around NZ$1,700 per person, including food, lodging, and guide services. Supplemental fees are commonly charged for single riders.

Adventure South. For a tour of the best purpose-built trails that take in mountains and lakes, you can't go past Adventure South with its experienced team of guides and local know-how. ⊠ *29 Iversen Terr., Christchurch* ☎ *03/942–1222* ⊕ *www.adventuresouth.co.nz.*

New Zealand Pedaltours. New Zealand Pedaltours operates on both islands, with tours of 2 to 37 days. Tour options include the Coromandel Peninsula, the Southern Alps, and the Central Otago Rail Trail. ⊠ *56 Tawa Rd., Kumeu, Auckland* ☎ *09/585–1338, 09/585–1339* ⊕ *www.pedaltours.co.nz.*

Pacific Cycle Tours. This family company offers small group tours taking in the best of what's on offer or a trip tailored to your needs. ⊠ *14 Kennaway Rd., Unit 3, Christchurch* ☎ *27/776–2018* ⊕ *www.bike-nz.com.*

Canoeing

Season: Year-round, best October–April.

Best Locations: Whanganui River, North Island.

Cost: From NZ$80 per person for single-day tours to NZ$225 per person for five-day trips. Tents, sleeping bags, and bedrolls can be rented for an additional fee.

Blazing Paddles Canoe Adventures. Blazing Paddles Canoe Adventures runs one- to five-day trips on the Whanganui River, during which you can ride mild rapids, and see waterfalls, pristine forests, and birdlife. Overnight stays are spent camping or in huts, depending on the trip. Blazing Paddles has a provisional OutdoorsMark safety rating and now holds a DOC concession for self-catered guiding trips on the Whanganui River. ⊠ *1033 State Hwy. 4, Taumarunui* ☎ *07/895–5261, 0800/252–946* ⊕ *www.*

Cross-Country Skiing

Season: July–September.

Best Location: Aoraki (Mt. Cook) and Wanaka, South Island.

Cost: Around NZ$850 for two to five days, NZ$1,170–NZ$1,700 for five days high on Mt. Cook alpine skiing, which includes equipment, meals, hut accommodation, a guide, and transport.

Alpine Recreation Canterbury. In winter (July–September), Alpine Recreation Canterbury runs multiday backcountry skiing trips on the glaciers of Aoraki/ Mount Cook and Westland national parks and in the Two Thumb Range above Lake Tekapo, with terrains to suit all reasonably fit skiers. In the national parks, alpine and telemark tours typically start with a flight to the alpine hut that becomes your base; from there the group sets out each day. In the Lake Tekapo High Country, you hike three hours to a private hut, from which you do day tours. Snowshoeing tours are also possible from here. In summer (November–April), Alpine Recreation Canterbury runs guided treks, mountaineering courses, and guided ascents in Aoraki/Mount Cook and Westland national parks. They have their own private hut straight opposite the mighty Caroline Face of Mt. Cook, which is used for the Aoraki Mt. Cook Trek, the Ball Pass Crossing, and climbing courses. ⊠ 8 Erebus Pl., Lake Tekapo, Christchurch ☏ 03/680–6736, 0800/006–096 ⊕ www. alpinerecreation.com.

Diving

Season: Year-round.

Best Locations: Bay of Islands, Poor Knights Islands, Great Barrier Island, Goat Island Marine Reserve, and the Coromandel Peninsula, North Island. Also, Milford Sound, South Island.

Cost: A two-dive day trip without rental gear runs about NZ$150, with gear around NZ$240.

Paihia Dive Hire and Charter. The company operates in the Bay of Islands and will visit the sunken Greenpeace ship *Rainbow Warrior,* among others. ⊠ *Paihia* ☏ *09/402–7551, 0800/107–551* ⊕ *www. divenz.com.*

Yukon Dive. Pacific Hideaway Charters runs dives at the Poor Knights Islands, Mokohinau Islands, and the coastal regions around Tutukaka—all of which are home to manta rays, large kingfish, and lots of other sea life. Day trips include tea, coffee, and snacks, as well as kayaks to borrow if you want to stay on the surface. ⊠ *Marina A8, Tutukaka* ☏ *09/434–4506, 0800/693–483* ⊕ *yukon. co.nz/pacifichideaway.*

Fishing

Licenses and Limits: Different regions require different licenses when fishing for trout, so check at the local tackle store or visit *fishandgame.org.nz.* Fees are approximately NZ$124 per year, but at most tackle shops, you can purchase a daily or weekly license. No license is needed for saltwater fishing.

Season: Varies by region.

Best Locations: Countrywide.

Cost: Big-game fishing: NZ$300 per person, per day. Heli-fishing: from NZ$560 per person, per day. Trolling and fly-fishing for lake trout: from NZ$90 per hour (one to four people). Charter costs vary widely.

NORTH ISLAND

Blue Ocean Charters. ⊠ *Tauranga Bridge Marina, Tauranga* ☎ *0800/224–278* ⊕ *www.blueocean.co.nz.*

Brett Cameron Central Plateau Fishing. When the need for chasing trout arises Brett Cameron will find the best spots. ⊠ *Taupo* ☎ *27/681–4134* ⊕ *www.cpf.net. nz.*

Te Ra Charters. ⊠ *Whangamata* ☎ *07/865–8681* ⊕ *tera.whangamata.co.nz.*

Hiking

Season: October–March for high-altitude walks, year-round for others.

Best Locations: Any of the national parks or New Zealand's 10 Great Walks.

Cost: Two- to five-day guided hikes start at NZ$2,850. Prices for longer and custom hikes vary widely.

Hiking New Zealand. Although based near Christchurch, Hiking New Zealand has hiking tours to suit everyone on both islands, from 5 to 20 days. ⊠ *1 Good St., Rangiora* ☎ *0800/697–232, 03/310–8188* ⊕ *www.hikingnewzealand.com.*

SOUTH ISLAND

Alpine Guides Ltd. ☎ *03/435–1834* ⊕ *www. alpineguides.co.nz.*

Guided Walks New Zealand Ltd. ⊠ *159 Gorge Rd., Unit 29, Queenstown* ☎ *03/442–3000, 0800/832–226* ⊕ *www. nzwalks.com.*

Marlborough Sounds Adventure Company. ⊠ *London Quay, Picton* ☎ *03/573–6078* ⊕ *www.marlboroughsounds.co.nz.*

Ultimate Hikes. ⊠ *The Station Bldg., Duke St. Entrance, Queenstown* ☎ *03/450–1940* ⊕ *www.ultimatehikes.co.nz.*

Wild West Adventure Co. ⊠ *8 Whall St., Greymouth* ☎ *03/768–6649, 0800/946–543* ⊕ *www.fun-nz.com.*

Horse Trekking

Season: All year-round on the North Island; may be weather dependent on the South Island.

Best Locations: Northland and the Coromandel Peninsula on the North Island, Nelson and Canterbury high country on the South Island.

Cost: Prices range from about NZ$125 for two hours to NZ$240 for a day trip, or NZ$500 for overnight; contact outfitters for specifics on shorter or multiday trips.

SOUTH ISLAND

Cape Farewell Horse Treks. ⊠ *23 McGowan St., Puponga* ☎ *03/524–8031* ⊕ *www. horsetreksnz.com* ⊠ *From NZ$80.*

Dart Stables Glenorchy. ⊠ *58 Coll St., Glenorchy* ☎ *0800/474–3464, 03/442–5688* ⊕ *www.dartstables.com.*

NORTH ISLAND

Pakiri Beach Horse Rides. ⊠ *317 Rahuikiri Rd., Pakiri Beach, R.D. 2, Wellsford* ☎ *09/422–6275* ⊕ *www.horseride-nz. co.nz* ⊠ *NZ$175 half day, NZ$299 full day, including packed lunch.*

Rafting

Season: Mainly October–May.

Best Locations: Rotorua and Taupo on the North Island, Canterbury and Queenstown on the South Island.

Cost: From NZ$125 for two hours to NZ$140 per person for three-hour trips; heli-rafting from NZ$240 per person, three-day trips from NZ$700 per person.

SOUTH ISLAND

Rangitata Rafts. ⊠ *Rangitata Gorge Rd., Peel Forest, Geraldine, South Canterbury* ☎ *0800/251–251* ⊕ *www.rafts.co.nz* ✉ *From NZ$210.*

Wet 'n' Wild Rafting Company. Wet 'n' Wild Rafting Company rafts several of the North Island's rivers: the Rangitaiki (Grade II–III, great for first timers), Kaituna (Grade IV–V, with the 21-foot waterfall), Wairoa (Grade IV–V, an ultimate white-water playground), Motu (Grade III–V, with wilderness camping for two to four days), and Mohaka (Grade III–V, with two to four days of camping and fishing). From $100. North Island. ⊠ *2 White St., Rotorua* ☎ *07/349–3191, 0800/462–7238* ⊕ *www.wetnwildrafting.co.nz.*

Sailing

Season: Year-round.

Best Locations: Bay of Islands, Auckland and Wellington on the North Island, upper and lower South Island, including the Marlborough Sounds.

Cost: Bay of Islands from NZ$90 for a day trip to NZ$700 to NZ$850; Doubtful Sound from NZ$1,750 for five days; Fiordland National Park from NZ$3,700 for eight days.

SOUTH ISLAND

Abel Tasman Sailing Adventures. ⊠ *46 Martin St., Nelson* ☎ *03/547–6666, 0800/467–245* ⊕ *www.sailingadventures. co.nz.*

Heritage Expeditions. ⊠ *53 Montreal St., Christchurch* ☎ *03/365–3500* ⊕ *www. heritage-expeditions.com.*

Sea Kayaking

Season: December–May.

Best Locations: Northland, the Coromandel Peninsula, and Whanganui River in the North Island; Marlborough Sounds, Kaikoura, Abel Tasman National Park, and Stewart Island's Paterson Inlet.

Cost: From NZ$80 for a half-day excursion; contact kayaking outfitters for price information for longer trips.

NORTH ISLAND

Coastal Kayakers. Coastal Kayakers runs sea-kayaking excursions in the Bay of Islands, from four- to six-hour guided trips to Waitangi or Haruru Falls to more leisurely three-day expeditions. On the overnight trips, you might camp on a deserted island after exploring lagoons, sea caves, and sandy beaches; you'll have time to swim, snorkel, or fish along the way. North Island. ⊠ *Paihia* ☎ *09/402–8105* ⊕ *www.coastalkayakers. co.nz* ✉ *From NZ$85 half day to NZ$685 for 3 days.*

New Zealand Sea Kayaking Adventures. New Zealand Sea Kayaking Adventures offers fully provisioned 3-, 5-, 7-, and 10-day guided sea-kayaking–camping trips in the Bay of Islands. ⊠ *Waitangi* ☎ *09/402–8596* ⊕ *www.nzkayaktours. com* ✉ *From $NZ800.*

What to Read and Watch Before You Go

THE LUMINARIES BY ELEANOR CATTON

Young author Eleanor Catton penned this ambitious, 800-page novel that went on to win the UK's prestigious Man Booker Prize. Organized into astrologically inspired sections, the book's intriguing characters meet each other during an 1860s gold rush on the South Island's West Coast, when many Europeans flocked to the area after word spread that two Māori men had struck gold.

TOP OF THE LAKE

This eerie television show about sordid crimes in a gorgeous region of New Zealand (shot mostly in Queenstown and Glenorchy on the South Island) was a BBC Original that's also currently available on Netflix. Its binge-worthy, cliffhanger episodes and creepy plot are responsible for many lost nights of sleep. In a stunning performance (but with a questionable New Zealand accent), Elizabeth Moss plays a troubled detective with mysterious issues around returning home for the first time. The show takes place in a remote mountain town and centers on the mysterious pregnancy of a 12-year-old girl.

HUNT FOR THE WILDERPEOPLE

The story of a Māori preteen and his unlikely foster father's adventure in the Bush is a feel-good, laugh-out-loud choice for anyone looking to venture to New Zealand. The heartwarming film takes you on a single-camera trek through the Central Plateau and Waitak-ere Ranges of the Auckland region. Director Taika Waititi's other film Boy, a coming-of-age story in Waihau Bay, is worth seeing as well.

THE LORD OF THE RINGS SERIES

You'd have to be living under a rock not to know that Peter Jackson's film adaptations of JRR Tolkien's fantasy book series were filmed exclusively throughout New Zealand. Today Lord of the Rings super-fans visit New Zealand just to experience the real-life Middle-earth that surrounds them, even inspiring guided tours and other LOTR-specific tourism to pop up in recent years. Even if you aren't obsessed, the six movies (the three in the original trilogy and the three in The Hobbit trilogy that came after) are a fun way to get psyched about a trip to the only land that could re-create such a fantasy world.

TO THE IS-LAND BY JANET FRAME

Perhaps New Zealand's most celebrated and prolific female writer, Janet Frame wrote dozens of novels, short story collections, poems, and other works. Her autobiographies (To the Is-Land, followed by An Angel at My Table) start with her childhood in 1920s New Zealand. Her fascinating, somewhat volatile life is marked by poverty, psychiatric (mis)treat-ment and hospitalizations, and eventual outstanding literary achievement.

POUNAMU POUNAMU BY WITI IHIMAERA

Witi Ihimaera's short stories are about the Māori people on the East Coast of New Zealand, both those living in traditional rural communities and those transitioning to urban environments. Ihimaera and others started a wider trend for Māori art and literature, helping the Māori as a whole to become better recognized and celebrated by mainstream (European) New Zealand and internation-al cultures.

THE BONE PEOPLE BY KERI HULME

In her novel that won the Man Booker Prize in 1984, Keri Hulme creates a mov-ing mystery full of complex characters and themes of love, loss, isolation, and grief. With her mixed cast of characters, outsiders, and recluses of both European and Māori identities, Hulme tells a larger story of New Zealand's historical relations.

THE WHALE RIDER BY WITI IHIMAERA

First a novel by Māori writer Witi Ihimaera and then a 2003 film, *The Whale Rider* is a glimpse into the Māori community and its heritage and how it has evolved in the modern era. It tells the story of a 12-year-old Māori girl who wants to follow in the tradition of her ancestor (the "Whale Rider") and become a warrior and leader but is prohibited by her elders because of her gender. True to the book's specific setting, the movie version was filmed in the community of Whangara, on the Northeast coast of the North Island.

ISLAND OF THE LOST BY JOAN DRUETT

A book of nonfiction pieced together from memoirs and historical accounts, *Island of the Lost* tells the stories of two shipwrecks on New Zealand's Auckland Island, occurring months apart from each other in 1864. Through these survival tales (both the successes and failures), the reader discovers the harsh environment, rare flora and fauna, and all elements of life on this unique island.

NOBODY IS EVER MISSING BY CATHERINE LACEY

In Catherine Lacey's raw and emotional novel, a young American woman—haunted by her past and confused about her present—escapes life by hopping on a plane to New Zealand, planning to traverse a country she knows little about. The beauty of the prose is enough to get lost in itself, but it's also fun to discover New Zealand alongside the narrator as she hitchhikes across the country, treks the cities and wilderness, and meets local personalities along the way.

THE CHRONICLES OF NARNIA SERIES

Director and New Zealand native Andrew Adamson took filming back to his home country when creating the movie versions of author C.S. Lewis's Chronicles of Narnia, the beloved children's fantasy series. The tales begin with *The Lion, the Witch, and the Wardrobe* (2005), when a family of children in post–World War II London escape to a faraway, enchanted land and adventure ensues. A grand scope of New Zealand serves as a backdrop (with a lot of special effects in the foreground), including scenes in Flock Hill, Woodhill Forest, Waitaki District, and Purakaunui Bay.

THE PIANO

A bleak and unruly 19th-century New Zealand sets the background for this eerie love story that went on to win multiple Oscars, including Best Actress and Best Supporting Actress for Holly Hunter and a young Anna Paquin. Director Jane Campion explores ideas of class barriers, British imperialism, and challenges to antiquated British ideals on the "wild" island, and received critical acclaim for the movie's artsy strangeness and talented dramatic performances.

WELLINGTON PARANORMAL

A follow-up to Taika Waititi and Jemaine Clement's very funny vampire/werewolf mockumentary *What We Do in the Shadows* finally found its way onto American television in 2021. This show follows a group of clueless Wellington police officers as they investigate the supernatural goings-on in the nation's capital.

Chapter 2

TRAVEL SMART

Updated by
Stuart Freeman

★ **CAPITAL:**
Wellington

POPULATION:
4,854,031

LANGUAGE:
English, Māori

$ **CURRENCY:**
New Zealand dollar

COUNTRY CODE:
64

⚠ **EMERGENCIES:**
111

DRIVING:
On the left

ϟ **ELECTRICITY:**
230-40V/50Hz; electrical
plugs have two flat prongs
in a V

TIME:
16 hours ahead of New York

WEB RESOURCES:
NZ Tourism:
www.tourismnewzealand.
com

NZ Tourism Guide:
www.tourism.net.nz

The New Zealand Herald:
www.nzherald.co.nz

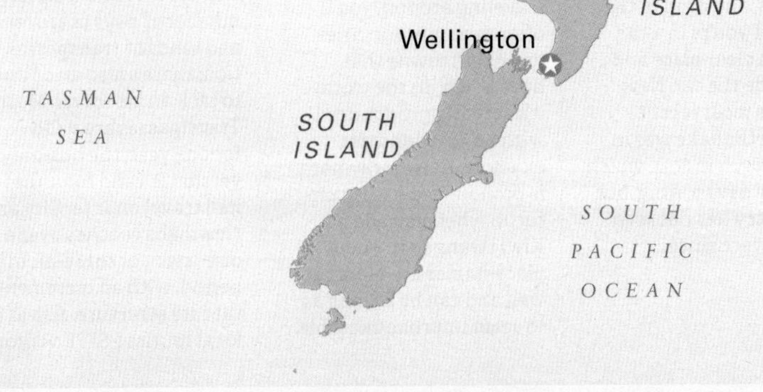

NEW
ZEALAND

Auckland

NORTH
ISLAND

Wellington

*TASMAN
SEA*

*SOUTH
ISLAND*

*SOUTH
PACIFIC
OCEAN*

Know Before You Go

IT HELPS TO KNOW WHEN THINGS ARE CLOSED
Almost everything except for a few gas stations, shops selling essentials, and emergency facilities closes on Christmas Day, Good Friday, Easter Sunday, and the morning of ANZAC Day (April 25). On other public holidays many museums, attractions, and transportation systems have reduced schedules.

KNOW WHAT TO DO IF AN EARTHQUAKE HAPPENS

It's nothing to be super concerned about, safety-wise, but earthquakes do happen in this small country constantly. There's a chance you might experience a small earthquake while here at least once, so it's important to know what safety precautions to take in the event one does occur. The biggest safety tips are to have an earthquake plan with your fellow travelers, stay indoors until the shaking stops and it's safe to exit, take cover under a desk or table, and stay away from windows and bookcases or anything that can fall on you. If you're outdoors, move to a clear spot away from buildings and trees, and drop to the ground; if you're in a car, drive to a clear place and stay inside the car. New Zealand's most recent major earthquake was in Christchurch in 2011, which was quite devastating, but the country has not seen one as severe since.

GET TO KNOW SOME VOCABULARY/ PRONUNCIATION

Kiwi English can be mystifying. The colloquialisms alone, not to mention rural slang, can make things puzzling. Known as "cow cockie" talk, this is what you'll hear when "girls" refers to someone's cows, and "gummies" (galoshes) are the favored footwear. It can be helpful to look up a list of slang locals use, so you don't get your verbs and nouns mixed up. People often refer to getting drunk as getting "pissed," so it doesn't always mean someone is angry. New Zealanders refer to dinner as "tea," and afternoon as "arvo." Things are also often pronounced differently here. When traveling around, you'll often see signs for cities and small towns that have a "wh" in the word; it's actually pronounced with an "F" sound: for example, Kaiwharawhara is pronounced kai-futuh-futuh when you add a Kiwi twang to it. Many place-names are Māori as well and can be so long as to seem unpronounceable.

(In fact, one of these can claim itself as the longest place-name in the world.) The biggest communication glitch between New Zealanders and visitors often involves the Kiwis' eloquent use of understatement. This facet of Kiwi culture is both blessing and curse. Everything sounds relaxed and easygoing, but if you're trying to judge something like distance or difficulty, you may run into trouble. No matter how far away something is, people often say it's "just down the road" or "just over the hill." Ask specific questions to avoid a misunderstanding. It pays to learn a little Te Reo, the Māori language, since words and phrases from it are often casually dropped into conversation by New Zealanders. Most frequent is the ubiquitous welcome, *"kia ora,"* that you'll hear as soon as you enter the country.

PASSES CAN HELP YOU SAVE MONEY

Look into the New Zealand Travelpass to save money by combining bus, ferry, and train costs. The Travelpass has no fixed itineraries and gives you 3,000 different stops to choose from. You choose from a certain number of days of travel and kinds of transportation; there's also an option to tack on air travel. Most Travelpasses are valid for one year; the bus-only version is valid for unlimited travel on InterCity and Newmans coaches over a one-, two-, or three-month period, with an incremental-rate structure. Ask at a local tourist i-SITE visitor information center about hotel and local transportation packages that include tickets to major museum exhibits or other special events.

DON'T MIX UP NEW ZEALAND AND AUSTRALIA

You'll find in your travels that many people don't quite know the difference between Kiwis and Ozzies. Since New Zealand is close to Australia and the two do have several cultural aspects in common, they can easily get mixed up. However, there are differences in the accents, and the indigenous cultures are drastically different. Be careful not to assume the two cultures are that much alike, as New Zealanders are a proud folk and appreciate when people realize that although their country is small, it's still distinct and ripe with great wine, mountain ranges, and an amazing rugby team.

NEW ZEALAND SUN IS STRONGER THAN MOST PLACES SO BRING SUNSCREEN

You won't notice it at first, but once you stay out in the sun on a summer day in New Zealand, you'll begin to feel just how much sharper the sun's rays are. It's important to wear sunglasses especially if your eyes are sensitive to sunlight. There isn't a direct hole in the ozone layer over New Zealand, but the thinning layer does send pockets of ozone-depleted air over certain parts of the country starting in the spring. Certain days can hit

you harder than others, so keep yourself protected at all times.

BE RESPECTFUL OF MĀORI CULTURE

As New Zealand's indigenous people, the culture of the Māori is embedded throughout the fabric of the country. The history between the native Māori and the European colonizers is long, and often fraught with violence. Recent years have seen a wonderful resurgence in Māori culture and pride, but there are still debates regarding the legal ownership of the land. Tourists especially should be respectful toward Māori history, culture, and tradition. If you don't know anything about the Māori prior to your trip, it's helpful to do some quick reading on the airplane before you land. For instance, the *marae*, the area in front of a Māori meetinghouse, should not be entered unless you are invited or unless it's in use as a cultural center. Only use the traditional *hongi* (touching foreheads and nose in greeting) if someone else initiates it. You're likely to see a lot of Māori culture on your trip; the Māori Haka is a ceremonial dance or challenge used to intimidate rivals or opponents with chants, the stomping of feet, and extreme facial expressions. The national rugby teams perform it before a game to demonstrate their strength and power to the opposite team. It is also performed at funerals as a memorial to someone's spirit.

THERE ARE STRICT RULES ABOUT WHAT YOU CAN BRING INTO THE COUNTRY

New Zealand has stringent regulations governing the import of weapons, foodstuffs, and certain plant and animal material. Most stringent is the agricultural quarantine. New Zealand is highly dependent on its agriculture and horticulture industries and cannot risk unwanted introduction of pest plants or animals or disease. The authorities don't want any nonnative seeds (or popcorn kernels or honey) haplessly transported into the country. You must declare even a single piece of fruit, and all camping and hiking gear must also be declared and inspected at customs. You'll be hit with an instant NZ$400 fine if you're caught bringing in fruit. And be truthful about your camping gear because they *will* want to take a look at it, unravel your tent and sleeping bag, and check for grass and muck. Do yourself a favor and make sure any camping gear and hiking boots are reasonably clean when entering the country. If you are unsure, simply declare it on the immigration card. An official will ask what you're declaring and if it's okay (like chocolate, for example), he'll send you straight through.

Getting Here and Around

Air

Most visitors will arrive in New Zealand via airplane, typically into Auckland International Airport. Although air travel within New Zealand can be expensive compared with bus travel, the one-way fare system does make it easy to get around, especially if you don't want to spend all your time on the road. These days, booking your domestic flights in conjunction with your international flight won't necessarily save you any money, but it can help if connecting flights are running late—they will hold your next flight for you if possible. Some airlines give great deals if you add stopovers to your flight itinerary. You'll need to stop in at a Pacific destination like Tahiti or Fiji for a limited time before heading to New Zealand. Check with the airline and see what they're offering; make sure that New Zealand is included in Pacific deals because sometimes it's the one exception. Qantas has a low-budget airline called Jetstar, which serves trans-Tasman and between major New Zealand hubs Auckland, Christchurch, Wellington, and Queenstown. When booking domestic flights with either Jetstar or Air New Zealand make sure you read the fine print regarding baggage allowance, as the cheaper fares include zero checked baggage. If you hold an international student identification card, you'll save even more. But make sure you check in well before time! Jetstar is notorious for turning away passengers if they arrive even one second after the cutoff time.

From New York to Auckland (via Los Angeles) flights take about 19 hours; from Chicago, about 17 hours; from Los Angeles to Auckland (nonstop), about 12 hours. From the United States and Canada, you will have to connect to a New Zealand–bound flight in Los Angeles, San Francisco, Houston, or Vancouver.

AIRPORTS

The major airport is Auckland International Airport (AKL). It is usually a bit cheaper to fly into and out of this airport, but the supplemental fees for flights to Wellington (WLG) or Christchurch (CHC) are reasonable. New Zealand's airports are relatively compact and easy to negotiate.

Auckland's international and domestic terminals are in separate buildings, a 10-minute walk apart. Free bus shuttles run constantly (however, after an incoming long-haul flight you may find that the walk and fresh air is great for the soul!). Christchurch International Airport is the main gateway to southern tourism destinations, though flying direct to Queenstown is a popular option from Australia.

New Zealand has a dense network of domestic air routes, so hopping from one area to another is fairly easy, if not inexpensive. Air New Zealand partners with other international airlines and serves some smaller regional airports, so you can make these flight arrangements when booking your international flight. If you are sure of your dates well ahead of time, it's worth checking Air New Zealand's Grab a Seat program for one-off domestic specials. Fares between the main cities (Auckland, Wellington, Christchurch, and Queenstown) can be reasonable, but others are often more expensive. For other cities, it's worth checking the websites of smaller regional airlines (Sounds Air and Chathams Air, for example), that have picked up routes the bigger airlines have deemed not worthwhile.

Jetstar, Qantas' low-cost operation, operates primarily on the main trunk routes connecting Auckland, Wellington, Christchurch, and Queenstown.

FLIGHTS

Air New Zealand flies two to three times a day from Los Angeles to Auckland and is the only carrier that extends a daily nonstop flight from San Francisco to Auckland. Qantas flies from Los Angeles to New Zealand daily, mostly through Sydney. United and Air Canada, affiliates of Air New Zealand, connect from points in North America to Los Angeles. Fiji Airways connects from Los Angeles through Nadi, Fiji, with Auckland, Wellington, and Christchurch.

Within New Zealand, Air New Zealand and Jetstar compete on intercity trunk routes, along with smaller airlines Sounds Air and Air Chathams, which fly several intercity routes. Several airlines provide services to Australia: trans-Tasman flights are available from Auckland, Wellington, Christchurch, Dunedin, and Queenstown.

Boat

To travel between the North Island and the South Island, take either the Interislander or Bluebridge ferry between Wellington and Picton. Both ferries carry cars. They also connect with KiwiRail trains. A free shuttle is available between the railway station and the Interislander ferry terminal in Wellington. The Bluebridge terminal is right across the road from the station. The Picton railway station is a few minutes' walk from the ferry terminals. Both ferries travel four to five times a day. Standard one-way passenger fare can be as much as NZ$70, but there are off-peak deals to be had for as low as NZ$39. The fare for a medium-size sedan starts at NZ$175 (including driver). Be sure to ask about specials, including ferry-train package deals through KiwiRail, when you book.

Schedules are available at i-SITE visitor information centers around the country. Most will arrange Interislander and Bluebridge ferry bookings. You can also check schedules and fares and book online via the Interislander and Bluebridge websites. Some fares allow you to make schedule changes up to the last minute and guarantee a full refund if you cancel prior to check-in. Discount fares can be booked once in New Zealand; these have some restrictions. No matter how you go about it, it's a good idea to reserve in advance, especially during holiday periods.

Bus

New Zealand is served by an extensive bus network. The InterCity Group operates the main bus lines, InterCity and Newmans. Some Newmans and InterCity bus routes overlap, but Newmans tends to have fewer stops and sticks to the key tourism routes, for example Christchurch to Queenstown and the West Coast. InterCity buses, on the other hand, cover more remote areas.

There are also many regional bus services. For instance, Bottom Bus, operated by Travel Head First, runs from Dunedin through the Catlins to Southland, Queenstown, and Fiordland; while Atomic Travel links Christchurch with Dunedin.

Take a hop-on, hop-off bus if you prefer a more flexible itinerary, typically valid for 12 months. InterCity offers this, along with "backpacker-target" companies like Kiwi Experience and Stray Bus. Some passes cover all of New Zealand, whereas others are limited to specific regions. Most of the backpacker buses have affiliations with accommodations and activities and can offer priority bookings and special deals.

Getting Here and Around

FARES AND PASSES

Fares vary greatly. A standard full fare between Auckland and Wellington is NZ$97 but can be obtained for as low as NZ$34. A certain number of seats are sold at a discounted rate, so book your tickets as early as possible, especially during the holidays. Individual company's websites are the best way to find out about special fares.

Look into the various flexible passes that allow coach travel over a set route in a given time frame, usually three or six months. You can travel whenever you like, without paying extra, as long as you stick to the stops covered by your pass. The Flexipass is sold in blocks of time during which you're eligible to travel on regular InterCity bus routes. This is such a good deal that locals even use this pass for their daily commute. Typically valid for a year, you can hop on and off, changing your plans without a penalty at least two hours prior to your departure. You must schedule in advance, as independent bus ticketing windows don't track your Flexipass hours.

There is also the New Zealand TravelPass, which allows unlimited travel on buses and trains and on the Interislander ferries that link the North and South Islands. Kiwi Experience and Stray Bus also visit some pretty cool destinations with special accommodations not found on the mainstream traveler networks—remote farming settlements, small town pubs, and Māori *marae* (villages), for example.

🚗 Car

Nothing beats the freedom and mobility of a car for exploring. Even if you're nervous about driving on the "wrong" side of the road, driving here is relatively easy. Many rental cars will have a sticker right next to the steering wheel reading "stay to the left." Having said this, as tourism numbers increased prior to COVID, so, too, did the number of driving accidents involving tourists. Tourism organizations have prepared a voluntary Code of Practice to help rental vehicle companies advise their clients, and the Drive Safe website (*www.drivesafe.org.nz*) gives some handy tips.

Remember this simple axiom: drive left, look right. That means keeping to the left lane, and when turning right or left from a stop sign, the closest lane of traffic will be coming from the right, so look in that direction first. By the same token, pedestrians should look right before crossing the street. Americans and Canadians can blindly step into the path of an oncoming car by looking left as they do when crossing streets at home. You'll find yourself in a constant comedy of errors when you go to use directional signals and windshield wipers—on Kiwi roads it's the reverse of what you're used to.

RENTAL CARS

Japanese brands dominate rental agencies in New Zealand. Most major agencies also offer higher-end options, for example convertibles and esteemed European models such as BMWs. Domestic agency Smart Car Rentals specializes in luxury rentals such as Mercedes and Audi convertibles. Most Kiwi cars these days are automatic, though some stick shifts (manual) are included in rental fleets, so specify if you prefer an automatic.

Many Kiwi companies (the largest is Maui-Rentals) rent a wide selection of small campers and larger motor homes. Most major international car rental companies operate here; there are also reputable domestic agencies. Rates in New Zealand begin at about NZ$35 a day and NZ$320 a week—although you can sometimes get even cheaper deals on economy cars with unlimited mileage. This does not include tax on car rentals, which is 12.5%. Reserve a vehicle well in advance if renting during holiday seasons, especially Christmas.

Most major international companies (and some local companies) have a convenient service if you are taking the ferry between the North and South Islands and want to continue your rental contract. You simply drop off the car in Wellington and on the same contract pick up a car in Picton, or vice versa. It saves you from paying the fare for taking a car across on the ferry (though you will have to organize your luggage into carry-ons). Your rental contract is terminated only at the far end of your trip, wherever you end up. In this system, there is no drop-off charge for one-way rentals, making an Auckland–Queenstown rental as easy as it could be. Check for rates based on a south-to-north itinerary; it may be less expensive as it's against the normal flow. Special rates should be available whether you book from abroad or within New Zealand.

In New Zealand your own driver's license is acceptable. Still, an International Driver's Permit is a good idea; it's available from the American Automobile Association. These international permits are universally recognized, and having one in your wallet may save you problems with the local authorities. For most major rental companies in New Zealand, 21 is the minimum age for renting a car. With some local rental companies, however, drivers under 21 years old can rent a car but may be liable for a higher deductible. Children's car seats are mandatory for kids under seven years old. Car-rental companies may ask drivers not to take their cars onto certain (rough) roads, so ask about such restrictions.

ROAD CONDITIONS

Roads are well maintained and generally not crowded (except for leaving major cities at peak holiday weekends). In rural areas, you may find some unpaved roads. On most highways, it's easier to use the signposted names of upcoming towns to navigate rather than route numbers.

Due to the less-than-flat terrain, many New Zealand roads are "wonky," or crooked. So when mapping out your itinerary, don't plan on averaging the speed limit of 100 kph (62 mph) too often. Expect two or three lanes; there are no special multi-occupant lanes on the major highways. In areas where there is only one lane for each direction, cars can pass, with care, while facing oncoming traffic, except where there is a double-yellow center line. Rural areas still have some one-lane roads. One-lane bridges are common. (For more on these, *see* Rules of the Road.)

Dangerous overtaking, speeding, failing to signal when turning, tailgating, and driving slowly in passing lanes are all problems on New Zealand highways.

GASOLINE

On main routes you'll find stations at regular intervals. However, if you're traveling on back roads where the population is sparse, don't let your tank get low—it can be a long walk to the nearest farmer.

Unleaded gas is widely available and often referred to as 91. High-octane unleaded gas is called 95. The 91 is usually a couple of cents cheaper than 95; most rental cars run on 91. Virtually all gas stations will have staff on hand to pump gas or assist motorists in other ways; however, they tend to have self-service facilities for anyone in a hurry. These are simply operated by pushing numbers on a console to coincide with the dollar value of the gas required.

Getting Here and Around

When you pump the gas, the pump will automatically switch off when you have reached the stated amount. Or push "fill" and the pump will stop when the tank is full.

Credit cards are widely accepted. Mostly you can pay at the counter inside the station after you fill your tank, although a few stations—perhaps victims of previous dishonesty—now request payment first.

ROADSIDE EMERGENCIES

In the case of a serious accident, immediately pull over to the side of the road and phone (111). Except on city motorways, emergency phone boxes are not common; you may have to rely on a cellular phone. You will find New Zealanders quick to help if they are able to, particularly if you need to use a phone. Minor accidents are normally sorted out in a calm and collected manner at the side of the road. However, "road rage" is not unknown. If the driver of the other vehicle looks particularly angry or aggressive, you are within your rights to take note of the registration number and then report the accident at the local or nearest police station.

The New Zealand Automobile Association (NZAA) provides emergency road service and is associated with the American Automobile Association (AAA). If you are an AAA member, you will be covered by the service as long as you register in person with an NZAA office in New Zealand and present your membership card with an expiration date showing it is still valid. NZAA advises that you register before you begin your trip.

Should you find yourself at a panel beater (repair shop) after a prang (minor car accident), talking about your vehicle might end up sounding like more of an Abbott and Costello routine if you're not prepared with the appropriate vehicle vernacular. For instance, you might hear the panel beater say, "Geez mate! Doing the ton on loose metal when it was hosing down? You have a chip in the windscreen, the fender has to be reattached under the boot, and your axle is munted. Pop the bonnet and let's take a look." Translation: "Wow! Driving so fast on a gravel road in the rain? You chipped the windshield, the bumper needs to be reattached under the trunk, and the axle is broken. Pop the hood."

RULES OF THE ROAD

The speed limit is 100 kph (62 mph) on the open road, 50 kph (31 mph) in towns and cities, and 70 kph (44 mph) or 80 kph (50 mph) in some "in between" areas. Watch for the signs that show where these change. A circular sign with the letters LSZ (Limited Speed Zone) means speed should be governed by prevailing road conditions but still not exceed 100 kph (62 mph). Speed cameras, particularly in city suburbs and on approaches to and exits from small towns, will snap your number plate if you're driving too fast. Fines start at about NZ$60 for speeds 10 kph (6 mph) over the speed limit. (If you're driving a rental, the company will track you down for payment.) It's easier and safer for everyone to obey the speed limit.

New Zealand law states that you must always wear a seat belt, whether you are driving or are a passenger. As the driver, you can be fined for any passenger not wearing a seat belt or approved child restraint if under the age of seven. If you are caught without a seat belt and you are clearly not a New Zealander, the result is likely to be a friendly but firm warning. Drunk drivers are not tolerated in New Zealand. The blood alcohol limit is 250 micrograms (mcg) of alcohol per liter of breath. This equates to about 1½ standard drinks, but everyone reacts differently. It's safest to avoid driving altogether if you've had a drink. If you are caught driving over the limit you will possibly be taken to the nearest police station to dry out and be required to pay a high fine. Repeat offenses or instances of causing injury or death while under the influence of alcohol are likely to result in jail terms.

When driving in rural New Zealand, cross one-lane bridges with caution—there are plenty of them. A yellow sign with parallel black lines will usually warn you that you are approaching a one-lane bridge, and another sign will tell you whether you have the right-of-way. A rectangular blue sign with a bigger white arrow on the left side of a smaller red arrow means you have the right-of-way, and a circular sign with a red border and red arrow on the left side of a white arrow means you must pull over to the left and wait to cross until oncoming traffic has passed. Even when you have the right-of-way, slow down and take care. Roundabouts can be particularly confusing for newcomers. When entering a roundabout, yield to all vehicles coming from the right. A blue sign with a white arrow indicates that you should keep to the left of the traffic island as you come up to the roundabout. In a multilane roundabout, stay in the lane closest to the island until ready to exit the circle. You must indicate left just before you exit.

You can only pass on the left if there are two or more lanes on your side of the center line or if the vehicle ahead is signaling a right turn. At all other times, you must pass on the right, and only when you have enough clear road to do so. When you encounter fog, try putting your headlights on low beam; this sometimes helps as high beams refract light

and decrease visibility. It is illegal to drive with only your parking lights on.

In cities and towns, the usual fine for parking over the time limit on meters is NZ$10–NZ$15. In the last few years "pay-and-display" meters have been put up in cities. You'll need to drop a couple of dollars' worth of coins in the meter, take the dispensed ticket, and put it in view on the dashboard of your car. Alternatively look for the parking lot number on the street beside your car and enter that into the nearest machine, along with your money. The fine for running over the time for these meters runs about NZ$12, but if you don't make any attempt at all to pay, the fine will be at least NZ$40 and you may risk being towed. So carry a few coins at all times—any denomination will usually do (gold coins only in Auckland and Wellington). Credit cards also work in some machines. Make sure to observe all "no parking" signs, especially at peak commuter times in cities, when parking on some busy streets is not permitted (signs will show this). If you don't, your car is highly likely to be towed away. It will cost about NZ$100 to NZ$200 to have the car released, and most tow companies won't accept anything but cash. For more road rules and safety tips, check the New Zealand Transport Agency website, *www.nzta.govt.nz.*

TRAFFIC
The only cities with a serious congestion problem during rush hour are Auckland and Wellington, particularly on inner-city highways and on- and off-ramps. Avoid driving between 7:30 am and 9 am and 5 pm and 6:30 pm. It is also worth taking this into account if you have important appointments or a plane to catch. Give yourself a spare 30 minutes to be on the safe side. Traffic around Christchurch also builds up at these times, and has been particularly problematic since the 2011

Getting Here and Around

earthquake damaged many roads. Also, as the city is rebuilt, many roads become closed or changed to one-way. Even the locals get confused (and bemused).

🚢 Cruise

Cruise companies are increasingly drawn to Auckland and Wellington's superb harbors, as well as to the gorgeous scenery, nature tourism, culture, food, and wine found in places such as the Bay of Islands, Tauranga, Napier, Marlborough Sounds, Akaroa, Dunedin, Fiordland, and Stewart Island. World Cruise itineraries with Crystal Cruises and Regent Seven Seas Cruises now include New Zealand. But some of the best cruising programs are those that concentrate entirely on the South Pacific and combine New Zealand with destinations such as Fiji, New Caledonia, Tonga, Samoa, and Australia. Generally, such cruises start and finish in Auckland and visit South Pacific islands in between, or they travel around New Zealand then cross the Tasman Sea to visit Australian east coast ports.

P&O Cruises runs a couple of cruises out of Auckland to the South Pacific. Another choice is Holland America Line with its cruises around New Zealand, Australia, and the South Pacific.

🚆 Train

Don't rely on trains to get you around; train travel in New Zealand is limited to three routes operated by Kiwi Rail Scenic Journeys and commuter services in Wellington and Auckland. That said, the three long journeys are indeed scenic. They include the daily TranzAlpine Express, a spectacular ride over Arthur's Pass and the mountainous spine of the South Island between Greymouth on the West Coast and Christchurch on the east. The Coastal Pacific runs from Christchurch along the stunning Kaikoura coast (between mountains and sea), to Marlborough wine country and Picton. This service recommenced in the summer of 2018, after two years of rebuilding following a devastating 2016 earthquake, and the journey now showcases the incredible sea floor uplift that occurred in the quake. The Coastal Pacific runs daily between October and April and a few days a week through winter months (timetable varies). The Northern Explorer travels from Wellington to Auckland, departing Auckland on Monday, Thursday, and Saturday and Wellington Tuesday, Friday, and Sunday.

The trains do leave and arrive on time as a rule. They have one class, with standard comfortable seats and a basic food service selling light meals, snacks, beer, wine, and spirits. Special meals (diabetic, wheat free, or vegetarian) can be arranged, but you have to order at least 48 hours before you board the train. Most carriages have large windows from which to view the spectacular passing scenery, and you'll hear a commentary on passing points of interest. Most trains also have a viewing carriage at the rear.

Travelers can purchase a New Zealand Travelpass for unlimited travel by train, bus, and Interislander ferry for a variety of periods. Senior citizens (over 60) get a 20% discount with proof of age. You can obtain both schedules and tickets at i-SITE visitor information centers and at train stations. Reservations are advised, particularly in the summer months. Book at least 48 hours in advance.

Essentials

Dining

The New Zealand dining scene comes from a long tradition of Māori staples, like fish, birds, and root vegetables, typically cooked slowly in an underground oven known as a *hāngi*. With the Europeans came livestock (sheep, cattle, and pigs) and a meat-and-potato diet. But the past few decades have seen a move towards farm-to-table and local fare, with farmers and consumers quickly developing a taste and reputation for sustainable, seasonal dishes. The food here is sometimes described as "Pacific Rim" or "Pacific Rim fusion"—that is, European-style mainstays with Asian and Pacific Island influences.

New Zealand's population has become far more diverse over the past decade, and this has resulted in a far more global look to the dining scene—particularly in Auckland and Wellington. If you have a hankering for spicy Thai, sushi with fresh New Zealand ingredients, or a creamy Italian pasta dish you won't have any trouble finding it.

Burgers are a staple for a quick bite. However, you'll find there's a whole lot more than two all-beef patties and a bun—two of the most popular fillings are beetroot and a fried egg. Cheese on burgers (and sandwiches) is often grated bits sprinkled on top. Another Kiwi snack staple, meat pies, is sold just about everywhere. The classic steak-and-mince fillings are getting gussied up these days with cheese or mushrooms. And who could forget good ol' fish-and-chips in this former British colony? Appropriately called "greasies," this mainstay is often made of shark but called lemon fish or flake. These days, many "takeaway" outlets give you the opportunity to upgrade to a more expensive fish species. You might notice bowls by the cash registers

of takeout shops containing packets of tartar sauce or tomato sauce (ketchup). These are usually not free for the taking; they cost about 50¢ each. Be aware that "bacon" might consist of a thick blubbery slice of ham or a processed fatty, pink, spongy substance. If you love your bacon streaky and crisp, politely inquire what kind of bacon they serve before ordering a BLT.

When in New Zealand, taste the lamb. No matter where you go in the country, it's sure to be on the menu along with locally farmed beef. Cervena, or farm-raised venison, is another local delicacy available all over New Zealand. Don't miss a Māori *hāngi*. This culinary experience is most likely to be available in conjunction with a cultural show or marae visit. The traditional preparation involves steaming meat, seafood, and vegetables for several hours in a large underground pit. Also be sure to try the locally grown *kūmara,* or sweet potato. Some Kiwi folk view muttonbird (the cute name for young sooty shearwaters, harvested from their burrows on little islands around Stewart Island) as a special treat, but others balk at its peculiar smell and strong flavor. It is an acquired taste, but if you're an adventurous eater it's definitely one to try.

Of course, seafood is a specialty, and much of the fish is not exported so this is your chance to try it. The tastiest fish around include snapper in the North and blue cod (not a true cod relative) in the South. Grouper (often listed by its Māori name of *hāpuku*), and marine-farmed salmon are also menu toppers, as is whitebait, the juvenile of several fish species, in the whitebait-fishing season of spring. Like many places, New Zealand has been subject to over-fishing, and some species (although they may appear on the menu) are best avoided

Essentials

for conservation's sake. Terakihi and orange roughy are two of the fisheries under pressure. As for shellfish: try the Bluff oysters (in season March–August), Greenshell mussels (also known as green-lipped or New Zealand green mussels), scallops, crayfish (spiny lobster), and local clamlike shellfish, *pipi* and *tuatua*.

Some restaurants serve a fixed-price dinner, but the majority are à la carte. Remember that "entrée" in Kiwi English is the equivalent of an appetizer. Increasingly, restaurants are offering smaller, tapas-style plates for sharing. It's wise to make a reservation and inquire if the restaurant has a liquor license or is "BYOB" or "BYO" (Bring Your Own Bottle)—a few places have both. This only pertains to wine, not bottles of beer or liquor. Be prepared to pay a corkage fee, which can be up to NZ$10. Many restaurants add a 15% surcharge on public holidays. Employers are required by law to pay staff a higher wage during holidays. This amount will be itemized separately on your bill.

For information on food-related health issues, see Health.

RESTAURANT HOURS
Hotel restaurants serve breakfast roughly between 7 and 10; cafés and restaurants often serve breakfast/brunch to 11 am, or even an "all-day breakfast." Lunch usually starts about noon and is over by 3. Dinners are usually served from 6 pm, but the most popular dining time is around 7 to 8. Restaurants in cities and resort areas will serve dinner well into the night, but some places in small towns or rural areas still shut their doors at around 8.

Unless otherwise noted, the restaurants listed in this guide are open daily for lunch and dinner.

RESERVATIONS AND DRESS
We only mention reservations specifically when they're essential or when they are not accepted. For popular restaurants, book as far ahead as you can (a week or more) and reconfirm as soon as you arrive. Large parties should always call ahead to check the reservations policy. We mention dress only when men are required to wear a jacket or a jacket and tie.

Attire countrywide is casual; unless you're planning to dine at the finest and more conservative of places, men won't need to bring a jacket and tie. At the same time, the most common dinner attire is usually a notch above jeans and T-shirts.

Embassies and Consulates
In Auckland, the U.S. Consulate is open from 8:30 until around 5:30 on weekdays (closed last Wednesday of each month). In Wellington, the U.S. Embassy is open weekdays 8:15 am to 5 pm.

✚ Health
All visitors to New Zealand must have a valid proof of COVID-19 vaccination and/or a booster; while the need and frequency of boosters is still being discussed in the medical community, it's important to verify the most recent requirements with your physician before you travel.

The most common types of illnesses are caused by contaminated food and water. In New Zealand that really shouldn't be an issue. New Zealand has high hygiene standards and strict health regulations when it comes to serving food and beverages in shops, restaurants, cafés, and bars. The tap water is fine to drink. Locals do it all the time.

General health standards in New Zealand are high, and it would be hard to find a more pristine natural environment. The major health hazard in New Zealand is sunburn or sunstroke. Even people who are not normally bothered by strong sun should cover up with a long-sleeve shirt, a hat, and pants or a beach wrap. At higher altitudes you will burn more easily, so apply sunscreen liberally before you go out—even for a half hour—and wear a visor or sunglasses.

Dehydration is another serious danger that can be easily avoided, so be sure to carry water and drink often. Limit the amount of time you spend in the sun for the first few days until you are acclimatized, and avoid sunbathing in the middle of the day.

There are no venomous snakes, and the only native poisonous spider, the *katipo,* is a rarity. The whitetail spider, an unwelcome and accidental import from Australia, packs a nasty bite and can cause discomfort but is also rarely encountered (and easily identified by its white tail). One New Zealander you will come to loathe is the tiny black sand fly, common mainly in the western half of the South Island, which inflicts a painful bite that can itch for several days. In other parts of the country, especially around rivers and lakes in the evenings, you may be pestered by mosquitoes. Be sure to use insect repellent.

One of New Zealand's rare health hazards involves its pristine-looking bodies of water; as a precaution don't drink water from natural outdoor sources. Although the country's alpine lakes might look like backdrops for mineral-water ads, some in the South Island harbor a tiny organism that can cause "duck itch," a temporary but intense skin irritation. The organism is found only on the shallow lake margins, so the chances of infection are greatly reduced if you stick to deeper water. Streams can be infected by giardia, a waterborne protozoal parasite that can cause gastrointestinal disorders, including acute diarrhea. Giardia is most likely contracted when drinking from streams that pass through an area inhabited by mammals (such as cattle or possums). There is no risk of infection if you drink from streams above the tree line.

Less common, but a risk nevertheless, is the possibility of contracting amoebic meningitis from the water in geothermal pools. The illness is caused by an organism that can enter the body when the water is forced up the nose. The organism is quite rare, but you should avoid putting your head underwater in thermal pools or jumping in them. Also remember not to drink geothermic water.

OVER-THE-COUNTER REMEDIES
Popular headache, pain, and flu medicines are Nurofen (contains ibuprofen), Panadol (contains acetaminophen), and Dispirin (contains aspirin). Dispirin often comes as large tabs, which you must dissolve in water. Many Kiwi households and wheelhouses have a green tube of Berocca, the soluble vitamin supplement often taken the morning after a big night out.

Lodging
You'll find a wide variety of accommodations in New Zealand, from youth-oriented hostels to quaint B&Bs to breathtaking luxury lodges. Tourism New Zealand publishes an online accommodation directory listing all properties that are accredited by Qualmark, the national tourism–quality assurance organization.

Essentials

While most reputable properties are Qualmark registered, some outstanding places to stay are not.

BED-AND-BREAKFASTS

There are some helpful resources on the Web for researching and booking B&B choices. On websites such as those maintained by the Bed and Breakfast Association, you'll find hundreds of listings and advertisements for reputable B&Bs throughout the country. Heritage & Character Inns of New Zealand specializes in higher-end B&Bs.

Once in New Zealand you will find the *New Zealand Bed & Breakfast Book* in most major bookstores, or you can look at their listings online for free. It lists about 1,000 B&Bs, but be aware that property owners, not independent writers, provide the editorial copy.

HOME AND FARM STAYS

If you think green acres is the place to be, New Zealand has plenty of them. Home and farm stays provide not only comfortable accommodations, but a chance to experience the countryside and the renowned Kiwi hospitality. Most operate on a B&B basis, though some also serve evening meals. Farm accommodations vary from modest shearers' cabins to elegant homesteads. Some hosts offer day trips, as well as horseback riding, hiking, and fishing. For two people, the average cost ranges from NZ$90 to NZ$400 per night, including meals. Check farmstay accommodations on Tourism New Zealand's website for options.

Farm Helpers in New Zealand (FHINZ) advertises dozens of positions throughout the country where you can stay for free in exchange for working on a farm. Tasks include fruit picking, gardening, and light carpentry.

Homestays, the urban equivalent of farm stays, are less expensive. Many New Zealanders seem to have vacation homes, called "baches" in the North Island, "cribs" in the South Island; these are frequently available for rent. New Zealand Vacation Homes lists houses and apartments for rent on both the North and South Islands. Baches and Holiday Homes to Rent Ltd. publishes an annual directory of rental homes throughout the country, with color photos for each listing.

MOTELS

Motels are popular accommodations, and most provide comfortable rooms with excellent self-service kitchen facilities for NZ$70–NZ$195 per night. Unlike in the United States, motels in New Zealand are not always below the standard of hotels. Many are set up like stylish apartments, with living and kitchen areas as well as bedrooms. Some motels are called "motor lodges." Accommodations with more basic facilities are called "serviced motels." The Motel Association of New Zealand (MANZ) is an independent organization with nearly 1,000 members. Its website allows you to find properties by region or by motel name.

MOTOR CAMPS

The least expensive accommodations are the tourist cabins and flats in most of the country's 400 motor camps, or holiday parks as they are now described. Many of these also offer excellent motel and apartment units, as well as camping and powered sites. Tourist cabins provide basic accommodation and shared cooking, laundry, and bathroom facilities. Bedding and towels are usually provided. A notch higher up the comfort scale, tourist flats provide fully equipped kitchens and private bathrooms. Tent sites and powered caravan or motor home sites usually cost less than NZ$50 and overnight rates for cabins range anywhere from NZ$50 to NZ$100. More fully equipped tourist flats will cost NZ$80 to NZ$200.

Nightlife

New Zealand is well known for its wines, particularly whites such as sauvignon blanc, riesling, pinot gris, and chardonnay. The country has also gained a reputation for red wines such as cabernet sauvignon, pinot noir, and merlot. The main wine-producing areas are Hawke's Bay, Wairarapa, Marlborough, Nelson, Waipara (north Canterbury), and Central Otago. Restaurants almost without exception serve New Zealand products on their wine list.

When ordering a beer, you'll get either a handle (mug), a one-liter jug (pitcher) with glasses, or a "stubby" (small bottle). You might need to request a glass if you don't want to glug straight from the bottle (depending how casual the bar is). Two large mainstream breweries, DB and Lion, produce their own products along with smaller, well-known brands that initially started as independent breweries, such as Mac's, Monteith's, and Speight's. They also dispense international brands Steinlager, Stella Artois, Heineken, and more. More popular in recent years, however, are boutique microbreweries and craft beers. Innovation, international awards, and ever-changing brews are the features of brands where even the brewery names are interesting, for example Garage Project, Parrotdog, Lakeman, and 8 Wired Brewing. Each brand has its own fan base, and the good pubs will have at least a couple of ever-changing taps serving up these tasty brews. Most restaurants and liquor stores also sell beers from Australia, Europe, and other parts of the world. Some of the beer in New Zealand, especially the craft beers, is stronger than the 4% alcohol per volume brew that is the norm in the United States. Many go up to 7% or 8% alcohol per volume, so check that number before downing your usual number of drinks.

Beer and wine can be purchased in supermarkets, specialized shops, and even little corner suburban shops—seven days a week. People under 18 are not permitted by law to purchase alcohol, and shops, bars, and restaurants strictly enforce this. If you look younger than you are, carry photo identification to prove your age.

Packing

In New Zealand, be prepared for weather that can turn suddenly and temperatures that vary greatly from day to night, particularly at the change of seasons. Wear layers. You'll appreciate being able to remove or put on a jacket. Take along a light raincoat and umbrella, but remember that plastic raincoats and non-breathing polyester are uncomfortable in the humid climates of Auckland and its northern vicinity. Many shops in New Zealand sell lightweight and mid-weight merino wool garments, which are expensive but breathe, keep you warm, and don't trap body odor, making them ideal attire for tramping (hiking). Don't wear lotions or perfume in southern places like Southland, either, because they attract mosquitoes and other bugs; carry insect repellent. Sand flies seem drawn to black and dark blue colors (so they say). Bring a hat with a brim to provide protection from the strong sunlight (*see* Health) and sunglasses for either summer or winter; the glare on snow and glaciers can be intense. There's a good chance you'll need warm clothing in New Zealand no

Essentials

matter what the season; a windbreaker is a good idea wherever you plan to be.

Dress is casual in most cities, though top resorts and restaurants may require a jacket. Some bouncers for big city bars will shine a flashlight on your shoes; if you like these kinds of places bring some spiffy spats. In autumn, a light wool sweater or a jacket will suffice for evenings in coastal cities, but winter demands a heavier coat—a raincoat with a zip-out wool lining is ideal. Comfortable walking shoes are a must. You should have a pair of what Kiwis call "tramping boots," or at least running shoes if you're planning to trek and rubber-sole sandals or canvas shoes for the beaches.

🌐 Passports and Visas

For American travelers, a valid passport is required for traveling to New Zealand, but a separate tourist visa is not required for stays of less than three months. For other countries, visas might be required; check before you go. However, to enter New Zealand, your passport must be valid for at least three months after your planned departure date.

➕ Safety

New Zealand is generally safe for travelers, but international visitors have been known to get into trouble when they take their safety for granted. Use common sense, particularly if walking around cities at night. Stay in populated areas, and avoid deserted alleys. Although New Zealand is an affluent society by world standards, it has its share of poor and homeless, and violent gangs and drug problems do exist. Avoid bus and train stations or city squares and parks late at night.

Hotels furnish safes for guests' valuables, and it pays to use them. Don't show off your wealth, and remember to lock doors of hotel rooms and cars. Sadly, opportunist criminals stake out parking lots at some popular tourist attractions. Put valuables out of sight under seats or lock them in your trunk *before* you arrive at the destination.

Most visitors have no trouble and find New Zealanders among the friendliest people in the world. Nine times out of 10, offers of help or other friendly gestures will be genuine.

Women will not attract more unwanted attention than in most other Western societies, nor will they be immune from the usual hassles. In cities at night, stick to well-lighted areas and avoid being totally alone. Hotel staff will be happy to give tips on any areas to avoid and the times to avoid them. New Zealand is relatively safe for women, but don't be complacent: female travelers have been victims of sexual assault in New Zealand. Hitchhiking is not recommended, especially for solo females.

New Zealand is generally very safe and accepting for LGBTQ travelers, with the major cities in particular being very friendly and having their own vibrant communities (same-sex marriage has been legal in New Zealand since 2013). As with most countries in the world, it is smart to practice caution when in more rural areas.

💲 Tipping

Tipping is not as widely practiced in New Zealand as in the United States or Europe, but in city restaurants and hotels it's appreciated if you acknowledge good service with at least a 15% tip. Tour guides and drivers are also used to receiving some gesture, even though it isn't mandatory.

Taxi drivers will appreciate rounding up the fare to the nearest NZ$5 amount, but don't feel you have to do this. The Uber app gives an opporuntiy to tip in New Zealand (as elsewhere). Porters will be happy with a NZ$1 or NZ$2 coin. Most other people, like bartenders, theater attendants, gas-station attendants, or barbers, will probably wonder what you are doing if you try to give them a tip. The nice thing about this is good service in New Zealand is given because the person means it, not because they're aiming for a good tip.

📍 Visitor Information

Tourism New Zealand is a government agency that markets New Zealand internationally. Their North American office is in Santa Monica. They have a website (*newzealand.com*) that lists all you'll want or need to know about your New Zealand holiday. There are also 30 locally funded Regional Tourism Organizations (RTOs) based throughout the country, some of these also market internationally, and they run most of the i-SITE visitor centers. Many of these have computerized booking systems in place, so rather than driving from lodge to B&B to hotel, making inquiries, the i-SITE can be a good place to instantly discover which places are vacant. They also offer knowledgeable, independent advice about local attractions, activities, and transport. These centers are marked with blue signs and a white lowercase letter *i*.

📅 When to Go

High Season: It's best to visit from October to April, especially in alpine areas. The summer holidays (mid-December to February) can be crowded, with scarce car rentals and accommodations and expensive flights.

Low Season: June through September (winter) is the least expensive time to visit New Zealand, although flights from the United States may not be at their lowest. Prices in ski areas do remain high June through August, but accommodations on weekdays will not be hard to come by.

Value Season: March to May and September to November, fall and spring respectively, offer the best combination of temperature, weather, and moderate prices. One exception is Easter weekend, when many families take vacations.

Speak Like a Local

From the moment you begin your New Zealand (or Aotearoa, as you'll learn in the airport) adventure, you'll confront the mélange of Māori words, Briticisms, and uniquely Kiwi phrases that make the language vibrant, but perhaps a bit hard for American ears to navigate.

New Zealand is a bilingual nation, as reflected in its national anthem. Although Māori isn't a conversational language, a basic knowledge of it is essential for understanding phrases and the meaning of place-names, as well as the pronunciation of certain words or place-names.

■ TIP➜ **For a crash course in the best way to pronounce New Zealand place-names, the best thing to do is watch the weather report on the news.**

Talking Kiwi is not as daunting as Māori pronunciations for those with the English language under their belt. New Zealanders tend to use the Queen's English, colored up with their unique brand of abbreviated slang. Most Kiwi turns-of-phrase are easy to unravel—a *car park* is a parking lot, for example. Others, like *dairy* (a convenience or corner store), can be confused with American terminology. Only occasionally will you find yourself at a complete loss (with words like *jandal*, for example—Kiwi for flip-flop), and even then New Zealanders will be happy to set you right. Below are common Māori and Kiwi phrases that you'll likely hear throughout the country.

MĀORI PRONUNCIATION

Knowing how to pronounce Māori words can be important while traveling around New Zealand. Even if you have a natural facility for picking up languages, you'll find many Māori words to be quite baffling. The West Coast town of Punakaiki (pronounced poon-ah-*kye*-kee) is relatively straightforward, but when you get to places such as Whakatane,

the going gets tricky—the opening *wh* is pronounced like an *f*, and the accent is placed on the last syllable: "fa-ca-tawn-*e*." Sometimes it is the mere length of words that makes them difficult, as in the case of Waitakaruru (why-*ta*-ka-ru-ru) or Whakarewarewa (fa-ca-*re*-wa-*re*-wa). You'll notice that the ends of both of these have repeats—of "ru" and "rewa," which is something to look out for to make longer words more manageable. In other instances, a relatively straight-forward name like Taupo can sound completely different than you expected (Toe-paw). Town names like Waikanea (*why*-can-eye) you'll just have to repeat to yourself a few times before saying them without pause.

The Māori *r* is rolled so that it sounds a little like a *d*. Thus the Northland town of Whangarei is pronounced "fang-ah-day," and the word *Māori* is pronounced "mah-*aw*-dee," or sometimes "mo-dee," with the *o* sounding like it does in the word *mold,* and a rolled *r*. A macron indicates a lengthened vowel. In general, *a* is pronounced *ah* as in "car"; *e* is said as the *ea* in "weather." *O* is pronounced like "awe," rather than *oh,* and *u* sounds like the *u* of "June." *Ng,* meanwhile, has a soft, blunted sound, as the *ng* in "singing." All of this is a little too complicated for those who still choose not to bother with Māori pronunciations. So in some places, if you say you've just driven over from "fahng-ah-ma-*ta*," the reply might be: "You mean 'wang-ah-*ma*-tuh'." You can pronounce these words either way, but more and more people these days are pronouncing Māori words correctly.

MĀORI GLOSSARY
COMMON MĀORI WORDS
Aotearoa: Land of the long white cloud (New Zealand's Māori name)

Haere mai: Welcome, come here

Haere rā: Farewell, good-bye

Haka: "Dance," implies history, life-force, rhythm, words and meaning of the haka, made internationally famous by the All Blacks, who perform it before each match

Hāngi: Earth oven, food from an earth oven, also used to describe a feast

Hongi: Press noses in greeting

Hui: Gathering

Iwi: People, tribe

Ka pai: Good, excellent

Kai: Food, eat, dine

Karakia: Ritual chant, prayer, religious service

Kaumātua: Elder

Kia ora: Hello, thank you

Koha: Customary gift, donation

Kūmara: Sweet potato

Mana: Influence, prestige, power

Marae: Traditional gathering place, sacred ground

Moko: Tattoo

Pā: Fortified village

Pākehā: Non-Māori, European, Caucasian

Pounamu: Greenstone

Rangatira: Chief, person of rank

Reo: Language

Tāne: Man

Tangata whenua: People of the land, local people

Taonga: Treasure

Tapu: Sacred, under religious restriction, taboo

Wahine: Woman

Waiata: Sing, song

Waka: Canoe

Whakapapa: Genealogy, cultural identity

Whānau: Family

KIWI GLOSSARY
COMMON KIWI WORDS

Across the ditch: Over the Tasman Sea in Australia (Australians are called Aussies)

Bach: Vacation house (pronounced *batch*)

Cabbage: Stupid

Crook: Sick

Fanny: Woman's privates (considered obscene)

Footie: Rugby football

Gutted: Very upset

Kiwi: A native, brown flightless bird; the people of New Zealand; or the furry fruit

Knackered: Tired

Nappie: Diaper

Pissed: Drunk

Sealed road: Paved road

Shout: Buy a round of drinks

Sticking plaster or plaster: Adhesive bandage

Stuffed up: Made a mistake

Sweet as: All good

Ta: Thanks

Torch: Flashlight

Track: Trail

Tramping: Hiking

Whinge: To whine

Great Itineraries

Best of the North Island, 8 to 10 Days

It can be difficult to decide which island to focus on, but this much is true: each of the islands is uniquely memorable, so no matter where you go, you will bring home a story. You will find volcanic springs, worm caves, and subterranean excitement on the North Island. Most of your time can be spent exploring the busy cities and close-to-ground activities. It's generally quicker and easier to get from place to place by car. If you travel by bus, consider adding a few hours to the itinerary, since buses make frequent stops and weave in and out of towns.

Fly in: Auckland Airport (AKL)

Fly out: Auckland Airport (AKL)

DAYS 1 AND 2: AUCKLAND

After a long international flight, stretch your legs and invigorate your circulation with a walk around the city center, with perhaps stops at **Auckland Museum** and **Auckland Domain** or **Albert Park**. Head to the harbor (or "harbour") and take a ferry ride round-trip between Auckland and Devonport for a great view of the city from the water. Have an early dinner and turn in to get over the worst of the jet lag.

On your second day, you'll have more wind in your sails to explore the City of Sails. Depending on your interests, head to **Kelly Tarlton's Antarctic Encounter and Underwater World**, the **New Zealand National Maritime Museum**, the **Auckland Art Gallery**, **Weta Workshop Unleashed**, **The All Blacks Experience**, or the **Parnell** neighborhood for window-shopping. If you're feeling energetic, you can even do a bit of kayaking (or just sunbathing) at **Mission Bay** or **Karekare Beach.**

DAYS 3 AND 4: WAITOMO AND ROTORUA

Waitomo is known for what's beneath the surface—intricate limestone caves filled with stalactites, stalagmites, and galaxies of glowworms. If this is up your alley, get an early start from **Auckland** to arrive here before 11 am and sign up for a cave tour. Afterward, continue on to **Rotorua,** which seethes with geothermal activity. In the late afternoon you should have time for a walk around the town center, strolling through the **Government Gardens,** and perhaps also **Kuirau Park.** If you decide to skip the **Waitomo** worms, you can zip straight down from Auckland to Rotorua. In addition to the town proper, visit some of the eye-popping thermal areas nearby, such as **Waikite Valley Thermal Pools,** or **Waimangu Volcanic Valley**. At night, be a guest at a *hāngi*, a Māori feast accompanied by a cultural performance. On the next day, you can either see some of the outlying thermal areas or continue south to **Taupo.** Another option is to take a detour to **Hobbiton**, the movie set that stood in for the Shire in the Lord of the Ring movies, located an hour northwest of Rotorua (1½ hours north of Taupo) in the town of Matamata. Even if you're not a fan of the books or movies, it's still a magical experience to explore the Hobbit holes and have a second breakfast. **Logistics:** 3–3½ hours by car.

DAY 5: TAUPO

Midway between Auckland and Wellington, the resort town of **Taupo**, on its giant namesake lake, is the perfect base for a day full of aquatic activities. If you're at all interested in trout fishing, this is the place to do it. You can also bathe in the volcanic springs in the park that is open to the public night and day. **Logistics:** 1–1½ hours by car.

DAY 6: NAPIER

The small town of **Napier** is an art deco period piece; after a devastating Richter 7.9 earthquake in 1931, the center of town was rebuilt in the distinctive style, and it's been carefully preserved ever since. Take a guided or self-guided walk around the heritage (historically significant) neighborhood. If you have a car, drive out of town and visit one of the 30-odd wineries around **Hawke's Bay.** In the afternoon, take a drive to the top of **Te Mata Peak,** or visit nearby towns **Hastings** or **Havelock North.** Otherwise, hang out at the waterfront or visit the aquarium. **Logistics:** 1½–2 hours by car.

DAYS 7 AND 8: WELLINGTON

New Zealand's capital, **Wellington,** is a terrific walking city, and there's even a cable car to help you with the hills. The big cultural draw is **Te Papa Tongarewa**— the Museum of New Zealand, which, with five floors and great interactive activities for kids, can take a full day to explore. You may wish to spend the rest of your first day here along the waterfront, winding up with dinner in the area. Be sure to check out the entertainment listings, too; you could be in town during one of the many festivals or catch a cool local band. On your second day, explore more of the urban highlights, like the **City Gallery** and the **Museum of Wellington City & Sea,** followed by a bit of browsing on the main shopping drags or a trip up into the hills to the **Botanic Garden.** If you'd prefer more time out in the country and have a car, drive up the **Kapiti Coast** and book to visit **Kapiti Island Nature Reserve,** or sip acclaimed pinot noir in the wine center of **Martinborough. Logistics:** 4–5 hours by car.

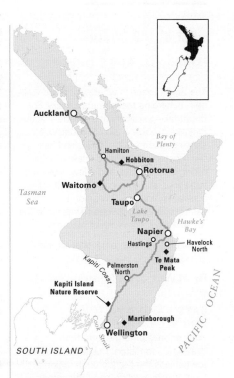

OTHER TOP OPTIONS

With at least one more day at your disposal, you could squeeze in one of the following destinations. **The Tongariro Crossing,** a challenging but spectacular daylong hike, could be added to your Taupo stay. You'll "tramp" up close to three volcanoes: **Tongariro, Ngauruhoe,** and **Ruapehu.** If you have two days and are keen on swimming with dolphins or doing some diving, loop up to **Paihia,** a small seaside town and gateway to the **Bay of Islands,** after your initial two days in Auckland. You can dip into the mellow, rural **Coromandel Peninsula,** perhaps the gateway town of **Thames,** before going south to Rotorua. Most places on the Coromandel are within 1 to 1½ hours' drive from the Thames township.

Great Itineraries

Best of the South Island, 10 to 13 Days

The South Island is where you'll find yourself recharging that camera battery. For breathtaking scenery and daredevil activities like skydiving, skiing, exotic wildlife viewing, and trekking, this island has the most to offer. Spend a few days on a biking or hiking trip, and a few days on a wine tour, and you've got yourself quite a suitable itinerary. Driving on this island can take longer between towns since the roads weave in and out of mountains.

Fly in: Wellington International Airport (WLG)

Fly out: Wellington International Airport (WLG)

DAYS 1 AND 2: PICTON AND BLENHEIM

Walk or drive onto the ferry from Wellington to Picton. This small seaside township is the Marlborough region's main commercial port and the gateway to the gorgeously scalloped coastline of **Marlborough Sounds.** Hop on a mail boat, which makes stops at coves and islands along the Sounds; take a day walk along the famous **Queen Charlotte Track** for spectacular water views; or join a kayak tour (you might just see some seals and dolphins as you paddle around). Have dinner along the foreshore and turn in early.

The next morning, head out of town to the **Blenheim** region, where the rolling hills are covered with grapevines and filled with scores of wineries. Stop in for tastings at esteemed spots like the **Seresin Estate, Cloudy Bay,** or **Allan Scott Wines**; if you've made reservations, you might also be able to dine at **Herzog** or

Hunter's Garden Cafe. Be sure to pick up a few bottles of wine and olive oil to take with you.

DAY 3: KAIKOURA

Get an early start and continue down the South Island's eastern coast to the seaside settlement of **Kaikoura,** where you can go whale-watching, reef diving, swimming with dolphins or seals, or stay on land and indulge in a big crayfish lunch ("Kaikoura" actually means "meal of crayfish" in the Māori language). **Logistics:** 1–3 hours by car.

DAYS 4 AND 5: CHRISTCHURCH

Three significant earthquakes rocked **Christchurch,** the South Island's largest city, in 2010 and 2011. The city center and some outlying suburbs were significantly damaged and are still in the process of being rebuilt. Nevertheless, "The Garden City" still lives up to its name: after you arrive from Kaikoura, spend the afternoon strolling around 395-acre **Hagley Park** and the neighboring **Christchurch Botanic Gardens,** a sprawling wonderland with more than 10,000 exotic and indigenous plants. Or take a punt on the meandering **Avon River,** followed by a coffee at a local café. For a two-day stay, fit in a couple of hours at the **International Antarctic Centre,** or spend the day in **Akaroa,** swimming with the endangered Hector's dolphins or enjoying the French-influenced atmosphere. The next morning, get an early start to make the push to Queenstown. **Logistics:** 2 hours from Kaikoura.

DAYS 6 THROUGH 8: QUEENSTOWN

Depending on your appetite for adventure, **Queenstown** may be the focus of your South Island trip. Take the plunge with **AJ Hackett Bungy,** free-fall on the **Shotover Canyon Swing,** try a jet boat ride, or go rafting. As the town is set on **Lake Wakatipu** with the jagged peaks of the **Remarkables** mountains around it, you won't lack for scenic distractions. If you're interested in the area's gold-mining history, detour to nearby **Arrowtown** and see the **Lake District Museum & Gallery.** If the area looks familiar, you're not dreaming: many scenes from the Lord of the Rings film trilogy were shot here. **Logistics:** 5–6 hours by car.

DAYS 9 AND 10: FIORDLAND NATIONAL PARK

Follow your extreme sports adventure with some extremely splendid landscapes. At **Milford and Doubtful sounds** in **Fiordland National Park,** deep green slopes fall steeply down to crystalline waters. Rare species live in the unique underwater environment here, so try to visit the **Milford Deep Underwater Observatory.** Drink in the views by catamaran, by kayak, or by flightseeing. Whatever you do, don't forget your rain gear and bug repellent! If pressed, you could visit Milford Sound, a long day's trip from Queenstown.

■TIP➔ **The road to Milford Sound can be a bit precarious. You can get more out of taking a bus through Fiordland National Park as the bus driver also serves as a tour guide and stops at various attractions. The bus trip is 4–5 hours, and you can ogle the mountains from the windows.**

OTHER TOP OPTIONS

With more time in your schedule, build in a couple of low-key days to offset the thrills-and-chills outdoor activities. After you arrive at Picton, you can drive or take a bus to Nelson, a relaxed waterfront town that's a good base for arts-and-crafts shopping and wine tasting. One fun stop is the **World of Wearable Art & Classic Cars Museum.** If ice is on your

mind and you're willing to brave rainy conditions, push on down the rugged West Coast, stopping at the **Pancake Rocks**—columns of limestone resembling stacks of pancakes—on your way to the **Fox** or **Franz Josef Glacier** in **Westland Tai Poutini National Park.** Their flow rates are up to 10 times the speed of most valley glaciers. (To do this, plan on three days, as it's a long drive, and you'll want at least one full day at the glaciers).

Contacts

Air

AIRPORTS Auckland International Airport. ☎ *09/275–0789* ⊕ *www. aucklandairport.co.nz.* **Christchurch International Airport.** ☎ *03/358–5029* ⊕ *www.christchurchairport.co.nz.* **Queenstown Airport.** ✉ *Sir Henry Wigley Dr., Queenstown* ☎ *03/450–9031* ⊕ *www. queenstownairport.com.* **Wellington International Airport.** ☎ *04/385–5100* ⊕ *www.wellingtonairport. co.nz.*

Boat

CONTACTS Bluebridge. ☎ *0800/844–844 toll-free in New Zealand* ⊕ *www. bluebridge.co.nz.* **Interislander.** ☎ *644/498–3302 in U.S., 0800/802–802 toll-free in New Zealand* ⊕ *www.greatjourneysofnz.co.nz.*

Bus

CONTACTS Atomic Travel. ☎ *03/349–0697 in NZ* ⊕ *www.atomictravel.co.nz.* **Bottom Bus.** ☎ *03/477–9083* ⊕ *www. travelheadfirst.com.* **InterCity.** ☎ *09/583–5780* ⊕ *www.intercity.co.nz.*

Flexipass. ⊕ *www. intercity.co.nz/bus-pass/ flexipass.* **Kiwi Experience.** ☎ *09/336–4286* ⊕ *www. kiwiexperience.com.* **Newmans.** ☎ *09/583–5780* ⊕ *www.intercity.co.nz.* **Stray Bus.** ☎ *09/526–2140* ⊕ *www.straytravel.com.*

Car

LOCAL COMPANIES New Zealand Transport Agency. ☎ *0800/822–422 toll-free in New Zealand, 06/953–6200* ⊕ *www. nzta.govt.nz.* **Smart Car Rentals.** ☎ *09/307–3553, 0800/458–987 toll-free in New Zealand* ⊕ *www. smartcarrental.co.nz.*

MAJOR AGENCIES
Avis. ☎ *09/526–2847, 0800/655–111 toll-free in New Zealand* ⊕ *www. avis.co.nz.* **Budget.** ☎ *0800/283–438 toll-free in New Zealand, 800/472–3325 toll-free in U.S. for international reservations* ⊕ *www.budget.co.nz.* **Hertz.** ☎ *0800/654–321 toll-free in New Zealand, 03/9698–2555 international* ⊕ *www.hertz. co.nz.* **Thrifty Rental Cars.** ☎ *0800/737–070 toll free in New Zealand* ⊕ *www. thrifty.co.nz.*

Train

Great Journeys of New Zealand. ☎ *04/495–0775, 0800/802–802 toll-free in New Zealand for bookings* ⊕ *www.greatjourneysofnz.co.nz.* **InterCity Travel Centres.** ☎ *09/583–5780 in Auckland, 03/365–1113 in Christchurch, 04/385–0520 in Wellington* ⊕ *www. intercity.co.nz/travel-info.*

Embassies and Consulates

CONTACTS U.S. Embassy. ✉ *29 Fitzherbert Terr., Thorndon* ☎ *04/462–6000* ⊕ *newzealand.usembassy. gov.*

Visitor Information

CONTACTS Tourism New Zealand. ✉ *501 Santa Monica Blvd., Los Angeles* ☎ *310/395–7480 in U.S., 09/914–4780 in New Zealand* ⊕ *newzealand.com.*

TRAMPING NEW ZEALAND

Tramping (hiking) in the backcountry is a sacred Kiwi pastime. Pristine coastal beaches, meandering rivers, glaciated peaks, steaming volcanoes, isolated lakes, cascading waterfalls, and lush native forest are often just an hour's drive from the major cities. You can "get amongst it" all with short walks, one-day tramps, or multiday hikes.

Many of New Zealand's best tramps are within the 13 national parks. The Department of Conservation (DOC) manages these parks and additional lands totaling over 5 million hectares, almost 30 percent of New Zealand. DOC maintains a range of tracks, walkways, huts, and campgrounds throughout these areas.

The Great Walks are the ten most renowned hiking (though one is technically a canoeing route) tracks, which traverse the country's volcanic plateau beaches, temperate rainforest, fjords, and mountain ranges. The most famous, Milford Track, is commonly called "the finest walk in the world." Collectively the Great Walks see over 86,000 trampers annually.

However, hundreds of other tracks and routes crisscross the country, ranging from grueling week-long, self-guided adventures to mellow, half-hour strolls through native bush. Often on these tracks you'll have the scenery to yourself. The range of difficulty and variety of terrain means almost anyone can experience tramping in New Zealand.

(above) Milford Track

PLANNING TIPS

■ During summer book accommodations well in advance, especially for the Milford Track.

■ DOC lowers fees from May to September. However, alpine tracks may be impassable or closed.

■ To avoid crowds, skip popular day walks such as the Tongariro Alpine Crossing over long weekends.

■ Many tracks require transport. Book in advance through local tour operators.

BEST ONE-DAY HIKES

You don't need to commit to a three-day trek in order to see New Zealand by foot. These one-day hikes will give you a sense of New Zealand's landscapes sans huts and tents.

Tongariro Alpine Crossing: Explore the central North Island's alpine scenery, steaming fumaroles, volcanic craters, and brilliant emerald lakes on the country's most popular day walk. In summer the hike is somewhat strenuous, though not technically difficult. In winter it requires high-alpine experience. Hikers generally walk from Mangatepopo to Ketetahi, with side trips to the summits of Ngauruhoe and Tongariro.

Abel Tasman National Park: The park's easily-accessible, golden-sand coastlines require limited fitness. Perhaps the best of the many day walks on the Abel Tasman Coast Track is from Totaranui to Separation Point, where seals are visible in winter and autumn. Water taxis from Marahau transport visitors to a number of different points along the track.

Fiordland National Park: There are a number of short walks from the roadside on the drive to Milford Sound. These range from easy to difficult and from 30-minutes to a day. Key Summit (medium) and Gertrude Saddle (difficult) take in some of New Zealand's most amazing mountain scenery. Don't miss Bowen Falls, an easy 30 minute walk along Milford Sound's foreshore.

Queenstown: A number of day walks start at Glenorchy at Lake Wakatipu's north end. You can access short sections of the Routeburn, Caples, and Greenstone tracks, where alpine scenery is the star. The walk to Routeburn Falls is particularly spectacular, well graded, and of medium difficulty.

(Top left) Hollyford Track, Fiordland National Park
(Right) Routeburn Falls, Mt. Aspiring National Park
(Bottom left) Anchorage Hut, Abel Tasman National Park (Opposite page) Routeburn Track

GREAT WALKS

ISLAND TRACK	DIFFICULTY	ACTIVITIES / ATTRACTIONS
LAKE WAIKAREMOANA TRACK, Te Urewera National Park (Ch. 6) 46 km (28.5mi), 3–4 days	Moderate. The toughest part is the climb from lake edge to Panekiri Bluffs. Heavy rain, mosquitoes and sandflies are common.	Much of the track runs through podocarp forest. Track condition is generally good. The best views are from Panekiri Bluffs. See a variety of birds: kaka, parakeets, paradise ducks, whiteheads, fantails, silvereyes, morepork (native owl) kiwi. Don't miss the short uphill side trip to Korokoro waterfall. Advance booking advised.
TONGARIRO NORTHERN CIRCUIT, Tongariro National Park (Ch. 6) 41 km (25 mi), 3–4 days	Moderate. Take good gear especially for the toughest section, the "Staircase." Do not attempt the track in rain or snow. Volcano erruptions are possible; stay back from steam vents.	This is one of New Zealand's best walks, with wonderful alpine and volcanic vistas, warm blue-green lakes, and steam vents, but mountains are often in heavy clouds. You'll see Mt. Ngauruhoe—a.k.a Mt. Doom in the Lord of the Rings films.
WHANGANUI JOURNEY, Whanganui National Park, near Taumarunui (Ch. 9) Full trip: 145 km (90 mi,) 5 days Short trip: 88 km (54.5 mi,) 3 days	Moderate. Those with experience can swim, canoe, and kayak. Be prepared for rain and floods.	Although a river journey, Whanganui is a Great Walk, and there is a 3-day version from Whakahoro to Pipiriki. The Whanganui river takes a twisting path to sea; en route, expect narrow gorges, high cliffs, waterfalls, and glowworm grottos. Tieke Marae has good huts and facilities, but you'll follow Māori protocol; *koha* (a gift of money) will be expected. Book trips and hire kayaks in advance from operators in Turangi, Taumaruni, or Ohakune.
ABEL TASMAN COAST TRACK, Abel Tasman National Park, near Nelson (Ch. 9) 54 km (34 mi), 3–5 days	Moderate. In autumn and winter, walking and weather conditions are good and the track is less crowded.	Follow the coast across beautiful golden-sand beaches, rocks, and regenerating rain forests (with nikau palms, ferns, and forest giants). The two estuaries are only passable around low tide. You may spot seals and penguins.
HEAPHY TRACK, Kahurangie National Park, near Nelson (Ch. 9) 78 km (48 mi), 4–6 days	Moderate. The most difficult section is between Brown and Perry Saddle huts. While normally a drier area, it does rain on the western slopes.	The track begins in dense beech and podocarp forest in north; continues up to snow tussock plateaus; and descends into palm-studded forests, rugged West Coast beaches. See birds, including kiwis and pipits, along one of the country's finest routes. This is primarily a summer route; snow can block the track in winter.

ISLAND TRACK	DIFFICULTY	ACTIVITIES/ATTRACTIONS
PAPAROA TRACK, Paparoa National Park (Ch. 9) 55 km (34 mi), 2–3 days	Moderate. Paparoa National Park averages over 200 inches of rain a year, so prepare for some wet weather and the occasional high winds.	New Zealand's newest Great Walk takes you through the Paparoa Range, past lush rain forests, limestone cliffs, and subtropical palms. Explore the area's unique mining history while enjoying gorgeous sunsets from the Moonlight Tops Hut and expansive views of the Tasman Sea. It was also designed to be equally accessible to cyclists.
ROUTEBURN TRACK, Mount Aspiring and Fiordland National Parks (Ch. 11) 32 km (20 mi), 2–3 days	Moderate. Heavy rain, clouds, snow, and ice can be factors. On mountaintops, winter avalanches are possible.	Travel in either direction through beech forest and onto exposed mountaintops for spectacular scenery. In summer flowers, many unique to New Zealand, cover the alpine slopes. You'll need good equipment to travel this route.
MILFORD TRACK, Fiordland National Park, near Te Anau (Ch. 11) 54 km (33.5 mi), 4–5 days	Moderate. There are two strenuous climbs, one with a very steep descent. It frequently rains. Beware of avalanche conditions at Mackinnon Pass in winter.	You can only hike in one direction (south to north) along New Zealand's most popular track. Clinton River (often muddy) crosses Mackinnon Pass, goes through alpine meadows, and passes waterfalls, including NZ's highest, Sutherland Falls. Thick forests bookend the track, and lots of *kea* (mountain parrots) greet trampers. Sandfly repellent is a must; book at least four months ahead.
KEPLER TRACK, Fiordland National Park, near Te Anau (Ch. 11) 60 km (37 mi), 3–4 days	Moderate. Day one includes a steep climb from lake to tops.	The hike goes through beech forests to sometimes snow-covered tussock tops with wonderful views in clear weather. Geology buffs will appreciate this trek, especially Mt. Luxmore. Detour to Iris Burn waterfall, 20-minute walk from Iris Burn hut.
RAKIURA TRACK, Rakiura National Park, Steward Island (Ch. 12) 36 km (22 mi, including road walk), 3 days	Moderate. There are two short uphill climbs. Be prepared to get muddy in the wet changeable weather. Expect mosquitoes and sand flies.	Follows the coastline through beech forest, subalpine scrub, and remote beaches. Mt. Anglem, a 3–4 hour side trip (one-way), provides wonderful views. Birdlife includes kiwi, bellbirds, *tūī*, fantails, and parakeets. You may see seals and penguins. Hut tickets are required; there's some camping. Pack extra food and insect repellent.

WHAT TO BRING

Weather in New Zealand is unpredictable to say the least, so it is extremely important to be prepared and to carry the right equipment. In the mountains you should prepare for cold, wet weather year-round; in the north you can generally travel a little lighter, but there is nothing worse than walking for five hours shivering and wet because you forgot a decent jacket.

Tramping gear is widely available throughout New Zealand for rental or purchase, but is usually more expensive than in the United States. You must declare all used camping and hiking equipment on arrival. The Ministry of Agriculture and Fisheries (MAF) will inspect and sterilize your equipment, which is usually available for immediate collection. By not declaring your gear you risk not only a hefty fine but also the fragile New Zealand ecosystem, which is extremely susceptible to invasive foreign species.

The equipment you carry and the fitness required depends hugely on where you are heading and how long and at what time of year you're going. In general you should carry:

■ A good-quality three-season hiking tent (for overnighters).

■ Tramping clothes, i.e., polypropylene underwear, fleece, etc.

■ Warm sleeping bag in the winter (year-round in the South Island).

■ Personal first-aid kit and insect repellent.

■ Topographic maps (widely available throughout the country). Though not required for the majority of marked tracks, they should be carried when venturing into the back country.

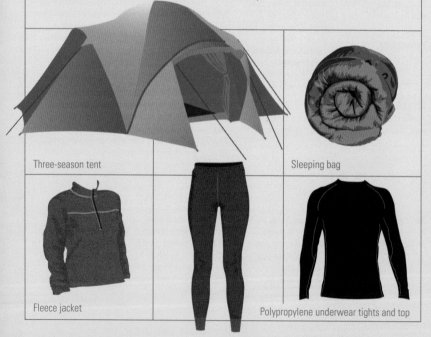

Three-season tent

Sleeping bag

Fleece jacket

Polypropylene underwear tights and top

WHAT TO WEAR

BASE LAYER: Wear lightweight thermal underwear, preferably polypropylene or other moisture wicking synthetic fabric.

MID LAYER: Fleece, wool, or synthetic jer (preferable for their lighter weight and rapid drying time) go over the base layer. This layer should keep you warm when wet (no cotton sweatshirts).

BACKPACK: Take a sturdy, comfortable pack that fits you well. Take a larger pack for longer tracks. Strong canvas fabric is best.

GAITERS: If walking through thick mud, water, or snow, tramping gaiters (covers for your shoes and pants) are a must.

The key thing to remember is layering. Wearing multiple layers of clothing allows you to rapidly adjust to changing temperatures and different exertion levels. Modern synthetic fabrics are preferable for their lightweight, quick drying times, and ability to keep you warm when wet.

HAT AND GLOVES: Bring a warm hat and gloves made from wool or synthetic.

SUN PROTECTION: Bring a sunhat and sunglasses.

OUTER LAYER: A water- and windproof outer layer is necessary. In addition to a jacket bring overtrousers for many tracks, especially in the winter.

TROUSERS/SHORTS: Strong synthetic fabrics are best because they dry quickly when wet. No jeans!

SOCKS: Wool or synthetic hiking socks to keep your feet warm.

FOOTWEAR: The most important part, boots should be strong, sturdy, and waterproof. For longer, more rugged tramps full leather boots are best, but on shorter tramps and day walks lightweight fabric boots are often sufficient.

CHOOSING YOUR TRACK

Pick your hike based on the type of experience you're looking for and the time of year you plan on visiting. The DOC has five classifications for walks to help you decide which tracks are best suited for your experience and fitness level.

Short Walks: These easy walks last up to an hour along an even, graded surface and are suitable for all fitness levels.

Walking Tracks: These easy to moderate walks take from a few minutes to a day on reasonably well-formed but occassionally steep tracks. They are clearly signposted and suitable for people with low to moderate fitness. You may need light hiking boots in winter.

Easy Tramping Tracks: These single or multiday, signposted tracks for people of moderate fitness are well formed but may be steep and muddy. Wear light hiking boots. This category includes all the Great Walks.

Tramping Tracks: Trampers need good fitness and moderate back country experience, including navigation and survival skills, to walk these challenging single or multiday unformed trails. Generally marked with poles or rock cairns, trails may include unbridged river crossings. Appropriate equipment, sturdy hiking boots, and preparation are required.

Route: You need a lot of backcountry survival and navigational experience, a high level of fitness, sturdy hiking boots and equipment, and preparation for these treks through natural terrain. Tracks may have basic markings, but trampers should be self-sufficient.

Visit DOC's information offices, in all major towns and the national parks, for information and lists of experienced guides, and to register your intentions. Inexperienced trampers should consider guided trips, which remove some of the organizational hassle and provide additional safety. Guides are generally friendly and extremely knowledgeable, and group trips are a great way to meet other travelers.

HUTS

DOC maintains a network of over 950 backcountry huts throughout New Zealand's conservation areas that are available for a small fee. Accommodations range from basic 4-person shelters offering a roof and a mattress to 20-person buildings complete with cooking facilities, toilets, lights, and heating. It's best to book huts well in advance. Book huts on the DOC Web site or by contacting the local DOC office. During the busy months custodians check for payment; however in the off season, respect the honesty system. Fees keep these places pristine and accessible to the public.

Chapter 3

AUCKLAND

Updated by
Richard Pamatatau

⊙ Sights	🍴 Restaurants	🛏 Hotels	🛍 Shopping	🍸 Nightlife
★★★☆☆	★★★★★	★★★★☆	★★★★☆	★★★★★

WELCOME TO AUCKLAND

TOP REASONS TO GO

★ **Boating and Sailing:**
Aucklanders love boating.
You can join them on a
commuter ferry, a sail-
boat, or a racing yacht.

★ **Cuisine and Café Culture:**
You'll find some of the
country's finest restau-
rants, plus bistro bars,
noodle houses, and vibrant
neighborhood eateries.

★ **Year-round Golf:**
Auckland has more than
20 golf courses, from
informal to challenging
championship level. The
Muriwai Golf Club fronts
a great surf beach.

★ **Art and Culture:** The
award-winning Auckland
Art Gallery, Auckland
Museum, theater com-
panies, and live music
scene draw crowds.

★ **Gorgeous Beaches:** The
West Coast's black-sand
beaches attract surfers
from around the world.
The safest swimming
is on the East Coast.
Takapuna Beach and
Mission Bay are good
places to swim but are
very crowded on a sunny
day. Remember to swim
between the flags and
slather on the sunscreen.

1 **City Center and
Parnell.** The main pulse
of the city is the water-
front and Queen Street.
To the east, Parnell has
historic buildings, good
restaurants, and water
views from its park "The
Domain."

2 **Ponsonby.** Explore
narrow streets lined with
wooden Victorian villas.
The main strip is lined
with hip cafés, bars,
restaurants, and local
designer clothing stores.

3 **Western Springs.** A
park and suburb west of
Auckland, as well as its
eponymous bubbling
springs, this makes a nice
retreat from the city.

4 **Devonport.** Across
Waitemata Harbour, this
suburb favored by the
well-to-do has great views
of the harbor, cafés, and a
grand dame hotel.

5 **Hauraki Gulf Islands.**
Rangitoto, Waiheke,
Rakino, and Motutapu
have great walking and
nature sites while
Waiheke offers wineries,
restaurants, and an
Easter Jazz Festival.

6 **Greater Auckland.** The
area surrounding
Auckland runs for 57
miles from north to south,
with everything from
parks and dormant volca-
nic cones to beaches and
forests.

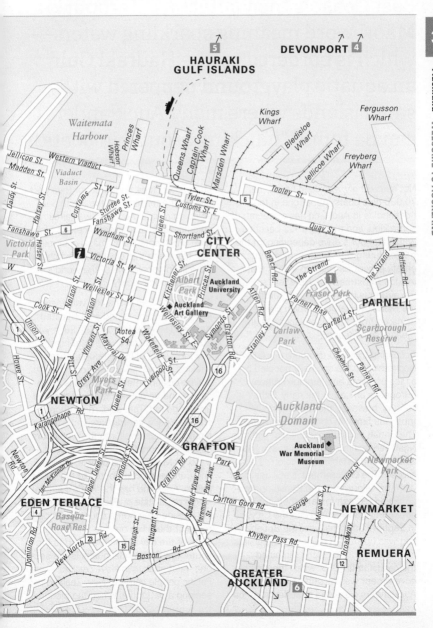

HAURAKI GULF ISLANDS 5

DEVONPORT 4

Kings Wharf

Fergusson Wharf

Waitemata Harbour

Princes Wharf

Hobson Wharf

Queens Wharf

Captain Cook Wharf

Marsden Wharf

Bledisloe Wharf

Jellicoe Wharf

Freyberg Wharf

Jellicoe St.

Madden St.

Western Viaduct

Viaduct Basin

Daldy St.

Halsey St.

Fanshawe St.

Customs St. W

Sturdee St.

Fanshawe St.

Wyndham St.

Customs St. E

Tyler St.

Tooley St.

Quay St.

6

Victoria Park W

Halsey St.

Fanshawe St.

Victoria St. W

Nelson St.

Hobson St.

Wellesley St. W

Queen St.

Shortland St.

CITY CENTER

Beach Rd.

The Strand

The Strand

Barbour Rd.

Fraser Park

PARNELL

Cook St.

Union St.

Kitchener St.

Albert Park

Princes St.

Auckland University

Allen Rd.

Parnell Rise

Garfield St.

Scarborough Reserve

1

Howe St.

Vincent St.

Pitt St.

Mayoral Dr.

Wellesley St. E

Auckland Art Gallery

Symonds St.

Stanley St.

Carlaw Park

Cheshire St.

Parnell Rd.

Aotea Sq.

Wakefield St.

Liverpool St.

16

16

Grafton Rd.

Auckland Domain

NEWTON

Grays Ave.

Myers Park

Queen St.

1

Karangahape Rd.

GRAFTON

Park Rd.

Auckland War Memorial Museum

Newmarket Park

Newton Rd.

Ian McKinnon Dr.

Upper Queen St.

Symonds St.

Grafton Rd.

Seafield-View Rd.

Claremont St.

Park Ave.

Carlton Gore Rd.

George St.

Morgan St.

Titoki St.

NEWMARKET

EDEN TERRACE

4

Basque Road Res.

New North Rd.

23

Burleigh St.

15

Nugent St.

Boston Rd.

1

Khyber Pass Rd.

Broadway

12

REMUERA

Dominion Rd.

GREATER AUCKLAND

6

i

Auckland is called the City of Sails, and visitors flying in will see why. On the East Coast is the Waitemata Harbour—a Māori word meaning sparkling waters—which is bordered by the Hauraki Gulf, an aquatic playground peppered with small islands where many Aucklanders can be found "mucking around in boats."

Not surprisingly, Auckland has some 70,000-plus boats. About one in four households in Auckland has a seacraft of some kind, and there are 102 beaches within an hour's drive depending on the traffic; during the week many are quite empty except for the two weeks that include Christmas and New Year's. Even the airport is by the water; it borders the Manukau Harbour, which also takes its name from the Māori language and means "solitary bird."

According to Māori tradition, the Auckland isthmus was originally peopled by a race of giants and fairy folk. When Europeans arrived in the early 19th century, however, the Ngāti-Whātua tribe was firmly in control of the region. The British began "negotiations" with the Ngāti-Whātua in 1840 to purchase the isthmus and establish the colony's first capital. (The Government is still dealing with the fallout from the British negotiations and redress for land theft continues between Ngāti-Whātua and the Crown.) In September of that year the British flag was hoisted to mark the township's foundation, and Auckland remained the capital until 1865, when the seat of government was moved to Wellington. Aucklanders expected to suffer from the

shift; it hurt their pride but not their pockets. As the terminal for the South Sea shipping routes, Auckland was already an established commercial center. Since then urban sprawl and massive immigration has made this city of approximately 1.6 million people one of the world's largest geographically.

A couple of days in the city will reveal just how developed and sophisticated Auckland is—the Mercer City Survey 2018 saw it ranked as the third-highest city for quality of life—though those seeking a New York in the South Pacific will be disappointed. Auckland is more get-up and go-outside than get-dressed-up and go-out. That said, most shops are open daily, central bars and a few nightclubs buzz well into the wee hours, especially Thursday through Saturday, and a mix of Māori, Pacific people, Asians, and Europeans contributes to the cultural milieu. Auckland has the world's largest single population of Pacific Islanders living outside their home countries, though many of them live outside the central parts of the city and in Manukau to the south. The Samoan language is the second most spoken in New Zealand. Most Pacific people came to New Zealand seeking a better life. When the plentiful, low-skilled work that attracted them dried up, the dream soured, and the population has suffered with poor health and education. Luckily, policies are now addressing that, and change is slowly coming. The Pacifica Festival in March is the region's biggest cultural event, attracting thousands to Western Springs with fantastic food, stunning performances, and art and craft from the region. The annual Pacific Island Secondary Schools' Competition, also in March, sees young Pacific Islander and Asian students compete in traditional dance, drumming, and singing. This event is open to the public.

At the geographical center of Auckland city is the 1,082-foot Sky Tower, a convenient landmark for those exploring on foot and some say a visible sign of the city's naked aspiration. The Waitemata Harbour has become better known since New Zealand staged its first defense of the America's Cup in 2000 and the successful Louis Vuitton Pacific Series in early 2009. The first regatta saw major redevelopment of the waterfront and more work is currently underway with the Cup challenge being held in 2021. The area, where many of the city's most popular bars, cafés, and restaurants are located, is now known as Viaduct Basin or, more commonly, the Viaduct. A recent expansion has created another area, Wynyard Quarter, which is packed with eateries.

GETTING ORIENTED

The drive from the airport is often slow as the city's road network is being revamped to accommodate rapid population growth. As you leave the airport, you'll pass some dramatic landscapes along with sculpture and industrial parks before you hit Auckland proper. The suburban landscape is dominated by the city's 50 or so volcanic hills. Many of these hills have been set aside as parks, some with livestock and all with great views from their summits, which can be

reached on foot. The Auckland region is geographically diverse, and Auckland city sits on an isthmus between Waitemata Harbour (to the east) and Manukau Harbour (to the southwest). At its narrowest point the isthmus is only 1 km (½ mile) wide. The Orakei and Panmure basins, which are east of the city, are actually large craters that have been invaded by the sea. There's plenty of outdoor activity on the easy rolling terrain outside the central suburban areas and in some of the city's big parks. The many islands of the Hauraki Gulf, off Auckland's East Coast, are a must; ferries go to most at least once a day.

These days, Auckland is still considered too bold and brash for its own good by many Kiwis who live "south of the Bombay Hills," the geographical divide between Auckland and the rest of New Zealand (barring Northland). "Jafa," an acronym for "just another f—ing Aucklander," has entered the local lexicon; there's even a book out called *Way of the Jafa: A Guide to Surviving Auckland and Aucklanders.* A common complaint is that Auckland absorbs the wealth from the hard work of the rest of the country. Aucklanders might reply that they produce more economic benefit than the rest of the country combined. But these internal identity squabbles aren't your problem. You can enjoy a well-made coffee in almost any café, or take a walk on a beach—knowing that within 30 minutes' driving time (depending on the traffic) you could be cruising the spectacular harbor, playing a round at a public golf course, or even walking in subtropical forest while listening to the song of a native *tūī* bird.

Planning

Getting Here and Around

AIR

Auckland International Airport (AKL) lies 21 km (13 miles) southwest of the city center, about a 30-minute drive away depending on traffic. It has adopted a "quiet airport" policy, so it doesn't use loudspeakers to announce boarding times. Look for flight info on screens, which abound.

A free inter-terminal bus links the international and domestic terminals from 6 am to 10 pm. Otherwise, the walk between the two terminals takes about 10 minutes. Luggage for flights aboard the two major domestic airlines, Air New Zealand and Qantas Airways, can be checked at the international terminal.

Air New Zealand and Jetstar, Qantas's budget airline, are the main domestic carriers serving Auckland. Air New Zealand connects with 20 domestic cities a day and makes about 10 flights a day to Australia. Jetstar also connects Auckland with many cities and complements Qantas's cross-Tasman service; Jetstar is now competing with Air New Zealand on some regional flights. It can have unpredictable service and requires check-in one hour before departure.

CONTACTS Auckland International Airport. ⊠ *Ray Emery Dr.* ☎ *09/275–0789* ⊕ *www.aucklandairport.co.nz.*

AIRPORT TRANSFERS

The SkyBus (NZ$18 one-way; NZ$32 round-trip) leaves the international terminal on a regular basis, 24 hours a day. You can request a stop at any bus stop or hotel along the 60-minute route between the airport and the Ferry Building in downtown Auckland. The bus leaves the Ferry Building at 20-minute intervals between 5 am and 6 pm, and then every 30 minutes until the morning. It's the best option if you don't need to rent a car and don't want to pay for a taxi.

Limo Hire Auckland runs between the airport and the city (NZ$350 one-way or NZ$650 return); it's an expensive but good service if you value privacy, comfort, and speed. Taxi fare to the city is NZ$90 to NZ$100. Super Shuttle has service between the airport and any address in the city center (NZ$20 per person); it's a popular service because of the cost, but it's very slow. Allow an hour's traveling time.

CONTACTS Limo Hire Auckland. ⊠ *Auckland* ☎ *09/948–2554* ⊕ *www.limohire-auckland.co.nz.* **SkyBus.** ⊠ *Auckland International and Domestic Airport, Ray Emery Dr.* ☎ *0800/759–287* ⊕ *www.sky-bus.co.nz.* **SuperShuttle.** ☎ *09/522–5100* ⊕ *www.supershuttle.co.nz.*

BUS (WITHIN AUCKLAND)

The easily recognizable red, green, and orange Link Buses circle the inner city and close suburbs every 10 minutes between 6 am and 7 pm weekdays, and then every 15 minutes until about 11:30 pm. Weekend service runs from 7 am to 6 pm. The route includes the Britomart Centre between Customs and Quay streets, Queen Street, Parnell, Newmarket (near the Auckland War Memorial Museum), Ponsonby, and Karangahape Road. The fares range from NZ$1 for the inner city to NZ$4.50 for the close suburbs. You can pay in cash using change or else buy a Hop prepay card available widely.

Auckland's bus and train network offers a joint electronic ticket. If you're not feeling intrepid, hire a car or take a taxi. For travel farther afield, Auckland Transport offers bus services as far north as Orewa on the Hibiscus Coast and south to Pukekohe. You can buy a range of day passes from the ferry office. The information office at Britomart provides maps and timetables.

CONTACTS Information Office. ✉ *137 Quay St., City Center* ☎ *09/365–9914 public service number* ⊕ *www.aucklandnz. com/visit/discover/i-SITE-Visitor-Information-Centres.*

BUS (TO AND FROM AUCKLAND)

The Sky City Coach Terminal is the hub for InterCity Coaches and Newmans Coaches. InterCity links Auckland to most other major cities at least once a day. Newmans has daily routes to Wellington daily via Hamilton and Taupo, and to Rotorua and Napier. Kiwi Experience goes to many more out-of-the-way destinations such as the East Cape; the "Funky Chicken" round-trip pass allows you to hop on and off where you please along the route. The buses depart from the Parnell office.

CONTACTS InterCity Coaches. ✉ *Auckland* ☎ *09/583–5780* ⊕ *www.intercity.co.nz.* **Kiwi Experience.** ☎ *09/336–4286* ⊕ *www. kiwiexperience.com.* **Sky City Coach Terminal.** ✉ *102 Hobson St., City Center* ☎ *09/583–5780* ⊕ *www.intercity.co.nz.*

CAR AND TAXI

Auckland traffic is unpredictable due to a road network groaning under the pressure of a rapidly growing population. An incident on any part of the road network leads to gridlock across the whole city. Local rush hours last from 5:30 to 10 am and then 3 to 7 pm, but if it's raining add an hour at least. Massive road upgrades are underway across the motorway system, so traffic can be disrupted at any time. The main motorways all have convenient city turnoffs, but watch the signs carefully. The main road into and out of Auckland is State Highway 1. Off-ramps are clearly marked. Most areas have meter parking where you can pay by credit card. Fines are hefty if you overstay your time.

Auckland taxi rates vary with the company. Most are around NZ$2 per km (½ mile), but some charge as much as NZ$4. Flag-fall, when the meters start, is usually NZ$2. The rates are listed on the driver's door. Most taxis accept major credit cards.

TAXI CONTACTS Alert Taxis. ✉ *Auckland* ☎ *09/309–2000* ⊕ *www.alerttaxis. co.nz.* **Auckland Cooperative Taxi Service.** ✉ *Auckland* ☎ *09/300–3000* ⊕ *www. cooptaxi.co.nz.* **Corporate Cabs.** ✉ *Auckland* ☎ *09/377–0773* ⊕ *www.corporatecabs. co.nz.*

FERRY

Auckland has 13 different ferry lines operated by three different companies, Fullers, Belaire, and SeaLink (the only company that carries cars). Certain destinations in Auckland, including Devonport and the Hauraki Gulf Islands, can only be reached by ferry, including popular Waiheke and its popular vineyards. Most of these services operate from the downtown Ferry Terminal building on Quay Street, but SeaLink offers ferry service from several places; always verify the starting point of the car ferry you intend to take. All the other passenger ferries operate from one of the central ferry docks.

CONTACTS Belaire Ferries. ✉ *Quay St.* ⊕ *www.belaire.co.nz.* **Fullers.** ✉ *Quay St.* ⊕ *www.fullers.co.nz.* **SeaLink.** ✉ *Quay St.* ⊕ *www.sealink.co.nz.*

TRAIN

KiwiRail, New Zealand's train operator, has a terminal and booking office at the **Britomart Transportation Centre,** on the harbor end of Queen Street. Service leaves Auckland for Wellington Monday, Thursday, and Saturday at 7:45 am and returns Tuesday, Friday, and Sunday.

CONTACTS Britomart Transport Centre. ✉ *Queen Elizabeth Sq., Queen and Quay Sts.* ☎ *0800/467–536* ⊕ *www.britomart. co.nz.*

Hotels

As New Zealand's gateway city, Auckland has most of the large international chain hotels, as well as a range of comfortable bed-and-breakfasts. Many of the large brand-name hotels cluster around the central business district (CBD), whereas B&Bs are found in trendier neighborhoods. Many of the best are in suburbs close to the city center like Devonport and Ponsonby.

November to March are the busiest months for Auckland hotels, so it pays to book by August to ensure you get your first choice. All the major hotels have parking at a price while a number of the B&Bs offer parking as part of your lodging package. Wi-Fi access is standard. B&B owners offer insider knowledge on what's best close by, and many will make reservations or other arrangements for you. Only the hotels tend to have air-conditioning, but this isn't a problem when you can fling open the windows and let in the fresh air.

Restaurant and hotel reviews have been shortened. For full information, visit Fodors.com. Restaurant prices are the average cost of a main course at dinner, or if dinner is not served, at lunch. Hotel prices are the lowest cost of a standard double room in high season, including 12.5% tax.

WHAT IT COSTS in New Zealand Dollars			
$	$$	$$$	$$$$
RESTAURANTS			
under NZ$15	NZ$15–NZ$20	NZ$21–NZ$30	over NZ$30
HOTELS			
under NZ$125	NZ$125–NZ$200	NZ$201–NZ$300	over NZ$300

Planning Your Time

You can get around city center and the suburbs close to the harbor like Ponsonby, Devonport, and Parnell, on foot, by bus, and by ferry. Elsewhere, Auckland is not as easy to explore. The neighborhoods and suburbs sprawl from the Waitemata and Manukau harbors to rural areas, and complicated roads, frequent construction, and heavy traffic can make road travel a challenge. Still it's best to have a car for getting between neighborhoods and some city center sights. What might look like an easy walking distance on a map can turn out to be a 20- to 30-minute hilly trek, and stringing a few of those together can get frustrating.

If you're nervous about driving on the left, especially when you first arrive, purchase a one-day Link Bus Pass that covers the inner-city neighborhoods and the CBD or, for a circuit of the main sights, a Discovery Pass. Take a bus to get acquainted with the city layout. Getting around Auckland by bus is easy and inexpensive. The region's bus services are coordinated through the Auckland Transport. You can buy electronic Hop cards that can be used on buses, trains, and ferries, and its website can provide door-to-door information, including bus route numbers, to most places in the greater Auckland area. Timetables are available at most information centers.

Restaurants

Princes Wharf and adjoining Viaduct Quay, an easy stroll from the city's major thoroughfare, Queen Street, offer dozens of eateries in every style from cheap-and-cheerful to super-posh. High Street, running parallel to Queen Street on the Albert Park side of town, is a busy café and restaurant strip. Vulcan Lane, between Queen and High streets, has some pleasant bars. Asian immigrants have created a market for a slew of cheap noodle and sushi bars throughout the inner city; the more crowded, the better.

Outside the city center, the top restaurant areas are a 10-minute bus or cab ride away on Ponsonby and Parnell roads. Dominion and Mt. Eden roads in the city, as well as Hurstmere Road in the seaside suburb of Takapuna (just over the Harbour Bridge) are also worth exploring. The mix is eclectic—Indian, Chinese, Japanese, Italian, and Thai eateries sit alongside casual taverns, pizzerias, and high-end restaurants.

Tours

Several companies run city orientation tours or special-interest excursions outside town.

BUS TOURS

InterCity's TravelPass (*0800/222–146*) provides set itineraries on comfortable buses and commentary on the passing scenery. For the independent traveler, the InterCity Flexipass lets you travel where and when it suits you. Based on hours of travel, it lets you hop on and off and stay as long as you like. Passes are valid for 12 months from activation.

Explorer Bus

BUS TOURS | This yellow double-decker stops at 18 city attractions; you can hop on and off anywhere along the way. Buses begin at the Ferry Building between 9 and 4 daily. Buy tickets with a range of options—such as a museum or zoo—visit from the driver, at the Fullers office in the Ferry Building, or online. ⊠ *Ferry Bldg., Queen's Wharf, 30 Custom St.* ☎ *0800/439–756* ⊕ *www. explorerbus.co.nz* ⊠ *From NZ$45; family pass NZ$100.*

Grayline Tours

BUS TOURS | If you are making Auckland your base to explore the region, Grayline offers a range of tours from a morning bus trip to see the main city sights to a trip to see Hobbiton in Matamata. If you want to venture farther afield but still return to Auckland, you can take in the sights and smells of Rotorua as well as visit glow worm caves in the Waikato region. All of these bus tours leave from Hobson Street, behind the Sky City Hotel, though complimentary hotel pick-up can be arranged. ⊠ *Sky City Coach Terminal, 102 Hobson St.* ☎ *09/583–5764* ⊕ *www.graylinetours.co.nz* ⊠ *From NZ$75.*

MĀORI CULTURAL TOURS

Potiki Adventures

CULTURAL TOURS | This company cultivates an air of intimacy with its small groups and friendly, open tour guides. You'll travel to Waiheke Island by ferry for an experience that includes a trip around the island, a visit to an ancient fortified village, a weaving demonstration, an olive oil tasting, and the chance to hear and play Māori musical instruments. Lunch is at one of the many cafés on the island. Potiki also offers customized private tours that include meeting Māori artists and visiting galleries; these tours can also include an overnight stay at a *marae* (meetinghouse). Potiki is also able to organize custom tours for groups. ⊠ *68 Ocean Rd., Waiheke Island, Hauraki Gulf Islands* ☎ *09/372–3477, 21/422–773* ⊕ *www.potikiadventures.co.nz* ⊠ *From NZ$175, excluding ferry fares.*

TIME Unlimited

CULTURAL TOURS | You'll have the time of your life on any of the tours offered by TIME Unlimited. The company integrates Māori culture with activities like kayak-fishing and trail walking and can arrange an overnight stay at a marae (meetinghouse). TIME, through its concessions with the Department of Conservation and Māori tribes, can take you to places often out of reach of other tours, and they will customize a tour to meet your specific needs and time frame. Transport is in late-model Mercedes vehicles. ⊠ *17b Farnham St.,*

Parnell ☎ 09/846–3469, 027/846–369 ⊕ www.newzealandtours.travel ✉ From NZ$275.

WILDERNESS TOURS
Bush and Beach Ltd.
ADVENTURE TOURS | Whether you are a Lord of the Rings fan, an outdoor adventurer, or a wine buff, you'll find something from Bush and Beach to meet your needs and time frame. Tours range from a quick-ish tour of Lord of the Rings Hobbiton set to a full-day excursion that includes the rain forest plus black-sand West Coast beaches, wineries, and a visit to where Jane Campion's *The Piano* was filmed. There are also tours of Great Barrier Island in the Hauraki Gulf. Custom tours are also available. ⊠ *Auckland* ☎ 09/837–4130 ⊕ www.bushandbeach. co.nz ✉ From NZ$80.

WINE TOURS
Fine Wine Tours
SPECIAL-INTEREST TOURS | The five-hour West Auckland tour takes in several wineries and includes lunch at one of them and, weather permitting, a visit to a black-sand beach. The full-day Waiheke Island tour covers a number of wineries and lunch. Tour host Phil Parker is an authority on New Zealand wines, and he has published a guide to the country's wine regions. Custom tours can be arranged. You will be picked up and delivered back to your accommodation. ⊠ *Auckland* ☎ 09/845–6971, 21/626–529 ⊕ www.insidertouring.co.nz ✉ From NZ$159 per person.

NZWinePro Auckland Wine Tours
SPECIAL-INTEREST TOURS | This company offers tours for those who are pushed for time with a four-hour tour to an all-day experience that mixes wine tasting with views and nature. Depending on your taste and time, your host will take you to the wine-growing areas to Auckland's north and west, plus Waiheke Island. If you are interested in a particular variety, a tour can be customized. There's even an "on the way to the airport" visit to a well-known winery that takes three hours. The Matakana Coastal Getaway Wine Tour is popular with its inclusion of cheese, chocolate, and a visit to an ancient tree. ⊠ *417a Tamaki Dr.* ☎ 09/575–1958, 21/464–469 ⊕ www. nzwinepro.co.nz ✉ From NZ$75.

Visitor Information

Need some travel advice? Drop in at one of Auckland's many i-SITEs and other visitor centers. Employees will help plan trips, provide sightseeing information, and point you toward a well-priced lunch.

CONTACTS Auckland International Airport Visitor Centre. ⊠ *Ray Emery Dr., next to arrivals exit, ground fl., International terminal* ☎ 09/275–0789 ⊕ www.aucklandiste.com. **Auckland i-SITE Visitor Centre.** ⊠ *Atrium, Sky City, Victoria and Federal Sts.* ☎ 09/365–9918 ⊕ www.aucklandiste.com.

When to Go

Auckland's weather can be unpredictable, but don't let that put you off. There is always something to do whatever the weather. The warmest months are December through April and a sun hat is a good idea. Winter is between July and October. It can be humid in summer and quite chilly in winter. It often rains, so be prepared.

City Center and Parnell

Auckland's city center includes the working port area, much of it reclaimed from the sea in the latter half of the 19th century. While it's easy to walk around this area, some of the best views can be marred by the container and car import terminal, which is behind a large red iron fence. Successive city administrators neglected Auckland's older buildings, too, so Queen Street and its surroundings are a mix of glass-tower office buildings and a dwindling number of older, some say more gracious, properties. Tucked away on Lorne and High streets, running parallel with Queen Street, are good examples of the city's early architecture, now home to the shops of some of New Zealand's leading fashion designers. The central business district (CBD) has been energized by a residential surge since the late 1990s and a move to create pedestrian-friendly strips, which is boosted by apartment development and an influx of Asian students. The Auckland Domain and Parnell areas have the city's preeminent museums and art gallery as well as historic homes and shops. Parnell was Auckland's first suburb, established in 1841, and is a good place to look for arts and crafts or to sample some of Auckland's most popular cafés, bars, and restaurants.

A dozen "city ambassadors" patrol the city center on weekdays between 8:30 and 5, providing directions and answering questions. They're identified by their yellow-and-gray uniforms with "ambassador" written on their tops in red.

 Sights

Albert Park
CITY PARK | FAMILY | These 15 acres of formal gardens contain a mix of established and seasonal plantings, a fountain, and statue- and sculpture-studded lawns. They are a favorite of Aucklanders, who pour out of nearby office buildings and two adjacent universities to eat lunch and lounge under trees on sunny days. Good cafés at the universities serve well-priced takeout food and coffee. The park is built on the site of an 1840s–50s garrison, which kept settlers apart from neighboring Māori tribes. On the park's east side, behind Auckland University's general library, are remnants of stone walls with rifle slits. The park is home to festivals throughout the summer and the Auckland Art Gallery is on its edge.

✉ Bounded by Wellesley St. W., Kitchener St., Waterloo Quad, City Center ⛝ Free.

★ Auckland Art Gallery Toi o Tāmaki
ART MUSEUM | The modernist addition to the Auckland Art Gallery has breathed life and light into a structure built in the 1880s. The soaring glass, wood, and stone addition, which some say looks like stylized trees, both complements and contrasts with the formal château-like main gallery. A courtyard and fountain space at the front is home to ever-changing works. The gallery, adjacent to Albert Park, has some 15,000 items dating from the 12th century but also shows innovative and challenging contemporary art that draws big crowds. Historic portraits of Māori chiefs by well-known New Zealand painters C.F. Goldie and Gottfried Lindauer offer an ethnocentric view of people once seen as fiercely martial. Goldie often used the same subject repeatedly—odd, considering his desire to document what he considered a dying race. New Zealand artists Frances Hodgkins, Doris Lusk, and Colin McCahon are also represented here, and there are shows and performances. The gallery has made a tilt to offering more international exhibitions so check with the website for the latest show. Free collection tours are given at 11:30 and 1:30. The café is hip and busy, and the gift shop offers a range of books, original artworks, and keepsakes. ✉ 5 Kitchener St., at Wellesley St. E., City Center ☎ 09/379–1349 ⊕ www. aucklandartgallery.com ⛝ Free, except for special exhibits.

Auckland Domain
CITY PARK | FAMILY | Saturday cricketers, Sunday picnickers, and any-day runners are some of the Aucklanders who enjoy this rolling, 340-acre park—not to mention loads of walkers, often with dogs. Running trails range from easy to challenging, and organized 10-km (6-mile) runs occur throughout the year. The Domain contains some magnificent sculpture as well as the domed

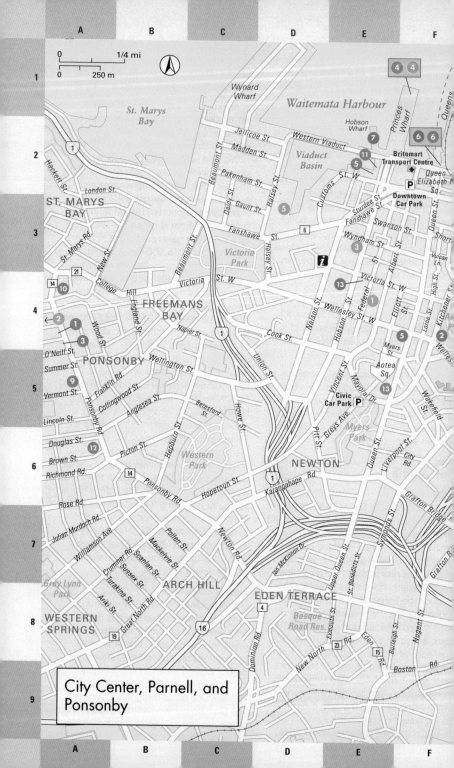

City Center, Parnell, and Ponsonby

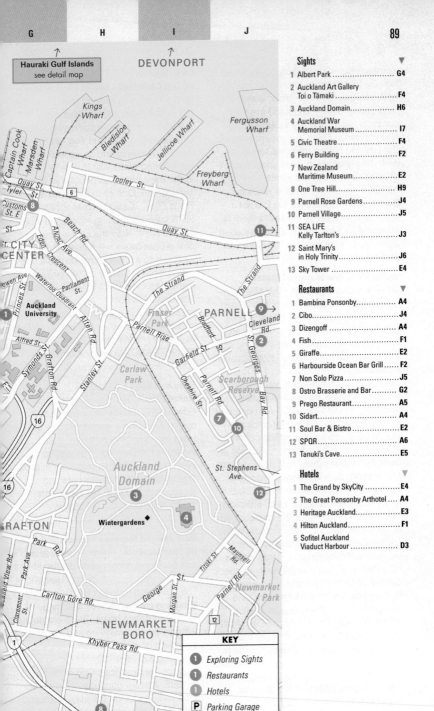

Sights ▼

1 Albert Park **G4**
2 Auckland Art Gallery
  Toi o Tāmaki **F4**
3 Auckland Domain................. **H6**
4 Auckland War
  Memorial Museum **I7**
5 Civic Theatre **F4**
6 Ferry Building **F2**
7 New Zealand
  Maritime Museum................. **E2**
8 One Tree Hill...................... **H9**
9 Parnell Rose Gardens............**J4**
10 Parnell Village......................**J5**
11 SEA LIFE
  Kelly Tarlton's **J3**
12 Saint Mary's
  in Holy Trinity......................**J6**
13 Sky Tower **E4**

Restaurants ▼

1 Bambina Ponsonby................ **A4**
2 Cibo.................................**J4**
3 Dizengoff **A4**
4 Fish **F1**
5 Giraffe..............................**E2**
6 Harbourside Ocean Bar Grill **F2**
7 Non Solo Pizza **J5**
8 Ostro Brasserie and Bar.......... **G2**
9 Prego Restaurant.................. **A5**
10 Sidart................................ **A4**
11 Soul Bar & Bistro **E2**
12 SPQR **A6**
13 Tanuki's Cave.......................**E5**

Hotels ▼

1 The Grand by SkyCity **E4**
2 The Great Ponsonby Arthotel **A4**
3 Heritage Auckland.................**E3**
4 Hilton Auckland.................... **F1**
5 Sofitel Auckland
  Viaduct Harbour **D3**

KEY

1 *Exploring Sights*
1 *Restaurants*
1 *Hotels*
P *Parking Garage*
i *Tourist Information*

Wintergardens (open daily 10–4), which houses tropical and seasonally displayed hothouse plants. In summer, watch the local paper for free weekend-evening concerts, which usually include opera and fireworks. There are superb views of the city and harbor from the top of the park. Take a bottle of wine and a basket of goodies and join the locals—up to 300,000 per show. ■TIP➔ While the Domain is safe during the day it is not a place to be at night unless you're there for a concert with a big crowd. ⊠ Entrances at Stanley St., Park Rd., Carlton Gore Rd., and Maunsell Rd., Parnell.

★ Auckland War Memorial Museum

HISTORY MUSEUM | FAMILY | The Māori artifact collection here is one of the largest in the world, housed in a Greek Revival building in one of the city's finest parks, with views to match. Must-sees include a fine example of a pātaka (storehouse), a fixture in Māori villages, and Te Toki a Tapiri, the last great Māori waka (canoe). Made of a single log and measuring 85 feet long, it could carry 100 warriors, and its figurehead shows tremendous carving. To learn more about Māori culture, attend one of the performances, held at least three times daily, that demonstrate Māori song, dance, weaponry, and the haka (a ceremonial dance the All Blacks rugby team has adopted as an intimidating pregame warm-up). The museum also holds an exceptional collection of Pacific artifacts and hosts high-quality visiting or issue-specific exhibitions. If you want a bit of talk and music in the evening check out the once-a-month panel discussion followed by live music known as Late at the Museum. The museum is also home to two cafés. On Anzac Day (April 25), thousands gather in front of the museum in a dawn service to recognize the gallantry of the country's servicemen and-women. ⊠ Auckland Domain, Park Rd., Parnell ☎ 09/309–0443 ⊕ www. aucklandmuseum.com ⬙ NZ$28.

Civic Theatre

NOTABLE BUILDING | FAMILY | This extravagant art nouveau movie theater was the talk of the town when it opened in 1929, but nine months later the owner, Thomas O'Brien, went bust and fled, taking the week's revenues and an usherette with him. During World War II, a cabaret show in the basement was popular with Allied servicemen. One of the entertainers, Freda Stark, is said to have appeared regularly wearing nothing more than a coat of gold paint. Now the café at the front of the Civic bears her name. When you sit down to a show or movie you'll see a simulated night sky on the ceiling and giant lions with lights for eyes on stage. The theater is host to an ever-changing roster of movie premieres, intimate rock concerts, live theater, and dance parties. ⊠ Queen and Wellesley Sts., City Center ☎ 09/309–2677 ⊕ www.aucklandlive. co.nz/venue/the-civic.

Ferry Building

MARINA/PIER | This magnificent 1912 Edwardian building continues to stand out on Auckland's waterfront. It's still used for its original purpose, launching ferries to Devonport as well as to Waiheke and other Hauraki Gulf islands. The building also houses bars and restaurants. ⊠ Quay St., City Center ⊕ nzhistory.govt.nz/media/photo/ auckland-ferry-building-and-tees.

New Zealand Maritime Museum

HISTORY MUSEUM | FAMILY | New Zealand's rich seafaring history is on display at this marina complex on Auckland Harbour. The collection includes Pacific and Māori seagoing canoes as well as a range of European sailing boats. There are detailed exhibits on early whaling and a superb collection of yachts and ship models, including KZ1, the 133-foot racing sloop built for the America's Cup challenge in 1988. A scow conducts short harbor trips twice a day on Tuesday, Thursday, and weekends, and there's a wharf-side eatery. ⊠ Eastern Viaduct, Quay St., City

Did You Know?

Although the Ferry Building was built in the Edwardian style, a new section of piers evokes a ship anchored behind the original structure. Look for the curved sail-shape roof and smokestack-like turrets.

One of the best walks to take in Auckland is to the summit of One Tree Hill, an extinct volcano and the site of three Māori pā (fortifications).

Center ☎ *09/373–0800* ⊕ *www.maritimemuseum.co.nz* ✉ *NZ$53.*

One Tree Hill

VIEWPOINT | FAMILY | The largest of Auckland's extinct volcanoes and one of the best lookout points, One Tree Hill, or Maungakiekie, was the site of three Māori *pā* (fortifications). It used to have a single pine tree on its summit, but that was attacked several times by activists who saw it as a symbol of colonialism, and in 2000 it was taken down. Sir John Logan Campbell, the European founding father of the city, is buried on the summit. There is fantastic walking and running in the surrounding acreage known as Cornwall Park, with avenues of oaks, a kauri plantation, and an old olive grove. Or just take a mat and read under an old tree. Free electric barbecue sites are also available. Because the park is a working farm of sheep and cattle, you'll need to be wary of cows with their calves along the paths. There's also a cricket club with old-style seating, where you can watch a game in summer, and a pavilion where you can buy refreshments. ✉ *Greenlane Rd. W, Parnell* ☎ *9/630–8485* ⊕ *www.cornwallpark.co.nz.*

Parnell Rose Gardens

GARDEN | FAMILY | When you tire of boutiques and cafés, take 10 minutes (or more) to gaze upon and sniff this collection of some 5,000 rosebushes. The main beds contain mostly modern hybrids, with new introductions planted regularly. The adjacent **Nancy Steen Garden** has antique varieties. And don't miss the incredible trees. There is a 200-year-old *pohutukawa* (puh-hoo-too-*ka*-wa), whose weighty branches touch the ground and rise up again, and a *kanuka* that is one of Auckland's oldest trees. In summer it's a popular site for wedding photographs. ✉ *85 Gladstone Rd., Parnell* ✉ *Free.*

Parnell Village

NEIGHBORHOOD | The lovely Victorian timber villas along the upper slope of Parnell Road have been transformed into antiques shops, designer boutiques, cafés, and restaurants. Parnell Village is the creation of Les Harvey, who saw the potential of the old, rundown shops and houses and almost single-handedly snatched them from the jaws of the developers' bulldozers in the early 1960s by buying them, renovating them, and leasing them out. Today, this village of trim pink-and-white timber facades is one of the most delightful parts of the city. At night, the area's restaurants and bars attract Auckland's well-heeled set. ✉ *Parnell Rd. between St. Stephen's Ave. and Augustus Rd., Parnell* 🌐 *www.parnell.net.nz.*

St. Mary's in Holy Trinity

CHURCH | This Gothic Revival wooden church was built in 1886 by the early Anglican missionary Bishop Selwyn. The craftsmanship inside the kauri church is remarkable, down to the hand-finished columns. One of the carpenters left his trademark, an owl, sitting in the beams to the right of the pulpit. If you stand in the pulpit and clasp the lectern, you'll feel something lumpy under your left hand—a mouse, the trademark of another of the craftsmen who made the lectern, the so-called Mouse Man of Kilburn. The story of the church's relocation is also remarkable. St. Mary's originally stood on the other side of Parnell Road, and in 1982 the entire structure was moved across the street to be next to the new church, the Cathedral of the Holy Trinity. ✉ *Parnell Rd. and St. Stephen's Ave., Parnell* 🌐 *www.holy-trinity.org.nz* 🎫 *Free.*

★ SEA LIFE Kelly Tarlton's

AQUARIUM | **FAMILY** | This harborside marine park—the creation of New Zealand's most celebrated undersea explorer and treasure hunter—offers a fish's-eye view of the sea. A transparent tunnel, 120 yards long, makes a bewitching circuit past moray eels, lobsters, sharks, and stingrays. You can also have an encounter with King and Gentoo penguins and their keepers in their icy abode, and take home photos to prove it. This attraction is popular and limited to four people a day so it pays to book ahead. ✉ *Orakei Wharf, 23 Tamaki Dr., 5 km (3 miles) east of downtown Auckland, Auckland* ☎ *09/531–5065* 🌐 *www.kellytarltons.co.nz* 🎫 *NZ$41* 🕓 *Closed Tues. and Wed.*

Sky Tower

OBSERVATORY | **FAMILY** | This 1,082-foot beacon is the first place many Aucklanders take visiting friends to give them a view of the city. Up at the main observation level, glass floor panels let you look past your feet to the street hundreds of yards below. Adults step gingerly onto the glass, while kids delight in jumping up and down on it. Through glass panels in the floor of the elevator you can see the counterweight of the **Sky Jump,** a controlled leap off the 630-foot observation deck that provides an adrenaline rush. ✉ *Victoria and Federal Sts., City Center* ☎ *09/912–6000* 🌐 *www.skycity.co.nz* 🎫 *NZ$32.*

🍴 Restaurants

★ Cibo

$$$$ | **MODERN NEW ZEALAND** | When you are in the mood for superb food without any drama head to Cibo. The name means "good food" in Italian, and it is apt for this restaurant, which has been around for more than 20 years. **Known for:** exceptional wine list; the best place for a long lunch; excellent innovative Italian food. [$] *Average main: NZ$50* ✉ *91 St. Georges Bay Rd., Parnell* ☎ *09/303–9660* 🌐 *www.cibo.co.nz* 🕓 *Closed Sun. and Mon. No lunch Sat.*

★ Fish

$$$$ | **NEW ZEALAND** | This light-filled restaurant with floor-to-ceiling glass looks across the harbor to trendy Devonport and the Bayswater boat marina. The menu is based on high-quality fresh local produce, particularly fish and meat cooked to perfection. **Known for:** excellent views; superb seasonal and local dishes; bright and buzzy ambience. [$] *Average main: NZ$50* ✉ *Hilton Auckland,*

New Zealand Snacks 🍴

Hokey-Pokey Ice Cream. Go for the full-fat version of this vanilla ice cream dotted with toffee bits.

Kūmara Fries. Packed with potassium and fiber, *kūmara* fries are guilt-free delicious snacks. The kūmara, or sweet potato, has a rich heritage as a Māori food staple. Red, gold, and orange varieties are plentiful in New Zealand today. Orange is the sweetest, especially good fried and served with sweet chili sauce and sour cream. These fries are soft rather than crunchy.

Pavlova. Like the ballerina for whom it was named, this national dessert is feather light—a meringue topped with fruit, sauce, and fresh cream. The confection is essentially hollow, but it forms the tough core of one of the many Kiwi and Aussie rivalries: who invented it and named it after Anna Pavlova? So far, Kiwis have the edge: their recipe predates the Australian one by six years.

Whitebait Fritters. The Kiwi passion for this seafood, a smeltlike fish caught as juveniles as they head upriver to spawn, is so intense that the media reports the start of whitebait season. Find the pancake-size fritters at markets or as a daily special in cafés. Strict controls and high demand make it a delicious and pricey delicacy.

Princes Wharf, 147 Quay St., City Center ☎ 09/978–2000 🌐 www.fishrestaurant.co.nz.

★ Giraffe

$$$$ | NEW ZEALAND | FAMILY | Located in the buzzy heart of the Viaduct, Giraffe unites the best local foods with flair and fun. It's open from breakfast until late and whether you are a meat eater or a vegan, the menu will leave you satisfied. **Known for:** relaxed atmosphere with great service; regularly changing menu of high-quality food; locally focused wine list. [$] *Average main: NZ$50 ✉ Viaduct Harbour, City Center ☎ 09/358–1093 🌐 www.girafferestaurant.co.nz.*

Harbourside Ocean Bar Grill

$$$$ | SEAFOOD | Overlooking the water from the upper level of the restored Ferry Building, this seafood restaurant is an Auckland institution that draws foodies and families alike. It serves seasonal New Zealand seafood on a menu that references a number of cuisine styles. **Known for:** stunning harbor views; high-quality seafood; unique and tasty meat options, including venison. [$] *Average main: NZ$50 ✉ Ferry Bldg., Quay St., City Center ☎ 09/307–0486 🌐 www.harbourside.co.*

Non Solo Pizza

$$$$ | ITALIAN | FAMILY | If you've had a busy day and want to roll on and be surrounded by animated diners this place is for you. The food can be ordered individually or with bowls to be shared by the table. **Known for:** fabulous desserts; delicious pizza; great range of pastas. [$] *Average main: NZ$45 ✉ 259 Parnell Rd., Parnell ☎ 09/379–5358 🌐 www.nonsolopizza.co.nz ⏲ Closed Mon.*

Ostro Brasserie and Bar

$$$$ | MODERN NEW ZEALAND | Housed in the artfully renovated Seafarers Building overlooking the harbor, Ostro has a buzzy bar, superb food, and some of the best people-watching in Auckland. Enjoy lunch, dinner, or something in-between in a relaxed brasserie style. **Known for:** waterfront views; seasonal menu of New Zealand classics; excellent wine list. [$] *Average main: NZ$50 ✉ Seafarers*

Bldg., Tyler St., Auckland ☎ *09/302–9888* ⊕ *www.seafarers.co.nz.*

★ Soul Bar & Bistro

$$$$ | NEW ZEALAND | There's always something to see at the Soul Bar and Bistro, which fronts the Viaduct Basin on the harbor. The menu is modern with a traditional twist and changes to match the season, but you will always find something good, whether your interest is in fresh fish, meat, or something from the plant family. **Known for:** outside seating on terrace; sensational wine list; hip atmosphere. $ *Average main: NZ$60* ⊠ *Viaduct Harbour, City Center* ☎ *09/356–7249* ⊕ *www.soulbar.co.nz.*

Tanuki's Cave

$$$$ | JAPANESE | A flight of dimly lighted stairs leads down to this buzzing Japanese yakitori and sake bar. The oblong bar is usually jammed with film-festival types, the young art and fashion crowd, or classical music lovers eating before a concert in the nearby Town Hall. **Known for:** hip crowds; Japanese small plates; wide range of sake. $ *Average main: NZ$40* ⊠ *319B Queen St., City Center* ☎ *09/379–5151* ⊕ *tanuki.co.nz/* ⊗ *No lunch.*

 ## Hotels

At the time of updating, several of Auckland's largest and most prominent hotels were being used as COVID-19 isolation facilities and were not available to the general public for updating. That list includes the following hotels, which Fodor's has recommended in the past: Crowne Plaza Auckland (*auckland. crowneplaza.com*), Grand Millennium Auckland (*www.millenniumhotels.com*), the Pullman Auckland (*pullman.accor. com*), and the Stamford Plaza (*www. stamford.com.au*). It is likely that these hotels will reopen to regular guests in early 2022, when quarantine requirements are lifted in New Zealand, though it is uncertain at this writing when the reopening might happen.

The Grand by SkyCity

$$$ | HOTEL | FAMILY | A bonus of staying at this central city hotel is the specially commissioned artwork by top New Zealand artists hanging in the soaring lobby. **Pros:** gorgeous design throughout; close to the city center; excellent restaurants. **Cons:** noisy at night; can be busy with conferences; expensive valet parking. $ *Rooms from: NZ$250* ⊠ *90 Federal St., City Center* ☎ *09/363–7000* ⊕ *www. skycitygrand.co.nz* ⤳ *316 rooms* ⦿| *No Meals.*

Heritage Auckland

$$$$ | HOTEL | FAMILY | This hotel in a former department store unites the historical with the contemporary. **Pros:** rooftop pool; close to city center; delicious restaurant. **Cons:** often busy with conference-goers; limited Wi-Fi; not all rooms have great views. $ *Rooms from: NZ$450* ⊠ *35 Hobson St., City Center* ☎ *09/379–8553* ⊕ *www.heritagehotels. co.nz* ⦿| *No Meals* ⤳ *467 rooms.*

★ Hilton Auckland

$$$$ | HOTEL | Standing on the end of Princes Wharf, the Hilton resembles the cruise ships that dock alongside it, with white walls and neutral furnishings in chic rooms that allow your eyes to drift to the great views. **Pros:** close to central city and ferry terminal; lovely views; decent on-site eating and drinking. **Cons:** wharf can be busy with revelers; ships mooring nearby can be noisy; some may find the short walk from town a hassle. $ *Rooms from: NZ$450* ⊠ *Princes Wharf, 147 Quay St., City Center* ☎ *09/978–2000* ⊕ *www. hilton.com* ⦿| *No Meals* ⤳ *201 rooms.*

Sofitel Auckland Viaduct Harbor

$$$ | HOTEL | This waterfront hotel presents the customer with both luxury and a friendly environment, as well as views of the ever-changing Viaduct Basin from some rooms. **Pros:** well situated, with waterside dining; close to Victoria Park; excellent rooms. **Cons:** no free parking; breakfast not included; Viaduct area can be noisy. $ *Rooms from: NZ$450*

✉ *21 Viaduct Harbour Ave., City Center* ☎ *09/909–9000* ⊕ *www.sofitel-auckland. com* ⇌ *172 suites* ⦿ *No Meals.*

Nightlife

COMEDY

Classic Comedy & Bar

COMEDY CLUBS | Auckland's main venue for live comedy has established itself on the international circuit with many well-known acts coming here to perform along with the best of New Zealand's rising talent. In April the venue hosts the International Laugh Festival. ✉ *321 Queen St., City Center* ☎ *09/373–4321* ⊕ *www.comedy.co.nz* ☞ *Check the website for what's on.*

 Performing Arts

MUSIC AND OPERA

Aotea Centre

CONCERTS | **FAMILY** | Auckland's main venue for the performing arts and medium-size conferences is in the center of the city and often mounts free art exhibitions in its public spaces. There is a good café on the steps leading into the main foyer. The New Zealand Opera performs three annual main-stage seasons here, accompanied by either the Auckland Philharmonia Orchestra or the New Zealand Symphony Orchestra. Check the website to find out what's on. ✉ *Aotea Sq., 50 Mayoral Dr., City Center* ☎ *09/309–2677* ⊕ *www.aucklandlive. co.nz/venue/aotea-centre.*

Auckland Town Hall

ARTS CENTERS | The New Zealand Symphony and Auckland Philharmonia Orchestras perform here in the Great Hall, which holds up to 1,529 people on three levels. Some say it has some of the finest acoustics in the world. It also features the largest musical instrument in the country, the Town Hall Organ. More intimate concerts take place in the Concert Chamber. Check the website for the latest concert schedule. ✉ *303 Queen St., City Center* ☎ *09/309–2677* ⊕ *www.aucklandlive.co.nz/venue/ auckland-town-hall.*

Civic Theatre

ARTS CENTERS | This theater hosts many performances by international touring companies and artists. Check the website for the most up to date schedule. ✉ *Queen and Wellesley Sts., City Center* ☎ *09/309–2677* ⊕ *www.aucklandlive. co.nz/venue/the-civic.*

Shopping

ART GALLERIES

Artspace

ART GALLERIES | This independent contemporary gallery shows both international and local artists plus occasionally hosts talks and seminars. The most up to date list of events and shows is on the gallery's website. ✉ *300 Karangahape Rd., City Center* ☎ *09/303–4965* ⊕ *www. artspace.org.nz.*

Masterworks

ART GALLERIES | This gallery exhibits and sells contemporary New Zealand art, glass, ceramics, and jewelry and is the place to go if you are looking for something different. Its location on Upper Queen Street is an easy walk from the center of town. Masterworks holds some 15 group and individual exhibitions a year, including student work, and will pack and ship any item purchased. ✉ *71 Upper Queen St., City Center* ☎ *09/373–5446* ⊕ *www.masterworksgallery.co.nz* ⊗ *Closed Sun. and Mon.*

BOOKS

Unity Books

BOOKS | If you are after New Zealand–related books, travel, and fiction, this is the place for you. Smart staffers will help you find that special text. ✉ *19 High St., City Center* ☎ *09/307–0731* ⊕ *www. unitybooks.co.nz.*

CLOTHING AND ACCESSORIES

★ Fingers

JEWELRY & WATCHES | This store showcases unique contemporary pieces by about 45 New Zealand artists who work with fine metals and stones to create beautiful jewelry. Many of the artists have works in the New Zealand National Collection, and customers who purchased items at an early stage of a maker's career are being rewarded with significant increases in value. Look out for works that combine precious metal with more mundane materials like rocks, seashells, or even plastic. ✉ *2 Kitchener St., City Center* ☎ *09/373–3974* ⊕ *www.fingers.co.nz.*

★ Zambesi

WOMEN'S CLOTHING | Always among the top New Zealand designers, this fashion label run by an informed family team has always charted its own course. You'll find its garments for men and women are never dated and are worn by very influential people who want a look that is both strong and understated. ✉ *56 Tyler St., near Britomart, City Center* ☎ *09/303–1701* ⊕ *www.zambesistore.com.*

SOUVENIRS AND GIFTS

★ Pauanesia

SOUVENIRS | The sign hanging above this gift shop sets the tone—the letters are shaped from *paua* shell, which resembles abalone. You'll find one-off bags, place mats, picture frames, cushions, jewelry, and many other handmade items. ✉ *35 High St., City Center* ☎ *09/366–7282* ⊕ *www.pauanesia.co.nz.*

 Activities

BOATING AND SAILING

Fullers

BOAT TOURS | To get a sense of Auckland, the Auckland skyline, and the size of Sky Tower, take a 1½-hour Auckland Harbour cruise that leaves from the Ferry Building. Commentary runs while the boat passes the Harbour Bridge, Devonport's naval base, and Bean Rock Lighthouse. There's a brief stopover on Rangitoto Island in the Hauraki Gulf. Various day tours of Waiheke Island are also available. ✉ *Ferry Bldg., 99 Quay St., Auckland* ☎ *09/367–9111* ⊕ *www.fullers.co.nz* ✈ *From NZ$68.*

★ Sail NZ

SAILING | No experience is necessary to sail on America's Cup yachts with Sail NZ. Help sail with a racing crew or relax while they do the work. For more thrills, participate in the America's Cup Match Racing trip, a two-hour experience that includes practice drills followed by a race against other yachts with a race crew. If you want a more relaxed activity, the company has a range of options that allow you to see the harbor without the pressure of racing. There are lunch and dinner options. ✉ *Viaduct Harbour, Auckland* ☎ *09/359–5987* ⊕ *www.explore-group.co.nz/en/unique-experiences/americas-cup-sail-auckland* ✈ *From NZ$190.*

BUNGY JUMPING

AJ Hackett Bungy—Auckland Harbour Bridge

LOCAL SPORTS | The only bungy (New Zealand spelling for bungee) jumping in Auckland, this company operates off the Harbour Bridge year-round. The Harbour Bridge Experience is a 1½-hour bridge climb with commentary on the history of the bridge and the region. Needless to say, views from the bridge walk are outstanding. There are three trips a day, and reservations are essential. ✉ *Westhaven Reserve, 105 Curran St., Herne Bay, Auckland* ☎ *09/360–7748* ⊕ *www.bungy.co.nz* ✈ *From NZ$104 for the walk, NZ$132 for the bungy.*

SPORTS VENUES

Eden Park

SPECTATOR SPORTS | The city's major stadium is the best place (in winter) to see New Zealand's sporting icon: the All Blacks, one of the best rugby teams in the world. More frequently, it sees

Rugby Madness

Rugby evolved out of soccer in 19th-century Britain. It was born at the elitist English school of Rugby, where in 1823 a schoolboy by the name of William Webb Ellis became bored with kicking a soccer ball and picked it up and ran with it. Rugby is similar to American football, except players are not allowed to pass the ball forward and they wear no protective gear. There's a World Cup for the sport, every four years since 1987.

Rugby developed among the upper classes of Britain, whereas soccer remained a predominantly working-class game. However, in colonial New Zealand, a country largely free from the rigid class structure of Britain, the game developed as the nation's number-one winter sport. One reason was the success of New Zealand teams in the late-19th and early-20th centuries. This remote outpost of the then British empire, with a population of only 750,000 in 1900, was an impressive rugby force, and it became a source of great national pride. Today, in a country of 4-plus million, the national sport is played by 250,000 New Zealanders at the club level.

The top-class rugby season in the southern hemisphere kicks off in February with the Super 15, which pits professional teams from provincial franchises in New Zealand, South Africa, and Australia against one another. New Zealand's matches are generally held in main cities, and you should be able to get tickets without too much trouble. The international season runs from June to late August. This is your best chance to see the national team, the All Blacks, and the major cities are again the place to be. National provincial championship games hit towns all over the country from late August to mid-October. A winner-takes-all game decides who attains the domestic rugby Holy Grail, the Ranfurly Shield. If you can't catch a live game, you can always join a crowd watching a televised match at a local pub or sports bar. There is also a growing number of women playing rugby here, including at the professional level.

the Auckland Blues, a Super 15 rugby team that plays professional franchise opponents from Australia, South Africa, and other parts of New Zealand. Cricket teams arrive in summer. For information on sporting events, check out *What's On Auckland*, a monthly guide available from the Auckland i-SITE Visitor Centre. ⊠ *Reimers Ave., Auckland* ⊕ *www.edenpark. co.nz.*

Ponsonby

Some of the city's best cafés are on Ponsonby Road. Breakfast is a specialty because of the high demand from locals looking to grab a coffee and something to eat before heading to a glass tower, media company, or studio downtown. It's difficult to single out any café as all are pretty good because the competition and expectations are high. If you are an architecture buff wander the streets and look at how smart renovation brings modern living and life to former working-class homes.

🍴 Restaurants

Bambina Ponsonby

$$$ | **INTERNATIONAL** | **FAMILY** | This café is part of the Ponsonby Road old guard and has been serving its loyal customers for over 20 years. The menu offers breakfast staples like eggs and bacon, but you can also mix it up with coconut yogurt, muesli, and superb salads at lunchtime. **Known for:** classic Auckland café experience; great coffee; fresh seasonal food. *[$] Average main: NZ$30 ✉ 268 Ponsonby Rd., Ponsonby ☎ 09/360–4000 🌐 www.bambinaponsonby.co.nz 🕓 No dinner.*

★ Dizengoff

$$ | **ISRAELI** | One of the area's most popular breakfast and lunch places, Dizengoff serves hearty Jewish (but not kosher) food to an eclectic clientele. The coffee is among the best around, and there is an ever-changing selection of New Zealand art. **Known for:** perfect chicken salad; superb scrambled eggs and veal sausages; long waits especially on weekends. *[$] Average main: NZ$20 ✉ 256 Ponsonby Rd., Ponsonby ☎ 09/360–0108 🕓 No dinner.*

★ Prego Restaurant

$$$$ | **ITALIAN** | It's no mean feat being the longest-running restaurant in Ponsonby, where the locals and their guests are fussy. The broad Italian menu includes wood-fired pizzas and good pasta. **Known for:** noisy and bustling atmosphere; great wine list; superb modern Italian food. *[$] Average main: NZ$39 ✉ 226 Ponsonby Rd., Ponsonby ☎ 09/376–3095 🌐 www.prego.co.nz.*

★ Sidart

$$$$ | **MODERN NEW ZEALAND** | This spot and its tasting menus bring modern cooking to a whole new level. The chefs take a slew of the finest ingredients and combine them in ways that will delight and astound the most jaded palate. **Known for:** beautiful city views; innovative use of produce; new recipes offered at Tuesday night test kitchen. *[$] Average main: NZ$150 ✉ Three Lamps Plaza, 283 Ponsonby Rd., Ponsonby ☎ 09/360–2122 🌐 www.sidart.co.nz 🕓 Closed Sun. and Mon.*

SPQR

$$$$ | **ITALIAN** | This former motorcycle shop is one of the best places on Ponsonby Road for people-watching. The excellent food is largely Italian, and it's known for its thin-crust pizzas. **Known for:** fun outdoor seating; excellent food and wine; hip (sometimes too hip) ambience. *[$] Average main: NZ$50 ✉ 150 Ponsonby Rd., Ponsonby ☎ 09/360–1710 🌐 www.spqrnz.co.nz.*

🛏 Hotels

The Great Ponsonby Arthotel

$$$ | **B&B/INN** | Local original art gives this villa hotel on a quiet street off Ponsonby Road a special touch. **Pros:** central Ponsonby location; friendly and relaxed atmosphere; tasty breakfast included. **Cons:** half an hour walk to the city; sophisticates may find it a bit too homey; rooms on the smaller side. *[$] Rooms from: NZ$290 ✉ 30 Ponsonby Terr., Ponsonby ☎ 09/376–5989 ✍ info@greatpons.co.nz 🌐 www.greatpons.co.nz 🍽 Free Breakfast 🛏 13 rooms.*

Western Springs

Western Springs Park is both a suburb and a park in the inner west part of Auckland. It takes its name from the lake there, fed by a natural spring. Today the park, which houses the zoo and the Museum of Transport and Technology, is home to Pacifica, the giant culture, food, and art festival that takes place in summer, generally in March. The speedway sometimes hosts rock concerts.

The lake, which is full of eels, swans, and ducks, has many surrounding paths popular with dog walkers and joggers alike. See native plants and wild fowl,

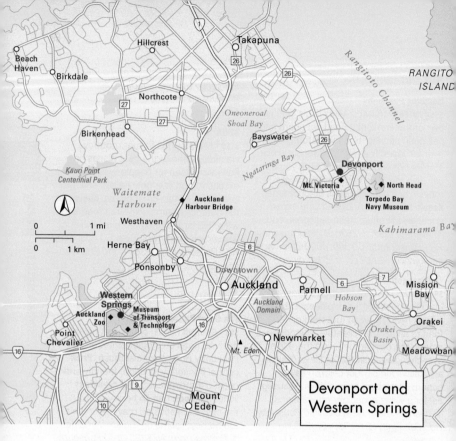

including native pūkeko, teal, Australian coot, and shovelers, around the shores and wetlands.

Across the road from Western Springs is the Chamberlain Park Golf Course, which is open to the public. Western Springs is a good place to read a book or have a picnic.

◉ Sights

Auckland Zoo

ZOO | FAMILY | Since the 1990s, this zoo, 6 km (4 miles) west of Auckland, has focused on providing its animals with the most natural habitats possible, as well as on breeding and conservation. To catch a glimpse of New Zealand flora and fauna, spend time in the New Zealand Native Aviary, where you walk among the birds, and the Kiwi and Tuatara Nocturnal

House. A number of music events are held in summer on the zoo grounds. ✉ *Motions Rd., Western Springs* ✛ *By car, take Karangahape Rd. (which turns into Great North Rd.) west out of city, past Western Springs. Take right onto Motions Rd. Buses from city stop opposite Motions Rd.* ☎ *09/360–3805* ⊕ *www. aucklandzoo.co.nz* ✉ *NZ$24.*

Museum of Transport & Technology

SCIENCE MUSEUM | FAMILY | Six km (4 miles) west of Auckland, this is a fantastic place for anyone with a technical bent. A fascinating collection of vehicles, telephones, cameras, locomotives, steam engines, and farm equipment is a tribute to Kiwi ingenuity. The aviation collection includes the only surviving Solent flying boat. One of the most intriguing exhibits is the remains of an aircraft built by New Zealand aviation pioneer

Robert Pearse. There is a reproduction of another he built in which he made a successful powered flight around the time the Wright brothers first took to the skies. The flight ended inauspiciously when his plane crashed into a hedge. But Pearse, considered a wild eccentric by his farming neighbors, is recognized today as a mechanical genius. MOTAT, as the museum is called, also has the scooter that former Prime Minister Helen Clark once rode. ⊠ *825 Great North Rd., off Northwestern Motorway (Rte. 16), Western Springs* ☎ *09/846–0199* ⊕ *www. motat.org.nz* ✉ *NZ$19.*

Activities

BIKING

★ Adventure Cycles

BIKING | This outfit can provide maps of biking routes that avoid pitfalls such as traffic and roadwork (and there's always roadwork in Auckland). Bikes can be rented for a day or a month. A full range of related gear, like panniers, helmets, and lights can also be rented. Though the company does not organize bike tours, it provides as much information as needed. ⊠ *9 Premier Ave., Western Springs* ☎ *09/940–2453* ⊕ *www.adventure-auckland.co.nz/adventurecycles* ✉ *Bike rentals from NZ$30 per day* ⊙ *Closed Tues. and Wed.*

GOLF

Chamberlain Park Golf Course

GOLF | This 18-hole public course in a parkland is a five-minute drive off the Northwestern Motorway (Route 16) from the city. It's a popular course with open fairways, controlled rough, and big old-specimen trees. The course is popular with the first tee at 6 am. Because it is publicly owned you don't need membership anywhere else to play, but call ahead to book because Chamberlain Park is busy. The club shop rents clubs, shoes, and carts. It's one of the cheapest golf courses in Auckland, and because it's on volcanic rock, the course holds up in wet weather. ⊠ *46 Linwood Ave., Western Springs* ☎ *09/815–4999* ⊕ *www.chamberlainpark.co.nz* ✉ *From NZ$30* 🏌 *18 holes, 5553 yards, par 69.*

Devonport

The 20-minute ferry to Devonport provides a fine view of Auckland's busy Waitemata Harbour. Originally known as Flagstaff, after the signal station on the summit of Mt. Victoria, Devonport was the first settlement on the north side of the harbor. Later the area drew some of the city's wealthiest traders, who built their homes where they could watch their sailing ships arriving with cargo from Europe. Aucklanders have fixed up and repopulated its great old houses, laying claim to the suburb's relaxed and moneyed seaside aura.

The Esplanade Hotel is one of the first things you'll see as you leave the ferry terminal. It stands at the harbor end of Victoria Road, a pleasant street for stopping at a shop, a bookstore, or a café; pick-up some fish-and-chips to eat under the giant Moreton Bay fig tree on the green across the street.

GETTING HERE AND AROUND

Various companies serve Waitemata Harbour; one of the best and least expensive is Fullers. The ferry terminal is on the harbor side of the Ferry Building on Quay Street, near the corner of Albert Street. Boats leave here for Devonport Monday through Thursday 6:15 am–11 pm, Friday and Saturday 6:15 am–1 am, and Sunday 7:15 am–10 pm at half-hour intervals, except for one 45-minute interval between the 9:15 am and 10 am sailings. From 8 pm Monday through Thursday and from 7 pm on Sunday they sail on the hour. The cost is NZ$12 round-trip.

FERRY INFORMATION Fullers Booking Office. ⊠ *Ferry Bldg., Quay St., Auckland* ☎ *09/367–9111* ⊕ *www.fullers.co.nz.*

Sights

Mt. Victoria

VIEWPOINT | FAMILY | Long before European settlement, this ancient volcano was the site of a Māori pā (fortified village) of the local Kawerau tribe. On the northern and eastern flanks of the hill you can still see traces of the terraces once protected by palisades of sharpened stakes. Don't be put off by its name—this is more molehill than mountain. The climb is easy and the views are outstanding. Mt. Victoria is signposted on Victoria Road, a few minutes' walk from the Esplanade Hotel. ✉ *Kerr St., Devonport* ✥ *Off Victoria Rd.*

North Head

MILITARY SIGHT | Jutting out from Devonport into Auckland's harbor, the position of an ancient Māori defense site was enough to convince European settlers that they, too, should use North Head for strategic purposes. Rumor has it that veteran aircraft are still stored in the dark, twisting tunnels under the Head, but plenty of curious explorers have not found any. You can still get into most tunnels (they're safe), climb all over the abandoned antiaircraft guns, and get great views of Auckland and the islands to the east. It's one of the best places to watch yacht racing on the harbor. North Head is a 20-minute walk east of the ferry terminal on King Edward Parade, left onto Cheltenham Street, and then out Takarunga Road. The visitor information center can say when the local folk-music club will have events in one of the old bunkers. ✉ *Takarunga Rd., Devonport.*

Torpedo Bay Navy Museum (*National Museum of the Royal New Zealand Navy*)

HISTORY MUSEUM | The role of New Zealand's navy is recognized in this small museum. Also known as Te Waka Huia O Te Taua Moana O Aoteoroa, or Torpedo Bay Navy Museum, it holds a trove of material that reflects the country from a naval perspective. You'll see not only predictable naval material like firearms, swords, and militaria but also memorabilia from those connected to the Navy. ✉ *64 King Edward Parade, Torpedo Bay, Devonport* ☎ *09/445–5186* 🌐 *www.navymuseum.co.nz* 🎟 *Free; donations welcome.*

Restaurants

Manuka

$$$ | NEW ZEALAND | FAMILY | A corner on Devonport's main street is a good place to people-watch and rest after exploring, and Manuka is a relaxed spot with wooden tables and stacks of newspapers and magazines. Wood-fired pizzas are available all day, with toppings ranging from classic pepperoni to smoked chicken, Brie, and roasted cashews. **Known for:** home-style baked goods; great coffee; delicious pizza. [$] *Average main: NZ$30* ✉ *49 Victoria Rd., Devonport* ☎ *09/445–7732* 🌐 *www.manukarestaurant.co.nz.*

Hotels

Esplanade Hotel

$$ | HOTEL | FAMILY | Commanding the corner opposite the pier, this turn-of-the-20th-century Edwardian baroque-revival hotel is the first thing you see when approaching Devonport by ferry. **Pros:** good restaurant; stunning views; charming decor. **Cons:** road access into Devonport can be slow; poor parking lot; outside environment can be busy and noisy. [$] *Rooms from: NZ$150* ✉ *1 Victoria Rd., Devonport* ☎ *09/445–1291* 🌐 *www.esplanadehotel.co.nz* 🛏 *17 rooms* 🍴 *Free Breakfast.*

Peace and Plenty Inn

$$$ | B&B/INN | FAMILY | Antiques give this lovely B&B a mix of luxury and simplicity. **Pros:** lovely environment; good location in Devonport; great breakfast. **Cons:** at least 30 minutes from the central city; accessing Devonport by car can be problematic; some may find the antiques too fussy. [$] *Rooms from: NZ$265* ✉ *6 Flagstaff*

Rangitoto Island emerged from the sea in a dramatic volcanic eruption 600 years ago.

Terr., Devonport ☎ *09/445–2925* ⊕ *www. peaceandplenty.co.nz* ➡ *7 rooms* ¶◎¶ *Free Breakfast.*

💼 Shopping

Takapuna Market
MARKET | FAMILY | The Takapuna parking lot comes alive on Sunday mornings, with organic cheese, meat, vegetables, home-made jams, small goods, and a slew of sweet and savory items from boutique bakers on sale. There's also clothing from young designers. ✉ *Corner Lake Rd. and Anzac St., Devonport* ☎ *021/127–2529.*

Hauraki Gulf Islands

More than 50 islands lie in the Hauraki Gulf, forming the Hauraki Gulf Marine Park, managed by the Department of Conservation (DOC). Many of the islands are nature reserves, like Hauturu, Little Barrier, home to endangered plants and birds, and public access to these is restricted. Others like TiriTiri Matangi

are public reserves that can be reached by ferry, and a few are privately owned. Rakino is also popular, but you will need to pack a lunch.

GETTING HERE AND AROUND
Fullers operates ferries year-round to Rangitoto daily at 9:15 and 12:15, departing the island at 12:45 and 3:30. The fare is NZ$29 round-trip; boats leave from the Ferry Building. Fullers also arranges Volcanic Explorer tours, which include a guided ride to the summit in a covered carriage. It's NZ$60 for the tour and ferry ride, and you must book in advance.

Fullers ferries make the 35-minute run from the Ferry Building to Waiheke Island from 5:30 am to 11:45 pm at a cost of NZ$36 round-trip. Return ferries leave every hour on the hour, and every half hour at peak commuter times. Buses meet ferries at the Waiheke terminal and loop the island. If you're planning on going farther afield on the island, you can purchase an all-day bus pass from Fullers Booking Office (NZ$9 to Oneroa, Palm Beach, Onetangi, and Rocky Bay), but you need to take the 10 am ferry (return time optional). Fullers also provides tours, after which passengers may use their ticket to travel free on regular island buses that day. Note that crossings can be canceled if seas are rough and that ferries are very crowded on busy holiday weekends.

SeaLink runs car and passenger ferries to Waiheke, leaving from Halfmoon Bay in the east of the city. The round-trip fare is NZ$152 per car, plus NZ$36.50 for each adult. On Waiheke you can also take a shuttle to beaches or vineyards; Waiheke Shuttles has reliable service, but it pays to book well ahead in summer.

FERRY AND BUS INFORMATION SeaLink.
✉ *Ara-Tai Dr., Halfmoon Bay, Auckland* ☎ *09/300–5900* ⊕ *www.sealink.co.nz.* **Waiheke Shuttles.** ✉ *Auckland* ☎ *09/372–2966* ⊕ *www.waihekeshuttles.co.nz.*

 Sights

Great Barrier Island
ISLAND | FAMILY | Also known as Aotea, Great Barrier Island is the largest in the gulf with a population of around 1,100, and is mostly agricultural. It's popular with surfers—particularly Awana Beach—and the population swells in summer as the boating crowd moves in, mooring in its many sheltered bays. Access is by ferry, air, or yacht. ✉ *Aotea Great Barrier, Hauraki Gulf Islands* ☎ *0800/997–222* ⊕ *www.greatbarrierislandtourism.co.nz.*

Passage Rock Wines
WINERY | On the eastern end of Waiheke Island, this vineyard in its own little valley with a view to Passage Rock has pricey and highly regarded wines. It's especially known for chardonnays, viogniers, and syrahs. The vineyard has a good bistro that is very popular with locals, but be sure to check the opening hours. Tastings are only offered in the afternoons. ✉ *438 Orapiu Rd., Waiheke Island, Ostend* ☎ *09/372–7257* ⊕ *www.passagerock.*

co.nz ⊙ *Winery closed Mon. and Tues. Bistro closed Mon.–Fri.*

★ Rangitoto Island
ISLAND | When Rangitoto Island emerged from the sea in a series of fiery eruptions 600 years ago, it had an audience: footprints in the solidified ash on its close neighbor Motutapu Island prove that Māori people watched Rangitoto's birth. It is the largest and youngest of about 50 volcanic cones and craters in the Auckland volcanic field, and scientists are confident it will not blow again. During the 1920s and '30s hundreds of prisoners built roads and trails on the island, some of which are still used as walkways. Small beach houses were erected by families in the early 20th century. Many were pulled down in the 1970s before their historical significance was recognized. Thirty-two remain, and a few are still used by leaseholders, who are allowed to use them during their lifetimes. (Afterward, they'll be relinquished to the DOC). The island's most popular activity is the one-hour summit walk, beginning at Rangitoto Wharf and climbing through lava fields and forest to the peak. At the top, walkers are rewarded with panoramic views of Auckland and the Hauraki Gulf. Short detours lead to lava caves and to the remnants of a botanical park planned in 1915. Wear sturdy shoes and carry water because parts of the walk are on exposed lava flows, which are hot in the sun. You can swim at Islington Bay and at the Rangitoto Wharf in a specially made pool. ✉ *Rangitoto Island, Hauraki Gulf Islands* ⚓ *Take the ferry from Central Auckland* ⊕ *rangitoto. co.nz.*

★ Stonyridge Vineyard
WINERY | This vineyard has followers all over the world. The Stonyridge Larose, made from the classic Bordeaux varieties, is excellent and the vintage often sells out. Reservations for lunch at the Veranda Café, which uses local produce including olive oil and wine, are essential.

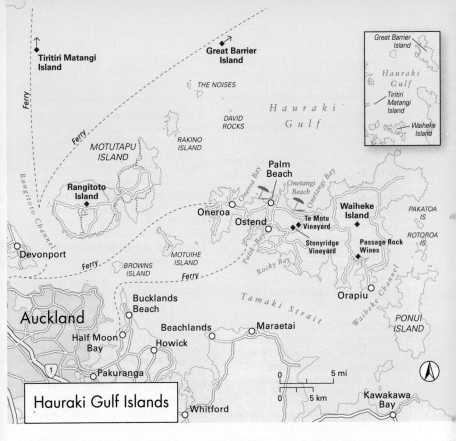

Tiritiri Matangi Island

Great Barrier Island

THE NOISES

Hauraki Gulf

DAVID ROCKS

RAKINO ISLAND

MOTUTAPU ISLAND

Rangitoto Channel

Rangitoto Island

Palm Beach

Oneroa Bay

Onetangi Beach

Onetangi Bay

Oneroa

Ostend

Waiheke Island

PAKATOA IS

Te Motu Vineyard

ROTOROA IS

Stonyridge Vineyard

Passage Rock Wines

Devonport

MOTUIHE ISLAND

BROWNS ISLAND

Putiki Bay

Rocky Bay

Waiheke Channel

Orapiu

Bucklands Beach

Tamaki Strait

Maraetai

PONUI ISLAND

Auckland

Beachlands

Half Moon Bay

Howick

Pakuranga

1

0   5 mi

0   5 km

Hauraki Gulf Islands

Whitford

Kawakawa Bay

Great Barrier Island

Hauraki Gulf

Tiritiri Matangi Island

Waiheke Island

This place is popular with the helicopter-in crowd. ✉ 80 Onetangi Rd., Waiheke Island, Ostend ☎ 09/372–8822 ⊕ www.stonyridge.com.

★ **Te Motu Vineyard**

WINERY | The friendly Dunleavy family started planting vines in 1989. Now its Te Motu Bordeaux blend, which is made only when conditions are right, is on the wine list at many Michelin-starred restaurants in France. The winery gives tastings, but it's best to call first to check for times. Don't be fooled by the restaurant's name, the Shed; it caters to a fussy clientele for its grown-on-site garden-to-plate cooking. The wine list, which always features Te Motu wines from the heritage cellar, changes monthly. Reservations are essential. ✉ 76 Onetangi Rd., Waiheke Island, Onetangi ☎ 09/372–6884 ⊕ www.temotu.co.nz

🍴 Tastings from NZ$20 ⊗ Winery and restaurant closed Mon.–Wed.

★ **Tiritiri Matangi Island**

WILDLIFE REFUGE | You can see rare native birds up close at Tiritiri Matangi, a bird sanctuary open to the public and accessible by ferry from Auckland or Gulf Harbour on the Whangaparoa Peninsula. Gentle, well-maintained, signposted trails lead to the top of the island and the oldest lighthouse in the gulf, still in operation. The island is free from predators, and the birds are unafraid. Tiritiri is home to at least 18 takahe, large blue-and-green flightless birds with red beaks that are part of a nationwide breeding program for the rare species; you can usually spot them eating grass near the lighthouse. ✉ Tiritiri Matangi, Hauraki Gulf Islands ⊕ www.tiritirimatangi.org.nz

Volcano Views

Auckland is built on and around 48 volcanoes, and the tops provide sweeping views of the city.

Mt. Eden. This is the highest volcano on the Auckland isthmus. Several bus tours include this central site, but you have to walk to the summit. It's a popular spot at night when the city's lights below make a spectacular show, and many go there to canoodle or even propose. At the base of the mountain is Mount Eden village, known for its good places to eat and shop at boutique stores. *www.mounteden. co.nz*

One Tree Hill. One Tree Hill, the largest of Auckland's extinct volcanoes, was the site of an early Māori settlement. The surrounding park is great for picnics and running or walking. *www.cornwallpark.co.nz*

Rangitoto Island. Rangitoto Island has an even better vista than One Tree Hill. This volcano emerged from the sea 600 years ago, no doubt much to the wonder of the Māori people living next door on Motutapu Island. Take a ferry to the island; then take a short ride on a covered carriage towed by a jeep or walk to the top to get a 360-degree view of the city and the Hauraki Gulf islands. There are paths around the island along which you can take a peek at some holiday homes. *www.rangitoto.org*

It's thought that Māori settled on the volcanoes beginning in the 14th century, taking advantage of the fertile soils. There's evidence that in the 16th century the Māori used the cones as defensive pā (fortified villages). Remains of complex earthworks can be seen on Mt. Eden and One Tree Hill, where Māori cleared volcanic stone to develop garden plots and formed the terraces that are features of pā.

⛴ *Ferry NZ$82 round-trip, guided walks NZ$10.*

★ **Waiheke Island**

ISLAND | FAMILY | Once a sleepy summer vacation retreat and hippie haven with beach houses dotting its edges, Waiheke is now home to 35 vineyards (many the passion projects of their owners), architecturally impressive holiday homes owned by the well heeled, and old-school tiny weekend escapes. The island has earned an international reputation for its vineyards, and many local cafés stock Waiheke wines unavailable elsewhere. The annual Waiheke Jazz Festival at Easter attracts renowned overseas performers. From the ferry landing at Matiatia Wharf you can walk five minutes to the small town of Oneroa, the island's hub, with its shops, cafés, bars, and real estate agents. Another minute's walk gets you to Oneroa Beach, one of the most accessible beaches. The north-facing beaches—sheltered bays with little surf—are the best for swimming. The most popular is Palm Beach, 10 minutes by bus from Oneroa. Around the rocks to the left is Little Palm Beach, one of Auckland's three nudist beaches. Another great beach, Onetangi, is on the north side of the island, 20 minutes from Matiatia by bus. Whakanewha Regional Park, on the south side, is a lovely bush reserve leading down to a half-moon bay. You can hike and picnic here, and the wetlands are home to rare birds such as the New Zealand dotterel. You can get to the park from Oneroa by shuttle bus. If you go in summer or on weekends, it pays to get ferry tickets early as the island draws big crowds on fine days.

🍴 Restaurants

Mudbrick Vineyard and Restaurant
$$$$ | **EUROPEAN** | This vineyard produces a small portfolio of whites and reds, many of which never make it off the island. The menu emphasizes seasonal, high-quality food and caters to all tastes. **Known for:** excellent lamb; exceptional local wine; stunning views. [$] *Average main: NZ$70* ✉ *Church Bay Rd., Hauraki Gulf Islands* ☎ *09/372–9050* 🌐 *www.mudbrick.co.nz.*

Vino Vino
$$$$ | **MEDITERRANEAN** | **FAMILY** | Waiheke's longest-running restaurant perches on Oneroa's main street, with a large all-weather deck overlooking the bay. The platters—Mediterranean, grilled (with Italian sausages and calamari), or seafood—are perennial favorites. **Known for:** gorgeous views; eclectic menu; good wine list. [$] *Average main: NZ$50* ✉ *3/153 Ocean View Rd., Oneroa, Hauraki Gulf Islands* ☎ *09/372–9888* 🌐 *www.vinovino.co.nz.*

🛏 Hotels

The Boatshed
$$$$ | **HOTEL** | If you feel like staying in a "lighthouse" without being responsible for the ships, the two-story turret suite at The Boatshed may be the place for you, though there are other options, and dinner can be a well-earned add-on. **Pros:** excellent food; gorgeous location with bay views; lovely rooms and decks. **Cons:** some find the rooms small; pricey; rooms close together. [$] *Rooms from: NZ$2390* ✉ *Tawa and Huia Sts., Little Oneroa, Waiheke Island, Hauraki Gulf Islands* ☎ *09/372–3242* 🌐 *www.boatshed.co.nz* 🔑 *7 rooms* 🍽 *Free Breakfast.*

🏃 Activities

KAYAKING

Ferg's Kayaks
KAYAKING | **FAMILY** | Instead of taking the ferry to Rangitoto, why not paddle? Ferg's Kayaks leads guided trips to the island twice daily, leaving at 9:30 am and 5:30 pm. The round-trip takes about six hours, including two to paddle each way and one to climb the volcano. On the later trip you paddle back in the dark toward the city lights. Booking is essential, and trips are dependent on weather and numbers. ✉ *12 Tamaki Dr., Auckland* ☎ *09/529–2230* 🌐 *www.fergskayaks.co.nz* 🎟 *From NZ$160.*

Ross Adventures
KAYAKING | **FAMILY** | There's more to Waiheke Island than relaxed beaches and wineries. Half-day, full-day, and overnight kayaking trips take paddlers past coastal cliffs and inlets. Explore caves, beaches, and Māori pā sites, and have coffee and snacks or lunch at a private beach depending on the day's route. Half- and full-day trips include swimming and snorkeling, and you may spot blue penguins or dolphins as you kayak. ✉ *Matiatia Wharf, Ocean View Rd., Auckland* ☎ *09/372–5550* 🌐 *waihekeadventurecentre.co.nz* 🎟 *From NZ$125.*

Greater Auckland

West Auckland has black-sand KareKare and Muriwai beaches, the former with a famous gannett bird colony, as well as vineyards. North Auckland includes Takapuna Beach, a ritzy seaside suburb.

👁 Sights

Babich Wines
WINERY | The Babich family has been making wine in New Zealand since 1916, beginning first in the far north, where Josip Babich joined his brothers from Croatia and planted grapes near the gum

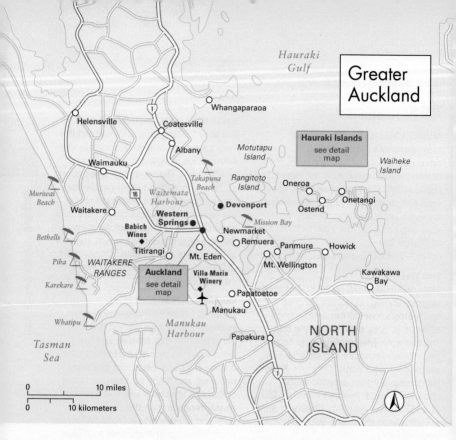

Hauraki Islands
see detail
map

Greater Auckland

Hauraki
Gulf

Whangaparaoa

Helensville
Coatesville

Albany

Waimauku

Motutapu
Island

Rangitoto
Island

Waiheke
Island

Muriwai
Beach

Takapuna
Beach

Oneroa

Onetangi

Waitakere

Waitemata
Harbour

Devonport

Ostend

Babich
Wines

Western
Springs

Mission Bay

Bethells

Newmarket

Titirangi

Remuera

Panmure

Howick

Piha

WAITAKERE
RANGES

Mt. Eden

Mt. Wellington

Karekare

Auckland
see detail
map

Villa Maria
Winery

Kawakawa
Bay

Whatipu

Papatoetoe

Manukau

Tasman
Sea

Manukau
Harbour

Papakura

NORTH
ISLAND

fields. The 72-acre Henderson cellar site has a range of tastings and snacks; years ago it was amid farmland but now is almost surrounded by houses as the population in west Auckland has grown. ✉ 15 Babich Rd., Henderson, Waitakere City, Auckland ☎ 09/833–7859 ⊕ www. babichwines.co.nz ⊙ Closed Sun.

🏖 Beaches

KareKare
BEACH | FAMILY | Film buffs will recognize KareKare and its black sand from the dramatic opening scenes of *The Piano*. Its size means you will never feel hemmed in, even in the peak summer months when it attracts big visitor numbers despite the steep road access. You'll need to pack a lunch as there are no shops. The pounding waves make for great swimming and surfing, but

again, go in only when the surf patrol is operating as there are strong rips and undertows. Fit walkers should explore the southern end of the beach. You can venture past the point but only go at low tide because getting back is difficult when the tide comes in. The sunsets are spectacular anytime of year. **Amenities:** lifeguards in summer; parking (free); toilets. **Best for:** sunset; surfing; swimming; walking. ✉ *KareKare Rd., Auckland.*

Mission Bay
BEACH | FAMILY | About 10 minutes' drive from the central city, Mission Bay off Tamaki Drive draws the crowds year-round and summertime can see families and community groups from all of Auckland picnicking side by side. Dining options run the gamut from fast food to formal-ish restaurants. Three extremely good ice cream parlors and an

abundance of good coffee round out the culinary options, and it's not uncommon to see long lines at each joint and then people eating sitting on the seawall. Be aware though it can get very busy in summer and finding a place to park can be a nightmare. **Amenities:** food and drink; parking; showers; toilets. **Best for:** sunrise; swimming. ⊠ *Tamaki Dr., Auckland.*

Muriwai Beach

BEACH | FAMILY | The black sand of Muriwai Beach is a must for those exploring the West Coast. Combine a trip here with a visit to any of the many wineries in the area. The beach is great for surfing, kitesurfing, walking, and swimming, but don't venture into the water if the surf patrol is not operating, and always swim between the red and yellow flags. It is a great spot for a long walk and in summer it draws huge crowds. In winter you may be accompanied by wild winds, but it's still enjoyable if you're warmly dressed. Alternatively, get up-close-and-personal with the local gannet colony from the DOC viewing platforms; you can see the chicks in December and January. **Amenities:** food and drink; lifeguards in summer; parking; showers; toilets. **Best for:** sunset; swimming; walking. ⊠ *Motutara Rd., Auckland.*

Takapuna Beach

BEACH | FAMILY | You'll see some of New Zealand's most expensive houses along Takapuna Beach on Auckland's North Shore. If architecture (or being nosey) isn't your thing, it's a safe swimming beach in summer and there are many picnic areas, but be sure to check the water quality signs at its entrances first; after heavy rains, the water can be polluted with rain run-off. It's good for walking and in the mornings and evenings it's where the well-sneakered walk their pooches. Sailors, kayakers, and triathletes all use this beach for training. Stand-up paddle boarding is also very popular here. The many cafés in Takapuna township are two minutes away from the sand. **Amenities:** food and drink; parking; showers; toilets; water sports. **Best for:** sunrise; swimming; walking. ⊠ *The Promenade, Auckland.*

🍴 Restaurants

★ The Food Vault

$$ | MODERN NEW ZEALAND | The freshbaked goods, plumber's breakfast (a hearty plate of eggs, hash browns, sausage, bacon, mushrooms, and anything else the chef adds), and coffee make this a great place to spend a morning. The atmosphere is friendly, with customers ranging from cyclists stopping for a fix to locals looking for a hearty breakfast or lunch. **Known for:** house-baked goods; sourdough and brioche bread; excellent coffee. Ⓢ *Average main: NZ$20* ⊠ *10 Matua Rd., Huapai, Auckland* ☎ *09/412–5085* ⊕ *www.thefoodvault.co.nz.*

🛍 Shopping

West Coast Gallery Piha

ART GALLERIES | It's well worth driving the winding road to this West Coast beach to see work by some 200 artists living in the region. There's everything from paintings, ceramics, sculpture, and jewelry to photography, glasswork, books, and CDs. Prices range from NZ$20 or NZ$30 to thousands of dollars. The gallery hosts regular events and occasional themed art projects that get locals involved. ⊠ *Seaview Rd., Piha* ☎ *09/8128 029* ⊕ *www.westcoastgallery.co.nz* ⊙ *Closed Mon.–Wed.*

🏃 Activities

GOLF

Gulf Harbour Country Club

GOLF | Designed by Robert Trent Jones Jr. (some say the world's finest designer of classic golf courses), this course is about 40 minutes north of Auckland (if the traffic is flowing) on the East

Coast's Whangaparaoa Peninisula. Some have called it the Pebble Beach of New Zealand, and there's a dress code here: collared shirts, golf slacks or shorts, and no metal spike shoes with socks. The first nine holes are hilly while the last nine offer amazing views of the Hauraki Gulf. Winter specials are posted on the website. After a round, take a stroll around the Gulf Harbour Marina to look at the range of yachts and launches. ⊠ *Gulf Harbour Dr., Rodney District, Auckland* ☎ *09/428–1380* ⊕ *www.gulfharbourcountryclub.co.nz* ✉ *NZ$130* ⚲ *18 holes, 7000 yards, par 72.*

Muriwai Golf Club

GOLF | A 40-minute drive (depending on traffic) northwest of the city brings you to this links course near a bird sanctuary, with outstanding views of the coast, even from the "19th hole." Because the links are on sandy soil, they can be played even if the rest of Auckland is sodden, and the course is often home to tournaments and training. If your partner is not a golfer there are some great beach and forest walks close by. ⊠ *Coast Rd., Muriwai Beach, Auckland* ☎ *09/411–8454* ⊕ *www.muriwaigolfclub.co.nz* ✉ *NZ$120* ⚲ *18 holes, 6800 yards, par 72.*

Titirangi Golf Club

GOLF | Designed by renowned golf architect Alister MacKenzie, this is one of the country's finest (and oldest) 18-hole courses. The club was established in 1909 and takes pride in its rolling fairways and challenging bunkers and greens. Golfers might be distracted by the magnificent setting and specimen trees. Non-members are welcome to play provided they contact the course in advance (and get through the painful automated phone system). Once booked, you must show evidence of membership at an overseas club, and the dress code must be adhered to. Tailored shirts and pants are a must and no beachwear of any kind is allowed. ⊠ *Links Rd., Waitakere City, Auckland* ☎ *09/827–3967* ⊕ *www.titirangigolf.co.nz* ✉ *NZ$200* ⚲ *18 holes, 6600 yards, par 70.*

Chapter 4

NORTHLAND AND THE BAY OF ISLANDS

Updated by
Richard Pamatatau

4

👁 **Sights**
★★★☆☆

🍴 **Restaurants**
★★☆☆☆

🛏 **Hotels**
★★☆☆☆

🛍 **Shopping**
★☆☆☆☆

🍸 **Nightlife**
★☆☆☆☆

WELCOME TO NORTHLAND AND THE BAY OF ISLANDS

TOP REASONS TO GO

★ **Boating and Fishing:** Take a cruise to an island, whale-watch, swim with dolphins, or fish with the Bay of Islands as the hub.

★ **Bountiful Beaches:** Most Northland beaches are safe for swimming. On the 90 Mile Beach you can swim in both the Tasman Sea and the Pacific Ocean. Experienced surfers head to Shipwreck Bay for great waves.

★ **Coastal Views:** Take the Old Coast Road to Russell for superb views of islands and (almost) hidden bays and places to picnic.

★ **Superb Diving:** Dive at the Poor Knights Islands, known for their huge variety of subtropical fish, or the wreck of the Greenpeace vessel *Rainbow Warrior,* sunk by French agents in 1985.

★ **Walking and Hiking:** Superb bushwalking (hiking) provides a close look at ancient kauri trees (a local species of pine) and interesting birds, such as *tūī* (too-ee), fantails, and wood pigeons.

The northernmost part of New Zealand features on its East Coast, a stunning collection of islands known, fittingly, as the Bay of Islands. The West Coast, from Dargaville to Cape Reinga seems empty, and the unassuming little towns along the way and the lumbering *Kohu Ra Tuama* Hokianga Harbour ferry contrast with the luxurious lodges and fancy yachts around the Bay of Islands. No matter where you are in the North, you're never far from the water and a combination of coastline, rolling pastures, and ancient native forest.

1 Warkworth. This small town with a working-class history is a good stopping point for visitors to the nearby Goat Island marine reserve.

2 Whangarei. The only city in Northland has an interesting Māori past and an up-and-coming artistic present. Work is underway to complete a museum designed by Austrian artist Friedensreich Hundertwasser, whose house has the biggest collection of his works outside his home country.

3 Hokianga and the Kauri Coast. This quiet area has small towns and access to gorgeous giant kauri trees in Waipoua State Forest.

4 Paihia and Waitangi. The small town of Paihia is the main vacation base for the region, while Waitangi holds one of the country's most important historic sites.

5 Russell. This relaxed and charming beach town has a fascinating Wild West–like history.

6 Kerikeri. Considered the cradle of the nation, most of New Zealand's earliest history can be traced back to this small town. It is now known for its citrus and kiwifruit production and farmers' market.

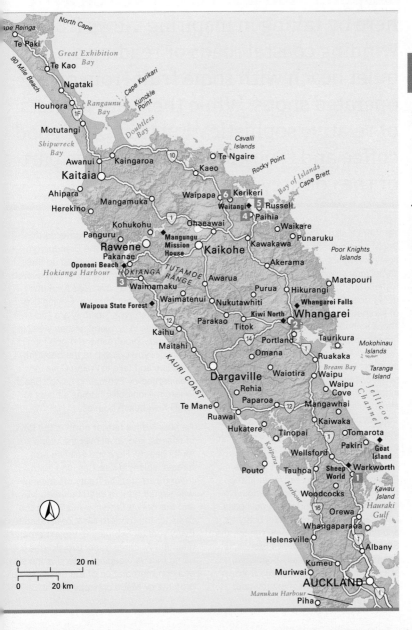

Northland is the place to go when you seek more than great restaurants and shopping. You'll be best served on a trip here by taking in inspiring views from winding coastal roads or reading on a quiet beach with some fruit from owner-operated shops. While there are pockets of relative sophistication that offer good coffee and fancy food, much of this part of the country is about the views.

Yet there's also a rawness to the North. Social tensions are exacerbated by political neglect and high unemployment, particularly among the area's Māori population, but the scenery is truly majestic, going from rugged to pastoral in a matter of kilometers. You will notice the change about an hour after leaving the sometimes-confusing jumble that makes up Auckland. With the city behind you the air starts to clear and you can see what some call the Northland light. The lack of industry in Northland alongside a declining population means less pollution, and may account for the fact that it seems brighter the farther north you go, even on overcast days.

The Tasman Sea to the west and the Pacific Ocean to the east meet at the top of North Island at Cape Reinga. No matter what route you take, you'll pass farms and forests, marvelous beaches, and great open spaces. Even though the East Coast, up to the Bay of Islands, is Northland's most densely populated, often with cashed-up migrants from bigger cities, it still feels uncrowded.

The first decision on the drive north comes at the foot of the Brynderwyn Hills. Turning left will take you up the West Coast through areas once covered with forests and now used for either agriculture or horticulture. Driving over "the Brynderwyns," as they are known, takes you to Whangarei, the only city in Northland. If you're in the mood for a diversion, you can slip to the beautiful coastline and take in Waipu Cove, an area settled by Scots, and Laings Beach, where million-dollar homes sit next to small Kiwi beach houses.

An hour's drive farther north is the Bay of Islands, known all over the world for its beauty. Here you will find lush forests, splendid beaches, and shimmering harbors. The Treaty of Waitangi was signed here in 1840 between Māori and the British Crown, establishing the basis for the modern New Zealand state. Every year on February 6, the extremely beautiful Waitangi Treaty Ground (the name means weeping waters) is the site of a commemoration of the treaty, and of protests by Māori unhappy with it.

Continuing north on the East Coast, the agricultural backbone of the region is even more evident and a series of winding loop roads off the main highway leads to beaches that are both beautiful and isolated where you can swim, dive, picnic, or just laze. The West Coast is even less populated, and the coastline is rugged and windswept. In the Waipoua Forest, you will find some of New Zealand's oldest and largest kauri trees (although a disease has recently spread, affecting the trees and closing some trails to them); the winding road will also take you past mangrove swamps.

Crowning the region is the spiritually significant Cape Reinga, the headland at the top of the vast stretch of 90 Mile Beach, from where it's believed Māori souls depart after death. Today Māori make up roughly a quarter of the area's population (compared with the national average of about 15%). The legendary Māori navigator Kupe was said to have landed on the shores of Hokianga Harbour, where the first arrivals made their home. Many different *iwi* (tribes) lived throughout Northland, including Ngapuhi (the largest), Te Roroa, Ngāti Wai, Ngāti Kuri, Te Aupouri, Ngaitakoto, Ngāti Kahu, and Te Rarawa. Many Māori here can trace their ancestry to the earliest inhabitants.

MAJOR REGIONS

Northland. *Te Tai Tokerau,* or Northland, with its no-frills, tiny, friendly towns and high rates of unemployment, is extremely different from the affluent Bay of Islands. However, the scenery is just as stunning. But without the infrastructure that goes along with organized tourism you will feel a little off the beaten path (in addition, many New Zealanders joke that cannabis cultivation fuels a giant hidden economy). Heading north from Auckland, you'll reach **Warkworth** first, a low-key base for stops like Goat Island and nearby wineries. Heading farther north, the largest town is **Whangarei,** which serves as the main center for the region.

On the west coast, you'll find the area known as **Hokianga Harbour** and its harbor along with the **Kauri Coast,** which features the unique kauri trees of Waipoua State Forest.

The Bay of Islands. This sweep of coastline is home to 144 islands amid a mild, subtropical climate and excellent game-fishing waters. That combination makes the Bay of Islands ideal—with a slew of things to do while visiting. You can base yourself in popular **Paihia,** take in history at **Waitangi** and **Kerikeri,** or relax at the nearby beaches of low-key **Russell.**

Planning

Getting Here and Around

BOAT AND FERRY

Three passenger boats cross between Paihia and Russell, with departures at least once every 20 minutes in each direction from 7:20 am to 10:30 pm from Paihia, and 7 am to 10 pm from Russell. The one-way fare is NZ$6. Or, join the car ferry at nearby Opua, about 5 km (3 miles) south of Paihia. It operates from 6:50 am to 9:50 pm, with departures at approximately 10-minute intervals from either shore. The last boat leaves from Okiato on the Russell side at 9:50 pm. The one-way fare is NZ$13 for car and driver plus NZ$1 for each adult passenger. Buy your tickets on board (cash only). Save time by crossing the Hokianga Harbour between Rawene and Kohukohu (with or without a car) by ferry.

BUS

Taking a bus is a cheap and also easy alternative to driving. Several companies serve all but the most out-of-the-way spots. InterCity runs several times daily between Auckland and the Bay of Islands and connects to the other Northland centers at least once a day. Auckland to

Paihia takes about 4½ hours depending on traffic and to Kerikeri about 5½ hours.

CAR

It's best to see Northland's many lovely bays, sandy beaches, and worthwhile sights by car. Take your time though as Northland roads are generally just two lanes wide, with many one-lane bridges in remote areas. Take care on the narrow—and often unsealed—roads that thread through the region. Don't risk a drive along 90 Mile Beach; the quicksand and tides can leave you stuck, and your rental car insurance won't cover any accidents here. You can easily find a tour company to take you along 90 Mile Beach in a range of vehicles.

From Auckland, drive up the East Coast on State Highway 1 and return down the West Coast on Highway 12 (or vice versa), but make sure to check out smaller, winding coastal roads with their stunning coastlines and dramatic island views.

Hotels

Northland accommodations vary from basic motels to luxury lodges. Hosts, particularly in the bed-and-breakfasts, are eager to share their local knowledge and are a great resource on less-obvious attractions. Paihia is considered a hub for Northland and has plenty of vacation apartments, standard motels, and luxury venues. You'll also find a range of B&Bs and lodges in places like Russell.

High season runs from December through March. Some lodges have shoulder seasons in April and May, and September and October. Overall, room rates drop between May and October, though many places also close for a break.

Restaurant and hotel reviews have been shortened. For full information, visit Fodors.com. Restaurant prices are the average cost of a main course at dinner or, if dinner is not served, at lunch. Hotel prices are the lowest cost of a standard double room in high season.

WHAT IT COSTS in New Zealand Dollars			
$	$$	$$$	$$$$
RESTAURANTS			
under NZ$15	NZ$15–NZ$20	NZ$21–NZ$30	over NZ$30
HOTELS			
under NZ$125	NZ$125–NZ$200	NZ$201–NZ$300	over NZ$300

Planning Your Time

Plan to spend three days in Northland. On Day 1 take in the main town of Paihia, and then catch the ferry to Russell for lunch and sightseeing. Drive north on the second day, stopping at beaches and Cape Reinga, where you can view the meeting of the Tasman Sea and the Pacific Ocean. Meander back via the Hokianga on Day 3 by winding south through the forests along the West Coast to Kohukohu. Ferry south across serene Hokianga Harbour to Rawene. From Opononi, closer to the harbor's mouth, continue down the Kauri Coast to the Waipoua Forest. From there, Highway 12 runs to Brynderwyn, where you rejoin State Highway 1 about an hour north of Auckland.

Restaurants

Seafood abounds in the north with scallops and oysters farmed throughout the region, though occasional sewerage scares and algae blooms put them off-limits. Snapper and kingfish are available year-round, and marlin and broad-bill swordfish are abundant between January and June. The region also prides itself on its local produce.

People eat earlier in Northland than in the cities, with restaurants filling around 7. Dress is casual—jeans are acceptable in all but the most upscale lodges. From May through September, many restaurants close or reduce their opening hours, some to four nights a week. October sees regular hours resume. There is a growing coffee culture in the north.

Visitor Information

Local visitor bureaus, many known as i-SITEs, have information on the whole region, with more extensive information on their particular environs. Destination Northland, a regional tourism organization, is a good resource for the entire region (*www.northlandnz.com*).

When to Go

Snow doesn't fall in the "winterless north," but it can get cool and wet. The best time to go is between mid-November and mid-April; peak season is December through March. During the quiet months of July and August it can be quite rainy. For game fishing, arrive from February to June.

Warkworth

59 km (36 miles) north of Auckland.

A sleepy town on the banks of the Mahurangi River, Warkworth was established in 1853. With lime mined from the local river, it became the first cement-manufacturing site in the southern hemisphere. Today, race-boat building and refitting are the main industries, though slowly boutique food producers are opening up shop. Warkworth also serves as a service town for the surrounding farms and market gardens. It's a convenient stopping point en route to the nearby Goat Island marine reserve or the superb vineyards at Matakana.

GETTING HERE AND AROUND

There are two ways to get to Warkworth: bus or car. It's on the major bus routes north, and all you need to do is let the driver know where you want to get off. InterCity has ticketing options that let you explore, as well as regular service. However, bus travel can be limiting because attractions are spread out. For more flexibility rent a car and rove the countryside more freely, especially if you are heading to Matakana to explore the wineries. The area has about 100 white-sand beaches that are easy to get to and often deserted.

VISITOR INFORMATION
CONTACTS Warkworth Visitor Information Centre. ✉ *1 Baxter St., Warkworth* ☎ *09/425–9081* ⊕ *www.matakanacoast.co.nz.*

Sights

Goat Island
BEACH | FAMILY | Take a trip to the Goat Island (also known as Te Hawere-a-Maki Marine Reserve), where fishing is prohibited and marine life has returned in abundance. Prominent species include blue *maomao* fish, snapper, and cod. It does get crowded here, and midweek is best. You can put on a snorkel and get up-close-and-personal with a school of maomao. The beach area is good for a picnic as well. Another fun activity is to take a glass-bottom boat tour. Just as the name promises, Glass Bottom Boat takes a glass-bottom boat around the island and gives you an aquarium eye view of waters teeming with fish. If the weather isn't ideal, there is an inner reef trip. Call ahead, because trips don't run if there is too much of a swell. You can also rent flippers, masks, and snorkels if you want to get in the water. To get to Goat Island head toward Leigh, 21 km (13 miles) northeast of Warkworth. From Leigh, take a left turn and follow the signs for a couple of miles. If you arrive by 10 am, you should avoid the masses

especially midweek and in winter. If you want to stay the night, there are camping grounds nearby; the Warkworth Visitor Centre will direct you. ⊠ *Goat Island Rd.* ⊕ *www.discovergoatisland.co.nz.*

SheepWorld

FARM/RANCH | FAMILY | Head for Sheep-World about an hour north of Auckland for a taste of life on a typical New Zealand sheep farm. Twice a day demonstrations show working farm dogs rounding up sheep before the shearers take over. An ecotrail meanders through the bush, providing information on native trees, birds (and their calls), and *weta* (large, ugly—yet impressive—native insects). On the weekends, the farm dogs even herd ducks. Children can take pony rides, and, in August, bottle-feed lambs. Depending on the weather there is also eel feeding. ⊠ *324 State Hwy. 1, Warkworth* ☎ *09/425–7444* ⊕ *www. sheepworldfarm.co.nz* 🎫 *NZ$59.*

Warkworth Museum

HISTORY MUSEUM | FAMILY | For a glimpse of Northland's pioneering past pay a visit to the Warkworth District Museum. It's a must if you are interested in learning about how smaller settlements in New Zealand developed. This eclectic collection includes Māori artifacts plus farming and domestic implements from the early days of the European settlement including tools used to dig for kauri gum. Rotating textile displays cover clothing and lace dating to the late 1700s. There is also a display of a school dental clinic—what Kiwi children called the "murder house." Outside is a collection of old buildings, including a bushman's hut and an army hut used by Americans stationed at Warkworth during World War II. ⊠ *Tudor Collins Dr., Warkworth* ☎ *09/425–7093* ⊕ *warkworthmuseum. co.nz* 🎫 *NZ$7.*

Whangarei

127 km (79 miles) north of Warkworth, 196 km (123 miles) north of Auckland.

The main center in Northland is the Whangarei (*fahng*-ar-ay) District; Whangarei Harbour was traditionally a meeting place for Māori tribes traveling south by *waka* (canoe). The full Māori name of the harbor, Whangarei Terenga Paraoa, means "swimming place of whales" but is also interpreted as "the meeting place of chiefs." Europeans started to settle in the area from the mid-1800s; now it's a town of roughly 45,000 people, rooted in the agriculture, forestry, and fishing industries. Boatbuilding is a traditional business, manufacturing everything from superyachts to charter boats. There is also a growing community of artists who have retreated to the North where housing is cheaper. The mouth of the harbor is dominated by the volcanic peaks of Whangarei Heads, atop Bream Bay. The drive from town to the Whangarei Heads takes about 20 minutes heading out on Riverside Drive, past mangrove-lined bays. At the Heads are stunning white-sand beaches and coves with safe swimming as well as several hikes, including up the peaks of Mt. Manaia.

GETTING HERE AND AROUND

Whangarei is about two hours by car from Auckland on State Highway 1 depending on weather, traffic, and road conditions. On busy holiday weekends it can take as long to get out of the city as people head to holiday homes on the coast. Bus services also travel this route but take longer as they stop at many small towns along the way.

You can fly from Auckland to Whangarei, but factoring arriving at the airport and checking in, it's often quicker to drive to Whangarei. There is no train service.

The Treaty of Waitangi

The controversial cornerstone of New Zealand's Māori and Pākehā relations is the 1840 Treaty of Waitangi, the first formal document that bound the Māori to the British crown. This contract became the basis for Britain's claim to the entire country as its colony.

In the mid-1830s, Britain became increasingly concerned about advances by French settlers and the inroads made by the New Zealand Company, a private emigration organization. The British government had an official Resident at Waitangi, James Busby, but no actual means to protect its interests. In 1835, Busby helped orchestrate an alliance among more than 30 North Island Māori chiefs.

In 1840, Captain William Hobson arrived in Waitangi to negotiate a transfer of sovereignty. Hobson and Busby hurriedly drew up a treaty in both English and Māori, and presented it to the Māori confederation on February 5, 1840. On the following day, about 40 chiefs signed the treaty.

But there were significant differences between the Māori and English versions. In the first article, the English version said the Māori would cede sovereignty to the Queen of England. But the Māori translation used the word *kāwanatanga* (governorship), which did not mean that the Māori were ceding the right to *mana* (self-determination).

The second article guaranteed the chiefs the "full, exclusive and undisturbed possession of their lands, estates, forests, fisheries, and other properties," but granted the right of preemption to the crown. The Māori translation did not convey the crown's exclusive right to buy Māori land, which caused friction over the decades that continues to this day. The third article granted the Māori protection as British citizens—and thus held them accountable to British law.

After the initial wave of signatures at Waitangi, signatures were gathered elsewhere on the North Island and on the South Island. In spring 1840, Hobson claimed all of New Zealand as a British colony. He had not, however, gotten signatures from some of the most powerful Māori chiefs, and this came back to haunt the crown during the Land Wars of 1860.

What wasn't confiscated after the Land Wars was taken by legislation. In 1877, Chief Justice Prendergast ruled that the treaty was "a simple nullity" that lacked legal validity because one could not make a treaty with "barbarians." At first European contact, 66.5 million acres of land was under Māori control, but by 1979 only 3 million remained—of mostly marginal lands.

The battle to have the treaty honored and reinterpreted is ongoing. In 1973, February 6 was proclaimed the official Waitangi Day holiday. From the get-go, the holiday sparked debate, as Māori activists protest the celebration of such a divisive document. The Waitangi Tribunal was established in 1975 to allow Māori to rule on alleged breaches of the treaty, and, in 1985, the tribunal's powers were made retrospective to 1840. It has its hands full, as the claims continue to be one of New Zealand's largest sociopolitical issues. The treaty is now in the National Archives in Wellington.

Did You Know?

According to Māori legend, the dead leap off the Pōhutukawa tree at Cape Reinga's point to begin their trip to the underworld. Turbulent waters churn below, where the Pacific Ocean and the Tasman Sea meet.

Sights

Claphams Clocks—The National Clock Museum

OTHER MUSEUM | FAMILY | If you want to while away some time, this clock museum is the place for you. About every conceivable method of telling time is represented. The collection of more than 1,500 clocks includes primitive water clocks, ships' chronometers, and ornate masterworks from Paris and Vienna. Ironically, the one thing you won't find here is the correct time. If all the bells, chimes, gongs, and cuckoos went off together, the noise would be deafening, so the clocks are set to different times. ✉ *Town Basin, Dent St., Whangarei* ☎ *09/438–3993* 🌐 *www.claphamsclocks.com* 🎫 *NZ$10.*

Kiwi North

MUSEUM VILLAGE | FAMILY | Minutes out of town, this 61-acre park is home to a nocturnal kiwi house, several Heritage buildings, and the Whangarei Museum. The museum has some 40,000 items in its collection including fine examples of pre-European Māori cloaks, *waka* (canoes), and tools. Photographers will love the early pictures of the area. You can also check out Glorat, an original 1886 kauri homestead, and the world's smallest consecrated chapel, built in 1859 from a single kauri tree. On the third Sunday of every month and on selected "Live Days" (call for dates), you can cruise around the park on model reproductions of steam and electric trains, as well as on a full-size diesel train. ✉ *500 State Hwy. 14, Maunu, Whangarei* ☎ *09/438–9630* 🌐 *www.kiwinorth.co.nz* 🎫 *Park free; Kiwi House and Whangarei Museum NZ$20.*

Reyburn House Art Gallery

ART GALLERY | This is the oldest kauri villa in Whangarei. It is home to the Northland Society of Arts and regularly hosts exhibitions from New Zealand artists. Original works from well-known artists are available for purchase. The permanent collection focuses on the 1880s to the present, and several well-known New Zealand artists are represented. ✉ *Town Basin, Reyburn House La., Whangarei* ☎ *09/438–3074* 🌐 *www.reyburnhouse.co.nz* 🎫 *By donation.*

Whangarei Falls

WATERFALL | FAMILY | The falls are a lovely picnic spot, located on Ngunguru Road, 5 km (3 miles) northeast of town. Viewing platforms are atop the falls, and a short trail runs through the local bush. ✉ *12 Ngunguru Rd., Glenbervie, Whangarei* 🌐 *www.whangareifalls.co.nz* 🎫 *Free.*

Whangarei Town Basin

MARINA/PIER | People often bypass Whangarei on their way to the Bay of Islands. It's easy to see why, as the town has a confusing traffic system, but if you can brave it, the area known as the Whangarei Town Basin is worth a look. The marina is now a haven for visiting yachts and has cafés, restaurants, galleries, and crafts shops. There's parking behind the basin off Dent Street. ✉ *Dent St., Whangarei* 🌐 *www.wdc.govt.nz.*

Restaurants

★ Tonic

$$$$ | FRENCH | This eatery draws diners with cuisine that fuses fresh local produce with an international flair. The local love for Tonic is intense, so be prepared to wait for a table. **Known for:** big local crowds; innovative cuisine; great NZ-heavy wine list. [$] *Average main: NZ$32* ✉ *239a Kamo Rd., Whangarei* ☎ *09/437–5558* 🌐 *www.tonicrestaurant.co.nz* ⏲ *No lunch.*

Hotels

Chelsea House

$$ | B&B/INN | This beautiful renovated villa offers three lovely rooms that will remind you of a relative's comfortable country house. **Pros:** tasty breakfasts; cozy decor;

The Poor Knights Islands

Jacques Cousteau once placed the Poor Knights Islands among the world's top 10 dive locations. Underwater archways, tunnels, caves, and rocky cliffs provide endless opportunities for viewing many species of subtropical fish. On a good day you'll see soft coral, sponge gardens, gorgonian fields, and forests of kelp.

Two large islands and many islets make up the Poor Knights, remnants of an ancient volcanic eruption 12 nautical miles off the stunning Tutukaka coast, a half-hour drive east of Whangarei. The ocean around them is a marine reserve, extending 800 meters (½ mile) from the islands. Indeed the islands themselves are a nature reserve; landing on them is prohibited.

At 7.9 million cubic feet, Rikoriko Cave, on the southern island's northwest side, is one of the world's largest sea caves. It's known for its acoustics. Ferns hang from its roof, and underwater cup coral grows toward the rear of it. (Normally found at depths of 200 meters, the cave light has tricked the coral into thinking it is deeper). Visibility at the Poor Knights is between 20 and 30 meters, but in Rikoriko Cave it goes up to 35 to 45 meters.

A dense canopy of regenerated *pohutukawa* covers the islands, flowering brilliant scarlet around Christmas time. Native Poor Knights lilies cling to cliff faces, producing bright red flowers in October. Rare bellbirds (*koromikos*) and red-crowned parakeets (*kakarikis*) thrive in the predator-free environment. Between October and May, millions of seabirds come to breed, including the Buller's shearwaters that arrive from the Arctic Circle. But possibly the most distinguished resident is the New Zealand native *tuatara*, a reptile species from the dinosaur age that survives only on offshore islands.

New Zealand fur seals bask on the rocks and feed on the abundant fish life, mostly from July to October, and year-round dolphins, whales, and bronze whaler sharks can be seen in the surrounding waters. In summer you can see minke and rare Bryde's whales, too. In March stingrays stack in the hundreds in the archways for their mating season.

Conditions rarely prevent diving, which is good year-round. That said, don't expect the same experience you'll get diving off Australia's Great Barrier Reef. There aren't as many colorful fish, and the water is cooler. In October, the visibility drops to about 18 to 20 meters because of a spring plankton bloom, though this attracts hungry marine life. The best places for novices are Nursery Cove and shallower parts of the South Harbour.

4

Northland and the Bay of Islands **WHANGAREI**

lovely environment. **Cons:** 20-minute walk to town; some may find it a bit basic; no guest cooking facilities. $ *Rooms from: NZ$135* ⊠ *83 Hatea Dr., Whangarei* ☎ *09/437–7115* ⊕ *www.chelsea-house. co.nz* ⌖ *3 rooms* ⊘ *Free Breakfast.*

Lodge Bordeaux

$$$ | **B&B/INN** | **FAMILY** | With obvious references to France (but in a very Kiwi way), Lodge Bordeaux offers comfortable and stylish accommodations. **Pros:** smart decor; big rooms; nice outdoor spaces. **Cons:** on a busy state highway; slightly clinical; no dining on-site. $ *Rooms*

Scuba divers examine the notoriously friendly subtropical fish in the Poor Knights Islands Marine Reserve.

from: NZ$270 ⊠ *361 Western Hills Dr., Whangarei* ☎ *09/438–0404* ⊕ *www. lodgebordeaux.co.nz* ➳ *15 rooms* ❌ *Free Breakfast.*

Shopping

★ Burning Issues Gallery

CRAFTS | Burning Issues Gallery is one of the best places in Northland to buy locally made arts and crafts and work from some of the country's best artisans. Look for beautifully carved *pounamu* (New Zealand greenstone) and bone pendants. The silver and gold jewelry and small ceramic items are perfect for tiny take-home gifts. ⊠ *8 Quayside, Town Basin, Whangarei* ☎ *09/438–3108* ⊕ *www. burningissuesgallery.co.nz.*

Quarry Craft Co-op Shop

CRAFTS | A cooperative of local craftspeople, including jewelers, potters, wood turners, and weavers, runs the Quarry Craft Co-op Shop. You will find unique crafts, including jewelry made from kauri gum. The cooperative also runs courses—some only a day long—so check the website; you might end up making your own souvenir. The co-op is also home to residential craftspeople dedicated to preserving the art of wood turning and hand-printing. ⊠ *21 Selwyn Ave., Whangarei* ☎ *09/438–1215* ⊕ *www. quarryarts.org.*

Activities

DIVING

Dive Tutukaka

DIVING & SNORKELING | Dive trips with Dive Tutukaka to the spectacular Poor Knights Islands include rented gear. Lunch is extra but inexpensive. You can also sail on *The Perfect Day,* a 70-foot luxury multilevel boat between November and April. This trip includes a half day of sightseeing, with the option to go kayaking, snorkeling, and diving. Free transfers to and from Whangarei are provided. ⊠ *Poor Knights Dive Centre, Marina Rd., Tutukaka* ☎ *09/434–3867* ⊕ *www.diving.co.nz* ✉ *Trips from NZ$2319.*

Hokianga and the Kauri Coast

85 km (53 miles) west of Paihia.

A peaceful harbor continues inland into the Hokianga region. It's a quiet area with small towns, unspoiled scenery, and proximity to the giant kauri trees on the Kauri Coast, a 20-minute drive south on Highway 12. Here the highway winds through Waipoua State Forest, then stretches south to Kaipara Harbour. Giant golden sand dunes tower over the mouth of Hokianga Harbour, across the water from the twin settlements of Omapere and Opononi. Opononi is the place where Opo, a tame dolphin, came to play with swimmers in the mid-1950s, putting the town on the national map for the first and only time in its history. A statue in front of the pub commemorates the much-loved creature.

GETTING HERE AND AROUND
The best way to get to the Hokianga is to drive. From Auckland turn left at the bottom of the Bryderwyn Hills and follow the road. There is generally one bus service a day from Auckland, and no air or train service. Be prepared to take your time. Unfortunately, there is a lot of work being done on these roads, so both construction work and farm vehicles can slow your journey.

VISITOR INFORMATION
CONTACTS Hokianga Visitor Information Centre. ✉ *29 State Hwy. 12, Omapere* ☎ *09/405–8869* ⊕ *www.northlandnz. com.*

 Sights

Dargaville
TOWN | Sixty-four kilometers (40 miles) south of the Waipoua Forest along the Kaihu River, you'll come to sleepy Dargaville, once a thriving river port and now a good place to stock up if you're planning to camp in any of the nearby forests. It has some good craft stores, too. The surrounding region is best known for its main cash crop, the purple-skinned sweet potato known as *kūmara.* You'll see field after field dedicated to this root vegetable. ✉ *Dargaville* ☎ *09/439–4975* ⊕ *www.dargaville.co.nz.*

Māngungu Mission House
NOTABLE BUILDING | The 1838 Māngungu Mission House is an overlooked stop on the tourist trail. Although Waitangi is the most famous site of New Zealand's founding document, this unassuming spot, which looks out over Hokianga Harbour, was the scene of the second treaty signing. Here, on February 12, 1840, the largest gathering of Māori chiefs signed the Treaty of Waitangi (73 chiefs, compared with about 40 at the signing in Waitangi). The house is now a museum, furnished with pre-treaty missionary items, including portraits, photographs, and furniture. ✉ *Motukiore Rd., Hokianga Harbour, Horeke* ☎ *09/407–0470* ⊕ *www. mangungumission.co.nz* 🎫 *NZ$10.*

★ Matakohe Kauri Museum
MUSEUM VILLAGE | South of Dargaville is Matakohe, a pocket-size town with this singularly outstanding attraction. The museum's intriguing collection of artifacts, tools, photographs, documents, and memorabilia traces the story of the pioneers who settled this area in the second half of the 19th century—a story interwoven with the kauri forests. The furniture and a complete kauri house are among the superb examples of craftsmanship. One of the most fascinating displays is of kauri gum, the transparent lumps of resin that form when the sticky sap of the kauri tree hardens. This gum, which was used to make varnish, can be polished to a warm, lustrous finish that looks remarkably like amber—right down to the occasional insects trapped and preserved inside—and this collection is the biggest in the world. Volunteers Hall contains a huge kauri slab running

from one end of the hall to the other, and there is also a reproduction of a cabinetmaker's shop, and a chain-saw exhibit. The Steam Saw Mill illustrates how the huge kauri logs were cut into timber. Perhaps the best display is the two-story replica of a late 1800s to early 1900s boardinghouse. Rooms are set up as they were more than 100 years ago; you can walk down the hallways and peer in at the goings-on of the era. If you like the whirring of engines, the best day to visit is Wednesday, when much of the museum's machinery is started up. ✉ *5 Church Rd., Matakohe* ☎ *09/431–7417* 🌐 *www.kaurimuseum.com* 🎟 *NZ$25.*

★ **Waipoua State Forest**

FOREST | Kauri forests once covered this region, and Waipoua State Forest contains the largest collection of the remaining trees although many are currently under threat from a disease known as Kauri Dieback. Because of this, always check with the center to see if the forest is open the day you visit. If it is open, a short path leads from the parking area on the main road through the forest to **Tane Mahuta,** "Lord of the Forest," and the largest tree in New Zealand. It stands nearly 173 feet high, measures 45 feet around its base, and is 1,200 to 2,500 years old. The second-largest tree, older by some 800 years, is **Te Matua Ngahere,** about a 20-minute walk from the road. If you have a few hours to spare you can visit Te Matua Ngahere and other trees of note. Head to the Kauri Walks parking lot about a mile south of the main Tane Mahuta parking lot. From there you trek past the **Four Sisters,** four kauri trees that have grown together in a circular formation, then the **Yakas Tree** (named after an old kauri-gum digger), and Te Matua Ngahere. The forest has a campground—check at the visitor center before you pitch a tent. Facilities include toilets, hot showers, and a communal cookhouse. When it's wet, you may spot large kauri snails in the forest. Also, the successful eradication of predators such as weasels and stoats has led to a rise in the number of kiwis in the forest. You'll need a flashlight to spot one because the birds only come out at night. The Waipoua campground and Waipoua Visitor Centre is managed by Te Iwi O Te Roroa, the local Māori tribe. ✉ *Waipoua Visitor Centre, 1 Waipoua River Rd., Waipoua* ☎ *09/439–6445* 🌐 *www.kauricoast.com/waipoua-forest-visitors-centre.*

Hotels

★ **Waipoua Lodge**

$$$$ | **B&B/INN** | Renovations of this 100-year-old kauri farmhouse and its buildings have created a sophisticated and relaxing place to stay in the northern end of the North Island. **Pros:** beautiful gardens; excellent food; peaceful, gorgeous location. **Cons:** on the pricey side; might be too isolated for some; not located on the beach. [$] *Rooms from: NZ$450* ✉ *State Hwy. 12, Waipoua* ☎ *09/439–0422* 🌐 *www.waipoualodge.co.nz* 🛏 *4 suites* 🍴 *Free Breakfast.*

Paihia and Waitangi

69 km (43 miles) north of Whangarei.

As the main vacation base for the Bay of Islands, Paihia is an unremarkable stretch of motels at odds with the quiet beauty of the island-studded seascape. With its handful of hostels, plus the long and safe swimming beach, it's popular with a young backpacker crowd. Most of the boat and fishing tours leave from the central wharf, as do the passenger ferries to the historic village of Russell. The nearby suburb of Waitangi, however, is one of the country's most important historic sites. The Treaty Grounds, a lovely nearby park, was where the Treaty of Waitangi, the founding document for modern New Zealand, was signed.

The main Bay of Islands visitor bureau, in Paihia, is open daily. There is a really

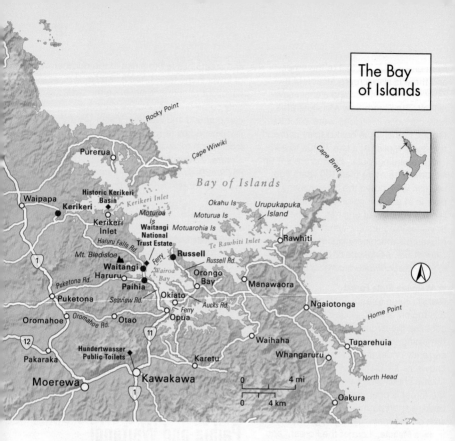

Bay of Islands

good toilet facility at the southern end of the strip.

GETTING HERE AND AROUND

BUS DEPOT Paihia. ✉ *Paihia Central, 69 Marsden Rd., Paihia* ☎ *09/402–7345* 🌐 *www.northlandnz.com.*

VISITOR INFORMATION

CONTACTS Bay of Islands Visitor Information Centre Paihia. ✉ *The Wharf, Marsden Rd., Paihia* ☎ *9/0800 363 463* 🌐 *www. northlandnz.com.*

◉ Sights

The Hundertwasser Public Toilets

NOTABLE BUILDING | On the main street of Kawakawa, a nondescript town just off State Highway 1 south of Paihia, stand surely the most outlandish public toilets in the country—a must-go even if you don't need to. Built by Austrian artist and architect Friedensreich Hundertwasser in 1997, the toilets are fronted by brightly colored ceramic columns supporting an arched portico, which in turn supports a garden of grasses. There are no straight lines in the building, which is furnished inside with mostly white tiles, punctuated with primary colors, and set in black grout (something like a Mondrian after a few drinks). Plants sprout from the roof. If you sit in one of the cafés across the road you can watch the tourist buses stop so the visitors can take pictures of the facilities. ✉ *Gillies St., Kawakawa* 🌐 *www.bay-of-islands-nz.com/hundertwasser.shtml.*

Mt. Bledisloe

VIEWPOINT | **FAMILY** | On the National Trust Estate beyond the Treaty Grounds, Mt. Bledisloe showcases the splendid view across Paihia and the Bay of Islands. The

Women perform a POI dance at the Māori National Festival in Waitangi, which commemorates the signing of the Treaty of Waitangi.

handsome ceramic marker at the top showing the distances to major world cities was made by Doulton in London and presented by Lord Bledisloe in 1934 during his term as governor-general of New Zealand. The mount is 3 km (2 miles) from the Treaty House, on the other side of the Waitangi Golf Course. From a small parking area on the right of Waitangi Road, a short track rises above a pine forest to the summit. ⊠ *Mt. Bledisloe, Waitangi.*

★ Waitangi National Trust Estate
HISTORIC SIGHT | Take in a major site in New Zealand's history at the northern end of Paihia to gain a better understanding of the turbulent relationship between Māori and the British colonizers. The Treaty House on Waitangi Treaty Grounds is a simple white-timber cottage and was prefabricated in New South Wales for British resident James Busby, who arrived in New Zealand in 1832. Busby had been appointed to protect British commerce and put an end to the brutalities of the whaling captains

against the Māori, but he lacked the judicial authority and the force of arms necessary to impose peace. The real significance of the Treaty House lies in the events that took place here on February 6, 1840, the day the Treaty of Waitangi was signed by Māori chiefs and Captain William Hobson, representing the British crown. The treaty was the first formal document that bound the Māori to the British crown, and it became the basis for Britain's claim to the entire country as its colony. The visitor center presents the events that led to the Treaty of Waitangi. You'll also be able to experience *kapa haka*, a live Māori cultural performance. The center also displays Māori artifacts and weapons, including a musket that belonged to Hone Heke Pokai, the first Māori chief to sign the treaty, who would later go on to attack the British in their stronghold at Russell. From the visitor center, follow a short track (trail) through the forest to Ngatoki Matawhaorua (ng-ga-to-ki ma-ta-*fa*-oh-*roo*-ah), a Māori

Continued on page 136

CARVING

Although pre-European Māori did not have a written language, their traditional carvings served as a historical record. Every piece has a *kaupapa* (story), which can be read by those who know how. The shape of the heads, position of the body, and surface patterns work together to commemorate important events.

MĀORI ART

Kiwi culture weaves together Māori and *Pākehā* (European) traditions. Māori symbols crop up in everything from the popular whale's tail pendants to a major airline's modernized koru logo. Likewise, today Māori art melds traditional storytelling with modern concerns.

It wasn't always this way, but since the 1970s there has been a resurgence of, and interest in, Māori culture throughout New Zealand. Days begin with the Māori greeting, "kia ora," literally "be well," offered by Māoris and Pākehā alike. Kiwis cheer the world-famous All Blacks rugby squad when they perform the haka—that fierce warrior dance that intimidates opposing teams.

There has even been a renaissance in Māori arts, crafts, and body art. Weavers gather by the hundreds to participate in the hui workshop. Reviving an ancient tradition, they work their *harakeke* (flax) materials into baskets and skirts.

Tens of thousands of spectators attend the biannual Māori performance competition at the Te Matatini arts festival. In Rotorua, the center of modern Māori life in New Zealand, there are nightly traditional chants and *hāngi* feasts. Galleries all over New Zealand celebrate works of contemporary artists who express strong or glancing Māori influences in their pieces, and visitors and locals alike mimic traditional Māori *moku*, or tattoos.

Although some people see this as unfair cultural appropriation, many Māori artisans see this integration as essential to preserving their culture.

Above: Whare *runanga* (meeting house), Waitangi

TRADITIONAL ART

Traditional Māori art is symbolic, not literal, and recurring motifs appear on meeting houses, in jewelry, and on other objects. Some shapes and symbols come from nature, others represent ancestors or the geographical region of an *iwi*, or tribe.

Hei Matau—The fish hook is a popular talisman for safe journeys over water. It also represents prosperity.

Hiku—New Zealanders frequently wear the whale's tail, which is a sign of strength and speed.

Koru—The curled fern frond symbolizes beginnings or life, as well as peace and strength.

Hei Tiki—The small human figure with a tilted head depicts a fetus in the womb and symbolizes fertility.

MASKS

North Island styles of face mask include Tai Tokerau, Tai Rawhiti, and Rongowhakaata, and are distinguished by the parallel, angular lines framing the eyes. Koruru, found in the mid-North Island area, are masks characterized by rounded, bulging eyes. The point at the top of the Taranaki mask symbolizes Mount Taranaki. In the Coromandel area, look for telltale paua shell eyes in the Pare Hauraki and hollow eye sockets in the Te Whanau a Apanui. The Te Arawa Māori, who live between Rotorua and Lake Taupo, make Ruru masks with pointed ears representing a small owl.

WOOD CARVING

Whakairo (carving) holds an important place in Māori culture; it functions as both an art form and a historical record. Each line and shape has meaning, and each design connects the physical object with mana, or spiritual power. Intricately carved Māori meeting houses and raised storehouses, seen on both islands, demonstrate the Māori practice of designing and patterning objects to imbue them with the spirits of ancestors. For an excellent example, visit the meeting house and war canoe on the Treaty of Waitangi grounds on the North Island.

Apprentice carvers spend upwards of ten years learning their craft.

TEKOTEKO AND OTHER OBJECTS

This ancestral face on an archway greets visitors to a marae.

Tekoteko, carved human figures, adorn Māori meeting houses, homes, and, traditionally, canoe prows. These symbolic ancestors' defiant stances, protruding tongues, and weapons ward off intruders. Other carved items include ceremonial war paddles (*wahaika*), spears (*taiaha*), treasure boxes, and sticks. Look for these carvings at a marae or in museums and galleries.

PAINTINGS (KOWHAIWHAI)

Decorative patterns, called *kowhaiwhai*, are considered less sacred than wood carvings or tattoo-making and can be done by anyone. Find these temporary designs on meeting-house ridgepoles and rafters, canoe bottoms, and paddles. The standard black, white, and red paints mimic the colors produced by red ochre, white clay, and charcoal, the materials used by Māori ancestors. Designs can represent speed and swiftness or hospitality and strength.

Above: The koru symbol is common in Māori style painting.

MĀORI TA MOKO

Unlike contemporary ink tattoos, traditional Māori *moku* (tattoos) were literally carved into the body with a tool called an uhi, filled with soot from burnt plants or caterpillars, and covered with leaves to heal.

Only those of high rank wore facial tattoos, and they were recognized by these patterns rather than by the natural features we use to describe people today. Segments of the face were reserved for identifying features related to the social rank of the wearer's family; for example, sections on each side of the face depicted the ancestry from the mother's and father's sides.

Markings also commemorated important events in a person's life and, except for some tribes that had tattoos on their legs and buttocks, were confined to the face. Women's tattoos were, and still are, limited to an outline around the lips and thin lines from the lips down the chin. This pattern is still worn in ink tattoos today.

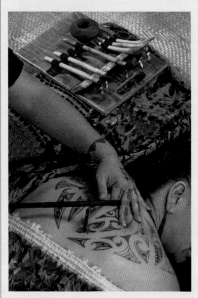

Today, talented Ta Moko artists continue the deeply spiritual traditions of ancient Māori tattooing.

MODERN MĀORI ART

Contemporary Māori artists work in every medium, including music, weaving, crafts, film, and visual entertainment, and often contain subtle cultural references or overt interpretations of historic symbols.

Museums, such as the comprehensive **Museum of New Zealand Te Papa Tongarewa** (in Wellington), the **Auckland Art Gallery Toi o Tāmaki**, and the tiny **Suter Art Gallery** (in Nelson), exhibit a range of art that may include portraits of Māori and their Ta Moku from the last century or modern, mixed-media art by pan-Pacific artists commenting on current events.

Contemporary artwork with traditional Māori influences

MĀORI JEWELRY AND SOUVENIRS

Māori symbols are common in contemporary pendants that are crafted of plastic and wood and hung on a braided cord. More expensive versions are made of greenstone (jade), once used for chisels and weaponry, or bone. These necklaces are popular souvenirs.

Traditional Māori pendant carved from greenstone (jade)

Many contemporary artists take the idea of these traditional pendants and reinterpret motifs in fresh ways. A modern necklace may reference a pattern from a chief's cloak or hint at the fish hook without mimicking the pattern. While such jewelry may come in greenstone, some artists work with metals like silver or gold instead.

Modern angular and traditional rounded wooden treasure boxes, called wakahuia, incorporate Māori symbols.

Contemporary textile artists blend traditional materials such as flax, tree bark pigments, and feathers with nontraditional colors to craft modern purses and wall hangings.

Popular souvenirs include greenstone, ceramics, synthetic feathers, decorative flax designs, replicas of paddles and war clubs, clothing, and jewelry. The Toi Iho certifies that items were produced by Māori artists (🌐 *www.toiiho. co.nz*). Not all Māori artists participate in the program; check carefully for authenticity.

This girl wears a greenstone pendant.

BUYING MĀORI ART

Woven Kete *pikau* (backpack)

Māori ceramics with traditional motifs

WHERE TO BUY

Those seriously interested in Māori art and culture should visit Rotorua. Creative Rotorua (🌐 *www.creativerotorua.org.nz*) is an umbrella organization that links to arts organizations, performances, various area artists, and the local Māori Arts Trail, which maps out studios you can visit. If your trip coincides with Te Matatini, a dance showcase as well as the largest Māori arts festival in the world, scour the booths for authentic crafts (🌐 *www.tematatini.org.nz*).

If Rotorua isn't on your itinerary, seek out Māori galleries in Christchurch, Queenstown, Auckland, Wellington, and Whangarei. The Te Papa Museum in Wellington has a range of Māori-influenced New Zealand artworks, jewelry and prints. Most museum shops have reproductions of pieces in the collection and rare art books.

HOW TO CHOOSE

Buy what you like or choose a depiction of a place you visited. The connection you feel to a piece and its beauty should motivate, not whether the piece might have resale value. If quality is important, seek authentication from a dealer.

CUSTOM MADE FOR YOU

New Zealand's small population and informal atmosphere allow for direct contact with artists. Visit their studios, attend a workshop, or chat with them about their pieces. Most artisans and craftspeople will happily custom-make a piece to forward to you at home. There are also dozens of online shops offering various Māori-themed wares if you regret not making a purchase after you return. By purchasing directly from the artist you'll get a one-of-a-kind piece, but don't expect a discount.

USEFUL WEB SITES
🌐 *www.maoriart.org.nz*

The Moko, or facial tattoo, on this carved figure displays ancestral and tribal messages that apply to the wearer. These messages represent the wearer's family, sub-tribal and tribal affiliations, and his place within these social structures. This carving commemorates an ancestor.

war canoe. ⊠ *Waitangi Rd., Waitangi* ☎ *09/402–7437* ⊕ *www.waitangi.org.nz* ✉ *NZ$50.*

Restaurants

Charlotte's Kitchen
$$$$ | **INTERNATIONAL** | This busy restaurant is named after Charlotte Badger, one of the first European women to live in New Zealand; legend says she was actually a pirate. It's pricey, but worth it for the delicious Japan-inspired seafood, seasonal vegetables, wood-fired pizza, and also gorgeous views from its location at the end of the wharf. **Known for:** good pizza selection; tasty cocktails; excellent oysters. $ *Average main: NZ$34* ⊠ *69 Marsden Rd., Paihia* ☎ *09/402–8296* ⊕ *www.charlotteskitchen.co.nz.*

Hotels

Abri
$$ | **HOTEL** | These freestanding studio apartments resemble tree houses and provide lovely sea views from the bush behind the Paihia beachfront. **Pros:** beautiful decor; close to town; friendly hosts. **Cons:** you're on your own for food; no beach or pool; some room views are better than others. $ *Rooms from: NZ$199* ⊠ *10–12 Bayview Rd., Paihia* ☎ *09/402–8003* ⊕ *www.abriapartments.co.nz* ⇄ *3 rooms* ⊚ *No Meals.*

Copthorne Hotel and Resort Bay of Islands
$$ | **HOTEL** | The biggest hotel north of Auckland and a favorite with tour groups, this complex sprawls along a peninsula within walking distance of the Treaty House. **Pros:** French-provincial style; lovely location; most rooms have a terrace or patio. **Cons:** limited Wi-Fi (that you have to pay for); often full of conference-goers; some rooms need refreshing. $ *Rooms from: NZ$175* ⊠ *Tau Henare Dr., Waitangi* ☎ *09/402–7411* ⊕ *www.millenniumhotels.com/en/bay-of-islands/copthorne-hotel-and-resort-bay-of-islands* ⇄ *145 rooms* ⊚ *No Meals.*

Paihia Beach Resort and Spa
$$$$ | **RESORT** | **FAMILY** | A large *pohutukawa* tree stands next to the heated saltwater pool in front, and all of the rooms have bay views, a deck or patio, and a large whirlpool tub in the bathroom. **Pros:** close to town; excellent spa; stunning views. **Cons:** breakfast not included; decor a bit dated; some road noise. $ *Rooms from: NZ$610* ⊠ *116 Marsden Rd., Paihia* ☎ *09/402–0111* ⊕ *www.paihia-beach.co.nz* ⇄ *21 rooms* ⊚ *No Meals.*

Activities

Getting out on the water is a highlight of the Bay of Islands whether on the ferry crossing from Paihia to Russell or on a guided trip such as the world-famous Hole in the Rock cruise. The coastal areas are also lovely places to stroll, especially in summer.

BOATING

Carino NZ Sailing and Dolphin Adventures
BOATING | Get close to dolphins (primarily bottlenose) and penguins. Passengers on the 50-foot purpose-built red catamaran can just relax or pitch in with sailing. This full-day trip includes a barbecue lunch at one of the islands, weather permitting, and a full cash bar is on board. This company has a permit that allows guests to swim with dolphins. The tours do not run in the winter months. ⊠ *Paihia Wharf Marsden Rd., Paihia* ☎ *09/402–8040* ⊕ *wildlifecruises.co.nz* ⊗ *Closed Jun.–Sept.* ✉ *From NZ$140.*

★ Fullers
BOATING | Cruises and sea-based adventure trips depart daily from both Paihia and Russell. The most comprehensive sightseeing trip is the six-hour, summer-only Best of the Bay Supercruise aboard a high-speed catamaran. You'll follow about half of what was once called the "Cream Trip" route, but nowadays, instead of picking up cream from farms, the boat delivers mail and supplies to vacation homes. Fullers also visits

Urupukapuka Island, once home to a *hapu* (subtribe) of the Ngare Raumati Māori. Little is known about their life, but there are numerous archaeological sites. It's also the only one to go to Otehei Bay, one of the island's most spectacular bays. On this particular trip, the boat stops for 1½ hours on the island, where you can go kayaking, take a short hike, or have lunch at the Zane Grey Café. The trip also takes in the Hole in the Rock, a natural hole at sea level in Piercy Island that boats pass through if the tide is right. During winter there is a shorter trip that is mostly focused on finding dolphins. If you prefer to travel under sail, try the the gaff-rigged schooner *R. Tucker Thompson,* which Fullers also operates. ✉ *Maritime Bldg., Marsden Rd., Paihia* ☎ *09/402–7421* ⊕ *www.dolphincruises. co.nz* ✆ *From NZ$120.*

DIVING

The Bay of Islands has some of the finest scuba diving in the country, particularly around Cape Brett, where the marine life includes moray eels, stingrays, and grouper. The wreck of the Greenpeace vessel *Rainbow Warrior,* bombed and sunk by French agents in 1985, is another underwater highlight. The wreck was transported to the Cavalli Islands in 1987 and is now covered in soft corals and jewel anemones; it's full of fish life. Water temperature at the surface varies from 16°C (62°F) in July to 22°C (71°F) in January. From September through November, underwater visibility can be affected by a plankton bloom.

Yukon Dive

SCUBA DIVING | This company with a highly experienced team will take you around two significant sunken ships: the Greenpeace vessel *Rainbow Warrior* plus the former Royal New Zealand Navy vessel *Canterbury,* and farther afield if required. It offers trips for accredited divers and has rental equipment. The unaccredited can sign up for dive courses, but snorkeling is also on offer. ✉ *7 Williams Rd., Paihia* ☎ *21/261–1779* ⊕ *www. yukon.co.nz* ✆ *From NZ$200 (including equipment).*

Russell

4 km (2½ miles) east of Paihia by ferry, 13 km (8 miles) by road and car ferry.

Russell is regarded as the "second" town in the Bay of Islands, but it's far more interesting, and pleasant, than Paihia. Hard as it is to believe, sleepy little Russell was once dubbed the "Hellhole of the Pacific." In the mid- to late 19th century (when it was still known by its Māori name, Kororareka) it was a swashbuckling frontier town, a haven for sealers and whalers who found the East Coast of New Zealand to be one of the richest whaling grounds on Earth.

Tales of debauchery abound. British administrators in New South Wales were sufficiently concerned to dispatch a British resident agent in 1832 to impose law and order. After the Treaty of Waitangi, Russell was the capital until 1844, when the Māori chief Hone Heke, disgruntled with newly imposed harbor dues and his loss of authority, cut down the flagstaff flying the Union Jack above the town three times before attacking the British garrison. Most of the town burned to the ground in what is known as the Sacking of Kororareka. Hone Heke was finally defeated in 1846, but Russell never recovered its former prominence, and the seat of government was shifted first to Auckland, then to Wellington.

Today Russell is a delightful town of timber houses and big trees that hang low over the seafront, framing the yachts and game-fishing boats in the harbor. The relaxed vibe can best be absorbed in a stroll along the Strand, the path along the waterfront. There are several safe swimming beaches, some in secluded bays, as well as the aptly named Long Beach, over the hill from the township.

GETTING HERE AND AROUND

The road between Russell and Paihia is long, winding, and tortuous. A better and faster way to travel between the two is by passenger ferry, which leaves from the Russell Wharf, or by car ferry, which departs from Okiato, about 9 km (5½ miles) southwest of town.

VISITOR INFORMATION

CONTACTS Russell Information Centre. ✉ *Russell Wharf, Russell* ☎ *09/403–8020* 🌐 *www.russellinfo.co.nz.*

Sights

Christ Church

CHURCH | One of the donors to the construction of New Zealand's oldest church was Charles Darwin, who at that time in 1835 was making his way around the globe on board the HMS *Beagle*. Behind the white picket fence that borders the churchyard, gravestones tell a fascinating and brutal story of life in the colony's early days. Several graves belong to sailors from the HMS *Hazard* who were killed in this churchyard by Hone Heke's warriors in 1845. Another headstone marks the grave of a Nantucket sailor from the whaler *Mohawk*. As you walk around the church, look for the musket holes made when Hone Heke besieged the church. The interior is simple and charming—embroidered cushions on the pews are examples of a still-vibrant folk-art tradition. ✉ *Church and Robertson Sts., Russell.*

Pompallier Mission

NOTABLE BUILDING | **FAMILY** | New Zealand's oldest industrial building, the Pompallier Mission, at the southern end of the Strand, was named after the first Catholic bishop of the South Pacific. Marist missionaries built the original structure out of rammed earth, because they lacked the funds to buy timber. For several years the priests and brothers operated a press here, printing Bibles in the Māori language. From December through April you can visit independently, but from May to November the mission organizes tours at set times. The gardens are beautiful. ✉ *5 The Strand, Russell* ☎ *09/403–9015* 🌐 *www.pompallier.co.nz* 🎫 *NZ$15.*

Restaurants

★ The Gables Restaurant

$$$$ | **MODERN NEW ZEALAND** | One of Russell's oldest buildings (built in 1847) is home to an up-to-the-minute kitchen, serving the finest cuts of meat, fresh fish, and imaginative vegetarian options. The atmosphere is calm, the wine list decent, and the service is on point. **Known for:** great seafood; smart seasonal cooking; lively atmosphere. [$] *Average main: NZ$40* ✉ *19 The Strand, Russell* ☎ *09/403–7670* 🌐 *www.thegablesrestaurant.co.nz.*

Hotels

★ Arcadia Lodge

$$$ | **B&B/INN** | This B&B, perched over Matauwhi Bay a few minutes' walk from town, had been supported for more than 100 years by whale vertebrae, which served as the backbones of this turn-of-the-20th-century home. **Pros:** lovely rooms; decadent breakfast; spectacular views. **Cons:** no other meals besides breakfast are served; finding the parking lot is tricky so follow the directions on the website; no beach access or pool. [$] *Rooms from: NZ$255* ✉ *10 Florance Ave., Russell* ☎ *09/403–7756* 🌐 *www.arcadialodge.co.nz* 🛏 *5 rooms* 🍴 *Free Breakfast.*

Duke of Marlborough Hotel

$$$ | **HOTEL** | This waterfront hotel is a favorite with the yachting fraternity, for whom ready access to the harbor and the bar downstairs are the most important considerations. **Pros:** fun crowds; prime waterfront position; good restaurant. **Cons:** little privacy; can be too close to the action; quite noisy. $ *Rooms from: NZ$285* ✉ *35 The Strand, Russell* ☏ *09/403–7829* ⊕ *www.theduke.co.nz* ⇌ *26 rooms* ⫚ *No Meals.*

 Activities

FISHING
Major Tom Charters

FISHING | Chase game fish such as marlin, kingfish, *hapuka* (grouper), snapper, broadbill, and tuna. Trips begin at 4 hours, but you can also book a full day, with a maximum of four anglers and lunch (hopefully you catch dinner) or a three-day trip with overnight stays. Fish caught that is of legal size is filleted and packaged for you to take with you. Equipment is provided, and the team will pick you up and deliver you back to your accommodations. ✉ *Russell Wharf, Russell* ☏ *274/341074* ⊕ *www.majortom. co.nz* ⛴ *4-hour trips from NZ$135 per person, full-day trips from NZ$1800 for four people, 3-night trips from NZ$5500.*

HIKING
There are several pleasant walks around the Russell area; the most challenging—and spectacular—is the 16.3-kilometer (10-mile) **Cape Brett Tramping Track** out to the lighthouse. It costs NZ$40 to walk the track, and you can stay in a hut for NZ$15 a night; book either at the Department of Conservation website (*www.doc.govt.nz*). You must book and pay in advance, as this is a popular walk. It is not for the unfit or inexperienced, and good shoes and all weather gear are a must. Check with the Russell Information Centre on the wharf or the DOC website for updates. For a shorter jaunt on your own (an hour each way), follow the **Whangamumu Walking Track** to the remnants of a whaling station. Many relics such as an old boiler and vats are still left at the station.

Kerikeri

20 km (12 miles) north of Paihia.

Kerikeri is often referred to as the cradle of the nation because so much of New Zealand's earliest history, especially interactions between Māori and Europeans, took place here. A major citrus and kiwifruit growing area, it was once principally a service town for the whole mid-north region. Though newcomers have flocked to Kerikeri for its low-key lifestyle, it still feels like a small town. The Sunday farmers' market is a treat.

The **Kerikeri Proctor Library,** open weekdays 8 to 5, and Saturday from 9:30 to 2, is the only place in Kerikeri that provides visitor information, and it's far less extensive than other bureaus.

GETTING HERE AND AROUND
Kerikeri is about four hours' drive from Auckland following State Highway 1 though significant road works may add time to the journey. Buses connect from Auckland directly and from the other centers. There is also a good airport with regular flights, but it is expensive to fly, particularly from Auckland. There is no train service.

VISITOR INFORMATION
CONTACTS Kaitaia Visitor Information Centre. ✉ *At South and Matthews Rd.,* ☏ *09/408–9450* ⊕ *www.northlandnz. com.*

 Sights

Kerikeri Mission Station

HISTORIC SIGHT | **FAMILY** | The station, which includes the 1821 Mission House and the Stone Store, provides a fascinating and rare look at pretreaty New Zealand. Kemp House, otherwise known as Mission House, has gone through many changes since 1821, but ironically, a major flood in 1981 inspired its "authentic" restoration. The flood washed away the garden and damaged the lower floor, and during repair much information about the original structure of the house was revealed. Its ground floor and garden have been restored to the style of missionary days, and the upper floor retains its Victorian decoration. Stone Store, New Zealand's oldest stone building, is a striking example of early colonial architecture. Designed by Wesleyan missionary John Hobbs and built by an Australian convict stonemason between 1832 and 1836, the Store was meant to house New Zealand mission supplies and large quantities of wheat from the mission farm at Te Waimate. When the wheat failed, the building was mainly leased as a kauri gum-trading store. The ground floor is still a shop. The upper stories display the goods of a culture trying to establish itself in a new country, such as red Hudson Bay blankets, which were sought after by Māori from the *pā* (hilltop fortification), forged goods, steel tools, an old steel flour mill, and tools and flintlock muskets—also prized by local Māori. Guided tours are available; bookings are essential. ⊠ *Kerikeri Historic Basin, Kerikeri Rd., Kerikeri* ☎ *09/407–9236* ⊕ *www. heritage.org.nz* 🎟 *NZ$15.*

Kororipo Pā

HISTORIC SIGHT | Across the road from the Kerikeri Basin's Stone Store is a path leading to the historic site of Kororipo Pā, the fortified headquarters of legendary chief Hongi Hika. The chief visited England in 1820, where he was showered with gifts. On his way back to New Zealand, during a stop in Sydney, he traded many of these presents for muskets. Having the advantage of these prized weapons, he set in motion plans to conquer other Māori tribes, enemies of his own Ngapuhi people. The return of his raiding parties over five years, with many slaves and gruesome trophies of conquest, put considerable strain between Hongi Hika and the missionaries. Eventually, his warring ways were Hongi's undoing. He was shot in 1827

and died from complications from the wound a year later. Untrained eyes may have difficulty figuring out exactly where the pā (Māori fortification) was, as no structures are left. The pā was built on a steep-sided promontory between the Kerikeri River and the Wairoa Stream. ⊠ *Kororipo Pā, Kerikeri* ☎ *09/407 0300* ⊕ *kororipo.co.nz.*

Te Ahurea

MUSEUM VILLAGE | FAMILY | Formerly called simply "Rewa's Village," this museum re-creates a *kāinga* (unfortified fishing village) where local Māori lived in peaceful times. In times of war they took refuge in nearby Kororipo Pā. In the village are good reproductions of the chief Hongi Hika's house, the weapons store, and the family enclosure, as well as two original canoes dug up from local swamps and original *hāngi* stones found on-site, which were heated by fire and used to cook traditional Māori feasts. A "discoverers garden" takes you on a winding path past indigenous herbs and other plants; information is posted describing the uses of each plant. ⊠ *1 Landing Rd., Kerikeri* ☎ *09/407–6454* ⊕ *teahurea.co.nz* 🎟 *NZ$20; tours from NZ$30* 🕐 *Closed Mon.*

Restaurants

★ Fishbone Café

$$$ | CAFÉ | The proprietors of this outfit take food, coffee, and hospitality seriously. It's an oasis of superb food and well worth a stop on a trip through the North. **Known for:** local charm; excellent coffee; great wine list. 🟦 *Average main: NZ$25* ⊠ *88 Kerikeri Rd., Kerikeri* ☎ *09/407–6065* ⊕ *www.fishbonekerikeri. co.nz* 🕐 *No dinner.*

★ Marsden Estate Winery and Restaurant

$$$$ | ECLECTIC | Named after the missionary Samuel Marsden, who planted New Zealand's first grapevines in Kerikeri in 1819, this family-run winery is a popular breakfast and lunch spot and for good

Northern Northland

Above the Bay of Islands Northland are many small communities. For many the big attraction is **90 Mile Beach**, a 100-km (60-mile) or so long clear stretch of golden sand running up North Island's tip. You access it from Kaitaia, a vibrant town with an extremely good café—Birdies—where the omelets are not only delicious, they will set you up for the day. If you want to travel the beach, take a tour; the beach is virtually off-limits to independent travelers, as, thanks to quicksand and incoming tides, rental-car insurance won't cover you here.

Just out of Kaitaia are the beaches at Ahipara and Shipwrecks. Surfers love the long lines and almost perfect waves here. Many surfers head south around the point for even better waves and fewer people.

Cape Reinga, at the peninsula's end, is a sacred Māori area. They believe that spirits depart for the underworld by sliding down the roots of the headland's gnarled *pohutukawa* tree (reputed to be 800 years old) and into the sea. A much-photographed solitary lighthouse stands here.

You can easily drive into the Far North, barring 90 Mile Beach. From the Bay of Islands on State Highway 10 you'll reach Mangonui, a former whaling port on the southeast side of **Doubtless Bay.** Beach lovers should head for the Karikari Peninsula, on Doubtless Bay's northwestern side. From Doubtless Bay it's less than a half-hour drive west to Awanui, near the service town of Kaitaia. Fill your gas tank in one of these two towns, then head north on Highway 1. The last few miles to Cape Reinga aren't paved.

reason. The seasonal menu is eclectic and is built around fresh, local produce. **Known for:** terrace seating; excellent seasonal cuisine; high-quality wine. $ *Average main: NZ$40* ✉ *Wiroa Rd., Kerikeri* ☎ *09/407–9398* 🌐 *www.marsdenestate.co.nz* ⏲ *No dinner.*

Hotels

★ Kauri Cliffs Lodge

$$$$ | **ALL-INCLUSIVE** | **FAMILY** | Several holes of a par-72 championship golf course sweep past this luxurious cliff-top lodge, which is truly outstanding and (for a price) offers space and excellent food for an all-inclusive rate. **Pros:** all the amenities you can imagine including pool, spa, and beach access; absolute luxury; superb scenery. **Cons:** expensive; possibly overwhelming for first-timers; dress code on the strict side. $ *Rooms from: NZ$1730* ✉ *139 Tepene Tablelands Rd., Matauri Bay* ☎ *09/407–0010* 🌐 *www.kauricliffs.com* 🛏 *22 suites.*

Kauri Park

$$ | **HOTEL** | **FAMILY** | This small cluster of chalets is a notch above the usual, with contemporary style and a magnificent setting among fruit trees adjacent to farmland. **Pros:** lovely location; relaxed and friendly atmosphere; beautiful rooms. **Cons:** no on-site restaurant; not within walking distance of town; some rooms on the small side. $ *Rooms from: NZ$190* ✉ *512 Kerikeri Rd., Kerikeri* ☎ *09/407–7629* 🌐 *www.kauripark.co.nz* 🛏 *9 units* 🍴 *No Meals.*

Paheke

$$ | **B&B/INN** | An enormous cedar of Lebanon stands in front of this gracious 1864 kauri homestead; both the tree and

the house are listed with the Historic Places Trust. **Pros:** stunning grounds; good value; relaxing atmosphere. **Cons:** some rooms share a bathroom; not close to town; might be too old-fashioned for some. [$] *Rooms from: NZ$150* ✉ *State Hwy. 1, Ohaeawai* ☎ *09/405–9623* 🌐 *www.paheke.co.nz* 🛏 *3 rooms* 🍴 *Free Breakfast.*

Shopping

Kerikeri Farmers' Market
MARKET | FAMILY | If you're in Kerikeri on a Sunday, head to the market to sample and buy the best the region has to offer, from music to fresh produce, local wines, cheeses, preserves, oils, and handmade soaps. Grab a locally roasted coffee and wander among the stalls. ✉ *Parking lot, off Hobson Ave., Kerikeri* 🌐 *www.bayofislandsfarmersmarket.co.nz.*

Makana Confections
CHOCOLATE | FAMILY | The hand-made confections at this boutique are fabulous. Favorites include the macadamia butter toffee crunch; chocolate-coated, locally grown macadamias; and liqueur truffles. Alongside the lineup of classic sweet treats like truffles and citrus jelly squares are some sugar-free items. ✉ *504 Kerikeri Rd., Kerikeri* ☎ *09/407–6800* 🌐 *www.makana.co.nz.*

Activities

GOLF

Carrington
GOLF | This tournament-quality course, which meanders along 100 acres of coastline, shares the land with its eponymous winery and Carrington Resort, a luxury lodge. It's popular with the corporate set or well-heeled golfers wanting to play in the country for a long weekend. ✉ *Matai Bay Rd., Karikari Peninsula* ☎ *09/408–1049* 🌐 *www.carrington.co.nz/golf* 🎟 *From NZ$135, club rentals NZ$20* ⛳ *18 holes, 7267 yards, par 72.*

★ **Kauri Cliffs**
GOLF | The spectacular championship course at Kauri Cliffs has four sets of tees to challenge every skill level. Fifteen holes have views of the Pacific, and six are played alongside the cliffs. Kauri Cliffs is approximately 45 minutes' drive from Kerikeri though many people fly in by helicopter. ✉ *139 Tepene Tablelands Rd., Matauri Bay* ☎ *09/407–0010* 🌐 *www.robertsonlodges.com/the-lodges/kauri-cliffs* 🎟 *From NZ$330* 🕒 *Closed Tues. and Wed.* ⛳ *18 holes, 7139 yards, par 72.*

Chapter 5

COROMANDEL AND THE BAY OF PLENTY

Updated by
Stuart Freeman

👁 **Sights**
★★★☆☆

🍴 **Restaurants**
★★☆☆☆

🛏 **Hotels**
★★☆☆☆

🛍 **Shopping**
★☆☆☆☆

🍸 **Nightlife**
★☆☆☆☆

WELCOME TO COROMANDEL AND THE BAY OF PLENTY

TOP REASONS TO GO

★ **Beach Bounty:** The seemingly endless coastline here is replete with forest-fringed inlets, sprawling sand dunes, and many of the country's most popular beaches.

★ **Vistas:** From Coromandel's coastal cliffs to the Bay of Plenty's volcanic peak, Mauao, great views abound.

★ **Walking and Hiking:** Climb Mauao (The Mount) for stunning coastal views, or take a forest walk to swim in a lagoon formed by Kaiate Falls. Coromandel Forest Park has a network of trails.

★ **Cycling and Gold:** Explore gold-mining history as you ride the gentle Hauraki Cycle Trail, through forested Karangahake and Waikino gorges.

★ **Watery Wonders:** Dive or snorkel in the region's marine reserves, or swim with dolphins. Charter a deep-sea fishing trip, or kayak beneath glow-worms by moonlight.

1 Thames. Coromandel's oldest town and current agricultural center.

2 Tapu-Coroglen Road. Gateway to the gorgeous Rapaura Watergardens.

3 Coromandel Town. The birthplace of the New Zealand gold rush.

4 Colville and Beyond. Coromandel's northmost (and wildest) reaches.

5 Whitianga. A great base for water activities.

6 Around Hahei. Home to the best beaches in the region.

7 Tairua. Another great base for area beaches.

8 Whangamata. A harborside town and summer hotspot.

9 Waihi to Paeroa. The southernmost part of Coromandel.

10 Katikati. Home to a collection of murals depicting the area's fraught history.

11 Tauranga. The Bay of Plenty's biggest city and one of the country's sunniest spots.

12 Whakatane. An important small town for Māori history.

13 Whakarri (White) Island. An eerie island containing New Zealand's most active volcano.

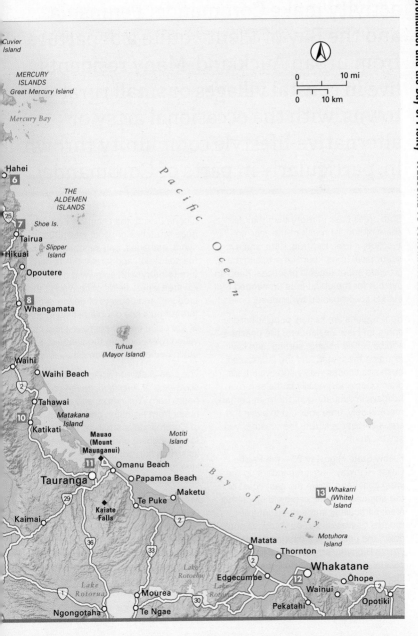

Beautiful sandy beaches, lush native forests, and some steamy geothermal activity make Coromandel Peninsula and the Bay of Plenty quite a departure from urban Auckland. Many residents live in coastal villages or small rural towns, with the occasional artsy or alternative-lifestyle community thrown in, particularly in parts of Coromandel.

Both areas bask in more than their fair share of sun for much of the year, so avocado, citrus, kiwifruit, nuts, and even subtropical fruits flourish here, and many growers adopt organic practices. Keep an eye out for the ubiquitous unmanned fruit stands accompanied by "honesty boxes."

Both regions are hugely popular holiday spots for New Zealanders: the beaches and bays, the fishing, surfing, and kayaking on the water, and the land-based bush and coastal walks and cycle trails draw people, especially in the summer holidays in January. Join them or, perhaps more wisely, time your trip to avoid the crowds—rest assured, the weather will still be warm.

Follow State Highway 25—the Pacific Coast Highway—as it meanders up the west coast and down the east coast of the peninsula. Traffic can build up on this road, particularly in the busy summer months or weekends. As you drive south down the peninsula's east coast, the Pacific Highway stretches out to the coastal plains and forests of the Bay of Plenty.

From the Bay of Plenty's northern gateway of Katikati as far as Whakatane and Ōhope Beach, the coastline consists of huge stretches of sand, interrupted by rivers, estuaries, and sandbars. Inland, the soil is rich and fertile; this is horticulture territory with sprawling canopies of kiwifruit vines, fields of corn and other produce, and pockets of dense native forest. You'll see people fishing in some of the bays, but others have strict conservation rules; signs in the shape of a fish outline whether you can fish.

The area is about two to three hours southeast of Auckland, seven to nine hours from Wellington, and one to two hours from Hamilton and Rotorua. Many of Coromandel's small settlements are former logging ports. Bay of Plenty, with its strong horticultural focus (in particular kiwifruit), is dotted with small rural towns fanning out from Tauranga's large port.

MAJOR REGIONS
Coromandel. Coromandel Peninsula beckons from the Hauraki Plains like a big lizard lying in the sun—the dark forest on the central mountainous spine promising more than just pretty pictures. When you arrive at the peninsula you'll be surprised how lush the forest growth is, wonder at how the road hugs the coast literally feet

above the water, and understand why people like living here. As with so many other lands "discovered" by Europeans, Coromandel was looted for its valuable resources: kauri trees, then kauri gum from the peninsula's forests, and finally gold from the southern hills and around Waihi and Coromandel towns in the 1870s. Relative quiet since the 1930s has allowed the region to recover its natural beauty and attract many life-styler types. In the 1960s and 1970s, dairy farms and orchards sprang up, as did communes, spiritual retreats, and artists' communities. The population is now a mix of artists, those who appreciate the country lifestyle (and the easy access to organic food), and a growing number of Aucklanders looking for a weekend or retirement home.

A craggy range of forest-covered peaks rises sharply to almost 3,000 feet and dominates the center of the peninsula. The west coast cradles the tidal Firth of Thames, and along the east coast the Pacific has carved out a succession of beaches and inlets separated by rearing headlands. Because of its rich soil, the peninsula has many spectacular gardens; some are open to the public. From the town of Thames, the gateway to the region, State Highway 25 will take you up the western coast of the peninsula to the Tapu-Coroglen Road, Coromandel Town, and Colville. Heading south on the eastern peninsula, you'll pass the towns of Whitianga, Hahei, Tairua, Whangamata, and the many beaches surrounding them. The southernmost part of the peninsula stretches between the towns of Waihi and Paeroa.

The Bay of Plenty. People refer to the Bay of Plenty as New Zealand's food bowl—as in plenty of food. Some of the most fertile land for fruit and vegetables is found in the region, and seafood is abundant. Coming from Coromandel, the first main area you'll hit is Katikati, and from there, you'll find the central city base of

the bay, Tauranga and its associated port, Mount Maunganui. Both have retained a relaxed vacation-town vibe despite ongoing expansion. From here and from the next major town along this coast, Whakatane, you can take day trips to beaches, the bush, and fly over volcanic White Island. "Laid-back sophistication" is an apt description of what this region can offer its visitors.

The Bay of Plenty also has a significant Māori history; this is the first landing place of *Takitimu, Tainui, Arawa,* and *Mataatua,* four of the seven Māori migration *waka* (canoes) that arrived in New Zealand from the Polynesian Pacific Islands, and from what they call their traditional homeland, Hawaiki. These first arrivals formed the ancestral base for the Māori tribes of the Tauranga region: Ngāti Ranginui, Ngāti Te Rangi, and Ngāti Pūkenga.

Planning

Getting Here and Around

AIR
There are some tiny airstrips along Coromandel Peninsula and a commercial airport at Tauranga and Whakatane. A number of scenic-flight operators offer trips over the region.

CONTACTS Air Chathams. ☎ 0800/580–127 ⊕ www.airchathams.co.nz. **Air New Zealand.** ☎ 0800/737–737 ⊕ www. airnewzealand.co.nz.

BUS
Go Kiwi Shuttles links Auckland, Auckland Airport, and towns of Coromandel, and also offers personal charters. InterCity Coachlines also serves the area.

CONTACTS Go Kiwi Shuttles. ☎ 0800/446–549 ⊕ www.go-kiwi.co.nz. **InterCity Coachlines.** ☎ 0800/222–146 toll free in New

Zealand, 09/583-5780 in New Zealand
⊕ *www.intercity.co.nz.*

CAR

The best way to explore the region is by car. Most roads are well-maintained and clearly signposted (albeit some can be narrow and winding), and a car gives you the freedom to explore attractions such as short walks and waterfalls along side roads.

There are two main ways to drive to Coromandel from Auckland. First take the Southern Motorway, following signs to Hamilton. Just as you get over the "Bombay Hills," turn left onto State Highway 2 (it's clearly signposted to Coromandel); then take the turnoff to State Highway 25, signposted between the small towns of Maramarua and Mangatarata. Follow the signs to Thames. Allow 1½ to 2½ hours for the 118-km (73-mile) journey. An arguably more scenic—though longer—way is to detour off the Southern Motorway at Manurewa, travel through Clevedon, and follow the Seabird Coast, past tiny Kaiaua village, Miranda thermal springs, and alongside the Firth of Thames, home to thousands of seabirds attracted here to the internationally recognized Ramsar wetland of Miranda. From Thames, State Highway 25 is the main loop that travels around the peninsula, and, though winding, the road is in good condition.

To reach the Bay of Plenty from Auckland, take the Southern Motorway, following signs to Hamilton. Just past the "Bombay Hills," turn left onto State Highway 2, and stay on Highway 2 all the way to Tauranga, driving through Paeroa, the scenic Karangahake Gorge (stop for walks and photos), Waihi, and Katikati on the way. The driving time between Auckland and Katikati is around 2 hours, 40 minutes. Between Auckland and Tauranga, it's at least 3 hours, 15 minutes.

FERRY

CONTACTS 360 Discovery. ☎ *0800/360–3472* ⊕ *www.fullers.co.nz.*

Auckland ferry company Fullers operates the 360 Discovery ferry service from downtown Auckland to Coromandel, daily during peak summer holiday season, five days per week during the rest of the summer, and three days a week during winter. The sailing takes just under two hours and travels via Waiheke and Rotoroa islands to Hannafords Wharf, 7 km (4 miles) from Coromandel Town. A free shuttle service operates into the town.

Hotels

Like mellow places around the world, you'll find plenty of comfortable bed-and-breakfasts and stylish motels, but both Coromandel and Bay of Plenty also have a sprinkling of luxe boutique lodges tucked away in the forest or along coastal coves. In peak season, from October through March, advance booking is essential across the board, and many of the better places have long-term customers who book as much as a year in advance.

Restaurant and hotel reviews have been shortened. For full information, visit Fodors.com. Restaurant prices are the average cost of a main course at dinner or, if dinner is not served, at lunch. Hotel prices are the lowest cost of a standard double room in high season.

WHAT IT COSTS in New Zealand Dollars			
$	$$	$$$	$$$$
RESTAURANTS			
under NZ$15	NZ$15–NZ$20	NZ$21–NZ$30	over NZ$30
HOTELS			
under NZ$125	NZ$125–NZ$200	NZ$201–NZ$300	over NZ$300

Planning Your Time

Set aside four to five days and get a rental car as Bay of Plenty and Coromandel need to be approached with flexibility. These regions have much to provide in a relatively small area. Allow for five-minute stops at the beach to become long coastal walks. Likewise, the many forest walks can be as challenging as you choose—from an hour to a whole day or overnight. You can approach the journey many ways, perhaps as a coastal exploration from Auckland along the "Seabird Coast," home to Miranda, an internationally recognized wetland on the Firth of Thames—then cross the fertile farmland of the Hauraki Plains to the base of Coromandel Peninsula. From here, try a loop of the peninsula that begins in Thames and ends in Whangamata, then continue along the coast to Bay of Plenty, Tauranga, and Whakatane. And be patient—the curvy roads challenge many drivers, especially tourists in campervans.

Restaurants

There are many dining options across Coromandel and the Bay of Plenty. You can buy fruit from roadside orchard stalls and takeout from fish-and-chips joints as well as visit cafés serving sandwiches, burgers, and espresso coffee, right through to fine-dining affairs. Even when restaurants are formal in appearance, diners and hosts tend toward a relaxed country-casualness. Restaurant owners make a point of using the region's abundant resources, like fruit from local orchards and shellfish from nearby mussel and scallop farms.

Dinner service begins about 6 pm in the winter and around 7 pm during the summer months, though many places have "all-day menus." In peak season, most places keep serving until at least 9 pm. For many restaurants, reservations are a good idea, especially in the summer

around Coromandel. In winter, phone ahead to check if the restaurant will stay open.

Tours

Coromandel Adventures
GUIDED TOURS | If you don't have your own transport, that's not a problem. Coromandel Adventures will happily drive you to any or all of the area's major sights or simply from town to town. The small company has a range of tailor-made tours that will show you the best and some secret spots of Coromandel, including the northern peninsula tip and beautiful Hot Water Beach and Cathedral Cove on the eastern side. Check the website for online specials. ✉ *480 Driving Creek Rd., Coromandel* ☎ *0800/462–676 toll-free in NZ only, 07/866–7014* ⊕ *www.coromandeladventures.co.nz* ✈ *From NZ$25.*

Visitor Information

The Coromandel, Katikati, Tauranga, Thames, Pauanui, Tairua, Waihi, Whakatane, Whangamata, and Whitianga visitor centers are open daily between at least 10 and 4. For tidal information, check the back page of the *New Zealand Herald* newspaper. *Tait's Fun Maps* of Coromandel, Thames, and Whitianga are not drawn to scale, but they clearly mark roads and main attractions. Pick up a copy at almost any hotel, tour-operator office, or visitor center, or check the official website for Destination Coromandel (*www.thecoromandel.com*).

When to Go

These regions are well loved for their beaches, and they are crowded between December and February when the hot summer weather draws thousands of holiday makers; sleepy seaside towns become filled with city folk with a tourist surge during the weeks around

Christmas and the New Year. Don't overlook the off-season (March through September). The weather's usually sunny, climate is temperate, prices are lower, and locals have more time to chat. Some of the more hardy locals swim whatever the weather.

Thames

120 km (75 miles) southeast of Auckland.

The peninsula's oldest town, Thames has evolved from a gold-mining hotbed in the late 1800s to an agricultural center. Locals have a saying that when the gold ran out, "Thames went to sleep awaiting the kiss of a golden prince—and instead it awoke to the warm breath of a cow." The main street was once lined with nearly 100 hotels (that is bars—gold mining and logging was thirsty work, and only hotels could serve alcohol). Only a handful of these hotels still operate, but the town and environs provide glimpses of the mining era. In 1872, two towns, Grahamstown in the north and Shortland in the south, merged to form Thames, and many locals still refer to upper Thames as Grahamstown. Thames today is also the gateway to Kauaeranga Valley, part of Coromandel Forest Park, home to waterfalls, kauri groves, and the dramatic Pinnacles formations. Pinnacles Hut is a popular overnight hiking destination (advance booking required). Thames is also the northern entry point for the two- to four-day Hauraki Rail Trail. This is part of Nga Haerenga, the New Zealand Cycle Trail. The 173-km (107-mile) trail travels in part on former railway lines, including tunnels (the grade is easy), and explores farmland, the coast around Thames, gold-mining history, and the scenic Karangahake Gorge.

GETTING HERE AND AROUND

If you're not driving, you can take a public bus to Thames from Auckland, Hamilton, Tauranga, or any of the smaller towns on the main road en route from these cities. If you're coming from the nearest big city, a bus ticket shouldn't cost you more than about NZ$30–NZ$42.

You can pick up a rental car at the Auckland airport and drive on down to Coromandel, or you can take a bus and rent a car when you arrive in Thames. At the Thames i-SITE Information Centre, located right where the bus deposits you, ask for rental car advice.

BUS CONTACTS Bus Depot. ⊠ *Thames i-SITE Visitor Infomation Centre, 200 Mary St., Thames* ☎ *07/868–7284.*

CAR RENTALS Saunders Rentals. ⊠ *201 Pollen St., Thames* ☎ *0800/111–110* ⊕ *www.saundersmotorgroup.co.nz.*

VISITOR INFORMATION
CONTACTS Thames i-SITE Visitor Centre. ⊠ *200 Mary St., Thames* ☎ *07/868–7284* ⊕ *www.thamesinfo.co.nz.*

 ## Sights

Goldmine Experience
NOTABLE BUILDING | Take a guided experience to learn about one of the richest gold strikes in the world. The tour includes a 40-minute underground tour of an 1868 stamper battery. Wear sturdy footwear, as it can be muddy. Advanced booking is recommended. ⊠ *Corner of State Hwy. 25 and Moanawataiari Creek Rd., Thames* ☎ *07/868–8154* ⊕ *www. goldmine-experience.co.nz* ☒ *NZ$15.*

Thames Historical Museum
HISTORY MUSEUM | This tiny, volunteer-run museum contains photographic displays of the 1860s gold-rush and logging industries, re-creations of period rooms from the 1800s, and information on the area's first Māori inhabitants and early European settlers. A nice feature on the grounds is the memorial garden, with period roses and other flora that settlers commonly planted; it's a lovely place to rest and reflect. ⊠ *Pollen and Cochrane Sts., Thames* ☎ *07/868–8509* ⊕ *www.*

thameshistoricalmuseum.weebly.com 🖾 *NZ$5* ⊙ *Closed Thurs.*

Thames School of Mines Mineralogical Museum

SCIENCE MUSEUM | From the mid-1800s, the School of Mines was an internationally recognized institution, teaching all aspects of mining. A diploma from here guaranteed a job anywhere in the world. The museum was established in 1900 to exhibit geological samples. The school closed decades ago, but the museum's still kicking, displaying those turn-of-the-20th-century rock specimens along with scales, models of stamper batteries, and other gold-mining paraphernalia. 🖾 *Brown and Cochrane Sts., Thames* 🕾 *07/868–6227* ⊕ *www.nzmuseums. co.nz/collections/3309* 🖾 *NZ$10.*

The Treasury Research Centre and Archives

ARCHIVE | The two buildings that host this historical collection could not be more contrasting, with The Treasury housed in the historic Carnegie Library and the adjacent Archives in an industrial-style complex constructed in 2014. Operated by the Coromandel Heritage Trust, this is the place to go if you want to conduct serious research into the history of the region. Among the resources here are old newspapers and photographic collections, cemetery records, and maps. However, it's only open from 11 am to 3 pm. 🖾 *705 Queen St., Thames* 🕾 *07/868-8827* ⊕ *www.thecoromandel.com/explore/ the-treasury* 🖾 *NZ$5 per hour (research fee)* ⊙ *Closed Fri.–Sun.*

🍴 Restaurants

The Junction Hotel

$$$ | NEW ZEALAND | FAMILY | Within one of the few hotels remaining from the gold rush days, you'll find classy pub grub in a convivial atmosphere. The Grahamstown Bar Diner (GBD) is the main restaurant bar, serving everything from breakfast and lunch to bar snacks and pizzas to evening main courses. **Known for:** late

night music on weekends; decent burgers and fish-and-chips; great tapas menu. 💲 *Average main: NZ$25* 🖾 *700 Pollen St., Thames* 🕾 *07/868–6008* ⊕ *www. thejunction.net.nz.*

Oh Sista

$ | NEW ZEALAND | One of Thames's newest cafes, this place comes with a good pedigree (having been opened by the team who previously ran another popular dining spot in town) and has quickly gained a local following. Rainbow vegetarian tart with pesto and ricotta, butterscotch scones, and sticky bao buns are available alongside more traditional offerings such as cornish pasties. **Known for:** changing blackboard specials; hot and tasty soups, including a vegan green velvet variety; handy main-street location. 💲 *Average main: NZ$12* 🖾 *501A Pollen Street, Thames* 🕾 *07/280-0297* ⊙ *Closed Sun.*

Hotels

Coastal Motor Lodge

$$ | HOTEL | Set amid 3 acres of gardens, with native bushwalks to the rear of the property and the Thames coast just across the road, this is a spacious, scenic spot to stay as you enter Coromandel. **Pros:** obliging hosts; close to Thames; lovely views. **Cons:** need to book well ahead in summer; basic furnishings; on a main road. 💲 *Rooms from: NZ$172* 🖾 *608 Tararu Rd., Thames* 🕾 *07/868–6843* ⊕ *www.stayatcoastal.co.nz* 🛏 *16 units* 🍽 *No Meals.*

Grafton Cottage & Chalets

$$ | APARTMENT | FAMILY | These six independent units set amid a hillside garden overlooking the sea offer a relaxing ambience and great sunsets. **Pros:** friendly hosts; great views; peaceful garden setting. **Cons:** some steps and stairs to access units; steep driveway; few minutes' drive to town and a steep climb home if you choose to walk. 💲 *Rooms from: NZ$180* 🖾 *304 Grafton Rd., Thames*

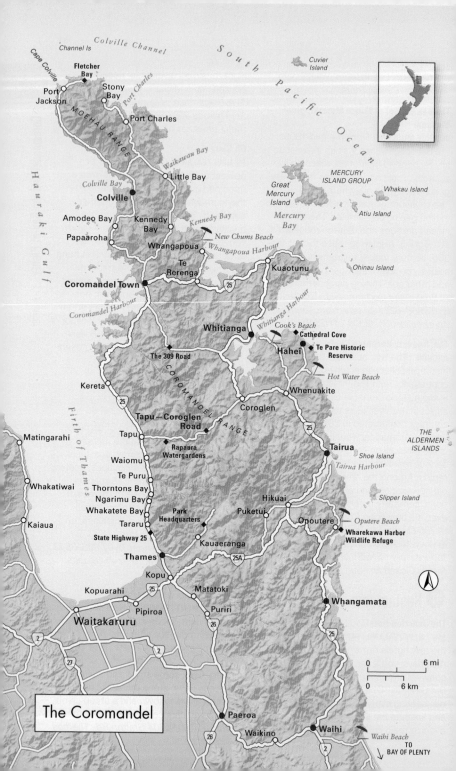

The Coromandel

☎ *07/868–9971* ⊕ *www.graftoncottage.co.nz* ⊙ *No Meals* ⇆ *6 units.*

🛍 Shopping

Bounty Store

CRAFTS | This design store–cum–gallery is Thames's best option for buying local arts and crafts, including jewelry, pottery, weaving, and paintings. ⊠ *754 Pollen St., Thames* ☎ *07/868–8988.*

Grahamstown Saturday Market

MARKET | On Saturday morning, the northern end of Thames's main street is transformed into a bustling market. Stalls line the street, with vendors selling local organic produce, cheeses, and beverages as well as antiques, jewelry, and arts and crafts. Every Saturday of the month, there's a dedicated craft market, too. ⊠ *Upper Pollen St., Thames.*

Activities

Short walks and longer day and overnight forest treks are a big attraction, especially in Kauaeranga Valley. Camping is also popular in the valley or at coastal camping grounds. On the water, try fishing around the mussel and scallop farms, or bird-watching.

HIKING

★ Coromandel Forest Park—Kauaeranga Valley

HIKING & WALKING | This area of the forest park has more than 20 walking trails that offer everything from a 15-minute stroll to an overnight trek. The hike to the interesting Pinnacles formations is a steep climb yet probably the most popular walk in the park; the trek from the trailhead to the Pinnacles hut takes three hours one-way. From the hut you can continue (about one hour one-way) to the Pinnacles and a viewpoint that spans both coasts, the Firth of Thames and Pacific Ocean. An overnight in Pinnacles hut costs NZ$15; you need to reserve it either through a DOC visitor center or

online (*booking.doc.govt.nz*). You can hike back via the three-hour-long Webb Creek trail or come down the longer (four-hour) alternative route, the Billy Goat track. Always read the signs at the start of the track to check their state. Summer holiday season is busy, so book well ahead. Generally, midweek is less crowded than weekends throughout summer. There are also delightful camping areas along the valley floor (from NZ$10; powered sites should be booked in advance). To reach Kauaeranga Valley, head south from Thames and on the outskirts of the town turn left on Banks Street, then right on Parawai Road, which becomes Kauaeranga Valley Road. Thirteen kilometers (8½ miles) from Thames you'll come to the DOC Visitor Centre, which is open from 8:30 to 4 (possibly later in summer, give them a call first). The visitor center offers up-to-date information on track conditions and camping facilities, educational displays, and information on many other Coromandel walks or hikes to places such as Fantail Bay, Cathedral Cove, or Opera Point. You can also check with them about track closures, initiated in late 2018 to prevent the spread of kauri dieback disease among the native trees. ☎ *07/867–9080* ⊕ *www.doc.govt.nz.*

★ Sleeping God Canyon

HIKING & WALKING | One of New Zealand's lesser known yet most epic outdoor and cultural adventures is set in a steep, forested canyon in Coromandel Forest Park. Not for the faint-hearted, you'll rappel, zip line, jump, water slide, and swim down and through a series of waterfalls and pools, a total 300-meter (984 foot) descent. You're in safe hands as the guides are professional, experienced, and DOC-approved operators. On the 45-minute bush hike/climb to reach your jump-off point, they will share the Māori history about this special place they know as Atuatumoa. All equipment and lunch are included. Transport is offered from Thames and Hamilton. An adventurous spirit is essential. ⊠ *1160 Kauaeranga*

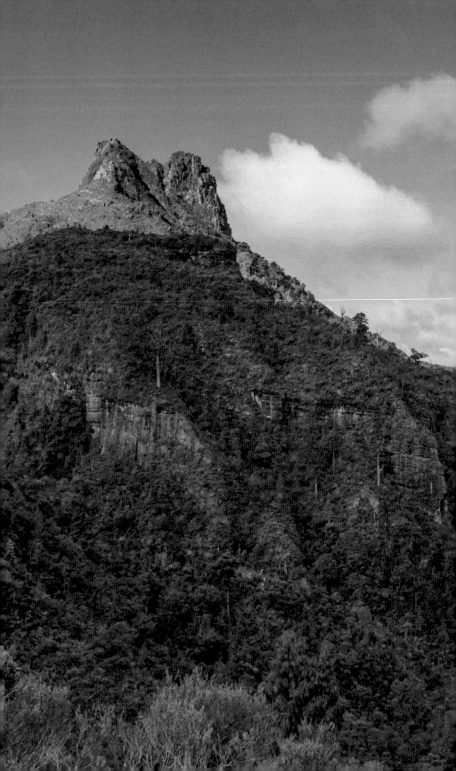

Valley Rd., Thames ☏ *0800/422–696*
🌐 *www.canyonz.co.nz* ✉ *From NZ$270.*

Tapu–Coroglen Road

25 km (16 miles) north of Thames.

The Coromandel Ranges drop right down to the seafront State Highway 25 as it winds up the west coast of the peninsula. When you top the hills north of Kereta on the way to Coromandel Town, mountains, pastures, and islands in the Firth of Thames open before you. It's quite wonderful to watch the sunset from this part of the coastal highway. Some of the vantage points along the way offer opportunities for stunning photographs. The area is popular with landscape painters.

The 28-km-long (17-mile-long), intermittently paved Tapu–Coroglen Road turns off State Highway 25 in the hamlet of Tapu to wind into the mountains. It's a breathtaking route where massive tree ferns blanket the roadside hills. Take it slowly: stretches of the road are quite narrow with access for only one vehicle. Signs indicate these places.

GETTING HERE AND AROUND

About 6½ km (4 miles) from Tapu you come to the magical Rapaura Watergardens. Travel another 3½ km (2 miles) along the road and pull over to climb the 187 steps up to the huge, 1,200-year-old Square Kauri, so named for its unusual square shape. At 133 feet tall and 30 feet around, this is the 15th-largest kauri in New Zealand. From a tree-side platform there is a splendid view across the valley to Mau Mau Paki, one of the peaks along the Coromandel Range. While this road continues east, winding through remote forest and farmland to the peninsula's east coast, your best bet might be to return to the west and continue exploring along the peninsula's west coast, to Coromandel Town.

 ## Sights

Rapaura Watergardens

GARDEN | Explore this 64-acre private estate, nurtured for more than 40 years with lush lawns, garden beds, and native forest and adorned with ponds, streams, waterfalls, fountains, and garden art. Trails lead through seasonal displays of primulas and spring bulbs, azaleas, rhododendrons, camellias, lilies, hydrangeas, and water lilies. Vegetable gardens supply Koru, the highly recommended garden café known for its wholesome house baking and local Coromandel produce. Rapaura also offers self-catering accommodations in either a Boutique Lodge or Garden Cottage. ✉ *586 Tapu–Coroglen Rd., 6 km (4 miles) east of Tapu, Tapu* ☏ *07/868–4821* 🌐 *www.rapaura.com* ✉ *NZ$15* ⊙ *Café closed May–Sept.*

Coromandel Town

60 km (38 miles) north of Thames, 29 km (18 miles) northwest of Whitianga.

Coromandel Town became the site of New Zealand's first gold strike in 1852 when sawmill worker Charles Ring found gold-bearing quartz at Driving Creek, just north of the town. The find was important for New Zealand because the country's workforce had been severely depleted by the gold rushes in California and Australia. Ring hurried to Auckland to claim the reward that had been offered to anyone finding "payable" gold. The town's population soared, but the reef gold could be mined only by heavy and expensive machinery. Within a few months, Coromandel resumed its former sleepy existence as a timber town—and Charles Ring was refused the reward.

Nowadays, Coromandel is a popular vacation town but manages to retain a low-key charm even when SUVs and campervans fill the streets. With 19th-century buildings lining both sides of its single main street, an active artists' collective, and the requisite fish-and-chips shops at either end, you could not find a truer example of a relaxed and slightly hippie Kiwi town. The local mussel farms mean that mussels are served every which way, from smoked-mussel pies to chowder.

GETTING HERE AND AROUND

As with every town on the Coromandel Peninsula, you can arrange to be dropped off or collected by Go Kiwi Shuttles or InterCity. There is no rental car company in Coromandel Town, so if you decide you want to get around by yourself, you'll need to rent a car in the neighboring towns of Thames or Whitianga.

BUS CONTACTS Bus Depot. ✉ *Coromandel Town Information Centre, 85 Kapanga Rd., Coromandel* ☎ *07/866–8598.*

TOURS

Coromandel Adventures

GUIDED TOURS | Coromandel Adventures offers daily, customized tours of the region and will pick you up in Coromandel Town. They can arrange anything from regional transportation and transfers to multi-day trips including overnight accommodations. ✉ *Coromandel* ☎ *0800/462–676 toll-free in NZ only, 07/866–7014* 🌐 *www.coromandeladventures.co.nz* 🎫 *From NZ$25.*

VISITOR INFORMATION

Coromandel Town Information Centre

✉ *85 Kapanga Rd., Coromandel* ☎ *07/866–8598* 🌐 *www.coromandeltown.co.nz.*

If local walks are your thing, head to the Coromandel Town Information Centre and ask for a photocopy of their Coromandel Town booklet that shows the town's walking trails.

👁 Sights

Driving Creek Railway

TRAIN/TRAIN STATION | **FAMILY** | The late Barry Brickell's narrow gauge railway, built so the potter could access special clay found at the top of a steep forested slope, has become a major tourist attraction. Trains make several one-hour trips each day, taking in a viaduct, three tunnels, a spiral, and a switchback through native forest, eventually climbing to the Eyefull Tower and viewing platform. The railway also funds a reforestation program and a 1.6-acre fenced wildlife sanctuary. The latest on-site addition is Coromandel Zip Line Tours, a three-hour experience encompassing eight zip lines. Advanced booking is advised; it's essential during peak summer months. ✉ *380 Driving Creek Rd., Coromandel* ☎ *07/866–8703, 0800/267-6947 toll free in New Zealand* 🌐 *www.drivingcreek.nz* 🎫 *NZ$35 rail tour, NZ$127 zip line.*

🍴 Restaurants

Coromandel Mussel Kitchen

$$$ | **SEAFOOD** | Recently reopened just to the south of Coromandel Town, this restaurant is well sign-posted but also easy to spot by the historical mussel barge at the main entrance. It sets the tone for a place that makes the local delicacy the star of the show, including delicious half-shell mussels or mussel pots served with bread. **Known for:** both indoor and outdoor dining; fresh mussels in all varieties; seafood souvlaki with scallops, prawns, and mussels. [$] *Average main: NZ$30* ✉ *20 309 Rd., Coromandel* ☎ *07/866-7727* 🌐 *www.musselkitchen.co.nz* 🕒 *Closed Mon.–Wed. No dinner.*

Pepper Tree Restaurant and Bar

$$$$ | **NEW ZEALAND** | The standout restaurant in town showcases local produce, shellfish, fish, lamb, and beef. Lunch easily segues into dinner in the sheltered courtyard or in front of the fire, depending on the season. **Known for:**

signature prime rib steak; other Coromandel shellfish like oysters and scallops; mussels (steamed or in chowder). [$] *Average main: NZ$40* ✉ *31 Kapanga Rd., Coromandel* ☎ *07/866–8211* 🌐 *www.peppertreerestaurant.co.nz.*

★ UMU Café

$$ | CAFÉ | Like many places to eat on the peninsula, this casual café does a roaring trade with mussels and seafood. But lots of Kiwi café foods are also here, like full breakfasts, salads, and pies, while the dinner menu serves all the classics. **Known for:** fair-trade coffee; fish and mussel chowders; house-baked cakes. [$] *Average main: NZ$17* ✉ *22 Wharf Rd., Coromandel* ☎ *07/866–8618.*

Hotels

Anchor Lodge

$$$ | HOTEL | Offering a range of rooms for all budgets, the accommodations at Anchor Lodge are all well-equipped, cozy, and clean, boasting views of Coromandel Harbour and native forest. **Pros:** free bikes available; wide choice of accommodations to suit range of travelers; heated swimming pool and whirlpool. **Cons:** no elevator; outward appearance is underwhelming; Wi-Fi can be inconsistent. [$] *Rooms from: NZ$220* ✉ *448 Wharf Rd., Coromandel* ☎ *07/866–7992* 🌐 *www.anchorlodgecoromandel.co.nz* 🛏 *25 rooms* 🍴 *No Meals.*

Buffalo Lodge

$$$ | B&B/INN | This private lodge perched on a busy hillside just out of Coromandel Town has great views across the Hauraki Gulf. **Pros:** splendid breakfasts; multilingual host; lots of privacy. **Cons:** no pool; stairs, but no elevator; town is a short drive away. [$] *Rooms from: NZ$225* ✉ *860 Buffalo Rd., Coromandel* ☎ *07/866–8960* 🌐 *www.buffalolodge.co.nz* ⏲ *Closed Apr.–Oct.* 🛏 *4 rooms* 🍴 *Free Breakfast.*

Coromandel Top 10 Holiday Park

$$$ | RESORT | FAMILY | Whether you choose a luxury villa, cottage, self-catering motel room, cabin, or powered campervan site, you can enjoy the amazing facilities at this park, which include a large swimming pool, barbecues with indoor/outdoor dining, laundry, and fish- and boat-cleaning facilities for fishers. **Pros:** short walk to excellent restaurants; a family haven with plenty of fun activities; Wi-Fi throughout. **Cons:** on the main road; crowded with families in summer; be wary of a room too close to the fish-cleaning bay. [$] *Rooms from: NZ$300* ✉ *636–732 Rings Rd., Coromandel* ☎ *0800/267–646 New Zealand only, 07/866–8830* 🌐 *www.coromandeltop10.co.nz* 🍴 *No Meals* 🛏 *24 rooms.*

Shopping

The Source

ART GALLERIES | This local arts collective gallery sells jewelry, pottery, clothing, sculpture, and more. There's an outdoor courtyard where you'll find recycled metal items, as well as huge ceramic works inspired by native plants. Everything, including the largest sculptures, can be broken down for shipping overseas. ✉ *31 Kapanga Rd., Coromandel* ☎ *07/866–7345.*

Activities

Fishing and forest walks are what most outdoorsy people do around here. Or, if fishing isn't your thing—simply cruising through the little islands to see the mussel farms is a great scenic, and social, thing to do.

FISHING

Mussel Barge Snapper Safaris

FISHING | FAMILY | Mussel farms are big business in the Coromandel, and fishing for tasty snapper that gather around these marine farms can be rewarding—and exciting. Ride out on one of the mussel barges, and try your luck. Cruises

The farmland outside of Coromandel Town stretches in every direction.

last four to five hours and depart daily at 7 am and 1 pm from Sugar Loaf Wharf, Te Kouma, 7 km (4½ miles) south of Coromandel Town. There's shelter and a barbecue on board; fishing lines can be rented and bait pre-ordered. ⊠ *Hannafords Wharf, Te Kouma Rd., Coromandel* ☎ *07/866–7667* ⊕ *www.musselbargesafaris.co.nz* ✉ *NZ$60 per person (Min. of 8 bookings required).*

Top Catch: Bait, Tackle, Advice
FISHING | This company can arrange fishing trips to suit all levels aboard local boats. They also sell all the fishing gear you need. Advice is given freely, and although this might be one of a national chain of fishing shops, the insight is definitely local. ⊠ *2 Kapanga Rd., Coromandel* ☎ *07/866–7397* ⊕ *www.topcatch. co.nz.*

HIKING
Hike & Bike Coromandel
BIKING | Run by locals Leeanne and Gavin Jeffcoat, this company offers a full-day tour and hike along the coast of the northern Coromandel Peninsula and a cycling excursion along the Tokatea Trail in the Coromandel Range. Hourly to multiday bike rental is available, and luggage can be stored at the operator's Coromandel Town location while you head off on an adventure. ⊠ *105 Wharf Rd., Coromandel Town* ☎ *0800/287– 432 Toll free in New Zealand, 07/866– 8175* ⊕ *www.hikeandbike.co.nz* ✉ *Biking tours from NZ$120 per person (self-guided).*

Kauri Block Track
HIKING & WALKING | On a clear day, head up to the Kauri Block Track (1½ hours round-trip), which provides panoramic views over the town, harbor, and coast. Follow the main road to Coromandel Town's western outskirts, where a signpost points out the start of the trail at 356 Wharf Road. The trail goes through native and regenerating bush then a side track leads to a Māori pā (fortified village) site on the summit, with spectacular views. The trail continues down through the bush and emerges onto Harbour View Road, which you follow back to

town. ✉ *356 Wharf Rd., Coromandel*
⊕ *www.doc.govt.nz* ✉ *Free*.

Long Bay Scenic Reserve and Kauri Grove
HIKING & WALKING | A gentle 40-minute
walk (one-way) leads to Tucks Bay and a
beautiful beach. Pack a picnic and enjoy a
relaxing afternoon. The track starts at the
end of Long Bay Road, at the Long Bay
Motor Camp (about 3 km [2 miles] from
Coromandel Town). En route it passes
through a grove of young kauri trees (and
one much bigger, older kauri that happily
evaded the early loggers). Either return
the way you came, or head across Tucks
Bay and follow the coastal track back to
the motor camp. ✉ *3200 Long Bay Rd.,
Coromandel*.

WALKING TOURS
Boom, Bust & Beyond
WALKING TOURS | FAMILY | These herit-
age walking tours are run through the
Coromandel Town Information Centre
with each of the local guides adding
their own personality to the experience.
They run on weekends from 11:30 am,
but extra tours are often available in the
summer, and private tours can often be
arranged on request. A lot of the focus
is on the area's gold-mining history. ✉ *74
Kapanga Rd., Coromandel* ☎ *07/866–
8598* ⊕ *www.coromandeltown.co.nz*
✉ *NZ$20*.

Colville and Vicinity

30 km (19 miles) north of Coromandel.

Get closer to the very north of the Coromandel Peninsula—with its rugged coastline, delightful coves, and pastures—and
take the 30-minute drive from Coromandel up to Colville. The town has a grocery
store–gas station, post office, community
hall, and café. For something different,
there is an interesting Buddha shrine, or
stupa, by the Mahamudra Buddhist Centre on the drive in and public toilets with
a mosaic worthy of a picture. Colville is
the gateway to some of the peninsula's

most untamed landscape. Maps of the
area are available in Coromandel at the
Town Information Centre and in Colville
at the General Store.

GETTING HERE AND AROUND
Other than driving to Colville, you can
get here by bus or with a small touring
company like Coromandel Adventures,
which offers excursions and shuttle
transport around the area from its base in
Coromandel Town.

 Sights

Fletcher Bay
BEACH | Beyond Colville, a twisty, gravel
road will take you to Fletcher Bay, the
northernmost end of the peninsula. (It's
impossible to fully circumnavigate the
peninsula by road). To reach Fletcher
Bay, turn left at a T-junction about 5 km
(3 miles) north of Colville. This road
follows the west coast to a stunning
sandy beach at Port Jackson, then
continues along the cliff-top and down
to Fletcher Bay, a smaller, sandy cove
banked by green pasture rolling down
to the beach. It's 60 km (38 miles) from
Coromandel—a 1¼-hour drive. There's
a small camping ground here, tracks
and beaches to explore, and a great
kayaking spot. From Fletcher Bay, hikers
can follow the signposted Coromandel
Coastal Walkway, an old bridle trail along
the very northeastern tip of Coromandel
Peninsula, down to Stony Bay. It's a
charming three- to four-hour walk, partly
along clifftops with grand views across
to the Mercury Islands, and at times
dipping down to secluded, forest-fringed
beaches.

Restaurants

Hereford 'n' a Pickle
$ | MODERN NEW ZEALAND | The meat and
produce in this café and store all come
from the owner's very own farm, Kairau-
mati Hereford Stud. The meat is processed on-site, the sausages are made

from an old family recipe, and the free-range eggs, honey, vegetables, jams, and pickles are all homegrown. **Known for:** pickles and chutneys; house-made baked goods; pure homegrown Hereford beef burgers. $ *Average main: NZ$10* ✉ *2318 Colville Rd., Colville* ☎ *07/866–6937* ⊕ *www.kairaumatipolledherefords.com.*

 Hotels

Anglers Lodge Motel and Holiday Park

$$ | **HOTEL** | A friendly, family-run business offers appealing cabins, motel units, and campervan and tent sites nestled off the main road at Amodeo Bay. The beach is just over the road, and it's a fisherman's paradise. **Pros:** spotless facilities; friendly operators; stunning location with great views. **Cons:** gets very busy during Easter and lodge's annual fishing competition; far from town; must book well ahead for summer. $ *Rooms from: NZ$140* ✉ *Amodeo Bay, 1446 Colville Rd., Colville* ☎ *07/866–8584* ⊕ *www.anglers.co.nz* ⦿ *No Meals* ⤳ *13 units.*

★ Tangiaro Kiwi Retreat

$$$ | **HOTEL** | It's quite a drive to get here, but there are not many places where you can stay in simple, understated luxury and hear kiwi calls at night. **Pros:** massage therapist's hut and hot tub in the bush; prolific birdlife—some 50 kiwi live in the local reserve; close to great beaches and forest walks. **Cons:** long winding drive (or expensive helicopter) to get there; birdsong might wake you early; far from shops. $ *Rooms from: NZ$220* ✉ *1299 Port Charles Rd., Coromandel* ☎ *07/866–6614, 0800/826–4276* ⊕ *www.kiwiretreat.co.nz* ⦿ *No Meals* ⤳ *14 rooms.*

 Shopping

★ Colville General Store

STORE/MALL | Colville's classic counter-culture General Store is run by a local co-operative. It sells foodstuffs (there's a well-stocked organic section), wine, beer, and gasoline. It's kind of like the general store that used to be in all country areas. It's also the northernmost supplier on the peninsula, so don't forget to fill your tank. ✉ *2314 Colville Rd., Colville* ☎ *07/866–6805.*

Whitianga

46 km (29 miles) southeast of Coromandel.

Between forest-clad hills and the sea on Coromandel's eastern coast is the main township on this side of the peninsula. Here the beachfront is lined with motels and hostels, all within walking distance of shops and the ferry across Whitianga Harbour to Flaxmill Bay and Cooks Beach. Many people use the town as a base for fishing or boating trips, and others stock up for camping at nearby beaches. In summer it hosts some great rock music and jazz shows, and people use it as a base for enjoying the region's gorgeous beaches.

If you're driving between Whitianga and Coromandel and the sun is shining, make time to head north toward Whangapoua. Park your car, grab your swimsuit, and make the 30-minute trek over to New Chums Beach, a native forest–fringed bay of golden sand. It's accessible only by foot, and you have to wade through an estuary to get there, but the beautiful and secluded beach (rated by locals as among the top 101 things to do in New Zealand) is one of the country's worst-kept secrets.

The Whitianga i-SITE Visitor Centre can help you choose an excursion and has a full list of the many B&Bs in the area.

GETTING HERE AND AROUND
Unless you're driving or on a charter flight from Auckland, the bus is the only way to get to Whitianga (with the exception of those stalwart few who are conquering the Coromandel by bicycle). Bus

companies stop at the Whitianga i-SITE Visitor Centre.

A nice way to explore Flaxmill Bay or Whitianga (if you're based at either of these points) is to leave your car near the dock and take the NZ$5 (NZ$7 round-trip) ferry across and explore the beaches or cafés, depending on which side you end up, on foot. Or for NZ$1.50 extra, take your bike along.

CONTACTS Whitianga. ✉ *Whitianga i-SITE Visitor Information Centre, 66 Albert St., Whitianga* ☎ *07/866–5555* ⊕ *www. thecoromandel.com.*

TOURS
Ocean Leopard Tours
BOAT TOURS | Explore the area's dramatic volcanic coastline from the comfort of a sleek, purpose-built craft that gets right up against sea cliffs, blowholes, and even into sea caves. Skipper Justin has years of experience in showing off his favorite local haunts. His covered boat keeps the rain and sun at bay without spoiling the views. Trips, which leave from both Whitianga Wharf and Ferry Landing (across the estuary), include one-hour and two-hour options (snorkeling can also be added). Booking ahead is essential in summer. ☎ *07/866–4990* ⊕ *www.ocean-leopardtours.co.nz* ⊠ *From NZ$70.*

Sea Cave Adventures
BOAT TOURS | This company uses a smaller boat that can get you into the sea caves and blowholes (weather and tide dependent) as well as showcase all the sheer volcanic coastal cliffs and white-sand beaches. The skipper knows the best spots, and you can shelter from the sun under the boat's awning. Two-hour trips leave from Whitianga Wharf at 8, 11, 2, and 4:30 (one hour each). Reservations are recommended. ⊠ *Whitianga Wharf, Whitianga* ☎ *0800/806–060* ⊕ *www.sea-caveadventures.co.nz* ⊠ *From NZ$90.*

FESTIVALS
Held every September, the annual **Whitianga Oceans Festivals** (*www.oceansfestival.co.nz*) celebrates Whitianga seafood and is one of the region's main events. It was previously branded as a scallops festival but has been renamed to reflect the growing need to protect the scallop stock in the area. Stalls serve a variety of seafood prepared every which way, and there are music performances, kids' activities, and cook-offs. Even though that's only early spring here, the vibes are warm enough. Keep an eye on the website, as tickets sell quickly.

VISITOR INFORMATION
CONTACTS Whitianga i-SITE Visitor Centre. ⊠ *66 Albert St., Whitianga* ☎ *07/866–5555* ⊕ *www.thecoromandel.com.*

◉ Sights
The Lost Spring
HOT SPRING | There are spas, and then there is The Lost Spring: thermal pools set in the middle of town yet landscaped as if they're lost in the forest. The Lost Spring taps into 16,000-year-old mineral water drawn from more than 2,000 feet below ground and now filling a man-made haven of steaming lagoons, waterfalls, and quartz-studded caves. Lie back in the water, and watch native birds eating berries from the trees and ferns while waiters deliver snacks, juices, beer, wine, or cocktails to the water's edge. There's also a restaurant and day spa (be sure to book ahead). ⊠ *121 A Cook Dr., Whitianga* ☎ *07/866–0456* ⊕ *www.thelostspring. co.nz* ⊠ *From NZ$40* ⊗ *Pools closed Mon.–Thurs. Spa and restaurant closed Mon.–Wed.* ☞ *14 and older only.*

🍴 Restaurants

Cafe Nina
$ | **CAFÉ** | Jasmine vines cloak the front porch of this adorable 1890 miner's cottage. Folks come here for breakfast

and lunch every day of the week, and you might have to wait a bit during holiday time, but locals think it's worth it. **Known for:** lots of locals; classic breakfasts, including a great eggs Benedict; seafood chowder. $ *Average main: NZ$14* ⊠ *20 Victoria St., Whitianga* ☎ *07/866–5440* ⊘ *No dinner.*

Salt Restaurant and Bar

$$$ | **NEW ZEALAND** | Put a slightly upscale yet still casual restaurant in a popular local hotel, with a waterside location in a vacation town, and you've got this can't-miss dining spot. There is casual pub dining in the bars, but Salt, with its alfresco dining by the palm-edged marina, is the star. **Known for:** steamed mussels; slow-roasted lamb sharing plate; great raw bar with oysters and ceviche. $ *Average main: NZ$30* ⊠ *1 Blacksmith La., Whitianga* ☎ *07/866–5818* ⊕ *www.facebook.com/Saltbarandrestaurant* ⊘ *Closed Mon. and Tues. No lunch.*

 ## Hotels

Admiralty Lodge

$$$ | **MOTEL** | A mile from the town center, but only across the road from Buffalo Beach, this is a good spot if you're planning on a few days beachside. **Pros:** beach location; great views; big swimming pool. **Cons:** included breakfast is at café a few minutes' drive away; right beside the road; not close to shops. $ *Rooms from: NZ$290* ⊠ *69–71 Buffalo Beach Rd., Whitianga* ☎ *07/866–0181, 0508/236–472* ⊕ *www.admiraltylodge.co.nz* ⦿ *Free Breakfast* ⇱ *18 rooms.*

Beachfront Resort

$$$ | **B&B/INN** | You can step out of this tiny, family-run property's garden onto a breathtaking beach. **Pros:** powerful showers; stunning location; direct beach access. **Cons:** no air-conditioning; few minutes' walk out of town; need to book well in advance for summer. $ *Rooms from: NZ$300* ⊠ *111–113 Buffalo Beach Rd., Whitianga* ☎ *07/866–5637* ⊕ *www.beachfrontresort.co.nz* ⇱ *8 rooms* ⦿ *Free Breakfast.*

Crow's Nest Apartments

$$ | **APARTMENT** | While this three-level apartment-style accommodation bears little resemblance to a ship's lookout, it does provide a handy and comfortable base from which to explore the area. **Pros:** covered parking on site; 20 meters (22 yards) from beach; friendly owners with local knowledge. **Cons:** can be noisy because of late night revelers from town; not all rooms have beach and ocean views; some rooms can be too bright at night due to proximity to security lights. $ *Rooms from: NZ$ 200* ⊠ *18-20 Mill Rd., Whitianga* ☎ *07/869-5979* ⊕ *www.crowsnestwhitianga.co.nz* ⦿ *No Meals* ⇱ *15 rooms.*

Oceanside Motel

$$$ | **B&B/INN** | Stylish studio suites or one-bedroom units overlook the beach here. **Pros:** kayaks and guest barbecue available; stunning sea views from upstairs rooms; friendly hosts. **Cons:** upstairs rooms with a view are more expensive; small bathrooms in some units; no air-conditioning. $ *Rooms from: NZ$250* ⊠ *32 Buffalo Beach Rd., Whitianga* ☎ *07/866–5766* ⊕ *www.oceansidemotel.co.nz* ⇱ *9 rooms* ⦿ *No Meals.*

Activities

Fishing, swimming, and diving are popular activities around this seaside town. There's kayaking along the dramatic coastline, with its rock arches and caves, or cruising the clear waters in a glass-bottom boat. Inland, old miner's trails now make interesting forest walks.

BOATING, FISHING, AND DIVING

Cathedral Cove Scenic Cruises

BOATING | Skipper Ken has a wealth of knowledge about the local history, geology, and marine life, and he'll share it all with you as he shows you the special spots of this spectacular coastline. He even has an underwater camera installed on his boat, so you can check out the fish without getting wet, or you can jump right in and snorkel. Tours leave daily from Whitianga Wharf (with Ferry Landing pick-ups possible). Reservations are recommended. ⊠ *Whitianga Wharf, Whitianga* ☎ *0800/888–688* ⊕ *www.cathedralcovecruises.co.nz* ⊠ *From NZ$70.*

Cave Cruzer

BOATING | The Cave Cruzer gives you an unusual spin on an ex-Navy rescue boat, exploring Cathedral Cove, blowholes, and sea caves, with time for snorkeling if you wish. At one point, you'll head into a cave, and your guides will provide a surprising acoustical demonstration. Two trip options are the standard 2- to 2½-hour Scenic and Sound and the 1-hour Express. There's no shade on this boat, but there's lots of personality. ⊠ *Whitianga Wharf, Esplanade, Whitianga* ☎ *07/866–3311* ⊕ *www.cavecruzer.co.nz* ⊠ *From NZ$70.*

Glass Bottom Boat

BOATING | On these cruises to Te Whanga-nui-A-Hei Marine Reserve, get in the water with a snorkel or simply sit on board and watch the marine life through the vessel's glass bottom. Informed guides discuss the formation and history of the land, Captain Cook's explorations here during the 1700s, the earliest Māori settlers Ngāti Hei, and the more recent history of Narnia film locations. Several trips daily (year-round, weather permitting) leave from Whitianga Wharf. The trips take two hours, and advanced booking is essential. ⊠ *Esplanade, Whitianga Wharf, Whitianga* ☎ *07/867–1962* ⊕ *www.glassbottomboatwhitianga.co.nz* ⊠ *From NZ$105.*

Hahei

57 km (35 miles) southeast of Coromandel, 64 km (40 miles) northeast of Thames.

The beaches, coves, and seaside villages around Hahei make for a great day of exploring—or lounging. If you're craving a true beach vacation, consider basing yourself in Hahei rather than in Whitianga. From Hahei, you can easily reach Cathedral Cove, the Purangi Estuary, Cooks Beach, and Flaxmill Bay (where the little passenger ferry crosses to Whitianga township). The famous Hot Water Beach is only minutes away.

GETTING HERE AND AROUND

If you're day-tripping from Whitianga, take the five-minute ferry ride (which leaves every hour, NZ$15 each way) across to Flaxmill Bay and explore by foot. Alternatively, follow State Highway 25 south from Whitianga. The road takes you past the Wilderland Community's roadside stand (selling organic produce and delicious honey from a community-run organic farm) and on a loop around to Hahei, Cooks Beach, and Flaxmill Bay. If you want to explore Cathedral Cove, you can walk the steepish track, or simply catch a water taxi off the beach at Hahei.

CONTACTS Cathedral Cove Water Taxi.
☎ *027/919–0563* ⊕ *www.cathedralcove-watertaxi.co.nz.*

Sights

Cathedral Cove (*Te Whanganui-a-Hei*)
VIEWPOINT | The Cathedral Cove rock arch is possibly the most visited feature in Coromandel. The two-hour return walk is steep, and the water at the cove is usually calm and clear, so good for swimming and snorkeling. To get there, travel along Hahei Beach Road, turn right toward town and the sea, and then, just past the shops, turn left onto Grange Road and follow the signs. In the height of summer

Swimmers enjoy the blue waters in Te Whanganui-a-Hei (Cathedral Cove) Marine Reserve, Coromandel Peninsula.

the parking lot at the trailhead is closed and a shuttle bus (NZ$5 return) takes you from Hahei Village. Or you can walk from the northern end of Hahei Beach, adding a 20-minute climb. Another option is to jump on the Cathedral Cove Water Taxi that buzzes from Hahei Beach to Cathedral Cove in a few minutes. Or you could paddle there with Cathedral Cove Kayaks. A good plan is to visit outside peak summer holiday season, January in particular. ☒ *Trail head car park, End of Grange Rd.*

★ **Colenso Country Café and Shop**

RESTAURANT | FAMILY | A cottage café and craft shop are set in a garden full of citrus and olive trees and kitchen herbs. The café serves soups, moreish country-style pies, salads, and an ever-changing variety of cakes, scones, muffins, slices, and Devonshire teas. In the shop you can procure tasty chutneys, jams, organic honey, and giftware. The open grassy space, play area, and tame donkeys make this an especially good place to stop with kids. It's located on State Highway 25

just south of the Hahei turnoff on the way to Tairua. ☒ *State Hwy. 25, Whenuakite* ☎ *07/866–3725* ⊘ *Closed Tues. and Wed.*

Te Pare Historic Reserve

VIEWPOINT | The headland at the south end of Hahei Beach is the site of two former Māori pā (fortified villages). Although no trace remains of the defensive terraces and wooden spikes that once ringed the cliffsides, the stunning outlook, which made it an ideal defensive site in years past, remains. At high tide, the blowhole at the foot of the cliffs adds a booming bass note to the sound of waves. To reach the actual pā site, follow the red arrow down the hill from the parking area at the end of Pa Road. After some 50 meters (164 feet), take the right fork through a grove of giant *pohutukawa* trees, then go through a gate and across an open, grassy hillside. You can also pick up the trail onto the headland from the southern end of Hahei Beach at mid- to low tide. ☒ *End of Pa Rd., Hahei.*

Beaches

Cooks Beach

BEACH | This beach lies in Mercury Bay, so named for Captain James Cook's observation of the transit of the planet Mercury in 1769. The beach is notable for the captain's landfall, the first here by a European. It's a beautiful expanse of white sand backed by a growing sprawl of vacation homes. Forest-covered headlands overlook each end (take the walking track to Shakespeare Cliff Scenic and Historic Reserve, on the northern headland for the view). The beach is a safe family swimming spot, likely to be crowded in peak summer months (January) and delightfully quiet at other times of the year. Along with private vacation homes, B&Bs and a holiday park with campsites and cabins are located near the beach. **Amenities**: food and drink; parking; toilets. **Best for:** sunrise; swimming; walking. ✉ *Marine Parade, Cooks Beach, Coromandel.*

Hot Water Beach

BEACH | This wild and potentially dangerous surf beach is incredibly popular for its under-the-sand thermal spring. By scooping a shallow hole in the sand, you can create a pool of warm water; the deeper you dig, the hotter it becomes. The phenomenon occurs only at low- to mid-tide, so time your trip accordingly. In summer you'll be joined by hundreds of other spade-toting, wannabe bathers—plan your visit outside of busy January if you can. Hot Water Beach is well signposted off Hahei Beach Road from Whenuakite (fen-oo-ah-kye-tee). If you need to while away some time before the tide goes out, there are a couple of beachside cafés, plus the Moko Artspace gallery to browse. ■ **TIP→ Only swim in the lifeguard-patrolled areas; the beach is notorious for drownings; however, nearby Hahei Bech is one of the finest and safest on this coast. Amenities:** food and drink; parking (fee); showers; toilets. **Best for:** surfing; walking. ✉ *Hot Water Beach Rd., Coromandel.*

Restaurants

★ Eggsentric Café

$$$$ | **ECLECTIC** | In addition to great food, this restaurant has a community-hub feel thanks to live music sessions, poetry readings, film nights, and a summer sculpture symposium. The dinner menu reaches beyond standard café fare, and there's also a great range of classic breakfasts and fresh baked goods. **Known for:** community art and music; scallops, chowders, and other seafood; tasty desserts. [$] *Average main: NZ$31* ✉ *1049 Purangi Rd., Flaxmill Bay* ☎ *07/866–0307* 🌐 *www.eggsentriccafe.co.nz* 🕓 *Closed Mon. and May–Sept.*

Go Vino

$$ | **MODERN NEW ZEALAND** | This café's small shared plates feature an eclectic fusion of Asian and classic European flavors with a strong Kiwi touch. Try the tea leaf salad, Burmese-style, with roasted soy beans, peanuts, *kawakawa* (a pepper-flavored native plant), cabbage, and tomato; ostrich and beef cheek; or the braised octopus with nectarines. **Known for:** dessert platters; great pizzas; selection of fusion dishes. [$] *Average main: NZ$18* ✉ *19 Captain Cook Rd., Cook's Beach* ☎ *07/867–1215* 🌐 *www.govino.co.nz* 🕓 *Closed Tues. and Wed.*

The Vessel

$$$ | **PIZZA** | This restaurant is "nautically themed" and really means it; the bar and kitchen are both housed in shipping containers. The atmosphere is casual to the extreme, so come in your swimwear if you feel comfortable doing so, and order some locally inspired pizzas. **Known for:** plenty of outdoor seating for sunny days; Kahawai Keeper, which is topped with smoked fish, capers, red onion, and few other goodies; good burgers and salads. [$] *Average main: NZ$24* ✉ *35b Captain Cook Rd., Cooks Beach Village*

☎ *07/866-0773* 🌐 *www.thevessel.co.nz* 🕐 *Closed May–Sept.*

Hotels

The Church Accommodation

$$ | HOTEL | Set amid gardens and native bush and connected by winding paths are these character-filled studios and cottages. **Pros:** range of accommodations; free Wi-Fi throughout; lovely garden. **Cons:** can be shady and cool in winter; must book well ahead in summer; at least 10-minute walk to the beach. [$] *Rooms from: NZ$195* ✉ *87 Hahei Beach Rd., Hahei* ☎ *07/866–3533* 🌐 *www.thechurchhahei.co.nz* 🕐 *Closed a few wks mid-winter* 🍴 *No Meals* 🛏 *12 rooms.*

Tatahi Lodge

$$$ | HOTEL | This lodge offers a range of accommodations (and prices) and is a four-minute walk from the beach. **Pros:** close to cafés, brewery, and beach; self-catering options; good for budget travelers. **Cons:** gets busy with young backpackers; can feel a bit crammed; some units lack privacy (and private bathrooms). [$] *Rooms from: NZ$215* ✉ *9 Grange Rd., Hahei* ☎ *07/866–3992* 🌐 *www.tatahilodge.co.nz* 🍴 *No Meals* 🛏 *10 units.*

Wairua Lodge

$$$ | B&B/INN | Rain-forest retreat describes this place well: four stylish double rooms and one two-bedroom apartment are nestled on a 15-acre property with native forest, bushwalks, streams, and hidden swimming holes for your enjoyment. **Pros:** fantastic river swimming; treetop bathhouse; divine location. **Cons:** have to book the balcony bath in one-hour timeslots; no shops close by for catering; some unpaved road access. [$] *Rooms from: NZ$205* ✉ *251 Old Coach Rd., Hahei* ☎ *07/866–0304* 🌐 *www.wairualodge.co.nz* 🍴 *Free Breakfast* 🛏 *5 rooms.*

Activities

Cathedral Cove Dive and Snorkel Hahei

DIVING & SNORKELING | Cathedral Cove Dive and Snorkel Hahei offers beginner, advanced, and dive-master courses, as well as daily dive trips in the Te Whanganui-a-Hei Marine Reserve, Cathedral Cove, and around the outer islands and pinnacles. Most dive sites are a 10-minute boat ride away. They also rent snorkels and give tips on the best spots to go snorkeling. ✉ *48 Hahei Beach Rd., Hahei* ☎ *07/866–3955* 🌐 *www.hahei.co.nz/diving.*

★ **Cathedral Cove Kayak Tours**

KAYAKING | FAMILY | A stunning way to explore this spectacular volcanic coastline is by sea kayak. This company is happy to work with beginners and families, and they pride themselves on showing off places you're unlikely to find on foot. Paddle straight off Hahei Beach and along to famous Cathedral Cove (they're the only kayak company licensed to land here) and be served a cappuccino—and that's just the standard trip. They take groups of eight in double kayaks. Other options, weather permitting, include a full-day paddle (think caves and blowholes) and a remote coastal tour. ✉ *88 Hahei Beach Rd., Hahei* ☎ *07/866–3877, 0800/529–258* 🌐 *www.kayaktours.co.nz* 🎟 *From NZ$125.*

Hahei Explorer

BOATING | *Hahei Explorer*, a sturdy, eight-seater rigid inflatable boat, explores this volcanic coastline's sea caves, blowhole, beaches, headlands, and spectacular Cathedral Cove. One-hour trips depart directly off Hahei Beach (the southeastern end) six times daily (four in winter). Booking ahead is essential; be sure to arrive 15 minutes before departure. ✉ *Hahei* ✣ *South end of beach* ☎ *07/866–3910 in New Zealand,* ☎ *0800/268-386 toll free in New Zealand* 🌐 *www.haheiexplorer.co.nz* 🎟 *NZ$105.*

Tairua

28 km (18 miles) south of Hahei, 37 km (23 miles) north of Whangamata.

Tairua is one of the larger communities along the coast. It's also one of the prettiest, framed by an estuary, harbor, and hills. The twin volcanic peaks of Paku rise beside the harbor, and there's an ocean beach close by. Because State Highway 25 is the town's main road, Tairua is also a convenient stop en route to other seaside spots around Whitianga and Hahei. The five-minute ferry ride from Tairua across the harbor to the vacation homes of Pauanui takes you to the immediate area's best beach. The ferry runs hourly throughout most of the summer (NZ$5 round-trip). If you're here at the end of February you can get fully immersed, literally, in the Tairua Wet & Wild weekend, involving lots of watersports fun. For year-round activities and maps check out the Pauanui and Tairua information centers.

GETTING HERE AND AROUND

If you're based in Thames, Tairua is an easy drive across the base of the Coromandel Peninsula along State Highway 25A. Otherwise, whether you're heading up or down the eastern side of the Coromandel, you can't miss it. The information center, just down the first road to the right after you cross the bridge coming into town, is a good place to stop in and get your bearings.

VISITOR INFORMATION

CONTACTS Pauanui Information Centre. ✉ *23 Centreway, Pauanui* ☎ *07/864–7101.* **Tairua Information Centre.** ✉ *2 Manaia Rd., Tairua* ☎ *07/864–7575* 🌐 *www.tairua.co.nz.*

Sights

Wharekawa Harbour Wildlife Refuge

WILDLIFE REFUGE | Take a detour to the dazzling, white-sand Opoutere Beach and Wharekawa Harbour Wildlife Refuge, reached by a five-minute drive off State Highway 25, turning left 8½ km (5 miles) south of Tairua. The road follows the Wharekawa Estuary to a parking lot. From here cross a wooden footbridge and follow the trail for 10 minutes through the forest to the long white beach. Much of the estuary and headland area here is a wildlife refuge, a breeding ground for shorebirds, including the endangered New Zealand dotterel. Take care not to enter fenced areas as these protect the barely visible eggs that lie in shallow nests in the sand. For more information, ask at the Tairua or Whangamata information center. 🎫 *Free.*

Restaurants

Manaia Café and Bar

$$$$ | **ECLECTIC** | This spacious, centrally located café–restaurant can get busy with both visitors and locals. Breakfast kicks off at 9 am with all the standard Kiwi options. **Known for:** art and craft store next-door; woodfire pizzas; breakfast waffles. [$] *Average main: NZ$31* ✉ *228 Main Rd., Tairua* ☎ *07/864–9050* 🌐 *www.manaia.co.nz.*

Surf and Sand

$ | **SEAFOOD** | A classic New Zealand takeout experience, this is the spot to get a quintessential Kiwi-style beachside lunch or dinner of fish, shellfish, chips (fries), and burgers. When the fish (battered or crumbed) and chips are done well, they're not too greasy or fatty. **Known for:** battered Coromandel oysters; classic New Zealand fish-and-chips; kūmara (sweet potato) fries. [$] *Average main: NZ$12* ✉ *Shop 7, Main Rd., Tairua* ☎ *07/864–8617.*

Hotels

Blue Water Motel

$$$ | MOTEL | These bright and cheery self-contained units are at the southern end of Tairua, across the street from a small sandy beach. **Pros:** outstandingly helpful hosts; simple and charming decor; close to the beach. **Cons:** beside the main road; a bit cramped; there are steps to some rooms. $ *Rooms from: NZ$220* ✉ *213 Main Rd., Tairua* ☎ *07/864–8537* ⊕ *www.bluewatermotel. co.nz* ⤳ *10 units* ❄ *No Meals.*

Grand Mercure Puka Park Resort

$$$$ | HOTEL | This hillside hideaway, managed by the international Accor hotel chain, is nestled in native bushland near Pauanui Beach. **Pros:** pool, tennis court, and bikes are among amenities; upscale and well-appointed; close to the beach. **Cons:** access to rooms not easy on steep paths (call for a golf cart); somewhat formal for the region; steep climb uphill from the beach. $ *Rooms from: NZ$347* ✉ *Mount Ave., Pauanui* ☎ *07/864–8088* ⊕ *www.pukapark.co.nz* ❄ *No Meals* ⤳ *48 rooms.*

Pacific Harbour Villas

$$$ | HOTEL | With a grand Pacific-style portico, this resort property on the main street in Tairua looks like a tropical island getaway. **Pros:** well-priced; tropical island ambience; good location. **Cons:** Wi-Fi not free; not all villas have a harbor view; cable television in lobby only. $ *Rooms from: NZ$298* ✉ *223 Main Rd., Tairua* ☎ *07/864–8581* ⊕ *www.pacificharbour. co.nz* ❄ *No Meals* ⤳ *31 rooms.*

Whangamata

37 km (23 miles) south of Tairua, 60 km (38 miles) east of Thames.

The Coromandel Ranges back Whangamata (fahng-a-ma-*ta*), another harborside town, with a population of around 3,500.

Once a town of modest houses, it's been discovered by city people wanting to work remotely from the beach, and some mighty big homes have now been constructed here. The harbor, surf beaches, mangroves, and coastal islands are glorious. In summer, the population more than triples. It's a great spot for deep-sea fishing, and for surfers its bar break creates some of the best waves in New Zealand. For classic- and muscle-car enthusiasts, the Whangamata Beach Hop held each year around March is a must-go. You'll see amazing classic cars and listen to some of the best rock-and-roll bands around. In February, British cars and bikes are a feature during the Brits at the Beach festival.

GETTING HERE AND AROUND

Whangamata is Coromandel's last coastal port of call as you travel southward into the Bay of Plenty. If you're only passing through, but you've got a couple of hours to spare, check out some of the short bush walks in the area, or, of course, head down to the beach.

VISITOR INFORMATION

CONTACTS Whangamata Information Centre. ✉ *616 Port Rd., Whangamata* ☎ *07/311-4102* ⊕ *www.thecoromandel. com/towns/whangamata.*

Restaurants

Neros Bar & Eatery

$$$ | ITALIAN | FAMILY | Come to this indoor–outdoor bistro for casual evening dining loosely billed as Italian with pizza, pastas, and risotto on the menu. There's also a great range of Kiwi-modern mains that feature salmon, steak, pork, and the local fish catch. **Known for:** Thai curries; wine menu with a focus on New Zealand wines; pizzas. $ *Average main: NZ$22* ✉ *711 Port Rd., Whangamata* ☎ *07/865–6300* ⊕ *www.neros.co.nz* ⊘ *Closed Mon. and Tues. No lunch.*

SixfortySix

$$ | **CAFÉ** | This café boasts of being the friendliest place in town, and the day-long crowds support the claim. Inside, you'll find good coffee, fresh pastries, and a paper roll menu (as they call it) listing fresh, wholesome breakfasts and lunches like house-smoked salmon, salads, and classic burgers. **Known for:** alfresco dining; spiced breakfast bircher museli; quality Kokako roast coffee. [$] *Average main: NZ$18* ✉ *646 Port Rd., Whangamata* ☎ *07/865–6117* 🌐 *www.sixfortysix.co.nz* ⏲ *No dinner Wed.–Fri.*

Hotels

Brenton Lodge

$$$$ | **B&B/INN** | Looking out over Whangamata and the islands in its harbor from your hillside suite, you'll feel rested and pampered, especially after being greeted with fresh flowers, fruit, and handmade chocolates. **Pros:** peaceful setting; breathtaking views; pool and hot tub. **Cons:** some stairs to negotiate; no air-conditioning; a little too far from town to walk home in the evening. [$] *Rooms from: NZ$470* ✉ *2 Brenton Pl., Whangamata* ☎ *07/865–8400* 🌐 *www.brentonlodge.co.nz* ⏲ *Closed Jun. and Jul.* 🛏 *4 suites* 🍴 *Free Breakfast.*

Pipinui Motel

$$$ | **MOTEL** | Tucked away down a quiet street, yet just a two-minute walk to Whangamata marina and a 10-minute walk to the beach, this motel has two studios and two one-bedroom units, all self-contained with modern kitchens, big bathrooms, peaceful pastel colors, and small private decks. **Pros:** good location; modern and spacious; well-serviced. **Cons:** breakfast not included; if you want to stay around Christmas you'll need to book months ahead; a bit expensive for what you get. [$] *Rooms from: NZ$235* ✉ *805 Martyn Rd., Whangamata* ☎ *07/865–6796* 🌐 *www.pipinuimotel.co.nz* 🍴 *No Meals* 🛏 *5 rooms.*

Activities

The beach is where it's at here. Surfers and swimmers share the waves. Farther offshore, big-game fishing is popular.

SURFING

Whangamata Surf Shop

SURFING | If you're looking for a quick introduction to the sport, check out the Whangamata Surf Shop, owned by legendary surfing family the Williams (daughter Ella is a former World Junior Champ and now follows the WLS QS Tour). Located in the center of town, the shop has surfboards and boogie boards for rent. If you want to learn what to do with them, they'll send you off for a surfing lesson with their friends down on the beach (at Access 8) who run the Whangamata Surf School. ✉ *634 Port Rd., Whangamata* ☎ *07/865–8252* 🌐 *www.whangamatasurfshop.co.nz* 🎟 *NZ$80 (1 hr, including instructor and surfboard).*

WALKING

Kiwi Dundee Adventures

HIKING & WALKING | Former Department of Conservation worker John Rich and his wife, Rose, recently purchased this long-established company and, along with their small family of expert, friendly Kiwi guides, offer personalized tours throughout New Zealand. However, they have a special focus on the history, nature, and spectacular scenery of their home region, Coromandel. The team's unbridled enthusiasm for the region rubs off on anyone who takes a Kiwi Dundee tour. There are one-day or three-day walks and tours, plus 14- to 20-day tours all over New Zealand if you'd like more. ✉ 200 Mary St., Thames ☎ *07/865–8809* 🌐 *www.kiwidundee.co.nz.*

Wentworth Valley

HIKING & WALKING | Regenerating forest, gold-mine history, and the 150-foot-high Wentworth Falls are all features along short walks in the hills of southern

Coromandel Forest Park, behind Whangamata. There's also a Department of Conservation campsite in the valley and lots of swimming holes for cooling off on hot summer days. From Whangamata township drive south on State Highway 25 for 2½ km (1½ miles). Turn right off the highway into Wentworth Valley Road. The trail starts at the road's end. ⊠ *Wentworth Valley Rd., Whangamata* ☎ *07/865–7032* ⊕ *www.wentworthvalleycamp.co.nz.*

Waihi to Paeroa

Waihi is 30 km (18.6 miles) south of Whangamata, 20 km (12.4 miles) from Paeroa.

Southern Coromandel is bounded by the historic and scenic Karangahake Gorge and smaller, adjoining Waikino Gorge. State Highway 2 wends its way through the forest-covered, gorged terrain from the small farming town of Paeroa to the gold-mining center of Waihi. While the towns are just 20 km (12.4 miles) apart, there is much to see and do along the way. Try to give yourself some time to explore the forest walks to old mining sites, batteries, and tunnels. Better still, take a bike ride on the Hauraki Rail Trail (including through the tunnels). Check out the gold-mining history in Waihi. If you're not beached-out after Coromandel, head to beautiful Waihi Beach, 11½ km (7 miles) from Waihi.

Gold mining has helped shape the history of this region. From the late 1800s to early 1900s, hundreds of miners toiled in both underground and open-pit mines. You can reflect on their efforts at heritage sites and in museums, and you can even visit a working mine, as mining still continues in Waihi.

Today, a new rush of people comes here to explore the walking trails and heritage mining sites and tunnels, to cycle the Hauraki Rail Trail and the Goldfields Heritage Railway, and to visit the cafés and wineries.

GETTING HERE AND AROUND

If you've headed south down the east coast of the Coromandel, Waihi is your last port of call before you arrive at the Bay of Plenty. Consider a break here, or at least a detour to the west on State Highway 2. This will lead you into the Waikino, then Karangahake Gorge in Coromandel Forest Park, and then into open farmland country and Paeroa township. InterCity runs daily bus services to the region.

BUS CONTACTS InterCity. ☎ *09/583–5780* ⊕ *www.intercity.co.nz.*

VISITOR INFORMATION

CONTACTS Paeroa Information Hub. ⊠ *101 Normanby Rd., Paeroa* ☎ *07/862–8636* ⊕ *www.thecoromandel.com.* **Waihi i-SITE Visitor Centre.** ⊠ *126 Seddon St., Waihi* ☎ *07/863–9015* ⊕ *www.golddiscovery-centre.co.nz.*

 Sights

Gold Discovery Centre and Gold Mine Tour
HISTORY MUSEUM | FAMILY | New owners Karen and Eddie Morrow manage both this and the Waihi information center (in the same location), and their enthusiasm is infectious. You can head underground to the interactive museum for an explanation of the region's gold-mining history. The roof is lined with timbers as if you are in a real mine shaft. You can operate a compressor drill; fire the explosives; learn about local geology and the role of stamper batteries in extracting gold from rock; and understand the social upheavals of striking miners, unions, and bosses. If you want to see the real thing, take a tour (1½ hours) to Waihi's still-working mine. Bike rental is also available here. ⊠ *126 Seddon St., Waihi* ☎ *07/863–9015* ⊕ *www.golddiscoverycentre.co.nz* ⎘ *From NZ$28; tours from NZ$44.*

Goldfields Railway

TRAIN/TRAIN STATION | FAMILY | This half-hour, 7-km (4½-mile) heritage-train journey into the Karangahake Gorge follows part of the former Waihi to Paeroa line, built in 1905 after five years of challenging construction in the steep gorge country. The train travels from historic Waihi Railway Station to the Waikino Station Café (with great house-made baked goods). Travel one-way or round-trip, or bring your bike—from Waikino to Paeroa, the former railway line now forms part of the Hauraki Rail Trail for bikers and walkers. Train reservations are recommended. ✉ *30 Wrigley St., Waihi* ☎ *07/863–9020* 🌐 *www.waihirail.co.nz* 🎫 *From NZ$15.*

Martha Mine

MINE | In the center of Waihi, gaze in awe into the huge open pit of the Martha Mine, one of the world's most significant gold and silver mines of its time. Since the late 1800s, thousands of miners worked here, extracting 174,000 kilograms of gold and more than a million kilos of silver. Cross the road from the Waihi i-SITE Visitor Information Centre to the Cornish Pumphouse (relocated here) for a glimpse into the pit, and perhaps walk around the Pit Rim Walkway (5 km/3 miles). For a more insightful experience book a trip with Gold Discovery Tours. ✉ *Seddon St., Waihi.*

Beaches

Waihi Beach

BEACH | Nineteen km (12 miles) north of Katikati, Waihi Beach is ideal for swimming and surfing and has access to numerous walkways. With 9 km (5½ miles) of sweeping white sand, the beach is one of the region's safest for swimming, surfing, and kayaking, and is particularly popular in peak summer (January). A surf club offers beach patrols at the beach's northern end and in summer at the far Bowentown end in the south, although you'll find people splashing about all along the long white stretch. Don't miss the drive to the top of the Bowentown heads at the southern end of Waihi Beach. This is an old Māori pā (fortified village) with stunning views. A short but steep walk from here leads to Cave Bay directly below the viewing point .■ **TIP→ Don't swim at Cave Bay; there are dangerous currents here.** The Waihi Beach township encompasses restaurants and shops, and there is a full range of accommodations, from holiday parks to boutique lodges. **Amenities:** food and drink; lifeguard; parking; toilets; waters sports. **Best for:** sunrise; surfing; swimming; walking; windsurfing. ✉ *The Esplanade, Waihi Beach* 🌐 *www.waihibeachinfo.co.nz.*

Restaurants

★ Bistro at the Falls Retreat

$$$$ | MODERN NEW ZEALAND | It might be way out in the bush, but this restaurant could stand proud in any big city. Dine inside or out, beneath the trees, and watch the chefs in the open kitchen adding wood to the pizza oven or creating contemporary cuisine with organic-farmed beef and lamb and vegetables straight from the garden. **Known for:** vegetarian salads; spicy chicken pizza (and other pizzas); sharing platters. [$] *Average main: NZ$33* ✉ *25 Waitawheta Rd., Karangahake Gorge* ☎ *07/863–8770* 🌐 *www.fallsretreat.co.nz* 🕓 *Closed Mon. and Tues. Apr.–Oct. (approximately).*

Down Thyme Restaurant and Cafe

$$$ | MEDITERRANEAN | Mediterranean food and ambience are the focus at this quiet restaurant tucked away on the edge of town. The finest local produce, organic where possible, is matched with quality international and local craft beers and wines. **Known for:** Mediterranean-style risottos; house-made ice cream; Angus beef cheeks. [$] *Average main: NZ$29* ✉ *31 Orchard Rd., Waihi* ☎ *07/863–8980* 🌐 *www.downthyme.nz* 🕓 *Closed Mon. No lunch Tues.*

The Refinery

$ | **CAFÉ** | Hidden down a side street (look for the sign on the main street), you'll find this gourmet home-cooking surprise. This café gem serves breakfasts, muffins, scones, cakes, and shortcakes alongside build-your-own bagels and counter "sammies" crammed with choices of grilled meats, haloumi (salty cheese of goat and sheep's milk), and vegetables. **Known for:** historic building; best bagels in the region; cornbread Reuben grilled sandwiches. [$] *Average main: NZ$13* ✉ *5 Willoughby St., Paeroa* ☎ *07/862–7678* 🌐 *www.the-refinery.co.nz* 🕒 *Closed Mon. and Tues.*

Hotels

Manawa Ridge

$$$$ | **B&B/INN** | A luxury retreat built with artistic architectural flair to exacting eco-standards (recycled beams, mud brick, and straw-bale walls), this lodge stands on a farm ridge top with 360-degree views over the Pacific Ocean and Coromandel. **Pros:** gourmet breakfasts; hospitable hosts; 360-degree farm, forest, and coastal views. **Cons:** no facilities or shops so you're committed to in-house dining; 9 km (5½ miles) out of town; rustic quirkiness may not suit all tastes. [$] *Rooms from: NZ$950* ✉ *267 Ngatitangata Rd.* ☎ *07/863–9400* 🌐 *www.manawaridge.co.nz* 🍴 *Free Breakfast* 🛏 *3 suites.*

Activities

BICYCLING

★ Hauraki Rail Trail

BIKING | **FAMILY** | Join the Kiwi families discovering this gently graded 160-km (100-mile) bike trail. There are six stages: from Waihi, a 24-km (15-mile) segment follows the old railway line through scenic Karangahake Gorge to Paeroa. Heritage gold-mine sites, bridges, and tunnels are part of the drama, so bring a flashlight, and call at a country café en route. You can even ride the Goldfields Railway train along with your bike for the first stretch. From Paeroa the trail crosses Hauraki Plains farmland for 34 km (21 miles) to Thames. The southern 60-km (37-mile) stage includes more farmland riding, south from Paeroa to Te Aroha then the Waikato town of Matamata. Or, from Thames, you can follow the Shorebird Coast around internationally important wetland site the Firth of Thames for 55 km (34 miles) to Kaiaua. The Hauraki Rail Trail is one of the Nga Haerenga-New Zealand Cycle Trails' "Great Rides." ✉ *Karangahake Gorge* 🌐 *www.haurakirailtrail.co.nz.*

HIKING

Karangahake Gorge Walks

HIKING & WALKING | **FAMILY** | Rivers, waterfalls, and steep, forest-sided ravines, plus old railway tunnels and gold-mining sites, can all be explored on the walkways in Karangahake Gorge. The trails are well-maintained by the Department of Conservation (DOC) and designed to showcase the best natural and heritage features. Recommended are Rail Tunnel Loop (one hour) and Waikino Historic Walkway (three to four hours, round-trip). Some routes are shared with bikers on the Hauraki Rail Trail, but there's plenty of room. Look for the large riverside parking lot and DOC signs partway through the gorge, opposite Moresby Road (to tiny Karangahake Village). Most trails begin across a footbridge from here. DOC camping spots and good cafés are also in the area. Pick up a DOC brochure at local i-SITE Visitor Information Centres. ✉ *Karangahake* 🌐 *www.doc.govt.nz.*

Katikati

62 km (39 miles) southeast of Thames, 35 km (22 miles) northwest of Tauranga.

The small town of Katikati was founded by Irish Protestant settlers in the 1870s. Long before the Irish arrived, Māori

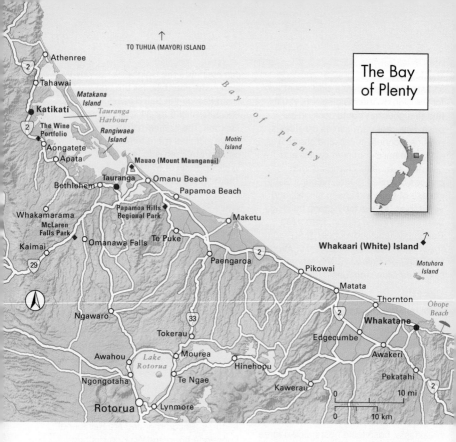

↑
TO TUHUA (MAYOR) ISLAND

The Bay of Plenty

Bay of Plenty

Athenree

Tahawai

Matakana Island

Katikati

Tauranga Harbour

The Wine Portfolio

Rangiwaea Island

Motiti Island

Aongatete

Apata

Mauao (Mount Maunganui)

Tauranga

Omanu Beach

Bethlehem

Papamoa Beach

Whakamarama

Papamoa Hills Regional Park

McLaren Falls Park

Maketu

Kaimai

Omanawa Falls

Te Puke

Whakaari (White) Island

Paengaroa

Pikowai

Motuhora Island

Matata

Thornton

Ohope Beach

Ngawaro

33

Whakatane

Tokerau

Edgecumbe

Awakeri

Awahou

Mourea

Hinehopu

Pekatahi

Lake Rotorua

Ngongotaha

Te Ngae

Kawerau

Rotorua

Lynmore

0   10 mi

0   10 km

---

had recognized the area's potential for growing food crops. These days, fruit-growing—particularly kiwi and avocado—keeps the Katikati economy afloat, perhaps providing one (of many) explanations for Katikati's name, "to nibble" in Māori. Katikati's most noticeable features are the more than 70 murals and sculptures around town that depict its history. Another interesting attraction is the Haiku Pathway, a walking trail studded with haiku-etched boulders. The path starts on Katikati's Main Street and leads down to the river. Pick up a map of the route at the visitor information center.

GETTING HERE AND AROUND

While remaining on the Pacific Coast Highway, head south from Coromandel toward the Bay of Plenty. At Waihi, State Highway 25 switches and becomes State Highway 2. The next town you'll meet

along State Highway 2 is Katikati, better known for its agricultural bounty than as a beach or fishing town (though the sea is very close by).

VISITOR INFORMATION

CONTACTS Katikati Visitor Information Centre. ✉ *36 Main Rd., Katikati* ☎ *07/549–5250* ⊕ *www.katikati.org.nz.*

 Sights

Lindemann Road Lookout

VIEWPOINT | For great views over the Bay of Plenty, drive a couple of minutes north of Katikati on State Highway 2 to Lindemann Road. The lookout is signposted at the turn off. Drive 3½ km (2 miles) to the road's end and the lookout. The road is good but narrow in parts; you'll find a map embedded in rock to help orient you. If the weather is clear you might see volcanic White Island to the south. Self-contained campervans can stop here overnight.

The Wine Portfolio

WINERY | A handsome, Dutch cape–style building will probably attract your attention, just south of Katikati on Highway 2. Originally built for Morton Estate Wines, it now houses the cellar door of wine-making business Wine Portfolio. The boutique, specialist winery produces vintages from grapes grown in leading New Zealand wine regions Hawke's Bay and Marlborough. Here's your chance to sample the country's best wines, all in one place. ✉ *Leveret Estate, 2389 State Highway 2, Katikati* ☎ *07/552–0795* 🌐 *www.wineportfolio.co.nz.*

🍴 Restaurants

Orchard House Cafe

$$$ | **CAFÉ** | Just off the road but with a backdrop of fruit trees, this is a fitting place to stop for breakfast or lunch in an area known for its fresh produce. A tasty vegetarian choice is the "Figotten Shroom" (balsamic mushrooms on a potato rosti stack with spinach and a dollop of fig jam). **Known for:** good children's menu; plenty of off-road parking, with room for campervans and motorhomes; early closing (at 3 pm). [$] *Average main: NZ$25* ✉ *603 State Hwy. 2, RD3 Katikati* ✣ *6 km (4 miles) north of Katikati* ☎ *07/549–1924* 🌐 *www.orchardhouse-cafe.co.nz* 🕒 *Closed Mon. and Tues. No dinner.*

The Talisman Hotel

$$$ | **NEW ZEALAND** | The 1876-built Talisman Hotel offers quality pub fare, with a focus on using local produce where possible. You'll meet the locals here, be it over brunch, lunch, or dinner, where your meal could be anything from crammed-full burgers to confit duck leg. **Known for:** impressive wine pairings; wood-fire pizzas; twice cooked ribs in sticky sauce. [$] *Average main: NZ$29* ✉ *7–9 Main Rd., State Hwy. 2, Katikati* ☎ *07/549–3218* 🌐 *www.talismanhotel.co.nz.*

🛏 Hotels

★ Matahui Lodge

$$$$ | **B&B/INN** | This lodge on 6 acres of manicured gardens and vineyards is an outstanding example of the boutique home-hosted properties popping up in this region. **Pros:** substantial breakfasts; good wine list; lovely gardens. **Cons:** books up quickly; some rooms have stair access; a little far from town for some. [$] *Rooms from: NZ$475* ✉ *187 Matahui Rd., 9 km (5½ miles) south of Katikati* ☎ *07/571–8121* 🌐 *www.matahui-lodge.co.nz* 🛏 *3 suites* 🍽 *Free Breakfast.*

Tauranga

216 km (134 miles) southeast of Auckland.

The population center of the Bay of Plenty, Tauranga is one of New Zealand's fastest-growing cities. Along with neighboring town Whakatane, this seaside city also rates as one of the country's sunniest spots. Unlike most local towns, Tauranga doesn't grind to a halt in the off-season, because it has one of the busiest ports in the country, and the excellent waves at the neighboring beach resort of Mount Maunganui—just across Tauranga's harbor bridge—always draw surfers and vacationers.

GETTING HERE AND AROUND

Whether you self-drive, catch a bus, or fly, getting to Tauranga is simple. Air New Zealand flies daily from major cities throughout New Zealand to Tauranga Airport. By road, Tauranga is about a 50-minute drive northeast of Rotorua. From Auckland, allow three hours for the drive south. You can travel either on State Highway 2 through the southern Coromandel and northern Bay of Plenty regions (slightly longer but arguably more scenic) or on State Highway 1 to Waikato then State Highway 29, which crosses over the Kaimai Ranges—a steep-ish but scenic drive through farmland and native forest. InterCity buses travel daily to Tauranga from Auckland, Hamilton, and Rotorua. The Tauranga bus depot is in the city center, close to shops and accommodations.

Once you are here, major and clearly signposted roads lead from Tauranga to coastal resorts, Mount Maunganui and Papamoa, and south through kiwifruit orchard country to Whakatane. A toll expressway bypasses some of these places, for example, Te Puke, should you be in such a hurry on your vacation. Local bus company Bay Bus (sometimes called the Bay Hopper) travels regularly between Tauranga and regional towns including Mount Maunganui, Te Puke, Katikati, and Whakatane. Activity operators, for example, swim with dolphins, kayaking, fishing, and walking tours, are mostly based in or close to the city and will collect you from your accommodations.

BUS CONTACTS Bay Bus. ⊠ *Tauranga* ☎ *0800/422–9287* ⊕ *www.baybus.co.nz.* **InterCity Tauranga Depot.** ⊠ *Wharf St., Tauranga* ☎ *07/578–8103* ⊕ *www.intercity. co.nz.*

VISITOR INFORMATION
CONTACTS Tauranga i-SITE Visitor Information Centre. ⊠ *103 The Strand, Tauranga* ☎ *07/578–8103* ⊕ *www.bayofplentynz. com.*

 Sights

To explore the town center, start at The Strand, where palm trees separate the shops from the sea. Bars, restaurants, and cafés line The Strand and nearby side streets. If you're interested in the beachier side of Tauranga, head 8 km (5 miles) east out of the city center and over the Harbour Bridge to Mount Maunganui. Here, you'll find one of the

best surf spots in the country along the 20-km (12½-mile) shoreline, a sheltered, harborside swimming spot, as well as shopping, restaurants, and walking trails up and around the prominent, small, and dormant volcano Mauao (Mt. Maunganui or, as locals say, The Mount).

★ Mauao (Mt. Maunganui)
BEACH | FAMILY | This dormant volcano is the region's visual icon; its rocky cone stands sentinel, 761 feet high at the end of the peninsula that boasts one of New Zealand's best swimming and surfing areas. White-sand beaches with rolling surf stretch for miles away from Mauao. Trails on Mauao include an easy walk around its base and the more strenuous summit climb. To get to Mauao, head toward it along any road running parallel to the beach. The Mount Maunganui area gets crowded around Christmas and New Year's Eve, so consider early or late summer (or even winter) for your visit. Beach walks or exploring Mauao is a delight at any time, and the sidewalk cafés are always open.

McLaren Falls Park
CITY PARK | FAMILY | Four hundred and ninety-four acres of parkland, alongside a gentle flowing river that tumbles over the small McLaren Falls, make a great spot for a picnic or driving break. Picnic tables, coin-operated barbecues, and toilets are located throughout. Walks include a 10-minute easy bushwalk to the falls and more strenuous walks to lookouts on Pine Tree Knoll or The Ridge. It's located a 15-minute drive south of Tauranga off State Highway 29, one of the main roads into Tauranga. ⊠ *State Hwy. 29, Tauranga* ☎ *07/578–8103.*

Papamoa Hills Regional Park
RUINS | FAMILY | A 45-minute climb through this 108-acre regional park will take you to the summit of a former Māori pā that dates back to 1460. It's one of the earliest archaeological sites in the region. From the parking lot the trail is clearly marked: you climb through pine

Did You Know?

The Bay of Plenty is perhaps best known for its dormant volcano called Mauao, or Mt. Maunganui. A hike to the top gives you a bird's-eye view of the surrounding beaches. This is also one of the sunniest regions in all of New Zealand.

forest, then open farmland. Stop for the views, if not to catch your breath. The park is a 20-km (12½-mile) drive east of Tauranga (en route to Whakatane). You'll need to get off the tolled expressway for access. If traveling from Tauranga, take the Papamoa exit and then follow the signs indicating the free road to Te Puke. Go past Welcome Bay Road and look for Poplar Lane on the right. The parking lot is at the end of Poplar Lane. ✉ *Poplar La., Papamoa Hills.*

🍴 Restaurants

Harbourside
$$$$ | **MODERN NEW ZEALAND** | The food and the view will vie for your attention here, as you dine on contemporary New Zealand cuisine. The menu is created largely from local artisan products, and you can admire Tauranga Harbour from the stunning waterfront location. **Known for:** several duck dishes; excellent harbor views; grill menu of local, organic cuts. [$] *Average main: NZ$35* ✉ *Old Yacht Club Bldg., 150 The Strand, Tauranga* ☎ *07/571–0520* 🌐 *www.harboursidetauranga.co.nz.*

Izakai Bar and Eatery
$$$ | **JAPANESE FUSION** | The Bayfair Shopping Centre may seem an unlikely place to find one of the area's most innovative restaurants, but this is well worth seeking out. Izakai combines Māori ingredients and cooking styles with Japanese cuisine, so you'll find *hāngi*-style pork belly and watercress with ramen (noodles); smoked kahawai with cabbage fritter, Tokoyaki sauce, and pickled red onion; and creamed *paua* (local shellfish) and prawn gyoza (dumplings). **Known for:** interesting cocktail selection; some tables left available for walk-ins; fig and manuka honey ice cream. [$] *Average main: NZ$25* ✉ *Bayfair Shopping Centre, 19 Girven Rd., Mount Manganui, 3116 Bay of Plenty* ☎ *07/572-0484* 🌐 *www.izakai.co.nz.*

Macau Restaurant and Lounge
$$$ | **ASIAN FUSION** | Fresh flavors right from Asia are blended with the best of local New Zealand meats, seafood, and vegetables at this popular-with-the-locals waterfront eatery. As with current restaurant trends, small plates are made for sharing, so you can enjoy a blast of flavors and just keep ordering until you're full. **Known for:** banquet-style menu options; crying tiger grilled beef sirloin; steamed buns, spring rolls, and dumplings. [$] *Average main: NZ$27* ✉ *59 The Strand, Tauranga* ☎ *07/578–8717* 🌐 *www.dinemacau.co.nz.*

Mount Bistro
$$$$ | **NEW ZEALAND** | The high prices set this restaurant apart from other local options, but then again so does the food: in the open-plan kitchen, nationally renowned chef Stephen Barry fuses quality indigenous meats, seafood, and produce with Pacific Rim flavors. À la carte menu choices range from small tapas to share and appetizers (which can also be requested in a slightly larger portion size) to full main courses. For those who inevitably want a taste of all the desserts, there's a tasting platter. **Known for:** dessert tasting platter; signature flambé seafood dish; multicourse degustation menu. [$] *Average main: NZ$35* ✉ *6 Adams Ave., Mount Maunganui* ☎ *07/575–3872* 🌐 *www.mountbistro.nz* 🕒 *Closed Mon. No lunch.*

Postbank Restaurant and Bar
$$$$ | **MODERN NEW ZEALAND** | The modern fusion menu has chapter-like descriptions, a nod to the quiet, library theme of this stylish eatery in the historic Postbank building. In what is undoubtedly one of the resort town's premier dining experiences, the dishes blend Mediterranean and Asian influences with top New Zealand produce. **Known for:** reservations required; marinated Ora king salmon; good wine list. [$] *Average main: NZ$36* ✉ *82 Maunganui Rd., Tauranga*

📞 *07/575–4782* ⊕ *www.postbank.co.nz* 🕐 *Closed Sun. No lunch Sat.–Thurs.*

☕ Coffee and Quick Bites

★ Rosie and Breadhead

$ | BAKERY | FAMILY | There's a vintage retro feel at this unassuming café that belies the amazing fresh-baked goods produced within. Cabinets are crammed with pastries, breads, cakes, panini and other sandwiches, and some truly fantastic cakes like the passionfruit curd cake. **Known for:** local vibe; great coffee; classic Kiwi sausage rolls. $ *Average main: NZ$12* ⊠ *50 9th Ave., Tauranga* 📞 *07/928–1112* ⊕ *www.bayofplenty.live/venues/rosie-and-breadhead.*

Sidetrack Cafe

$ | CAFÉ | At the base of Mauao and across the street from the beach, this bustling café is a great place for breakfast or lunch after a climb or swim. Grab a table (there are more outside than in) for a blueberry muffin, blue cheese scone, a falafel, a salad, or a dense chocolate brownie. **Known for:** excellent coffee; tasty muffins and pies; smoothies to go. $ *Average main: NZ$12* ⊠ *1 Marine Parade, Mount Maunganui* 📞 *07/575–2145* 🕐 *No dinner.*

🛏 Hotels

Clarence Tauranga

$$$ | HOTEL | Dating from 1903, the Edwardian-style building that now houses this stylish, luxurious hotel was originally the local post office, behind whose grand facade (check out the French antique tiles that line the roof) lie some of the city's most luxurious lodgings as well as two excellent restaurants. **Pros:** free parking; friendly, attentive staff; espresso coffee machines in rooms. **Cons:** bar sometimes closes early if it's a quiet night; road-side rooms can be a bit noisy (no double glazing on the windows); air-conditioning in room slightly

noisy. $ *Rooms from: 255* ⊠ *51 Willow St., Tauranga, Bay of Plenty* 📞 *07/574–8200* ⊕ *www.clarencetauranga.co.nz* 🍽 *No Meals* 🛏 *10 rooms.*

Harbour City Motor Inn

$$ | MOTEL | This bright, modern inn features spacious, self-contained studio and one-bedroom units, all with cooking facilities; you can also order breakfast (full or continental) to be delivered. **Pros:** bathrooms have spa baths; central location; units have cooking facilities. **Cons:** no outdoor spaces; built around a parking lot; basic design. $ *Rooms from: NZ$190* ⊠ *50 Wharf St., Tauranga* 📞 *07/571–1435* ⊕ *www.taurangaharbourcity.co.nz* 🍽 *No Meals* 🛏 *20 rooms.*

Hotel on Devonport

$$$ | HOTEL | This luxurious hotel in central Tauranga has earth-tone guest rooms that look out either over the city or the harbor. **Pros:** access to the adjacent private members' club; smart design; modern architecture. **Cons:** not all rooms have sea views; slightly impersonal vibe; secure parking lot costs extra and must be booked in advance. $ *Rooms from: NZ$300* ⊠ *72 Devonport Rd., Tauranga* 📞 *07/578–2668* ⊕ *www.hotelondevonport.net.nz* 🍽 *Free Breakfast* 🛏 *38 rooms.*

Papamoa Beach Resort

$$ | RESORT | FAMILY | This resort complex has the widest range of accommodations in the area, and they're all on the beach, about a 10-minute drive from the Mount Maunganui crowds. **Pros:** on the beach; spacious rooms; affordable options. **Cons:** can be noisy; gets busy in summer; range of accommodation can be confusing (just choose beachside). $ *Rooms from: NZ$155* ⊠ *535 Papamoa Beach Rd., Tauranga* 📞 *07/572–0816, 0800/461–222* ⊕ *www.papamoabeach.co.nz* 🍽 *No Meals* 🛏 *38 units.*

For a relaxing swim, take a dip in the saltwater pools at Mount Hot Pools.

Trinity Wharf

$$$ | HOTEL | Perched over the edge of Tauranga Harbour, this is one of the city's higher-end hotels. **Pros:** handy location not far from airport; fantastic views; comfortable, spacious rooms. **Cons:** some rooms have parking-lot views; 10-minute walk into the city center; traffic noise. $ *Rooms from: NZ$250* ✉ *51 Dive Crescent, Tauranga* ☎ *07/577–8700* ⊕ *www.trinitywharf.co.nz* ⬎ *120 rooms* ⫶⊙⫶ *No Meals.*

 Activities

Surfing, swimming, kayaking, dolphin-watching, fishing, big-game fishing—yes, it's mostly on the water that visitors (and locals) enjoy the outdoors around here. There are great short walks around estuaries and to viewpoints.

HELICOPTER TOURS
Adventure Helicopters
AIR EXCURSIONS | If you think this is a scenic place on the ground, take in the view from a helicopter. Adventure Helicopters offers flights from 10 minutes (around Mount Maunganui) to 40 minutes (the Kaimai Classic over the ranges). Their most popular trip is the half-hour Bay Explorer that takes in the Papamoa Hill, skirts the Kaimai Ranges, then heads back with views of Matakana Beach and Mount Maunganui. Exclusive lodge transfers, plus private charters focusing on food and wine in the area, are also available. ✉ *Tauranga Airport Hangar 1, 240 Aerodrome Rd., Mount Maunganui* ⊕ *www.adventurehelicopters.co.nz* ✈ *From NZ$135 (10-min.), from NZ$350 (30-min.).*

KAYAKING
★ Waimarino Glowworm Kayaking
KAYAKING | FAMILY | For an excellent regional experience, paddle into the night to a magical canyon filled with the lights of thousands of tiny glowworms. You don't need kayaking expertise; after a taste of local wines and cheeses at dusk, you'll be guided on a gentle, two-hour

paddle across Lake McLaren to the glowworms. Floating in the dark and the silence (everyone has to be quiet or the glowworms "turn off") is quite something. Tours last about 3½ hours and include 15-minute shuttles to the lake from Waimarino Adventure Park. Times change so check the website. If your time in the area is limited, hire a kayak by the hour during the day and explore the park itself at leisure, or take advantage of the various family-orientated offerings like water slides, paddle boarding, climbing walls, and picnic facilities. ⊠ *36 Taniwha Pl., Wairoa River, Bethlehem, Tauranga* ☎ *07/576–4233* ⊕ *www.waimarino.com* 🖥 *From NZ$130* ⊗ *Closed May–early Oct.*

SURFING
Hibiscus Surf School
SURFING | FAMILY | Where better to learn to surf than on one of New Zealand's premier surfing beaches? These dudes reckon that by the end of your first two-hour lesson, you'll actually be riding the waves. They take care of everyone, from beginner to advanced, from daily lessons to multiday packages; they also rent surfboards, paddle boards, and any other gear you need. They're on Mount Maunganui's Main Beach—look for the red Hibiscus Surf trailer parked across from Leisure (Moturiki) Island. ⊠ *Main Beach, Mount Maunganui* ☎ *027/279–9687* ⊕ *surfschool.co.nz* 🖥 *From NZ$99.*

SWIMMING
Mount Hot Pools
SPAS | FAMILY | Heated saltwater bathing is reputed to be a great healer, and these pools offer just that, nestled beneath Mauao (Mt. Maunganui). The complex includes a cooler pool with marked lanes for anyone who wants some serious exercise, but most visitors prefer to soak in the hotter saltwater pools. The four pressure water spouts are fun, too. If that's not enough, book a session with one of the in-house massage therapists.

There's also a slightly not-so-hot pool for the kids, and private pools are available. ⊠ *9 Adams Ave., Mount Maunganui* ☎ *07/577–8551* ⊕ *www.mounthotpools. co.nz* 🖥 *From NZ$18.*

SWIMMING WITH DOLPHINS
Swimming with dolphins is a big summer activity in the Bay of Plenty. Most cruises leave from the Tauranga Bridge Marina. Advanced booking is essential and should be arranged at least one day prior. The Department of Conservation licenses and regularly inspects operators and sets limits on the number of boats allowed around any pod of dolphins.

Dolphin Seafaris
WILDLIFE-WATCHING | FAMILY | A completely wild and natural encounter on a purpose-built dolphin-viewing vessel is what you'll get with this company. All guides are qualified marine biologists, so you'll be educated, too, and there's a chance of seeing other marine mammals (orcas perhaps) as well as dolphins. Strict rules mean all encounters are on the dolphins' terms, but guests do get to swim with them 85% of the time. Wet suits and snorkels are provided. Trips leave at 8 am and return around 1 pm. Be sure to book ahead of time. The season runs from November to April. ⊠ *Berth D1, Bridge Marina, Tauranga* ☎ *07/577–0105, 0800/326–8747* ⊕ *www.nzdolphin.com* 🖥 *From NZ$99.*

Orca Wild Adventures
WILDLIFE-WATCHING | Orca refers to the name of the vessel used on this company's trips, but you are also quite likely to see the real thing while out on the water. The company offers dolphin swimming, transport to nearby Mayor Island, and dive charters. ⊠ *101 Te Awanui Dr., Tauranga* ☎ *022/467-2269* ⊕ *www.orcawildlifeadventures.co.nz* 🖥 *From NZ$100.*

Whakatane

100 km (62 miles) southeast of Tauranga.

For yet another chance to laze in the summer haze, Whakatane (fah-kah-*tah*-ne) is regularly rated as the North Island's sunniest town. The harbor here was a landfall site of *Mataatua,* one of the first migratory Māori canoes, and the fertile hinterland was among the first areas of the country to be farmed.

GETTING HERE AND AROUND

Whakatane is an easy one-hour drive down the Tauranga Eastern Link Expressway from Tauranga (NZ$2 toll) or, if you want to see more attractions, about 1½ hours on the old SH2. Whichever you choose you'll travel along a spectacular stretch of coast. Keep your eyes on the road—it's easy to lapse when you've got such spectacular ocean scenery.

BUS DEPOT InterCity Whakatane Depot. ✉ *Quay and Kakahoroa Sts., on The Strand, Whakatane* ☎ *0800/942–528* ⊕ *www.intercity.co.nz.*

VISITOR INFORMATION

CONTACTS Whakatane i-SITE Visitor Information Centre. ✉ *Quay and Kaka-horoa Sts., on The Strand, Whakatane* ☎ *07/306–2030, 0800/942–528* ⊕ *www. whakatane.com.*

Sights

★ Mataatua Māori Marae

NOTABLE BUILDING | Mataatua, one of the most beautiful carved *wharenui* (meetinghouses) in Māoridom, endured a 130-year-long indignity: it was dismantled; carted to museums around New Zealand, Australia, and England; and rebuilt in various forms. In 2011, the house was returned home to the local Ngāti Awa people and restored. For a truly enriching cultural experience, let these people host you, explain their protocols, and share their history (including song, chants, and an outstanding light show).

They'll also take you for a short coastal walk, tell the story of their ancestors, and show you where they first landed in Aotearoa (New Zealand). ✉ *105 Muriwai Dr., Whakatane* ☎ *07/308–4271* ⊕ *www. mataatua.com* ✉ *From NZ$49.*

Whakatane Observatory

OBSERVATORY | If you've a hankering to see the stars from an antipodean perspective, check out the Whakatane Observatory, up on a hill above the town. With no city lights to obscure the view, the skies here rate among the clearest in the country. Showings are obviously weather dependent; however, on a good night you will see in stark clarity sights such as the "jewel box," a cluster of multicolor stars near the Southern Cross. Nighttime presentations are informal and informative, led by local astrologer Norm Izett. ✉ *22 Hurinui Ave., Whakatane* ☎ *07/308–6495* ⊕ *nzastronomy.co.nz/ operators/whakatane-astronomical-society* ✉ *NZ$15* ☉ *Closed Sat.–Mon., Wed., and Thurs.*

Beaches

★ Ōhope Beach

BEACH | FAMILY | The region's most popular and safest swimming beach is the 11-km (7-mile) laid-back Ōhope, just a 10-minute drive east of Whakatane. Pohutuka-wa Avenue, Ōhope's main road, runs parallel to the beach, flanked by native *pohutukawa* trees, private homes, and grazing cows. You can stay in the Top 10 Holiday Park or choose from a range of holiday homes, motels, apartments and B&Bs. There's lots to do here: fishing off the beach, surfing, and walking the Nga Tapuwae o Toi trail are just a few options. **Amenities:** food and drink; lifeguards; parking (free); toilets. **Best for:** surfing; swimming; walking. ✉ *Pohutukawa Ave., Whakatane* ⊕ *www.whakatane.com.*

🍴 Restaurants

Café 4u

$$ | **CAFÉ** | Salted-caramel, white-chocolate, and creme-custard donuts are among the decadent favorites at this central Whakatane café. However, sandwiches and savory pies are other options from the cabinet, and you can order from a full breakfast and lunch menu for something cooked freshly on site. **Known for:** central location close to shops; great coffee; house-made cereal for breakfast. [$] *Average main: NZ$15* ✉ *93 The Strand, Whakatane* ☎ *07/308–6549* 🌐 *www.whakatane.com/taste/cafe-4u* ⏲ *No dinner.*

White Island Café

$$ | **NEW ZEALAND** | At the base of Moutohora Island Tours, run by Ngati Awa Tourism, this place specializes in breakfast and lunch. The café opens up from 7 am to 2 pm, and its right by the water, as good an excuse as any to try the delicious seafood chowder with its mix of prawns, calamari, fish, and mussels. **Known for:** tasty scones; great coffee; selection of egg dishes. [$] *Average main: NZ$15* ✉ *15 The Strand E, Whakatane* ☎ *07/308–9588, 0800/733–529* 🌐 *www.moutohora.co.nz* ⏲ *No dinner.*

☕ Coffee and Quick Bites

The Bean Cafe and Roastery

$ | **CAFÉ** | Mellow jazz might be playing in the background, local art graces the walls, and the retro couches and armchairs are great spots to chill out and enjoy a coffee, which is freshly roasted every day in the café. Snack options include bagels with any filling you desire, egg and bacon rolls, sandwiches, cakes, and slices. **Known for:** excellent bagels; in-house coffee roasting; quirky and arty decor. [$] *Average main: NZ$14* ✉ *72 The Strand, Whakatane* ☎ *07/307–0494* 🌐 *www.thebeancafe.co.nz* ⏲ *No dinner.*

🛏 Hotels

Ataahua Ruru

$$$$ | **B&B/INN** | Check into this canopy camping operator, and you'll have 14 acres of bush-covered land to yourself, but there is one permanent canvas tent here, which sleeps two, with access to buildings containing a kitchenette and bathrooms. **Pros:** delicious house-cooked breakfast; abundant bird life; board games and books available for downtime. **Cons:** at least a 10-minute drive to nearest shops and restaurants; limited capacity and availability; breakfast is the only meal available. [$] *Rooms from: NZ$350* ✉ *Hoterini St., Wainui, Whakatane* 🌐 *www.canopycamping.co.nz/ataahua-ruru* 🍴 *Free Breakfast* 🛏 *1 unit.*

Moanarua Beach Cottage

$$ | **HOUSE** | Hosts Miria and Taroi Black provide true Māori *manaakitanga* (hospitality) and a cultural homestay experience. **Pros:** close to beach; kayaks available to rent; welcoming, relaxed environment. **Cons:** minimum two-night stay December–April; may be too far off-the-beaten-track for some; not luxurious. [$] *Rooms from: NZ$180* ✉ *2 Hoterini St., Ōhope Beach* ☎ *07/312–5924* 🌐 *www.moanarua.co.nz* 🛏 *1 2-bedroom cottage* 🍴 *Free Breakfast.*

White Island Rendezvous

$$ | **MOTEL** | This motel is across the road from the marina and within walking distance of town. **Pros:** friendly hosts; on-site café; clean and relaxed. **Cons:** one room upstairs with no elevator; thin walls in units and loud plumbing; seagulls can be noisy. [$] *Rooms from: NZ$150* ✉ *15 The Strand E, Whakatane* ☎ *07/308–9588, 0800/242–299* 🌐 *www.whiteislandrendezvous.co.nz* 🍴 *No Meals* 🛏 *27 rooms.*

Activities

Fishing, diving, and swimming with dolphins and seals are popular activities in the Whakatane area. The water surrounding White (Whakaari) Island and Whale (Moutohorā) Island has some great dive sites, with volcanic formations and abundant marine life. The Whale Island sanctuary is home to many endangered native species.

DOLPHIN- AND SEAL-WATCHING
Dolphin and Seal Encounters
WILDLIFE-WATCHING | FAMILY | For close encounters of the mammalian kind, these local experts take you on a three- to four-hour cruise from Whakatane Wharf. First you'll check out the dolphins (they give a 97% success rate of finding them), then you'll head to Whale Island where the seals might jump off the rocks and swim out to meet you. Wet suits and snorkels for swimming with the dolphins and seals are provided, or you can just watch. From November through March, cruises run twice daily, usually from 8:30 am or 1:30 pm, weather and passenger numbers permitting. ⊠ 96 The Strand, Whakatane ☎ 0800/354–7737, 07/308–2001 ⊕ www.diveworks-charters. com ☜ From NZ$130.

FISHING AND DIVING
Diveworks
FISHING | FAMILY | Offering specialist diving and fishing trips, Diveworks has an afternoon fishing venture that is especially suited to families. Rods, bait, and filleting the fish you might catch are all included. There's also a full-day option for chasing game fish. Dive trips include the opportunity to view the teeming marine life in the area, and there are also excursions focused on swimming near and observing dolphins. ⊠ 96 The Strand, Whakatane ☎ 0800/354–7737, 07/308–2001 ⊕ www.diveworks-charters. com ☜ Fishing trips from NZ$90, dolphin encounters from NZ$160.

HIKING
The native forest reserves around Whakatane provide a range of bush walks and hiking trails. The 6-km (4-mile) walkway called Nga Tapuwae o Toi (The Footprints of Toi) is named for a descendant of Tiwakawaka, one of the first Māori to settle in New Zealand. In total it takes about four hours, and it's also divided into eight shorter walks that take you past historic pā (fortified village) sites, along the coastline and the Whakatane River, around Kohi Point (which separates Whakatane from Ōhope), and through the Ōhope and Makaroa Bush Scenic Reserves. These shorter sections range from one to three hours. No guide is necessary, and the i-SITE visitor information center in Whakatane stocks free trail maps. The main trailhead starts from Canning Place, behind the Whakatane Hotel on the corner of George Street and The Strand. Follow the steps up the cliff, and you'll be at the beginning of the trail. For an easier wander (30 minutes round-trip), start at the west end of Ōhope Beach and head over to Otarawairere, a delightful secluded cove.

WILDLIFE WATCHING
Moutohorā (Whale Island) Sanctuary Tours
WILDLIFE-WATCHING | FAMILY | Cruise to this island wildlife reserve, home of endangered species such as kiwi, saddleback, parakeet, and *tuatara*. The trip, run by Ngati Awa Tourism, involves a 15-minute boat ride each way and a four-hour guided tour on the island. Highlights include a visit to a kokeno (New Zealand fur seal) colony and a chance to swim at a secluded hot water beach. Your ticket includes a fee that supports the Department of Conversation's work on Moutohorā. The tour runs on weekends only. ⊠ 15 The Strand East, Whakatane, Whakatane ☎ 07/308–9588 in New Zealand, 0800/733-529 toll free in New Zealand ⊕ www.moutohora. co.nz ☜ NZ$120 ⊙ Closed Mon.–Fri.

Whakatane Kiwi Trust Night Walks

BIRD WATCHING | FAMILY | Kiwi are prospering around the region due to local community conservation efforts, and there is every chance you will hear their calls at night or even spot one, especially if you are there in the best kiwi viewing season from April to June. The Whakatane Kiwi Trust operates walks into Ōhope Scenic Reserve and Mokorua Bush Scenic Reserve regularly during these months, but you do need to check the schedule and book ahead. The probability of seeing these shy nocturnal birds is improving, though not guaranteed. Regardless of that, the knowledgeable guides will ensure you have an enjoyable and educational experience on these walks. The trust also operates Kids Night Walks of Discovery, but check with them for specific dates. ⊠ *Whakatane* ⊕ *www. whakatanekiwi.org.nz* ✈ *From NZ$23* ⊘ *Closed Jul.–Mar.*

Whakaari (White) Island

49 km (29 miles) off the coast of Whakatane.

With its billowing plumes of steam, the active volcano Whakaari (White) Island is New Zealand's only active marine volcano—and New Zealand's most active volcano overall. On December 9, 2019, it showed off its power with dire consequences, when an eruption killed 22 of the 47 people on the island at the time. It is now completely closed to visitors. Steam issues continuously from the many fumaroles (vents) and from the central crater, and the area reeks of sulfur. The island itself is eerie but exquisite, with fluorescent sulfuric crystal formations and boiling mud pools, but it can now only be viewed from the air or out at sea. Boats can usually get fairly close and can circumnavigate the island, but be aware that this could change at any time depending on volcanic activity.

TOURS

From Whakatane or Tauranga, you can fly over the island on a fixed-wing plane. You can no longer land on the island or visit by boat.

White Island Flights

AIR EXCURSIONS | Take a close look at the steaming island volcano from a safe distance. This company flies fixed-wing aircraft to and over the island and its crater (they can't land). It's an option to consider if the weather is too rough for the boat trip. Flights last one hour, or you could book a double whammy and buzz across to see the chasm of Mt. Tarawera. This volcano, near Rotorua, famously erupted in 1886, burying nearby Māori settlements. ⊠ *216 Aerodome Road, Whakatane* ☎ *0800/944–834* ⊕ *www. whiteislandflights.co.nz* ✈ *From NZ$249.*

Chapter 6

EAST COAST AND THE VOLCANIC ZONE

6

Updated by
Richard Pamatatau

Sights	Restaurants	Hotels	Shopping	Nightlife
★★★★☆	★★☆☆☆	★★★☆☆	★★☆☆☆	★★☆☆☆

WELCOME TO EAST COAST AND THE VOLCANIC ZONE

TOP REASONS TO GO

★ **Hiking and Walking:** The central North Island has great trails, including the famed Tongariro Alpine Crossing in Tongariro National Park (which stood in for Mordor in the Lord of the Rings movies).

★ **Māori Ceremonial Feasts:** Rotorua may be the best place in New Zealand to indulge in the traditional Māori feast known as a *hāngi* where the food is wrapped and cooked on hot stones in the ground.

★ **Soaking:** In Rotorua and Taupo, thermal springs are on tap. Soak in your own thermal bath in some Rotorua lodgings or take advantage of public facilities like the Polynesian Spa.

★ **The Shire:** Fans of the Lord of the Rings and The Hobbit movies should make their way to one of New Zealand's most popular tourist attractions: Hobbiton, the movie set that brought the famed hobbits' home to life.

★ **Fishing:** Central North Island is trout-fishing country. Local guides know the best spots to nab a catch.

1 Rotorua. A geothermic wonderland and one of the world's first spa towns.

2 Nearby Rotorua. Gorgeous countryside filled with Māori history and a little place called Hobbiton.

3 Taupo. A town on Lake Taupo's northeastern shore that doubles as a major outdoor activities center and one of the best places in the world for rainbow-trout fishing.

4 Tongariro National Park. Three volcanic peaks dominate the oldest and most popular national park in New Zealand.

5 Napier. A coastal city that was devastated by an earthquake in 1931 and rebuilt in colorful art-deco style.

6 Hawke's Bay. A popular vacation area and producer of some of the country's best wines.

7 Gisborne. A mostly quiet, rural place with undiscovered wineries and some important New Zealand history.

8 Te Urewera National Park. A rugged and remote park, with the biggest area of native forest on the North Island.

White Island

Motiti
Island

Cape Runaway   Midway Point

Hicks Bay

Te Araroa

35

Maketu

Puke

Motuhora
Island

Bay of Plenty

Te Kaha

Omaio

Tikitiki

Ruatoria

Thornton

Whakatane

Torere

Aorangi   Whareponga

30

Kawerau

Pekatahi

Opotiki

Kutarere

Waioeka

Waipiro
Te Puia

Tokomaru
Bay

Lake
Tarawera

Matahi

Oponae

Motu

EASTLAND

35

Mangatuna

Waiotapu

Galatea

Matawai

Rakauroa

2

Te Karaka

Tolaga Bay

38

Murupara

Te Whaiti

8

Te Urewera
National Park

Hexton

Whangara

7

Manutuke

Gisborne

angitaiki

Tiniroto

5

Pohokura

Tuai

Omahanui

Te Reinga

38

Marumaru

Tarawera

Rangiahua

Frasertown

2

Te Haroto

Ohinepaka

Wairoa

Nuhaka

Oraka Beach

Waihua

Table Cape

Te Pohue

Tutira

Long Point

MAHIA
PENINSULA

Tangoio

Hawke
Bay

Portland Island

Hawke's Bay

6

Rissington

Bay View

Napier

5

Otamauri

Matapiro

Omahu

Hastings

Kereru

50

Tikokino

RAUKUMARA RANGE

HUIARAU RANGE

South Pacific Ocean

0   20 mi

0   20 km

When you get to Rotorua, after a trip through the rolling, sheep-speckled fields of the Waikato and the wild Mamaku Ranges, the aptly named "Sulfur City"—with its mud pots, geysers, and stinky air—comes as a complete surprise. Rotorua, the mid-island's major city and Māori hub, has been a tourist magnet since the 19th century, when Europeans first heard of the healing powers of local hot springs.

South of Rotorua is the small town of Taupo; it stands alongside the lake of the same name (Australasia's largest) and is the geographical bull's-eye of the North Island. From the lake, you'll have a clear shot at Ruapehu, the island's tallest peak and a top ski area, and its symmetrically cone-shape neighbor, Ngauruhoe. Ruapehu dominates Tongariro National Park, a haunting landscape of craters, volcanoes, and lava flows that ran with molten rock as recently as 1988. As part of the Pacific Ring of Fire (a zone that's earthquake- and volcanic-eruption prone), the area's thermal features remain an ever-present hazard—and a thrilling attraction.

Southeast of Lake Taupo lies Hawke's Bay and the laid-back art deco town of Napier. Laze the days away drinking at the local vineyards, or, to truly get off the beaten path, head north to Gisborne; it's the easygoing center of isolated Eastland, the thick thumb of land that's east of Rotorua.

MAJOR REGIONS

The Rotorua Area. Home of geothermal unrest and oddities, Rotorua today is almost entirely a product of the late 19th-century fad for spa towns; its elaborate bathhouses and formal gardens date to this era. You'll find surreal wonders that include limestone caverns, volcanic wastelands, steaming geysers, and bubbling ponds. Nearby Māori communities offer a fascinating look into the region's most ancient living history as well as beautiful natural landscapes. The area is also where you can most easily access one of the world's most unique landscapes of all: the hobbits' Shire. You can find it within Hobbiton, the former movie set where many scenes from the Lord of the Rings movies were filmed.

Lake Taupo and Tongariro National Park. Fishing and water sports are popular activities in Lake Taupo, New Zealand's largest lake, and on the rivers running into it. The area also has its share of geothermal features. The town of Taupo is the best base for exploring the lake area while Tongariro National Park, dominated by three volcanic peaks, has some great otherworldly hiking trails.

Napier and Hawke's Bay. On the shores of Hawke Bay (Hawke Bay is the body of water, Hawke's Bay is the region), you'll find a fabulous architectural anomaly: the town of Napier, a time capsule of colorful art deco architecture. The countryside here is thick with vineyards, as this is one of the country's major wine-producing areas.

Gisborne and Eastland. Traveling to Eastland takes you well away from the tourist track on the North Island. Once here, you will find rugged coastline, beaches, dense forests, gentle nature trails, and small, predominantly Māori communities. Gisborne is the area's largest town. Above it juts the largely agricultural East Cape, a sparsely populated area ringed with stunning beaches; inland lies the haunting beauty of Te Urewera National Park.

Planning

Getting Here and Around

AIR
Air New Zealand offers daily direct flights from Wellington, Auckland, and Christchurch to Napier and Rotorua; direct flights from Wellington and Auckland also land in Gisborne. Budget carrier Jetstar serves Napier with direct flights from Auckland.

CONTACTS Air New Zealand. ⊠ *185 Fanshawe St., Central City* ☎ *0800/737–000, 09/357–3000* ⊕ *www.airnewzealand. co.nz.* **Jetstar.** ⊠ *Auckland Airport Terminal D, Ray Emory Dr., Auckland* ☎ *0800/800– 995* ⊕ *www.jetstar.com/nz.*

BUS
InterCity provides regular bus service for the entire region. Comfortable, reasonably priced, and efficient, it's particularly useful to backpackers and people who are in no particular hurry. The Napier-to-Auckland trip takes 8 hours, Napier–Rotorua is 3½ hours, Napier–Taupo is 2¼ hours, and Napier–Wellington is 6 hours. Frequent local services go between Napier and Hastings. There's also a daily bus to Gisborne from either Auckland, via Rotorua, or from Wellington, via Napier.

CAR
The best way to travel in this region is by car. Rotorua is about three hours from Auckland (could be more than four if you leave Auckland during the rush hour or if there is a motorway holdup). Take Highway 1 south past Hamilton and Cambridge to Tirau, where Highway 5 breaks off to Rotorua. Roads in this region are generally in good condition.

The main route between Napier and the north is Highway 5. Driving time from Taupo is two hours, five if you're coming straight from Auckland. Highway 2 is the main route heading south; it connects Hastings and Napier; from Wellington, driving time is 4½ hours to the former, 5 hours to the latter.

The most direct route from the north to Gisborne is to follow State Highway 2 around the Bay of Plenty to Opotiki, Eastland's northern gateway, then continue to Gisborne through the Waioeka Gorge Scenic Reserve. The drive from Auckland to Gisborne takes seven hours. South from Gisborne, continuing on Highway 2, you pass through Wairoa, about 90 minutes away, before passing Napier, Hawke's Bay, and Wairarapa on the way to Wellington.

TRAIN
Northern Explorer, a scenic 10-hour train connecting Auckland and Wellington, stops at National Park Village and Ohakune. The journey from Wellington

passes over five high viaducts. The train from Auckland goes around the remarkable Raurimu Spiral, where the track rises 660 feet in a stretch only 6 km (3½ miles) long.

CONTACTS Northern Explorer. ⊠ *Auckland Strand Railway Station, Ngaoho Pl., Parnell* ☏ *0800/872–467 bookings and enquiries* ⊕ *www.greatjourneysofnz. co.nz.*

Hotels

Accommodations range from super-expensive lodges to multistory hotels and budget motels. Bed-and-breakfast establishments—whether in town centers or in the depths of the countryside where you can succumb to the silence, curl up and read a book, or cast a fly in a quiet stream—are another excellent option.

Rotorua has lodgings in all price ranges. If you're willing to stay out of the town center, you can find bargain rates virtually year-round. In both Rotorua and Taupo, many hotels and motels give significant discounts on their standard rates off-season, from June through September. For stays during the school holidays in December and January, book well in advance. Also note that peak season in Tongariro National Park and other ski areas is winter (June–September); summer visitors can usually find empty beds and good deals. Many places, even the fanciest lodges, don't have air-conditioning, as the weather doesn't call for it.

Restaurant and hotel reviews have been shortened. For full information, visit Fodors.com. Restaurant prices are the average cost of a main course at dinner or, if dinner is not served, at lunch. Hotel prices are the lowest cost of a standard double room in high season.

WHAT IT COSTS in New Zealand Dollars			
$	$$	$$$	$$$$
RESTAURANTS			
under NZ$15	NZ$15–NZ$20	NZ$21–NZ$30	over NZ$30
HOTELS			
under NZ$125	NZ$125–NZ$200	NZ$201–NZ$300	over NZ$300

Planning Your Time

Start in Rotorua and then head down to Taupo and the national park region. If trout fishing is your game, stop at Turangi. Napier and Hastings, with Hawke's Bay, are home to excellent wineries and not to be missed. Prepare for a lengthy drive to Gisborne and the East Cape, and if you have the time (allow for 2½ hours each way, and don't forget to fill the tank in Wairoa), take the rugged side road to Lake Waikaremoana. Make sure to save one day for a quick trip to Hobbiton, outside of Rotorua.

North Island's East Coast and volcanic zone include some of the country's most popular attractions. Plenty of excellent tours and bus routes hit most highlights, but having your own vehicle gives you the flexibility to seek out an untrammeled scenic spot or that lesser-known-but-outstanding winery.

Information centers known as i-SITEs are found throughout the region. They supply free information and brochures on where to go and how to get there, available accommodations, car rentals, bus services, restaurants, and tourist venues. The centers often serve as bus and tour stops, too.

Restaurants

Rotorua has the area's most diverse dining scene. You can order anything from Indian to Japanese fare, or, for true local flavor, try a Māori *hāngi* (a traditional meal cooked in an earth oven or over a steam vent). Hawke's Bay is another hot spot: its winery restaurants emphasize sophisticated preparations and food-and-wine pairings. Around Eastland, which is so laid-back it's nearly horizontal, the choices are simpler, and you'll be treated with the area's characteristic friendliness. One thing you won't find on any menu is fresh trout. Laws prohibit selling this fish, but if you catch a trout, chefs at most lodging establishments will cook it for you.

Dressing up for dinner, or any other meal, is a rarity, expected at only the most high-end lodges and restaurants.

When to Go

November through mid-April is the best time to visit Central and Eastern North Island. The weather is generally balmy and everything is open. This is also the season for vineyard festivals, so keep an eye on local calendars. Try to avoid the school holidays (from mid-December to late January), when the roads and hotels get clogged with Kiwi vacationers. To see the gannet colony at Cape Kidnappers, you need to go between October and April, when the birds are nesting and raising their young.

Hawke's Bay and Gisborne can be remarkably mild in winter; Rotorua and Taupo, however, can get quite cold and wet. If you want to do some skiing, you can hit the slopes of Tongariro National Park from June through October, but you will be competing with families if you are there during the school break.

Rotorua

227 km southeast of Auckland by car.

Visitors tend to have a love-hate relationship with Rotorua (ro-to-roo-ah). Millions of them—both from New Zealand and abroad—flock in each year, sometimes embracing and sometimes ignoring the unashamedly touristy vibe that has earned it the nickname Rotovegas. In either case, there's no denying that Rotorua has long capitalized on nature's gifts. After all, the influx is nothing new. The "Great South Seas Spa," as the city was once known, ranks among the country's oldest and busiest tourism ventures and has been luring vacationers since the late 19th century.

Rotorua's Māori community traces its ancestry to the great Polynesian migration of the 14th century through the Arawa tribe, whose ancestral home is Mokoia Island in Lake Rotorua. The area is steeped in Māori history and legend—for hundreds of years, they have settled by the lake and harnessed the geological phenomena, cooking and bathing in the hotpools. Today there are still many places where you can soak in the naturally heated water—and soak up the traditional Māori atmosphere.

Whakarewarewa, at the southern end of Tryon Street, is the most accessible of these places and also the most varied. "Whaka," as the locals call it, has two parts (the Living Thermal Village and Te Puia), both of which give firsthand exposure to the hotpools and Māori culture. The community was founded by people who moved here from Te Wairoa after the eruption in 1886.

GETTING HERE AND AROUND

Air New Zealand runs daily direct flights from Wellington, Auckland, and Christchurch to the Rotorua Regional Airport (ROT). It's located 10 km (6 miles) from the city center on Highway 33. Taxi fare into the city is NZ$25 to NZ$30.

You could also arrange for a ride (NZ$26) with Super Shuttle; call ahead for a reservation.

In regular traffic, you can drive here from Auckland in about 3 hours; it will take about 5½ to come from Wellington. If you don't have your own vehicle, InterCity provides long-distance bus service.

The city itself is easy to navigate as streets follow a neat grid pattern. Entering Rotorua from Taupo, Fenton Street (the wide main drag) starts around Whakarewarewa. For about 3 km (2 miles), it's lined with lodgings until just before it reaches the lakefront, where shops and restaurants dominate. The Rotorua i-SITE Visitor Information Centre at 1167 Fenton is a good first stop; facilities include a tour-reservation desk and a map shop operated by the Department of Conservation.

AIRPORTS Rotorua Regional Airport. ⊠ *837 Te Ngae Rd., Rotorua* ☎ *7/345–8800* ⊕ *www.rotorua-airport.co.nz.*

AIRPORT TRANSFERS Rotorua Taxis. ⊠ *8/1209 Hinemaru St., Rotorua* ☎ *7/349-6248* ⊕ *www.rotoruataxis.co.nz.*

BUS DEPOT Rotorua Bus Depot. ⊠ *1167 Fenton St., Rotorua* ✢ *Adjacent to the Rotorua i-SITE Visitor Information Centre* ⊕ *www.rotoruanz.com.*

TOURS
HELICOPTER TOURS
Volcanic Air

Helicopters and floatplanes fly from the Volcanic Air office on the Rotorua lakefront. Trips include over-city flights, crater-lake flights, and excursions to Orakei Korako/Mt. Tarawera. The floatplane trip over the Mt. Tarawera volcano is extremely popular, and custom trips are available. ⊠ *Lakefront Dr., Rotorua* ☎ *07/348–9984* ⊕ *www.volcanicair.co.nz* 🖫 *From NZ$265.*

VISITOR INFORMATION
Rotorua i-SITE Visitor Information Centre
⊠ *1167 Fenton St., Rotorua* ☎ *07/348–5179* ⊕ *www.rotoruanz.com.*

 Sights

Government Gardens
GARDEN | Heading south from Lake Rotorua takes you to the Government Gardens, which occupy a small peninsula. The Māori call this area Whangapiro (fang-ah-*pee*-ro, "evil-smelling place"), an appropriate name for these gardens, where sulfur pits bubble and fume behind manicured rose beds and bowling lawns. The high point is the extraordinary neo-Tudor Bath House. Built as a spa at the turn of the 20th century, it is now the Rotorua Museum but currently closed to the public for seismic strengthening (reopening at the earliest in 2025). However, free daily garden tours are still offered at 11, 1, and 2 weekdays, 11 and 2 weekends. ⊠ *Government Gardens, Oruawhata Dr., Rotorua* ☎ *07/350–1814* ⊕ *www. rotoruamuseum.co.nz* 🖫 *Gardens free.*

Kuirau Park
CITY PARK | FAMILY | This public park is a local hot spot—literally. Mud pools and hot springs sit alongside the flower beds, which at times are almost hidden by floating clouds of steam. You can wander around or join the locals soaking their weary feet in shallow warm pools. Because this thermally active place can change overnight, keep to the paths. ⊠ *Kuirau St., south from Lake Rd., Rotorua* ⊕ *www.newzealand.com/int/feature/ kuirau-park* 🖫 *Free.*

St. Faith's
CHURCH | A short walk north from the Rotorua lakefront brings you to the Māori *pā* (fortress) of Ohinemutu, the region's original Māori settlement. It's a still-thriving community, centered on its *marae* (meetinghouse) and St. Faith's, the lakefront Anglican church. The interior of the church is richly decorated with carvings

Hāngi: A Traditional Māori Feast

Rotorua is the best place to experience a *hāngi*, a traditional Māori feast featuring food cooked over steaming vents or hot stones. Several local venues offer the opportunity for you to try this slow-cooked treat, paired with a concert—an evening that may remind you of a Hawaiian luau.

As a *manuhiri* (guest), you'll typically get the full treatment, beginning with a *powhiri*, the awe-inspiring Māori welcome that generally includes the *wero* (challenge), the *karanga* (cries of welcome), and the *hongi*, or the pressing together of noses and sharing of breath/life-force, an age-old Māori gesture that shows friendship and trust.

While the meal cooks, a show begins with haunting harmonious singing, foot stamping, and *poi* twirling (rhythmic swinging of balls on strings). The performance is always followed by food, glorious food. The lifting of the *hāngi* will produce pork, sometimes lamb and chicken, *kūmara* (sweet potato), vegetables, and maybe fish and other seafood, followed by dessert.

Cultural enclaves like **Whakarewarewa—The Living Māori Village** (*17 Tryon St.; 07/349–3463; www.whakarewarewa. com NZ$63*) and **Te Puia** (*Hemo Rd.; 07/348–9047; www.tepuia. com; NZ$128*) are only two of the places where you can get a true taste of local flavor.

The **Holiday Inn Rotorua** (*10 Tryon St.; 07/348–1189; rotorua.holidayinn. com; NZ$69*) also has an excellent cultural performance and *hāngi*; and the **Matariki Hāngi and Concert** at the **Novotel Rotorua Lakeside Hotel** (*Tutanekai St.; 07/346–3888; www.accorhotels.com; From NZ$39*) combines an informative, enthusiastic show with ample, delicious food.

---

inset with mother-of-pearl. Sunday services feature the sonorous, melodic voices of the Māori choir. The service at 9 am is in Māori and English. Visitors looking rather than attending a service pay a modest admission fee. ✉ *Tunohopu St., Rotorua* ⊕ *www.stfaithsrotorua.co.nz* ✉ *NZ$5.*

Te Puia

STATE/PROVINCIAL PARK | FAMILY | The grounds here are home to silica terraces, mud pools, and the Pohutu Geyser (the largest active one in the southern hemisphere). Te Puia also contains the New Zealand Māori Arts & Crafts Institute, where you can watch skilled carvers and weavers at work. Don't miss the Nocturnal Kiwi House, where you might spot one of New Zealand's beloved national birds. Day passes include a guided tour; packages with extras like a cultural performance or *hāngi* feast are also available. ✉ *Hemo Rd., Rotorua* ☎ *07/348–9047* ⊕ *www.tepuia.com* ✉ *From NZ$39* ⊘ *Closed Mon. and Tues.*

Whakarewarewa—The Living Māori Village
MUSEUM VILLAGE | FAMILY | For an introduction to Māori life, visit this authentic village. On a guided tour you'll see thermal pools where villagers bathe, boiling mineral pools, and natural steam vents where residents cook. You can add on a cultural performance and *hāngi* meal to complete the experience. Arts and crafts are available at local shops in case you want to take home a memento. ✉ *17 Tryon St., Rotorua* ☎ *07/349–3463* ⊕ *www.whakarewarewa.com* ✉ *From NZ$41.*

Hotels

★ Holiday Inn Rotorua

$$ | **HOTEL** | From the massive but welcoming entrance foyer with its huge stone fireplace to the lake views from the tower wing, this hotel spells class. **Pros:** complimentary shuttle service to town; good accommodations at all levels; a Māori concert and *hāngi* on the premise. **Cons:** it's close enough to Whakarewarewa to get more than a whiff of the local vapor; breakfast not included; can be crowded with conference attendees. [$] *Rooms from: NZ$190* ✉ *10 Tryon St., Rotorua* ☎ *07/348–1189* 🌐 *www.rotorua.holidayinn.com* 🛏 *206 rooms* 🍴 *No Meals.*

Princes Gate Hotel

$$$ | **HOTEL** | This ornate timber hotel was built in 1897 on the Coromandel Peninsula; its large, wonderfully appointed guest rooms were transported here in 1920. **Pros:** excellent afternoon tea; elegant and sophisticated; has an air of old-fashioned charm. **Cons:** if you want clinical and modern it's not for you; you'll feel you have to whisper in the lounge; some may find it twee. [$] *Rooms from: NZ$220* ✉ *1057 Arawa St., Rotorua* ☎ *07/348–1179* 🌐 *www.princesgate.co.nz* 🛏 *50 rooms* 🍴 *No Meals.*

Regal Palms 5 Star City Resort

$$$ | **RESORT** | **FAMILY** | The well-appointed studio, one-bedroom, and two-bedroom suites at this resort, located 2 km (1 mile) from downtown Rotorua sit amid spacious grounds. **Pros:** lovely day spa; good recreational facilities; roomy accommodations. **Cons:** there may be some traffic noise; you'll need to take the car to town; breakfast not included. [$] *Rooms from: NZ$280* ✉ *350 Fenton St., Rotorua* ☎ *07/350–3232* 🌐 *www.regalpalms.co.nz* 🛏 *44 suites* 🍴 *No Meals.*

Shopping

★ Āhua

CRAFTS | **FAMILY** | Te Puia was established in 1963 to preserve Māori heritage and crafts. At the institute you can watch master wood-carvers and expert flax weavers at work and see New Zealand greenstone (jade) sculpted into jewelry. The institute's shop and gallery, called Āhua, sells fine examples of this work, and the prices ranging from a few hundred dollars for simple carved pieces to thousands of dollars for museum-quality sculptures and other crafted pieces reflect the quality and amount of workmanship. ✉ *Hemo Rd., Rotorua* ☎ *07/348–9047* 🌐 *www.tepuia.com* 🕒 *Closed Mon. and Tues.*

Mountain Jade

CRAFTS | Look for beautifully made, high-quality jade items in this bright, spacious shop. ✉ *1288 Fenton St., Rotorua* ☎ *07/349–1828* 🌐 *www.mountainjade.co.nz.*

Simply New Zealand

SOUVENIRS | This spot stocks an excellent range of New Zealand gifts and souvenirs from carved greenstone or jade to woven bags and more. ✉ *1105 Pukuatua St., Rotorua* ☎ *07/348–8273* 🌐 *www.simplynewzealand.co.nz.*

Activities

BOATING

Kawarau Jet

BOAT TOURS | **FAMILY** | This company, which is best known for jet boat trips on Lake Rotorua, has extended its offerings to include parasailing adventures and hot springs excursions. The team goes out of its way to make sure you have a safe, memorable experience. ✉ *Memorial Dr., Rotorua* ☎ *07/343–7600* 🌐 *www.katoalakerotorua.co.nz* 🎟 *From NZ$125.*

Lakeland Queen

BOAT TOURS | FAMILY | Licensed for 300 passengers, the *Lakeland Queen*, a genuine stern-wheel paddle ship, has breakfast, lunch, and dinner cruises. One popular trip includes an onboard barbecue. The ship is often used for music events ranging from traditional jazz and singing to funk and DJs spinning at the desk, so check for special cruises on the website. ⊠ *Memorial Dr., Rotorua* 🕾 *07/348–0265* ⊕ *www.lakelandqueen. com* 🖃 *1-hour cruises from NZ$19.50, meal cruises from NZ$49.*

SPAS

★ Polynesian Spa

SPAS | FAMILY | Considered one of the best spas of its kind, the Polynesian Spa has a wide choice of mineral baths available, from large communal pools and family pools to small, private baths for two. You can also treat yourself to a massage or spa treatments; for a scenic soak, the Lake Spa has exclusive bathing in shallow rock pools overlooking Lake Rotorua. ⊠ *Hinemoa St., Rotorua* 🕾 *07/348–1328* ⊕ *www.polynesianspa. co.nz* 🖃 *Private pool NZ$38.95 per ½ hr; lake spa NZ$59.95; family shared pool from NZ$10* ☉ *Closed. Mon. and Tues.*

Rotorua Environs

The countryside near Rotorua includes magnificent untamed territory with lakes and rivers full of some of the largest rainbow and brown trout on Earth. From here down through Taupo and on into Tongariro National Park, fishing is a booming business. So if you're dreaming of landing the "big one," this is the place to do it. It's also where you'll find one of New Zealand's most popular man-made attractions: Hobbiton, the film set that recreated the Shire for the Lord of the Rings movies.

GETTING HERE AND AROUND

Most of the sights outside the Rotorua city area can be reached from State Highway 30, which branches right off Fenton Street at the southern corner of town. The Buried Village is accessed from Highway 30; farther east, you reach the airport, lakes Rotoiti and Rotoma, and Hell's Gate. Keeping on Fenton Street will lead to Lake Road and back onto Highway 5, which goes to Paradise Valley, Fairy Springs Road, and farther out of town to Ngongotaha and the Agrodome. If you don't have a car, sightseeing buses operated by Geyser Link Shuttles will transport you to a number of thermal sites in the area, Waimangu and Waiotapu among them; buses leave from Rotorua's i-SITE center on Fenton Street.

BUS CONTACTS Geyser Link Shuttles.
🕾 *0800/304–333* ⊕ *booking.headfirsttravel.com/geyserlink.*

Sights

Buried Village of Te Wairoa

RUINS | FAMILY | At the end of the 19th century, Te Wairoa (tay-why-*ro*-ah, "the buried village") was the starting point for expeditions to the pink-and-white terraces of Rotomahana, on the slopes of Mt. Tarawera. As mineral-rich geyser water cascaded down the mountainside, it formed a series of baths, which became progressively cooler as they neared the lake. In the latter half of the 19th century, these fabulous terraces were the country's major attraction, but they were destroyed when Mt. Tarawera erupted in 1886, burying the village of Te Wairoa under a sea of mud and hot ash. The village has since been excavated, and of special interest is the *whare* (*fah*-ray, "hut") of the *tohunga* (priest) Tuhoto Ariki, who predicted the destruction. An interesting museum contains artifacts, photographs, and models re-creating the day of the disaster, and a number of small

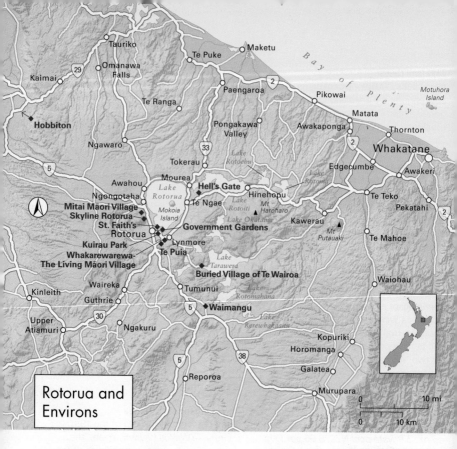

Rotorua and Environs

dwellings remain basically undisturbed beneath mud and ash. A path circles the excavated village, then continues on as a delightful trail to the waterfall, the lower section of which is steep and slippery in places. Te Wairoa is 14 km (9 miles) southeast of Rotorua. ⊠ 1180 Tarawera Rd., Rotorua ☎ 07/362–8287 ⊕ www. buriedvillage.co.nz ⊠ NZ$30.

Hell's Gate

HOT SPRING | FAMILY | Located 15 km (9 miles) east of Rotorua, Hell's Gate is arguably the most active thermal reserve in the area. Its 50 acres hiss and bubble with steaming fumaroles and boiling mud pools. Among the attractions here is the Kakahi Falls, reputedly the largest hot waterfall in the southern hemisphere, where, according to legend, Māori warriors bathed their wounds after battle. Warm mud pools are available for public bathing; at the Hellsgate Mud Spa, you can soak in a mud bath or try a *mirimiri* (a traditional Māori massage). ⊠ *State Hwy. 30, Tikitere* ☎ *07/345–3151* ⊕ *www. hellsgate.co.nz* ⊠ *NZ$99 for a package that includes a tour and spa in either a mud bath or thermal pool.* ☞ *Check the website for closures.*

★ Hobbiton

FILM/TV STUDIO | FAMILY | Even if you're not an aficionado of Lord of the Rings and The Hobbit movies, a delve into this magic, pretend world of the Shire of Mid-dle-earth (aka the Hobbiton movie set) is rather fascinating. Guides will escort you along the paths of the 12-acre set, stopping at little Hobbit houses set into the hillsides. Along the way, they share secrets about how the movies were made and explain incredible, intricate details of the set design. Like the thirsty

Scenery in Middle-earth

Some of the most striking elements of the Lord of the Rings films weren't created by special effects—they were the astonishing views of New Zealand's countryside. The film crew traveled all over the country, so there are dozens of locales to tempt you to stop and dream awhile.

On the North Island, you can visit a handful of hobbit homes in rural Matamata (*www.hobbitontours.com*). The volcanic peaks and blasted terrain of Tongariro National Park provided the setting for Mordor. Tackle one of the park's walking trails to see the otherworldly hot springs, lava rocks, and craggy peaks like Ruapehu, the films' Emyn Muil. Take the spectacular Tongariro Crossing trek to pass Ngauruhoe, the volcano the hobbits Frodo and Sam braved as Mount Doom.

Wellington, the film production's home base, is also the hometown of the director, Peter Jackson. Here the orcs, trolls, and the horrible Balrog all came to life, created by Weta Workshop and the production company Three Foot Six (named for the height of a hobbit). Weta's has had its hands full with other major films, including Jackson's *King Kong*. Local wags dub the capital "Wellywood."

The Hutt Valley, east of Wellington, saw plenty of hobbit action. During filming a huge polystyrene castle towered over a quarry by the Western Hutt road. Unsuspecting drivers would pass by Minas Tirith and the fortress of Isengard, where the wizard Gandalf was betrayed and imprisoned. Stay on Highway 2 to reach the beautiful Kaitoke Regional Park, used for the Elven city of Rivendell and a perfect place to picnic on the riverbank.

On the South Island, Highway 6 unrolls south to glacier country. Stop at Franz Josef and look for Mt. Gunn, where the beacon burned. Carving through the magnificent landscape, the road leads on to Wanaka, where the ghastly ringwraiths gave chase to Arwen and Frodo.

The breathtaking White Mountains, or Remarkables, at Queenstown were the background for the Ithilien Camp, the giant statues of the Pillars of Argonath, and other scenes. From nearby Glenorchy, you can hire a horse and ride to Paradise, seen as the Elven Lothlórien forest. Farther south, near Te Anau, the brooding silence of the lake district was shot as the Midgewater Marshes, and is prime trout-fishing territory.

Hobbits, you'll enjoy finishing up at the Green Dragon Inn for an exclusively brewed beverage. The standard tour lasts two hours. Meal packages can be added, and transport can be arranged from nearby Matamata and Rotorua. Hobbiton is one of New Zealand's most visited attractions, and reservations are essential for all tours. To think this was once just another New Zealand sheep farm. ✉ *501 Buckland Rd., Matamata* ☎ *07/888–1505*

⊕ *www.hobbitontours.com* ✉ *From NZ$89.*

★ Mitai Māori Village

MUSEUM VILLAGE | Rewind time by spending an evening at Mitai Māori Village, where you can listen to the harmonious chant of traditionally clad warriors as they paddle a *waka* (war canoe) along the Wai-o-whiro stream, then watch a top-notch cultural show, and enjoy a delicious

The geothermal activity at Waimangu keeps the water of Inferno Crater Lake at a boil.

hāngi feast. Getting the chance to see glowworms on a short, guided bush walk is a bonus. ⊠ *196 Fairy Springs Rd., Rotorua* ☎ *07/343–9132* ⊕ *www.mitai. co.nz* ⊠ *NZ$123* ☞ *Check the website for information.*

Skyline Rotarua

VIEWPOINT | FAMILY | A 2,900-foot cable-car system carries you up Mt. Ngongotaha for spectacular views over Lake Rotorua. At the summit, 1,600-feet above sea level, there's a café, a restaurant, and a souvenir shop. As an alternative, try the luge track, where you can take hair-raisingly fast rides on wheeled bobsled-like contraptions (you can also go slowly; a braking system gives you full control of your speed). The track runs partway down the mountain, winding through the redwood trees; from the bottom, you can return to the summit on a separate chairlift. For further thrills, consider zip-lining or mountain biking. ⊠ *Fairy Springs Rd., Rotorua* ☎ *07/347–0027* ⊕ *www.skyline. co.nz* ⊠ *Gondola NZ$35, gondola and luge NZ$52* ☞ *Check the website for events.*

★ Waimangu

VOLCANO | When Mt. Tarawera erupted in 1886, destroying Rotomahana's terraces, not all was lost. A volcanic valley emerged from the ashes, extending southwest from Lake Rotomahana. It's consequently one of the world's newest thermal-activity areas, encompassing the boiling water of the massive Inferno Crater, plus steaming cliffs, bubbling springs, and bush-fringed terraces. A path (one–two hours) runs through the valley down to the lake, where a shuttle bus can get you back to the entrance. You can also cap your trip by taking a cruise on the lake itself. Waimangu is 26 km (16 miles) southeast of Rotorua; to reach it, take Highway 5 south (Taupo direction) and look for the turn after 19 km (12 miles). ⊠ *587 Waimangu Rd., Rotorua* ☎ *07/366–6137* ⊕ *www.waimangu.co.nz* ⊠ *From NZ$50* ☞ *The park staff also offer customised trips.*

Hotels

★ **Solitaire Lodge**

$$$$ | HOTEL | Nestled in native bush on a private peninsula, the luxurious Solitaire Lodge commands extensive views over Lake Tarawera and the legendary mountain. **Pros:** high-end wine and food; quiet, secluded class in superb surroundings; diverse collection of activities offered. **Cons:** remote location comes at a high price; no swimming pool; no golf course. $ *Rooms from: NZ$2300* ⊠ *16 Ronald Rd.* ☎ *07/362–8208* ⊕ *www.solitaire-lodge.co.nz* ⦿ *All-Inclusive* ⌁ *11 suites.*

 Shopping

Amokura Glass

GLASSWARE | This artist-run hot glass studio and gallery offers live demonstrations four days a week at 12:30 pm. Its collection includes a mix of high-end sculpture, glass tapestries, and souvenirs. ⊠ *2 Amokura St., Rotorua* ☎ *07/349–0096* ⊕ *www.amokuraglass.com* ⦿ *Closed Tues. and Thurs.*

 Activities

The trout fishing in area lakes, streams, and rivers is some of the finest in the world. For outdoor enthusiasts and photographers wanting action shots there is also no shortage of activities such as trail biking, white-water rafting, and bungy jumping.

BIKING

Planet Bike

BIKING | FAMILY | First-timers and experts alike will find the perfect mountain-bike adventures with Planet Bike. You can ride for a couple of hours or several days, and some tours combine biking with rafting, kayaking, indoor climbing, or horseback riding. A full-day rental (helmet included) starts at NZ$60, depending on the bike. For those wanting an easier ride the company offers E-bikes but demand is high. ⊠ *8 Waipa Bypass Rd., off Waipa State*

Mill Rd., Rotorua ☎ *7/346–1717* ⊕ *www. planetbike.co.nz.*

FISHING

If you want to keep the trout of a lifetime from becoming just another fish story, go with a registered guide. Prices vary, but expect to pay about NZ$130–NZ$160 per hour for a fishing guide and a 20-foot cruiser that takes up to six passengers. The minimum charter period is two hours; gear and tackle are included in the price. A one-day fishing license costs NZ$20 per person and is available on the boat. (You'll need a special license to fish in the Rotorua area and in Taupo). For general information about local lake and river conditions, check with the Rotorua i-SITE Visitor Information Centre..

RAFTING AND KAYAKING

The Rotorua region has rivers with Grade III to Grade V rapids that make for excellent white-water rafting. For scenic beauty—and best for first-timers—the Rangitaiki River (Grades III–IV) is recommended. For experienced rafters, the Wairoa River has exhilarating Grade V rapids. The climax of a rafting trip on the Kaituna River is the drop over the 21-foot Okere Falls, among the highest to be rafted by a commercial operator anywhere. The various operators run similar trips on a daily schedule, though different rivers are open at different times of year, depending on water levels. All equipment and instruction are provided, plus transportation to and from the departure points—which can be up to 80 km (50 miles) from Rotorua. Prices vary depending on the run and the river; many operators sell combination trips.

Kaitiaki Adventures

WHITE-WATER RAFTING | FAMILY | The well-qualified team at Kaitiaki Adventures leads daily rafting trips on the Kaituna River. For a variation on the theme, try white-water sledging—you'll shoot the rapids on a specially designed plastic raft the size of a boogie board, and then soak in a natural hotpool; the cost is NZ$119 to

NZ$209, gear included. ✉ *1135 Te Ngae Rd., Rotorua* ☎ *0800/338–736* ⊕ *www.kaitiaki.co.nz* ✉ *From NZ$119.*

River Rats

KAYAKING | FAMILY | Day trips to the main rivers are organized by River Rats; adventure packages are available, too, as well as kayaking. ✉ *391 State Hwy. 33, Mourea* ☎ *07/345–6543, 0800/333–900* ⊕ *www.riverrats.co.nz* ✉ *From $129.*

Taupo

82 km (51 miles) south of Rotorua, 150 km (94 miles) northwest of Napier.

The tidy town of Taupo is the base for exploring Lake Taupo, the country's largest lake. Its shores are backed by volcanic mountains, and in the vicinity you'll see more of the geothermal activity that characterizes this zone. Water sports are popular here—notably sailing, cruising, and waterskiing—but Taupo is best known for fishing. The town is the rainbow-trout capital of the universe: the average Taupo trout weighs in at around 4 pounds, and the lake is open year-round. Meanwhile, the backpacker crowd converges on Taupo for its adventure activities. The town has skydiving and bungy jumping opportunities, and white-water rafting and jet boating are available on the local rivers.

GETTING HERE AND AROUND

Taupo is four hours from Auckland, depending on traffic, taking Highway 1 the whole way. It's 70 minutes from Rotorua, also via Highway 1. If you are coming by bus, InterCity Buses has daily service to Taupo from Auckland (approximately 5 hours) and from Rotorua (1 hour and 20 minutes).

Within the town, streets are laid out in a grid pattern. Busy Lake Terrace runs along the waterfront; it turns into Tongariro Street as it heads north, crossing the Waikato River and the gates that control the flow of water from the lake. Heu Heu, the main shopping street, runs from the traffic lights on Tongariro Street.

BUS DEPOT Taupo Bus Depot. ✉ *Taupo i-SITE Visitor Information Centre, 30 Tongariro St., Taupo* ☎ *07/348–0366* ⊕ *www.lovetaupo.com.*

TOURS
BOAT TOURS
Barbary

BOAT TOURS | The 1920s yacht *Barbary,* believed to have once been the property of golden-age film star Errol Flynn, has been given an eco-makeover so that it can use an electric motor when the wind is too light to sail. On offer are short cruises departing daily at 10:30, 2, and 5. They take in giant carvings on a lakefront cliff face and, depending on the weather, let you swim off the boat when it's moored. On board, you can help hoist the sails or just sit back and dream in one of the big beanbags. ✉ *Berths 9, 10 Redoubt Rd., Taupo* ☎ *07/378–5879* ⊕ *www.sailbarbary.com* ✉ *From NZ$49.*

Maid of the Falls

BOAT TOURS | Board the *Maid of the Falls* for a Huka Falls cruise. The boat leaves from Aratiatia Dam, 10 km (6 miles) north of Taupo, at 10:30, 12:30, and 2:30; a 4:30 trip is added in summer. The vessel has a viewing platform on the front and takes you up close to the falls, which push a huge amount of water through a narrow gap in the rocks. ✉ *630 Aratiatia Rd., Taupo* ☎ *0800/7377–3454* ⊕ *www.hukafallscruise.co.nz* ✉ *NZ$42 adult, NZ$15 child, family packages are available.*

BUS TOURS
Paradise Tours

BUS TOURS | Bus tours operated by this outfit visit attractions in and around Taupo, including Huka Falls and Craters of the Moon. If you are a Lord of the Rings fan, the company offers a trip to Hobbiton. ✉ *Taupo* ☎ *21/7378–9955*

⊕ *www.paradisetours.co.nz* ⛵ *From NZ$109.*

VISITOR INFORMATION

CONTACTS Taupo i-SITE Visitor Information Centre. ⊠ *30 Tongariro St., Taupo* ☎ *07/376–0027* ⊕ *www.greatlaketaupo. com.*

 Sights

Aratiatia Dam

DAM | The Waikato River is dammed along its length; the first construction is the Aratiatia Dam, 10 km (6 miles) northeast of Taupo. The river below it is virtually dry most of the time, but three times a day (at 10, noon, and 2), and four times a day in summer (October–March, also at 4), the dam gates are opened and the gorge is dramatically transformed into a raging torrent. Watch the spectacle from the road bridge over the river or from one of two lookout points a 15-minute walk downriver through the bush. To access the dam from Taupo, turn right off Highway 5. ⊠ *Aratiatia Rd., Taupo.*

Craters of the Moon

NATURE SIGHT | **FAMILY** | The construction of the local geothermal project had an impressive—and unforeseen—effect. Boiling mud pools, steaming vents, and large craters appeared in an area now known as Craters of the Moon. A marked walkway snakes for 3 km (2 miles) through the belching, sulfurous landscape, past boiling pits and hissing crevices. The craters are up Karapiti Road, across from the Huka Falls turnoffs on Highway 1, 3 km (2 miles) north of Taupo. ⊠ *171 Karapiti Rd., Taupo* ☎ *0276/564– 684* ⊕ *www.cratersofthemoon.co.nz* ⛵ *NZ$8.*

Huka Falls

WATERFALL | The Waikato River thunders through a narrow chasm and over a 35-foot rock ledge at Huka Falls. The fast-flowing river produces almost 50% of the North Island's required power, and its force is extraordinary, with the falls dropping into a seething, milky-white pool 200 feet across. The view from the footbridge is superb; for an even more impressive look, both the *Maid of the Falls* and vessels operated by Hukafalls Jet get close to the maelstrom. The falls are 3 km (2 miles) north of town; to reach them, turn right off Highway 1 onto Huka Falls Road. ⊠ *Huka Falls Rd., Taupo.*

Huka Prawn Park

FARM/RANCH | **FAMILY** | This prawn farm is a curious mix of cheesy and fascinating. Check out the holding tanks where prawns are bred in specially heated river water (in some, baby prawns eat out of your hand). You can also catch your own prawns using a small rod and fishing line, or just buy some on site; either way you can have them cooked and served as you like in the adjoining café. ⊠ *Huka Falls Rd., Wairakei Park, Taupo* ☎ *07/374–8474* ⊕ *www.hukaprawnpark.co.nz* ⛵ *NZ$30.*

Orakei Korako

NATURE SIGHT | **FAMILY** | Even if you've seen enough bubbling pools and fuming craters to last a lifetime, the thermal valley of Orakei Korako is still likely to captivate you. Geyser-fed streams hiss and steam as they flow into the waters of the lake, and a cream-and-pink silica terrace is believed to be the largest in the world since the volcanic destruction of the terraces of Rotomahana. At the bottom of Aladdin's Cave, the vent of an ancient volcano, a jade-green pool was once used by Māori women as a beauty parlor, which is how the name Orakei Korako (A Place of Adorning) originated. The valley is 37 km (23 miles) north of Taupo, via Highway 1, and takes about 25 minutes to reach by car; you could always see it en route to or from Rotorua, which lies another 68 km (43 miles) northeast of the valley. ⊠ *494 Orakeikorako Rd., Reporoa* ☎ *07/378–3131* ⊕ *www.orakeikorako. co.nz* ⛵ *NZ$42.*

Taupo Museum

ART MUSEUM | **FAMILY** | You'll find Māori treasures and contemporary art on

Kayakers paddle the Waikato River, New Zealand's longest waterway.

display at this museum. The volcanic eruptions that have shaped the area are also chronicled. The star attraction, however, is the glorious Ora Garden, which was granted Garden of National Significance status in 2011. ✉ *Story Pl., Taupo* ☎ *07/376–0414* 🌐 *www.taupodc.govt.nz/community/taupo-museum* 🎫 *NZ$5.*

🍴 Restaurants

★ The Bistro
$$$$ | EUROPEAN | This joint aims for simple but nice and has fittingly become an impressive but unpretentious eatery. Large cylindrical lamp shades brighten the modern interior, creating a contemporary bistro vibe; the food follows suit, focusing on what's fresh and seasonal. **Known for:** standard European fare with a local twist; excellent pork belly; good wine list. [$] *Average main: NZ$45* ✉ *17 Tamamutu St., Taupo* ☎ *07/377–3111* 🌐 *www.thebistro.co.nz* 🕒 *No lunch.*

★ Brantry Restaurant
$$$$ | CONTEMPORARY | The menu is updated seasonally at this converted 1950s town house on a suburban street not far from the shores of Lake Taupo. Owners Prue and Felicity Campbell know what they're doing and use the best local ingredients to make delicious things to satisfy all palates. **Known for:** unique wines; ever-changing innovative menu; high-quality ingredients. [$] *Average main: NZ$40* ✉ *45 Rifle Range Rd., Taupo* ☎ *07/378–0484* 🌐 *www.thebrantry.co.nz* 🕒 *Closed Mon. No lunch Tues.–Thurs.*

★ The Replete Food Company
$$ | CAFÉ | FAMILY | This café draws the crowds for breakfast and lunch thanks to its outside tables and excellent food. In the morning, try the Complete Replete Breakfast: honey-cured bacon, tomato relish, poached eggs, roasted field mushrooms, and grilled focaccia. **Known for:** New Zealand dishes with an Asian twist; popular breakfast spot; tasty coffee. [$] *Average main: NZ$16* ✉ *45 Heu*

Heu St., Taupo ☎ 07/377–3011 🌐 www.replete.co.nz ⏲ No dinner.

Hotels

Cascades Lakefront Motel

$$$ | **APARTMENT** | This lakeside motel offers comfortable rooms with great views. **Pros:** great views; on the lakeside with a safe beach; heated pool. **Cons:** units near road may get some traffic noise; 3 km (2 miles) from town center; uninspiring decor. [$] *Rooms from: NZ$300 ✉ 303 Lake Terr., just south of State Hwy. 5 (Napier) turnoff, Taupo ☎ 07/378–3774 🌐 www.cascades.co.nz 🍴 No Meals 🛏 24 units.*

★ Huka Lodge

$$$$ | **HOTEL** | **FAMILY** | Set on 17 blissful acres, this riverfront lodge is one of the country's finest and has seen its fair share of prominent guests over the years. **Pros:** gorgeous setting; one of the world's best lodges with a knowing and established clientele; excellent range of activities. **Cons:** prices are per person per night; perfection does not come cheap; fixed dinner times. [$] *Rooms from: NZ$2400 ✉ 77–105 Huka Falls Rd., Taupo ☎ 7/378–5791 🌐 www.hukalodge.co.nz 🛏 25 suites 🍴 All-Inclusive.*

The Pillars

$$$$ | **B&B/INN** | This modern, Mediterranean-style country manor features four large en suite rooms, a spacious guest lounge, a conservatory, and patio areas where a complimentary evening drink can be enjoyed. **Pros:** delightful, friendly hosts; pool and tennis court; free Wi-Fi. **Cons:** encouragement to socialize with other guests isn't for everyone; you need transport to see the sights; no restaurant or bar on site. [$] *Rooms from: NZ$395 ✉ 7 Deborah Rise, Bonshaw Park, Taupo ☎ 07/378–1512 🌐 www.pillarstaupo.co.nz 🍴 Free Breakfast 🛏 4 suites.*

Activities

The Central North Island region is an absolute must for anyone keen on hunting, fishing, canoeing, hiking, or just about any other outdoor activity.

BUNGY JUMPING

Taupo Bungy

LOCAL SPORTS | Plunge from a cantilevered platform that projects out from a cliff 150 feet above the Waikato River. You can go for the "water touch" or dry versions. Even if you have no intention of "walking the plank," go and watch the jumpers from the nearby lookout point, 1 km (½ mile) north of town. Jumps are available daily from 9 to 5. *✉ 202 Spa Rd., off Tongariro St., Taupo ☎ 07/377–1135, 0800/888–408 🌐 www.taupobungy.co.nz 🎟 From NZ$180.*

FISHING

There is some great fishing in the Taupo area and a large number of guides with local expertise who work the Tongariro River and the lake. High season runs from October to April. Costs are usually around NZ$250 for a half day and include all equipment plus a fishing license (note that you need a special license to fish here and in Rotorua). Book at least a day in advance.

Chris Jolly Outdoors

FISHING | Staffed by people with a love of the outdoors, this company can take you mountain biking, hiking, hunting, cruising, and, of course, fishing. Try fly-fishing or cast for trout on a chartered boat trip. A half-day fly-fishing expedition includes all your equipment. *✉ Berth 4, Taupo Boat Harbour, Ferry Rd., Taupo ☎ 07/378–0623, 0800/252–628 🌐 chrisjolly.co.nz 🎟 Half-day trips NZ$570 for two people.*

Mark Aspinall

FISHING | Fly-fish for rainbow and brown trout with Mark Aspinall. He will organize a custom trip to meet your needs and collect you from wherever you are staying, but it's important to book well in advance, especially in summer. A half-day or full-day trip includes all gear; full-day trips include lunch. ✉ *Taupo* ☎ *021/500–384* ⊕ *www.markaspinall.com* ✉ *Half-day trips from NZ$300, full-day trips with lunch from NZ$550.*

JET BOATING
Hukafalls Jet
BOATING | For high-speed thrills on the Waikato River, take a ride with Hukafalls Jet. Its jet boats spin and skip between the Aratiatia Dam and Huka Falls multiple times per day. Trips last 30 minutes. ✉ *200 Karetoto Rd., Taupo* ☎ *07/374–8572* ⊕ *www.hukafallsjet.com* ✉ *From NZ$99.*

RAFTING
Rafting New Zealand
RAFTING | The Wairoa and Mohaka rivers are accessible from Taupo, as are the Rangitaiki and the more family-friendly Tongariro. Rafting New Zealand provides transportation, wet suits, equipment, and much-needed hot showers at the end. ✉ *41 Ngawaka Pl., Taupo* ☎ *07/386–0352, 0800/865–226* ⊕ *www.raftingnewzealand.com* ✉ *From NZ$139.*

SKYDIVING
Call at least one day in advance to arrange your jump—weather permitting—and expect to pay NZ$249–NZ$339 per, more if you want to add on a video or other mementos to commemorate your experience.

Taupo Tandem Skydiving
SKYDIVING | For a thrill—along with a bird's-eye view of Taupo—try Taupo Tandem Skydiving. Jumps start at 9,000 feet and go up to 18,500 feet. ✉ *Anzac Memorial Dr., Taupo* ☎ *07/377–0428, 0800/826–336* ⊕ *taupotandemskydiving.com* ✉ *From NZ$199.*

Tongariro National Park

110 km (69 miles) southwest of Taupo.

Tongariro offers a spectacular combination of dense forest, wild open countryside, crater lakes, barren lava fields, and rock-strewn mountain slopes. Its rugged beauty and convenient location, almost in the center of the North Island, make it the most popular and accessible of New Zealand's parks.

GETTING HERE AND AROUND
The park is best reached by car. The approach from the north is along Highway 4 on the park's western side; turn off at the village of National Park for Whakapapa. Coming from the south, turn off State Highway 1 at Waiouru for Ohakune. From Taupo to the park, follow State Highway 1 south and turn off at Turangi onto State Highway 47. The roads are generally good; however, snow and ice can be a problem around the park in winter.

It's difficult to reach Tongariro National Park by public transport, though InterCity does run a daily bus in summer (mid-October–April) between Taupo, Whakapapa, and National Park village; the trip takes around 1½ hours. Numerous local shuttle operators also provide transportation for hikers to and from the park.

Northern Explorer, a scenic train that links Auckland and Wellington, stops at National Park village and Ohakune; it travels southbound on Monday, Thursday, and Saturday and northbound on Tuesday, Friday, and Sunday.

Whakapapa, on the north side of Ruapehu, is the only settlement within the park with services, and it is the jump-off point for the Whakapapa ski slopes. The second ski area is Turoa, and its closest town is Ohakune, which is just beyond the southern boundary of the park. Both towns keep their doors open for hikers

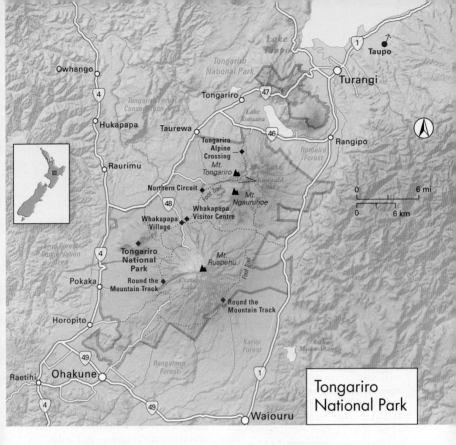

Tongariro National Park

and other travelers when the snow melts. The Tongariro National Park Visitor Centre is the best place to get maps, guides, and, if needed, hut passes. If you want to do some online research, the Department of Conservation's website (www.doc.govt.nz) is another helpful resource.

TOURS

Tongariro Expeditions

This outfit runs a shuttle to Tongariro National Park from the Taupo, Turangi, and Tongariro Base Camp and Ketetahi car park in summer. Only guided trips, which include gear and return transportation, are available in winter. There is an additional charge for gear as many of the walks are through challenging terrain. You will be picked up, and all bookings are made online. ⊠ Taupo ☎ 21/07 377–0435

⊕ www.tongariroexpeditions.com
☉ Shuttle from NZ$35.

VISITOR INFORMATION

CONTACTS Tongariro National Park Visitor Centre. ⊠ Whakapapa Village, State Hwy. 48, Mt. Ruapehu, Tongariro National Park ☎ 21/07 892–3729 ⊕ www.doc.govt.nz.

 Sights

Tongariro National Park

MOUNTAIN | Tongariro National Park is the oldest national park in New Zealand and the largest on the North Island. Gifted to the nation by the Ngāti Tuwharetoa people in 1887, this stunning mountainous region provided much of the dramatic scenery for the Lord of the Rings films, where its jagged volcanic landscape most famously stood in for Mordor. The

Planning Your Trip to Tongariro

Best Time to Go

Your best window for decent weather is November through March, and the busiest time is between Christmas and New Year. Keep in mind, however, that even during summer you may feel like you're experiencing all four seasons in a single day, with weather ranging from hot and sunny to cool and rainy, and even snowy at higher elevations. In winter, cold alpine conditions are not uncommon. Suitable clothing should always be carried and sensible footwear worn.

Best Activities

Hiking and Tramping. The Tongariro Alpine Crossing has been described as the best one-day walk in the world. Approach it with the expectation that sudden changes of weather, even during summer, are always possible. There are numerous other trails covering the area and various types of accommodations, from cheap backpacker campgrounds to lodges and at least one first-class hotel. Most of these will organize transport to get the keen walkers to places where hikes can vary from an hour to several days. The longer trails will have huts to provide basic overnight stopovers.

Horseback Riding. Horses were brought to New Zealand by white settlers in 1814, and within a few years herds of feral horses were common. One, known as the Kaimanawa Wild Horses, established itself on the Central Plateau, virtually under the eastern shadow of Mt. Ruapehu. For a number of years they have been confined to a protected area, and travelers often catch a glimpse of these horses from Desert Road, State Highway 1.

Skiing. June through October (give or take a week or two, depending on conditions), the slopes of Mt. Ruapehu come to life with hundreds of skiing and snowboarding enthusiasts. On occasion the runs have to be cleared when the mountain's crater lake threatens to overflow, but this hasn't decreased the area's popularity. The combined fields of Turoa and Whakapapa form the largest ski slope in New Zealand and have brought a measure of prosperity to the once sleepy villages of National Park and Ohakune.

Viewing Volcanoes. Massive and downright awesome, Tongariro, Ngauruhoe, and Ruapehu dominate from whichever direction you approach, and the views from Desert Road are a photographer's dream. If you travel from the south on State Highway 1 on a clear day, the first glimpse of Ruapehu as the road crests will take your breath away. Farther north on the same road, the enormous, almost perfectly truncated, cone-shaped bulk of Ngauruhoe looms alongside a series of hairpin bends.

park has a spectacular combination of dense forest, wild open countryside, crater lakes, barren lava fields, and rock-strewn mountain slopes. Its rugged beauty and convenient location, almost in the center of the North Island, make it the most popular and accessible of New Zealand's parks. Three volcanoes, Tongariro, Ngauruhoe, and Ruapehu, tower above its Central Plateau overlooking miles of untamed country that stretch to the West Coast on one side and the aptly named Desert Road on the other. The volcanoes are no sleeping giants: Tongariro is the least active, but Ngauruhoe and Ruapehu have both erupted in recent years. In 1995, 1996, and again in 2007, Ruapehu spewed ash, created showers of rock, and released lahars (landslides of volcanic debris) that burst through the walls of the crater lake. The park is famed for its hiking trails, but the weather can change very quickly here so be sure to be prepare for the day with good outdoor gear and plenty of food. ✉ *State Hwy. 48, Tongariro National Park* 🌐 *www.nationalpark.co.nz.*

Hotels

Chateau Tongariro
$$$$ | HOTEL | Built in 1929, this French neo-Georgian-style property in Whakapapa hosts everyone from well-heeled movie types to people who tramp and ski by day, then switch their clothing to dress in heels or jacket and tie for the evening. **Pros:** superb views; classy, restful place; enormous lounge area has a welcoming open fire and billiard table. **Cons:** long way from the nearest town; views are often obstructed by mist; may be seen as stuffy. [$] *Rooms from: NZ$350* ✉ *99 State Hwy. 48, Mt. Ruapehu, Tongariro National Park* ☎ *07/892–3809, 0800/242–832* 🌐 *www.chateau.co.nz* 🍴 *No Meals* 🛏 *116 rooms.*

En Route: Turangi

Straddling State Highway 1 between National Park village and Taupo sits the small town of **Turangi.** A regular stopover for motorists on the main north–south route, its number-one attraction is trout fishing on some of the world's most productive rivers, but there is also great local walking, kayaking, and white-water rafting. Hotpools are also close by. The **Turangi i-SITE Visitor Information Centre** (*07/386–8999, www.greatlaketaupo.com*) is on Ngawhaka Place, Turangi.

Discovery Lodge
$$$ | APARTMENT | FAMILY | The only tourist lodging in the park to give a panoramic view of three active volcanoes is this friendly complex, only minutes from the ski slopes. **Pros:** good food; handy to the village; close to the start of the Tongariro Alpine Crossing and their shuttle gets you there quite early. **Cons:** breakfast not included; a long way from shops; not a good range of shuttle times to the crossing. [$] *Rooms from: NZ$280* ✉ *State Hwy. 47, Whakapapa Village* ☎ *07/892–2744, 0800/122–122* 🌐 *www.discovery.net.nz* 🍴 *No Meals* 🛏 *22 rooms.*

Activities

HIKING

The best one-day itinerary is indisputably the **Tongariro Alpine Crossing.** The 19.4-km (12½-mile) walk starts and finishes in different places, so make arrangements for drop-off and pickup points. Several firms and most lodgings will organize this at a reasonable charge. Check on the condition of the trail before you depart—there have been geological disturbances, and, as a result, some parts of the track may not be accessible.

Starting at Mangatepopo, the one-way crossing is a spectacular seven- to nine-hour hike up and over the namesake mountain, passing craters, the evocatively named Emerald Lakes, old lava flows, and hot springs. It's a harsh environment for vegetation, but you'll spot moss and lichens and occasional wetland plants. It's a steep climb to the Mangetepopo Saddle, which lies between Tongariro and Ngauruhoe, but the views on a clear day can seem endless. For the adventurous, an unmarked track leads to the top of Mt. Ngauruhoe (Mount Doom if you're a Lord of the Rings fan). It's very steep and estimated to be a three-hour trip; adding this excursion requires a high level of fitness. The main trail proceeds to the south crater of Tongariro to a ridge leading up Red Crater. Here you can often smell sulfur. Rising 6,120 feet, the Red Crater's summit is the highest point of the Tongariro Alpine Crossing. From here the trail has a lot of loose stones and gravel and is extremely rough underfoot as it descends down to three smaller water-filled craters known as the Emerald Lakes (so named for their brilliant greenish color). The trail then continues across Central Crater to the Blue Lake to lead across the North Crater and downhill all the way to the Ketetahi Hut, where you'll be glad to sit and take a breather. Afterward, hike on to the springs of the same name; these are on private land, which the trail artfully skirts, but their steam cloud is impossible to miss. From here it's pretty much all downhill through tussock slopes to the start of the bush line and a long descent through forest to your pickup at the end.

Although children and school groups commonly do the hike, it is not to be taken lightly. Prepare yourself for rapidly changing weather conditions by bringing warm and waterproof clothing. Wear sturdy footwear, and carry food, plenty of water, sunblock, and sunglasses—and don't forget a hat. Also, be careful not to get too close to steam vents; the area around them can be dangerously hot. From late November to May, you'll be sharing the trail with many other hikers. In the colder months, it's really only for experienced winter hikers who can deal with snow and ice; some transport companies will take you only if you have an ice axe and crampons. It is recommended that you get up-to-date trail and weather conditions from the Department of Conservation's Tongariro National Park Visitor Centre before starting out. A number of trail transport operators provide shuttles to and from the Tongariro Alpine Crossing. Many of the motels and lodges in National Park village can also arrange transport.

The longest hikes in the park are the three-day **Northern Circuit,** which goes over Tongariro and around Ngauruhoe, and the four-day **Round-the-Mountain Track,** which circles Ruapehu. There are trailside huts throughout the park to use on overnight trips. You'll need to buy a hut pass at the visitor center; check for costs as they vary depending on the time of year. During the "Great Walks Season" (the third week in October to the last week in April), huts musts be booked ahead; otherwise it's first come, first served. Gas stoves are available in the huts. You can also tackle short half-hour to two-hour walks if all you want is a flavor of the region. A 90-minute round-trip trek to the Tawhai Falls via the **Whakapapanui Track** takes you through the forest, and a two-hour round-trip to Taranaki Falls showcases subalpine scenery.

With all of these tracks it is vital to carry the right gear as weather can suddenly change.

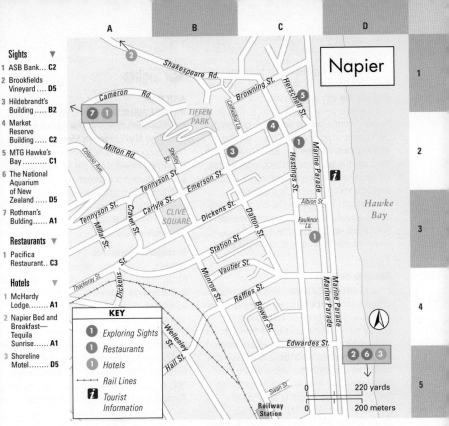

KEY

- 1 Exploring Sights
- 1 Restaurants
- 1 Hotels
- ┼─┼ Rail Lines
- 🄸 Tourist Information

0 ——— 220 yards
0 ——— 200 meters

SKIING

Mt. Ruapehu Ski Slopes

SKIING & SNOWBOARDING | FAMILY | Combined, the Mt. Ruapehu ski slopes add up to New Zealand's most extensive skiing and snowboarding area. Whakapapa, on the mountain's north side, has more than 30 groomed trails, including beginners' slopes. Turoa, on the south side, has a half-pipe. Ski season generally runs from June through October, depending on snow conditions. Full-day, all-mountain lift passes are available as are lessons and rental equipment. In summer, lifts operate depending on weather for those wanting to enjoy a little alpine sightseeing. ✉ Taupo ⊕ www.mtruapehu.com.

Napier

150 km (94 miles) southeast of Taupo, 345 km (215 miles) northeast of Wellington.

The earthquake that struck Napier at 10:46 am on February 3, 1931, was—at 7.8 on the Richter scale—the largest quake ever recorded in New Zealand. The coastline was wrenched upward several feet. Almost all of the town's brick buildings collapsed, and many people were killed on the footpaths as they rushed outside. The quake triggered fires throughout town, and with water mains shattered, little could be done to stop the blazes that devoured the remaining wooden structures. Only a few buildings survived (the Public Service Building with its neoclassical pillars is one), and the death toll was well over 100.

The surviving townspeople set up tents and cookhouses in Nelson Park and then tackled the city's reconstruction at a remarkable pace. In the rush to rebuild, Napier went mad for art deco, the bold, geometric style that had burst on the global design scene in 1925. Now a walk through the art deco district, concentrated between Emerson, Herschell, Dalton, and Browning streets, is a stylistic immersion. The decorative elements are often above the ground floors, so keep your eyes up. It's this style that fuels much of the town's cultural activity.

TOURS
Absolute de Tours
SPECIAL-INTEREST TOURS | This company offers a range of visits and walking tours that include tastings of award-winning honey, wine, and local beers. Some tours include food (and platters can be ordered at other venues), and there is always the option of a customized itinerary by hosts who know the area and its delights. At some vineyards, there is an additional tasting charge. ⊠ 112 Avenue Rd., Greenmeadows ☎ 06/844–8699 ⊕ www.absolutedetours.co.nz ✉ From NZ$110.

Art Deco Trust
SPECIAL-INTEREST TOURS | The Trust leads excellent themed tours that highlight Napier's architectural heritage. A one-hour walk starts daily at 10 am from the Napier i-SITE Visitor Information Centre; a two-hour version, which includes an audiovisual introduction, starts at 2 pm from the Art Deco Centre. You can also arrange a private tour in a vintage car. DIY types can pick up the Trust's Art Deco Tour Map, which plots a self-drive route through Napier and Hastings. ⊠ Art Deco Centre, 7 Tennyson St., Napier ☎ 09/835–0022 ⊕ www.artdeconapier.com ✉ From NZ$28; private tours from NZ$200.

VISITOR INFORMATION
CONTACTS Napier i-SITE Visitor Information Centre. ⊠ 100 Marine Parade, Napier ☎ 06/834–1911 ⊕ www.napiernz.com.

Sights
ASB Bank
NOTABLE BUILDING | One of Napier's more notable buildings is at the corner of Hastings and Emerson streets. The Māori theme on the lintels is probably the country's finest example of kowhaiwhai (rafter) patterns decorating a European building. The traditional red, white, and black pattern is also continued inside around a coffered ceiling. ⊠ 100 Hastings St., Napier.

Brookfields Vineyards
WINERY | One of this region's most attractive wineries features rose gardens and a tasting room that overlooks the vines. The chardonnay and pinot gris are usually outstanding, but the showpiece is the reserve cabernet sauvignon–merlot, a powerful red that ages well. Syrah grapes are proving spectacular as is the Brookfields Hillside syrah. ⊠ 376 Brookfields Rd., Napier ✛ From Napier, take Marine Parade toward Hastings and turn right on Awatoto Rd. Follow it to Brookfields Rd., and turn left. Signs will point to the winery. ☎ 06/834–4615 ⊕ www.brookfields-vineyards.co.nz ✉ Free.

Hildebrandt's Building
NOTABLE BUILDING | Hildebrandt's has an excellent frieze, which is best viewed from across Dalton Street. The original owner was a German who migrated to New Zealand—hence the German flag at one end, the New Zealand at the other; the wavy lines in the middle symbolize the sea passage between the two countries. ⊠ 90 Tennyson St., Napier.

Market Reserve Building
NOTABLE BUILDING | On Tennyson and Hastings, this was the first building to rise after the earthquake. Its steel metal frame was riveted, not welded, so that the construction noise would give residents the message that the city was being rebuilt. The bronze storefronts with their "crown of thorns" patterned leaded

glass are original. ✉ *28 Tennyson St., Napier.*

★ MTG Hawke's Bay

ART MUSEUM | This complex, also known as the Hawke's Bay Museum, is home to a museum, a theater, and an art gallery. The museum component's curatorial team is engaged, and the exhibitions ponder a range of local and international issues, so you might see a temporary display devoted to an exploration of memory alongside a cutting-edge digital presentation. There's also a significant collection of newspaper reports, photographs, and audiovisuals that re-create the suffering caused by the 1931 earthquake, plus a unique collection of artifacts—including vessels, decorative work, and statues—relating to the Ngāti Kahungunu Māori people of the East Coast. ✉ *1 Tennyson St., Napier* ☎ *06/835–7781* 🌐 *www.mtghawkesbay.com* 🎟 *Free.*

★ National Aquarium of New Zealand

AQUARIUM | **FAMILY** | Stand on a moving conveyor that takes you through the world of sharks, rays, and fish. Environmental and ecological displays showcase tropical fish, sea horses, tuatara, and other creatures. For an additional fee you can get up close and personal with penguins. There is also a kiwi enclosure where these birds can be seen in ideal viewing conditions. ✉ *Marine Parade, Napier* ☎ *06/834–1404* 🌐 *www.national-aquarium.co.nz* 🎟 *NZ$23.*

Rothman's Building

NOTABLE BUILDING | A little over a kilometer (½ mile) north of the central core stands one of the area's finest deco edifices. The 1932 structure has been totally renovated and its original name reinstated: the National Tobacco Company Building. It has a rose theme on the stained-glass windows and on a magnificent glass dome over the entrance hall. ✉ *1 Ossian St., Napier.*

🍴 Restaurants

★ Pacifica Restaurant

$$$$ | **NEW ZEALAND** | Enter this weathered blue bungalow to experience the innovative cooking and fresh produce Pacifica brings to the New Zealand dining scene. The five-course degustation menus with matched wine change daily and reflect the chef's creativity and commitment to using the finest local products. **Known for:** great wines; fresh seafood and pasta; two excellent (but pricey) tasting menus. [$] *Average main: NZ$65* ✉ *209 Marine Parade, Napier* ☎ *06/833–6335* 🌐 *www.pacificarestaurant.co.nz* 🕒 *Closed Sun. and Mon. No lunch.*

🛏 Hotels

McHardy Lodge

$$$$ | **B&B/INN** | The gardens at this historic mansion, high on Napier Hill, have panoramic views of the Pacific Ocean and the splendid Kaweka Ranges. **Pros:** heated pool and full-size billiard table; grand mansion feel; fabulous views. **Cons:** hard uphill walk from town center; can be hard to find on a dark night; need to book evening meals ahead of time. [$] *Rooms from: NZ$625* ✉ *11 Bracken St., Napier* ☎ *06/835–0605* 🌐 *www.mchardylodge.co.nz* 🛏 *6 rooms* 🍽 *Free Breakfast.*

Napier Bed and Breakfast—Tequila Sunrise

$$$ | **B&B/INN** | **FAMILY** | This modern hilltop residence with sweeping views over the countryside and ocean was purpose-built as a B&B. **Pros:** quality accommodations; quiet atmosphere; complimentary wine made on premises. **Cons:** decor a little old-fashioned; long way from restaurants; 20-minute drive to town. [$] *Rooms from: NZ$295* ✉ *123 Eskridge Dr., Napier* ☎ *06/836–7373* 🌐 *www.napierbandb.co.nz* 🛏 *4 suites* 🍽 *Free Breakfast.*

Shoreline Motel
$$ | **MOTEL** | The rooms at this Marine Parade place are well-appointed and well-equipped; each comes with its own hot tub, a flat-screen TV, and free Wi-Fi. **Pros:** free off-street parking; close to town; many rooms have sea views. **Cons:** two flights of outside stairs to top units; often full in the holiday season; main road can be noisy. [$] *Rooms from: NZ$195* ✉ *377 Marine Parade, Napier* ☎ *06/835–5222* 🌐 *www.shorelinenapier.co.nz* 🛏 *38 rooms* 🍴 *No Meals.*

Shopping

Art Deco Centre
OTHER SPECIALTY STORE | Napier's Art Deco Trust takes its role as an arbiter of the movement's style and maintains a perfectly laid-out shop that sells everything from table lamps to ceramics, as well as a selection of hats, toys, jewelry, rugs, and wineglasses. Aficianados of art deco will find a range of reproduction items here that speak to the era without eye-watering prices. ✉ *7 Tennyson St., Napier* ☎ *06/835–0022* 🌐 *www.artdeconapier.com.*

★ Opossum World
OTHER SPECIALTY STORE | This fascinating spot sells opossum products and houses a mini museum about the opossum's effects on New Zealand's environment. Fur items include hats, gloves, and rugs; a soft blend of merino wool and opossum fur is also made into sweaters, scarves, and socks. ✉ *106 Hastings St., Napier* ☎ *06/835–7697* 🌐 *www.opossumworld.com.*

Hawke's Bay

320 km (205 miles) northeast of Wellington, 165 km (100 miles) southeast of Taupo.

Bounded by the Kaweka and Ruahine ranges, Hawke's Bay is known as the fruit basket of New Zealand. You can't travel far without seeing a vineyard or an orchard, and the region produces some of the country's finest wines. Roughly 25 years ago, a dry, barren area known as the Gimblett Gravels was about to be mined for gravel. Then an enterprising vine grower took a gamble and purchased the land. The stony soil turned out to be a boon for grapevines because it retains heat, and now several wineries benefit from its toasty conditions. Chardonnay is the most important white variety here; you'll also find sauvignon blanc, Bordeaux varieties, and syrah.

On the coast east of Hawke's Bay is Cape Kidnappers, a fascinating spot that is home to as many as 20,000 gannets. To the south, you'll find Hastings, which is blessed with art deco buildings, and adorable Havelock North (known locally as "the Village"), with the Te Mata Peak rising dramatically beyond.

Farther south, a hill near Porangahau is the place with the longest name in the world. Take a deep breath and say, "Taumatawhakatangihangakoauauotamateaturipukakapikimaungahoronukupokaiwhehuakitanatahu." If that's too difficult to memorize, just remember it as "the place where Tamatea, the man with the big knees who slid, climbed, and swallowed mountains, known as land-eater, played his flute to his loved one," and it should be no problem at all.

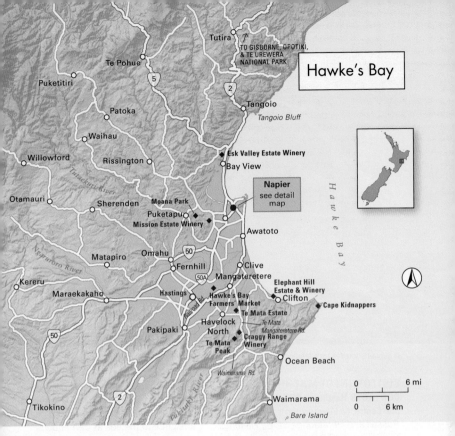

Hawke's Bay

To Gisborne, Opotiki, & Te Urewera National Park

Tutira
Te Pohue
Puketitiri
Patoka
Waihau
Willowford
Rissington
Tangoio
Tangoio Bluff
Esk Valley Estate Winery
Bay View
Napier
see detail map
Otamauri
Sherenden
Moana Park
Puketapu
Mission Estate Winery
Awatoto
Matapiro
Omahu
Fernhill
Clive
Mangateretere
Kereru
Hastings
Elephant Hill Estate & Winery
Clifton
Cape Kidnappers
Maraekakaho
Hawke's Bay Farmers' Market
Te Mata Estate
Havelock North
Te Mata
Mangateretere Rd.
Pakipaki
Craggy Range Winery
Te Mata Peak
Ocean Beach
Waimarama Rd.
Tikokino
Waimarama
Bare Island
Hawke Bay

0 ____ 6 mi
0 ____ 6 km

GETTING HERE AND AROUND

Distances here are comparatively short: Hastings, for instance, is only 18 km (11 miles) south of Napier, so driving is the optimal way to get around.

TOURS

Gannet Beach Adventures

SPECIAL-INTEREST TOURS | Make the most of your trip to the Cape Kidnappers gannet colony by boarding a trailer towed by a 1949 Minneapolis-Moline tractor. Along the way, you'll hear commentary about the geological features of this amazing coastline. Tours lasting about four hours run daily, October through late April. Depending on the time of year you'll see eggs or chicks or birds about to depart for foreign shores. Tours depart approximately two hours before low tide from Clifton Reserve; transport from the Napier or Hastings i-SITE is available. ⊠ 475 Clifton Rd., Clifton, Te Awanga, Napier 🕾 06/875–0898 ⊕ www.gannets. com ✉ From NZ$55.

Gannet Safaris Overland

SPECIAL-INTEREST TOURS | This outfit runs a four-wheel-drive bus to Cape Kidnappers from its base, just past Te Awanga. The three-hour tour includes commentary and stops within a few feet of the gannets— no walking required. Buses leave daily at 9:30 and 1:30, September through April. Advance booking is essential; transportation from Napier or Hastings can be arranged at extra cost. ⊠ 396 Clifton Rd., Clifton, Te Awanga, Napier 🕾 06/875–0888 ⊕ www.gannetsafaris.co.nz ✉ From NZ$88 (4-person minimum) ☞ Personalized tours can be arranged.

A gannet comes in for a landing on the rocks of Cape Kidnappers in Hawke's Bay.

 Sights

Cape Kidnappers

BEACH | This outstanding spot is believed to be the only mainland gannet sanctuary in existence. It was named by Captain James Cook after local Māori tried to kidnap the servant of his Tahitian interpreter, Tupaia. Gannets—large white seabirds with black-tipped flight feathers, a golden crown, and a wingspan that can reach 6 feet—generally nest only on remote islands. But between October and April, thousands of them build their nests here, hatch their young, and prepare them for their long migratory flight. Watching them dive for their dinner is particularly impressive: when the birds find a shoal of fish, they fold their wings and plunge straight into the sea at tremendous speed. You can walk to the sanctuary along the beach from Clifton, but check with the i-Site first—from time to time rock fall makes the walk dangerous, and you can't go at high tide. Clifton is about 24 km (15 miles) south of Napier. The 8-km (5-mile) walk must begin no earlier than three hours after the high-tide mark, and the return journey must begin no later than four hours before the next high tide. Tidal information is available at area i-SITE Visitor Information Centres. A rest hut with refreshments is near the colony. ✉ *Cape Kidnappers, 468 Clifton Rd., Clifton* ☎ *06/834–3111* ⊕ *www.doc.govt.nz/parks-and-recreation/places-to-go/hawkes-bay/places/cape-kidnappers-gannet-reserve.*

★ Craggy Range Winery

WINERY | Situated by a small lake with the towering Te Mata Peak beyond, this vineyard has a stellar backdrop. The wines include single-varietal chardonnay, merlot, and syrah; a predominantly merlot blend called Sophia; and a pinot noir dubbed Aroha. You can sample wines at the cellar door; leave time to linger over a meal at Terroir, a French-inspired restaurant overlooking the lake. ⌧ *253 Waimarama Rd., Havelock North* ☏ *06/873–7126* ⊕ *www.craggyrange. com* ⌧ *Tastings NZ$10 (refundable with purchase of bottle).*

Elephant Hill Estate & Winery

WINERY | Blending contemporary architecture with the traditional aspect of wine making, this stunning estate overlooks jagged rows of vines with expansive views from the terrace taking in the ocean and Cape Kidnappers. Sip a glass of wine in the sunken lounge, or enjoy a meal in the ultramodern dining room—it's an unforgettable experience. You can also stay in the winery's boutique accommodation. ⌧ *86 Clifton Rd., Hawke's Bay* ☏ *06/872–6073 winery, 06/872–6073 restaurant* ⊕ *www.elephanthill.co.nz.*

★ Esk Valley Estate Winery

WINERY | Winemaker Gordon Russell produces merlot, syrah, and blends with cabernet sauvignon, merlot, cabernet franc, and malbec in various combinations, including a rare and expensive red simply called The Terraces. White varieties include chardonnay, sauvignon blanc, riesling, verdelho, chenin blanc, and pinot gris. Look for the Winemakers Reserve versions of chardonnay, syrah, and merlot-malbec blend to find out what he has done with the best grapes from given years. The vineyard's position, in a sheltered valley overlooking the Pacific, ensures it captures full sun; it's located 12 km (8 miles) north of Napier, just north of the town of Bay View before Highways 2 and 5 split. ⌧ *745 Main Rd., Bay View* ☏ *06/872–7430* ⊕ *www.eskvalley. co.nz* ⌧ *NZ$20 for a four-wine tasting.* ☾ *Closed Sun. and Mon.*

Hastings

TOWN | Napier's twin city doesn't have the same concentrated architectural interest as Napier. But the 1931 earthquake also did a great deal of damage here, and buildings in its center exhibit similar art deco flourishes. The Westerman's Building, on the corner of Russell and Heretaunga, is one prime example; it now houses the town's i-SITE center. Hastings is 18 km (11 miles) south of Napier, down Highway 2.

Hawke's Bay Farmers' Market

MARKET | **FAMILY** | For picnic supplies, visit the Hawke's Bay Farmers' Market. It's held at the A&P Showgrounds on Sunday from 8:30 to 12:30. Local products include handmade cheese, breads, ice cream, and fruit. This is also a good place to people-watch. ⌧ *Kenilworth Rd., Hastings* ☏ *027/697–3737* ⊕ *hawkesbay-farmersmarket.co.nz.*

★ Mission Estate Winery

WINERY | Surrounded by gardens, this classic winery—the country's oldest and set up by Catholic missionaries—stands in the Taradale hills overlooking Napier. Dating back to 1851, it deserves to be added to your "must-see" list. Award-winning wines, including the Mission Jewelstone range, can be bought or tasted at the cellar door. Learn more about the mission's history by joining one of the twice-daily tours, or order a meal in the on-site restaurant, which serves lunch and dinner daily (take a seat on the terrace for a terrific view of the vineyard and Napier). Also check out the website—the winery occasionally hosts concerts by big-name performers. ⌧ *198 Church Rd., Taradale* ✛ *To get here, leave Napier by Kennedy Rd., heading southwest from the city center toward Taradale. Just past Anderson Park, turn right onto Avenue Rd., and continue to its end at Church Rd.* ☏ *06/845–9350* ⊕ *www.mission-estate.co.nz* ⌧ *Free.*

Moana Park

WINERY | At this boutique producer, specific wine styles are selected and handcrafted from each vintage, based on its Gimblett Gravels and Dartmoor Valley vineyards. All grapes are grown on either organic or sustainable sites and are vegan approved. Platters of local produce are available; you're also welcome to bring along a picnic as there are plenty of tables on the lovely grounds. ✉ *530 Puketapu Rd., Taradale* ☎ *06/844–8269* 🌐 *moanaparkcellar.co.nz* 🕓 *Closed Mon.–Wed.*

★ Te Mata Estate

WINERY | This is one of New Zealand's oldest and best family-owned wineries. Coleraine, a rich but elegant cabernet–merlot blend named after the much-photographed home of the owner, John Buck, is considered the archetypal Hawke's Bay red. Bullnose syrah, Elston chardonnay, and Cape Crest sauvignon blanc show similar restraint and balance. If there's any Zara viognier open (it's made only in tiny quantities), try it—it's excellent. ✉ *349 Te Mata Rd., Havelock North* ✣ *From Napier, head south on Marine Parade through Clive, and turn left at the Mangateretere School. Signs will then lead you to Te Mata Rd. and the estate.* ☎ *06/877–4399* 🌐 *www.temata.co.nz* 🎫 *Tastings NZ$8.*

Te Mata Peak

VIEWPOINT | It's possible to gaze across the plains to Napier and the rumpled hills beyond from this famed local viewpoint. The summit is a 15-minute (signposted) drive along Te Mata Peak Road from the village of Havelock North. ✉ *Te Mata Peak Rd., Havelock North.*

🍴 Restaurants

Jarks Cityside

$$$ | **CONTEMPORARY** | **FAMILY** | On sunny days, you can sit outside on the patio here and enjoy the varied menu. In winter, a large fireplace warms the rustic interior, and candles on the tables enhance the scene. **Known for:** friendly local vibe; seasonal produce; cheesecake of the day. [$] *Average main: NZ$30* ✉ *118 Maraekakoho Rd., Hastings* ☎ *06/870–8333* 🌐 *www.jarks.co.nz* 🕓 *Closed Sun.*

Rose & Shamrock

$$$ | **IRISH** | **FAMILY** | This lovely old-world pub in the heart of Havelock North has the largest selection of tap beer in Hawke's Bay. The pints mix with reasonably priced pub fare, including Scotch fillet, Irish sausages, and hearty beef-and-Guinness pie. **Known for:** good standard pub food; fun trivia night; friendly atmosphere. [$] *Average main: NZ$26* ✉ *Napier Rd. and Porter Dr., Havelock North* ☎ *06/877–2999* 🌐 *www.roseandshamrock.co.nz* 🕓 *Closed Christmas Day.*

★ Terroir Restaurant

$$$$ | **FRENCH** | The massive cedar doors, high circular roof, and open wood fire give this well-regarded restaurant at Craggy Range Winery a rustic character. Although the menu is loosely country French, the "rustic" cuisine here is far from unsophisticated. **Known for:** twice-baked goat cheese soufflé; gorgeous views from the terrace; some of the best wine in the region. [$] *Average main: NZ$50* ✉ *Craggy Range Winery, 253 Waimarama Rd., Havelock North* ☎ *06/873–0143* 🌐 *www.craggyrange.com* 🕓 *Closed Mon. and Tues. Apr.–Oct. No dinner Sun.*

🛏 Hotels

Harvest Lodge

$$$ | **MOTEL** | **FAMILY** | Close to the center of Havelock North, this up-to-the-minute motel has spacious units with original artwork and comfortable king-size beds. **Pros:** spacious rooms; close to town; handy to restaurants and bars. **Cons:** may be some traffic noise; near busy road; breakfast not included. [$] *Rooms from: NZ$260* ✉ *23 Havelock Rd., Havelock North* ☎ *06/877–9500* 🌐 *www.*

Gisborne is one of New Zealand's more low-key wine regions, which means its wineries are less crowded.

harvestlodge.co.nz 🛏 *19 units* 🍴 *No Meals.*

Mangapapa Hotel

$$$$ | HOTEL | FAMILY | The 1885 grand residence of one of New Zealand's earliest entrepreneurs has been converted into a charming boutique hotel. **Pros:** excellent café; private and quiet; understated luxury. **Cons:** pricey; breakfast not included; grounds could use some maintenance in places. [$] *Rooms from: NZ$525* ✉ *466 Napier Rd., Havelock North* ☎ *06/878–3234* 🌐 *www.mangapapa.co.nz* 🛏 *12 suites* 🍴 *No Meals.*

Portmans Motor Lodge

$$ | MOTEL | Conveniently located near the center of Hastings, this motel has 20 modern units surrounding a spacious courtyard; 10 have whirlpool baths, and all are comfortably equipped. **Pros:** lovely pool; reasonably priced accommodations; really handy to town. **Cons:** pool isn't heated; some parking is a little cramped; decor not very charming. [$] *Rooms from: NZ$185* ✉ *401 Railway Rd., Hastings* ☎ *06/878–8332* 🌐 *www.portmans.co.nz* 🛏 *20 rooms* 🍴 *No Meals.*

Gisborne

210 km (130 miles) northeast of Napier, 500 km (310 miles) southeast of Auckland.

The Māori name for the Gisborne district is Tairawhiti (tye-ra-*fee*-tee), "the coast upon which the sun shines across the water," and Gisborne is indeed the first city in New Zealand to see the sunrise. With a population of just 30,000, it's hardly large, however, you'll need a day or so to get around properly. The landmark Town Clock stands in the middle of Gladstone Road. Nearby, in a house on Grey Street, Kiri Te Kanawa, New Zealand's world-famous opera diva, was born in 1944 (the house is no longer there).

Europeans settled the Gisborne area early in the 19th century. A plaque on the waterfront commemorates the first official sale—of an acre of land—on June

30, 1831. On that site, the first European house and store was reportedly erected (it's long gone, too).

GETTING HERE AND AROUND

Air New Zealand flies daily to Gisborne from Auckland and Wellington. The small Gisborne Airport (GIS) is about 5 km (3 miles) from the city center; you can catch a taxi in for NZ$20. InterCity buses also link Gisborne to Auckland and Wellington once per day.

Motorists should note that Gisborne is a long way from almost anywhere, but the coastal and bush scenery makes the drive wholly worthwhile. Most of the town's historical sights and other attractions are too spread out to explore by foot, and a car is needed for the spectacular countryside. The main driving approach is by State Highway 2, which becomes Gladstone Street as it enters the town.

AIRPORTS Gisborne Airport. ⊠ *Aerodrome Rd., Gisborne* ☎ *06/986–4800* ⊕ *www. eastland.co.nz/gisborne-airport.*

BUS CONTACTS Gisborne Bus Depot. ⊠ *Gisborne i-SITE Visitor Information Centre, 209 Grey St., Gisborne* ☎ *06/868–6139* ⊕ *tairawhitigisborne. co.nz.*

VISITOR INFORMATION

CONTACTS Gisborne i-SITE Visitor Information Centre. ⊠ *209 Grey St., Gisborne* ☎ *06/868–6139* ⊕ *tairawhitigisborne. co.nz.*

 Sights

Cook Landing Site National Historic Reserve

BEACH | This place has deep historical significance and contestation for New Zealanders. A statue of Captain James Cook, who first landed here on October 9, 1769, stands on Kaiti Beach, across the river southeast of the city center. It is both a site of protest and commemoration. The beach itself attracts interesting birdlife at low tide. ⊠ *Esplanade on south end of Turanganui River, Gisborne.*

Eastwoodhill Arboretum

GARDEN | FAMILY | Inspired by the gardens seen on a trip to England in 1910, William Douglas Cook returned home and began planting 160 acres. His brainchild became a stunning collection of more than 600 genera of trees from around the world. In spring and summer, daffodils mass yellow; magnolias bloom in clouds of pink and white; and cherries, crab apples, wisteria, and azalea add to the spectacle. The main trails in the park can be walked in about 45 minutes. Maps and self-guided tour booklets are available. Drive west from Gisborne center on State Highway 2 toward Napier, cross the bridge, and turn at the rotary onto the Ngatapa–Rere Road. Follow it 35 km (22 miles) to the arboretum. ⊠ *2392 Wharekopae Rd., Ngatapa* ☎ *06/863–9003* ⊕ *www.eastwoodhill.org.nz* ⊠ *NZ$15.*

Gisborne–Opotiki Loop

SCENIC DRIVE | Soak in the beauty of Eastland by driving the Provincial Highway 35 loop between Gisborne and Opotiki—it's one of the country's ultimate roads-less-traveled. The 330-km (205-mile) trip takes about five hours without stops. En route, rolling green hills drop into wide crescent beaches or rock-strewn coves, and small towns appear, only to fade into the surrounding landscape. Some scenic highlights are Anaura Bay, with rocky headlands, a long beach favored by surfers, and nearby islands; it is between Tolaga Bay and Tokomaru Bay, two former shipping towns. Tolaga Bay has an incredibly long wharf stretching over a white-sand beach into the sea, and Cooks Cove Walkway is a pleasant amble through the countryside past a rock arch. Farther up the coast in Tikitiki, you'll find both a gas station and an Anglican church full of carved Māori panels and beams. East of the small town of Te Araroa, which has the oldest *pohutukawa* (po-hoo-too-*ka*-wa) tree in the country, the coast is about as remote as you could imagine. At the tip of the cape, 21 km (13 miles) from Te Araroa, the East Cape Lighthouse promises fantastic views after a long, steep climb from the beach. Back toward Opotiki, Whanarua (fahn-ah-*roo*-ah) Bay is one of the most gorgeous on the East Cape, with isolated beaches ideal for a picnic and a swim. Farther on, there is an intricately carved Māori marae (meetinghouse) called Tukaki in Te Kaha. If you choose to spend a night along the loop, there are motels at various points on the cape and some superbly sited motor camps and backpacker lodges, though you'll need to be well stocked with foodstuffs before you set off. Gisborne's i-SITE Centre can provide information about lodging.

Millton Vineyard

WINERY | The first New Zealand facility to attain organic certification specializes in making fine wine from estate-grown grapes sourced from single vineyards and grown in the traditional manner using biodynamic techniques. It's a great place to sample, sit, and relax. The vineyard is signposted off State Highway 2, about 11 km (7 miles) south of Gisborne. ⊠ *119 Papatu Rd., Manutuke* ☎ *06/862–8680* ⊕ *www.millton.co.nz.*

Tairawhiti Museum

ART MUSEUM | FAMILY | With its Māori and *Pākehā* (non-native) artifacts and an extensive photographic collection, this small but interesting museum provides a good introduction to the region's history. A maritime gallery covers seafaring matters, and there are changing exhibits of local and national artists' work. The pottery displays are particularly outstanding. An on-site shop sells locally made items. Check out Wyllie Cottage before leaving the grounds (although it stands outside, it's part of the museum). Built in 1872, this colonial-style house is the oldest in town. ⊠ *Kelvin Park, 10 Stout St., Gisborne* ☎ *06/867–3832* ⊕ *www.*

tairawhitimuseum.org.nz ⊠ *NZ$5 Tues.– Sun.; free Mon.*

Te Poho o Rawiri Meeting House

NOTABLE BUILDING | One of the largest Māori marae (meetinghouses) in New Zealand has an intriguing interior with complex traditional carvings. One example is the *tekoteko,* a kneeling human figure with the right hand raised to challenge those who enter. There are also unusual alcoves and a stage framed by carvings; it's essentially a meetinghouse within a meetinghouse. Photography is not allowed inside. On the side of the hill stands the 1930s Toko Toro Tapu Church. You'll need permission to explore either site; contact the Gisborne i-SITE Visitor Information Centre. ⊠ *At Ranfurly St. and Queens Dr., Kaiti Hill* ⊕ *nzplaces.nz/place/ te-poho-o-rawiri-marae* ⊠ *Donations requested.*

Titirangi Domain

VIEWPOINT | This was the site of an extensive pā (fortified village), which can be traced back at least 24 Māori generations. It has excellent views of Gisborne, Poverty Bay, and the surrounding rural areas. Titirangi Recreational Reserve is a part of the Domain, and it makes a great place for a picnic or a walk. The Domain is south of Turanganui River. Pass the harbor and turn right onto Esplanade, left onto Crawford Road, then right onto Queens Drive, and follow it to several lookout points in the Domain where the views are extraordinary. ⊠ *Ranfurly St., Gisborne.*

🍴 Restaurants

The Rivers

$$$ | IRISH | FAMILY | A casual place to hoist a few pints while dining on hearty pub fare, the Rivers is popular with Gisborne locals. Stained-glass partitions separate the dining alcoves, which have brass chandeliers, dark woodwork, and green leather upholstery. **Known for:** central location; friendly atmosphere; great Irish pub food. [$] *Average main: NZ$25* ✉ *At Reads Quay and Gladstone Rd., Gisborne* ☎ *06/863–3733* 🌐 *www.therivers.co.nz.*

The Works Café & Winery

$$$$ | NEW ZEALAND | FAMILY | This eatery in the former Gisborne Freezing Works embraces its industrial roots (note the large driveshaft and pulleys on the brick walls). The menu builds on local products and seasonality, from cheeses to fruit, scallops to calamari. **Known for:** local wine; excellent panfried fish; cool atmosphere. [$] *Average main: NZ$35* ✉ *41 The Esplanade, Gisborne* ☎ *06/868–9699* 🌐 *www.theworksgisborne.co.nz.*

Hotels

Ocean Beach

$$ | MOTEL | FAMILY | A surfer's paradise, this Mediterranean-looking motel complex is a five-minute drive north of Gisborne, close to Wainui Beach. **Pros:** ideal situation for beach-type getaway; nice amenities; spacious rooms. **Cons:** breakfast not included; need transport into town; there may be traffic noise in the busy season. [$] *Rooms from: NZ$140* ✉ *7 Oneroa Rd., Wainui Beach, Gisborne* ☎ *06/868–6186* 🌐 *www.oceanbeach.co.nz* 🍴 *No Meals* 🛏 *15 rooms.*

Senator Motor Inn

$$ | MOTEL | FAMILY | Offering comfortable, modern accommodations with lovely views over the marina and inner harbor on one side and main-street shopping on the doorstep, this motel has an ideal location that ticks all the boxes. **Pros:** free Wi-Fi and off-street parking; great views; close to everything. **Cons:** proximity to street means it can be noisy; may be full in high season; no food available on site (but within walking distance of cafes). [$] *Rooms from: NZ$185* ✉ *2 Childers Rd., Gisborne* ☎ *06/868–8877* 🌐 *www.senatormotorinn.co.nz* 🍴 *No Meals* 🛏 *16 rooms.*

Activities

DIVING AND SNORKELING

★ Dive Tatapouri

DIVING & SNORKELING | Dean and Chrissie lead an extremely popular snorkeling excursion that lets you swim freely with stingrays, eagle rays, kingfish, crayfish, octopuses, and other ocean creatures. You'll get to observe, touch, and feed them in their natural habitat (wet suits, snorkels, and masks provided). If you'd rather not dive right in, try the Reef Tour. On this one you wade out to spy all manner of marine life. Huge rays slide up the rocks and put their head clear of the water; when you pop a morsel into their mouth, they take it gently, and then glide silently away (waders included). Tours are available year-round but are dependent on tides. Dive Tatapouri is 15 km (9 miles) north of the city, off State Highway 35. ✉ *Whangara Rd., Gisborne* ☎ *06/868–5153* 🌐 *www.divetatapouri.com* 🎫 *From NZ$55.*

FISHING

Touchwood Fishing Charter

FISHING | Albacore, yellowfin tuna, mako shark, and marlin along with the yellow-tail kingfish are prized catches from January to April (no license required). There are various operators who will help you land one—including Touchwood. Its boat has a full range of safety equipment, plus fish-finding electronics that help it target a number of species from the lesser-known hot spots around Gisborne. Group trips, which anyone can join, are typically offered at least twice a month (call for dates), but private charters are also available anytime; tackle and bait are included in all trips. ✉ *37a Massey Rd., Gisborne* ☎ *0274/305–701* 🌐 *touchwoodfishingchartersgisborne.co.nz* 🎫 *NZ$150 per person (based on party of 10), private charters from NZ$1765 per day.*

GOLF
Poverty Bay Golf Course

GOLF | This 18-hole championship course ranks among the top five in the country. Established in 1893, the links-style, par 72 course is one of the country's oldest and open for play daily to both members and non members. ⊠ *Lytton and Awapuni Rds., Elgin* ☎ *06/867–4402* ⊕ *www.gisbornegolf.co.nz* ✉ *NZ$45 for nonmembers* ⚐ *18 holes, par 72, 6593 yds.*

Te Urewera National Park

163 km (101 miles) west of Gisborne.

New Zealand's fourth-largest national park protects the biggest area of native forest remaining on the North Island. The ancestral home of the Tuhoe people, its main attraction is Lake Waikaremoana, which draws hikers, canoeists, and fishing enthusiasts from around the world.

GETTING HERE AND AROUND

Local bus service is extremely limited, so the best way to get around is by car. Campervans are also popular, as there is plenty of space for the outdoor style of living. Access to the park is from Wairoa, 100 km (62 miles) southwest of Gisborne down Highway 2. It's then another 63 km (39 miles) northwest from Wairoa along Highway 38 to Lake Waikaremoana. It gets busy here in summer.

VISITOR INFORMATION

CONTACTS Te Urewera Visitor Centre. ⊠ *6249 Lake Rd., State Hwy. 38, Aniwaniwa* ☎ *06/837–3803* ⊕ *www.ngaituhoe. iwi.nz.*

Sights

★ Te Urewera National Park

NATIONAL PARK | **FAMILY** | Remote Te Urewera National Park is rugged and mountainous. This park's outstanding feature is glorious Lake Waikaremoana ("sea of rippling waters"), a forest-girded lake with good swimming, boating, and fishing. The lake is encircled by a 50-km (31-mile) walking trail, which takes three or four days to complete; it's a popular trek, and the lakeside hiking huts are heavily used in the summer months. The Department of Conservation Visitor Centre at Aniwaniwa is stocked with maps and informative leaflets; staff will also give advice about other park walks, like the one to the Aniwaniwa Falls (30 minutes round-trip) or to Lake Waikareiti (five to six hours round-trip). All trails pass through spectacular countryside of high, misty ridges covered with silver and mountain beech. Waterfalls and streams abound, and on the lower levels the forest giants, *rimu, rata, kamahi, totara,* and *tawa* attract native birds like the New Zealand falcon, North Island brown kiwi, *kaka,* and *kokako.* A motor camp on the lakeshore, not far from the visitor center, has cabins, chalets, and motel units; in summer, a launch operates sightseeing and fishing trips from it. Note that there are areas of private Māori land within the park, so be sure to stay on marked paths. ⊠ *Te Urewera National Park, Gisborne* ⊕ *www.doc.govt.nz/parks-and-recreation/places-to-go/east-coast/places/te-urewera.*

Chapter 7

NORTH ISLAND'S WEST COAST

7

Updated by
Stuart Freeman

 Sights
★★★★☆

 Restaurants
★★★☆☆

 Hotels
★★★☆☆

 Shopping
★★☆☆☆

 Nightlife
★☆☆☆☆

WELCOME TO NORTH ISLAND'S WEST COAST

TOP REASONS TO GO

★ **Caving:** Beneath Waitomo, underground passageways, fossils, limestone formations, and glowworms await. Explore by walking, boating, "black-water" rafting, or rappelling.

★ **Kayaking and Canoeing:** Ideal for beginners, the Whanganui is New Zealand's longest navigable river. Paddling trips promise amazing scenery and historic Māori settlements.

★ **Walking and Hiking:** Take a short walk or multiday trek through the wetlands, alpine fields, and lowland rain forest of Egmont National Park.

★ **Surfing:** The black-sand surfing beaches here are among the world's best. Near Raglan try Whale Bay and Manu Bay; in Taranaki "Surf Highway 45" accesses premier breaks.

★ **Scenic Drives:** Rolling green farmlands, dense forests, mountain ranges, river gorges, and dramatic coastlines—you can see them all from the comfort of your car.

The region's landscape includes the majestic volcano, Mt. Taranaki; the gorges and wilderness of the Whanganui River; the underground wonders of the Waitomo Caves; world-renowned surfing beaches; two national parks; and a host of forest-covered conservation areas, along with highly productive farmland.

In the northwest, surfing town Raglan sits on a sparsely populated coastline, but it's an easy hour's drive from the region's main city, Hamilton. Waitomo is on the westward route to New Plymouth and the Taranaki region. While State Highway 1 traverses the center of the North Island, State Highway 3 travels the West Coast through the Taranaki bight to Whanganui, then meets again with State Highway 1 close to Palmerston North.

1 Raglan. This low-key small town is one of the region's top surfing spots, thanks to Manu Bay and Whale Bay.

2 Waitomo. This small village leads to the area's wondrous underground cave systems and the famed glowworms that live in their ceilings.

3 New Plymouth. The hub for one of the country's largest agricultural regions, New Plymouth also has a great arts scene and some of New Zealand's best gardens.

4 Egmont National Park. The star of New Zealand's second-oldest national park is the magnificent Mt. Taranaki.

5 Stratford. This eccentric town serves the surrounding farmland and features some beautiful gardens.

6 Whanganui. This river city is the main gateway to Whanganui National Park and the multitude of activities found along the Whanganui River.

7 Whanganui National Park. New Zealand's longest navigable river cuts through the single largest tract of lowland forest remaining on the North Island.

8 Palmerston North. This student-friendly city is a center for education and research in the area.

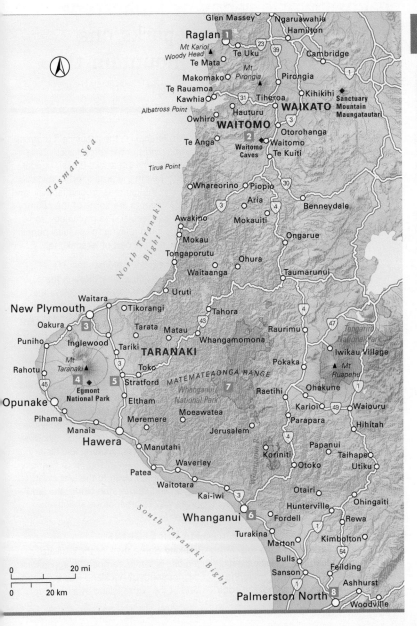

Tasman Sea

Glen Massey
Ngaruawahia
Hamilton
Raglan 1
Mt Kariol
Woody Head
Te Mata
Te Uku
23
39
Cambridge
Mt Pirongia
Makomako
Pirongia
1
Te Rauamoa
Kawhia
31
Tiheroa
Kihikihi
Sanctuary Mountain Maungatautari
Albatross Point
Hauturu
WAIKATO
Owhiro
WAITOMO
3
Te Anga
2
Otorohanga
Waitomo Caves
Waitomo
Te Kuiti
Tirua Point
Whareorino
Piopio
30
Aria
Awakino
Mokauiti
4
Benneydale
Mokau
Ongarue
Tongaporutu
Ohura
Waitaanga
Taumarunui
Uruti
Waitara
Tahora
4
New Plymouth
Tikorangi
Oakura 3
Tarata
Matau
43
Whangamomona
Raurimu
47
Tongariro National Park
Puniho
Inglewood
Tariki
Iwikau Village
Rahotu
Mt Taranaki
Toko
Pokaka
Mt Ruapehu
TARANAKI
3
45
4 5
Stratford
MATEMATEAONGA RANGE
7
Ohakune
1
Opunake
Egmont National Park
Eltham
Whanganui National Park
Raetihi
Pihama
Meremere
Moeawatea
Karioi
49
Waiouru
Manaia
Jerusalem
Parapara
Hihitah
Hawera
Manutahi
4
Papanui
Waverley
Koriniti
Taihape
Patea
Otoko
Utiku
Waitotara
Kai-iwi
3
Otairi
Ohingaiti
South Taranaki Bight
Whanganui 6
Hunterville
Fordell
Rewa
Turakina
1
Kimbolton
Marton
54
Bulls
Feilding
Sanson
Ashhurst
Palmerston North 8
Woodville

0   20 mi
0   20 km

The North Island's West Coast is all about landscape diversity: top surfing beaches; world-renowned limestone caves; and two national parks, one centered on a volcanic mountain, the other on a wilderness river.

The land is generally rural, ranging from lifestyle blocks (small farms under 10 acres that can't usually support commercial farming) to sheep-and-cattle farms located in remote, rolling hill country and a jumble of forest-covered mountain ranges. The long coastline is captivating: world-class surfing breaks meet sandy swimming beaches and craggy cliffs. Small cities and rural towns throughout the region provide a high level of sophistication for their size. They may have started as service communities, but delve deeper and you'll find galleries, art studios, farmers' markets, designer stores, museums, and funky cafés.

Waikato is a region of surprises. To the west are the famed surfing beaches of Raglan, guarded by ancient forest-covered volcanoes. In the south, 30 million years of nature's handiwork have created the Waitomo Caves, an underground spectacle that thousands of visitors now explore each year, be it by foot, boat, or rappelling rope. Don't be too quick to pass through the region's main city, especially if you are interested in gardens. Hamilton Gardens includes some of the most admired theme gardens in the country.

The Taranaki region sprang from the ocean floor in a series of volcanic blasts, creating that distinctive curve along the West Coast of the North Island. The cone of Mt. Taranaki is the province's dramatic symbol and the backdrop for climbing routes and hiking tracks (trails). Agriculture thrives in the area's fertile volcanic soil, and the gardens around Taranaki and New Plymouth are some of the country's most spectacular. The mythology and historic sites relating to the local people are an integral part of Taranaki, too.

Farther south, the Whanganui River wends its scenic way through the forest-covered ridges and valleys that encompass Whanganui National Park. The river is the first in the world to be given legal personhood status by the government, a designation that recognizes the river's physical and spiritual connection with the local *iwi* (tribe). Steeped in history, for centuries the river formed the "road" for the Māori who lived on its banks, and it was later a major route for tourists traveling by steamer. Today the river and surrounding national park draw canoeists, hikers, cyclists, and history buffs. As you veer inland, from river city Whanganui through to the Manawatu region and Palmerston North, the land gives way to prosperous sheep and cattle farms.

MAJOR REGIONS

Waikato. Some think of the Waikato region—a fertile, temperate, agricultural district south of Auckland—as the heartland of the North Island. It's home to

New Zealand's largest inland city (Hamilton) and some of the most important pre-European sites. Polynesian sailors first landed on the region's West Coast as early as the mid-14th century; by way of contrast, Europeans (mainly British) didn't settle here until the 1830s. In the 1860s, the Waikato's many tribes united to elect a king in an attempt to resist British encroachment. This King Movement, as it is known, is still a significant cultural and political force within Waikato Māoridom. Other regional attractions are the surfing hot spots and magnificent harbor of Raglan on the West Coast and the extraordinary cave formations at Waitomo.

New Plymouth and Taranaki. On a clear day, sometimes with a cover of snow, Mt. Taranaki (also known as Mt. Egmont) towers above green flanks of forest and farmland. The nearly perfectly symmetrical volcano forms the basis of Egmont National Park, sitting at the heart of the Taranaki region, and the province has shaped itself around it. Northeast of Taranaki, the provincial city of New Plymouth (known for climbing, hiking, surfing, fishing, and cultural museums) hugs the coast, and smaller rural towns like Stratford dot the roads that circle the mountain's base. Heading seaward, there's some 200 km (124 miles) of shoreline—complete with top surf breaks, beach walks, shipwrecks, seal colonies, small estuaries, and fishing spots—to discover along the Taranaki coast.

Whanganui, the Whanganui River, and Palmerston North. The Whanganui River, flowing through a vast, forest-covered wilderness from the central North Island mountains, is the focus here. At its mouth, Whanganui city was established when river travel was the main form of transport. Today, kayakers and jet boaters enjoy the scenic, historic, and wilderness experiences of Whanganui National Park. Palmerston North sits in the heart of farming country, an easy one-hour drive southeast of Whanganui. With a population of nearly 90,000, it ranks as New Zealand's seventh largest city. "Palmy," as it's affectionately known, is home to Massey University, and a youthful demographic helps keep it young at heart.

Planning

Getting Here and Around

AIR
Airports serve the main centers but driving or taking a bus is best for other areas. Air New Zealand operates flights daily from Auckland and Wellington to Hamilton, New Plymouth, and Palmerston North, as well as from Christchurch to New Plymouth and Palmerston North. Originair connects Palmerston North and Nelson, and Air Chathams connects Whanganui with Auckland.

CONTACTS Air Chathams. ☎ 0800/580–127 ⊕ www.airchathams.co.nz. **Air New Zealand.** ☎ 0800/737–000 ⊕ www.airnewzealand.co.nz. **Originair.** ☎ 0800/380–380 ⊕ originair.co.nz.

BUS
InterCity links all cities and towns throughout the region with regular daily service. Flexible travel passes let passengers stop off as they please along the way. The Waitomo Wanderer (now operated by Kiwi Experience) links Rotorua and Taupo with Waitomo, once daily each way. From Otorohanga, the Waitomo Shuttle (book in advance) connects with major bus and train arrivals.

CONTACTS InterCity. ☎ 09/583–5780, 0800/222-146 Toll free in New Zealand ⊕ www.intercity.co.nz. **Kiwi Experience.** ☎ 0800/364–286 ⊕ www.kiwiexperience.com.

CAR

Driving is the most flexible way to travel through this region. Roads are nearly all clearly signposted, and drivers pass through diverse and scenic landscapes of farmland, forest-covered ranges, and rugged coastline.

TRAIN

Northern Explorer, the scenic 10-hour Auckland–Wellington train, stops at Hamilton, National Park, Ohakune, and Palmerston North. It travels southbound on Monday, Thursday, and Saturday and northbound on Tuesday, Friday, and Sunday.

CONTACTS Northern Explorer.
☎ 0800/872–467 ⊕ www.greatjourney-sofnz.co.nz.

Hotels

Bed-and-breakfasts can be stylishly converted country homesteads; sometimes they're custom built. There are also luxury lodges and a wonderful range of self-catering villas and cottages (some on working farms, others with spectacular coastal locations, and a few deep in the forest-covered hinterland). National parks have mountain lodges, river lodges, basic backcountry huts, and camping spots managed by the Department of Conservation.

In tourist towns and larger cities, there's the full range of options: boutique hotels, standard hotels with basic rooms, motels with full kitchens, holiday parks with RV sites and sometimes apartment units, as well as backpacker hostels. Although hostels are generally budget options with shared facilities, an increasing number are modern and feature private en suite rooms.

Restaurant and hotel reviews have been shortened. For full information, visit Fodors.com. Restaurant prices are the average cost of a main course at dinner or, if dinner is not served, at lunch. Hotel prices are the lowest cost of a standard double room in high season.

WHAT IT COSTS in New Zealand Dollars			
$	$$	$$$	$$$$
RESTAURANTS			
under NZ$15	NZ$15–NZ$20	NZ$21–NZ$30	over NZ$30
HOTELS			
under NZ$125	NZ$125–NZ$200	NZ$201–NZ$300	over NZ$300

Planning Your Time

Whether surfing or just enjoying the harbor and bush walks, spare at least a couple of days for Raglan and another day or two for exploring the Waitomo Caves. From Waitomo, travel southwest to Taranaki, where two to three days would allow exploration of the gardens and museums, plus a beach trip and a short walk in Egmont National Park—allow longer for more serious hiking, climbing, or surfing adventures. Whanganui city is worth a day or two. A river jet boat or road trip provides a quick glimpse of the area. For an in-depth tour try a five-day kayak journey, then take a good day or two to absorb the university town of Palmerston North before heading on south to Wellington.

Restaurants

Throughout western North Island, provincial city restaurants and small, tourist-town cafés feature an overall sophistication you might not expect away from major urban centers: think wholesome and hearty fare, local organic produce, good espresso and loose-leaf teas, high-quality New Zealand wines, and local craft beers. Counter food is generally fresh salads, panini, filled rolls, sweet or savory pies, and homemade soups.

Dinner menus in the higher-end restaurants include the chef's latest creations using high-quality New Zealand eye fillet of beef (beef tenderloin), fish, lamb racks, pork fillets, and chicken. The best chefs change menus regularly to focus on fresh regional and seasonal ingredients. You will also find Indian, Thai, Malaysian, Japanese, Mexican, Turkish, and Italian restaurants, even in smaller centers. "Smart-casual" is about as formal as attire gets.

Visitor Information

Hamilton and Waikato Regional Tourism is a helpful regional resource. The regional tourism organization in Taranaki also maintains a website with local listings and event information.

CONTACTS Hamilton and Waikato Regional Tourism. ⊕ www.hamiltonwaikato.com. **Discover Taranaki.** ⊠ Stratford ⊕ www. taranaki.co.nz.

When to Go

Although the most popular period is from November through mid-April, most attractions can be enjoyed year-round. Spring is garden festival time in Taranaki. Summer is obviously warmer and great for swimming or surfing. However, the weather is often more settled during winter—unlike some South Island regions, it generally has no harsh snow or ice conditions to thwart travel—and there are fewer people.

Raglan

176 km (110 miles) south of Auckland, 44 km (27 miles) west of Hamilton.

It's hard to think of a more laid-back, welcoming spot than Raglan. On sheltered Raglan Harbour, and in the lee of the forest-covered volcano, Mt. Karioi, the tiny town owes its easygoing ways to the surfers drawn to the legendary breaks at Manu Bay, 8 km (5 miles) southwest of town, and Whale Bay, just beyond. The Raglan surf is featured in movies and regularly plays host to international competitions. When the surf's up, you can drive out to the parking areas above the sweeping bays to see scores of enthusiasts tackling what's reputed to be the world's longest, most consistent left-hand break.

Surfers have made this seaside village cool, and along the main drag, Bow Street, barefoot dudes in designer shades pad in and out of the hip café-bars or hang in the smattering of craft and surfwear shops; there is, however, much more to Raglan. The huge harbor, with its long Māori history, sandy beaches, and opportunities for kayaking, fishing, and relaxation, draws vacationers throughout the year.

GETTING HERE AND AROUND

The main road route to Raglan is from Hamilton, an hour away by car. Travelers from Auckland can turn off State Highway 1 at Ngaruawahia (10 minutes north of Hamilton) and follow State Highway 39 to Whatawhata to join the road from Hamilton. Turn right to Raglan. Buses to Raglan (NZ$9) run from Hamilton several times daily.

BUS CONTACTS Raglan Bus Depot. ⊠ Waikato District Library Raglan, 7 Bow St., Raglan ⊕ www.busit.co.nz.

VISITOR INFORMATION

CONTACTS Raglan i-hub Visitor Information Centre. ✉ *13 Wainui Rd., Raglan* ☎ *07/825–0556* ⊕ *www.raglan.org.nz.*

🍴 Restaurants

George's Beach Club

$$ | MODERN NEW ZEALAND | This restaurant is actually a short walk from the beach, but the atmosphere is right, if a little kitschy. Seafood is predominant on the menu (try the seafood chowder or the smoked kawahai fish cakes), but there's also an extensive selection of wood-fired pizzas. **Known for:** both indoor and outdoor dining; cold lager in the summer; mulled cider in the winter; tempura fish and chips with pickles and aioli. $ *Average main: NZ$20* ✉ *2 Bow St., Raglan* ☎ *07/825–0565* ⊕ *www.facebook.com/georgesbeachclubraglan.*

Iso Cafe and Bistro

$$$ | INTERNATIONAL | One of the newer eateries in town, Iso has established itself as a favorite with locals as well as the visiting surf set (it's connected to a surf shop). Bagels are a brunch special, along with the Ozone-brand coffee, but the restaurant really comes into its own in the evening when you can pick up a wine or locally brewed beer along with European-inspired fare such as tapas or pasta. **Known for:** outdoor seating on footpath; "Nasty Burger" with beef, bacon, caramelized onions, cheese, lettuce, tomato, pickles, and chimichurri aioli; good daily fish and meat specials. $ *Average main: NZ$30* ✉ *23 Bow St., Raglan* ☎ *021/198–7983* ⊕ *www.isobarraglan.co.nz* ☾ *Closed Wed.*

Orca Restaurant and Bar

$$$ | NEW ZEALAND | This waterside restaurant has big windows, big views, and big tasty menus. Brunch is served every morning, and dinner brings out the chef's creativity. **Known for:** excellent food and wine pairings; signature braised beef cheek with balsamic pickled onions and garlic mash; best dining views in Raglan (look for the orcas!). $ *Average main: NZ$22* ✉ *2 Wallis St., Raglan* ☎ *07/825–6543* ⊕ *www.orcarestaurant.co.nz.*

Rock-it Kitchen

$$ | MODERN NEW ZEALAND | FAMILY | Occupying a 100-year-old shearing shed, the funky, rustic Rock-it serves casual Kiwi fare and local Raglan Roast coffee. The menu is small but wholesome; try the all-day brunch, beef sliders, and soups for lunch, either inside or out on the huge deck. **Known for:** alternative access (you can paddle a kayak up the Wainui estuary to get here); aged prime Scotch fillet with truffle agria mash and smoked vine tomatoes; country atmosphere. $ *Average main: NZ$19* ✉ *248 Wainui Rd., Raglan* ☎ *07/825–8233* ⊕ *www.rockitraglan.co.nz* ☾ *No dinner Sun.–Thurs.*

★ The Shack

$$ | CAFÉ | At this buzzing corner café, surfers—here for the great coffee and organic, free-range food—cram the couches and Formica tables beneath walls decorated with hanging plants, surfboards and Raglan beach scenes. The menu is huge and the meals hearty, starting with breakfast at 8. **Known for:** gluten-free, paleo, and vegan options all available; locally sourced coffee, produce, and beverages; retro, casual beach vibe. $ *Average main: NZ$16* ✉ *19 Bow St., Raglan* ☎ *07/825–0027* ⊕ *www.theshackraglan.com* ☾ *No dinner Sun.–Wed.*

🛏 Hotels

Bow Street Studios

$$$ | APARTMENT | Right at the edge of town, with views over the harbor, you can choose from a two-bedroom historic cottage or several two-story apartment units, each with a king bed and a sunset view. **Pros:** all units have well-equipped kitchens; picturesque tree-lined grounds; quiet location at end of main street.

Raglan is known in surfing circles for its world-class breaks.

Cons: 2-story apartments not wheelchair-accessible; no on-site food of any kind; management is off-site, so getting immediate assistance can be difficult. [$] *Rooms from: NZ$240* ✉ *1 Bow St., Raglan* 🌐 *www.bowstreet.co.nz* 🍴 *No Meals* 🛏 *8 units.*

Raglan Sunset Motel

$$ | **MOTEL** | **FAMILY** | The location (a five-minute walk from town and from the harbor) and family-friendly facilities are key attractions here. **Pros:** free Wi-Fi throughout; lovely barbecue area; quiet yet close to shops and restaurants. **Cons:** beware nearby local fire brigade training on Wednesday evening; grounds not hugely spacious; covered parking is limited. [$] *Rooms from: NZ$180* ✉ *7 Bankart St., Raglan* ☎ *07/825–0050* 🌐 *www.raglansunsetmotel.co.nz* 🛏 *24 studios* 🍴 *No Meals.*

Activities

Surfing (with waves to attract both beginners and the world's top surfers), kite surfing, fishing, kayaking, paddle-boarding, and just cruising in the vast harbor are the big water-sport attractions. Coastal walks and forest walks, from one hour to one day, are also popular.

BOATING AND KAYAKING

★ Raglan Boat Charters

BOATING | In Raglan, the harbor is a star attraction, and distinctive harbor cruise experiences operate under the umbrella of Raglan Boat Charters. For a social two-hour sunset cruise, board the *Wahine Moe,* a 70-person purpose-built catamaran. It runs daily barbecue dinner cruises from December to April. A morning scenic harbor cruise is also on offer for the same price. Long-time skipper Ian Hardie knows his way around the harbor's tidal inlets and bays; you'll see forest reserves, historic habitation sites, isolated beaches, the "pancakes" (limestone outcrops), seabirds, and perhaps the pod of orca that occasionally visits. This morning tour runs all year, with times based on the tides. Reservations are essential for both cruises. ⊠ *92 Wallis St., Raglan* 🕾 *07/825–7873, 027/488–1215* ⊕ *www. raglanboatcharters.co.nz* 🖃 *From NZ$49.*

★ **Raglan Kayak and Paddleboard**
KAYAKING | There's no better way to explore huge Raglan Harbour than on nature's terms with Steve and Candide Reid and their enthusiastic guides. Local boy Steve searched the world for the perfect place to work on water, then realized it was back home. People of any age and ability are welcome on the daily guided trips, where the focus is on paddling with the tide and wind, swimming at secluded beaches, and great scenery. Trips run for two hours (featuring limestone landscapes) and three hours (including espresso and home-baked goodies). Kayak and paddleboard lessons and rentals are also offered. Tours are run from November through May. ⊠ *Bow St. Jetty, Raglan* 🕾 *07/825–8862* ⊕ *www.raglankayak.co.nz* 🖃 *From NZ$79* ⊘ *Closed Easter–Oct.*

SURFING

Raglan Surf Emporium
SURFING | If you're itching to hit the waves, stop by this top surfing store. Once a factory that produced high-performance boards for years, it now stocks homegrown boards as well as the leading brands. The shop also rents surfboards, wet suits, and boogie boards, and staffers pass along helpful tips. ⊠ *3 Wainui Rd., Raglan* 🕾 *07/282–0018* ⊕ *www.raglansurfemporium.com.*

★ Raglan Surfing School
SURFING | National surfing champions often work as instructors at the RSS. Two-hour group and private lessons are available for beginners (board and wet suit included). Rental gear is available from the RSS-operated trailer on Ocean (Ngarunui) Beach in summer. It is located a little out of town. ⊠ *5b Whaanga Rd., Whale Bay, Raglan* 🕾 *07/825–7873* ⊕ *www.raglansurfingschool.co.nz* 🖃 *From NZ$79.*

SWIMMING

Although the surf looks inviting at most of the West Coast beaches, there can be dangerous rips and undertows, so be careful where you take a dip. The safest spots around Raglan are Aroaro Bay (Wallis and Puriri streets), Te Kopua, and at Cox and Lorenzen bays during high tide. Call the Raglan iHub Knowledge Centre (*07/825–0556*) for tide times. In summer, lifeguards patrol the beach at Ocean (Ngarunui); to avoid the strong rips, swim between the flags.

WALKING AND HIKING

From Raglan, a number of walks and hikes give you wonderful views of the coastline and take you through splendid native bush. The closest and easiest is from the township itself through Wainui Bush Park to gorgeous Ocean (Ngarunui) Beach. You can climb above coastal bluffs to a lookout point and enjoy the drama of the kite surfers at play, or follow the beach for 6 km (4 miles), except during high spring tides. Ask for a brochure at the Raglan i-hub Visitor Information Centre.

Mt. Karioi
HIKING & WALKING | The trek up Mt. Karioi is steep but rewarding, with great views from the top. The Mt. Karioi Track, from Te Toto Gorge at Whaanga Road, climbs to a lookout and then on to the summit (3–3½ hours one-way). Expect chains and ladders to help you up bluffy bits, but make sure you bring good walking gear, too. Wairake Track, from Karioi Road, is a shorter, and not as challenging, summit option (2–3 hours one-way), but the views aren't quite as good. ⊕ *www.doc.govt.nz.*

Te Ara Kakariki (Kakariki Trails)

BIKING | FAMILY | These mountain biking trails have a few jumps and get high enough to provide expansive ocean views. However, they are not too difficult and are ideal for beginners and families. Grab a map at the Raglan i-hub Visitor Centre, which outlines each of the individual trails. Most of these can be combined with another trail depending how long you want to stay out. ✉ *Riria Kereopa Memorial Dr., Raglan.*

★ Waireinga/Bridal Veil Falls

HIKING & WALKING | A 15-minute shaded hike from the parking lot leads through native forest to the spectacle of the falls. Two viewing platforms are poised near the top of the 150-foot drop. This section of trail is wheelchair accessible. Another much steeper track continues to a midway viewing platform; from there a 10-minute trail descends to a bridge and viewing platform at the base of the falls. The tall trees and the sight of the water cascading over the hard basalt cliff justify the effort required for the return climb. The falls are 20 km (12 miles) south of Raglan via the Kawhia road. ⊕ *www.doc. govt.nz.*

Waitomo

80 km (50 miles) southwest of Hamilton, 65 km (41 miles) southwest of Cambridge, 150 km (95 miles) west of Rotorua.

Waitomo is a busy little village located a short drive from the main highway. Above ground, the surrounding hills are a mix of native bush and verdant farmland. Below ground, you'll find the region's famous cave systems, and Waitomo caters to the tourists who come to ogle them. Despite its small size—everything here is within walking distance—the village promises a good selection of cafés, a tavern, plus cave tour options ranging from gentle walking on well-lighted pathways to rappelling, tubing, and jumping down dark waterfalls.

The Waitomo Caves are part of an ancient seabed that was lifted and then spectacularly eroded into a surreal subterranean landscape of limestone formations, gushing rivers, and contorted caverns. The name, a combination of *wai* (water) and *tomo* (cave), refers to the Waitomo River that vanishes into the hillside here. Many of the amazing underground passages are still unexplored, but four major cave systems are open for guided tours: Ruakuri, Spellbound, Aranui, and Waitomo Glowworm Cave. Each has its own special characteristics, and you won't be disappointed by any.

After all, notable features include not only stalactites and stalagmites but also glowworms—the 1- to 2-inch larvae of *Arachnocampa luminosa,* which live on cave ceilings. They snare prey by dangling sticky filaments, trapping insects attracted to the light they emit. A single worm produces far less light than any firefly, but when massed in great numbers in the dark, it's like looking at the night sky in miniature. The guides who introduce you to all of this below-ground beauty may be descendants of local chief Tane Tinorau (who discovered Waitomo Glowworm Cave); they will certainly be local caving experts who have spent years exploring the amazing network of shafts and passageways around Waitomo.

GETTING HERE AND AROUND

Although it's in the countryside, Waitomo is close to State Highway 3, one of the major highways linking Waikato and Rotorua with Taranaki and Tongariro. Day-trippers wishing to see the caves can also take advantage of bus-tour packages offered by InterCity, which travels from Auckland or Rotorua.

If you'd rather ride the rails, the Auckland–Wellington *Northern Explorer* train stops in Otorohanga, 16 km (10 miles) from Waitomo. The Caves Shuttle and Taxi Service (NZ$12 per person) can be booked to meet the train and bring you into town; contact the Waitomo i-SITE Discovery Centre for bookings.

BUS CONTACTS Waitomo Bus Depot.
⊠ *Waitomo i-SITE Discovery Centre, Waitomo Village Rd., 21 Waitomo Caves Village, Waitomo.*

TRAIN CONTACTS Otorohanga Train Station. ⊠ *7 Wahanui Cres., Otorohanga.*

VISITOR INFORMATION

There are two visitor centers in Waitomo village. Waitomo Glowworm Caves Visitor Centre is managed by the company that owns access to the Waitomo Glowworm, Ruakuri, and Aranai caves. The independent Waitomo i-SITE Discovery Centre offers impartial advice to help you decide which tour is most suitable as well as bookings for all cave tours and other regional attractions. Bookings may also be made with the individual tour operators. The i-SITE Discovery Centre also houses the Waitomo Caves Museum for people who want insight into the caves without actually going underground (or before doing so). Entry is NZ$5.

CONTACTS Waitomo Glowworm Caves Visitor Centre. ⊠ *39 Waitomo Village Rd., Waitomo* ☎ *0800/456–922* ⊕ *www.waitomo.com.* **Waitomo i-SITE Discovery Centre.** ⊠ *21 Waitomo Village Rd., Waitomo Caves Village, Waitomo* ☎ *07/878–7640* ⊕ *www.waitomocaves.com.*

 Sights

Aranui Caves

CAVE | This is one of the smallest and prettiest cave systems in Waitomo. Eons of dripping water have sculpted a delicate garden of pink-and-white limestone here. Hour-long tours lead along boardwalks into tall, narrow chambers. Keep an eye out for the resident cave wetas; these

native insects grow up to 4 inches long, but don't worry—they will most likely hide if they sense you coming. Tours meet at the Ruakuri Visitor Centre at the top of Ruakuri Reserve on Tumutumu Road, 3 km (2 miles) beyond Waitomo Caves Village. Reservations are essential. ⊠ *Cave entrance at Ruakuri Reserve, Tumutumu Rd., Waitomo* ☎ *0800/456–922* ⊕ *www.waitomo.com* ☒ *Tours NZ$50; multicave tickets available.*

Ruakuri Cave

CAVE | To enter Ruakuri, visitors descend a dramatic, man-made spiral "drum passage," then go on to explore narrow, low-lit passages. Surrounded by magical limestone formations and the roar of hidden waterfalls, the way follows a dark underground river that twinkles with glowworm reflections. Tours are two hours (reservations suggested) and limited to 15 people. This is the longest cave-walking tour in Waitomo, but it's easily managed by people of reasonable fitness. All pathways are wheelchair-accessible. Tours meet at the Ruakuri Visitor Centre on Tumutumu Road. ⊠ *39 Waitomo Village Rd., Waitomo* ☎ *0800/228–464* ⊕ *www.waitomo.com* ☒ *NZ$74; multicave tickets available.*

Sanctuary Mountain Maungatautari

WILDLIFE REFUGE | Walk among some of the most ancient forests in the region at Maungatautari, where the Maungatautari Ecological Island Trust, in conjunction with the Department of Conservation, is carrying out one of New Zealand's many successful conservation stories. The trust has built a 50-km (31-mile) pest-proof fence around 8,400 acres of native forest, creating a refuge for some of New Zealand's rarest native species. Endangered birds, including the kaka bush parrot, kiwi, takahe, and saddleback, have been reintroduced here. The best place to start is at the Manu Tioriori Visitor Centre, which has information and refreshments; it's on the southern side

Did You Know?

Underground streams slowly dissolved limestone to form the Waitomo Caves over thousands of years. The water picked up lime and, as it moved, left deposits that eventually formed intricate, beautiful stalactites and stalagmites.

of the mountain at the end of Tari Road in Pukeatua, 32 km (20 miles) outside of Cambridge. From here you can explore on your own or take a short guided walk through the Southern Enclosure (1½-hours). Five kilometers (3 miles) of high-quality trails lead through forest to a 52-foot viewing tower in the treetops, where you can be one with the birds. Another guided walk explores Tautari Wetland (1½ hours). Both guided walks have an additional fee. Keen walkers can tackle the Over the Mountain trail, a full-day walk from one side to the other. It's a good spot to stop if you're driving off the main routes from Rotorua to Waitomo. ✉ *Tari Rd., Pukeatua, Cambridge* ☎ *07/870–5180* 🌐 *www.sanctuary-mountain.co.nz* 🎟 *NZ$20; guided walks from NZ$56.*

Spellbound Glowworm and Cave Tour

CAVE | This company offers three different underground experiences, all incorporating a gentle raft trip and close-up views of glowworms, and a short bush walk to the caves is a bonus. The raft trip, in Spellbound, explores a glowworm chamber that was filmed by Sir David Attenborough for the BBC. Te Ana o Te Atua (Cave of the Spirit) features limestone formations, fossils, and bones. Tours range from 1½ to 3½ hours and are limited to 12 people; advanced booking is advised. The shorter tours depart from a new base on Boddies Road, while the longer tours offer pick up and drop off from Waitomo Village. Private tours can be arranged. ✉ *334 Boddies Rd., Waitomo Village, Waitomo* ☎ *0800/773–552* 🌐 *www.glowworm.co.nz* 🎟 *From NZ$50.*

★ Waitomo Glowworm Cave

CAVE | The most "genteel" and perhaps famous of all the caves here was first officially explored in 1887 by local Chief Tane Tinorau and surveyor Fred Mace. They floated on a raft of flax stems, with candles for light, into the cave where the stream goes underground. Now visitors enter via a gentle pathway, explore the limestone cathedral (and, like opera diva Kiri Te Kanawa, are invited to test the amazing acoustics), then board a boat for a magical cruise beneath the "starry" glowworm-lit ceiling, floating out of the cave on the Waitomo River. Tours last 45 minutes and start at the Waitomo Glowworm Cave Visitor Centre. ✉ *39 Waitomo Village Rd., Waitomo* ☎ *0800/456–922* 🌐 *www.waitomo.com* 🎟 *Tours NZ$51; multicave tickets available.*

Waitomo Walkway

TRAIL | With its limestone features (fluted outcrops, arches, tunnels, and caves), open farmland, and native forest, the 5-km (3-mile) Waitomo Walkway is an interesting short trek. Start at the Waitomo i-SITE Discovery Centre and follow the path beside the Waitomo River. You can return the same way, or follow the road (a bit shorter). Alternatively, you can drive to Ruakuri Reserve (from the Village take Te Anga Road then Tumutumu Road), and just walk the 30-minute loop through natural rock tunnels, across cantilevered bridges, and beneath limestone bluffs. The trail is slippery following wet weather, and there are steep sections, so wear good walking shoes. **■ TIP→ Many people come after dusk for a free viewing of the local glowworms; bring a flashlight to find your way.** 🌐 *www.doc.govt.nz.*

🍴 Restaurants

★ HUHU Cafe

$$$ | **MODERN NEW ZEALAND** | This spot out in the country offers food up there in quality with the best urban-chic cafés. The contemporary New Zealand–style menu has a mix of smaller and larger plates that (mostly) stay under NZ$30. **Known for:** local Te Kuiti slow-cooked lamb shoulder; traditional rewana (Māori bread); good wine list for such a small and isolated place. [$] *Average main: NZ$28* ✉ *10 Waitomo Village Rd.,*

In the Waitomo Caves, you can take a boat ride through magical formations, where glowworms light up the ceiling and walls like stars.

Waitomo ☎ *07/878–6674* 🌐 *www.huhu-cafe.co.nz* 🕒 *Closed Mon. and Tues. No lunch Mon.–Fri.*

Twelve Tables Bar and Eatery
$$ | **CAFÉ** | Situated at Waitomo's General Store (which itself offers limited grocery items and souvenirs), this versatile eatery can serve as a café if you're just looking for a coffee with a scone or biscuit, but it also offers fresh cabinet-style food such as paninis and bagels that can be prepared on the spot, as well as a full menu for breakfast, lunch, and early dinner. Grab a comfortable and sunny spot near the window in the lounge-style seating area if you can, but there are plenty of standard tables and chairs. **Known for:** right next to i-Site; slow-cooked sheep shank; closing early (by 7 pm nightly). [$] *Average main: NZ$20* ✉ *15 Village Rd, Waitomo* ☎ *07/878–8613* 🌐 *www.waitomocaves.com.*

Hotels

★ Abseil Breakfast Inn
$$ | **B&B/INN** | Hosts John and Helen treat you like family when you stay in one of the comfortable rooms here; each comes with a local decor theme (bush, cave, farm, and swamp), superqueen bed, and a second deck entrance. **Pros:** rural views; quirky, helpful hosts; big and delicious breakfasts. **Cons:** not for those who like big, impersonal hotels; steep driveway; thin walls. [$] *Rooms from: NZ$180* ✉ *709 Waitomo Village Rd., Waitomo* ☎ *07/878–7815* 🌐 *www.abseilinn.co.nz* 🛏 *4 rooms* 🍴 *Free Breakfast.*

★ Waitomo Top 10 Holiday Park
$$ | **HOTEL** | **FAMILY** | Modern, clean, and rated Qualmark four-star-plus, this delightful holiday park in the heart of Waitomo Village offers tents, powered campervan sites, cabins, and a self-contained motel. **Pros:** friendly hosts; central location; spacious rural environment with great views of the surrounding forest. **Cons:**

kid-friendly environment may not suit everyone; likely to be busy in summer; by the main road (though it's quiet at night). [$] *Rooms from: NZ$190* ✉ *12 Waitomo Village Rd., Waitomo* ☎ *0508/498-666* 🌐 *www.waitomopark.co.nz* 🛏 *18 rooms* 🍴 *No Meals.*

Activities

CAVE ADVENTURES

Many of Waitomo's subterranean adventure tours involve black-water rafting—that is, floating through the underground caverns on inflated inner tubes, dressed in wet suits and equipped with cavers' helmets. Be prepared for pitch darkness and freezing cold water. Your reward is an exhilarating trip gliding through vast glowworm-lighted caverns, clambering across rocks, and jumping over waterfalls. There are also dry options. Some tours involve steep rappelling and tight underground squeezes. Each company runs several trips daily.

Kiwi Cave Rafting

SPELUNKING | Thrill-seekers can venture down below on a four-hour combo adventure that includes abseiling, black-water rafting, rock climbing, caving, and checking out the glowworms. ✉ *95 Waitomo Village Rd., Waitomo* ☎ *07/873-9149* 🌐 *www.blackwaterraftingwaitomo.co.nz* 🎟 *From NZ$125.*

The Legendary Black Water Rafting Company

SPELUNKING | Most adventurous types can handle the basic, three-hour Black Labyrinth trip, which finishes with a welcome hot shower and mug of soup back at base. Then there's the five-hour Black Abyss that includes an exhilarating abseil, zip line, and float under a canopy of glowworms. Although the guides and the underground scenery are great (you'll learn caving techniques from experts), these are staunch physical and emotional challenges and can be scary. Departure times depend on demand. ✉ *584 Waitomo Village Rd., Waitomo* ☎ *07/878-6219, 0800/456-922* 🌐 *www.waitomo.com* 🎟 *From NZ$55.*

★ Waitomo Adventures

SPELUNKING | Four different trips with these caving enthusiasts release serious adrenaline. A 328-foot rappel into the famous Lost World cave system is spectacular—not just for a thumping heart, but also for the underground landscape, illuminated by daylight sneaking in through a couple of surface openings. Other tours include TumuTumu Toobing (climbing, swimming, tubing, and rafting), Haggas Honking Holes (rappelling, rock climbing, and crawling), and the seven-hour Lost World Epic (rappelling, wading, swimming, and climbing). These caves are a little way out of the main Waitomo tourist center, beneath picturesque farmland. Families should check out the new Trollcave, a man-made attraction that provides one of the few child-focused activities in the region. ✉ *Waitomo Adventure Centre, 654 Waitomo Caves Rd., Waitomo* ☎ *07/878-7788, 0800/924-866* 🌐 *www.waitomo.co.nz* 🎟 *From NZ$425.*

New Plymouth

375 km (235 miles) south of Auckland, 190 km (120 miles) southwest of Waitomo, 163 km (102 miles) northwest of Whanganui.

New Plymouth serves as a hub for one of New Zealand's most productive dairy regions as well as a center for the gas and oil industries. This natural wealth translates into an optimistic outlook that is reflected in New Plymouth's healthy arts scene, an abundance of cafés and restaurants, and a lifestyle that maximizes the great outdoors.

The area has a strong Māori history and a strong history of Māori–European interaction, not all of it friendly. Before the arrival of Europeans in 1841, *kainga* (villages) and *pā* (fortified villages) spread along the coast. In the mid-1800s, land disputes between Māori and English settlers racked Taranaki. An uneasy formal peace was made between the government and local Māori tribes in 1881, and New Plymouth began to play its current role as a trading port. On the edge of the Tasman Sea, today's city is second to its surroundings, but its few surviving colonial buildings, cafés, stores, galleries, museums, and extensive parklands merit a day's exploration.

Taranaki is a productive agricultural region; layers of volcanic ash have created free-draining topsoil and the western, coastal location ensures abundant rainfall. What serves farmers also serves gardeners. Some of the country's most magnificent gardens, as rated by the New Zealand Gardens Trust, grow in the rich soil. Some, such as Pukekura Park, Pukeiti, and Hollard, are public, but many are private, open only by appointment and during the annual Taranaki Garden Festival and Taranaki Fringe Garden Festival. During these spring events, more than 100 splendid gardens celebrate the area's green-fingered excellence, particularly its rhododendrons.

GETTING HERE AND AROUND

Air New Zealand flies daily to New Plymouth from Auckland, Wellington, and Christchurch. New Plymouth Airport (NPL) is about 12 km (7½ miles) from the city center; expect to pay about NZ$50 for a taxi to town. Scott's Airport Shuttle runs a door-to-door service from the airport for NZ$24 (first person, plus NZ$4 each additional passenger); book ahead online or by phone.

Bus company InterCity provides a daily service linking New Plymouth, Stratford, and Hawera. Local service provider Citylink runs from New Plymouth to nearby Waitara and the surfing village of Oakura.

Travel by private car, however, is the best option for getting around New Plymouth and Taranaki. The roads are generally paved and in good condition. From the north, State Highway 3 passes through Te Kuiti, near Waitomo, and then heads west to New Plymouth. The highway continues south through Taranaki to Whanganui and onto Bulls, where it connects with State Highway 1. New Plymouth is a six- to seven-hour drive from Auckland and a five-hour drive from Wellington. If you're traveling west on a sunny afternoon, watch out for strong glare from the setting sun.

You can take in most of Taranaki in a couple of days, using New Plymouth as a base, but that would keep you on the run. Ideally, treat yourself to a leisurely week, choosing accommodations from fine lodges, B&Bs, motels, backpacker hostels, and holiday parks spread throughout the region.

AIRPORTS New Plymouth Airport. ✉ *192 Airport Dr., New Plymouth Taranaki* ☎ *06/759–6594* ⊕ *www.nplairport.co.nz.*

AIRPORT TRANSFERS Scott's Airport Shuttle. ☎ *06/769–5974, 0800/373–001* ⊕ *www.npairportshuttle.co.nz.*

BUS CONTACTS Ariki Street Bus Station. ✉ *19 Ariki St., City Center, New Plymouth* ☎ *0800/872–287.* **CityLink.** ☎ *0800/872–287* ⊕ *www.trc.govt.nz/ taranaki-bus-information.*

VISITOR INFORMATION

CONTACTS New Plymouth i-SITE Visitor Information Centre. ✉ *Puke Ariki, 65 St. Aubyn St., New Plymouth* ☎ *06/759– 0897* ⊕ *www.visitnewplymouth.nz.*

 Sights

Govett Brewster Art Gallery, Len Lye Centre
ART MUSEUM | This stunning architectural drama of twisted towers of glass and steel houses one of the country's leading modern art museums. Collections include New Zealand conceptual,

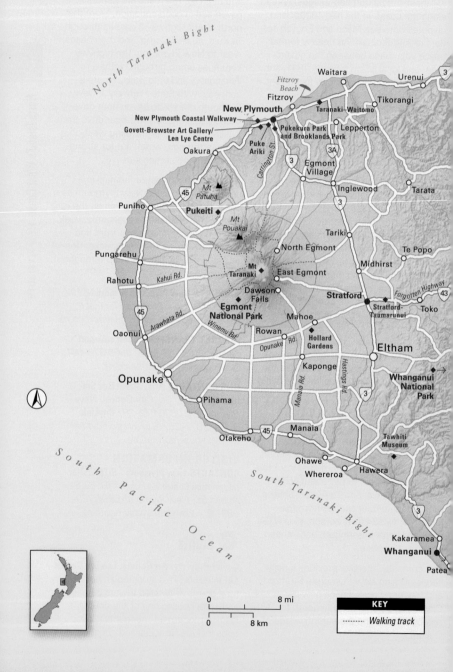

Around Mt. Taranaki

North Taranaki Bight

Waitara
Urenui
3
Fitzroy Beach
Fitzroy
New Plymouth
Taranaki–Waitomo
Tikorangi
New Plymouth Coastal Walkway
Govett-Brewster Art Gallery/
Len Lye Centre
Pukekura Park
and Brooklands Park
Lepperton
Puke Ariki
3A
Oakura
Cutfield St.
3
Egmont Village
Inglewood
Tarata
45
Mt Patuha
Puniho
Pukeiti
Mt Pouakai
Tariki
Te Popo
North Egmont
Midhirst
Pungarehu
Mt Taranaki
East Egmont
Stratford
Forgotten Highway
43
Rahotu
Kahui Rd.
Dawson Falls
Stratford–Taumarunui
Toko
45
Egmont National Park
Arawhata Rd.
Mahoe
Oaonui
Winemu Rd.
Rowan
Opunake Rd.
Hollard Gardens
Eltham
Opunake
Manaia Rd.
Kaponge
Hastings Rd.
Whanganui National Park
Pihama
3
45
Manaia
Tawhiti Museum
Otakeho
Ohawe
Whereroa
Hawera

South Pacific Ocean

South Taranaki Bight

3
Kakaramea
Whanganui
Patea

0   8 mi

0   8 km

KEY
------- Walking track

abstract, and contemporary pieces from the 1970s to today, along with visiting international exhibitions. Special features are the experimental film and kinetic art works of New Zealander Len Lye, who is internationally acclaimed for his Modernism and thought-provoking originality. ⊠ *42 Queen St., New Plymouth Taranaki* ☎ *06/759–6060* ⊕ *www.govettbrewster. com* ⊠ *NZ$15.*

New Plymouth Coastal Walkway

TRAIL | FAMILY | Step out of the city and onto the coast by taking a stroll or cycle along this gentle coastal path, which meanders for 13 km (8 miles), from Port Taranaki to Hickford Park (a rugby and bike park). It explores beaches and playgrounds, crosses rivers, passes by a golf course, and runs beneath the Wind Wand, a sculpture almost as iconic to New Plymouth residents as the Statue of Liberty is to New Yorkers. Created by the late New Zealand artist Len Lye, the red carbon-fiber tube stands 148 feet high and, like a conductor's baton, dances in the wind as Lye's tribute to what he called "tangible motion." Leaving the city confines the walkway crosses the startling white Te Rewa Rewa Bridge (Mt. Taranaki framed in the bridge's struts makes a great photo) into farmland and past the Waipu Lagoons, a wetland reserve.

★ Puke Ariki

HISTORY MUSEUM | The stories of Taranaki's compelling volcanic and cultural history are revealed here, in the region's heritage, research, and information center. From the landscape's violent volcanic formation and the tragic Māori versus English settler/soldier Land Wars to the discovery of natural oil and gas deposits and today's internationally acclaimed surfing culture, it's all here, including interactive science exhibits for children. Located across the road from the beach and popular Wind Wand kinetic sculpture, the in-house Arborio Café is worth a stop,

too, as demonstrated by the presence of locals. ⊠ *Puke Ariki Landing, 1 Ariki St., New Plymouth* ☎ *06/759–6060* ⊕ *www. pukeariki.com* ⊠ *Free.*

★ Pukeiti

GARDEN | FAMILY | Established by the Pukeiti Rhododendron Trust, these 900 acres of lush, native rain forest are surrounded by farmland. The Pukeiti (pooke-*ee*-tee) collection of 2,500 varieties of rhododendrons is the largest in New Zealand. Many were first grown here, such as the giant winter-blooming *R. protistum var. giganteum*, collected from seed in 1953 and now standing 15 feet tall, and the delightful Lemon Lodge and Spring Honey hybrids, which bloom in spring. *Kyawi*, a large red "rhodo," is the last to bloom, in April (autumn). Rhododendrons aside, there are many other rare and special plants here. All winter long the Himalayan daphnes fragrance the pathways. Spring-to-summer-growing candelabra primroses reach up to 4 feet; and, for a month around Christmas, spectacular 8-foot Himalayan *cardiocrinum* lilies bear heavenly scented, 12-inch, white trumpet flowers. There's a classy café on site and a self-guided Kids Treehouse Trail. Located 20 km (12½ miles) southwest of New Plymouth's center, Pukeiti is also a wonderful bird habitat. ⊠ *2290 Carrington Rd., New Plymouth* ☎ *06/765–7127* ⊕ *www.trc.govt.nz/ gardens/pukeiti* ⊠ *Free.*

Pukekura Park and Brooklands Park

CITY PARK | FAMILY | Together the lawns, lakes, gardens, and woodlands of these connected parks make up a 128-acre urban oasis. Each summer evening the Festival of Lights transforms the gardens and giant trees of **Pukekura Park** (annually from mid-December through January and during the March WOMAD Festival). Rowboats can be rented to explore the small islands and nooks and crannies of the main lake. The park also has massive botanical display houses and a fernery in caverns carved out of the hillside. The adjoining **Brooklands Park** is known for its ancient rain forest and exotic trees, such as giant copper beeches, pines, walnuts, and oaks. The Monterey pine, magnolia soulangeana, ginkgo, and native karaka and kohekohe here are the largest of their kind in New Zealand. A giant puriri tree is believed to be more than 2,000 years old. Brooklands is also home to the hugely popular Bowl of Brooklands, a natural amphitheater used for concerts and events, including international acts. Brooklands Zoo has farm animals, meerkats, monkeys, and an aviary. ⌂ *Park entrances on Brooklands Park Dr. and Liardet, Somerset and Rogan Sts., New Plymouth* ☎ *06/758–6060 for Brooklands Zoo only* ⌂ *Free.*

Taranaki–Waitomo

SCENIC DRIVE | Mt. Taranaki (Taranaki Maunga) is a receding presence in your rearview mirror as you head northeast up the Taranaki coast from New Plymouth on Highway 3. This is the most direct route to the Waitomo Caves and Hamilton, turning inland at Awakino, 90 km (56 miles) from New Plymouth. The Awakino Gorge, between Mahoenui and the coast, is appealing. Forest-filled scenic reserves are interspersed with stark, limestone outcrops and lush farmland. Look for well-worn sheep trails traversing the steep-sided hills. At the mouth of the Awakino River, little shacks dot the water's edge. These belong to seasonal fishers of the tiny migrating fish, whitebait. Awakino is worth a stop; the Awakino Hotel (*www.awakinohotel.com*) offers a friendly country pub experience, or you could turn off the main road by the hotel to find a sheltered picnic spot beneath the summer-flowering *pohutuka-wa* trees. A little farther along is Mokau. Between September and November, if the whitebait are running, delicious whitebait fritters might be on the menu at the two little cafés nearby. From Awakino to Waitomo, allow about an hour.

Beaches

Fitzroy Beach

BEACH | A reasonably exposed yet popular and easily accessible beach, Fitzroy is just 1½ km (1 mile) from the center of New Plymouth. You can even walk or ride there via the New Plymouth Coastal Walkway. Changeable surf makes it a bit wild, so be sure to swim between the patrol flags. There's interesting rock-pool exploring here and at other beaches along this coast, courtesy of the black sand and rocky outcrops. Expect crowds on hot summer days, when *pohutuka-wa* trees provide shade in some spots. **Amenities:** lifeguards (summer only); parking (free); toilets. **Best for:** surfing; swimming; walking. ⌂ *Beach St., Fitzroy.*

🍽 Restaurants

Arranged Marriage

$$ | INDIAN | The dosa (a filled, savory pancake) takes pride of place on the menu at this southern-Indian restaurant on New Plymouth's main street. The most traditional (and popular) option is the masala dosa (filled with seasoned potatoes, other vegetables, and mixed spices), but you can also get a number of variations, including one with mozzarella cheese for an "India meets Italy" combo. **Known for:** lentil doughnuts for starters; central location on main street; set menus available for two people or more. $ *Average main: NZ$15* ⌂ *77 Devon St. E., New Plymouth* ☎ *06/215–4488* ⊕ *www.arrangedmarriage.co.nz* ⊘ *Closed Mon.*

Caffe Windsor

$$ | NEW ZEALAND | Wholesome homemade food attracts both Taranaki locals and travelers to this character-filled village café housed in a circa-1878 butcher shop. The menu runs from breakfast through late lunch (i.e., 5 pm), with dinner only on Friday and Saturday nights. **Known for:** gourmet burger selection; waffles for breakfast; best baristas

for miles. $ *Average main: NZ$20* ✉ *1 Kelly St., Inglewood* ☎ *06/756–6665* ⊕ *www.caffewindsor.co.nz* ⊗ *No dinner Sun.–Wed.*

Social Kitchen

$$$ | CONTEMPORARY | The name says it all: this is the place to socialize with friends while sharing plates from the open kitchen. The food has been fired up with flavor in the South American–styled Mibrasa charcoal oven or slow-cooked to create delicious 12-hour smoked meats. **Known for:** charcoal-flavored foods all served with chimichurri; Sunday roasts; lively late dining (go early if you want quiet). $ *Average main: NZ$30* ✉ *40 Powderham St., New Plymouth* ☎ *06/757–2711* ⊕ *www.social-kitchen.co.nz* ⊗ *No lunch.*

Snug Lounge

$$ | JAPANESE FUSION | The casual yet stylish setup at this Japanese yakitori grill and cocktail bar is designed to bring people together, and it works. The menu focuses on small plates to share. **Known for:** alcohol-infused desserts; steamed buns, dumplings with assorted fillings, and spicy meat skewers; deep-fried kusiage delights. $ *Average main: NZ$18* ✉ *White Heart Hotel, 124 Devon St. W, New Plymouth* ☎ *06/757–9130* ⊕ *www. snuglounge.co.nz* ⊗ *No lunch Sat.–Thurs.*

 Hotels

★ Ahu Ahu Beach Villas

$$$ | HOUSE | These rustic yet chic studio and one-bedroom villas sit on a clifftop with stunning views of world-famous surf beach Oakura. **Pros:** eco-friendly; dramatic coastal views; handsome design. **Cons:** uphill walk returning from the beach; 15-minute drive to New Plymouth; no shops within walking distance. $ *Rooms from: NZ$260* ✉ *321 Ahu Ahu Rd., Oakura* ☎ *027/365–7739* ⊕ *www.ahu.co.nz* ⮑ *5 villas* ⦿ *No Meals.*

Ducks and Drakes Boutique Motel and Backpackers

$ | HOTEL | A place for travelers rather than party animals, Ducks and Drakes offers character, color, and modern accommodations within walking distance of shops, cafés, and Pukekura Park. **Pros:** friendly hosts; comfortable lounge; lots of cozy places to relax, indoors and outdoors. **Cons:** parking is tight and only for motel guests; old, steep staircase in main building; most rooms share bathrooms. $ *Rooms from: NZ$110* ✉ *48 Lemon St., New Plymouth* ☎ *06/758–0404* ⊕ *www. ducksanddrakes.co.nz* ⮑ *18 rooms* ⦿ *No Meals.*

Millennium Hotel New Plymouth Waterfront

$$$ | HOTEL | Stylish and modern, central New Plymouth's only waterfront lodging is handily placed next to the Puke Ariki Museum. **Pros:** proximity to the beach and Puke Ariki Museum; excellent hotel restaurant; nice views. **Cons:** not all rooms have tubs; not a lot of personality in guest rooms; port traffic rumbles past. $ *Rooms from: NZ$254* ✉ *1 Egmont St., New Plymouth* ☎ *06/769–5301* ⊕ *www. millenniumhotels.com* ⮑ *44 rooms* ⦿ *No Meals.*

Nice Hotel and Table

$$$ | HOTEL | Personable owner Terry Parkes has transformed this 19th-century heritage building into an opulent city retreat decorated with eclectic furnishings and contemporary art by leading Taranaki artists. **Pros:** fine in-house restaurant; boutique character; complimentary Netflix in rooms and port in the library. **Cons:** parking is difficult to find; reservations a must for hotel and restaurant; next to busy streets so can be noisy. $ *Rooms from: NZ$260* ✉ *71 Brougham St., New Plymouth* ☎ *06/758–6423* ⊕ *www.nice-hotel.co.nz* ⮑ *12 rooms* ⦿ *No Meals.*

Wai-iti Beach Retreat

$$ | APARTMENT | FAMILY | With a walkway and views straight onto a surf beach and about half an hour's drive north of New

Plymouth, the setting is the star of this comfortable self-contained accommodation. **Pros:** lively café with extensive menu for brunch and dinner during summer; friendly managers live on site; expansive grounds. **Cons:** no food available on site in winter (May to September); no lifeguards at the beach; closest shops about 10 minutes' drive away. $ *Rooms from: NZ$200 ⊠ 30 Beach Rd, Pukearuhe, New Plymouth ☎ 06/752–3276 ⊕ www. wai-itibeach.co.nz ⤳ 29 units (14 with shared baths).*

🛍 Shopping

Devon Street, which runs from Fitzroy in the east to Blagdon in the west, is New Plymouth's main shopping thoroughfare.

Et Vous

WOMEN'S CLOTHING | Thanks to leading New Zealand, Australian, French, Italian, Turkish, and Danish labels, this boutique has the best selection of designer clothing in town. It also stocks plus-size items, as well as European shoes. If you work up an appetite browsing, just wander through to the adjoining bakery and cafés. ⊠ *118 Devon St. W., New Plymouth ☎ 06/759–1360 ⊕ www. etvous.co.nz.*

Kina NZ Design + Art Space

CRAFTS | For magnificent locally made arts and crafts with an edge, visit Kina, which exhibits the works of Taranaki artists and carries contemporary design pieces, from jewelry to sculpture. ⊠ *101 Devon St. W, New Plymouth ☎ 06/759–1201 ⊕ www.kina.co.nz.*

Taranaki Hardcore

SPORTING GOODS | Designer Taranaki-themed clothing and quality surfboards are sold here, plus you can check the shop's webcam to see if the surf's up at nearby Fitzroy Beach. ⊠ *454 Devon St. E., New Plymouth ☎ 06/758–1757 ⊕ www.taranakihardcore.co.nz.*

🏃 Activities

Surfing is the big thing along the Taranaki coast, but the beaches and coastal walkways also draw swimmers, beachcombers, paddleboarders, and kayakers. Fishing, be it surfcasting from the shore, trailing a line from a boat, or netting the delicacy whitebait at stream mouths during the season, is also popular.

BIKING

Cycle Inn

BIKING | To ride the New Plymouth Coastal Walkway, rent a touring (aka road, not mountain) bike and a helmet at Cycle Inn. Expect to pay NZ$10 for two hours, NZ$20 for a full day. Electric bikes rent for NZ$30 (two hours) and NZ$50 (full day). Lockers are provided. ⊠ *133 Devon St., New Plymouth ☎ 06/758–7418 ⊕ www.cycleinn.co.nz.*

BOATING AND KAYAKING

★ **Chaddy's Charters**

BOATING | FAMILY | A classic one-hour trip in an old English lifeboat takes you direct from the boat shed into the water and out to Nga Motu–Sugar Loaf Islands, just offshore. You'll probably see seals, sea birds, maybe check lobster pots, and be thoroughly entertained by the informative and humorous commentary. Original owner Happy Chaddy sold the operation after many years to Carl Hayman, a former member of the much-loved national rugby team the All Blacks. Longer-duration fishing trips can be arranged. Rental kayaks and paddleboards are also available here. Note that the company sometimes takes a break in midwinter, so it pays to check ahead if you are traveling around July or August. ⊠ *Ocean View Parade, New Plymouth ☎ 06/758–9133 ⊕ www.chaddyscharters. co.nz ⤳ From NZ$40.*

SURFING

The coastal road between New Plymouth and Hawera is known as the **Surf Highway** for its popular surf beaches. To find the beaches, you'll need to take

Planning Your Visit to Egmont

Best Time to Go

December through March is the best time for walking, hiking, viewing alpine flowers, and making summit ascents. Experienced or guided mountaineers can snow- and ice-climb in July and August. Skiing is available July through September (depending on snow levels).

Best Ways to Explore

Take a Short Walk. Several gentle, well-signposted walking trails leave from the three main park entrances. Some top examples are Wilkies Pools, which takes in mountain streams, sculpted rocks, and goblin forest (1½-hour round-trip); Patea Loop, encompassing mountain cedar forest and stony riverbeds (two hours); and Potaema, with giant *rimu* and *rata* forest plus a vast wetland (20 minutes).

Take a Scenic Drive. Three main access roads lead into the park, climbing steeply (allow 10 to 20 minutes) up the mountain's forest-lined lower slopes and, in some areas, opening up stunning views. Short strolls along these roads enable you to appreciate the plants, trees, waterfalls, and streams. The interesting displays and photos at the main North Egmont Visitor Centre enhance the experience—as will the taste temptations in the café.

Take a Long Hike. The two- to three-day Pouakai Circuit explores all the park's landscapes: subalpine terrain, lava cliffs and gorges, the vast Ahukawakawa wetland, the tussock tops of the Pouakai Range, and lichen-covered goblin forest. The one-day Pouakai Crossing takes in much of the Pouakai Circuit and descends through forest to the western park boundary (transport shuttles required). Hiking around the mountain (four to five days) is another option, if you're keen to climb in and out of steep gullies and through mud. A second mountain loop above the tree line (three to four days) can be stunning in summer, icy in winter, and exposed to extreme weather at any time.

Climb the Mountain. The steep climb is a serious undertaking, especially with frequent bad weather. The mountain is sacred to the local Māori people, so they ask that climbers respect its spirituality and not clamber over the summit rocks. The main summer route (seven to eight hours round-trip) follows the northeast ridge. When there's no snow, it's all rock underfoot—slippery shingle or big tangled boulders. In winter, climbing is technical, requiring snow- and ice-climbing gear and expertise. Mountain guides can be hired in both winter and summer.

short detours off the main road and pass through rolling farmland down side roads to the coast. **Oakura,** a village 17 km (10 miles) southwest of New Plymouth, has one of the most popular surf beaches, with the added bonus of good cafés and crafts shops. Closer to New Plymouth, Fitzroy, East End, Back, and Bell Block beaches are all popular with surfers.

Opunake, in South Taranaki, has an artificial surf reef.

Beach Street Surf Shop

SURFING | This shop has all the equipment surfers need, and the team here will give you the lowdown on the hot spots in Taranaki. ⊠ *Fitzroy Beach, 39 Beach St., New Plymouth* ☎ *06/758–0400.*

Vertigo Surf

SURFING | In Oakura, this is the place to get the latest in surfing gear and advice on local conditions. A webcam shows what the Oakura Beach surf is doing at that moment. ⊠ 2 Tasman Parade, Oakura ☎ 06/752–7363 ⊕ www.vertigosurf. com.

Egmont National Park

North Egmont Visitor Centre is 26 km (16 miles) south of New Plymouth, Dawson Falls Visitor Centre is 68 km (42 miles) southwest of New Plymouth.

Rising 8,261 feet above sea level, Mt. Taranaki dominates the landscape of this national park. It's difficult not to be drawn toward it. The lower reaches are cloaked in dense and mossy rain forests; above the tree line, lower-growing tussocks and subalpine shrubs cling to spectacularly steep slopes. Taranaki is the mountain's Māori name. James Cook gave it its English name, Egmont, in 1770, to honor the Earl of Egmont, who supported his exploration. Both are officially acceptable today.

Mt. Taranaki is notorious for its changing weather conditions, and many climbers and hikers are caught with insufficient gear. On a clear day, from even the mountain's lower slopes you can see the three mountains of Tongariro National Park in the central North Island—and sometimes even as far as the South Island.

GETTING HERE AND AROUND

Three well-marked main roads provide access up the mountain and to walking trails, lodgings, and visitor centers. Egmont Road, the first mountain turnoff as you drive south from New Plymouth on State Highway 3, leads to the start of many walking trails and the **North Egmont Visitor Centre.** Drop in to peruse the

excellent displays and grab a bite at the small café. Pembroke Road, the second road up the mountain from State Highway 3, goes to the Ngati Ruanui Stratford Mountain House hotel, a few walking trails, and, a little farther on, **Stratford Plateau,** where there are stunning views and access to the mountain's small ski slope. A third turnoff (Manaia Road) turns right off Opunake Road coming from Stratford, and leads up the south side of the mountain to the **Dawson Falls Visitor Centre.**

You can book a local transport operator from New Plymouth through the New Plymouth i-SITE Visitor Information Centre.

VISITOR INFORMATION

CONTACTS Dawson Falls Visitor Centre. ⊠ Upper Manaia Rd., Kaponga, Egmont National Park ☎ 027/443–0248 ⊕ www. doc.govt.nz. **North Egmont Visitor Centre.** ⊠ 2679 Egmont Rd., Egmont National Park ☎ 06/756–0990 ⊕ www.doc.govt.nz.

👁 Sights

Egmont National Park

FOREST | Mt. Taranaki (8,261 feet), called Mt. Egmont by Captain Cook, is a steep, symmetrically shaped volcanic peak that dominates the region's landscape and weather. Egmont National Park was created in 1900 to protect the mountain and its surrounding forests. From a distance, the landscape looks simple; a cone-shaped mountain draped white with snow in winter and flanked by a near-perfect circle of forest. Look closer—or try walking on the park trails—and a different picture emerges. Thousands of years of volcanic buildup and erosion have crafted steep gullies and rivers, immense lava bluffs, unstable slips, and acres of moss-covered "goblin" trees and tall, ancient forest giants. It's a fascinating place to explore, and thankfully there are many ways of doing this no matter your level of fitness. Try a scenic drive up

Did You Know?

Thomas Dawson was the first European to discover this waterfall—when he almost fell over it. Despite the inauspicious beginning, he settled nearby and explored the land. Dawson Falls still bears his name.

one of the three access roads, explore the easy short trails around each of the three park entrances, or take a longer hike, staying in a park hut. The one-day Pouakai Crossing or two- to three day Pouakai Circuit explores all the park's landscapes: lava cliffs, wetlands, tussock tops, and goblin forests. (Always check with the DOC before heading out since some tracks are often temporarily closed due to erosion). Climbing the mountain is a serious undertaking for only experienced climbers, especially with frequent bad weather. The mountain is sacred to the local Māori people, so they ask that climbers respect this and not clamber over the summit rocks. In winter, climbing is for technically equipped and experienced climbers only.

 Hotels

Dawson Falls Mountain Lodge and Cafe

$$ | B&B/INN | A charming alpine-style building on the southern slopes of Mt. Taranaki, this 1896-built lodge offers stellar views of the coastline and native bush. **Pros:** quality cuisine; bush backdrop, waterfalls, and birdsong; superb hosts. **Cons:** no television; way out in the country; can be cold in rooms. $ *Rooms from: NZ$200* ⊠ *1890 Upper Manaia Rd., Kaponga, Dawson Falls* ☎ *06/765–5457* ⊕ *www.dawsonfalls.co.nz* ↪ *12 rooms* ⏴ *Free Breakfast.*

Ngati Ruanui Stratford Mountain House

$$ | HOTEL | High on the mountain, this hotel and restaurant has a deserved reputation for its dramatic setting and fine food. **Pros:** massage treatments available by reservation; dramatic mountain views; owned by local Māori people, Ngati Ruanui. **Cons:** long, steep drive to get here; can rain often on the mountain; no Wi-Fi in the rooms. $ *Rooms from: NZ$175* ⊠ *998 Pembroke Rd., E. Egmont, Egmont National Park* ☎ *06/765–6100* ⊕ *www.stratfordmountainhouse.co.nz* ⏴ *No Meals* ↪ *10 rooms.*

Activities

Whether your thing is climbing sheer rocky crags or taking a 10-minute stroll to a forest waterfall, you'll find something to wow you in this national park. Short walks to natural features, multiday hikes using park huts for accommodation, and the 18 km (11 mile) Pouakai Crossing are all popular. Summit climbs are notoriously dangerous, owing to the changeable weather, the mountain's steepness, and the loose unstable rock that surrounds it. In winter, technical expertise is a must. There's also a very basic slope for skiers.

HIKING

Top Guides

HIKING & WALKING | Take a half-day or full-day hiking trip showcasing the finest features of the park, escorted by guides with exceptional local knowledge and mountain experience. They will discuss with you what kind of adventure you would like, although the Pouakai Crossing is their signature day walk. They also offer shuttle transport from New Plymouth for those who want to walk independently on the 18-km (11-mile) trail. Rock climbing training courses are available. ☎ *027/270–2932* ⊕ *www.topguides. co.nz.*

SKIING

Manganui

SKIING & SNOWBOARDING | Owned by a small club, the sole ski slope on Mt. Taranaki only operates for 10 to 30 days each winter (June–October), based on snow conditions. The terrain is for intermediate and advanced skiers; nonmembers can buy daily tow passes. Note that facilities are limited, and it's a 20-minute walk from the parking lot to the ski area. ⊠ *Egmont National Park* ⊕ *www.skitaranaki.co.nz* ⏴ *Tow passes from NZ$50.*

Stratford

41 km (27 miles) southeast of New Plymouth.

Sitting under the eastern side of Mt. Taranaki, Stratford is a service town for surrounding farms. Its streets are named after characters from Shakespeare's works, and it has the first glockenspiel in New Zealand, which chimes four times a day. A number of the country's most interesting private gardens, including Hollard, thrive here in the rich volcanic soil. Because the town is at the junction of two highways, you'll likely pass through at some stage if you're exploring Taranaki.

GETTING HERE AND AROUND

Stratford is in central Taranaki, at the junction of State Highway 3, which passes through the region along the eastern side of Mt. Taranaki, and State Highway 43, aka the Forgotten World Highway. The town is just more than a 30-minute drive from New Plymouth. Daily bus service through Stratford, linking New Plymouth and Wanganui, is provided by InterCity; bookings can be made via i-SITE Visitor Information Centres.

BUS CONTACTS Stratford Bus Depot. ✉ *By Stratford i-SITE Visitor Information Centre, 56 Miranda St., Stratford.*

VISITOR INFORMATION

CONTACTS Stratford i-SITE Visitor Information Centre. ✉ *54 Miranda St, Stratford* ☎ *06/765–6708, 0800/765-6708* ⊕ *www. stratford.govt.nz.*

 ## Sights

Fenton Street Art Gallery, Cafe, and Gin Distillery

ART GALLERY | You can casually browse the art at this light and casual establishment, then sit down for a coffee or brunch (the beef pot pie is recommended) and be surrounded by the local works, or turn your attention to the gins and vodkas on sale. The owner, Stuart Greenhill, is also a published author; his murder mystery, *Dante Fog*, is on sale at the gallery. Don't restrict yourself to the main room; take a quick stroll down the corridors where you will find more interesting photos and paintings. ✉ *11 Fenton St., Stratford* ☎ *021/0299–2839* ⊕ *www.fentonartscollective.co.nz* ✍ *Free.*

★ Hollard Gardens

GARDEN | FAMILY | A 14-acre horticultural haven 16 km (10 miles) southwest of Stratford, Hollard Gardens encompasses native and exotic trees, rhododendrons, azaleas, camellias, and perennials. The 1920s vision of farmers Bernie and Rose Hollard, the gardens are now managed by the local council for all to enjoy. For families, there is a children's playground and a picnic area. Self-contained campervans can stay overnight. ✉ *1686 Upper Manaia Rd., off Opunake Rd., Kaponga* ☎ *0800/736–222* ⊕ *www.trc.govt.nz/ gardens/hollard-gardens* ✍ *Free.*

Stratford–Taumarunui

SCENIC DRIVE | Known as the Forgotten World Highway, Highway 43, heading northeast from Stratford, takes you on an intriguing, heritage-rich journey back in time as it winds through rolling farmland and dense rain forests to Taumarunui, the northern access point for the Whanganui River. You'll see few cars here, but there's no shortage of scenic sights. Highlights include Mt. Damper Falls (a side trip); spectacular views from three saddles and a lookout point; the steep, forest-filled Tangarakau Gorge; a road tunnel and historic railway; plus Whanganui River views. The 155-km (96-mile) highway is paved for all but 11 km (7 miles). Allow three hours, and be sure to fill your tank before leaving Stratford. If you need a break, drop into the vintage **Whangamomona Hotel** (*6018 Ohura Rd.*). More than a century old, it's the only place to stop for refreshments along the Forgotten World Highway. Travelers who

Did You Know?

Mt. Taranaki is one of the most symmetrical volcanic cones in the world. Its resemblance to Mt. Fuji won it a starring role in *The Last Samurai*.

don't feel like driving a car can sign on with **Forgotten World Adventures** (*www. forgottenworldadventures.co.nz*), an outfit that lets you "ride the rails"—golf carts mounted on a decommissioned railway line. The self-drive carts reach a top speed of 20 kph (12 mph) as you're led along 140 km (87 miles) of stunning track; guided trips from three hours to two days are available.

Tawhiti Museum

HISTORY MUSEUM | FAMILY | This isn't a boring old museum but rather an outstanding presentation of Taranaki's lively history. It's the creation of former schoolteacher-cum-historian Nigel Ogle, who has created life-size fiberglass figures and set them into historic scenes: dioramas depict the huge intertribal wars of the 1830s and European–Māori land wars of the 1860s, for example. More than 800 model warriors, none of them the same, have been created. In "Traders and Whalers," you glide by lantern light on a boat through an eerie world of traders and whalers and witness their first encounters with Māori tribes. Outside, Tawhiti Bush Railway highlights historical logging operations in Taranaki (runs the first Sunday of each month). Mr. Badger's Café, with its *Wind in the Willows* theme, and a quaint gift shop, can bring you back to the present. To reach the museum, in southern Taranaki, head south on State Highway 3 for 30 km (18 miles). It's a fascinating stop, but well off the beaten path. ✉ *401 Ohangai Rd., Hawera* ☎ *06/278–6837* ⊕ *www.tawhitimuseum.co.nz* 🎟 *Museum NZ$15, Traders and Whalers NZ$15, Bush Railway NZ$6* 🕘 *Closed Mon.–Sat. June–Aug.*

🛍 Shopping

Envirofur

HATS & GLOVES | This small but thriving business near Stratford is turning possum, a local environmental pest, into high-end items using all-natural tanning processes. Designer fur and leather products such as hats, rugs, coats, and scarves are sold. ✉ *1103 Opunake Rd., Mahoe* ☎ *06/764–6133* ⊕ *www.envirofur.co.nz.*

Whanganui

119 km southeast of Stratford.

A major gateway to Whanganui National Park, Whanganui is worthy in its own right. Its compact center has lively streets with shops and galleries, plus restored heritage buildings that harken back to colonial times and the busy trading days. The city is home to a vibrant arts community, and locals gather at the River Traders riverside market on Saturday morning for fresh produce and crafts. Recently the section of Drews Avenue between Rutland Street and Taupo Quay has been developed into a pedestrian-friendly arts precinct that is well worth spending a morning exploring. One of the centers here, Fine Arts Whanganui, is run by a collective of local artists. Restored riverboats cruise the river's lower reaches; gardens, parks, an interesting regional museum, and fine cafés and restaurants complete the picture.

GETTING HERE AND AROUND

Air Chathams flies here from Auckland three times a day (two on the weekend), landing at Whanganui Airport (WAG). The airport is located south of the river, approximately 4 km (2½ miles) from the center of Whanganui; you can catch a taxi in for about NZ$25.

If you're driving, Whanganui is three hours from Wellington; take State Highway 1 north to Sanson and Highway 3 west from there. From New Plymouth drive south on State Highway 3, allowing about 90 minutes for the journey. Access to the lower and middle reaches of the Whanganui River from the city is via the scenic Whanganui River Road—expect it to take two hours to drive from Whanganui to Pipiriki. Remember to keep left

A paddle steamer plies the Whanganui River.

on the narrow corners. For a scenic backcountry day trip, drive north up the Whanganui River Road, cut east along the minor road connecting Pipiriki to Raetihi, and then return down Highway 4, a paved though winding route through steep farmland and forest, to Whanganui. To reach the main kayak starting point, take Highway 4 north from Whanganui; it's a three-hour drive to Taumarunui, via Raetihi.

Note that the river is named Whanganui, the traditional spelling. The city can officially be spelled Wanganui or Whanganui, though nearly all businesses, agencies, attractions, and road signs now use the traditionally correct spelling of Whanganui.

AIRPORTS Whanganui Airport. ⊠ *Airport Rd., Whanganui* ☎ *06/348–0536* ⊕ *www. whanganuiairport.co.nz.*

BUS CONTACTS Whanganui Travel Centre. ⊠ *156 Ridgeway St., Whanganui* ☎ *06/345-4433.*

VISITOR INFORMATION

CONTACTS Whanganui i-SITE Visitor Information Centre. ⊠ *31 Taupo Quay, Whanganui* ☎ *06/349–0508* ⊕ *www.whanganui. govt.nz.*

 Sights

Durie Hill Lookout

VIEWPOINT | This lookout, Whanganui's most popular attraction, provides spectacular views, but reaching it—via an elevator that runs through the hill—is something else. First, you walk through a 700-foot tunnel to the elevator shaft, and the elevator concierge at the top will see you on camera and lower the elevator for you (there's a charge for the elevator each way in cash only). Alternatively, you can climb several hundred steps to the lookout, plus another 176 steps up the nearby Durie Hill Memorial Tower. ⊠ *Durie Hill, Whanganui* ☎ *NZ$2 each way (cash only).*

New Zealand Glassworks

STORE/MALL | Whanganui is regarded as the country's home for glass artisans; many of them exhibit internationally. This community studio is open for the public to watch some of these artists at work, join workshops (the half hour paperweight session is the most popular, but you need to check times and book in advance), and purchase their own stunning pieces from the retail gallery. ✉ *2 Rutland St., Whanganui* ☎ *06/927–6803* 🌐 *www.nzglassworks.com* 🎫 *Free.*

Virginia Lake

CITY PARK | The formal gardens here are a delight, and a gentle 25-minute stroll leads around the lake through woodlands and gardens. Take the time to check out the winter gardens. There's also a small café here. ✉ *110 Great North Rd., Whanganui* 🎫 *Free.*

***Waimarie* and Riverboat Centre**

HISTORY MUSEUM | The coal-fired paddle steamer, *Waimarie,* is one of the original riverboats that operated here. Sunk in 1954, it was salvaged from the river bed and restored in the 1990s. Throughout summer (late Oct.–early May) you can enjoy a historic, two-hour cruise, just like the old days. The Waimarie Centre displays photographs and related artifacts from the era when riverboats thrived here. Opening hours are variable at this volunteer operation; summer weekends are your best bet. ✉ *Waimarie Centre, 1A Taupo Quay, Whanganui* ☎ *06/347–1863, 0800/783–2637 Toll-free in New Zealand* 🌐 *www.waimarie.co.nz* 🎫 *Cruise NZ$45, museum by donation* 🕒 *Museum closed Tues. late Oct.–early May, closed Sun., Tues., Thurs., and Sat. early May–late Oct. No cruises early May–late Oct.*

Wairua

TRANSPORTATION | Rescued from the muddy riverbed and restored to first-class order, the classic little riverboat *Wairua* now makes regular two- and three-hour passenger trips upriver. Scheduled cruises depart year-round on Tuesday, Thursday, Saturday, and Sunday at 11 am. ✉ *1H Taupo Quay, opposite Moutoa Gardens, Whanganui* ☎ *0800/924–782* 🌐 *www.motorvesselwairua.co.nz* 🎫 *NZ$35* 🕒 *Closed Mon., Wed, Fri.*

★ Whanganui Regional Museum

HISTORY MUSEUM | This museum offers a superb overview of the region's history and one of the country's best collections of Māori artifacts. It contains *taonga* (Māori ancestral treasures) of the river people and re-creates 19th-century pioneer-town Whanganui. There's also Te Pataka Whakaahua (the Lindauer Gallery), featuring 19th-century paintings of Māori leaders by respected artist Gottfried Lindauer. Entry is free, but the museum offers guided tours for an extra charge if you want to gain more insight into the exhibits. ✉ *Queens Park, Watt St., Whanganui* ☎ *06/349–1110* 🌐 *www.wrm.org.nz* 🎫 *Free, guided tours NZ$10.*

🍴 Restaurants

Momiji Japanese Restaurant and Cafe

$$ | **JAPANESE** | Traditional Japanese food made with a mix of imported Japanese ingredients and fresh local produce is the star here. There's also a good selection of beer, sake, rice wine, and New Zealand beverages. **Known for:** sashimi and sushi with locally caught fish; bento boxes; Kirin beer on tap. [$] *Average main: NZ$20* ✉ *26 Victoria Ave., Whanganui* ☎ *06/345–0444* 🕒 *Closed Mon.*

Stellar Restaurant and Bar

$$ | **PIZZA** | This relaxed bar–restaurant specializes in pizzas, burgers, light meals, salads, and meaty main courses. It's also a music venue and hosts weekly quiz nights. **Known for:** nice craft beer selection; strong Kiwi vibe; late-night entertainment. [$] *Average main: NZ$19* ✉ *2 Victoria Ave., Whanganui* ☎ *06/345–7278* 🌐 *www.stellarbar.co.nz.*

Yellow House Café
$$ | **CAFÉ** | Join the locals at this cozy café, spread throughout the veranda, garden, and several intimate rooms of an old, mostly yellow villa. It serves a full breakfast/brunch menu with all the classics as well as wholesome, house-cooked lunches. **Known for:** bright and welcoming atmosphere; great tea selection; best brunch menu in town. [$] *Average main: NZ$18* ✉ *17 Pitt St., at Dublin St., Whanganui* ☎ *06/345–0083* ⏲ *No dinner.*

Coffee and Quick Bites

Article Cafe
$ | **CAFÉ** | The local newspaper used to be produced in this historic building, but the premises now house a friendly café that doubles as a retro clothes and arts store. A large communal wooden table takes pride of place near the streetside windows, so this is a great place to chat with locals or just people-watch while you enjoy a cup of organic, fair-trade coffee. **Known for:** lively atmosphere; location in Whanganui's emerging arts district; artisan breads. [$] *Average main: NZ$12* ✉ *Old Chronicle Building, 21 Drews Ave., Level 1, Whanganui* ☎ *027/752–2472* ⏲ *Closed Sun.–Tues.*

Hotels

Anndion Lodge
$$ | **HOTEL** | **FAMILY** | A blend of upscale "flashpacker" lodge rooms and stylish self-contained suites and apartments give visitors to the Anndion Lodge lots of flexibility. **Pros:** nice communal layout; well-equipped kitchen; river and grassy park area just across the road. **Cons:** backpacker area can get rowdy; short drive from downtown; beside busy main road. [$] *Rooms from: NZ$160* ✉ *143 Anzac Parade, Whanganui* ☎ *06/343–3593, 0800/343–056* 🌐 *www.anndionlodge.co.nz* 🍴 *No Meals* 🛏 *21 rooms.*

Aotea Motor Lodge
$$$ | **MOTEL** | Aimed primarily at business travelers, the spacious digs here, with their handsome yet comfy decor and convenient location are popular with tourists, too. **Pros:** close to supermarkets and fast-food restaurants; spacious rooms; amenities include double whirlpool baths. **Cons:** beside busy road; tight car parking spaces; cooked breakfast is not a good value. [$] *Rooms from: NZ$210* ✉ *390 Victoria Ave., Whanganui* ☎ *06/345–0303* 🌐 *www.aoteamotorlodge.co.nz* 🍴 *No Meals* 🛏 *28 rooms.*

★ **Iona Tiny House**
$$$ | **HOUSE** | This unusual accommodation started life on the South Island in 1924—as a boat—which the current owner found, moved to Whanganui, turned it on its side, and embedded it into a hill as an exclusive accommodation overlooking the river and city. **Pros:** relaxing riverside environment; very private; wide use of reclaimed timber. **Cons:** no kids under 12 allowed; no food on-site; two-night minimum stay. [$] *Rooms from: NZ$295* ✉ *52 Puketi Dr., Whanganui* ☎ *021/468–425* 🌐 *www.ionatinyhouse.nz* 🍴 *No Meals* 🛏 *1 house.*

151 on London
$$ | **MOTEL** | **FAMILY** | This upscale motel-style complex comes with a good selection of amenity-packed units. **Pros:** interesting rustic architectural theme; centrally located; high-quality amenities. **Cons:** breakfast not included in price; entrance is off a busy road (but hush glass keeps noise down); no bar or restaurant on-site. [$] *Rooms from: NZ$185* ✉ *151 London St., Whanganui* ☎ *06/345–8668* 🌐 *www.151onlondon.co.nz* 🍴 *No Meals* 🛏 *26 units.*

Rutland Arms
$$ | **B&B/INN** | Elegance and character team with modern amenities in this renovated Edwardian inn in the center of town. **Pros:** central location; very well heated for an old building; old-world

elegance. **Cons:** restaurant can be packed with locals; on busy main street, so some noise; no elevator. $ *Rooms from: NZ$160* ⌧ *Victoria Ave. and Ridgeway St., Whanganui* ☎ *06/347–7677* ⊕ *www. rutlandarms.co.nz* ⦶ *Free Breakfast* ⊸ *8 suites.*

 Nightlife

Porridge Watson
BARS | Located down a short, plant-lined lane off the arts precinct of Drew Street, a red door marks the entrance of this relatively new Whanganui bar. Open the door, and you'll be met by a large lounge setting that features pinball machines, long tables, lounge areas, leaners, a library, and a couple of stages. Decorations include chandeliers and disco balls, but somehow it seems to work. There is an extensive snack menu, but the main attractions are the wines and craft beers (mulled wine is a popular addition in the winter). Depending on which night you come, you could find anything from a poetry session to a live band or DJ playing. ⌧ *30 Drews Ave., Whanganui* ☎ *022/035–3877* ⊕ *www.facebook.com/ porridgewatson* ⊘ *Closed Tues. and Wed.*

Whanganui National Park

The Pipiriki access point is 77 km north of Whanganui, via the Whanganui River Rd., or 114 km north of Whanganui via State Hwy. 4.

The Whanganui, the longest continually navigable river in New Zealand, flows through one of the country's largest remaining areas of native lowland forest, much of which is protected in Whanganui National Park. Canoeing, jet boating, hiking, and mountain biking are the main recreational activities here.

GETTING HERE AND AROUND
Whanganui National Park, through which the eponymous river flows, is in the hinterland of the central North Island. The closest access points are Whanganui in the south and the township of Taumarunui to the north. The latter sits on State Highway 4 and is served by daily InterCity buses from Auckland and Wellington.

Traditional entry points for a Whanganui River journey are Taumarunui and the small settlements of Whakahoro and Pipiriki. To reach Whakahoro, turn off State Highway 4 at Owhango, just south of Taumarunui. Pipiriki is 27 km (17 miles) from Raetihi (also on State Highway 4) and 79 km (49 miles) from Whanganui, via the Whanganui River Road. Shuttle services for kayakers, hikers, mountain-bikers, and jet boat travelers are run by tourism operators based in the Whanganui/Ruapehu region, including the towns of Ohakune, National Park, Taumarunui, and Pipiriki.

BUS CONTACTS Taumarunui Bus Depot. ⌧ *Taumarunui i-SITE Visitor Information Centre, 116 Hakiaha St., Taumarunui* ☎ *07/895-7494.*

TOURS
Whanganui River Adventures
ADVENTURE TOURS | Ken and Josephine Haworth, who grew up on the river, run a Pipiriki-based company that offers jet boat tours to the Bridge to Nowhere, shorter trips to scenic highlights of the Drop Scene and Manganui o te Ao River, and jet boating/canoeing combo trips, plus river shuttle services for mountain bikers, canoers, and hikers. Tours range from 45 minutes to multiday adventures. They also operate a café and nicely landscaped campground with cabins, tents, and camper van sites on the grounds of the former Pipiriki School. ⌧ *Pipiriki Raetihi Rd, Pipiriki, Whanganui* ☎ *06/385–3246, 0800/862–743* ⊕ *www. whanganuiriveradventures.co.nz* ⛵ *Tours from NZ$80.*

Planning Your Trip to Whanganui

Best Time to Go

Anytime. Guided river trips gener-ally operate in summer; however, the climate is mild and a winter journey, while a little cooler and possibly wetter, is equally rewarding—and less crowded. The historic Whanganui River Road is open year-round.

Best Ways to Explore

Paddle the River. The Whanganui, New Zealand's most canoed river, is popular both for the terrain it transects and its suitability for beginners. Although the water flows through gorges and forested wilder-ness, its gradient is gentle and most of its 239 named rapids have little more than a 3-foot fall. The river is suitable for all kinds of craft, from kayaks to open-style Canadian canoes. Department of Conservation huts and campsites provide basic (but very scenic) riverside accommodations. Most people take a three- or five-day trip through the heart of the wilder-ness to Pipiriki, though paddling the lower reaches past historic Māori settlements is also appealing.

Take a Hike. Two three-day hiking trails (one is also a mountain-bike trail) traverse the park, and each has a distinctive character. Regen-erating forests along Mangapurua–Kaiwhakauka Track tell the story of failed farming attempts in these remote valleys. The old farming road was upgraded in 2010 and is now popular with mountain-bikers. In contrast, the Matemateaonga Track passes through the park's most pristine forested areas. Jet boats can be chartered for access to the river end of each walk.

Take a Drive. The narrow Whanganui River Road follows the water's lower reaches, climbing around bluffs and steep gullies and passing through historic Māori settlements. Heritage stops include an old flour mill, mission settlement, village churches, and traditional Māori *marae* (villages)—check with a local before venturing into these. You can drive yourself, or take the daily mail delivery tour from Whanganui.

Ride a Bike. Much of the Mountains to Sea—Nga Ara Tuhono Cycle Trail passes through Whanganui National Park. Remote, at times challenging, mountain-bike sections traverse the bluff-lined Kaiwhakauka and Mangapurua valleys. The last section follows the narrow, twisting, and very scenic Whanganui River Road before linking with off-road trails through Whanganui city to the sea. Jet boat shuttles can be booked for the 32-km (20-mile) section of river gorge that links two trail sections. Several companies offer packages including jet boat shuttles, accommodation, bike rentals, and a guide.

Jump in a Jet Boat. New Zealand ingenuity pioneered the planing jet boat, enabling fast, safe travel into the most remote, rapid-filled rivers. If your time is limited or you'd prefer not to paddle, take a jet boat trip into the heart of the national park. Tours, mostly run by family operators who have long associations with the river people, depart from settlements in the upper, middle, and lower reaches, and last from one hour to one day.

Whanganui Eco-stays

The Flying Fox has rustic yet comfortable cottages and glamping sites built from recycled timbers. The property, which is certified organic, is dotted with heritage fruit trees.

Accessible only by river, the **Bridge to Nowhere Lodge** is nestled on a small riverside patch of farmland. There's no electric power, but diesel generators, wood-fueled stoves, and helpful hosts provide all the comforts of home. They also offer jet boat and canoe trips. **Blue Duck Station** is a multifaceted operation that includes accommodations, a restaurant and café, river trips, and award-winning conservation work protecting endangered kiwi and blue duck species. Frontier Lodge is built to high eco-standards. Other lodges on the property cater to groups. Guests can partake in river, farm, and conservation activities.

All three lodges are set beside the Whanganui River and adjoin Whanganui National Park.

Whanganui River Road Mail Tour

ADVENTURE TOURS | Join the rural mail delivery run and enjoy a day of history and scenic splendor along the Whanganui River Road. Highlights include meeting the locals; visiting small Māori settlements with their traditional Māori ceremonial houses; exploring churches, including Jerusalem, where Mother Aubert founded the Home of Compassion; and a journey through steep farmland then the forest-covered hills and valleys of Whanganui National Park. From Pipiriki, a jet boat tour farther upriver can be arranged at extra cost. Pick-ups are from city accommodations, and reservations are essential. The company also offers cycling and tramping tours. ✉ 4/51 Abbot St., Gonville, Whanganui ☎ 06/344–4918 ⊕ www.whanganuitours. co.nz ✆ From NZ$63.

Whanganui Scenic Experience Jet

ADVENTURE TOURS | Mark and Claire Wickham, a pair of knowledgeable locals, offer two- to eight-hour jet boat tours that can include morning or afternoon tea stops at scenic and historic spots along the river. Trips start from the Wickham family farm, a 30-minute drive from Whanganui. If you have a little extra time to spend in the area, ask about customized journeys and longer trips, such as a three-day safari up the river. ✉ 1195 Whanganui River Rd., Whanganui ☎ 06/342–5599, 0800/945–335 ⊕ www.whanganuiscenicjet.com ✆ Tours from NZ$80.

VISITOR INFORMATION

CONTACTS Taumarunui i-SITE Visitor Information Centre. ✉ 116 Hakiaha St., Taumarunui ☎ 07/895–7494 ⊕ www. visitruapehu.com. **Whanganui i-SITE Visitor Information Centre.** ✉ 31 Taupo Quay, Whanganui ☎ 06/349–0508 ⊕ whanganuinz.com.

Sights

Whanganui River and Whanganui National Park

NATIONAL PARK | The Whanganui River starts high on the volcanic mountains of the central North Island, and travels 329 km (204 miles) to the sea. For several hundred years the tribe Te Atihau nui a Paparangi has lived along the riverbanks; they regard the waterway as their spiritual ancestor. To acknowledge this, the Whanganui became the first river in the world to be accorded legal personhood in 2017. The Whanganui flows through the heart of Whanganui National Park, through steep gorges and huge tracts of forested wilderness. The remoteness and beauty, culture and history, the river's relatively easy navigability, and forest trails and mountain bike tracks are the main draws to this national park. Scenic jet boat trips operate throughout the year from road access points along the river. Single and multiday kayak trips, both guided and independent, are extremely popular. The Whanganui Journey is, in fact, listed as one of New Zealand's famed Great Walks. Most visitors kayak in summer, but a river trip is feasible at any time. Two multiday walks and many shorter ones explore the lowland forest. Totaling 317 km (197 miles), the Mountains to Sea—Nga Ara Tuhono Cycle Trail traverses remote forest tracks (challenging for mountain bikes) and roads through Tongariro and Whanganui national parks from Mt. Ruapehu to the river's mouth; it can be ridden in stages. The river journey is also part of Te Araroa, the New Zealand Trail. ✉ *Whanganui National Park, Taranaki* 🌐 *www.doc.govt.nz.*

Whanganui River Road

SCENIC DRIVE | For a little slice of New Zealand, take a scenic and historic drive along the river's lower reaches by following the Whanganui River Road from the city of Whanganui. Turn left off State Highway 4 15 minutes north of the city. The narrow rural road follows the river for 79 km (49 miles) north, as far as Pipiriki. It passes several small villages and historic sites (ask a local before venturing into any traditional Māori villages). Interpretive signs are progressively being added along the route to help visitors uderstand what they are looking at. Be sure to keep left, drive slowly, and watch for wandering livestock. ✉ *Whanganui River Rd., Whanganui.*

Hotels

Bridge to Nowhere Lodge

$$ | **B&B/INN** | Roughly 30 miles upriver from Pipiriki, this private farm enclave can only be reached by jet boat or kayak. **Pros:** memorable wilderness experience; package rates include meals and jet boat transport; range of lodging styles. **Cons:** guest rooms quite basic, with shared bathrooms; remote location; river access only. [$] *Rooms from: NZ$160* ✉ *Whanganui National Park* ☎ *06/385–4622, 0800/480–308* 🌐 *www.bridgetonowhere.co.nz* 🕒 *Closed mid-May–Sept. Catered meals not available Sun.–Tues.* 🍴 *No Meals* 🛏 *8 rooms.*

The Flying Fox

$$$ | **APARTMENT** | Even just arriving here is an exceptional experience—whether by boat or the namesake Flying Fox, a cable car that carries you across to the remote, west bank of the Whanganui River. **Pros:** getting here is an adventure; river wilderness; eco-friendly and organic. **Cons:** native birdsong will probably wake you early; no cell phone reception; remote location. [$] *Rooms from: NZ$240* ✉ *Whanganui River Rd., Koriniti* ☎ *06/927–6809* 🌐 *www.theflyingfox.co.nz* 🍴 *No Meals* 🛏 *6 rooms.*

★ Frontier Lodge at Blue Duck Station

$$ | **RESORT** | This stylish, purpose-built lodge is set on Blue Duck Station, a multiuse tourism, farming, and conservation venture beside the Whanganui River. **Pros:** can hear kiwi calling at night; stunning New Zealand location; stylish, thoughtful building design. **Cons:** nearest shops about an hour drive; might be too remote for some; birdsong might wake you too early. [$] *Rooms from: NZ$195* ✉ *4265 Oio Rd., Owhango* ☎ *07/895–6276* 🌐 *www.blueduckstation.co.nz* 🕒 *Restaurant closed Jun.–Sept.* 🍴 *No Meals* 🛏 *3 rooms.*

Did You Know?

The Whanganui River is the longest continually navigable river in all of New Zealand, which makes it very popular with rafters and kayakers alike.

⚡ Activities

CANOEING AND KAYAKING

The main season for Whanganui River trips is between October and Easter; the busiest period is during the summer holidays (Christmas–January). Winter trips are also doable; the weather will be slightly colder, but you'll probably have the river to yourself. In summer, although there can be several hundred folks on the water at any one time, they are all moving in one direction, so a group can travel long periods without seeing another soul. The time they do come together is in the evenings, at park huts and campsites.

Travel on the river is generally in open, two-seater canoes or in kayaks. Tour options range from one-day picnic trips to five-day camping expeditions. What's known as the **Whanganui Journey** is regarded as one of ten "Great Walks" in New Zealand's national parks. Most people travel the river from Taumarunui to Pipiriki (a four- to five-day trip) or from Whakahoro to Pipiriki (three to four days). The latter is a true wilderness experience; there is no road access. A lower-river trip, from Pipiriki to Whanganui, passes through a mix of native forest, farmland, and several small communities and follows a road for much of the way.

To arrange a guided trip, contact a licensed commercial operator or the Whanganui office of the **Department of Conservation** (06/349–2100, www.doc.govt.nz). No experience is necessary as the Whanganui is considered a beginner's river; however, while it's definitely not a white-water adventure, the river should be respected. One or two rapids can play nasty tricks on paddlers, and the river can rise quickly to dangerous flood levels. Operators can supply all equipment, transfers, and the necessary hut and campsite passes, whether the trip is independently undertaken or guided and catered. Prices vary considerably according to the length and style of the journey, but you can expect to pay from about NZ$55 for a simple one-day outing and in the NZ$600 to NZ$800 range for an all-inclusive three-day excursion.

Canoe Safaris

CANOEING & ROWING | One of the most experienced companies with more than three decades running Whanganui River trips, these guides cater to everyone from families to septuagenarians. Their fleet ranges from kayaks to big open Canadian fur trapper–style canoes. Their campsite catering includes three-course dinners with wine; they'll also tell you about the natural fauna and history of the area. Fully guided trips include all equipment, including waterproof gear bags and a Department of Conservation User Pass. Kayak and canoe rentals and combo jet boat trips are also offered, plus they'll put you up pre- or post-trip nearby in their Ohakune lodge (at extra cost). ✉ 6 Tay St., Ohakune ☎ 06/385–9237, 0800/272–3353 ⊕ www.canoesafaris.co.nz ⌦ 5-day guided tour from NZ$1245.

Unique Whanganui River Experience

CANOEING & ROWING | Māori-owned and -operated, this company's three-, four-, and five-day tours concentrate on the cultural and historic aspects of the region as well as the stunning scenery and birdlife. You'll visit local *marae*, dine on *hāngi* meals with the locals, and learn about the fortified *pā* (strongholds) and trading stations along the way. ✉ 71 Carlton Ave., Tawhero, Whanganui ☎ 027/554–4426 ⊕ www.uniquewhanganuiriver.co.nz ⌦ From NZ$1150 for a five-day tour.

Whanganui River Canoes

CANOEING & ROWING | Canoe and kayak rentals with jet boat support, plus three- to five-day guided tours, are offered by Raetihi-based couple Ben and Rebecca. Ben is on the river most days in the summer, driving jet boats for his father's Bridge to Nowhere Lodge, so he'll be looking out for you. Rebecca's great-grandad was one of the first to map this river—his maps are still used by river travelers. The couple also owns Raetihi Holiday Park, 27 km (17 miles) from Pipiriki, so they can accommodate you pre- or post-trip if required. They'll also organize shuttles for hikers and mountain-bikers. ✉ *10 Parapara Rd., Raetihi* ☎ *06/385–4176, 0800/408–888* ⊕ *www. whanganuirivercanoes.co.nz* ✍ *From NZ$105.*

JET BOAT TOURS

If you fancy a faster-paced river adventure, consider a jet boat tour—you'll skim across the rapids, dodge the rocks, and see fantastic scenery. Note that Whanganui River rides are more about grand scenery and cultural history than the short, thrill-seeking ones offered by some southern-based operations. One of the most popular tours is a boat trip from Pipiriki to Mangapurua Landing, followed by a walk to the Bridge to Nowhere in the Mangapurua Valley. The valley was a farming settlement established in 1918 and abandoned in 1942, owing to the impossibly remote and rugged country. The old concrete bridge in the bush is a fascinating reminder. Jet boat companies also transport hikers to two national park hiking trails: the Matemateonga Track and the Mangapurua Track.

★ Blue Duck Station

BOATING | FAMILY | A standout farming, conservation, and tourism operation, you can take your pick here from a slew of activities. Options include jet boating or kayaking on the river, hiking in the national park, mountain-biking a remote forested section of the Mountains to Sea Heritage Trail, horseback-riding over the farm, taking a Bush Safari to learn about the conservation work protecting the habitats of kiwi and blue duck, or just relaxing by the river. Owner/operator Dan Steele is a Kiwi legend in tourism and conservation circles. ✉ *4265 Oio Rd., Owhango* ☎ *07/895–6276* ⊕ *www. blueduckstation.co.nz.*

Bridge to Nowhere

BOATING | Jet boats make the trip from Pipiriki to the Bridge to Nowhere as well as to other natural and historic sights. The company also offers a host of additional activities, including canoeing, canoe/jet boat combos, hiking, accommodations at the Bridge to Nowhere Lodge, and transport for mountain bikers tackling the Bridge to Nowhere section of the Mountains to Sea—Nga Ara Tuhono Cycle Trail. ✉ *Whanganui National Park* ☎ *0800/480–308* ⊕ *www.bridge-tonowhere.co.nz* ✍ *From NZ$130.*

★ Forgotten World Adventures

BOATING | These Taumarunui-based jet boat tours will bounce you over the more shallow rapids of the upper river. Their signature river trip is the eight-hour Bridge to Nowhere Tour; they will also do a shorter, one-hour spin for a minimum of four. You can also check out the company's unique Rail Cart Tours. Self-driving specially adapted golf carts travel on a disused railway line through hinterland forests and farms between the Whanganui River and Taranaki. Or do a combo of river/rail adventuring. ✉ *9 Hakiaha St., Taumarunui* ☎ *0800/7245–2278* ⊕ *www. forgottenworldadventures.co.nz* ✍ *From NZ$369* ⊙ *Closed Jun.–Sept.*

Palmerston North

145 km (87 miles) northeast of Wellington, 72 km (45 miles) southeast of Whanganui.

Palmerston North—or "Palmy" as the locals call it—is home to several major educational and agricultural research institutes, supporting sectors such as agrifood and agritech, health, education, distribution, logistics, and defense. With nearly 2,000 scientists calling it home (and 40% of the population studying or training), it's a place where bright minds flourish.

The biggest influence on the city is Massey University, one of the country's leading post-secondary institutions, which sits amid huge trees and lovely gardens just across the Manawatu River on Palmerston North's southern edge. The campus includes the Sport and Rugby Institute, which serves as a training facility for players on the All Blacks (New Zealand's revered national rugby team) and other elite athletes.

Drive ten minutes from the city center and you will find yourself in picturesque surroundings with various short walks and longer hikes, cycle routes, and mountain bike trails to explore. Popular options include Te Apiti Manawatu Gorge and Arapuke Mountain Bike Park. Rolling sheep and cattle farms, stunning gardens, and country homestay retreats are all in close proximity, nestling at the foot of the steep Ruahine Ranges.

GETTING HERE AND AROUND

The Palmerston North Airport (PMR) is 5 km (3 miles) northeast of the city. Air New Zealand serves it with daily direct flights from Auckland, Wellington, and Christchurch. Originair flies direct from Nelson. Ground transportation options to the city center include Super Shuttle (NZ$20) and Palmerston North Taxis (NZ$28–NZ$30).

The scenic *Northern Explorer* train also stops here as it travels between Auckland and Wellington.

If you're driving, Palmerston North is about two hours north of Wellington (allow more time during busy holiday weekends), and six to seven hours south of Auckland, following State Highway 1 through the central North Island. Whanganui is a one-hour drive to the northwest, and Napier is just under a three-hour drive to the northeast. While the traditional road to Napier is permanently closed due to rockslides, there are two options remaining: Saddle Road is

the quickest, and although it is winding the road is in good condition. A longer, but scenic, way around is the Paihiatua Track.

InterCity offers daily bus services from all major North Island communities. They arrive and depart from the Palmerston North i-SITE Visitor Information Centre. Activity in the city is centered on the streets around the Square. From there, you can easily explore the cafés, boutiques, art galleries, and museums on foot.

AIRPORTS Palmerston North Airport. ⊠ *Airport Dr., Palmerston North* ☎ *06/351–4415* ⊕ *www.pnairport.co.nz.*

AIRPORT TRANSFERS Palmerston North Taxis. ⊠ *Palmerston North* ☎ *06/355–5333* ⊕ *www.pntaxis.co.nz.* **Super Shuttle.** ⊠ *Palmerston North* ☎ *0800/748–885* ⊕ *www.supershuttle.co.nz.*

BUS CONTACTS Palmerston North Bus Depot. ⊠ *Palmerston North i-SITE Visitor Information Centre, The Square, Palmerston North.*

TRAIN CONTACTS Palmerston North Train Station. ⊠ *Matthew Ave., Palmerston North* ⊕ *www.railnewzealand.com.*

VISITOR INFORMATION

CONTACTS Palmerston North i-SITE Visitor Information Centre. ⊠ *The Square, Palmerston North* ☎ *06/350–1922, 0800/626–292* ⊕ *www.manawatunz.co.nz.*

Sights

★ Feilding

TOWN | For a look at an authentic New Zealand farming town visit Feilding, 20 km (12 miles) northwest of Palmerston North. The **Feilding Saleyards Guided Tour** is a classic experience. One of the largest livestock sale yards in the southern hemisphere, nearly 30,000 sheep and cattle are sold here every week. Every Friday at 11, a retired farmer will guide you (NZ$10, bookings essential) through the sheep pens and computerized cattle auction pavilion, and explain the secrets of a long-time New Zealand farming tradition. After the tour, visit the rustic Saleyards Café, where farmers meet for pie and chips or a toasted steak sandwich. Other local attractions in the Edwardian-style town square include the Friday morning farmers' market and the **Coach House Museum** that displays restored vehicles from the pioneering era (NZ$12). You could also putter about the town's bookshops, art galleries, and boutique movie theater, and café. From Feilding, Kimbolton Road passes through prime sheep-farming country to Kimbolton Village, 28 km (17 miles) away. Within a few minutes' drive of it are two outstanding gardens with rhododendrons and myriad other plants: **Cross Hills** (*crosshills.co.nz*; NZ$10; daily Sept.–May) and **Heritage Park Garden** (*heritagepark. co.nz*; NZ$7; daily year-round). ⊠ *Feilding & Distruct Information Centre, 61 Aorangi St., Feilding* ☎ *06/323–3318 Feilding & District Information Centre* ⊕ *www.feilding.co.nz* ⊘ *Information center is closed weekends.*

New Zealand Rugby Museum

OTHER MUSEUM | FAMILY | This museum—located upstairs in the Te Manawa complex—is worth a visit whether or not you're a rugby fan because it offers insight into a sport that many New Zealanders treat like a religion. The ever-growing collection of rugby memorabilia dates back to the start of this national game in 1870. Interactive components even let visitors "have a go"; you can kick, tackle, and jump in the lineout, testing your playing skills quite safely. ⊠ *326 Main St., Palmerston North* ☎ *06/358–6947* ⊕ *www.rugbymuseum. co.nz* ⊠ *NZ$13.*

Te Manawa

OTHER MUSEUM | FAMILY | This distinctive complex is divided into three sections that weave together the region's art,

science, and history, including natural history and the history of Rangitane, the local Māori people. For young ones, the Mind Science Centre, with its quirky interactive exhibits, is entertaining and educational. Regular touring exhibitions that visit here are also known for their quality. The art gallery has a strong focus on established and emerging artists from the local area, but you'll also find works from national and international artists. Te Manawa also houses the New Zealand Rugby Museum. ⊠ *326 Main St., Palmerston North* ☎ *06/355–5000* ⊕ *www. temanawa.co.nz* ⊠ *Life and Art galleries free; charges for some exhibitions.*

🍴 Restaurants

Brew Union Brewing Company

$$$ | MODERN NEW ZEALAND | FAMILY | A buzzy microbrewery, right in the center of the city, Brew Union serves a flexible menu of small plates, wood-fired pizzas, grills, salads, and burgers. Along with house-brewed beers, there are regular taps serving ales and ciders from craft brewers across New Zealand as well as a full selection of other beverages. **Known for:** lots of different spaces (communal, quiet, indoors, and covered outdoors); fresh house-brewed beers; tasty tapas. $ *Average main: NZ$25* ⊠ *41 Broadway Ave., Palmerston North* ☎ *06/280–3146* ⊕ *www.brewunion.co.nz.*

Café Cuba

$ | NEW ZEALAND | FAMILY | Just off the Square, funky Café Cuba is a perennially popular local haunt for breakfast, brunch, lunch, dinner, and after-show mingling. The menu is all classic, wholesome café fare, matched with laid-back background music. **Known for:** sweet treats like cheesecake; student community vibe; modern bubble and squeak (British breakfast) with bacon. $ *Average main: NZ$14* ⊠ *Cuba and George Sts., Palmerston North* ☎ *06/356–5750* ⊕ *www. cafecuba.co.nz.*

The Herb Farm and Cafe

$$ | CAFÉ | FAMILY | Wholesome, organic, and scrumptious food is served in a country café that's set in the middle of a 2-acre herb garden. The herbs grown here are served fresh with your food and are also used in the natural healing products manufactured on site. **Known for:** adjacent shop filled with healing herb products made on-site; spectacular herb garden; generous and fresh Kiwi breakfast and brunch classics. $ *Average main: NZ$19* ✉ *88 Grove Rd., Palmerston North* ☎ *06/326–8633* ⊕ *herbfarm.co.nz* ⊗ *No dinner.*

★ Local Café and Eatery

$$ | INTERNATIONAL | Though this café shares premises with a property brokerage office, it's not your usual pie and sandwich workplace diner. At lunchtime, people from all over town descend on the Local, and you are unlikely to get a table to yourself if you don't make a reservation. **Known for:** large windows and streetside location; fresh salads; noodle bowls with anything from tofu to prawns. $ *Average main: NZ$20* ✉ *240 Broadway Ave., Palmerston North* ☎ *06/280-4821* ⊕ *www.cafelocal.co.nz* ⊗ *No dinner.*

★ Nero Restaurant

$$$$ | MODERN NEW ZEALAND | Head to Nero for fine dining in a charming old Victorian-style villa on a quiet inner-city street. Chef and owner Scott Kennedy describes the cuisine as contemporary New Zealand, along with a touch of fusion to celebrate cultural diversity. **Known for:** quality service; diverse Asian flavors; 42-day whisky-aged Wagyu beef. $ *Average main: NZ$37* ✉ *36 Amesbury St., Palmerston North* ☎ *06/354–0312* ⊕ *www.cafenero.co.nz* ⊗ *Closed Sun. and Mon.*

 ## Hotels

Distinction Hotel Coachman

$$ | HOTEL | FAMILY | This large property has an array of hotel rooms and motel units, as well as a luxury villa. **Pros:** peaceful ambience in the garden; close to town; lots of options for types of rooms. **Cons:** can get busy with business meetings and functions; by main road so front guest rooms can be noisy; some decor is dated. $ *Rooms from: NZ$145* ✉ *140 Fitzherbert Ave., Palmerston North* ☎ *06/356–5065* ⊕ *www.distinctionhotelscoachman.co.nz* ⫶◯⫶ *No Meals* ⇲ *31 rooms.*

Distinction Hotel Palmerston North

$$ | HOTEL | The city's largest hotel occupies a 1927 heritage building (check out the cage-style elevator, one of the country's oldest). **Pros:** elevator access; in central city; good facilities. **Cons:** traffic noise; guest rooms lack character; not a lot of personality here. $ *Rooms from: NZ$160* ✉ *175 Cuba St., Palmerston North* ☎ *06/355–5895, 0800/554–490* ⊕ *www.distinctionhotelspalmerstonnorth.co.nz* ⇲ *85 rooms* ⫶◯⫶ *No Meals.*

Quest Palmerston North

$$ | HOTEL | This is a fairly standard apartment-style chain hotel, but it's the newest in town, and it's as close as you'll get to the central city. **Pros:** local restaurant charge-back scheme; close to town; laundry in every unit. **Cons:** no outdoor grounds or balconies; no on-site restaurant; gym is off-premises. $ *Rooms from: NZ$140* ✉ *109 Fitzherbert Ave., Palmerston North* ☎ *06/357–7676* ⊕ *www.questpalmerstonnorth.co.nz* ⫶◯⫶ *No Meals* ⇲ *41 rooms.*

Shopping

Palmerston North's shopping is concentrated around the Square; Broadway Avenue and the Plaza shopping centers are within easy walking distance. George

Street, which is also just off the Square, has a number of specialty shops, galleries, and cafés.

Bruce McKenzie Books

BOOKS | This is considered one of New Zealand's leading independent bookstores (and they are becoming a rare breed). ✉ *37 George St., Palmerston North* ☎ *06/356–9922* ⊕ *www.bmbooks. co.nz.*

Zimmerman Art Gallery

ART GALLERIES | This private art gallery displays and sells collections from specific artists it represents. It is well located directly opposite the city's public gallery in Te Manawa. ✉ *329 Main St., Palmerston North* ☎ *06/353-0122* ⊕ *www. zimmerman.co.nz* ☉ *Closed Sun.–Wed.*

⚫ Performing Arts

Several theaters in the city center host local and visiting productions.

The Stomach

MUSIC | If you're in the mood to catch a bit of the youth culture the city is known for, check out what's going on in this independent and alternative music venue. Bands routinely use the studio space to rehearse, but there are also regular shows open to the public, with acts and times listed on the venue's website. It's an all-ages place, so there's no alcohol served: the nonprofit society that runs the place is all about the music. You'll need a sense of adventure because the bands that play here don't tend to be household names. ✉ *84 Lombard St., Palmerston North* ☎ *06/359–0120* ⊕ *www.creativesounds.org.nz* 🎫 *NZ$20.*

Chapter 8

WELLINGTON AND THE WAIRARAPA

8

Updated by
Lesley Wild

 Sights
★★★★☆

 Restaurants
★★★★★

 Hotels
★★★★☆

 Shopping
★★★☆☆

 Nightlife
★★★★☆

WELCOME TO WELLINGTON AND THE WAIRARAPA

TOP REASONS TO GO

★ **Arts and Culture:** The national symphony, ballet, and opera are based here. The biennial New Zealand Festival of the Arts packs a three-week program with local and international acts that span drama, music, and dance.

★ **Eclectic Cuisine:** Be sure to enjoy the fruits of the capital's humming cuisine scene.

★ **Craft Beer and Wine:** Taste top award-winning tipples, from the expansive Wairarapa vineyards to the dozens of inner-city breweries.

★ **Walk on the Wild Side:** Take a self-guided roam through the lush green valley of the world's first urban eco-sanctuary to meet kiwi, *takahē*, and other famously feathered locals.

★ **The Waterfront:** Meandering along Wellington's waterfront is sublime on a sunny day. You can visit both the Museum of New Zealand Te Papa Tongarewa and the Wellington Museum for free.

1 Wellington. The capital of New Zealand offers good food, idyllic forests and an excellent art scene.

2 Akatarawa Valley. This steep valley is full of hidden gems, like the Staglands Wildlife Reserve.

3 Kapiti Coast. This gorgeous coastal area leads you to the arty beach town of Paekakariki.

4 Kapiti Island. One of Wellington's best-kept secrets, this protected island reserve has excellent hiking and nature tours.

5 Martinborough. This laid-back town is the center of the Wairarapa wine industry.

6 Palliser Bay and Cape Palliser. The southernmost part of the North Island coast has a seal colony and Putangirua Pinnacles Scenic Reserve.

7 Masterton and Around. Wairarapa's second-biggest city is dotted with interactive museums, imaginatively-designed parks and renowned vineyards.

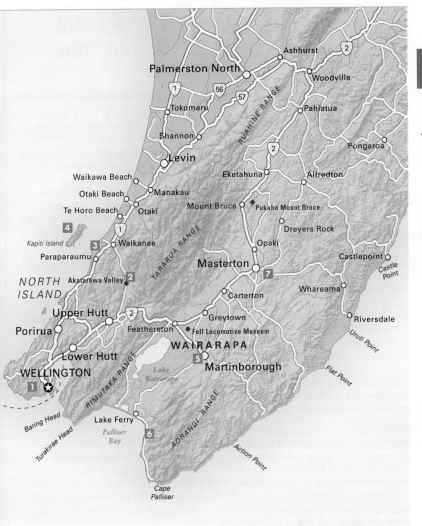

Palmerston North
Ashhurst
Woodville
Tokomaru
Pahiatua
Shannon
Pongaroa
Levin
Eketahuna
Alfredton
Waikawa Beach
Otaki Beach
Manakau
Mount Bruce
Pukaha Mount Bruce
Te Horo Beach
Otaki
Dreyers Rock
Kapiti Island
Waikanae
Opaki
Castlepoint
Paraparaumu
Castle Point
NORTH
ISLAND
Akatarawa Valley
Masterton
Whareama
Upper Hutt
Carterton
Porirua
Riversdale
Greytown
Featherston
Fell Locomotive Museum
Lower Hutt
WAIRARAPA
WELLINGTON
Martinborough
Lake Ferry
Palliser Bay
Baring Head
Turakirae Head
Cape Palliser
RUAHINE RANGE
TARARUA RANGE
RIMUTAKA RANGE
AORANGI RANGE
Lake Wairarapa
Uruti Point
Flat Point
Action Point

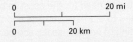

0   20 mi
0   20 km

Upon a panoramic backdrop of golden ranges, temperate forests, and a sweeping blue-green harbor, Wellington has developed the lively, friendly, and infectious spirit of a city coming into its own.

From Wellington's windswept heights, a clear winter's morning unveils snow-touched peaks, calm seas, and the scent of fresh coffee rising from the city. Mild summer nights are equally blissful, as the bright medallion moon cloaks the hillsides in silver, forming the stage for a lively night among the city lights.

For many, Wellington is ever-growing in its charm as a destination. The "cool" capital boasts lively arts, food, and nightlife scenes and is home to the country's most coveted festivals and events. During the day, you may find yourself drifting from coffee shops to art galleries, to the artisanal chocolate factory, to world-renowned museums and parks. By night, you might start off in a bustling restaurant, meander toward a craft beer or wine bar, and finish off the evening dancing to live jazz or settling into a quiet corner of a speakeasy.

Refreshingly, the city also offers many an opportunity to break from the bustle. On the waterfront, the first-class Museum of New Zealand Te Papa Tongarewa has many hands-on exhibits that are equally fascinating for children and adults. Or, if ambling through winding forest trails is more your pace, visit one of the many nature reserves to meet rare and colorful native species. In the summer evenings, be sure to head for the coast to be treated to dramatic sunsets and the odd sighting of whales, seals, and penguins.

Wellington and its adjacent Hutt Valley form the southern gateway to the Wairarapa, a region whose name has become synonymous with wine. Journey over the hills and coast along quiet byways from vineyard to vineyard for a day—or two, or three—of wine tasting. If wine isn't your thing, the Wairarapa is still worth an excursion for its markets, hiking trails, and fishing opportunities.

Wellington and the adjacent Wairarapa regions sit at the North Island's southern point, crested by the seldom-still waters of Cook Strait that divide the country's landmass. All main roads are northern-bound, separated by a mountain range that virtually tumbles into the strait. Road travel between the two regions is via the Hutt Valley and the winding Rimutaka Hill road. On the way, expect peaceful river scenery, green pleasant outlooks, and spectacular hilltop views.

MAJOR REGIONS

Outside of the city limits in **Greater Wellington,** you'll find an appealing variety of day trips, from exploring the rugged Akatarawa Valley to immersing oneself in the forests and beaches of the Kapiti Coast.

For some years, the rather daunting access road gave a sense of isolation to **The Wairarapa**. The emergence of the wine industry has, however, triggered a tourism boom. Red grape varietals flourish in the local soil, and as such, pinot noir is widely celebrated across the vines. Wairarapa wines are typically produced in small quantities, allowing vintners to experiment with flavor profiles, leading local vineyards to win international awards and admiration. These days, wine tastings, olive farms, and the twice-yearly Martinborough Fair are firmly established attractions. Aside from wine, the "Golden Shears" shearing competition, the Patuna Chasm Walk, and spectacular fishing spots also bring visitors over "The Hill." The towns of Martinborough and Masterton are good bases for exploring the region's wineries, while also providing easy access to the rugged beauty of Palliser Bay and the Tararua Ranges.

Planning

Make time to enjoy a relaxing day on the city's waterfront; it's a stone's throw from the city center. This area is flat and easily walkable, dotted with unique shops, museums, and restaurants. You don't need a car in the city, but to explore the vineyards of Wairarapa or the beaches of the Kapiti Coast, it's best to make a day trip of it and drive.

Getting Here and Around

AIR

Wellington International Airport (WLG) lies about 8 km (5 miles) from the city. Domestic carriers serving Wellington include Air New Zealand, Qantas, Jetstar, and Sounds Air. You can rent a car on site or catch a shuttle into town; a taxi or rideshare service from the airport to central Wellington costs about NZ$40.

AIRPORTS Wellington Airport. ⊠ Stewart Duff Dr., Rongotai ☎ 04/385–5100 ⊕ www.wellingtonairport.co.nz.

AIRLINES Air New Zealand. ⊠ Wellington ☎ 0800/737–000 ⊕ www.airnewzealand.

co.nz. **Jetstar.** ☎ 0800/800–995 ⊕ www.jetstar.com. **Qantas.** ☎ 0800/808–767 ⊕ www.qantas.com. **Sounds Air.** ☎ 0800/505–005 ⊕ www.soundsair.com.

AIRPORT TRANSFERS Super Shuttle. ⊠ Wellington ☎ 0800/748–885 ⊕ www.supershuttle.co.nz.

BOAT AND FERRY

The Interislander runs a ferry service between Wellington and Picton. Bookings are open up to six months in advance. Fares vary by time of year, ranging from NZ$56 to NZ$75 one-way per person; for a car and driver, fares are NZ$177 to NZ$330, depending on vehicle type and dimensions. Plan for a 4-hour journey, and arrive at least an hour prior to sailing time if traveling with a vehicle. For those without a car, a free bus to the ferry terminal leaves 50 minutes prior to departure times from Platform 9 at the Wellington Railway. Bluebridge Cook Strait Ferry vessels, *The Strait Feronia* and *The Straitsman,* sail up to four times per day between Wellington and Picton. Fares are NZ$54 to NZ$90 one-way per person, and NZ$174 to NZ$190 for a driver with a car up to 20 feet long. Most car-rental agencies offer North Island–South Island transfer programs.

CONTACTS Interislander. ⊠ Wellington ☎ 0800/802–802 ⊕ www.greatjourneysofnz.co.nz/interislander. **Bluebridge Cook Strait Ferry.** ⊠ Wellington ☎ 0800/844–844 ⊕ www.bluebridge.co.nz.

BUS

InterCity operates daily long-distance bus services, connecting Wellington to most other cities and major towns in New Zealand. Metlink runs the bus network in the wider Wellington region. A trip planner and live timetables are available via their app.

CONTACTS InterCity. ☎ 04/385–0520 ⊕ www.intercity.co.nz. **Metlink.** ☎ 0800/801–700 ⊕ www.metlink.org.nz. **Wellington Bus Depot.** ⊠ Bunny St. and Waterloo Quay, Wellington.

CAR

The main access to the city is via the Wellington Urban Motorway, which starts just after Highways 1 and 2 merge, a few miles north of the city center. The motorway links the city center with all towns and cities to the north.

Outside of the city, transportation options are very limited, so you'll need a car to properly explore the area. State Highway 2 runs north–south through the region between Napier and Wellington. From Wellington, you drive through Upper Hutt (the River Road bypasses the town), over the hills into the gateway town of Featherston. Highway 53 takes you to Martinborough; turn southwest here on Lake Ferry Road for Lake Ferry and Cape Palliser. Masterton is farther north along State Highway 2, roughly a 30-minute drive from Martinborough. The journey from Wellington to Martinborough takes about 75 minutes; Masterton is another 15. From Napier, Masterton is about three hours.

TRAIN

Metlink operates trains connecting the Wellington Railway Station with the Hutt Valley and Masterton. If you're a fan of scenic train trips, try the *Northern Explorer;* linking Wellington and Auckland, it stops in Paraparaumu, Palmerston North, Ohakune, National Park, Otorohanga (near Waitomo), Hamilton, and Papakura. The train travels southbound on Monday, Thursday, and Saturday and northbound on Wednesday, Friday, and Sunday.

CONTACTS Metlink. ☎ *0800/801–700* ⊕ *www.metlink.org.nz.* **Northern Explorer.** ☎ *0800/872–467* ⊕ *www.greatjourneysofnz.co.nz/northern-explorer.* **Wellington Railway Station.** ⊠ *Bunny St. and Waterloo Quay, Wellington.*

Hotels

Accommodations in Wellington range from no-frills backpacker hostels and motel units to sleek central hotels and classic bed-and-breakfasts in colonial-era villas.

As more people move into the city, serviced apartment-hotels are also gaining steam. Rates are significantly more expensive than those of the average motel, but they're a good option if you're planning to stay a while. Most of these apartment-hotel hybrids have weekend or long-term specials.

Lodgings generally do not have air-conditioning, but the temperate weather in Wellington rarely warrants it.

Restaurant and hotel reviews have been shortened. For full information, visit Fodors.com. Restaurant prices are the average cost of a main course at dinner or, if dinner is not served, at lunch. Hotel prices are the lowest cost of a standard double room in high season.

WHAT IT COSTS in New Zealand Dollars			
$	$$	$$$	$$$$
RESTAURANTS			
under NZ$15	NZ$15– NZ$20	NZ$21– NZ$30	over NZ$30
HOTELS			
under NZ$125	NZ$125– NZ$200	NZ$201– NZ$300	over NZ$300

Restaurants

In Wellington, restaurants, cafés, bars, and breweries spring up overnight like mushrooms. Although you'll never be without the classic meal of steak, fries, and ale, chefs returning from stints abroad have also embraced more adventurous fare. Chinese, Thai, Japanese,

Malaysian, Mexican, and Italian cuisines are all easy to find at high standards. Locally sourced food is also appearing in restaurants around the city—native produce might be paired with traditional seafood or made into sauces to accompany meat or sweet-potato dishes.

In rural areas outside Wellington, the wine industry has revolutionized local tables, with excellent dining and wine-tasting spots. In the Wairarapa, restaurants are winning a reputation for creative cuisine.

Generally, lunch runs from noon until 2, then some restaurants close for a few hours before opening for dinner around 5. On Monday, many restaurants are shuttered; however, no matter the day of the week, it's always wise to book a table. Dress codes are still really relaxed; jeans would rarely be frowned upon even at the top restaurants.

Visitor Information

There is a comprehensive information service for the city and surrounding districts—⊕ WellingtonNZ.com—which covers everything you need to know. The Wellington i-SITE Visitor Information Centre, on Wakefield Street, can provide you with brochures, tour bookings, theater tickets, and more.

CONTACTS Wellington i-SITE Visitor Information Centre. ☒ 111 Wakefield St., Wellington ☎ 04/802–4860 ⊕ www. wellingtonNZ.com. **WellingtonNZ.com.** ☒ Wellington ☎ 04/916–1205 ⊕ www. WellingtonNZ.com.

When to Go

November to mid-April is the best time weather-wise in the Wellington area. Most establishments are open year-round (apart from Christmas Day, New Year's Day, and Good Friday). In Wairarapa, book well ahead if you're traveling during the summer school holidays from mid-December to the end of January. From February to April, you can expect fewer crowds and many brilliant, warm days. Winters bring more rain, but they're rarely bitterly cold. Be prepared with waterproof layers for unpredictable weather and southerly gales, which are possible even during the summer.

FESTIVALS
CubaDupa
Every year, New Zealand's largest outdoor arts and music festival transforms the capital's cool Cuba Street for a weekend in late March. This free, family-friendly event is packed with an extraordinary variety of programmed entertainment. Quality food stalls from local restaurants also line the streets. ☒ Cuba Street, Wellington ⊕ www.cubadupa.co.nz.

Matariki
In late May or early June, Māori New Year begins with the first new moon after the appearance of Matariki (Pleiades). To celebrate, the Museum of New Zealand Te Papa Tongarewa hosts nine days of music, storytelling, and dance performances; events kick off with a ceremony at dawn. ☒ Museum of New Zealand Te Papa Tongarewa, 55 Cable St., Wellington ⊕ www.tepapa.govt.nz/visit/events.

The New Zealand Festival of the Arts
The country's major art showcase is held February through March on even-numbered years at venues across the city. A huge array of international talent in music, drama, dance, and visual media descends upon Wellington. Events fill up quickly; check online for program information, and book a month in advance if you can. ☒ Wellington ☎ 04/473–0149 ⊕ www.festival.nz.

Wellington on a Plate
Wellington's annual food festival hosts over 100 events, with local and visiting chefs creating special menus and experiences. New Zealand's largest beer festival, Beervana, kicks off the two-week

festival in early August. A major component of the festival is Burger Wellington, which sees more than 200 eateries competing to be ruled the Best Burger. ✉ *Wellington* ☎ *04/473–8044* ⊕ *www. visawoap.com.*

Wellington

Wellington, the seat of government since 1865, rests between the sea and towering hillsides. The city's landscape forms a natural arena with the harbor as its stage. Ferries carve patterns on the green water while preening seabirds survey the scene. Houses cascade down the steep hills, creating a vibrant collage of colorful rooftops against a spectacular green backdrop. An old brick monastery peers down on the marina—a jigsaw of masts and sails bobbing alongside the impressive Museum of New Zealand Te Papa Tongarewa. Modern high-rises gaze over Port Nicholson, one of the finest natural anchorages in the world. Known to local Māori as the Great Harbor of Tara, for its two massive arms that form the "jaws of the fish of Maui" (Maui being the name of a god from Māori legend).

Dominating the northern end of the waterfront, the Sky Stadium is home to rugby matches, bombastic festivals, and rock concerts. Stretching around and south of the stadium, Thorndon is known for its historic and idyllic streets that meet Parliament grounds and its characteristic "Beehive" building. From Parliament, Lambton Quay and Featherston Streets stretch southward as the main arteries of the central business district. Here, all roads lead toward the entertainment district of Victoria, Cuba, and Ghuznee Streets. The nightlife stretches on through the fabled Courtenay Place, meeting the broad sweep of Oriental Bay, a picturesque art deco suburb with cafés, a beach, and a wide promenade.

GETTING HERE AND AROUND

Wellington is a great walking city. The compact area around Lambton Quay and on Cuba Street is flat. A stroll along the waterfront around Oriental Bay provides outstanding sea views. If you head for the hills, take the cable car, and see the sights before strolling down.

For cyclists, designated bike lanes in and around Wellington are marked with a continuous white line and a white bike image on the pavement. More details about urban cycling are on the city's website.

Buses are an easy way to navigate the city, though service outside the city center is sporadic. In Wellington, buses are operated by several companies; for information on all routes and fares, contact **Metlink** (*0800/801–700, www. metlink.org.nz).* The main terminals are at the Wellington Railway Station (Bunny Street and Waterloo Quay) and Courtenay Place. For all inner-city trips, pay when you board the bus. Bus stops are marked with red-and-white signs. For longer stays, a Snapper card costs NZ$10 and offers good discounts and convenience.

You don't need a car to get around central Wellington—and you probably don't want one as the many one-way streets can frustrate drivers. Having one, however, is essential if you hope to fully explore the outer regions.

Taxi ride rates are NZ$3.50 on entry, then NZ$2.95 per 1 km (½ mile). Taxis idle outside the railway station and along Wakefield Street, Courtenay Place and Lambton Quay. Metlink operates trains connecting the Wellington Railway Station with the Hutt Valley and Masterton. If you're a fan of scenic train trips, try the *Northern Explorer;* linking Wellington and Auckland, it stops in Paraparaumu, Palmerston North, Ohakune, National Park, Otorohanga (near Waitomo), Hamilton, and Papakura. The train travels southbound on Monday, Thursday, and

Saturday and northbound on Wednesday, Friday, and Sunday.

TOURS
BOAT TOURS
East by West Ferry

BOAT TOURS | East by West Ferries runs a commuter service between the city and Days Bay, on the east side of Port Nicholson; it's one of the best value tours around. On the 10 am sailing, you can stop at Matiu/Somes Island; this former quarantine station makes a unique picnic spot on a warm afternoon. Just be sure to confirm your return pick-up time with the crew. Days Bay itself has a seaside village character, a lovely swimming beach, local craft shops, and great views of Wellington. Weekdays, the catamaran regularly departs Queens Wharf between 6:20 am and 7:05 pm. The return boats leave Days Bay roughly 30 minutes later. The sailing schedule is cut back on weekends and holidays, but additional Harbour Explorer Tours visit Seatoun Wharf. You can pick up tickets at the ferry terminal between 8 and 5; otherwise, tickets can be bought on board. All sailings may be canceled in stormy weather. ⊠ *Queens Wharf, Wellington* ☎ *04/499–1282, 04/494–3339* ⊕ *www.eastbywest.co.nz* ✉ *From NZ$12.*

BUS TOURS
Rover Rings Tours

GUIDED TOURS | As the base of production for the Lord of the Rings and The Hobbit films, there are many famous filming locations in and around Wellington. Rover Rings Tours offers half-day and full-day Lord of the Rings film location tours, with the full-day option including a picnic lunch and a tour of Weta Workshop. All leave from the i-SITE Visitor Information Centre, and advanced reservations are essential. ⊠ *Wellington* ☎ *04/471–0044* ⊕ *www.rtgl.co.nz* ✉ *From NZ$110.*

PRIVATE GUIDES
Black Cars

PRIVATE GUIDES | With an emphasis on luxury, these all-inclusive, upscale tours are offered in chauffeur-driven vehicles. Tours range from four to eight hours and can follow a set itinerary or a tailor-made experience. Private transfers and driver services are also available. ☎ *022/588–0085* ⊕ *www.blackcars.co* ✉ *From NZ$450 for two people.*

VISITOR INFORMATION
CONTACTS **Wellington i-SITE Visitor Information Centre.** ⊠ *111 Wakefield St., Wellington* ☎ *04/802–4860* ⊕ *www. wellingtonnz.com.*

◉ Sights

City Gallery Wellington
ART GALLERY | This gallery is internationally recognized for its striking showcases of contemporary art. The ever-changing program is filled with works from local and international artists, events, and tours. Visitors can view sometimes challenging, but always captivating work. ⊠ *Civic Sq., Wakefield St., Wellington* ☎ *04/913–9032* ⊕ *www.citygallery.org.nz* ✉ *Free (but there are charges for some special exhibits).*

★ Hannah's Laneway
STREET | FAMILY | This former factory—now foodie favorite—is packed to its industrial rafters with gastronomic gifts. During the day, you'll see boutique **Fix and Fogg** peanut butter sold upon slabs of toast from a window, **Lashing's** famously Vegemite-laced brownies, and the beloved bread from **Leed's Street Bakery**. Deeper into the laneway, your sense of smell will cartoonishly lead you to the **Wellington Chocolate Factory**, where you'll watch bars and truffles being made Wonka-style. In the evening, you'll find old and golden beer and pizza institutions, **Golding's Free Dive** and **Fortune Favours**, the literally "off-the-hook" cocktails from the **Hanging Ditch**, and the top award-winning casual dining restaurant, **Shepherd**. ⊠ *Leeds St., Wellington Central.*

8

Wellington and the Wairarapa WELLINGTON

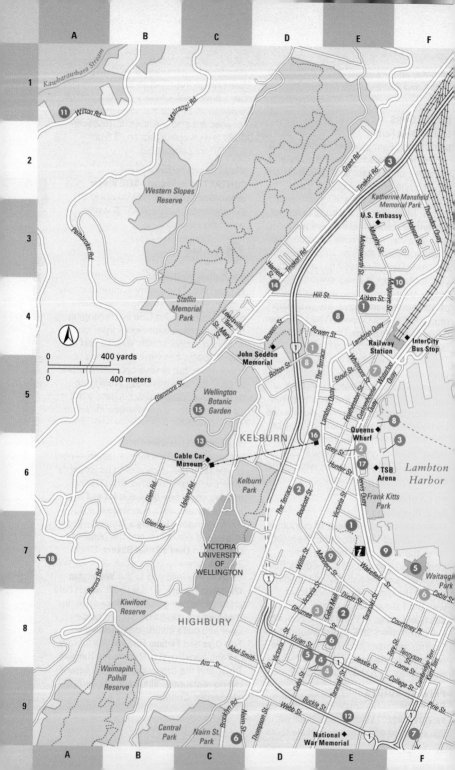

A B C D E F

1

Kawharawhara Stream

⑪ Wilton Rd.

Mairangi Rd.

2

Western Slopes Reserve

Grant Rd.

Tinakori Rd.

③

Katherine Mansfield Memorial Park

Thornton Quay

Hobson St.

3

Pembroke Rd.

U.S. Embassy ◆

Molesworth St.

Murphy St.

⑦
①

⑩

Aitken St.

Mulgrave St.

Stellin Memorial Park

Lewisville Terr.

St. Mary St.

Harriet St.

Tinakori Rd.

⑭

Hill St.

4

N

0   400 yards
0   400 meters

Bowen St.

Bowen St.

⑧

Lambton Quay

Railway Station

InterCity Bus Stop

John Seddon Memorial ◆

The Terrace

①

⑧

Bolton St.

Whitmore St.

Stout St.

⑦

Featherston St.

Customhouse Quay

Waterloo Quay

5

Glenmore St.

Wellington Botanic Garden

⑮

KELBURN

Lambton Quay

⑯

Queens Wharf ◆

⑧

② ③

Lambton Harbor

⑬

Cable Car Museum ◆

Grey St.

Hunter St.

⑰

TSB Arena ◆

6

Glen Rd.

Upland Rd.

Kelburn Park

The Terrace

Beaucroft St.

②

Jervis Quay

Frank Kitts Park

Glen Rd.

①

Victoria St.

⑨

Wakefield St.

ℹ

⑨

⑤

Waitangi Park

7

← ⑱

VICTORIA UNIVERSITY OF WELLINGTON

Willis St.

⑨

Manners St.

Cable St.

⑥

Raroa Rd.

Kiwifoot Reserve

③

Cuba Mall

②

Dixon St.

Taranaki St.

Courtenay Pl.

HIGHBURY

Ghuznee St.

⑥

8

Waimapihi Polhill Reserve

Ara St.

Abel Smith St.

Vivian St.

Victoria St.

⑤ ④

④

Jessie St.

Tory St.

Tennyson St.

Lorne St.

Cambridge Terr.

Kent Terr.

College St.

Cuba St.

Taranaki St.

9

Central Park

Nairn St.

Brooklyn Rd.

Nairn St.

⑥

Thompson St.

Buckle St.

Webb St.

⑫

National War Memorial ◆

①

①

Pirie St.

⑦

A B C D E F

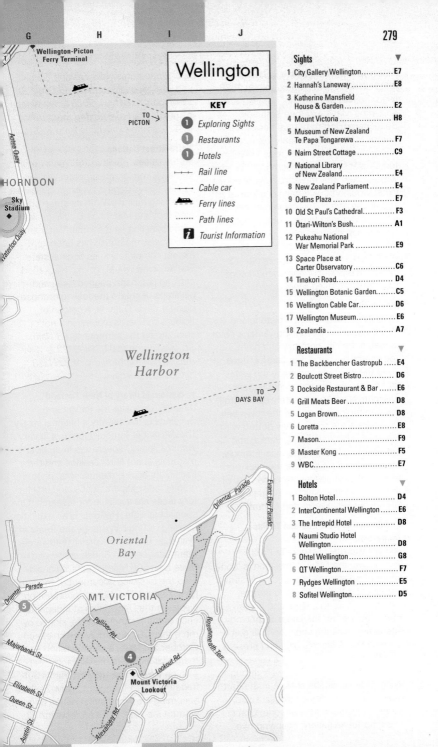

Wellington

KEY

- **1** Exploring Sights
- **1** Restaurants
- **1** Hotels
- Rail line
- Cable car
- Ferry lines
- Path lines
- **ℹ** Tourist Information

Katherine Mansfield House & Garden

HISTORIC HOME | The writer, born in 1888, lived the first five years of her life here. Katherine Mansfield (née Kathleen Beauchamp) left to pursue her career in Europe when she was only 20, but many of her short stories take place in Wellington. A year before her death in 1923, she wrote, "New Zealand is in my very bones. What wouldn't I give to have a look at it!" The house, which has been restored as a typical Victorian family home, contains furnishings, photographs, and videos that elucidate Mansfield's life and times. ⊠ 25 Tinakori Rd., Thorndon ☎ 04/473–7268 ⊕ www.katherinemansfield.com ⌨ NZ$10 ⊘ Closed Mon.

Mount Victoria

VIEWPOINT | Placed atop a historic and trendy suburb is a stunning vantage point to watch the city both day and night. You can take a short, but careful, drive up to the lookouts and enjoy the vistas that sweep across the whole region. Alternatively, take a leisurely uphill stroll through the pine forest of the town belt. These trails are sporadically dotted with outlooks, mountain biking tracks, and creatively crafted playgrounds. Fittingly, its tall twisted trees were the backdrop to a number of scenes from the Lord of the Rings trilogy, which are signposted. ⊠ Lookout Rd., Wellington Central.

★ Museum of New Zealand Te Papa Tongarewa

HISTORY MUSEUM | FAMILY | Te Papa Tongarewa (the Māori translation is "container of treasures") provides an essential introduction to the country's people, cultures, landforms, flora, and fauna. Bringing together the latest technology, interactive exhibits, and storytelling, it shares New Zealand's past and present. Whether you want to enter a carved *marae* (Māori meetinghouse), walk through living native bush, be shaken in the Earthquake House, or see a colossal squid, there's inspiration for everyone. Don't miss the **Toi Art gallery**; spanning two floors, it features New Zealand, Pacific, and international works. ⊠ 55 Cable St., Wellington ☎ 04/381–7000 ⊕ www.tepapa.govt.nz ⌨ Free; guided tours from NZ$20; some exhibitions from NZ$15.

Nairn Street Cottage

HISTORIC HOME | Built in 1858 as a family home by immigrant carpenter William Wallis, this cottage is Wellington's oldest remaining building. With its steep shingled roof and matchboard ceilings, kauri wood paneling, and somber Victorian wallpapers, the house has been kept almost completely in its original state. The spinning wheel, smoke-blackened cooking pot, hand-pegged rugs, and oil lamps re-create the feeling of those pioneer days. Outside, a garden of flowers and herbs blooms in a riot of color during the summer. ⊠ 68 Nairn St., Wellington ☎ 04/384–9122 ⊕ www.museumswellington.org.nz ⌨ NZ$8 ⊘ Closed weekdays.

★ National Library of New Zealand

LIBRARY | Opposite the Parliament Buildings is the country's national library. The Alexander Turnbull Library, a "library within a library," specializes in archival materials about New Zealand and the Pacific. Its books, manuscripts, photographs, newspapers, maps, and oral history tapes are available for research. One special highlight, He Tohu, is an exhibition housing Te Tiriti o Waitangi, the Treaty of Waitangi. This controversial 1840 agreement between the British crown and more than 500 Māori chiefs is considered the founding document of modern New Zealand. The oldest document on display is the Declaration of Independence of the Northern Chiefs, signed by more than 30 northern Māori chiefs on October 28, 1835, a confederation agreement that led up to the Waitangi treaty. Also on view is the 1893 Women's Suffrage Petition, which led to New Zealand becoming the world's first nation to grant women the vote. ⊠ 58 Molesworth St.,

The Museum of New Zealand Te Papa Tongarewa holds a wide variety of treasures documenting the country's cultural and natural history.

Thorndon ☎ *04/474–3000* ⊕ *www.natlib.govt.nz* 🎟 *Free* ⊘ *Closed Sun.*

New Zealand Parliament

GOVERNMENT BUILDING | The buildings that make up the Parliament complex include Parliament House with its Debating Chamber, a copy of the one in the British House of Commons right down to the Speakers Mace. Here legislation is presented, debated, and voted on. There is fine Māori artwork in the Māori Affairs Select Committee Room. The adjoining building is the Parliamentary Library. The neighboring Executive Wing is known for architectural reasons as The Beehive; it's where the prime minister and cabinet ministers of the elected government have their offices and hold cabinet meetings. Across the road at the corner of Whitmore Street and Lambton Quay, the Old Government Buildings, the largest wooden structure in New Zealand, is now home to Victoria University's law faculty. Tours start in The Beehive, and a guide explains the parliamentary process in detail. ✉ *1 Museum St., Wellington*

☎ *04/817–9503* ⊕ *www.parliament.nz* 🎟 *Free.*

Odlins Plaza

PLAZA/SQUARE | As the heart of the waterfront, the beat of Odlins drum depends on the season. In summer, the plaza is lined with market stalls and food trucks. Springtime sees many an art installation or pop-up theater battle the waterfront winds. In the colder months, food stalls return with warmer fare to feed ice skaters, sauna-goers, and the odd brave ocean diver. The plaza is also a great central location where the Museum of New Zealand Te Papa Tongarewa, the City Gallery, and Mount Victoria are all in easy reach. ✉ *21 Cable St., Wellington Central.*

Old St. Paul's Cathedral

CHURCH | Consecrated in 1866 in a style dubbed Colonial Gothic, the church is a splendid example of the English Gothic Revival style executed entirely in native timbers. Even the trusses supporting the roof transcend their mundane function with splendid craftsmanship. ✉ *34*

Mulgrave St., Thorndon ☎ *04/473–6722* ⊕ *www.oldstpauls.co.nz* ✉ *Free.*

Ōtari-Wilton's Bush

GARDEN | Devoted to gathering and preserving indigenous plants, Ōtari's collection is the largest of its kind. With clearly marked bushwalks and landscape demonstration gardens, it aims to educate the public and ensure the survival of New Zealand's unique plant life. While in the garden, you'll learn to identify forest plants, from the various *blechnum* ferns underfoot to the tallest trees overhead. An aerial walkway crosses high above the bush, giving an unusual vantage point over the gardens. Look and listen for the native birds that flock to this haven: the bellbird (*korimako*), New Zealand wood pigeon (*kereru*), and parson bird (*tūī*) among others. Take the No. 14 Wilton bus from downtown (20 minutes) and ask the driver to let you off at the gardens. ✉ *160 Wilton Rd., Wilton* ☎ *04/475–3245* ✉ *Free.*

Pukeahu National War Memorial Park

CITY PARK | This appropriately monumental space around the National War Memorial is the base for remembrance of New Zealand's experience in war. At the foot of the Tomb of the Unknown Warrior towers the carillon, whose bells ring across this city and echo in the memorial's Hall of Memories. Beyond the steps of the memorial is a wide plaza with reflective artworks and historical information. ✉ *Buckle St., Wellington Central* ⊕ *www.mch.govt.nz/ pukeahu-national-war-memorial-park.*

Space Place at Carter Observatory

OBSERVATORY | FAMILY | Lie back and watch an almost limitless range of virtual space journeys in the planetarium, or, on a clear night, view the heavens through the observatory telescope. Such experiences—plus state-of-the-art displays and a remarkable collection of artifacts that includes the oldest working telescope of its kind in the country—make this a popular stop. The observatory is only a two-minute walk from the top of the Kelburn Cable Car, and you can also wander up from the botanical gardens. ✉ *40 Salamanca Rd., Wellington* ☎ *04/910– 3140* ⊕ *www.museumswellington.org. nz* ✉ *NZ$14* ⊙ *Closed Mon., Wed., and Thurs.*

Tinakori Road

NEIGHBORHOOD | The lack of suitable local stone, combined with the collapse of most of Wellington's brick buildings in the earthquake of 1848, ensured the almost-exclusive use of timber for building here in the second half of the 19th century. Most carpenters of the period had learned their skills as cabinetmakers and shipwrights in Europe, and the sturdy houses on this street are a tribute to their craftsmanship. A few notables are the tall and narrow No. 304, Premier House, and the little doll-like cottages along the adjoining **Ascot Street**.

Wellington Botanic Garden

GARDEN | FAMILY | In the hills overlooking downtown is a concentration of splendidly varied terrain and forest. Native woodlands fill the garden's valleys, water-loving plants line its mountain streams, and the lawns brightly flourish with seasonal and annual blooms. The lovely **Lady Norwood Rose Garden** is in the northeast part of the garden. On a fine summer day, you couldn't find a better place to enjoy the fragrance of magnificent flowers. This rose garden is the most popular part of the Wellington Botanic Garden. Situated on a plateau, the formal circular layout consists of 110 beds, each planted with a single variety of modern and traditional shrubs. Climbing roses cover a brick-and-timber colonnade on the perimeter. Adjacent to the rose beds, the **Begonia House** conservatory is filled with delicate plants. If you don't want to walk up the hill, the Kelburn Cable Car can take you. Or catch the No. 2 bus (direction: Karori from Lambton Quay to the main (Glenmore Street) entrance. ✉ *Upland Rd. and Glenmore St., parking lot on Tinakori*

Rd., Wellington ☎ *04/499–1400* 🌐 *www.wellingtongardens.nz* 🎟 *Free.*

Wellington Cable Car

TRANSPORTATION | **FAMILY** | The Swiss-built funicular railway makes a short-but-sharp climb from among the shops on Lambton Quay to the highest point in the Wellington Botanic Gardens, the Kelburn Terminal. Once up there, you get great views across parks and city buildings to Port Nicholson. Sit on the left side during the six-minute journey for the best scenery. At the top, a small **Cable Car Museum** in the old winding house has a free display of restored cable cars and a splendid gift shop. ✉ *280 Lambton Quay, at Grey St. and Upland Rd., Wellington* ☎ *04/472–2199* 🌐 *www.wellingtoncablecar.co.nz* 🎟 *From NZ$5 (one-way).*

Wellington Museum

HISTORY MUSEUM | **FAMILY** | Smell the burlap sacks, hear the gulls, and see the (mechanical) rats scuttling around in this refurbished 1892 bond store, now a museum that portrays the history of the original Māori tribes and the European settlers who arrived around 1840. The displays cover work, leisure, crime, and education in Wellington. A steampunk-themed fourth-floor attic is not to be missed with its weird and wonderful exhibits. ✉ *The Bond Store, 3 Jervois Quay, Queens Wharf, Wellington* ☎ *04/472–8904* 🌐 *www.museumswellington.org.nz* 🎟 *Free.*

★ Zealandia

NATURE PRESERVE | **FAMILY** | Just minutes from downtown Wellington, more than 500 acres of forest have been transformed into a unique safe-haven for New Zealand's most endangered native species. A specially designed fence creates a cage-free eco-sanctuary for species that had disappeared from the mainland. Tuatara, New Zealand's unique "living fossil," are breeding, as are takahē and saddleback, which have both been brought back from the brink of extinction. Pick up a map and explore at your leisure, or join a 2-hour guided tour. The flashlight-led nighttime tour is very popular; departing about 30 minutes before sunset, it provides a glimpse into the nocturnal world—you might even spy a little spotted kiwi. ✉ *53 Waiapu Rd., Karori* ☎ *04/920–9213* 🌐 *www.visitzealandia.com* 🎟 *NZ$22; tours from NZ$55.*

🍴 Restaurants

The Backbencher Gastropub

$$$ | **NEW ZEALAND** | Right across the way from the Parliament buildings sits this landmark watering hole where politicians grab a cold beer after a hot debate. The walls have become a gallery of political cartoons and caricature puppets of government characters and well-known sports figures, while menu items are named after notable politicians. **Known for:** rubbing elbows with politicians; upscale pub cuisine; quirky decor. [$] *Average main: NZ$28* ✉ *34 Molesworth St., Wellington* ☎ *04/472–3065* 🌐 *www.backbencher.co.nz* 🕒 *Closed Sun.*

★ Boulcott Street Bistro

$$$$ | **BISTRO** | A well-respected institution on the Wellington dining scene, this old colonial-style house conveys tradition and class. The delightful bistro menu features long-standing dishes like the aged beef fillet with béarnaise sauce. **Known for:** simple yet well-rounded menu; excellent wine selection; cozy intimate setting. [$] *Average main: NZ$39* ✉ *99 Boulcott St., Wellington* ☎ *04/499–4199* 🌐 *www.boulcottstreetbistro.co.nz* 🕒 *No lunch Sat. and Sun.*

Dockside Restaurant & Bar

$$$$ | **NEW ZEALAND** | A wood-beam roof and oiled floorboards enhance the nautical vibe at this former warehouse on the wharf, and you can get close to the water on the large harborfront deck. Inside or out, it's a lively spot, particularly on Friday nights, and as expected, the menu features a broad range of fresh seafood. **Known for:** busy weekend nights;

Visitors dine alfresco in Courtenay Place, Wellington's entertainment center.

five-course degustation menu (book well in advance); prime waterfront location. $ *Average main: NZ$35* ✉ *Shed 3, Queens Quay, Jervois Quay, Wellington* ☎ *04/499–9900* ⊕ *www.dockside.co.nz.*

Grill Meats Beer
$$$ | BURGER | A relaxed and fun place to enjoy conversation and good food, the focus here is on the casual beer drinker rather than the aficionado. Each dish has a recommended beer to go with it; if you want to try something out of your comfort zone, staff are trained to help you expand your palate. **Known for:** chipotle-braised brisket fries; local sustainable produce; excellent beer pairings. $ *Average main: NZ$25* ✉ *227 Cuba St., Wellington* ☎ *04/801–8787* ⊕ *www. grillmeatsbeer.co.nz* ⊘ *Closed Mon. and Tues.*

★ Logan Brown
$$$$ | NEW ZEALAND | The imposing exterior and classical interior of this former bank building showcase the fact that this Wellington stalwart delivers exceptional dining in an unpretentious way. The menu highlights New Zealand's produce and exemplary wines; knowledgeable and friendly staff talk you through each dish, and there's an early bistro menu or a longer degustation menu if you want to make a night of it. **Known for:** local and sustainable ingredients; *paua* (abalone) ravioli; seven-course menu on Saturday. $ *Average main: NZ$40* ✉ *192 Cuba St., Wellington* ☎ *04/801–5114* ⊕ *www.logan-brown.co.nz* ⊘ *Closed Mon. and Tues.*

★ Loretta
$$$ | NEW ZEALAND | FAMILY | Adorned with its earthy-chic accents and wide wooden tables, Loretta makes a daily, but effortless transformation from a relaxed brunch spot to a bustling candle-lit restaurant. With their famously daily-evolving menu, brunches typically begin with smoothies and spritzers, waffles, and crumpets, each served with seasonal fruits. **Known for:** an extensive wine list available by the glass; daily-changing menu; an easy-going atmosphere great for families. $ *Average main: NZ$28* ✉ *181 Cuba St., Wellington Central*

☎ 04/384–2213 ⊕ www.loretta.net.nz
🕓 Closed Mon.

Mason

$$$$ | **MIDDLE EASTERN** | Tucked away in a nook of suburban Newtown, the deceptive frontage suggests Mason offers little else beyond a trendy wine bar. However, once you look beyond the local and organic wine and beer lists, you'll also find a celebration of Middle Eastern and Mediterranean cuisine. **Known for:** locally celebrated chef Matt Hawkes; friendly and attentive service; humming atmosphere. $ *Average main: NZ$35* ✉ 3 Wilson St., Newtown ⊕ barmason.co.nz 🕓 Closed Sun.–Tues. No lunch.

Master Kong

$$$ | **ASIAN** | **FAMILY** | Reveling in the lively waterfront atmosphere, Master Kong has a vibrant, fun, and sometimes spicy personality, both in its cuisine and its decor. The menu covers the most-beloved Asian street foods, ranging from fresh sake-cured salmon bites, to flavorful fusion-style dumplings, to Korean barbecue banquets. **Known for:** extravagant and creative cocktails; Peking duck pancake feast; bright and lively waterfront location. $ *Average main: NZ$25* ✉ 33 Customhouse Quay, Wellington Central ☎ 04/471–1776 ⊕ www.masterkong. co.nz.

WBC

$$$$ | **ASIAN FUSION** | An art-deco-era factory floor is now a popular fusion restaurant and local institution. Enjoying the large, elegant windows from its predecessor, WBC's dining hall has an open and airy atmosphere that balances the lively bustle from the open kitchen. **Known for:** excellent fresh seafood bar; sun-soaked art deco dining space; Asian-influenced menu. $ *Average main: NZ$39* ✉ 1st Floor., 107 Victoria St., Wellington Central ☎ 04/499–9379 ⊕ www.wbcrestaurant. co.nz 🕓 Closed Sun. and Mon.

 Hotels

Bolton Hotel

$$$ | **HOTEL** | Well-known to upscale business travelers, this independently owned hotel is great for extended stays, with some rooms containing full kitchen facilities and washer/dryers. **Pros:** large suites; lovely decor; quiet location. **Cons:** limited parking; some rooms overlook an old cemetery; no harbor views from most rooms. $ *Rooms from: NZ$269* ✉ 12 Bolton St., Wellington ☎ 04/472–9966 ⊕ www.boltonhotel.co.nz ❙⊙❙ No Meals ➷ 139 rooms.

InterContinental Wellington

$$$ | **HOTEL** | In the heart of the business district and a stone's throw from the waterfront, this landmark high-rise gets the details right. **Pros:** extra amenities like on-site spa; central location; great restaurant and lobby bar. **Cons:** gets expensive around events; some rooms have views of office buildings; can get booked up with corporate functions. $ *Rooms from: NZ$215* ✉ 2 Grey St., Wellington ☎ 04/472–2722 ⊕ www.intercontinental. com ➷ 236 rooms ❙⊙❙ No Meals.

The Intrepid Hotel

$$$ | **HOTEL** | Offering luxury loft-style rooms, the Intrepid Hotel brings home comforts to your inner-city stay. **Pros:** great central location; attentive and friendly service; modern and cozy loft-style decor. **Cons:** can be affected by loud street noise; some rooms lack views; smaller corridors, typical of heritage buildings. $ *Rooms from: NZ$280* ✉ 60 Ghuznee St., Wellington Central ☎ 04/830–0996 ⊕ www.theintrepidhotel. com ❙⊙❙ No Meals ➷ 18 rooms.

★ Naumi Studio Hotel Wellington

$$$ | **HOTEL** | With its stately heritage facade hiding a colorful whimsical interior, you'd think you've stumbled onto a set of a Wes Anderson film. **Pros:** brilliant bar and lounge area; strikingly exciting decor; attentive and friendly service. **Cons:** can be affected by loud street noise; smaller

rooms, typical of heritage buildings; some rooms lack views. [$] *Rooms from: NZ$220* ✉ *213-223 Cuba St., Wellington Central* ☎ *04/913–1800* 🌐 *www.naumihotels.com* 🍴 *No Meals* 🛏 *116 rooms.*

Ohtel Wellington

$$$ | **HOTEL** | In the iconic waterfront neighborhood of Oriental Bay, this boutique hotel is tailored to hose who enjoy a personalized and luxurious experience. **Pros:** attentive hosts; stylishly curated interior; quiet surroundings. **Cons:** some rooms not easily accessible for wheelchairs; not all rooms have waterfront views; brunch not served Monday and Tuesday. [$] *Rooms from: NZ$251* ✉ *66 Oriental Parade, Wellington* ☎ *04/803–0600* 🌐 *www.ohtel.nz* 🍴 *No Meals* 🛏 *10 rooms.*

★ **QT Wellington**

$$$ | **HOTEL** | With bold art on display everywhere you look, this hotel is for the hip and trendy. **Pros:** well-appointed rooms; wonderfully walkable location; one of the best restaurants in the city. **Cons:** some guests will be put off by the choice of art; can be affected by loud street noise; city-side rooms lack views. [$] *Rooms from: NZ$269* ✉ *90 Cable St., Wellington* ☎ *04/802–8900* 🌐 *www.qthotels.com* 🛏 *179 rooms* 🍴 *No Meals.*

Rydges Wellington

$$$ | **HOTEL** | Situated near several major Wellington landmarks, including the waterfront, this hotel makes navigating the city a breeze. **Pros:** indoor heated lap pool; upper-level suites enjoy beautiful harbor views; complimentary snacks served between 5 pm and 6 pm. **Cons:** poor views from many rooms; foyer bar can be crowded with locals; street front is a wind tunnel in bad weather. [$] *Rooms from: NZ$299* ✉ *75 Featherston St., Wellington* ☎ *04/499–8686* 🌐 *www.rydges.com* 🍴 *No Meals* 🛏 *280 rooms.*

Sofitel Wellington

$$ | **HOTEL** | In celebration of its proximity to the Wellington Botanic Garden, this sophisticated hotel has a strong but subtle floral theme throughout the rooms and shared spaces. **Pros:** large rooms with comfortable beds; excellent gym; lovely modern decor. **Cons:** no pool; limited parking; some rooms face an old cemetery. [$] *Rooms from: NZ$190* ✉ *11 Bolton St., Wellington* ☎ *04/472–2001* 🌐 *www.sofitel-wellington.com* 🛏 *129 rooms* 🍴 *No Meals.*

Nightlife

Wellington's after-dark scene splits between several main areas. The "alternative" set spends its time at **Cuba and Ghuznee streets'** funky gastropubs, bars, and cocktail lounges, which stay open until around 1 am during the week and about 3 am or later on weekends; cocktails are innovative, and the music is not top-40 radio.

Courtenay Place is home to the traditional drinking action with a selection of pubs, sports bars, and a few upscale establishments. It's packed on Friday and Saturday nights, especially when a rugby game is on, and the streets fill with beery couples in their late teens and early twenties lining up to get plastered (New Zealand's legal drinking age is 18).

In the **downtown business district**—between Lambton Quay and Manners Street—a couple of brewpubs and a few taverns cater to the after-work mob. Down by the harbor, a flashy corporate crowd hangs out in several warehouse-style bars, sipping martinis on weeknights and filling the dance floor on weekends.

BARS

CGR Merchant & Co.

COCKTAIL LOUNGES | Trading in uniquely infused rums and gins, this modern and cozy pirate den serves delicious, and sometimes unexpected, tipple treasures.

Did You Know?

Matiu/Somes Island in
Wellington Harbour was
a human and livestock
quarantine station until
1980 and served as an
internment camp during
both World Wars. Today
it is a tranquil wildlife
preserve with native
birds, reptiles, and plants.

44 Courtenay Pl., Floor 1, Wellington Central ☎ *04/384–6737* ⊕ *www.cgrmerchant.co.nz* ⊙ *Closed Mon. and Tues.*

Fortune Favours

BREWPUBS | Beckoning passers-by to the celebrated Hannah's Laneway, Fortune "favours" their patrons with a welcoming atmosphere, great food, and a huge range of craft beer, some of which is specially brewed on site. ⊠ *7 Leeds St., Wellington Central* ☎ *04/595–4092* ⊕ *www.fortunefavours.beer.*

Golding's Free Dive

BARS | With a comfortable but buzzing atmosphere and excellent beer selection, Golding's is a great place to spend an hour or two. There is geeky and Kiwi memorabilia on every wall. It's especially nice for solo travelers, whether you want to mingle or sit quietly and read. There's no food menu, but you can get some of the best pizza in town delivered from the pizza parlor next door. ⊠ *14 Leeds St., Wellington* ☎ *04/381–3616* ⊕ *www. goldingsfreedive.co.nz.*

Havana Bar

BARS | Find Havana's two iconic colorful cottages just off Cuba Street, walk down between them, and you'll find two doors. The quieter cottage on the left is their brilliant tapas restaurant. On the right, there's a well-stocked bar extending the length of the wooden dance floor. This spot is regularly packed when the jazz, rhythm, and funk musicians come to visit. For quieter drinks, you can cozy into a nook of the sheltered street-styled courtyard. ⊠ *32a-34 Wigan St., Wellington Central* ☎ *04/384–7039* ⊕ *www. havanabar.co.nz* ⊙ *Closed Sun. and Mon.*

Malthouse

PUBS | Modern with polished wood and plate glass aplenty, Malthouse's long bar with illuminated lettering is an attractive place to drink a pint. With 29 taps, the only problem is deciding where to start. ⊠ *48 Courtenay Pl., Wellington*

☎ *04/802–5484* ⊕ *www.themalthouse. co.nz.*

★ Night Flower

COCKTAIL LOUNGES | This hidden speakeasy offers special punches, crafted cocktails, and impeccable service. Look for the lion-head door knocker. ⊠ *55 Ghuznee St., Floor 1, Wellington Central* ☎ *04/385–4425.*

Whistling Sisters Brewery and Fermentery

BREWPUBS | Skipping away from the "hoppy" trend, the sisters brew cleaner craft beer. Their fermenting talents also extend to their menu of elevated versions of bar food. ⊠ *100 Taranaki St., Wellington Central* ☎ *04/381–3208* ⊕ *www.whistlingsisters.co.nz* ⊙ *Closed Mon.*

LIVE MUSIC AND DANCE CLUBS

★ The Rogue and Vagabond

LIVE MUSIC | With its bean bag lawn, wood-fired pizzas, and craft beers on tap, Rogue is the focal point for the city's summertime hum. When the sun goes down, it's the brilliant live funk, jazz, and pop shows that keep the patrons around. Find their packed schedule on their website or on the chalkboards outside. ⊠ *18 Garrett St., Wellington Central* ☎ *04/381–2321* ⊕ *www.rogueandvagabond.co.nz.*

San Fran

LIVE MUSIC | Upstairs from a small poster-plastered doorway is the capital's iconic chameleon cavern of a venue. This Cuba Street spot stages everything, including international metal bands, local comedians, sonic "experiences," and psychedelic blues groups. San Fran has perfected the essentials: a big bar, a vast dance floor, and great sound. ⊠ *171 Cuba St., Floor 1, Wellington Central* ☎ *04/801–6797* ⊕ *www.sanfran.co.nz* ⊙ *Closed Sun. and Mon.*

🎭 Performing Arts

For current event listings in Wellington, check the entertainment section of the *Dominion Post,* Wellington's daily newspaper. The website for Wellington Tourism (*www.WellingtonNZ.com*) also has up-to-date entertainment listings, covering everything from movies to theater and music. Buy tickets at Ticketek (*www.ticketek.co.nz*), situated in the Wellington i-SITE on Wakefield Street.

Bats Theatre

THEATER | Wellington's long-standing source for experimental, sometimes off-the-wall theater hosts a range of performances throughout the year, including stand-up, dance, and theater. There are three performance spaces and a small bar on site. ⊠ *1 Kent Terr., Te Aro* ☎ *04/802–4175* ⊕ *www.bats.co.nz.*

Circa Theatre

THEATER | Catch contemporary New Zealand pieces along with established masterworks from Harold Pinter to Oscar Wilde. It's on the wharf next to the Museum of New Zealand Te Papa Tongarewa. ⊠ *1 Taranaki St., Wellington* ☎ *04/801–7992* ⊕ *www.circa.co.nz.*

Michael Fowler Centre

ARTS CENTERS | Named after a former long-standing mayor, this venue regularly hosts shows ranging from the New Zealand Ballet to orchestral and pop concerts. ⊠ *111 Wakefield St., Wellington* ☎ *04/801–4207* ⊕ *www.venueswellington.com.*

Opera House

THEATER | Wellington's century-old Opera House has plush carpets and tiered seating. As the capital's main mid-size venue, its line-up consists of stage performances, musicals, and international comedy. ⊠ *111–113 Manners St., Wellington* ☎ *04/801–4231* ⊕ *www.venueswellington.com.*

TSB Arena

CONCERTS | Headlining tours head to this large indoor venue on the waterfront. ⊠ *Jervois Quay, Wellington* ☎ *04/801–4207* ⊕ *www.venueswellington.com.*

🧳 Shopping

The main downtown shopping area is the so-called **Golden Mile**—from Lambton Quay up to Willis and Victoria streets. Here you'll find department stores, designer clothes, shoes, books, outdoor gear, and souvenirs. For smaller, funkier boutiques, visit Cuba Street.

BOOKS

Arty Bee's Books

BOOKS | This friendly and locally owned store sells new and second-hand books with a strong focus on New Zealand fiction and nonfiction. ⊠ *The Oaks, 106 Manners St., Wellington* ☎ *04/384–5339* ⊕ *www.artybees.co.nz.*

Unity Books

BOOKS | Find a generous supply of New Zealand and Māori literature in this bright and spacious independent store. ⊠ *57 Willis St., Wellington* ☎ *04/499–4245* ⊕ *www.unitybooks.nz.*

CLOTHING AND ACCESSORIES

Deadly Ponies

HANDBAGS | Based on the gorgeous decor alone, this store focused on leather accessories is well worth a visit. The leather in their products is all ethically and locally sourced. ⊠ *28 Ghuznee St., Wellington* ☎ *04/802–5511* ⊕ *www.deadlyponies.com.*

Good As Gold

MIXED CLOTHING | Laidback streetwear meets high fashion in this independent family-owned store. It mixes some of the best-known global brands with local labels, so you'll find shelves well-stocked with the latest trends in clothing, sneakers, and accessories. ⊠ *20 Bond St., Wellington Central* ☎ *04/381–4653* ⊕ *www.goodasgoldshop.com.*

Jane Daniels

WOMEN'S CLOTHING | Here is a comprehensive range of Jane Daniels's New Zealand ladies' fashions. All pieces are locally manufactured from European fabrics. ⊠ *97c Customhouse Quay, Wellington*

☎ 04/473–7400 ⊕ www.janedaniels.co.nz ⊙ Closed Sun. and Mon.

Zambesi

MIXED CLOTHING | Well-established New Zealand designer Elisabeth Findlay whips up innovative and extremely wearable clothes. ✉ 103 Customhouse Quay, Wellington ☎ 04/472–3638 ⊕ www.zambesistore.co.nz.

DEPARTMENT STORE AND MALLS

David Jones

DEPARTMENT STORE | Locals were initially resistant to the arrival of this Australian giant, but they quickly came around when exposed to its range of high-end brands previously unavailable in Wellington. Featuring a lovely early-19th-century facade, this three-level department store is an absolute must for the discriminating shopper. There is a wide range of women's and men's fashion, perfume, household goods, and more. ✉ 165 Lambton Quay, Wellington ☎ 04/912–0700 ⊕ www.davidjones.com.

Old Bank Arcade

MALL | The Old Bank Arcade sits in the iconic neoclassical walls of the former Bank of New Zealand. The arcade is something of a fashion enclave, containing a slew of well-known boutiques, including New Zealand designers Taylor, Ricochet, and Ruby. There is classic jewelry at The Gold Exchange and delicious handmade sweets at de Spa Chocolatier. ✉ 233–237 Lambton Quay, at Customhouse Quay and Willis St., Wellington ☎ 04/922–0600 ⊕ www.oldbank.co.nz.

Victoria Street

MALL | Top New Zealand and local Wellington labels line Victoria Street and its little **Lombard Laneway**. Find phenomenal fragrances at World, chic and understated leather bags at Yu Mei, and luxury lingerie at Lonely. Further fashion can be found at Wilson Trollope, St. Fabiola, Juliette Hogan, Kilt, and Karen Walker's Playpark. Luckily, there are great coffee shops nearby to take a rest from retail therapy.

✉ Victoria St. and Lombard La., Wellington Central.

MARKETS

★ Harbourside Market

MARKET | **FAMILY** | On Sunday, between 7:30 am and 1 pm, folks flock to this outdoor food market on the waterfront. Organic produce, cheese, fresh fish and meats are the main draws. There's also a plethora of food trucks serving coffee and international street food. ✉ At Cable and Barnett Sts., Wellington ⊕ www.harboursidemarket.co.nz.

OUTDOOR EQUIPMENT

Gordon's Outdoors

SPORTING GOODS | This spot sells camping gear and outdoor clothing from international brands as well as footwear. ✉ Corner of Cuba and Wakefield Sts., Wellington ☎ 04/499–8894.

Kathmandu

SPORTING GOODS | Wellington is a fine place to stock up on camping supplies before hitting the great outdoors. Kathmandu carries its house brand of clothing and equipment. ✉ 1 Willis St., Wellington ☎ 04/472–0113 ⊕ www.kathmandu.co.nz.

SOUVENIRS

Kura Gallery

SOUVENIRS | Part gallery, part gift store, this establishment has a strong contemporary Māori current running through its merchandise. Some of the smaller, less-expensive items make unique souvenirs. ✉ 19 Allen St., Wellington ☎ 04/802–4934 ⊕ www.kuragallery.co.nz.

Greater Wellington

Located beside the airport, the movie-making town of Miramar sits 9 km (6 miles) southeast of Wellington. Extending north of the city, the Hutt Valley begins at the bay of Petone, 14 km (9 miles) from central Wellington, and stretches to Upper Hutt, 34 km (21 miles) from

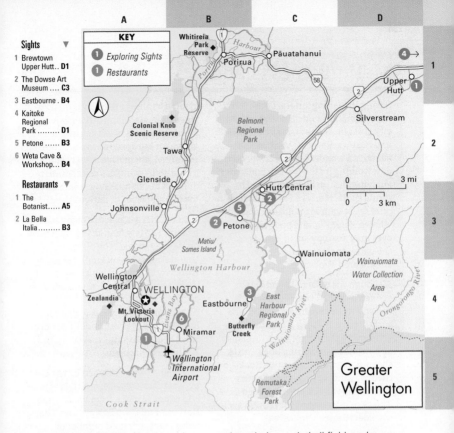

central Wellington. The southeast road from Petone leads to Eastbourne, a 24-km (15-mile) drive from the city.

Sights

★ Brewtown Upper Hutt

BREWERY | FAMILY | This sprawling tipple-town is an embodiment of a sunny summer's afternoon feeling. Brewtown is conveniently within walking distance from Upper Hutt train station. On site are five award-winning breweries and a whisky distillery, spread around a large green of picnic tables on which to enjoy the vast menus of elevated bar food. Guided tours are available and are a great way to get a behind-the-scenes look and taste of the best in town. All five senses, not just taste, are stimulated at Brewtown: also on-site is a raceway, an ice skating rink, a ten-pin bowling alley, a large trampoline

park, an indoor paintball field, and a multiplayer VR gaming station! Essentially a massive playground, Brewtown is incredibly family-friendly, so everyone can join the fun. ⊠ *23 Blenheim St., Upper Hutt* ⊕ *www.brewtown.co.nz* ☏ *NZ$165 for guided tours.*

The Dowse Art Museum

ART MUSEUM | FAMILY | Near Petone, this museum stages a changing array of exhibitions—including ones focused on extraordinary jewelry, fashion, photography, and ceramics—that showcase the creativity of New Zealand's artisans. ⊠ *45 Laings Rd., Lower Hutt* ☏ *04/570–6500* ⊕ *www.dowse.org.nz* ☏ *Free* ⊗ *Closed Mon.*

Eastbourne

NEIGHBORHOOD | FAMILY | From Petone, a winding road leads south about 10 km (6 miles) to the suburb of Eastbourne.

Matiu/Somes Island

Sitting in Wellington Harbour approximately 8 km (5 miles) from the city is Matiu/Somes Island Scientific and Historic Reserve. Visiting the island is a wonderful way to spend a day, walking its lively bush trails and enjoying the unrivaled views of its picnic spots. Many of the trails also offer great vantage points to spot whales, dolphins, and penguins. Sharp eyes may also spy small lizards on the paths, including the ancient and endangered Tuatara.

Although the 62-acre island was opened as a DOC reserve in 1995, it has an interesting history. From the early 1880s until 1980 it was used as a quarantine station for both humans and animals—including dogs, cattle, sheep, llamas, and other livestock—on their way into the country. During both world wars, it was also used as a place of internment for immigrants considered a security threat.

In 1981, Matiu/Somes Island became a project of the Royal Forest and Bird Protection Society. Volunteers began planting trees that year to replace vegetation that had previously been cleared to allow grazing for quarantined animals. Many other native plants that flourished before the arrival of Europeans have also been replanted, and native insects (such as the giant, wingless weta) reintroduced. The island is now a safe haven for many species of native fauna.

This is strictly a place to enjoy natural beauty. The few man-made structures on it today include the old quarantine station and gun emplacements from World War II—which were never used, and which remain on the southernmost summit of the island. An automated lighthouse, that was built in 1900, still sends out its southward beacon to ships traveling from Wellington Harbour.

The island can be reached by the East by West ferry service; multiple round-trip runs are made from Wellington Harbour and Days Bay per day. The boats carry a limited number of passengers to the island at a time, so it's never crowded. To enjoy the island coming alive at dusk, overnight camping and lodging options are available at *bookings.doc.govt.nz*.

Have an alfresco bite in its tiny shopping area before driving on to where the road eventually transforms into a 4-km (2½-mile) walking trail, following the coast to Pencarrow Head and its lighthouse, with views across the strait. There's a kiosk where you can rent a bike, or for more adventure, The Boatshed has kayaks and stand-up paddleboards for hire. ⊠ *Lower Hutt*.

Kaitoke Regional Park

FOREST | From Upper Hutt, continuing north on State Highway 2 takes you to the Wairarapa region. But if you have time to spare, stop into Kaitoke Regional Park. Just beyond Upper Hutt, it's a great camping and picnic spot with pleasant walks by the river. Lord of the Rings lovers can check out the corner of the forest that stood in for Rivendell, the great homeland of the elves. Trails, varying from 15-minute ambling loops to 3-hour hiking routes, all follow sections of the crystal-clear river, flanked by towering trees and native birdsong. ⊠ *Waterworks Rd., off State Hwy. 2, Upper Hutt* ☎ *0800/496–734 for rangers* ⊕ *www. gw.govt.nz/kaitoke* ⊠ *Free*.

Petone

TOWN | FAMILY | A 15-minute drive north of Wellington on State Highway 2—with magnificent harbor views all the way—leads you to the Hutt Valley and its namesake river. The Petone Esplanade, on the eastern side of the harbor, has good fishing from the wharf and is overlooked by houses clinging to steep bush-clad hills. On the waterfront, visit the small but interesting **Petone Settlers Museum**; it's open Wednesday through Sunday, 10–4. Housed in the historic Wellington Provincial Centennial Memorial building, the free museum stands near the 1840 landing site of New Zealand's first organized European settlement. Nearby, Jackson Street is home to many boutique shops and eateries. ✉ *Lower Hutt* ☎ *04/568–8373 museum* 🌐 *www.petonesettlers.org.nz* 🎟 *Free* 🕒 *Museum closed Mon. and Tues.*

★ **Weta Cave & Workshop**

FILM/TV STUDIO | FAMILY | The innovative designers and effects wizards at Weta have brought many high-profile movies to life. At Weta Cave, you get a fascinating "behind the scenes look" detailing the characters and equipment used in special effects for the Lord of the Rings and The Hobbit series, *Avatar, King Kong,* and many other award-winning films. Memorabilia (think models, limited-edition sculptures, books, posters, and T-shirts) is sold at the on-site shop. Departing from the Cave are your choice of two popular tours guided by industry experts. The workshop tour showcases original props, costumes, and the artists at work. The miniature effects tour explores how miniatures, lighting, and clever camerawork make for some of the most iconic shots in cinema history. You can also pre-book special interactive workshops to try your hand at sculpting, special effects make-up, and even making chain mail. ✉ *Corner of Weka St. and Camperdown Rd., Wellington* ☎ *04/909–4035* 🌐 *wetaworkshop.com* 🎟 *Cave free; guided tours from NZ$28; interactive workshops from NZ$69.*

🍴 Restaurants

The Botanist

$$$ | VEGETARIAN | FAMILY | Though right at home among the seaside cottages of Lyall Bay, this plant-based haven is anything but traditional. The Botanist offers tasty and innovative takes on traditionally meat-centered meals in a seasonally evolving menu. **Known for:** sheltered sunny courtyard; seaside views; 100% plant-based menu. [$] *Average main: NZ$22* ✉ *219 Onepu Rd., Wellington Central* ☎ *04/891–0198* 🌐 *thebotanistlyallbay.co.nz.*

★ **La Bella Italia**

$$$ | ITALIAN | FAMILY | On the otherwise sleepy Petone Wharf is a vibrant Italian trattoria, where prestigious awards, relics of family history, and shelves of the finest Italian ingredients cover the walls. This spot was awarded the prestigious Ospitalità Italiana quality-approved seal and is recognized as one of the top 70 Restaurants with Pizzeria in the World by Ristorazione Italiana. **Known for:** phenomenal salumeria; the award-winning bravo gubello salmon pizza; welcoming family atmosphere. [$] *Average main: NZ$26* ✉ *10 Nevis St., Petone* ☎ *04/566–9303* 🌐 *www.labellaitalia.co.nz* 🕒 *No dinner Mon. and Tues.*

🛍 Shopping

Whirlwind Design Store

SOUVENIRS | Let the wind blow you past the airport and into the movie-making suburb of Miramar. Here, local artists Nick Blake and Michelle Fyson specialize in making rustic-chic accessories for you, your home, and your garden. ✉ *9a Park Rd., Rongotai* 🌐 *www.whirlwinddesigns.com.*

Akatarawa Valley

40 km (25 miles) northeast of Wellington.

Winding through the steep bush-clad hills north of Wellington, the narrow road through Akatarawa Valley links the regions of Hutt Valley with the Kapiti Coast. Take care while driving this route. Akatarawa Road lives up to its namesake in the Māori language as a "place of tangled vines."

About 35 minutes north of Wellington on State Highway 2, turn left at the Brown Owl turnoff, north of Upper Hutt. About two minutes after the turnoff is Harcourt Park, terraced with picnic spot plateaus and playgrounds. The park was also used as a filming location for several scenes in the Lord of the Rings movies.

A kilometer (½ mile) farther on, a bridge spanning the junction of the Hutt and Akatarawa rivers leads into the heart of the Akatarawa Valley. Drive over the bridge, and look for the Bluebank Blueberry and Emu Farm on the left. Continue uphill on the winding road, and on the right is the Staglands Wildlife Reserve. From Staglands, it is around 7 km (4½ miles) to the summit, then the narrow road twists downhill. Look for the tiny wooden Church of St. Andrews and turn right immediately for the Reikorangi Potteries. The road continues for about 3 km (2 miles) and joins State Highway 1, where you can head back to Wellington; from here, you are about 45 minutes north of the city.

VISITOR INFORMATION

CONTACTS Upper Hutt i-SITE Visitor Information Centre. ⊠ *836 Fergusson Dr., Upper Hutt* ☎ *04/527–2168* ⊕ *www. huttvalleynz.com.*

 Sights

Bluebank Blueberry and Emu Farm

FARM/RANCH | FAMILY | This property produces delicious blueberries and is home to several emus, a large flightless bird. You can enter to visit the emus for free; you pay for the blueberries you pick (at a great rate). ⊠ *1301 Akatarawa Rd., Upper Hutt* ☎ *04/526–9540* ⊕ *www.bluebank. co.nz* ⊠ *Free* ⊗ *Closed Apr.–Dec.*

★ Staglands Wildlife Reserve

ZOO | FAMILY | Staglands offers visitors the opportunity to feed and freely interact with animals in a beautiful natural environment. As you wander around its 25 peaceful acres, you'll follow its weaving trails around rivers, forests, and paddocks. Take a tip-toe through the aviaries, and you'll be rewarded with famously funny encounters with the native kea and kaka parrots. At the stables, you'll meet goats, highland cows, and native *kunekune* pigs, who are always happy to exchange more petting for feed. If you want the complete cozy homestead experience, you can take a tractor-trailer ride or roast marshmallows on the outdoor fire pit. Be sure to also explore the nooks of the re-created Old Bush Settlement. Here, you may just stumble upon the whimsical wonderland of the secret garden. Take a climb to the Deer Park lookout and finish your visit with stunning views. ⊠ *2362 Akatarawa Rd., Upper Hutt* ☎ *04/526–7529* ⊕ *www. staglands.co.nz* ⊠ *NZ$24.*

Kapiti Coast

50 km (31 miles) north of Wellington.

A drive up the West Coast from Wellington is not to be missed. State Highway 1 leads you north, and at about 30 minutes out of the city, you see the coast at Paremata. From here you can continue on State Highway 1 straight up the Kapiti Coast, named for its view of Kapiti Island. Alternatively, you can take the longer—but infinitely more scenic—drive around the Pauatahanui Inlet, following the road along the ridge of the rugged, winding, and windy Paekakariki Hill, where stunning views of the coastline and Kapiti Island await. Both routes lead to Paekākāriki (pie-*kahk*-a-reeky), a small, artsy beach town.

VISITOR INFORMATION

CONTACTS Kapiti Coast Visitor Information. ✉ *Paraparaumu* ⊕ *www.kapiticoastnz. com.*

 ## Sights

Paekākāriki Escarpment Track

TRAIL | This 9.1 km (5.7 miles) cliffside trail has breathtaking views of the coast. With its step-climbs and swing bridges, this track is a little different from your typical "long walks on the beach." Most walkers drive to the Pukerua Bay Train station and catch the northbound train to the next stop, Paekākāriki, to walk the trail from north to south. ✉ *State Hwy. 1, Between Paekākāriki and Pukerua Bay, Paraparaumu.*

Queen Elizabeth Park

BEACH | FAMILY | Paekākāriki's draw is the shore, but it's also the main entry point for Queen Elizabeth Park. Covering more than 1,600 acres, the park is edged by sand dunes and swimmable beaches. Walking, horseback riding, and cycling are popular activities here. Of special interest is the WWII U.S. Marines memorial and display. ✉ *State Hwy. 1, Paraparaumu* ⊕ *www.gw.govt.nz/QEP.*

★ Southward Car Museum

OTHER MUSEUM | FAMILY | Housing the southern hemisphere's largest private car collection, this museum has more than 400 automobiles and 140 motorcycles, plus aircraft, vintage tools, and an old fire engine. Among the most popular are Marlene Dietrich's 1934 Cadillac Town Cabriolet, a 1915 Stutz Indianapolis race car, a gull-winged Mercedes-Benz, a 1950 Cadillac "Gangster Special" that had belonged to gangster Mickey Cohen, and an 1895 Benz Velo. ✉ *Otaihanga Rd., Paraparaumu* ☎ *04/297–1221* ⊕ *www. southwardcarmuseum.co.nz* ✉ *NZ$20.*

Kapiti Island

50 km (31 miles) north of Wellington and 5 km (3 miles) off the coast of Paraparaumu.

Paraparaumu is the departure point for one of Wellington's best-kept secrets: Kapiti Island. A protected reserve since 1897, the island is a fantastic place to hike. All pests have been eliminated from it, and birdlife—including saddlebacks, stitchbirds, and colonies of little spotted and South Island brown kiwi—is abundant. Don't be surprised if a curious and fearless *weka* bird investigates your day pack or unties your shoelaces. Climb to the Tuteremoana lookout point, which is more than 1,700 feet high, for stellar views.

The island's most famous inhabitant was Ngati Toa chief Te Rauparaha, who took the island by a ruse in 1822. From this stronghold, he launched bloodthirsty raids before he was captured in 1846. He died in 1849, but his burial place is a mystery. Old tri-pots (used for melting down whale blubber) on the island bear testimony to the fact that Kapiti was also used as a whaling station in the late 19th century.

The reserve is 5 km (3 miles) from the mainland. Sign on with a tour operator for the boat trip out; all depart from the Kapiti Boating Club, Paraparaumu Beach. Crossings are weather-dependent.

TOURS

Kapiti Explorer

GUIDED TOURS | This outfit offers scenic cruises to Kapiti, guided walks, and sea kayak trips around the island. Part of your admission fee goes to keeping Kapiti Island predator-free. ✉ *Kapiti Boating Club, Kapiti Rd., Paraparaumu* ☎ *04/866–2044* ⊕ *www.kapitiislandeco. co.nz* ✉ *Scenic cruise from NZ$80; guided walk from NZ$15; sea kayak combo from NZ$160.*

Kapiti Island Nature Tours

GUIDED TOURS | Sample genuine Māori hospitality with Kapiti Island Nature Tours. Options range from a day trip with an introductory talk, lunch, and a guided walk to an overnight stay with accommodations, three meals, and a kiwi-spotting night walk. Passage to the island and Department of Conservation park permits are included. ✉ *Kapiti Boating Club, Kapiti Rd., Paraparaumu* ☎ *0800/527–484* ⊕ *www.kapitiisland.com* ✉ *From NZ$184.*

Martinborough

70 km (44 miles) north of Wellington.

The pleasant town of Martinborough embodies the changes that have taken place in the Wairarapa as a result of the burgeoning wine industry. The town gets its name from its founder, John Martin, who, in 1881, laid out the streets in a union jack pattern, radiating from the square that forms the hub. Most restaurants and shops are on or close to the square.

To tap into the Wairarapa wine world, Martinborough is the place to come. More than 20 vineyards are within a few miles of it—an easy walk or bike ride to some and a pleasant drive to most.

GETTING HERE AND AROUND

During weekdays the roads are mostly quiet, ideal for cycling and relaxed motoring; however, driving on rural roads can be deceptive. Keep a sharp eye out for livestock movement—large herds of cattle or sheep can be just around that bend.

Weekends at virtually any time of the year can bring a flood of visitors. The first Saturday in February and March, the two Martinborough Fair Days, can see traffic jams for miles. On a good, sunny winter weekend, Wellington people regularly pop "over the hill" to sample a vineyard meal and a glass of vino. Plan your visit if you want to avoid the crowds.

VISITOR INFORMATION

CONTACTS Martinborough i-SITE Visitor Information Centre. ✉ *Corner of Cork and Texas Sts., The Square, Martinborough* ☎ *06/306–5010* ⊕ *www.wairarapanz.com.*

WHEN TO GO

The town's signature event, the **Martinborough Fair** (*www.martinboroughfair. org.nz*), packs the place with crafts stores and food stalls—regularly drawing crowds of thousands. The fair is typically held in the main square on the first Saturday of February and March; however, these dates can be subject to change, so be sure to check their website.

The **Toast Martinborough Wine, Food, and Music Festival** in November is also a major draw.

Sights

Ata Rangi Vineyard

WINERY | This family-owned and -managed winery makes exceptional chardonnay, sauvignon blanc, pinot noir, and Célèbre. For her hard work on the vines, Helen Masters won the 2019 title of New Zealand Winemaker of the Year. Tastings at their cellar door must be booked in advance through their website. ✉ *14 Puruatanga Rd., Martinborough* ☎ *06/306–9570* ⊕ *www.atarangi. co.nz* ✉ *Tastings free (with advance reservation).*

Cambridge Road

WINERY | With its eco-ethical philosophy, this winery produces high-quality wines using organic and biodynamic techniques. Try these natural and delicious wines for yourself on their sun-soaked porch alongside their well-paired platters. Tastings can be booked for any day of the week, or you can just walk in on the weekends. ✉ *32 Cambridge Rd., Martinborough* ☎ *06/306–8959* ⊕ *www. cambridgeroad.co.nz* ✉ *Tastings NZ$10.*

Olivo

FARM/RANCH | For a taste-bud-tickling exercise that doesn't involve grapes, head to Helen and John Meehan's olive grove, 3 km (2 miles) north of Martinborough. You can visit the grove and its 5 acres of gardens to learn how oils are produced. Tastings (and sales) of their extra-virgin and infused olive oils are encouraged. ✉ *136 Hinakura Rd., Martinborough* ☎ *06/306–9074* 🌐 *www.olivo.co.nz* 🎟 *Tours NZ$20* 🕒 *Closed weekdays Feb.–Dec.*

Palliser Estate

WINERY | Don't miss the white wines here—they're some of the best around. Of particular note is the sauvignon blanc, which is renowned for its intense ripe flavors, and the chardonnay, which is organically made in an elegant classic style. ✉ *76 Kitchener St., Martinborough* ☎ *06/306–9019* 🌐 *www.palliser.co.nz* 🎟 *Tastings NZ$5.*

★ Patuna Chasm Walk

TRAIL | Explore true backcountry New Zealand on a half-day trek. This four-hour hike starts with a typical Kiwi trail through native forest, before descending to the river floor. Here you'll discover the chasm's cathedral-like limestone halls and waterfalls. Be advised that most of the walk is in a river and can be steep or slippery. Pack a change of clothes and shoes for after the walk. Bookings are essential. ✉ *236 Haurangi Rd., Martinborough* ☎ *027/530–8883* 🌐 *www.patunafarm.co.nz* 🎟 *NZ$30* 🕒 *Closed Apr.–Nov.*

★ Poppies Martinborough

WINERY | Wine-lovers flock to Poppies for the stunning wines, picturesque views, and relaxed ambience. Their wines, crafted by old-world techniques, celebrate the beauty of simplicity and tradition. Visiting the tasting room, you can expect to sip on delectable wines paired with excellent platters, all while admiring the vineyard vista. Bookings are essential. ✉ *91 Puruatanga Rd, Martinborough* ☎ *06/306–8473* 🌐 *www.poppiesmartinborough.co.nz* 🎟 *Tastings NZ$10.*

Reid and Reid Craft Gin Distillery

DISTILLERY | The Reid brothers curate craft gins and vermouth from the unique flavors of New Zealand botanicals. Taste their range at their G&T garden bar, or contact them by email to take a tour through the distillery, which must be pre-booked through the company's web site. ✉ *145 Todds Rd., Martinborough* ✍ *admin@reidandreid.co.nz* 🌐 *www.reidandreid.co.nz.*

★ The Wine Bank

WINERY | For an all-weather, all-season exploration of Martinborough's vineyards, look no further than The Wine Bank. The Bank has an ATM-style automatic wine dispensary, a small kitchen, and a classy and comfortable lounge. The set-up makes for a relaxed experience, where you can select from over 60 local wines and try the ones you want, at your own pace. ✉ *1 Memorial Sq., Martinborough* ☎ *06/216–8276* 🌐 *www.thewinebank.nz* 🎟 *Free (you pay only for the wine you drink)* 🕒 *Closed Tues. and Wed.*

🍴 Restaurants

Tirohana Estate and Cellars Restaurant

$$$$ | **EUROPEAN** | The dark-tile floor and white tablecloths put this classy dining area way above the usual winery restaurant, and a wrought-iron door, black leather chairs, and polished-brass ceiling fan add to the aura. It's a prix-fixe dinner menu, and there is usually a lamb and a beef dish among their offerings. **Known for:** complimentary transfers from local accommodations; excellent wine-pairings; bread and butter pudding. [$] *Average main: NZ$32* ✉ *42 Puruatanga Rd., Martinborough* ☎ *06/306–9933* 🌐 *www.tirohanaestate.com.*

Union Square Bistro and Bar

$$$$ | **BISTRO** | Located and independently operated within the historic Martinborough Hotel, the decor here is understated yet comfortable. The classic bistro menu offers European favorites for lunch and dinner, with brunch on weekends. **Known for:** great gin menu; Michelin-starred chef; town center location. $ *Average main: NZ$32* ⊠ *Martinborough Hotel, Union Sq., Martinborough* ☎ *06/306–8350* ⊕ *www.unionsquare. co.nz.*

The Village Café

$$ | **NEW ZEALAND** | At this rustic barnlike café with a sunny outdoor courtyard, all the food is made from local ingredients. The cooks even smoke their own salmon and stuff their own sausages. **Known for:** plenty of space; hearty brunches; huge and varied menu. $ *Average main: NZ$17* ⊠ *6 Kitchener St., Martinborough* ☎ *06/306–8814* ☉ *No dinner.*

 ## Hotels

The Claremont

$$ | **HOTEL** | In a quiet rural area just outside the village center, this motel complex has a variety of stylishly modern units to suit a range of budgets. **Pros:** spacious rooms; quiet location out of the town center; good modern lodgings. **Cons:** you need to go into town for a restaurant; no swimming pool or activities; no air-conditioning. $ *Rooms from: NZ$155* ⊠ *38 Regent St., Martinborough* ☎ *06/306–9162* ⊕ *www.theclaremont. co.nz* ◎ *No Meals* ⇄ *23 rooms.*

The Martinborough Hotel

$$$ | **HOTEL** | Sitting on a corner of Martinborough Square, this vintage hotel was built in 1882 and has rooms that open onto either the veranda or the garden. **Pros:** lovely restaurant downstairs; historic charm; handy to everything. **Cons:** no air-conditioning; books up fast at peak times; some rooms affected by street noise. $ *Rooms from: NZ$279* ⊠ *10-12 Memorial Sq., Martinborough* ☎ *06/306–9350* ⊕ *www.martinboroughhotel.co.nz* ⇄ *20 rooms* ◎ *No Meals.*

Peppers Parehua

$$ | **RESORT** | Located next to a vineyard, luxurious Peppers Parehua enjoys a parklike setting. **Pros:** tennis court; modern luxury lodgings; outdoor pool. **Cons:** no air-conditioning; a long way from the bright lights; underwhelming breakfast. $ *Rooms from: NZ$240* ⊠ *52 New York St. W., Martinborough* ☎ *06/306–8405* ⊕ *www.peppers.co.nz* ⇄ *28 cottages* ◎ *No Meals.*

 ## Performing Arts

FESTIVALS

Toast Martinborough Wine, Food & Music Festival

ARTS FESTIVALS | Devoted to the hedonist's holy trinity, this festival occurs on the third Sunday of November. Thousands of tickets are typically sold within hours of their first release—you can get yours online through Ticketek (*www. ticketek.co.nz*). ☎ *06/306–9183* ⊕ *www. toastmartinborough.co.nz* ⊠ *NZ$85.*

Palliser Bay and Cape Palliser

Southwest of Martinborough: 25 km (16 miles) to Lake Ferry, 40 km (25 miles) to Putangirua Pinnacles, 65 km (40 miles) to Cape Palliser.

This, the most southerly part of the North Island's coast, can be a wild and desolate area in winter. Still, the lighthouse and seal colony at Cape Palliser are well worth seeing, as are the eerie rock formations in Putangirua Pinnacles Scenic Reserve. Wedged between the bay and a lagoon, Lake Ferry is a great spot to enjoy rugged scenery on a good day.

Continued on page 305

SEARCHING FOR MIDDLE-EARTH

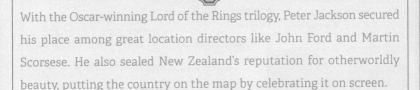

With the Oscar-winning Lord of the Rings trilogy, Peter Jackson secured his place among great location directors like John Ford and Martin Scorsese. He also sealed New Zealand's reputation for otherworldly beauty, putting the country on the map by celebrating it on screen.

The sets have long been struck, but New Zealand's vistas will inspire your imagination to fill in the castles, and creatures. It seems as if half the country was involved in filming, so you can always ask a local to tell a tale of Middle-earth. Or take a tour—elf ears are optional!

The Lord of the Rings series marked New Zealand scenery's star turn, but, like an aspiring actor, it has worked its way up, often as a stand-in for better-known, bigger names. Mountain peaks outside of Queen-

stown double for the Rockies in advertisements, and Mt. Taranaki on the North Island played Japan's Mt. Fuji alongside Tom Cruise in *The Last Samurai*.

Now, thanks to generous incentives and a favorable exchange rate, New Zealand has lured other large international productions such as The Chronicles of Narnia series and the upcoming Avatar sequels. And Jackson has given Tolkien fans three more reasons to celebrate with The Hobbit trilogy.

Above: Scene from *The Lord of the Rings: The Two Towers*

MIDDLE-EARTH

TONGARIRO NATIONAL PARK

The peaks near Mt. Ruapehu, the country's largest ski slope and its largest and most active volcano, played **Emyn Muil**; nearby Mt. Ngauruhoe starred as **Mount Doom.** Frodo and Sam tracked and caught Gollum on rocky cliffs here, and Gollum caught fish at Ohakune, a World Heritage Site.

MATAMATA, WAIKATO

Matamata stood in for **the Shire,** Bilbo Baggins's home and the starting point for Frodo's quest. The rolling hills are here, but those sod homes were struck; only the Hobbit holes are left. Tour with Hobbiton Tours for the backstory (⊕ *www.hobbitontours.com*).

WELLINGTON

Wellington served as home base for the cast and crew, and digital work was done here as well. Scenes of **the Shire, Rivendell**, and **Dunharrow** were all shot in Wellington and the suburbs of Upper and Lower Hutt. Wairarapa's Putangirua Pinnacles were the movie's **Paths of the Dead.**

Cape Reinga
Kerr Point

Bay of Islands

NORTHLAND

Whangarei

NORTH ISLAND

Great Barrier Island

Hauraki Gulf

Firth of Thames

Whangamata

Cape Runaway

Tauranga

Bay of Plenty

Hamilton

WAIKATO

Matamata

EASTLAND

Raglan

Rotorua

TE UREWERA NATIONAL PARK

Gisborne

Tasman Sea

Taupo

North Taranaki Bight

Lake Taupo

Ohakune

TONGARIRO NATIONAL PARK

Hawke Bay

New Plymouth

Mt. Taranaki

Mt. Ruapehu

Napier

Cape Egmont

TARANAKI

WANGANUI

HAWKE'S BAY

Wanganui

Palmerston North

MANAWATU

SOUTH PACIFIC OCEAN

WAIRARAPA

Upper Hutt

Lower Hutt

WELLINGTON

Putangirua Pinnacles

Cook Strait

SOUTH ISLAND

0		100 miles
0		100 km

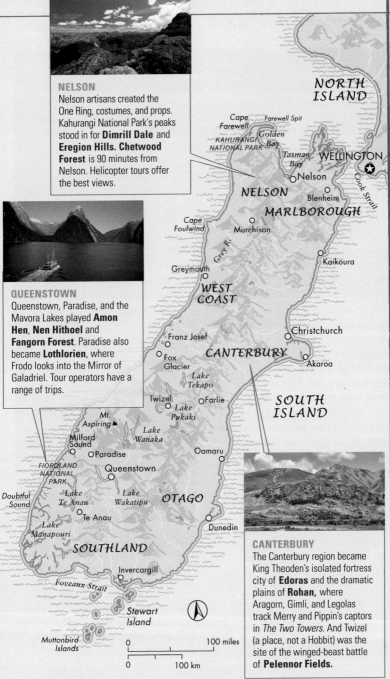

NELSON
Nelson artisans created the One Ring, costumes, and props. Kahurangi National Park's peaks stood in for **Dimrill Dale** and **Eregion Hills. Chetwood Forest** is 90 minutes from Nelson. Helicopter tours offer the best views.

QUEENSTOWN
Queenstown, Paradise, and the Mavora Lakes played **Amon Hen**, **Nen Hithoel** and **Fangorn Forest**. Paradise also became **Lothlorien**, where Frodo looks into the Mirror of Galadriel. Tour operators have a range of trips.

CANTERBURY
The Canterbury region became King Theoden's isolated fortress city of **Edoras** and the dramatic plains of **Rohan,** where Aragorn, Gimli, and Legolas track Merry and Pippin's captors in *The Two Towers*. And Twizel (a place, not a Hobbit) was the site of the winged-beast battle of **Pelennor Fields.**

NORTH ISLAND

WELLINGTON

Cook Strait

Cape Farewell

Farewell Spit

KAHURANGI NATIONAL PARK

Golden Bay

Tasman Bay

Nelson

NELSON

Blenheim

MARLBOROUGH

Cape Foulwind

Murchison

Grey R.

Kaikoura

Greymouth

WEST COAST

Franz Josef

Fox Glacier

CANTERBURY

Christchurch

Akaroa

Lake Tekapo

Twizel

Lake Pukaki

Farlie

SOUTH ISLAND

Mt. Aspiring

Lake Wanaka

Milford Sound

Paradise

Oamaru

FIORDLAND NATIONAL PARK

Queenstown

OTAGO

Doubtful Sound

Lake Te Anau

Lake Wakatipu

Te Anau

Lake Manapouri

Dunedin

SOUTHLAND

Invercargill

Foveaux Strait

Stewart Island

Muttonbird Islands

0   100 miles

0   100 km

TOURS OF THE RINGS

If you're familiar with the concept of "second breakfast," and know the difference between Smaug and a warg, you may want to break the bank for Nomad Safari's **Full Day Lord of the Rings Tour**, an all-day adventure that will take you to several filming locations in the vicinity of Queenstown (including those for some other major films). Or try their shorter half-day options to see sights near Queenstown or Glenorchy. You can drive to some locations on your own, but without a guide it may be difficult to "see" where the films were made (⊕ *nomadsafaris.co.nz*).

Hobbiton Movie Set Tours (⊕ *www. hobbitontours.com*) offers guided tours of the Hobbit Holes, the Green Dragon Inn, The Mill, and other structures from The Hobbit and Lord of the Rings sets that have been meticulously rebuilt. Based on a private farmland, The Hobbiton Movie Set is truly a journey into the Shire.

PRECIOUS MOMENTS

Many LOTR tours feature capes, swords, and flag replicas in the famous settings. Be sure to check out the Weta Cave in Wellington, the museum of the movies' special-effects team (⊕ *www.wetanz.com*).

(top) The leisurely two-hour ride across the river flats at Glenorchy (bottom) Mount Aspiring National Park

Sights

Cape Palliser

LIGHTHOUSE | FAMILY | Named by Captain Cook, Cape Palliser marks the eastern end of Palliser Bay. You cannot miss its candy-stripe classic lighthouse, which was erected in 1897. Climb the 250 (the sign says 258) wooden steps for terrific views up and down the wild coastline. Below the lighthouse, splashing in the surf are members of the North Island's only fur seal colony. Don't get too close for photos though; these animals are fiercely protective of their young. Department of Conservation rules require you to keep 20 meters (22 yards) from seals, so don't get between seals and pups, or seals and the ocean. To reach it from Martinborough, start at Memorial Square and turn left into Jellicoe Street, this becomes Lake Ferry Road. After 30 km (18½ miles), turn left at the Cape Palliser road sign; from here it is another 35 km (21½ miles) to the cape itself. You will pass the **Putangirua Pinnacles** on your left; after this, the road deteriorates and is unpaved in places. It is a stark and dramatic drive, though not particularly hard if you take care. The travel time from Martinborough is approximately 80 minutes. ✉ *Cape Palliser* 🎟 *Free*

Lake Ferry

TOWN | The tiny settlement of Lake Ferry sits beside Palliser Bay, 40 km (25 miles) northwest of Cape Palliser. The lake in question, called Onoke, is actually a salt lagoon formed by the long sandbank here. Vacation homes, fishing spots, and remarkable sunsets bring in the weekend Wellingtonian crowd. If you're coming from Martinborough, expect a 25-km (16-mile) drive through rolling sheep country.

Putangirua Pinnacles Scenic Reserve

NATURE SIGHT | Just before Lake Ferry, turn left (coming from Martinborough) at the sign for Cape Palliser and drive another 15 km (9 miles) around Palliser Bay to Te Kopi, where the Putangirua Pinnacles Scenic Reserve is protected from the hordes by its relative isolation. The spectacular rocks have been formed over the last 120,000 years as rains have washed away an ancient gravel deposit, and pinnacles and towers now soar hundreds of feet into the air on both sides of a stony riverbank. An hour-long loop walk from the parking area takes you along the riverbank to the base of the pinnacles. If you're feeling adventurous, a three- to four-hour bushwalk involves some steep climbs and magnificent vistas of the coast—as far off as the South Island on a clear day. Sturdy footwear and warm clothing are essential. The Pinnacles are an hour's drive from Martinborough. ✉ *Palliser Bay, Featherston* 🎟 *Free.*

Hotels

Lake Ferry Hotel

$ | HOTEL | This waterfront hotel is home to the North Island's southernmost pub, with breathtaking views across Cape Palliser to the South Island's Kaikoura Ranges. **Pros:** genuine local experience; if you like the feeling of being at the end of the Earth, this is for you; great food. **Cons:** only one room is en suite; don't expect the Ritz; can get crowded because it's the only place to stay in town. [$] *Rooms from: NZ$75* ✉ *2 Lake Ferry Rd., Lake Ferry* ☎ *06/307–7831* 🌐 *www.lake-ferryhotel.co.nz* 🛏 *10 rooms* 🍴 *Free Breakfast.*

★ Wharekauhau

$$$$ | HOTEL | A working sheep station meets bygone-era elegance at this unique coastal getaway, 90 minutes from Wellington; the 3,200-acre estate comes complete with an Edwardian-style main lodge surrounded by 16 guest cottages, each with a king-size bed, small patio, and open fireplace. **Pros:** luxurious spa using organic New Zealand products; on-site working farm; breakfast and dinner included in beautiful dining area. **Cons:** you won't want to move far from the fireplaces in rough weather; steep price; don't expect the nightlife to set you alight. 💲 *Rooms from: NZ$3795* ✉ *Wharekauhau Rd., Featherston* ☎ *06/307–7581* ⊕ *www.wharekauhau. co.nz* 🛏 *16 cottages* ❮❯❘ *Free Breakfast.*

Activities

CAMPING

On Kawakawa's 5,000 acres of rolling hills, **Kawakawa Station** (*2631 Cape Palliser Rd., 06/307–8989, www. kawakawastation.co.nz*) is a beautiful, self-contained glamping site, perfect for a private getaway. During the day, you'll enjoy being nestled among the hills of a quiet native manuka forest. At night, this remote spot really shines for its crystal-clear views of the stars. Even better, you can stay warm and cozy while stargazing, as the comfy queen bed sits under the tent's clear canopy. There is a separate, fully-enclosed cabin with full kitchen, dining, and bathroom facilities, including hot running water, towels, and pots and pans. The site can be fitted out for up to five adults to stay across two massive tents. Prices begin at NZ$250 per night for two people. The station also offers a popular three-day, three-night walk through farmland and bush from October to April. It's closed from April through the end of September.

Masterton and Environs

Masterton is 40 km (25 miles) northeast of Martinborough.

Masterton is Wairarapa's major population center, and, like Martinborough to the south, it's in a developing wine region. There's not much to do in the town, but it's a handy gateway for hiking in the nearby parks and on the coast. Popular annual events include the Hot Air Balloon Festival in early April and the Golden Shears sheep-shearing competition, usually held the first weekend in March.

State Highway 2 strings together a handful of eye-catching small towns on its way north past the Rimutakas. Farther north on the arrow-straight highway is Greytown, where well-preserved Victorian buildings now filled with cafés and boutiques line the main street. After a few miles, you'll reach Carterton, another small town with a handful of tempting stores.

GETTING HERE AND AROUND

Approached on State Highway 2, Masterton is about a 90-minute drive from Wellington. Trains operated by Metlink come here from Wellington via the Hutt Valley, making the trip up to six times per day. Metlink also provides a very limited local bus service, but you will need a car to explore the outlying areas.

BUS CONTACTS Masterton Bus Depot. ✉ *316 Queen St., Masterton.*

TRAIN CONTACTS Masterton Railway Station. ✉ *North end, Perry St., Masterton.*

VISITOR INFORMATION

CONTACTS Masterton i-SITE Visitor Information Centre. ✉ *10 Dixon St., Masterton* ☎ *06/370–0900* ⊕ *www.wairarapanz. com.*

Sights

Castlepoint

VIEWPOINT | An hour's drive east of Masterton along Te Ore-ore Road (which turns into the Masterton–Castlepoint Road), Castlepoint is perhaps the most spectacular site on the entire Wairarapa coast. Castle Rock soars 500 feet out of the sea, where below, in Deliverance Cove, you'll sometimes see seals playing in the surf.

Fell Locomotive Museum

OTHER MUSEUM | The tiny town of Featherston is worth a stop for the Fell Locomotive Museum. Along with photos, models, and memorabilia, it has the last remaining Fell locomotive in the world. Built in 1875 and expertly restored, the

engine is one of only six that clawed their way up the notorious Rimutaka Incline. The museum is open to the public on weekends, but tours can be booked for any day of the week. ✉ *Lyon and Fitzherbert Sts., Featherston* ☎ *06/308–9379* 🌐 *www.fellmuseum.org.nz* 🎫 *NZ$6* 🕘 *Closed Mon.–Fri. (but tours can be arranged any day with advance notice).*

★ Pūkaha Mount Bruce

NATURE PRESERVE | **FAMILY** | Head 30 km (19 miles) north of Masterton for a fine introduction to the country's wildlife. An easy trail through the bush (one hour, round-trip) takes you past aviaries containing rare, endangered, or vulnerable birds, including the takahē, a flightless species thought to be extinct until it was rediscovered in 1948. The real highlight, though, is the nocturnal habitat containing foraging kiwis, endearing little bundles of energy that are the national symbol. Here you can also view the only white kiwi in captivity; she glows in the dark, so you won't have to wait for your eyes to adjust to the gloom to see her. In addition to animal feedings and talks, Pūkaha offers a variety of tours and workshops that can be booked online. ✉ *85379 State Hwy. 2, Masterton* ☎ *06/375–8004* 🌐 *www.pukaha.org.nz* 🎫 *NZ$22.*

Tararua Forest Park

FOREST | For enjoyable bushwalks in gorgeous forests laced with streams, come to Tararua Forest Park. The Mount Holdsworth area at the east end of the park is popular for tramping. If you're in the mood for an alfresco lunch, the park also has picnic facilities. To get here turn off State Highway 2 onto Norfolk Road 2 km (1.2 miles) south of Masterton. Follow Norfolk Road for 16 km (10 miles) to the Mount Holdsworth Campsite. ✉ *End of Norfolk Rd., Mount Holdsworth Campsite, Masterton* ☎ *06/377–0700 for ranger office.*

🍴 Restaurants

The Farriers Bar & Eatery

$$$ | **MODERN NEW ZEALAND** | **FAMILY** | At The Farriers, you can watch the chefs in the open kitchen while waiting for your order to arrive. Much of the large menu is devoted to pub fare and wood-fired pizzas, all made from scratch, but interesting main courses tempt those with more ambitious appetites. **Known for:** courtyard for summer seating; popular with locals; basic, well-executed menu. [$] *Average main: NZ$25* ✉ *4 Queen St. N, Masterton* ☎ *06/377–1107* 🌐 *www.thefarriers.co.nz.*

Saint Sebastian

$$$ | **SEAFOOD** | Experience delicious and unique takes on *kaimoana* (seafood) in this pale blue monument to the sea. The restaurant specializes in home-style cooking and features locally sourced ingredients from the Wairarapa pastures to the coast of Palliser Bay. **Known for:** excellent service and ambience; great sharing plates; popular with locals. [$] *Average main: NZ$26* ✉ *109a Chapel St., Masterton* ☎ *06/216–1471* 🌐 *www.saintsebastian.co.nz* 🕘 *Closed Sun. and Mon.*.Masterton Restaurants

The White Swan Country Hotel Restaurant

$$$ | **NEW ZEALAND** | This former railway administration building was chopped into several pieces and relocated before being transformed into a grand country hotel. The menu changes seasonally and incorporates locally sourced meat and vegetables. **Known for:** good local wine selection; excellent veranda seating; great accommodations on site. [$] *Average main: NZ$29* ✉ *The White Swan Country Hotel, 109 Main St., Greytown* ☎ *021/539–528* 🌐 *www.thewhiteswanhotel.co.nz* 🕘 *Closed Tues.–Wed.*

Hotels

Copthorne Resort Solway Park Wairarapa
$$ | **HOTEL** | **FAMILY** | With 24 acres of landscaped grounds and gardens, this spot on the southern outskirts of Masterton is a large resort for a small town. **Pros:** good off-road parking; great restaurant; indoor pool, squash court, and golf driving range. **Cons:** can get crowded on weekends with special family rates; weekdays popular for corporate conferences; dated decor. [$] *Rooms from: NZ$180* ✉ *230 High St., Masterton* ☎ *06/370–0500* 🌐 *www.solway.co.nz* 🛏 *102 rooms* 🍴 *No Meals.*

★ **Kaituna Riverside Cottages**
$$$$ | **APARTMENT** | Tucked away in the Tararua Ranges, this serene off-grid getaway is only a scenic 20-minute drive from Masterton. **Pros:** locally sourced light breakfast and snacks; very comfy super-king beds; excellent service. **Cons:** no Wi-Fi; remote setting; not wheelchair-accessible. [$] *Rooms from: NZ$345* ✉ *407 Upper Waingawa Rd., Masterton* ☎ *021/254–6776* 🌐 *www.kaitunariversidecottages.com* 🕐 *Closed Jun.–Aug.* 🍴 *Free Breakfast* 🛏 *2 cottages.*

Shopping

★ **C'est Cheese Artisan Cheese & Deli**
FOOD | For any Wellingtonian's trip "over-the-hill," C'est Cheese is their first essential stop. The shelves are stocked with soft and hard cheeses, all made in-house from nearby milk supplies. Above all, C'est prioritizes matchmaking; they make the cheese, then they'll help you match it with their range of locally sourced goods that will complete your platter. ✉ *19 Fitzherbert St., Remutaka Hill, Featherston* ☎ *06/308–6000* 🌐 *www.cestcheese.co.nz* 🕐 *Closed Mon. and Tues.*

Kuripuni Village
MALL | This shopping village is a 10-minute walk from central Masterton. Among the cafés and bars, you'll find a local jewelry designer, a high-fashion clothing and perfume boutique, and a book shop. ✉ *430-460 Queen St., Masterton.*

Chapter 9

9

UPPER SOUTH ISLAND AND THE WEST COAST

Updated by
Gerard Hindmarsh

 Sights
★★★★★

 Restaurants
★★★☆☆

 Hotels
★★★☆☆

 Shopping
★☆☆☆☆

 Nightlife
★★☆☆☆

WELCOME TO UPPER SOUTH ISLAND AND THE WEST COAST

TOP REASONS TO GO

★ **Mountains, Glaciers, and Rain Forests:** Hiking, climbing, short rain forest and coastal walks, glacier walks, and scenic flights are all popular West Coast activities.

★ **Beaches:** Golden beaches and forest-fringed bays ring Upper South Island.

★ **Wildlife:** The Marlborough Sounds and Abel Tasman coast are home to several island sanctuaries where New Zealand seals and rare native bird species are protected. At Kaikoura, whales, dolphins, and ocean-traveling albatross come close to shore to feed.

★ **Wine:** In Marlborough and Nelson, the sunny-day–cool-night climate and diverse soil types mean grapes come off the vines plump with flavor.

★ **Mining Legacy:** Nelson, Marlborough, Murchison, Reefton, and the West Coast all have a strong legacy of mining, for gold and coal. This rich history comes alive in such places as the Denniston Mine near Westport.

1 Kaikoura. Whale-watching center.

2 Blenheim. Marlborough wine-making center.

3 Picton. A popular maritime town.

4 Havelock. Greenshell mussel capital.

5 Nelson. A good base to explore.

6 Around Nelson. National parks, crafts, and wine.

7 Motueka. National park gateway.

8 Abel Tasman National Park. The smallest.

9 Golden Bay and Tākaka. Stunning coast.

10 Farewell Spit. Bird sanctuary.

11 Kahurangi National Park. A Great Walk.

12 Nelson Lakes National Park. Glacial lakes.

13 Murchison. White-water rafting.

14 Westport. Gold rush boomtown.

15 Paparoa National Park. Otherworldly region.

16 Greymouth. Town rich in greenstone.

17 Hokitika. An artisan center.

18 Westland and Tai Poutini National Park. Two famous glaciers.

19 Ōkārito. Pristine wetland.

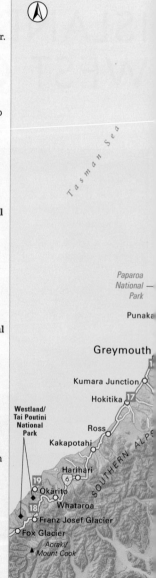

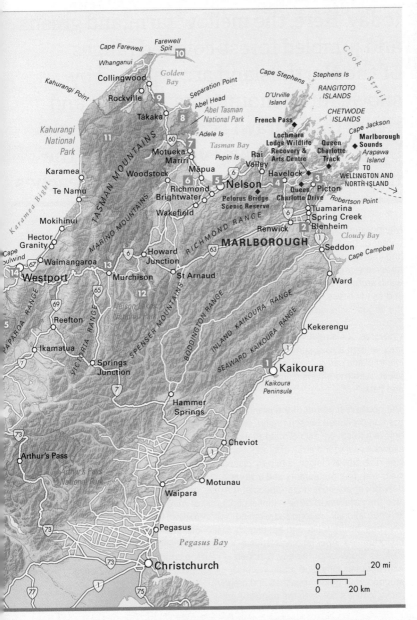

Cook Strait

Cape Farewell   Farewell Spit   **10**

Whanganui

Collingwood   Golden Bay

Kahurangi Point   Rockville   **9**   Separation Point

Cape Stephens   Stephens Is

Takaka   **8**   Abel Head   Abel Tasman National Park   D'Urville Island   RANGITOTO ISLANDS

Kahurangi National Park   **11**   Adele Is   French Pass   CHETWODE ISLANDS   Cape Jackson

Karamea   Motueka   **7**   Tasman Bay   Lochmara Lodge Wildlife Recovery & Arts Centre   Queen Charlotte Track   ♦ Marlborough Sounds   Arapawa Island   TO

Te Namu   Mariri   Pepin Is   Rai Valley   ♦   ♦   WELLINGTON AND NORTH ISLAND

Woodstock   Māpua   **5**   Havelock   **4**   Queen Charlotte Drive   Picton   ♦   **3**

Mokihinui   Richmond **6 1 6**   **5**   Nelson   Pelorus Bridge Scenic Reserve   Robertson Point

Hector   Brightwater   Wakefield   Renwick   Tuamarina   **2**   Spring Creek   Blenheim

Granity   Cape   Howard Junction   63   **MARLBOROUGH**   Seddon   Cloudy Bay

Waimangaroa   **14**   **13**   Murchison   St Arnaud   Ward   Cape Campbell

Westport   65   **12**   Nelson Lakes National Park

69   Reefton   Kekerengu

5   Ikamatua   Springs Junction   **1** ♦ Kaikoura

7   Kaikoura Peninsula

Hammer Springs

73   Cheviot

Arthur's Pass   Arthur's Pass National Park   1   Motunau

Waipara

73   Pegasus   Pegasus Bay

73   ○ Christchurch

77   1   75

0   20 mi
0   20 km

The South Island has been carved by ice, water, and tectonic uplift, and all these processes are still rapidly occurring today. Here, the mellow farmland greens and jumbled forest-covered ranges of the North Island are replaced by snowcapped mountains, glaciers, and rivers that sprawl across wide-shingle beds, drowned river valleys (along the northern coastlines), and golden beaches.

Marlborough occupies the northeast corner of the South Island. The bays and inlets of the Marlborough Sounds (these are the drowned river valleys) wash around bush-covered peninsulas and sandy coves. Marlborough is also the largest wine-growing region in New Zealand, with more than 30,000 acres of vineyards. It's a relatively dry and sunny area, and on a hazy summer day the inland plains can resemble the American West, with mountains rising beyond the arid flats.

The northwest corner of the island is the sun-drenched Nelson region, which enjoys a relatively mild climate that allows a year-round array of outdoor activities. The city of Nelson is a lively place to visit, with fine restaurants and a vibrant network of artists and craftspeople. It's also the gateway to three national parks, an internationally recognized wetland, beaches, hiking trails, and boating opportunities. Abel Tasman National Park, to the west of the city, is ringed with spectacularly blue-green waters studded with golden beaches and craggy rocks, and it's home to the popular Abel Tasman Coast Track. To the southwest is Kahurangi National Park, with unique karst marble mountains and the popular Heaphy Track. Farther to the south, Nelson Lakes National Park—with its glacial lakes, bushwalks, longer hiking trails, alpine passes, and snowcapped peaks—is a popular vacation spot for both Kiwi folk and overseas visitors.

After the gentler climes of Marlborough and Nelson, the wild grandeur of the West Coast is a dramatic contrast. The coastline is lashed by huge seas and drenching rains, and its beaches are littered with tons of bleached driftwood. When it rains, you feel like you're inside a fishbowl; then the sun bursts out, and you swear you're in paradise. (Always check local conditions before taking an excursion.) This region has a rich heritage of mining for gold and coal, as well as for milling, a legacy that has created a special breed of rough-hewn and powerfully independent locals—known to the rest of the country as Coasters—who occupy a special place in New Zealand folklore.

MAJOR REGIONS

Marlborough. This region is a contrast of two delights: the vineyards that cover wide open river valleys and shingle riverbeds and the sheltered, forest-lined waterways of the Marlborough Sounds. The Marlborough Sounds were first settled 700 to 900 years ago by the seafaring Māori people who named the area Te Tau Ihu O Te Waka a Māui ("the prow of Maui's canoe"). As legend has it, the great Maui fished up the North Island from his canoe via a jawbone hook with special powers. Consequently, the North Island is called Te Ika a Māui—"the fish of Maui." European settlers arrived in the early 1800s, mostly to hunt whales and seals. By the 1830s, the whale and seal population had dropped drastically, and the new settlers looked inland to farm the fertile river plains of the Wairau Valley, where Blenheim now stands. While surveyors were pressured to open territory for farming, local Māori were reluctant to part with more of their land and responded by sabotaging the surveyors' work and equipment.

Captain Arthur Wakefield, founder of an English settlement in Nelson, arrived to confront the two Māori chiefs leading the protests. A fracas flared up beside the Tuamarina River (now marked by a memorial on the roadside between Picton and Blenheim), resulting in 26 deaths, both Māori and European, including Captain Wakefield, and the daughter of noted chief Te Rauparaha. New Zealand's Governor Fitzroy later upbraided the English for their "impudent behavior" in what is now referred to as the "Wairau Affray." The land was later sold reluctantly by the Māori tribes, and, by 1850, the new settlers began farming.

Thirty years later, the unwittingly prescient Charles Empson and David Herd began planting red muscatel grapes among local sheep and grain farms. Their modest viticultural torch was rekindled in the next century by the Freeth family,

and, by the 1940s, Marlborough wineries were successfully producing port, sherry, and Madeira. In 1973, New Zealand's largest wine company, Montana, planted vines in Marlborough to increase the supply of New Zealand grapes. This was the beginning of the region's success with sauvignon blanc. Other vintners followed suit, and, within a decade, today's major players—such as Hunter's and Cloudy Bay—had established the region's international reputation. Marlborough now glories in being New Zealand's single largest area under vine, and many local growers sell grapes to winemakers outside the region. Blenheim, Picton, and Havelock are popular bases for winery and outdoor adventures.

The Northwest. The northern coast encompasses the massive sand spit, Farewell Spit; the sheltered, golden-sand bays of the Abel Tasman National Park; and the wide expanse of Tasman Bay. On the broad curve of Tasman Bay and backed by mountains, Nelson is a top area for year-round adventure. To the west beckon the forested bays and golden beaches of Abel Tasman and Golden Bay. To the south, the high peaks and glacial lakes and valleys of Nelson Lakes National Park draw hikers, climbers, fishers, kayakers, and sightseers. In the west are the tussock and karst rock mountains of Kahurangi, New Zealand's second largest national park. There's a climatic allure here as well: Nelson usually has more hours of sunlight than any other city in the country. New Zealanders are well aware of these attractions, and in December and January the region is swamped with vacationers. Apart from this brief burst of activity, you can expect the roads and beaches to be relatively quiet.

First settled by Māori hundreds of years ago, and originally named Whakatu, the area that is now Nelson city was chosen for its extremely sheltered harbor, good climate, and plentiful *kaimoana* (seafood).

These enticements later caught the eye of the entrepreneurial London-based New Zealand Company, and Nelson became the second town developed by that organization, with British immigrants arriving in the 1840s. These days Nelson is one of the country's chief fishing ports and a key forestry, orchard, hop-growing, wine-producing, and olive-growing area. This setting has long attracted creatively minded people, and a significant community of artists, craftspeople, and writers is settled in the countryside around Nelson. Westport and Murchison are other popular small towns in the area.

The West Coast. The coast is a long narrow strip of land hemmed between the Tasman Sea and the Southern Alps. Landscapes encompass subtropical rain forests in the north and icy, steep glaciers in the south, and Westland/Tai Poutini National Park is a part of the massive Te Wahipounamu/South West New Zealand World Heritage Area.

Māori, the first inhabitants, knew this area to be rich in *pounamu* (greenstone or jade). The Māori name for the South Island, Te Wai Pounamu, reflects this treasure. For hundreds of years the riverbeds, beaches, and mountain passes served as walking trails to access pounamu for intertribal trade, and you'll still hear references to "greenstone trails" throughout the area. Today, the rights to gather, craft, and sell pounamu sit exclusively with the South Island *iwi* (tribe) of Ngai Tahu. West Coast galleries sell their traditional and contemporary greenstone carvings. Early Pākehā (European) settlers carved out a hardscrabble life during the 1860s, digging for gold while constantly lashed by the West Coast rains. After the gold rushes, waves of settlers arrived to mine the vast coal reserves in the surrounding hills. Farmers and loggers followed. Although the gold has mostly gone and magnificent native forests are now protected from milling, the coal mining (to a lesser extent than

before) and farming remain. The towns along this stretch of coastline are generally no-frills rural service centers, though they make good bases for exploring the primeval landscape. These communities have also known mining tragedy: the most recent was at Pike River in late 2010, when 29 miners lost their lives in an underground gas explosion.

Near the southern glacier towns of Franz Josef and Fox, nature's spectacles are the high mountains, voluminous precipitation, and massive valleys of ice descending straight into rain forests (a combination also present on the southwest coast of South America). South of the glaciers, the road follows the coast, where majestic *kahikatea* rain forest grows closer to the ocean than anywhere else in New Zealand. On sunny days, the Tasman Sea can take on an almost transcendent shade of blue.

In 2000, New Zealand's Labour-led government legislated to end commercial logging of the West Coast's native forests. Since then, the local communities have been in flux, as residents turn to tourism, farming, and a now-struggling coal mining industry to sustain their livelihoods. But it's the environment that continues to determine the lifestyle here. Locals pride themselves on their ability to coexist with the wild landscape and weather. As a visitor, you may need a sense of adventure—be prepared for rain, swirling mist, and cold winter winds alternating with warm, clear days. "The Barber," Greymouth's infamous winter wind, blasts down the Grey River valley to the sea. The meteorological mix can mean that the glacier flight you planned at Franz Josef or Fox won't fly that day. So plan to stay an extra day, or more, as there are plenty of other things to do while you wait on the weather. Although the coast is well known for its rain, it also has clear, bright days when the mountains shine above the green coastal plains and the surf pounds onto sunny, sandy beaches. Often the best, most settled weather is in winter.

Planning

Getting Here and Around

AIR

Several daily Air New Zealand flights operate from Auckland and Wellington to Blenheim and Nelson, and from Christchurch to Nelson. Sounds Air flies smaller planes daily between Wellington and Blenheim, Picton, Nelson, and Westport. Origin Air flies from Nelson to Palmerston North and Hamilton. Hokitika is also serviced by Air New Zealand flights from Christchurch. Picton and Golden Bay are serviced by smaller commuter aircraft.

BUS

InterCity runs daily between Christchurch and Kaikoura, Picton, Blenheim, and Nelson a couple of times a day. Atomic Travel operates coaches between Christchurch, Blenheim, Picton, and Nelson and has a seat-booking arrangement with InterCity for the West Coast. Bus tickets can be booked directly or at information centers.

CAR

Roads through this region's mountain ranges and gorges can be narrow and winding, and a 160-km (100-mile) drive might take more than three hours. However, the roads are generally good, and there's always something to look at. There are a number of one-way bridges along the way. Check the road sign with two colorful arrows: if the arrow is red for your side of the road, that means you give way if traffic is coming the other way. Remember always to keep left. It can also be a long way between gas stations, so fill up when you can.

Nelson is about a two-hour drive from Picton. From Nelson, State Highway 6 runs southwest to the West Coast, then north to Westport, and south down the coast to the glaciers. At Haast, south of the glaciers, the road turns inland, and crosses the Haast Pass and leads to highways to Wanaka, Queenstown, and Central Otago. For the West Coast, count on at least seven hours solid driving (and photo stops) for the 458-km (284-mile) journey from Nelson to Franz Josef. (But seriously, don't even think about doing this in one haul. Take a few days.) For Nelson to Christchurch, allow up to five hours, whether you go through the mountains of the Lewis Pass or take the coastal route via Blenheim and Kaikoura. Heading direct west from Nelson, Highway 60 splits from State Highway 6 about 13 km (8 miles) out of the city, near Richmond, and continues to Motueka, Abel Tasman National Park, and Golden Bay.

Westport, gateway to the northern West Coast, is roughly a three-hour trip from Nelson on State Highway 6 or a five- to six-hour drive over Arthur's Pass on Highway 7 from Christchurch. State Highway 7 climbs from Arthur's Pass and across the backbone of the Southern Alps before winding steeply down through rain forest to the tiny town of Otira and on to the coastal river plains of the mid–West Coast.

Some car rental agencies have North Island–South Island transfer programs for their vehicles: you leave one car in Wellington, travel as a foot passenger, and pick another car up in Picton on the same contract. Others let you keep one car that you drive on and off the ferry; check first.

FERRY

Visitors traveling from the North Island can take either the Interislander or Bluebridge ferry from Wellington to Picton, the northern entrance to the South Island. The trip is scenic, especially through sheltered Tory Channel in the Marlborough Sounds, though Cook Strait itself can be rough at times. The one-way adult fare ranges from NZ$56 to NZ$80.

Ferries dock in Picton, right beside the township.

CONTACTS Bluebridge. ☎ *0800/844–844* ⊕ *www.bluebridge.co.nz.* **Interislander.** ☎ *0800/802–802, New Zealand only* ⊕ *www.greatjourneysofnz.co.nz.*

TRAIN

Two of New Zealand's three scenic rail journeys serve these regions. The West Coast is connected with Christchurch by the **TranzAlpine Express,** which ranks as one of the world's great rail journeys. The train crosses the Southern Alps between Christchurch and Greymouth, winding through southern beech forests and snow-covered mountains. In summer, the **Coastal Pacific** meets some Cook Strait ferry sailings and travels through Marlborough and along the scenic Kaikoura coast to Christchurch. Both trains are modern and comfortable, with panoramic windows and a no-frills dining and bar service.

CONTACTS Coastal Pacific Train. ☎ 0800/872–467 ⊕ www. greatjourneysofnz.co.nz. **The TranzAlpine Express.** ☎ 0800/872–467, New Zealand only ⊕ www.greatjourneysofnz.co.nz.

Hotels

Bed-and-breakfasts, farm stays, and homestays, all a variation on the same theme, abound in the South Island, many in some spectacular coastal and mountain environments. Your hosts will generally feed you great breakfasts and advise on where to eat and what to do locally. Other choices include boutique luxury lodges and hotels or less expensive but well-equipped motel rooms and backpacker lodges.

Locals generally take vacations from Christmas through January, so book early at these times. From April through November, everything settles down, and in most towns you can book at short notice. Heating is standard in virtually every room, especially in cooler southern regions, and most places around Nelson and Marlborough, which can be hot in summer, provide air-conditioning.

Restaurant and hotel reviews have been shortened. For full information, visit Fodors.com. Restaurant prices are the average cost of a main course at dinner or, if dinner is not served, at lunch. Hotel prices are the lowest cost of a standard double room in high season.

WHAT IT COSTS in New Zealand Dollars			
$	$$	$$$	$$$$
RESTAURANTS			
under NZ$15	NZ$15– NZ$20	NZ$21– NZ$30	over NZ$30
HOTELS			
under NZ$125	NZ$125– NZ$200	NZ$201– NZ$300	over NZ$300

Planning Your Time

Anything less than three or four days through Nelson and Marlborough and an additional three to four days on the West Coast will be too few. Don't be deceived by the maps; steep, winding roads slow down the drive times. Campervans proliferate on these roads in summer, and they tend to move slowly, so be patient and wait for a clear place to pass.

Restaurants

In Marlborough, visit a winery restaurant—there's no better way to ensure that your meal suits what you're drinking. Cloudy Bay clams are harvested here; salmon and Greenshell mussels are farmed in the Marlborough Sounds; and local crops—besides grapes—include cherries and garlic. In Kaikoura, try crayfish. The region is named after this delicacy (in Māori, *kai* means "food" and *koura* means "lobster"). Nelson is also famous for seafood, in particular scallops, as well as for fresh produce and, yes, for wine. On the West Coast, try the local delicacy whitebait fritters—a sort of omelet filled with the whitebait—tiny, young eel-like fish netted at river mouths as they migrate upstream in late spring.

Some restaurants in more remote tourist regions close in winter (June through August); others may curtail their hours. In summer, all doors are open, and it's best to make reservations. If a restaurant is open on a major holiday, it may add a surcharge to your bill.

Year-round, the restaurants and cafés around the glaciers and other remote spots can be quick to close their doors at night. Arrive by 8:30 (it's sometimes even earlier in winter) or you might go hungry. Some of the smallest towns—including Punakaiki, settlements in the Marlborough Sounds, and parts of outer Golden Bay—have few cafés and no general stores, so bring your own supplies.

Visitor Information

Every large, and most small, town has an information center or i-SITE office; watch for the blue-and-white "i" sign showing their location.

Several regional tourism organizations maintain helpful websites: Destination Marlborough (*www.marlboroughnz.com*), Nelson Tasman Tourism (*www.nelsontasman.nz*), Tourism West Coast (*westcoast.co.nz*), and Glacier Country Tourism Group (*www.glaciercountry.co.nz*). The Department of Conservation (*www.doc.govt.nz*) is the best source for national parks, forest parks, and scenic reserves.

When to Go

Nelson and Marlborough are delightful year-round, but beach activities are best from December to mid-March if you plan

to be in or on the water. From Christmas through January, some places can be busy with New Zealanders on their own vacations so book ahead. International tourists flock to the West Coast and glacier region throughout the summer. Snow generally covers the mountains from June through October. Don't let this stop you from driving through these regions; scenically they will look even more stunning. Sperm whales and dolphins live year-round off the coast of Kaikoura. Humpback whales visit in early winter. The pleasures of winter weather around the West Coast glaciers—clear skies and no snow at sea level—are a well-kept local secret. Look into local festival schedules; they occur year-round.

Kaikoura

129 km (81 miles) south of Blenheim, 182 km (114 miles) north of Christchurch.

With its marine wildlife and spectacular coastal location, the town of Kaikoura sits at the base of a peninsula that juts into the ocean from the east coast, and it is backed by the steep Kaikoura mountain range. In addition to its spectacular scenery, Kaikoura is famous for the abundant marine life that gathers here because of offshore sea canyons and the meeting of subtropical and cold southern sea currents, which support a rich and complex underwater food chain. Sperm whales feed closer to shore at Kaikoura than anywhere else in the world. Humpbacks, pilot whales, and orca join them during seasonal migrations. You are most likely to see the whales between October and August, though the sperm whales live here year-round. Joining the marine melee are dolphins and seals, and the birdlife is equally prolific. On a good day, Kaikoura is considered one of the world's best places for watching pelagic (oceangoing) birds, such as albatross, while Hutton's shearwaters, also oceanic travelers, nest only here, high in the craggy peaks of the Seaward Kaikoura Range. Ecotourism, whale-watching, bird-watching cruises, and swimming with dolphins and seals have become the backbone of Kaikoura's economy, attracting thousands of visitors each year. There has also been a whole new perspective to a Kaikoura visit since November 2016, when a 7.8 magnitude earthquake struck the region, thrusting the seabed upward 5 meters, and causing massive slips and landfalls along the coast. Seeing the physical changes and hearing the stories of the resilient locals are all now as much of the experience as watching whales and dolphins.

Kaikoura's main street runs close to the coast, behind a high, stony bank, protected from stormy swells. On the southern shoreline of the peninsula, a few minutes' drive away, is South Bay, the boarding point for whale-watching and dolphin-swimming operators.

GETTING HERE AND AROUND
Kaikoura township sits on State Highway 1, between Picton and Christchurch and the coastal route between Nelson and Christchurch. It's a 2½-hour drive south from Kaikoura to Christchurch and 2 hours north to Blenheim. The highway has reopened after suffering significant damage caused by the 2016 earthquake, but it's still currently subject to occasional closures and delays, especially in stormy weather.

InterCity runs daily buses between Christchurch, Kaikoura, Blenheim, Picton, and Nelson.

In summer, the Coastal Pacific train follows the coast from Christchurch to Picton, meeting with the Cook-Strait ferries. It stops at Kaikoura both ways.

TOURS
Kaikoura Short Walk
WALKING TOURS | This is a great one-hour guided walk looking at heritage and cultural highlights of the town. These include the Memorial Gardens,

Takahanga Marae (traditional home for the local *iwi* [tribe]), and a look at the incredible landscape changes and seabed lift that occurred as a result of the 2016 earthquake. Meet and book at the Kaikoura i-SITE Visitor Centre. ⊠ *West End, Kaikoura* 🕾 *027/435–3905* 🖃 *NZ$20.*

VISITOR INFORMATION
CONTACTS Kaikoura i-SITE Visitor Centre. ⊠ *West End, Kaikoura* 🕾 *03/319–5641* ⊕ *www.kaikoura.co.nz.*

Sights

Fyffe House
NOTABLE BUILDING | Kaikoura's oldest building, erected soon after Robert Fyffe's whaling station was established in 1842, is now a small museum. Partly built on whale-bone piles on a grassy rise overlooking the sea, the house provides a look at what life was like when people aimed at whales with harpoons rather than cameras. ⊠ *62 Avoca St., Kaikoura* 🕾 *03/319–5835* ⊕ *www.heritage.org.nz* 🖃 *NZ$10.*

Lavendyl Lavender Farm
GARDEN | Visitors are welcome to wander this working 5-acre farm, where rows of heavenly scented lavender stretch out against the stunning backdrop of the Seaward Kaikoura Range (catch the harvest from December to February). In the shop, lavender hangs from the ceiling and lavender mustards, chutneys, soaps, oils, and salves line the shelves. There's a café serving tea and coffee, ice creams, cold drinks, and a few lavender-flavor treats. They also have two rustic self-contained B&B cottages in the garden, which is just a 15 minutes' drive north of Kaikoura. ⊠ *268 Postmans Rd., Kaikoura* 🕾 *03/319–5473* ⊕ *www.lavenderfarm. co.nz* 🖃 *NZ$2* ⊗ *Closed Aug. and Sept.*

🍴 Restaurants

For a small place Kaikoura has an excellent choice of restaurants. But for a taste of the local crayfish visit one of the roadside caravans. On the coast north of town, Nin's Bin at Rakautara has a strong fan base. Crays come cooked or uncooked, or you may prefer to get your crayfish fix at a local café, though they are expensive even at a casual place. Also try the whitefish-like *groper* (grouper) and *terakihi,* or the shellfish, for example abalone, known here as *paua*.

Café Encounter

$$ | CAFÉ | Here's a bright outdoor eatery sharing space with the Dolphin and Albatross Encounter operations and a gallery/shop. Food is available off the all-day menu or from the cabinet; breakfasts and light lunches are appealing; and their cakes and slices are always tempting. **Known for:** big breakfasts before you hit the sea in pursuit of dolphins and seabirds; waterfront views; house-made baking. [$] *Average main: NZ$15* ✉ *96 The Esplanade, Kaikoura* ☎ *03/319–6777* 🕒 *No dinner.*

The Craypot

$$ | SEAFOOD | FAMILY | Sustainably caught seafood is the star at this casual, friendly café, but other menu offerings are equally appealing. Meals range from eggs, pancakes, and toasties for breakfast and brunch to lunch steaks, soups, and salads. **Known for:** board games to keep diners entertained; seafood chowder; Kiwi craft beer menu. [$] *Average main: NZ$20* ✉ *70 West End Rd., Kaikoura* 🕒 *No dinner.*

★ **Hislops Wholefoods Café**

$$$ | CAFÉ | This wholesome foodie café is a local institution, a few minutes' walk north of town and worth the trip. In the morning you'll find tasty free-range eggs and bacon, plus freshly baked, genuinely stone-ground whole-grain bread served with marmalade or their own honey. **Known for:** mountain and ocean views; house-made bircher and organic muesli bowls for breakfast; open fish sandwiches. [$] *Average main: NZ$24* ✉ *33a Beach Rd., Kaikoura* ☎ *03/319–6971* 🌐 *www.hislops-wholefoods.co.nz* 🕒 *Closed Mon. and Tues. No dinner.*

The Pier Hotel

$$$$ | NEW ZEALAND | In a two-story Victorian waterfront hotel overlooking Ingles Bay, one of Kaikoura's most dependable eateries serves traditional (albeit updated) New Zealand pub fare. The bar serves cheaper lunches and pub snacks if you're just looking to graze. **Known for:** mountain views; focus on seafood like chowders, lobster, and line-caught fish; vintage pub ambience. [$] *Average main: NZ$34* ✉ *1 Avoca St., Kaikoura* ☎ *03/319–5037* 🌐 *www.thepierhotel.co.nz.*

★ **The Store at Kekerengu**

$$ | CAFÉ | This big, indoor–outdoor café–restaurant overlooking a rolling surf beach on State Highway 1 makes one of the best road stops in the area (maybe even the whole country). You can choose lunch from a selection of prepared dishes or order from the menu. **Known for:** outdoor deck to enjoy the view while eating; location with wild coastal views and sprawling gardens and lawns; classic fish-and-chips. [$] *Average main: NZ$18* ✉ *5748 State Hwy. 1, Kekerengu* ✥ *64 km (40 miles) south of Blenheim* ☎ *03/575–8600* 🌐 *www.thestore.kiwi* 🕒 *No dinner.*

🛏 Hotels

Accommodations in Kaikoura are a mix of country lodges, motels, apartments, and holiday parks.

Alpine-Pacific Holiday Park

$ | APARTMENT | FAMILY | Just outside town, this nicely laid-out site has cabins, studios, and full motel units, plus powered campervan sites and campsites. **Pros:** bikes for rent; incredibly clean, tidy outfit layered down a terraced slope; hot tubs and heated pool. **Cons:** by main road so busy entrance/exit; small site can be crowded when full; no ocean views. $ *Rooms from: NZ$77* ✉ *69 Beach Rd.,* ☎ *03/319–6275, 0800/692–322 free in New Zealand* ⊕ *alpine-pacific.co.nz* ⇌ *22 units, 50 campsites* |O| *No Meals.*

★ Hapuku Lodge and Tree Houses

$$$$ | HOTEL | Luxurious tree houses are the star accommodations here, but there's also a main lodge with a restaurant and hotel-style rooms, plus the salubrious Olive House, a freestanding and self-contained three-bedroom suite featuring spacious dining, lounge, and bedroom areas and 360-degree views. **Pros:** gourmet breakfast and dinner included in rates; unique luxury accommodations; surf out the back window and snow out the front. **Cons:** out of town; stay in the main lodge if you can't manage stairs; tree house life not for everyone. $ *Rooms from: NZ$1600* ✉ *State Hwy. 1, at Station Rd., 12 km (8 miles) north of Kaikoura, Kaikoura* ☎ *03/319–6559, 0800/524–56872* ⊕ *www.hapukulodge. com* |O| *All-Inclusive* ☞ *Children not allowed in main lodge* ⇌ *10 rooms.*

Surfwatch Getaway Cottages

$$$ | APARTMENT | Located 12 minutes north of town, this property is perched high on the cliffs with spectacular Pacific Ocean views all the way to the horizon. **Pros:** lots of handcrafted furniture and wood detail; views from the B&B suite are exceptional; 5-acre property is also a small farm. **Cons:** opens off a fast stretch of coastal highway so take care crossing the road; really steep access road; out of town. $ *Rooms from: NZ$230* ✉ *1137 State Hwy. 1, Mangamaunu* ☎ *03/319–6611* ⊕ *surfwatch.co.nz* ⇌ *3 units* |O| *No Meals.*

The White Morph Heritage Collection

$$$ | APARTMENT | FAMILY | A waterfront view is hard to ignore—even more so on the rugged Kaikoura coast—and this rather fancy apartment-style lodge is just across the road from the beach and a few minutes' walk from the town

center. **Pros:** great location on Esplanade close to cafés and shops; well-designed, comfortable units with a taste of luxury; breakfast available in the neighboring Encounter Café. **Cons:** no elevator; on a busy road; not all units have sea views. $ *Rooms from: NZ$230* ✉ *92 The Esplanade, Kaikoura* ☎ *03/319–5014* ⊕ *www. whitemorph.co.nz* ⇌ *50 rooms* |O| *No Meals.*

Activities

December to March are the most popular months for whale-watching and swimming with dolphins or seals. Book well in advance.

BIRD-WATCHING

★ Albatross Encounter

BIRD WATCHING | Kaikoura is one of the leading pelagic (oceangoing) bird-watching destinations in the world. It's also one of the most accessible, as the birds come close to shore to feed. These boat tours provide an intimate encounter with several albatross species and the Hutton's shearwater, which disperses all around the world yet breeds only in the Seaward Kaikoura Range. Tours last 2½ hours. Longer specialist tours are available by arrangement. ✉ *96 The Esplanade, Kaikoura* ☎ *03/319–6777, 0800/733–365* ⊕ *www.albatrossencounter.co.nz* ▨ *From NZ$160.*

HIKING

Kaikoura Coast Track

HIKING & WALKING | This breathtakingly beautiful two-day walk provides uncrowded, unguided hiking and two nights in rustic yet comfortable accommodations along spectacular coastal farmland. You'll explore high cliffs, sandy beaches, an ancient buried forest, forested valleys, open tussock country, and farmland. Take binoculars to search out seals and seabirds. Expect about 13 km (8 miles) of walking each day. Bags are transferred so you only need to carry a day pack. The walks operate between October and April, and reservations are essential. The start point is a ¾-hour drive south of Kaikoura; public transport can drop you at the gate. ⊠ *356 Conway Flat Rd., Cheviot* ☎ *03/319–2715* ⊕ *www.kaikouratrack. co.nz* ⊠ *From NZ$230 per person, including bag transfers. Inquire about all-inclusive meal prices.*

Kaikoura Peninsula Walkway
HIKING & WALKING | FAMILY | Here great coastal scenery from the cliff tops is mixed with likely close encounters with seal and seabird colonies. The southern entry point is at South Bay, while the first section to Limestone Bay is wheelchair accessible. The northern access point, by the Point Kean parking lot, is where you are most likely to encounter seals; they can move fast so keep a safe distance. There are short (five-minute) walks to lookout points, or you can walk one long circuit from town, right around the coastline (up to three hours). ⊠ *Penisula Walkway, Kaikoura* ⊕ *www.doc.govt.nz.*

RAFTING
Clarence River Rafting
WHITE-WATER RAFTING | The Clarence is one of New Zealand's most geologically interesting and beautiful wilderness rivers. It follows a fault line between the Inland and Seaward Kaikoura ranges, through tussock-covered hills covering ancient limestone. The 2016 earthquake actually reshaped the valley, forming new lakes and rapids, adding huge interest to a river trip. This experienced local company is a good, safe option for you to explore these changes. They will organize the entire expedition, including gear, food, and helicopter access to the remote upper reaches. Half-day to multiday trips are offered, but only for group bookings. The rapids are "bouncy" up to grade two and suitable for families. ⊠ *3802 State Hwy. 1, Kaikoura* ☎ *03/319–6993* ⊕ *www.clarenceriverrafting.co.nz* ⊠ *Three-day trips from $1200* ⊙ *Closed May–Sept.*

SWIMMING WITH DOLPHINS AND SEALS
The dolphin- and seal-spotting opportunities are fantastic here. Although operators have led visitors to view and swim with dolphins and seals off the Kaikoura coast for years, and the animals may be familiar with boats, they are not tame. New Zealand fur seals are also common along this coast and, if you get into the water around the rock pools, you might spot crayfish and abalone as well. Pods of Dusky dolphins stay in the area year-round; you may even see them doing aerial jumps and flips.

Options to engage with seals and dolphins vary, and operators will explain these before you book. These creatures live in the wild, and all tours adhere strictly to Department of Conservation wildlife watching regulations. Some boat operators go quite a ways offshore, whereas others hug the coast. If you have any questions about the suitability of a trip, pipe up; these guys are happy to help. Guides can prime you with information on the local species and will be in the water with you. Wet suits and other gear are provided.

Dolphin Encounter
WILDLIFE-WATCHING | Swim with, or just watch from the boat, the Dusky dolphins that live around here. You'll be out in the deep ocean so you'll need to be confident in the water and, ideally, have some snorkeling experience. All tours adhere strictly to marine-mammal watching regulations. Tours operate three times a day through summer and twice a day in winter, but they can be canceled due to bad weather so prepare to be flexible. There is heavy demand so book well ahead. ⊠ *96 Esplanade, Kaikoura* ☎ *03/319–6777, 0800/733–365* ⊕ *www. dolphinencounter.co.nz* ⊠ *From NZ$105.*

Point Kean Sea Colony
WILDLIFE-WATCHING | You can drive to this seal colony just outside of town on the northern side of the Kaikoura Peninsula.

Whale-watchers delight in spotting a whale in the waters near Kaikoura.

Watch the seals in their natural habitat, lying in the sun or playing in the kelp-filled shallows. These are wild animals and can move fast, so don't approach closer than 30 feet. With seabirds wheeling above and waves breaking along the shore, this is a powerful place just minutes from the main street. Follow Fyffe Quay to the colony at the end of the road. ⊠ *Pt. Kean, Kaikoura.*

★ Seal Swim Kaikoura

WILDLIFE-WATCHING | New Zealand's original seal-swimming experience has both boat- and shore-based tours running daily from October to May. The swims (wetsuits and snorkels are provided) are in shallow, sheltered waters. You're virtually guaranteed to see New Zealand fur seals up close, and your guides will tell you lots of interesting facts about them. If the seals don't want get off the rocks to play in the water with you, the guides won't disturb them; you will, however, receive a 50% refund. ⊠ *58 West End, Kaikoura* ☎ *03/319–6182, 0800/732–579* ⊕ *www.sealswimkaikoura.co.nz* ✉ *Viewing* from NZ$60, Swimming with seals from NZ$120.

WHALE-WATCHING
★ Whale Watch Kaikoura

WILDLIFE-WATCHING | Sperm whales feed closer to shore at Kaikoura than anywhere else in the world. Humpbacks, pilot whales, and orcas pass by on annual migrations. See these marine giants on specialist whale-watching cruises operated by local iwi (tribe) Ngai Tahu. All interactions with whales adhere strictly to marine-mammal protection laws. Allow 3½ hours for the whole experience, 2¼ hours on the water. Check in at the Whaleway Station to be transported to your boat. Book well in advance. Should your tour miss seeing a whale, which is rare, you will get an 80% refund. No children under three are allowed. ■**TIP→ Take motion-sickness pills if you suspect you'll need them; even in calm weather, the sea around Kaikoura often has a sizable swell. Trips are subject to cancellation if the weather is particularly bad.** ⊠ *Whaleway Station Rd., Kaikoura*

☎ *03/319–6767, 0800/655–121* ⊕ *www.
whalewatch.co.nz* ✉ *From NZ$120.*

Wings over Whales

WILDLIFE-WATCHING | If you're in a hurry,
take a half-hour whale-viewing flight with
a guaranteed 95% success rate of spotting giant sperm whales and others that
pass by. Your small, fixed-wing aircraft
will drop to 450 feet for a closer view,
and your pilots will give an informative
commentary. The scenic coastal flight is
a bonus, and, of course, you won't get
seasick. Also, the planes can often fly
when it's too rough for the boats to go
out. ✉ *Kaikoura Airfield, State Hwy. 1,
Kaikoura* ☎ *03/319–6580, 0800/226–629*
⊕ *www.whales.co.nz* ✉ *From NZ$180;
shuttle to airfield NZ$10 if required.*

Blenheim

*29 km (18 miles) south of Picton, 120 km
(73 miles) southeast of Nelson, 129 km
(80 miles) north of Kaikoura.*

Many people come to Blenheim (pronounced *bleh*-num by the locals) for the
wine. There are dozens of wineries in
the area, some with stylish cellar doors
and restaurants, and Blenheim township
is developing fast, though it still has a
small-town veneer.

In 1973, the Montana (pronounced Mon-
taa-na here) company paid two California
wine authorities to investigate local
grape-growing potential on a commercial
scale. Both were impressed with what
they found. It was the locals who were
skeptical—until they tasted the first
wines produced. After that, Montana
opened the first modern winery in
Marlborough in 1977, although there had
been fledgling efforts over the past 100
years by pioneering wine growers. The
region now has more than 100 vineyards
and wineries. The Marlborough Wine and
Food Festival held in mid-February each
year celebrates the region's success in
suitable style.

Don't bury your nose in a tasting glass
entirely, though; the landscape shouldn't
be overlooked. The vineyards sprawl
across the large alluvial plains of the
Wairau River, backed by mountains.
From many points, you can see Mt.
Tapuae-o-Uenuku, which, at 9,465 feet,
is the highest South Island mountain
outside the Southern Alps. Blenheim is
a 30-minute drive from the Marlborough
Sounds to the north; it's 90 minutes
from the Nelson Lakes National Park to
the west. Looking closer, you can walk
off your winery excesses in the Wither
Hills Farm Park on the southern side
of town, where you can climb through
open farmland for a wide view across the
Wairau Plains.

GETTING HERE AND AROUND

Marlborough Airport (BHE), which is at
Woodbourne near Blenheim, is served
by Air New Zealand, with several
return flights daily from Wellington,
Christchurch, and Auckland. Local
airline Sounds Air flies daily to and from
Wellington to Marlborough Airport and to
Picton's small Koromiko Airport (PCN).

InterCity runs daily between
Christchurch, Picton, Blenheim, and
Nelson. The ride between Christchurch
and Blenheim takes about 4 to 5 hours,
from Christchurch to Picton 5 to 6 hours,
and from Picton to Nelson about 2½
hours. At Blenheim, buses stop at the
train station; at Picton, they use the
ferry terminal. Once in Marlborough, if
you're looking to explore the wineries
you'll find them easily, on roads laid out
more or less in a grid that extends from
close to Blenheim and across the Wairau
Plains. Rapaura Road is the central artery
route for vineyard visits; wineries cluster
around Jeffries and Jacksons roads, Fair-
hall, the area around Renwick village, the
lower Wairau Valley, and State Highway
1 south of Blenheim. To access the Marlborough Sounds, take either the road to
Picton, or head west on the main road to
Nelson and turn off at Havelock. The main

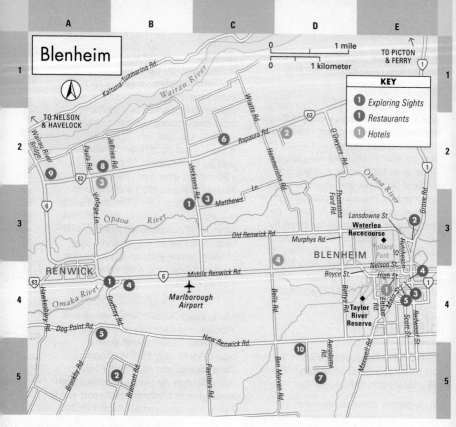

Blenheim

TO NELSON & HAVELOCK

TO PICTON & FERRY

KEY

1 Exploring Sights
1 Restaurants
1 Hotels

RENWICK

BLENHEIM

Marlborough Airport

Waterlea Racecourse

Taylor River Reserve

Pollard Park

Sights

1 Allan Scott Family Winemakers............. B3
2 Brancott Estate B5
3 Cloudy Bay Vineyards.................. C3
4 Fromm Winery B4
5 Highfield TerraVin...... A4
6 Hunter's Wines........... C2
7 Omaka Aviation Heritage Centre D5
8 The Vines Village A2
9 Wairau River Wines.... A2
10 Wither Hills Winery & Restaurant............ D5

Restaurants

1 Arbour.................... A4
2 Dodson Street Beer Garden.............. E3
3 Hakuna Matata Cafe E4
4 Raupo Cafe & Restaurant................ E4
5 Scotch Wine Bar E4

Hotels

1 Chateau Marlborough... E4
2 The Marlborough D2
3 Marlborough Vintners Hotel A2
4 St Leonards Vineyard Cottages...... D3

road inland from Renwick heads toward the West Coast and accesses Nelson Lakes National Park.

■ TIP→ Pick up a map of the Marlborough wine region at the Marlborough i-SITE Visitor Centre.

FESTIVALS AND EVENTS

Garden Marlborough

FESTIVALS | Marlborough's climate and soils encourage great gardens and this is one of the country's most popular garden festivals. For five days in November you can wander through inspiring and beautifully kept gardens, and partake in workshops and social events. Watch the website for bookings; tickets go on sale at least a couple of months ahead. ⊠ 92 High St., Blenheim ☎ 03/577–5500, 0800/627–527 ⊕ www.gardenmarlborough.co.nz.

TOURS

Bubbly Grape Wine Tours

FOOD AND DRINK TOURS | With a choice of times, wineries, and lunch stops, these tours are about as flexible as you can get. There's no minimum number of people required, and if you're into chocolate, owner Kerry will take you to a boutique chocolatier as well. Options include the Sauvignon Blanc Blended Tour (half day), Special Reserve Tour (full day), and Gourmet Lunch Wine Tour (full day). Tour prices include wine tastings. Pick up from your accommodations can be arranged. ☎ 0800/228–2253 New Zealand only, 027/672–2195 ⊕ www.bubblygrape.co.nz ⍟ From NZ$120.

VISITOR INFORMATION

CONTACTS Blenheim i-SITE Visitor Centre. ⊠ Blenheim Railway Station, 8 Sinclair St., Blenheim ⊹ Beside State Hwy. 1 ☎ 03/577–8080, 0800/777–181 ⊕ marlboroughnz.com.

◉ Sights

Marlborough is the flagship wine-growing region of New Zealand. Most famous for its sauvignon blancs, the region also produces top chardonnays, rieslings, and pinot noirs. Throughout Marlborough there are over 90 vineyards, many of which are open to the public and also offer fine cuisine at their on-site restaurants. Wine buffs can also take a guided tour through the wineries. Pick up a Wine Marlborough map (updated each year) from the i-SITE Visitor Centre, or visit Wine Marlborough (www.wine-marlborough.co.nz) for more information.

Allan Scott Family Winemakers

WINERY | One of the most respected Marlborough winemakers, Allan Scott launched his own company in 1990, and his whole family is now involved in the business. They make well-respected sauvignon blancs, chardonnays, pinot gris, pinot noirs, methode traditionelle (try the Blanc de Blancs), gewürztraminers, and rieslings (the last two are particularly good). The cellar door adjoins the indoor–outdoor Allan Scott Bistro, which opens out to a delightful herb garden. Marlborough salmon fillet and seafood chowder are menu classics (open for lunch only, closed in winter). ⊠ 229 Jackson's Rd., Blenheim ☎ 03/572–9054 ⊕ www.allanscott.com ⍟ Tastings from NZ$35 per person ⊘ Closed Mon. and Tues. No dinner at restaurant ⌖ 8-person min. for tastings.

Brancott Estate

WINERY | This estate is worth a visit not only for its history (the region's first sauvignon blanc grapes were planted here), but also for the striking views across Wairau Valley, the excellent restaurant (lunch only), and, of course, the wines. Both the sauvignon blanc and pinot noir have merit. Brancott also supports preservation of the rare New Zealand falcon (which helps vineyards by keeping the mice at bay). A Living Land

Falcon Encounter is offered here. You can also take a guided cycle tour through the vineyard. ⊠ *180 Brancott Rd., off New Renwick Rd., Blenheim* ⊕ *www.brancottestate.com.*

Cloudy Bay Vineyards

WINERY | Since its first vintage in 1985, Cloudy Bay has produced first-class sauvignon blanc, along with a range that includes an equally impressive Pelorus sparkling, chardonnays, pinot noirs, rieslings, pinot gris, gewürztraminers, and its unique barrel-aged Sauvignon Te Koko. Various tasting options are available, as are small plates of seasonal cuisine. Relax in the restful courtyard, or dine alfresco at Jack's Raw Bar, which offers clams and oysters matched with house wines. ⊠ *230 Jackson's Rd., Blenheim* ☎ *03/520–9147* ⊕ *www.cloudybay.co.nz* 🍷 *Tastings from NZ$10* ⊙ *Jack's Raw Bar closed Mon. and Tues.*

Fromm Winery

WINERY | Terroir over technology is the mantra at Fromm, one of Marlborough's smaller wineries known for its organic, sustainable growing principles. All grapes are handpicked. Fromm pioneered the local use of pinot noir and is also known for syrah, malbec, and merlot reserves. Visitors can enjoy cheese and meat platters with their tastings. ⊠ *15 Godfrey Rd., Renwick* ☎ *03/572–9355* ⊕ *www.frommwinery.co.nz* 🍷 *Tastings from NZ$10.*

Highfield TerraVin

WINERY | Sitting high on the Brookby Ridge, with spectacular views over the Wairau Plains, this winery is marked by a Tuscany-inspired tower that visitors are welcome to climb. Highfield produces first-class sauvignon blanc, pinot noir, chardonnay, and riesling; their best, however, is a sparkling Elstree Cuvée Brut. You can relax and enjoy this magnificent setting in the Mediterranean-style Highfield Terra Vin Vineyard Restaurant, which opens for lunch daily. ⊠ *27 Brookby Rd., Blenheim* ✦ *Omaka*

Valley ☎ *03/572–9244* ⊕ *www.highfield. co.nz* 🍷 *Tastings from NZ$5* ⊙ *Closed Jul. Closed Mon. and Tues. in June, Aug., and Sept.*

★ Hunter's Wines

WINERY | Jane Hunter is an internationally respected winemaker and a pioneer of wine making in Marlborough. A visit to her wine cellar, a restored old farm house, is a delight. You can also savor wine with an artisan cheese and meat board in the 5-acre garden, an environmental showpiece for the rare native plants it protects. There's also a regular artist-in-residence. Famous Hunter wines include the Kaho Roa (oak-aged sauvignon blanc), pinot noir, and the Miru Miru (Māori for "bubbles"). ⊠ *603 Rapaura Rd., Blenheim* ☎ *03/572–8489, 0800/486–837 New Zealand only* ⊕ *www.hunters.co.nz* ⊙ *Closed Mon. and Tues.*

★ Omaka Aviation Heritage Centre

HISTORY MUSEUM | **FAMILY** | War stories are brought to life with actual historic planes placed in settings dramatized by New Zealand's Oscar-winning special-effects teams Weta Digital and Wingnut Films. The planes are from famed director Sir Peter Jackson's collection. World War I–era planes, and the stories of their pilots, are showcased in the Knights of the Sky exhibition. Dangerous Skies focuses on aviation development during World War II. There's also a café and shop. ⊠ *Omaka Aerodrome, 79 Aerodrome Rd., off New Renwick Rd., Blenheim* ☎ *03/579–1305* ⊕ *www.omaka.org.nz* 🍷 *Exhibitions from $25.*

The Vines Village

MARKET | **FAMILY** | These artisan shops showcase wines alongside olive oils, fudge, homeware, quilts, ceramics, glassware, jewelry, and recipe books. Dine in the café, let the kids loose in the playground, or you can all just relax in the tranquil lakeside grounds. ⊠ *193 Rapaura Rd., Blenheim* ☎ *03/572-7170* ⊕ *www. thevinesvillage.co.nz.*

Many of New Zealand's wineries also come with picturesque scenery.

Wairau River Wines

WINERY | Phil and Chris Rose were among the first grape growers in the region, starting in 1978. Now the second generation of family helps produce award-winning sauvignon blanc and other excellent varietals under their own Wairau Valley label. The winery building is made from mud bricks and has two log fires in winter; in summer, you can relax on the sun-drenched lawns. Local produce features in the lunch restaurant adjacent to the cellar door. It's popular with the locals, so reservations are recommended. ✉ *11 Rapaura Rd., at State Hwy. 6, Blenheim* ☎ *03/572–9800* 🌐 *www.wairauriverwines.com.*

Wither Hills Winery & Restaurant

WINERY | From this impressive, three-story edifice of river rock, tiles, concrete, and wood, there's a commanding view across the Wairau Valley and the Wither Hills. Tastings include award-winning sauvignon blancs and rieslings. At the popular winery restaurant, guests can relax at alfresco tables, lounge on beanbags on the lawn, or opt for more formal seating inside. A "wine library" consists of vines of wine grape varieties grown in New Zealand—30 of them lined up across the front of the winery. ✉ *211 New Renwick Rd., Blenheim* ☎ *03/520–8284* 🌐 *www.witherhills.co.nz* 🎫 *Tastings from NZ$5.*

🍴 Restaurants

Arbour

$$$$ | **MODERN NEW ZEALAND** | A friendly and very stylish eatery, Arbour is innovative and critically acclaimed yet so laidback and hospitable. The quality produce is matched with quality local wine. **Known for:** dining in the kitchen alongside the chef; great desserts; degustation-style option for chef to create entire menu for you. [$] *Average main: NZ$59* ✉ *36 Godfrey Rd., Renwick* ☎ *03/572–7989* 🌐 *www.arbour.co.nz* 🕒 *Closed Sun.–Tues. and Jul. No lunch.*

Continued on page 338

In recent decades New Zealand has emerged as a significant presence on the international wine stage. The country's cool maritime climate has proven favorable for growing high-quality grapes, and winemakers now produce some of the world's best sauvignon blancs and pinot noirs, as well as excellent chardonnays and merlots.

Touring wineries in New Zealand is easy as vineyards stretch virtually the entire length of the country, and most properties have tasting rooms with regular hours. Even if you just sample wines at a shop in Auckland, here's how to get the most out of your sipping experience.

(top) pinot noir grapes on a vine
(right) Rippon Vineyard, Lake Wanaka, Otago

Wines of *New Zealand*

NEW ZEALAND WINES: THEN AND NOW

(top left) Nikola Nobilo was a New Zealand wine pioneer. (right) Central Otago vineyard
(bottom left) Ripe cabernet sauvignon grapes

A BRIEF HISTORY

The first grapes were planted by missionaries on the North Island of New Zealand in 1819, and a British official (and hobbyist viticulturist) James Busby was the first to make wine almost 20 years later. For the next 150 years, the country's vineyards faced the significant challenges of powdery mildew and phylloxera, a root-killing louse.

New Zealand's modern-day wine production started in the 1970s, as European varietals were planted and started to show promise. Pioneers like Lebanese immigrant Assid Corban of Corbans Wines, and Croatian immigrants Nikola Nobilo of Nobilo and Josip Babich of Babich Wines settled in Henderson Valley, near Auckland, and helped shape the future of New Zealand wine production, innovating with cultured yeast, stainless steel tanks, and temperature-controlled fermentation, which have become widespread practices in many of the world's wine regions.

TODAY'S WINE SCENE

Ever since the country's sauvignon blancs captured the imagination of British wine critics at a major international tasting in 1985, wine drinkers worldwide have clamored for this crisp, fruity wine. New Zealand wines are now exported to 80 countries, with Australia biting a 20 percent chunk out of the export share, followed by the U.K. and the United States.

New Zealand is a long, narrow country of 1,000 miles between the North and South Islands, with numerous microclimates and soil types, each suited to different varietals. Sauvignon blanc is eminently well matched to the South Island, particularly Marlborough, while chardonnay and pinot gris conveniently grow in most areas. Pinot noir—NZ's most-planted red grape—and riesling do best in Martinborough and on the South Island, with high-quality bottles coming from Marlborough, Nelson, Waipara, and Central Otago, the country's southernmost winegrowing area. Heavy-bodied red grapes like cabernet sauvignon, mer-

Grapevines at Babich Vineyard, one of New Zealand's largest wineries.

lot, malbec, and syrah excel in warmer Hawke's Bay and Auckland on the North Island.

As for the future, many winegrowers are playing around with new varieties, hoping to find the "next big thing." Gewürztraminer and viognier are already well established, while varieties like arneis and grüner veltliner are still rare. For red grapes, sangiovese and montepulciano show great promise, while zinfandel and tempranillo are making inroads.

NZ SAUVIGNON BLANC

Sauvignon blanc grapes

New Zealand is best known for its celebrated sauvignon blanc wines, but the varietal wasn't planted in the country until the 1970s.

In recent years, sauvignon blancs from Marlborough have become the worldwide benchmark for the varietal, with concentrated grassy, herbal, and floral notes. Compared to the sauvignon blancs of France, New Zealand's wines are more intensely perfumed, with fruitier flavors.

Neudorf Vineyards, Nelson, produces several well-regarded wines.

NEW ZEALAND'S WINE REGIONS

AUCKLAND. One of the country's original wine regions, this warm area produces high-quality reds, especially from Waiheke Island and Matakana.

GISBORNE. Distinctive chardonnays with peach and melon flavors are the specialty here. The region is also known for its spicy gewürztraminer wines.

MARTINBOROUGH. The area, which houses the Wairarapa subregion, is known for its rich pinot noirs and luscious cabernet sauvignons.

CLASSIC WINE TRAIL

For the ultimate touring experience, take a weeklong excursion down the Classic Wine Trail. The well-marked, 240-mile touring route passes through towns and rural routes full of attractions, like farmer's markets and restaurants, artist's studios and museums, and outdoor activities, including hiking trails, horse riding, and fishing rivers. Download the trail guide at ⊕ www.classicwine-trail.co.nz.

NORTHLAND

AUCKLAND
Auckland ○

NORTH ISLAND

Tasman Sea

BAY OF PLENTY

GISBORNE

WAIKATO

HAWKE'S BAY

○ Napier

○ Hastings

PACIFIC OCEAN

Classic Wine Trail

MARTINBOROUGH

○ Wellington

○ Blenheim

SOUTH ISLAND

HAWKES BAY. A geographically and climactically diverse wine region that produces many wines, such as chardonnay, merlot, and cabernet sauvignon.

NELSON. A small wine region about two hours from Marlborough wineries. The region produces chardonnay as its primary wine, followed by riesling.

MARLBOROUGH. The country's most important wine region, and the home of its world-class sauvignon blancs. Also common are chardonnay and riesling.

CANTERBURY. This region, which includes the up-and-coming Waipara Valley, is cool and dry, making it well suited to chardonnay and pinot noir. riesling and sauvignon blanc are also produced here.

NELSON

Tasman
Mountains

Wellington

Blenheim

MARLBOROUGH

Tasman
Sea

Southern Alps

Christchurch

CANTERBURY

PACIFIC OCEAN

SOUTH
ISLAND

Queenstown

OTAGO

Dunedin

OTAGO. This region is known for growing the world's southernmost grape vines. Its intensely concentrated pinot noirs have received great critical acclaim.

WINE-TASTING PRIMER

Ordering and tasting wine—whether at a winery, bar, or restaurant—is easy once you master a few simple steps.

LOOK AND NOTE

Hold your glass by the stem and look at the wine in the glass. Note its color, depth, and clarity.

For whites, is it greenish, yellow, or gold? For reds, is it purplish, ruby, or garnet? Is the wine's color pale or deep? Is the liquid clear or cloudy?

SWIRL AND SNIFF

Swirl the wine gently in the glass to intensify the scents, then sniff over the rim of the glass. What do you smell? Try to identify aromas like:

- **Fruits**—citrus, peaches, berries, figs, melon

- **Flowers**—orange blossoms, honey, perfume

- **Spices**—baking spices, pungent, herbal notes

- **Vegetables**—fresh or cooked, herbal notes

- **Minerals**—earth, steely notes, wet stones

- **Dairy**—butter, cream, cheese, yogurt

- **Oak**—toast, vanilla, coconut, tobacco

- **Animal**—leathery, meaty notes

Are there any unpleasant notes, like mildew or wet dog, that might indicate that the wine is "off"?

SIP AND SAVOR

Prime your palate with a sip, swishing the wine in your mouth. Then spit in a bucket or swallow.

Take another sip and think about the wine's attributes. Sweetness is detected on the tip of the tongue, acidity on the sides of the tongue, and tannins (a mouth-drying sensation) on the gums. Consider the body—does the wine feel light in the mouth, or is there a rich sensation? Are the flavors consistent with the aromas? If you like the wine, try to pinpoint what you like about it, and vice versa if you don't like it.

Take time to savor the wine as you're sipping it—the tasting experience may seem a bit scientific, but the end goal is your enjoyment.

WINE & FOOD PAIRING

Hospitality is a core value in Māori society, something you'll encounter in wineries and eateries.

New Zealand cuisine is influenced by Pacific Rim, Asian, and European flavors and traditions. The diversity of the cuisine and its wide variety of ingredients—beef, lamb, venison, pork, poultry, and seafood—makes for a number of interesting food and wine pairings.

Sauvignon blanc is delicious with shellfish and seafood, summer herbs, feta cheese, and salad greens.

Pinot noir complements mushroom-based dishes. Lighter wines are best paired with tuna and salmon, while heavier wines suit lamb, duck, venison, and game.

Cabernet sauvignon and **merlot** work well with steaks and minted lamb.

Chardonnay goes well with rock lobster.

Pinot gris matches beautifully with fresh salmon.

Riesling suits South Pacific-influenced dishes, such as seafood with coconut and lime.

Gewürztraminer is especially suited to lightly spiced Asian cuisine.

THE VISITING EXPERIENCE

Many wineries have cellar doors where wines can be sampled for free or for a nominal fee. Facilities vary from grandiose buildings to rustic barns. Most larger wineries are open daily, all year round, while boutique vintners may close from Easter until Labour Weekend (end of October). If a winery is closed, you may still be able to make an appointment. Regional winegrower associations publish wine trail guides detailing opening hours and other attractions, such as tours, dining options, and vineyard accommodations. Pick up a guide at a visitors center or local wine shop.

(Left) A tour of Marlborough vineyards could last for three hours to three days, depending on your stamina.

Dodson Street Beer Garden

$$ | NEW ZEALAND | In this cheery beer garden–restaurant, hearty ales and craft brews are matched with traditional German cuisine, pizzas, gourmet burgers, and Kiwi fare. If beer is your focus, you can also get a beer-tasting tray. **Known for:** busy crowds; pork knuckles, goulash soup, strudels, and other German classics; huge tap beer selection. $ *Average main: NZ$19* ✉ *1 Dodson St., Blenheim* ☎ *03/577–8348* ⊕ *www.dodsonstreet.co.nz.*

Hakuna Matata Cafe

$ | CAFÉ | Every town needs a darn good café, and this one is Blenheim's. The breakfast menu runs all day on the weekends, with all the standard Kiwi options like hotcakes, eggs, and muesli. **Known for:** vegetarian breakfasts; big hot chocolates, fresh smoothies, and great coffee; house-made cranberry and orange muesli. $ *Average main: NZ$14* ✉ *1C Main St., Blenheim* ☎ *03/579–5040* ⊕ *www.facebook.com/hakunamatata-cafewine* ⊗ *No dinner Tues.–Sun.*

Raupo Cafe & Restaurant

$$$ | NEW ZEALAND | Be it coffee and French pastries for breakfast, mussels and clams with a glass of wine for lunch, or a full à la carte dinner, the European chef and owners at Raupo will indulge you. Meals are light, healthy, organic, and locally sourced when possible. **Known for:** French influence on top local produce; riverside dining; patisserie on site. $ *Average main: NZ$28* ✉ *6 Symons St., Blenheim* ☎ *03/577–8822* ⊕ *www.saveur.co.nz.*

Scotch Wine Bar

$$$ | ECLECTIC | This contemporary-style wine bar and restaurant (with a wine shop next door) offers evening dining with tapas plates and some larger main courses. The menu changes weekly to encompass the freshest and most seasonal produce. **Known for:** 500-plus wines offered from temperature-controlled cellar; cool black booths and brick decor; shared plates. $ *Average main: NZ$21* ✉ *24-26 Maxwell Rd., Blenheim* ☎ *03/579–1176* ⊕ *www.scotchbar.co.nz* ⊗ *Closed Sat. and Sun. No lunch.*

 # Hotels

Chateau Marlborough

$$$ | HOTEL | The region's only Qualmark-rated five-star hotel offers a mix of suites, apartments, and studios, all luxuriously appointed, some with full kitchens, dining areas, and laundry, and some overlooking the gardens of Seymour Square. **Pros:** two-minute walk to town center; spacious guest rooms; off-street parking. **Cons:** conferences can make it a busy spot; feels a bit jammed into the site; big complex. $ *Rooms from: NZ$230* ✉ *95-117 High St, Blenheim* ☎ *03/578–0064* ⊕ *www.marlboroughnz.co.nz* ⇆ *80 rooms* ⦿ *No Meals.*

The Marlborough

$$$$ | B&B/INN | Follow a lavender-lined driveway to this 1901-built Victorian convent, now a luxury boutique hotel. **Pros:** handmade truffles on turn-down, muffins to take at check-out; 16 acres of vineyard and rambling, beautiful gardens; in the heart of Marlborough wine country. **Cons:** out in the country; only downstairs rooms are easily accessible to guests with limited mobility; beverage list could be more varied. $ *Rooms from: NZ$1250* ✉ *776 Rapaura Rd., Blenheim* ☎ *03/570–5700* ⊕ *www.themarlborough.co.nz* ⦿ *Free Breakfast* ⇆ *10 suites.*

Marlborough Vintners Hotel

$$ | HOTEL | Nestled on 6 acres of landscaped grounds, each of the 16 suites in the contemporary Tuscan-style villas enjoys views of the vineyards and gardens. **Pros:** good gym; delightful vineyard and Wither Hills views; self-contained restaurant on-site. **Cons:** no shops handy; weddings and small conferences can bring a crowd; country location not for everyone. $ *Rooms from: NZ$185* ✉ *190 Raupara Rd., Blenheim* ☎ *03/572–5094*

🌐 *www.mvh.co.nz* 🛏 *16 suites* 🍴 *No Meals.*

St. Leonards Vineyard Cottages

$$$ | **APARTMENT** | **FAMILY** | This rural retreat has four self-contained cottages dotted around an expansive rambling garden and surrounded by vineyards. **Pros:** tennis and petanque courts; sheep, deer, and chickens to amuse the kids; each accommodation is in a private setting. **Cons:** no shops nearby; have to drive to get to area restaurants; might be too rural for some. [$] *Rooms from: NZ$220* ✉ *18 St. Leonards Rd., just off State Hwy. 6, 3 km (2 miles) from Blenheim* ☎ *03/577–8328* 🌐 *www.stleonards.co.nz* 🍴 *Free Breakfast* 🛏 *4 units.*

Picton

29 km (18 miles) north of Blenheim, 110 km (69 miles) east of Nelson.

The maritime township of Picton (population 4,000) is a popular boating spot and has two sizable marinas, the smaller at Picton Harbour and the much larger at nearby Waikawa Bay. There's plenty to do in town, with craft markets in summer, cafés and bars, historical sites, and museums (including one on an old sailing ship), and trails through bushy scenic reserves to beaches and gorgeous lookouts over the Sounds. The Picton foreshore is a delightful parklike area looking up into Queen Charlotte Sound. It's a nice spot to wait for your ferry to the North Island and to watch the comings and goings of smaller pleasure craft and water taxis.

GETTING HERE AND AROUND

Picton lies at the head of Queen Charlotte Sound and is the arrival point for ferries from the North Island and summer-visiting international cruise ships. The town is the base for services and transport by water taxi to the popular Queen Charlotte Track, as well as to remote communities in the vast area of islands, inlets, and peninsulas of Queen Charlotte Sound.

Visitors from the North Island can take the Interislander or Bluebridge ferry from Wellington to Picton. Ferries dock in Picton wharf.

TOURS

Beachcomber Cruises

BOAT TOURS | Scheduled daily scenic and eco-cruises run throughout Queen Charlotte Sound and include the Mail Boat cruise, which explores all the way to the outer reaches. Help deliver mail and supplies to families living in these wild, remote spots. They can also take you to the Queen Charlotte Walkway for one-day or longer unguided walks and bike rides. Boats depart from the Picton waterfront throughout the day (tours, times, and prices vary according to the time of year; check the website). ✉ *London Quay, The Waterfront, Picton* ☎ *03/573–6175, 0800/624–526* 🌐 *www.beachcomber-cruises.co.nz* 🎟 *From NZ$81.*

Cougar Line

BOAT TOURS | Several water taxi trips operate daily through the Queen Charlotte Sound, dropping passengers (sightseers included) at accommodations and private homes. Scenic options range from three-hour morning and afternoon cruises to shorter trips for passengers in a hurry. Also on offer are walking–cruise combos, an early bird eco-cruise to Motuara Island bird sanctuary, and transport for Queen Charlotte Track walkers. Recommended is the Twilight Fish and Chips cruise. Reservations for all trips are essential at peak times and recommended at others. ✉ *The Waterfront, Picton* ☎ *03/573–7925, 0800/504–090* 🌐 *www.cougarline.co.nz* 🎟 *From NZ$85.*

Seafood Odyssea Cruise

BOAT TOURS | Cruise to a salmon farm on Queen Charlotte Sound on board the Marlborough Tour Company's 65-foot catamaran MV *Odyssea*. Enjoy a taste of smoked salmon and locally farmed oysters, washed down with a top sauvignon blanc. Three-and-a-half-hour afternoon cruises depart daily at 1:30 (October to April, otherwise four days a week) from Picton Marina. ⊠ *London Quay, Picton* ☎ *03/577–9997, 0800/990–800 New Zealand only* ⊕ *www.marlboroughtourcompany.co.nz* ⊜ *NZ$155.*

Sounds Connection

SPECIAL-INTEREST TOURS | If you like drinking wine and/or catching fish, let these folks guide you. Full-day and half-day tours are offered to Marlborough's most renowned wineries—and others less well known. The Gourmet Experience tour (November through April) combines a wine-and-food appreciation tour with behind-the-scenes glimpses and a four-course, wine-matched lunch. They also offer half-day and longer fishing charters in the Sounds with third-generation fishing guides. ⊠ *94 Wellington St., Picton* ☎ *03/573–8843, 0800/742–866* ⊕ *www. soundsconnection.com* ⊜ *From NZ$85.*

VISITOR INFORMATION

CONTACTS Picton i-SITE Visitor Centre. ⊠ *The Foreshore, Picton* ☎ *03/520–3113* ⊕ *marlboroughnz.com.*

 Sights

Edwin Fox Maritime Museum

NAUTICAL SIGHT | The preserved hulk of the *Edwin Fox* demonstrates just how young New Zealand's European settlement is. The ship was used in the Crimean War, transported convicts to Australia, and brought settlers to New Zealand. Now dry-docked, it serves as a museum, bringing to life the conditions the early immigrants faced. It has the honor of being the oldest surviving merchant ship in the world. ⊠ *Dunbar Wharf, Picton* ☎ *03/573–6868* ⊕ *www.edwinfoxsociety. com* ⊜ *NZ$15.*

Lochmara

RESORT | **FAMILY** | Take the short boat ride out to explore this delightful café, lodge, wildlife refuge, and art studio on

the shore of Lochmara Bay. Follow the bushwalks to see native gecko and the kakariki (a native parrot) being nurtured here as part of the lodge's wildlife recovery program. There's a pampering spa room and bathhouse above the beach, galleries of local art, and a sculpture trail. Artists-in-residence sometimes work here. Four-star chalets are suitable for couples and families, if you plan to stay longer. ⊠ *Lochmara Bay, Queen Charlotte Sound, Picton* ☎ *03/573–4554* ⊕ *www. lochmara.co.nz* ⊜ *Programs from NZ$50 per person* ⊙ *Closed mid-May–late Sept.*

Picton Heritage and Whaling Museum

HISTORY MUSEUM | Picton's seafaring history is captured with a wealth of memorabilia showcased in this quaint and worthy museum. The area was first a key Māori settlement called Waitohi, then an important whaling and sealing location for European immigrants in the early 19th century. Until 1860, all trade and travel was done by sea. ⊠ *9 London Quay, Picton* ☎ *03/573–8283* ⊕ *www.pictonmuseum-newzealand.com* ⊜ *NZ$5.*

Pelorus Bridge Scenic Reserve

FOREST | Halfway between both Picton and Nelson and Blenheim and Nelson, on State Highway 6, is this remnant of the native lowland forest that once covered the whole region. Easy walking trails explore the beech, podocarp (a species of evergreen), and broadleaf trees. In summer ,the crystal clear river is warm enough (just) for swimming (watch for the sand flies). There's also a rare colony of endangered long-tailed native bats that come to play round the streetlight at the bridge at night. This is an utterly delightful place to take a pause, especially with a campground and café both in the vicinity. ⊠ *Pelorus Bridge, State Hwy. 6, Havelock* ⊕ *www.doc.govt.nz.*

Queen Charlotte Drive

SCENIC DRIVE | The main road out of Picton, State Highway 1, heads directly to Blenheim. If you're heading west toward Havelock and Nelson, and don't mind

A launch cuts a swathe through the calm waters of Queen Charlotte Sound.

a slower, though much more scenic, route, Queen Charlotte Drive is for you. From Picton, the drive climbs the hill to the west of the town, then winds in and out of bays along the edge of Queen Charlotte Sound. Governor's, Momorangi, and Ngakuta bays are gorgeous spots for a picnic. The drive then cuts across to Pelorus and Keneperu sounds, and follows the water's edge to Havelock township. Cullen Point, a short walk near the Havelock end of the drive, leads to a good lookout point across Pelorus Sound. From Havelock you join State Highway 6, which leads to Nelson.

Restaurants

Le Café

$$$ | CAFÉ | Sitting outside Le Café on the waterfront you can look right down Queen Charlotte Sound and watch the local boats and the big Cook Strait ferries coming and going. Staffers source organic, local, and free-range foods wherever possible—your fish was probably landed on the wharf at the end of the street and,

if it's beef, they reckon they know the farmer. **Known for:** Continental European classics at dinner; great coffee; edgy vibe. $ *Average main: NZ$26* ✉ *London Quay, Picton* ☎ *03/573–5588* ⊕ *www. lecafepicton.co.nz.*

Cafe Cortado

$$$ | CAFÉ | South American and Mediterranean influences are paired with top Marlborough wines and craft range beers at this prime waterfront spot with a laid-back atmosphere. The fresh breakfasts will sufficiently fuel you up for a day out on the Sounds. **Known for:** sustainable sourcing; good selection of tapas; pizzas and breakfast burritos. $ *Average main: NZ$28* ✉ *Corner of High St. and London Quay, Picton* ☎ *03/573–5630* ⊕ *www. cafecortado.co.nz.*

Seumus' Irish Bar

$$$ | IRISH | This place definitely has the classic Irish bar vibe. Irish locals confirm they pour a good Guinness, plus there's lots of live music; it's not all Celtic, but it will get your toes tapping regardless. **Known for:** Sunday roasts; classic Irish pub menu; beef burgers and fries. $ *Average main: NZ$25* ✉ *25 Wellington St., Picton* ☎ *03/573–5050* 🌐 *www.seumusirishbar.co.nz* 🕑 *Closed Mon. and Tues.*

Hotels

Bay of Many Coves Resort

$$$$ | **RESORT** | A contemporary luxury waterfront lodge built to complement the surrounding native bush and seascape, the property's spacious suites and apartments are built into the hillside. **Pros:** health spa on site; idyllic spot in a sheltered, iconic Marlborough Sounds location; great views from every unit. **Cons:** built on a hillside so steepish paths (guests can request a golf cart); boat or foot access only; dining shared with day visitors and minimum stay requirement for two weeks over Christmas. $ *Rooms from: NZ$900* ✉ *Bay of Many Coves, Queen Charlotte Sound, Picton* ☎ *03/579–9771, 0800/579–9771* 🌐 *www.bayofmanycoves.co.nz* 🍴 *No Meals* 🛏 *11 apartments.*

Jasmine Court Motel

$$ | **HOTEL** | Stylish, well-sized guest rooms, with kitchenettes and en suite bathrooms, overlook the town to the main harbor. **Pros:** bike and luggage storage if you're off to walk the Queen Charlotte Track; parking outside your door; handy for an early morning ferry sailing. **Cons:** units a bit jammed into a small area; kids by arrangement only; often full in summer. $ *Rooms from: NZ$185* ✉ *78 Wellington St., Picton* ☎ *03/573–7110, 0800/421–999* 🌐 *www.jasminecourt.co.nz* 🛏 *19 rooms* 🍴 *No Meals.*

Sennen House

$$$ | **B&B/INN** | Private, boutique accommodation in an 1886 Victorian villa, this is one of Picton's most historic homes. **Pros:** understated luxury; two apartments have full kitchens and three have kitchenettes; sense of history. **Cons:** short winter close-down that varies year to year; ask for the downstairs rooms if you have limited mobility; no children under 13. $ *Rooms from: NZ$285* ✉ *9 Oxford St., Picton* ✥ *Follow western part of Oxford St. from Nelson Sq., crossing 2 roads, to reach property* ☎ *03/573–5216* 🌐 *www.sennenhouse.co.nz* 🍴 *Free Breakfast* 🛏 *4 suites.*

Whatamonga Homestay

$$$$ | **B&B/INN** | These are purpose-built guest apartments. **Pros:** friendly hosts share their kayaks and barbecue, for example; quiet and private; magnificent Marlborough Sounds environment with great views. **Cons:** particularly steep driveway with concealed exit; minimum two-night stay; away from township, need a vehicle. $ *Rooms from: NZ$390* ✉ *425 Port Underwood Rd., Waikawa Bay, Picton* ☎ *03/573–7193* 🌐 *www.whslbnb.co.nz* 🍴 *Free Breakfast* 🛏 *4 apartments.*

Activities

DOLPHIN-WATCHING TRIPS

★ E-Ko Tours

WILDLIFE-WATCHING | Swim with or watch dolphins with this knowledgeable Department of Conservation-permitted company. Rare Hector's dolphins, plus bottlenose, dusky, and common dolphins all frequent the Sounds. Orcas sometimes pay visits as well. Or engage with the prolific birdlife on Motuara Island, a wildlife reserve and home to rare and endangered species. Walk to the top of the island for a great view of the Sounds. Tour options include Dolphin Swim and View, Motuara Island Bird Sanctuary and Dolphin Cruise, and Bird Watchers Expedition, which includes close-up encounters with King shags. ✉ *1 Wellington St, Picton Foreshore, Picton* ☎ *03/573–8040, 0800/9453–5433* 🌐 *www.e-ko.nz* 🎟 *From NZ$129.*

HIKING

★ Marlborough Sounds Adventure Company

ADVENTURE TOURS | Kayaking, walking, biking, or all three, guided or independent, half-day or multiday trip—it's your choice with this local company of soft adventure pioneers. Their signature fully guided three-day trip combines walking, biking, and kayaking with meals and high-quality lodging taken care of and your luggage ferried ahead each day. The trip kicks off weekly from November through April. Other guided and independent options are available with all logistics taken care of, some including an ecotour of Motuara Island en route to the Queen Charlotte Track. ⊠ *The Waterfront, London Quay, Picton* ☎ *03/573–6078* ⊕ *www.marlboroughsounds.co.nz* ⊠ *From NZ$870 for 4-day freedom trip, multiday guided trips from $1995.*

★ Queen Charlotte Track

TRAIL | Picton is the entryway to the Queen Charlotte Track, which stretches 73.5 km (45 miles) along peninsulas, around inlets, and on ridgetops, playing hide-and-seek with the Marlborough Sounds along the way. The Department of Conservation provides a few camping areas, but there is also a variety of other accommodations, including backpacker hostels, lodges, and plush resorts. (Booking ahead for any type you choose is advised.) Boat companies Cougar Line or Beachcomber Cruises can drop you at various places for one- to four-day walks (guided or unguided). You can also mountain-bike on this track—it's the longest single track ride in New Zealand. (The outermost section, Ship Cove to Keneperu Sound, is closed to bikes from December 1 to February 28). The boat companies can deliver and retrieve you and your bike to and from points along the track. For walkers and bikers they'll also carry your luggage between overnight stops. Some of the track passes through private land. Track users must buy a Queen Charlotte Track Pass, which contributes toward track maintenance. The track has steep inclines and long drop-offs, and the weather can be unpredictable. It also gets busy in summer, and is part of Te Araroa, the Long Pathway

walking trail that runs the length of New Zealand. ■TIP→ **Though it's relatively easy to access, the track shouldn't be taken lightly.** ⊕ *www.qctrack.co.nz.*

KAYAKING

A great way to experience the Marlborough Sounds is by sea kayak—and the mostly sheltered waters of Queen Charlotte Sound are perfect for it.

★ Wilderness Guides

KAYAKING | These local experts offer guided walking, kayaking, and mountain-biking trips exploring the glorious Marlborough Sounds. Day and multiday trips are available, including fully catered and guided inn-to-inn walking or biking on the Queen Charlotte Track. Booking ahead is essential. Alternatively, they'll set you off to walk independently, organizing your accommodation and water taxi transport; the price varies depending on the standard of accommodation you choose. Or you can just hire their guiding expertise for a day walk, half-day kayak, or combinations of walking, kayaking, and biking. ⊠ *Picton Waterfront, London Quay and Wellington St., Picton* ☎ *03/573–5432, 0800/266–266 toll-free in New Zealand* ⊕ *www.wildernessguidesnz.com* ⊠ *From NZ$99 for ½-day guided kayak tour of Queen Charlotte Sound.*

Havelock

35 km (22 miles) west of Picton.

Known as the Greenshell mussel capital of the world (Greenshells are a variety of green-lipped mussel), Havelock is at the head of Pelorus and Keneperu sounds, and trips on the Pelorus Sound mail boat, *Pelorus Express,* depart from here. Pelorus Sound is larger than Queen Charlotte Sound but less accessible by commercial craft. Small, waterside Havelock (population 590) is a pretty place to stroll. Check out the busy little marina, shop in the few arts and crafts shops, and enjoy those mussels.

TOURS

Greenshell Mussel Cruise

BOAT TOURS | This cruise takes you into the largely untouched Kenepuru and Pelorus sounds, home of the world's largest Greenshell mussel farms. Your skipper will cruise to the black buoys that mark the farms, pull up ropes covered in great swathes of clinging mussels, and harvest them for your gourmet delight. You can enjoy the mussels onboard, steamed gently and washed down with a Marlborough sauvignon blanc. You'll also hear about the pioneering history of the region. Transfers are available from Blenheim and Picton. ☎ *03/577–9997, 0800/990–800 New Zealand only* 🌐 *www.marlboroughtourcompany.co.nz* 🎫 *NZ$125.*

Pelorus Mail Boat

BOAT TOURS | The *Pelorus Express* is a sturdy launch that makes a daylong trip around Pelorus Sound, delivering mail and supplies to residents, as it has since 1918. This is an excellent way to discover the waterway and meet the locals. You might also see dolphins, King shags, and a mussel farm. The boat leaves from Havelock daily November through April and on Monday, Wednesday, and Friday from May through October. Reservations are advised in summer. Bring your lunch; there is tea and coffee onboard. ✉ *Pier B, Havelock Marina, Havelock* ☎ *03/574–1088* 🌐 *www.themailboat.co.nz* 🎫 *NZ$130.*

Restaurants

The Mussel Pot

$$ | **SEAFOOD** | **FAMILY** | The locally farmed mussels are the stars in this quirky café although the other meals like fish, burgers, pastas, and salads, all served with local wines and craft beers, are also good. As for the mussels, you can order them steamed or grilled with amazing flavors and toppings. **Known for:** fish-and-chips; steamed mussels; mussel chowder. [$] *Average main: NZ$21* ✉ *73 Main Rd., Havelock* ☎ *03/574–2824* 🌐 *www.themusselpot.co.nz.*

★ Pelorus Bridge Café

$ | **CAFÉ** | This is definitely one of the best on-the-road cafés in the whole area. Friendly locals serve great breakfasts and wholesome, homemade lunches to both passersby and the campers in the adjacent Department of Conservation campsite. **Known for:** busy crowds in summer; house-made pies; alfresco tables in beautiful bush setting. [$] *Average main: NZ$9* ✉ *State Hwy. 6, at Pelorus Bridge, Havelock* ☎ *03/571–6019.*

Hotels

Raetihi Lodge

$$$$ | **HOTEL** | This grand old lodge has been given a thorough overhaul and overlooks the forest-covered hills and waterfront. **Pros:** absolute peace, quiet, and tranquility; in-house massage therapist; boating, country golf, or walking on nearby tracks all leisure options. **Cons:** hotel dining is your only option here; birdsong might wake you early; not easy to access in a hurry. [$] *Rooms from: NZ$330* ✉ *7124 Keneperu Rd., Keneperu Sound* ☎ *03/573–4300* 🌐 *raetihilodge.co.nz* 🕒 *Closed Apr.–Oct.* 🛏 *14 rooms* 🍴 *No Meals.*

Nelson

116 km (73 miles) west of Blenheim.

Relaxed, hospitable, and easy to explore on foot, Nelson has a way of always making you feel as though you should stay longer. You can make your way around the mostly two-story city in a day, poking into craft galleries and stopping at cafés, but two days is a practical minimum. You can also use Nelson as a base for a variety of activities within an hour's drive of the city itself.

GETTING HERE AND AROUND

Nelson Airport (NSN) is a small regional airport 10 km (6 miles) south of the city center. Air New Zealand links Nelson with Christchurch, Auckland, and Wellington a number of times each day. Sounds Air flies to and from Wellington three times a day with a scenic, low-level flight over the Marlborough Sounds, weather permitting. Originair connects Nelson with Palmerston North and Hamilton.

Geographically Nelson is quite isolated, and you'll climb a range of hills to approach from any direction. It's a 2½-hour drive from Westport, 5½ hours from Christchurch via the Lewis Pass, and 2 hours from Blenheim. From Nelson, head west to Motueka and on to reach Abel Tasman Park, Golden Bay, and Kahurangi National Park. There is a big hill to climb to reach Golden Bay, but the road is good, and it's well worth the trip.

InterCity buses run daily services between Christchurch, Blenheim, Nelson, and the West Coast.

ScenicNZ Abel Tasman runs buses from Nelson to Motueka and to Kaiteriteri and Marahau, gateways to Abel Tasman National Park. Golden Bay Coachlines buses run from Nelson and Motueka to Golden Bay townships and provide access to Abel Tasman National Park and Kahurangi National Park.

Many of the smaller routes cut their service frequency in winter, so double-check the schedules.

AIRPORT Nelson Airport. ⊠ *Trent Dr., Nelson* ☎ *03/547–3199* ⊕ *www.nelsonairport.co.nz.*

AIRPORT TRANSFERS Super Shuttle. ☎ *03/547–5782, 0800/748–885* ⊕ *www.supershuttle.co.nz.*

BUS Golden Bay Coachlines. ☎ *03/525–8352* ⊕ *www.goldenbaycoachlines.co.nz.* **ScenicNZ Abel Tasman.** ⊠ *27 Bridge St.* ☎ *03/548–0285* ⊕ *www.scenicnzabeltasman.co.nz* Ⓜ *Nelson.*

BUS DEPOT Nelson Bus Station. ⊠ *27 Bridge St., Nelson* ☎ *03/548–3290* ⊕ *www.nelson.govt.nz/nbus.*

TOURS

Bay Tours Nelson

SPECIAL-INTEREST TOURS | Local, knowledgeable guides run daily half- and full-day tours of wine trails, craft breweries, arts-and-crafts tours, plus scenic adventure and custom-designed tours by arrangement. Wine tours can include tastings and platters or full lunches, depending on your preference. ⊠ *30 Orakei St., Nelson* ☎ *03/540–3873, 0800/229–868* ⊕ *www.baytoursnelson.co.nz* 🎫 *From NZ$150, including wine tastings.*

Nelson Tours & Travel

DRIVING TOURS | Learn about the region's wines, winemakers, and artisan food producers with local guide (and fledgling winemaker), CJ. He offers a five-hour tour of selected local wineries. He'll also take you to the Marlborough vineyards, combine both regions into one tour, or customize tours to suit any special interests you might have. ☎ *0800/222–373 New Zealand only, 027/237–5007, 027/237–5007* ⊕ *www.nelsontoursandtravel.co.nz* 🎫 *From NZ$140.*

Wine Art and Wilderness

GUIDED TOURS | Premium, fully catered gourmet tours explore the Nelson region's wine, art, and wilderness. Your host, Noel, is a true wine buff, plus he knows several local artists, and will take you into their homes and studios. He once worked for the Department of Conservation and is licensed to guide in all three of the region's national parks. Whatever your interest, he has many options for full-day tours—check the website for the full line-up. ☎ *0800/326–868* ⊕ *www.wineartandwilderness.co.nz* 🎫 *From $325.*

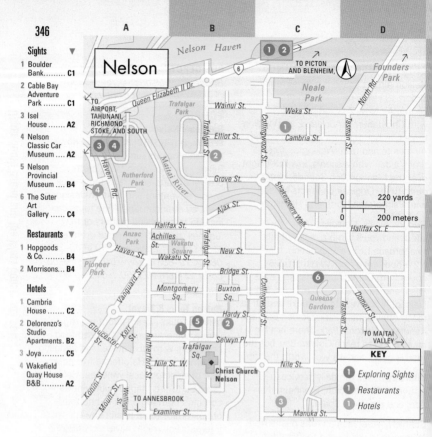

⊙ Sights

VISITOR INFORMATION

CONTACTS Nelson i-SITE Visitor Centre.
✉ *77 Trafalgar St., at Halifax St., Nelson* ☎ *03/548–2304* ⊕ *www.nelsontasman. nz.*

Once you arrive in Nelson get your bearings at the visitor center on the corner of Trafalgar and Halifax streets. The heart of town is farther up Trafalgar Street, between Bridge Street and the cathedral steps, also home to the region's museum. This area is lined with shops, and the block between Hardy Street and the cathedral steps is a sunny spot to enjoy a coffee. Lively Nelson Markets (produce and arts) are held at the Montgomery parking lot on weekend mornings (used goods and crafts) and on Wednesday you'll find the Nelson Farmers Market

selling fresh produce in Morrison Square. There are a few art stores and galleries on Nile Street, too. For a dose of greenery, the Queens Gardens are on Bridge Street between Collingwood and Tasman. You will find yourself, literally, in the center of New Zealand in this park.

A five-minute drive around the waterfront from town, Tahunanui Beach offers some of the safest swimming in the country. This long, open beach is perfect for watching the sky change during the sunset and is a favorite spot for paddleboarders and kite-boarders, with its rollicking summer sea breeze. There are also several bars and cafés here, and one of the country's largest campgrounds.

In the 1950s, the first potters were drawn by the abundant clays in the hills of the hinterlands. Over the decades not only potters, but painters, ceramicists, glass artists, and mixed-media practitioners have continued to enjoy the climate, colors, and inspiring light of the region. Many artists continue to work in Nelson and Golden Bay, and the locally published *Nelson Arts Guide* is available at local visitor centers, bookshops, some hotels and cafés, and online.

Boulder Bank

NATURE SIGHT | A defining Nelson landscape feature is the 13-km (8-mile) natural stone bank, built from the eroding Mackay Cliffs farther north along the coast. The sheltered harbor the bank created is essentially the reason the region was first settled by Māori. Later, an entry was cut through the boulders to allow larger ships into the harbor. A lighthouse on the Boulder Bank guided ships from the 1860s until the 1980s. As you look across from the Nelson waterfront consider that, for 27 years, a lighthouse keeper, his wife, and 10 children lived there on the isolated bank. Access today is via Boulder Bank Road off Atawhai Drive. It is a two- to three-hour walk each way. ⊠ *Boulder Bank Dr., Nelson.*

Cable Bay Adventure Park

LOCAL SPORTS | FAMILY | There's a ton of fun on this 1,600-acre farm a 10-minute drive from Nelson. The Skywire is a mile-long zip line (reportedly the world's longest) that zooms across a forest-filled gully. Quad bikes climb a bush-lined track for 14 exciting km (8½ miles) before reaching a grand, hilltop ocean view. Horse treks explore the entire farm taking in steep trails and stunning views; they can be tailored depending on your riding ability. Then there's paintball, Argo (all-terrain-vehicle) rides, and the Base Café to replenish at the end of it all. ⊠ *194 Cable Bay Rd., 10-minute drive north of Nelson, Nelson* ☎ *03/545–0304, 0800/157-300* ⊕ *www.cablebayadventurepark.com* ☜ *Thrill rides from NZ$95.*

Isel House

HISTORIC HOME | This grand house, in the delightful tree-filled Isel Park in Stoke,

was built for Thomas Marsden, one of the region's prosperous pioneers. It was Marsden who laid out the magnificent gardens surrounding the house, which include several towering California redwoods. The well-preserved stone house has had several rooms restored to their former glory and contains stories of Isel and its surroundings, interpreted in part by local artists. You'll also find original anecdotal material, family items, and a herbarium. For some visitors, the sprawling woodland gardens are the highlight of a visit here. ⊠ *16 Hilliard St., Isel Park, Stoke* ☎ *03/547–1347* ⊕ *www.nelsontasman.nz* ☜ *By donation.*

★ Nelson Classic Car Museum

OTHER MUSEUM | See a superb collection of 150 immaculate vintage cars from over 100 years of motoring, ranging from a 1908 Renault AX to classics of the 1950s—including Vauxhalls, Triumphs, and Cadillacs—through to the exquisite mastery of Ferrari and Jaguar. ⊠ *1 Cadillac Way, Annesbrook, Nelson* ⊹ *Off Quarantine Rd.* ☎ *03/547–4570* ⊕ *www.wowcars.co.nz* ☜ *NZ$19.*

Nelson Provincial Museum (*Pupuri Taonga o Tai Ao*)

HISTORY MUSEUM | On the site of New Zealand's first museum, the city's provincial museum explores the first Māori residents and early European settlements, the city's development as a port, and general events that shaped the region. Exhibits include a rare collection of Māori musical instruments. There are heritage pieces donated from private collections and regular visiting exhibitions. ⊠ *Hardy St. and Trafalgar St., Nelson* ☎ *03/548–9588* ⊕ *www.nelsonmuseum.co.nz* ☜ *NZ$5.*

The Suter Art Gallery (*Te Aratoi o Whakatu*)

ART MUSEUM | An impressive gallery for its size, Suter was bequeathed to the city of Nelson by Bishop Suter in 1899. In 1916 the gallery was significantly redeveloped and expanded. Collections include the watercolors of 19th-century artist John Gully; works of local Sir Toss Woollaston, a Nelson and New Zealand pioneer of modern art; British Modernism works by various artists; and ceramic pieces from local, nationally renowned artists. Visiting exhibitions change regularly. The gallery's popular café looks out over neighboring Queen's Gardens. ✉ *208 Bridge St., Nelson* ☎ *03/548–4699* 🌐 *www.thesuter.org.nz* 🎟 *Free.*

🍴 Restaurants

★ Hopgoods & Co.

$$$$ | MODERN NEW ZEALAND | Chef–owner Kevin Hopgood focuses on using regional produce and regularly wins national restaurant awards for this small, eponymously named bistro-restaurant. Along with the à la carte menu, Hopgoods offers a five-course degustation tasting spectacle, plus an ever-changing two- or three-course bistro-style menu on Monday and Tuesday. **Known for:** big crowds so reservations are a good idea; angus beef fillet; duck confit. [$] *Average main: NZ$40* ✉ *284 Trafalgar St., Nelson* ☎ *03/545–7191* 🌐 *www.hopgoods.co.nz* 🕓 *Closed Sun. No lunch.*

Morrisons

$$$ | ECLECTIC | FAMILY | Regional, artisanal produce is showcased at this upbeat, all-day café that's been around for more than 20 years. Wholesome breakfasts, lots of in-house baking, and a tasty lunch menu are the stars here. **Known for:** tasty, innovative children's menu; Moroccan eggs for breakfast; Atomic coffee matched with locally produced Oakland milk. [$] *Average main: NZ$22* ✉ *244 Hardy St., Nelson* ☎ *03/548–8110* 🌐 *www.morrisonstreetcafe.co.nz* 🕓 *No dinner.*

🛏 Hotels

Cambria House

$$$$ | B&B/INN | Built for a sea captain, this restored 1880s Victorian villa pairs antiques with modern fabrics and conveniences, so each bedroom has an en suite bathroom with shower; the three luxury rooms also have a separate bathtub. **Pros:** hospitable, helpful hosts; elegant old house in leafy surroundings; close to the Maitai River and riverside walkway. **Cons:** 10-minute walk to town and restaurants; tight off-street parking when at capacity (but plenty of street parking); decor a bit old-fashioned. [$] *Rooms from: NZ$325* ✉ *7 Cambria St., Nelson* ☎ *03/548–4681* 🌐 *www.cambria.co.nz* 🛏 *6 rooms* 🍽 *Free Breakfast.*

Delorenzo's Studio Apartments

$$$ | HOTEL | These spacious and stylish studio apartments have plenty of conveniences, including washer-dryers and very comfy leather lounger chairs. **Pros:** walking distance to restaurants, the cinema, and the riverside walk; great pool; lots of flashy appliances. **Cons:** dinner and breakfast not included with the price; a bit jammed into a small site; roadside units have some street noise. [$] *Rooms from: NZ$225* ✉ *43–55 Trafalgar St., Nelson* ☎ *03/548–9774, 0800/468–357* 🌐 *delorenzos.co.nz* 🛏 *25 suites* 🍽 *No Meals.*

Joya

$$ | B&B/INN | This heavenly spot encapsulates what Nelson is all about, with a focus on eco-values in its B&B room, a studio unit in the main house, and a delightful studio cottage in the garden with its own water garden and turf roof. **Pros:** multilingual and friendly host; patios with garden and city views; natural, organic ethos throughout. **Cons:** steep walk back from town; extremely steep driveway, need to park on the street; some rooms have shared bathrooms. [$] *Rooms from: NZ$190* ✉ *49 Brougham St., Nelson* ☎ *03/539–1350* 🌐 *www.joya.co.nz* 🍽 *Free Breakfast* 🛏 *3 rooms.*

Wakefield Quay House B&B

$$$$ | B&B/INN | This graceful villa has one of the best waterfront locations in town. **Pros:** evening drinks on the veranda with host; 180-degree views of mountains,

sea, and sunsets; easy walk to good waterfront restaurants. **Cons:** limited off-street parking; some road noise; minimum two-night stay. $ *Rooms from: NZ$380* ⊠ *385 Wakefield Quay, Nelson* ☎ *03/546–7275, 027/265–7547* ⊕ *www. wakefieldquay.co.nz* ⊙ *Closed June–Aug.* ⏐○⏐ *Free Breakfast* ⤴ *2 rooms.*

Nightlife

Nelson is known for its craft beers, so be sure to check out the local bars and their expansive beer menus.

The Free House

PUBS | FAMILY | Sorry, the ale isn't actually free here—the name means that this place isn't tied to any particular brewery, so you can try a range of craft beers from this very crafty beer region. Light meals are served from a food caravan, or you can bring your own food along (the one rule is no global-branded fast food). Eat with the locals in the garden—plates and blankets are provided. Oh, and it's in a former church, which adds another touch of uniqueness. ⊠ *95 Collingwood St., Nelson* ☎ *03/548–9391* ⊕ *www.thefree-house.co.nz.*

★ Sprig & Fern

PUBS | This locale is one of nine Sprig & Fern outlets throughout the Nelson region and Wellington, pouring 100% natural beers and ciders from the Nelson-based brewery. At the flagship bar, there is indoor and courtyard seating, a good bistro menu, and often live music on Saturday night. If you're looking for an even more casual tipple, the Sprig & Fern at nearby Milton Street is a true neighborhood bar set in an old villa. ⊠ *280 Hardy St., Nelson* ☎ *03/548–1154* ⊕ *www.sprigandfern.co.nz.*

Performing Arts

Nelson Arts Festival

FESTIVALS | A top music and performance event is the Nelson Arts Festival, usually held in October. It's a magnet for top-notch Kiwi and international acts. ⊕ *www.nelsonartsfestival.co.nz.*

Nelson Centre of Musical Arts

MUSIC | New Zealand's oldest music school is known for its excellent acoustics. Each year it hosts musical performances, local productions, and top national and international tours. Check the website for upcoming events that coincide with your visit. ⊠ *48 Nile St., Nelson* ☎ *03/548–9477* ⊕ *www.ncma.nz.*

Shopping

Talented artists live throughout the Nelson region, working full- or part-time in various media: ceramics, glassblowing, wood turning, fiber, sculpture, and painting. Not surprisingly there are many arts-and-crafts trails to follow, for which there is a brochure at the i-SITE Visitor Centre. There is also a colorful Monty's Sunday Market in the central city, where you'll find both new and preloved crafts and goods.

★ Jens Hansen Contemporary Gold & Silversmith

JEWELRY & WATCHES | Jens Hansen craftspeople have long been known for their skilled gold and silver jewelry creations. Contemporary pieces are handmade at the workshop/showroom, and many are set with precious stones or local pounamu (jade). The focus here changed when Jens crafted the precious "One Ring" of Lord of the Rings film trilogy fame. The original prototype is on display, and this is now the only place where an officially authorized replica ring can be purchased. ⊠ *320 Trafalgar Sq., Nelson* ☎ *03/548–0640* ⊕ *www.jenshansen.com.*

Nelson Markets

MARKET | Nelson is a market town, and Saturday morning's Nelson Market, in Montgomery Square, is one of the oldest in the country. It showcases the region's wealth of artists, craftspeople, and artisan food producers. Vintage items,

There's only one place to get an authentic replica of the One Ring—Jens Hansen Contemporary Gold & Silversmith in Nelson.

recyclables, and collectibles feature at Monty's Sunday Market, also in Montgomery Square. On Wednesday it's the local foodies' turn, selling their produce at the Nelson Farmers' Market in Morrison Square (*www.nelsonfarmersmarket. org.nz*). ✉ *Montgomery Sq., Nelson* ⊕ *www.nelsonmarket.co.nz.*

Activities

BIKING

The Tasman Great Taste Trail, one of the Nga Herenga New Zealand Cycle Trail rides, offers rides on largely flat terrain, exploring the vineyards, orchards, cafés, and coastal areas from Nelson to Kaiteriteri and along the Motueka River valley. You can ride it independently or with a guide, in sections or in a multiday package that includes all accommodations, bike rentals, and baggage-carrying services, with add-on options to walk or kayak in Abel Tasman National Park. You can also stop at the many cafés, wineries, craft beer breweries, beaches, orchards, and art galleries along the way; in fact,

many cycling companies incorporate tastings into their tour packages. You can even be met at the airport, your luggage swapped for a bike, and off you pedal. For more information, visit ⊕ *www. nzcycletrail.com.*

The Gentle Cycling Company

BIKING | A range of self-guided rides and themed rides (options include Great Taste Beer and Great Taste Wine, for example), independent bike and e-bike rentals, and multiday packages including accommodation is offered from these experienced local biking hosts. They provide all that you need: bikes, helmets, high-visibility vests, maps, and advice. They'll shuttle you and your bike to and from anywhere on the trail and pick you up from your accommodations. ■**TIP→ They're based in Stoke, just around the corner from McCashins Brewery and Café, so plan your ride to finish there.** ✉ *411 Nayland Rd., Stoke, Nelson* ☎ *03/929–5652, 0800/932–453 in NZ* ⊕ *www.gentlecycling.co.nz* ✉ *Bike rentals from NZ$50 full-day.*

Kiwi Journeys

BIKING | Bike rentals, day and multiday tour packages, and Māpua Ferry crossings (a vital link in the Great Taste Trail) are all provided by this highly experienced company. In addition to rides in the Māpua area, they also offer bike rentals from Nelson and Kaiteriteri Beach. They'll organize your West Coast Wilderness Trail adventure as well. ☒ *Māpua Wharf, 10 Aranui Rd., Nelson* ☎ *0800/292–538, 03/540–3095* ⊕ *kiwijourneys.co.nz* 🖙 *From NZ$45 half-day rental.*

Wheelie Fantastic

BIKING | Bike rentals, single-day and multiday rides, and luxury packages are all on offer from this experienced and knowledgeable outfit. They're based at Māpua but will deliver bikes and luggage wherever they're needed. ☒ *Community Hall, 72 Aranui Rd., Nelson* ☎ *0800/229–253 New Zealand only, 03/543–2255* ⊕ *wheeliefantastic.co.nz* 🖙 *From NZ$55 full-day rental.*

Māpua

Māpua is 22 km (14 miles) west of Nelson.

Though Nelson's a bustling city, it retains a rural quality. Overlooking Tasman Bay and the foothills of the Bryant and Richmond ranges behind, open farmland, national parks, and vineyards are within easy reach. State Highway 6 winds southwest from the city through the outlying suburb of Stoke and through to Richmond, a good-size neighboring town. The commercial and civic center of the Tasman District, Richmond, has a good library and a modest shopping mall.

Just beyond Richmond, State Highway 60 branches northwest off State Highway 6, heading coastward to Māpua. There's a wealth of vineyards along the strip toward Motueka, plus small farm and coastal communities with craft galleries and serious art studios tucked

into valleys that run inland. If on a day drive, detour back along the inland route through historic Upper Moutere, with its blackcurrant and hop gardens. If you carry on south without turning to Motueka, look out for the birthplace of scientist Ernest Rutherford, on the right as you're leaving the small town of Brightwater. Five minutes south of Richmond, the elaborate, atom-shape monument remembers this local boy's contribution to the world of nuclear science.

⊙ Sights

Heaphy Vineyards

WINERY | This boutique winery (formerly known as Kahurangi Vineyards), in the small village of Upper Moutere, was one of the region's first, developed by Hermann Seifried in the 1970s. Greg and Amanda Day now produce a good range of riesling, pinot gris, sauvignon blanc, chardonnay, and pinot noir under the exclusive Heaphy label. The cellar door is open all year for wine tastings with a range of Italian-style pizzas and platters to enjoy in the courtyard or banquet room during weekends or public holidays. ☒ *4 Sunrise Rd., Upper Moutere* ☎ *03/543–2983* ⊕ *www.facebook.com/heaphycellardoor.*

Hoglund Art Glass

STORE/MALL | One of New Zealand's longest-standing glass galleries is known internationally for its iconic collectible family of penguins as well as bold platters and vases. Their work creates a kaleidoscope of bright saturated colors and smooth curves. The gallery is open seven days; if the glassblowers are working during your visit, you can watch them at their craft. They don't do this every day, so call ahead to check. ☒ *52 Lansdowne Rd., Richmond* ☎ *03/544–6500* ⊕ *www.hoglundartglass.com* 🖙 *Free.*

Neudorf Vineyards

WINERY | Despite its tiny size, Neudorf has established an international reputation for its pinot noir, and chardonnay. Riesling, pinot gris, and sauvignon blanc are also highly regarded. The top wines wear the Moutere designation on the label, as the winery is in the Moutere Valley surrounded by acres of vineyards and hop gardens. The Moutere Chardonnay is regarded as the vineyard's signature wine. Artisan cheeses are served in summer, and they also stock olives, cheese, and oat crackers in the small deli to enjoy on the lovely grounds. ✉ *138 Neudorf Rd., Upper Moutere* ☎ *03/543–2643* 🌐 *www.neudorf.co.nz* 🎫 *Tastings from NZ$10* ⏲ *Closed Sat. and Sun. June–Sept.*

🍴 Restaurants

While exploring craft galleries in Māpua, check out Māpua Wharf for its smokehouse, craft brewery, and café, which overlooks the estuary and serves some great fish-and-chips. On the way to Māpua, you may also pass through Richmond, which is a larger service town with some good cafés.

The Apple Shed Kitchen and Bar

$$$ | **MODERN NEW ZEALAND** | The Māpua Wharf setting complements the food, and you can watch the boats go by while dining on quality produce (organic when possible) washed down with Nelson wines, ciders, and craft beers. All bread is baked in-house, the coffee is great, and the menu serves a mix of small and large plates. **Known for:** local fish and shellfish dishes; dining overlooking the water; Golden Beer craft beer from the brewery next door. [$] *Average main: NZ$26* ✉ *Māpua Wharf, Shed 3, Māpua* ☎ *03/540–3381* 🌐 *www.theappleshed.nz.*

🛏 Hotels

Throughout the Moutere, Māpua, and Motueka region there are a number of delightful B&Bs and boutique lodges for staying the night.

The Applepickers Cottages

$$$ | **APARTMENT** | Three self-contained cottages on the shoreline of the Waimea Estuary began life as apple pickers' cottages and have been refurbished in a pleasing rustic style. **Pros:** coastal reserve and bird habitat restoration project out your door; intimate waterfront setting and views; fresh farm eggs and fruit when available. **Cons:** could feel a bit isolated; minimum two-night stay; books up quickly. [$] *Rooms from: NZ$250* ✉ *43 Apple Valley Rd. E, Māpua* ☎ *03/540–2214* 🌐 *www.applepickers.nz* 🍴 *No Meals* ☞ *No children under 12* 🛏 *3 cottages.*

Te Koi the Lodge at Bronte

$$$$ | **HOTEL** | Nestled beside an estuary this estate features pure, simple luxury. **Pros:** right in the heart of wine country; bird-watching opportunities on the sand flats; excellent hosts with wide local knowledge. **Cons:** might be too buttoned up for some; very expensive; out in the country. [$] *Rooms from: NZ$760* ✉ *133 Bronte Rd. E, off State Hwy. 60, Māpua* ☎ *03/540–2422* 🌐 *www.tekoithelodge.com* ⏲ *Closed June–Sept.* 🍴 *Free Breakfast* 🛏 *5 suites.*

🛍 Shopping

Down at the Māpua Wharf you'll find an ice-cream store, a gardening store, ceramics and craft stores, galleries, a few restaurant–bars, and a microbrewery.

Cool Store Gallery

CRAFTS | In an old apple cool store (where apples were stored at cool temperatures after being picked), this gallery is filled with well-priced, New Zealand–made art and craft work. The work, produced by artists from the Nelson and West Coast regions, includes paintings, sculpture, textiles, paua-shell items, ceramics, glasswork, and jewelry. They can arrange to ship your hard-to-travel-with purchases home in one piece. ✉ *10 Aranui Rd., Māpua* ☎ *03/540–3778* 🌐 *www.coolstoregallery.co.nz.*

Motueka

50 km (31 miles) west of Nelson.

Motueka (mo-too-*eh*-ka) is a horticultural center—hops, kiwifruit, and apples are among its staples. As a major gateway to two national parks, Kahurangi and Abel Tasman, Motueka also attracts kayakers, hikers, and vacationers. The town sits at the seaward end of the Motueka Valley, close to the mountains of Kahurangi National Park. Like Golden Bay, Motueka is popular with the "alternative" communities around Nelson, and a few artisans and erstwhile hippies live alongside more traditional farming and orchard families. The hinterland is now also laced with vineyards, olive groves, and small, well-to-do farms often owned by absentee overseas owners. Many good cafés and places to stay are outside the town center, either in the sheltered inland valleys or out along the Abel Tasman coast and nearby bays, just north of town. South of town, the Motueka River is internationally known for its trout fishing, and the Great Taste Cycle Trail passes through the town.

GETTING HERE AND AROUND

Motueka is a 50-minute drive west of Nelson on State Highway 60. You can also arrive from the south along the Motueka Valley Highway, which leaves State Highway 6 at Kohatu, 50 minutes north of Murchison. From Motueka it's a one-hour drive over the Tākaka Hill to Golden Bay.

ScenicNZ runs coaches from Nelson to Motueka, Kaiteriteri, and Marahau. Golden Bay Coachlines travel from Nelson to Motueka and on to Tākaka, in Golden Bay.

VISITOR INFORMATION

CONTACTS Motueka i-SITE Visitor Centre. ✉ *20 Wallace St., Motueka* ☎ *03/528–6543* 🌐 *www.nelsontasman.nz.*

Sights

Motueka Valley

SCENIC DRIVE | If you are headed for the West Coast from Motueka, turn south onto Highway 61 at the very obvious Motueka Clock Tower, following the sign to Murchison. The road snakes through the Motueka Valley and follows the Motueka River, with green valley walls pressing close alongside. If this river could talk, it would probably scream, "Trout!" After the town of Tapawera, turn south on State Highway 6 at Kohatu Junction and continue to the West Coast.

Restaurants

Jester House Cafe

$$$ | CAFÉ | FAMILY | The locally sourced, mainly organic food at this funky place includes a raft of home baking, chutneys and dressings, and hearty country fare like chowders and salads. There's cozy indoor seating, and tables dotted throughout the garden and veranda. **Known for:** twice-baked three-cheese soufflé; family-friendly atmosphere; tame eels (to feed, not eat). [$] *Average main: NZ$21* ✉ *320 Aporo Rd.* ✣ *Follow Ruby Bay Scenic Dr.* ☎ *03/526–6742* 🌐 *www.jesterhouse.co.nz* ⏲ *Closed Sat.–Thurs.*

Riverside Café

$$ | ECLECTIC | FAMILY | Sprawling gardens make the perfect surrounding for this rambling, 160-year-old, colonial cottage where the menus are built around organic produce, which is all sourced locally, including from the Riverside Community, which owns and operates the café and its own farm. Menu choices range from stylish restaurant fare to French bistro-style with a range of salads and cakes. **Known for:** outdoor seating; breakfast until 3 pm; country ambience. [$] *Average main: NZ$18* ✉ *289 Main Rd., Upper Moutere along Inland Hwy., Lower Moutere* ✣ *South of Motueka* toward Upper Moutere ☎ 03/526–7447 ⊕ www.riverside.org.nz/cafe ⊗ No dinner Sun.–Thurs.

★ T.O.A.D. Hall

$$ | **CAFÉ** | At this café, shop, and produce market in a former church, enjoy breakfasts of French toast, free-range eggs Benedict, or free-range eggs cooked any way you like. Then stock up for your holiday travels from the food market. **Known for:** Townshend Brewery beers; fresh, wholesome local foods; wooden toys and furniture for sale made by the owners. $ *Average main: NZ$19* ⊠ *502 High St., Motueka* ☎ *03/528–6456* ⊕ *www. toadhallmotueka.co.nz* ⊗ *No dinner except in summer on Fri. and Sat.*

Hotels

Kairuru Farmstay Cottages

$$ | **HOUSE** | **FAMILY** | Halfway up the Tākaka Hill from Motueka, these homey cottages with timber interiors and verandas have all you need for a comfortable stay in the country. **Pros:** fantastic country base for area exploration; gorgeous views; a real Kiwi sheep and cattle farm, with tame animals for the kids to pat. **Cons:** a few gates to open and close as you drive in; long, narrow driveway onto the farm; steep 15-minute drive up the Tākaka Hill from Riwaka. $ *Rooms from: NZ$150* ⊠ *1014 State Hwy. 60, Tākaka Hill, Motueka* ☎ *03/528–8091, 0800/524– 787 New Zealand only* ⊕ *www.kairu- rufarmstay.co.nz* ❍| *No Meals* ➴ *2 cottages.*

Motueka River Lodge

$$$$ | **B&B/INN** | Tranquility, marvelous mountain views, and a superb standard of comfort are the hallmarks of this rustic lodge on 35 acres overlooking the Motueka River. **Pros:** Kiwi hosts who know and understand this part of the world; fishing rivers all around; all meals can be arranged, and they are superb. **Cons:** 50-minute drive from Nelson airport; out

in the countryside; closed June through August. $ *Rooms from: NZ$1200* ⊠ *Motueka Valley Hwy. (State Hwy. 61), Motueka* ☎ *03/526–8668* ⊕ *www. motuekalodge.com* ❍| *Free Breakfast* ➴ *5 suites.*

Motueka Top Ten Holiday Park

$ | **RESORT** | **FAMILY** | This premium Kiwi holiday park just steps from the center of town has top facilities and hosts. **Pros:** pizza truck on site; pool and hot tub; parklike setting. **Cons:** no views; can get crowded; not many options for food on site. $ *Rooms from: NZ$70* ⊠ *10 Fearon St., Motueka, Motueka* ☎ *03/528–7189, 0800/668–835* ⊕ *www.motuekatop10. co.nz* ❍| *No Meals* ➴ *35 units.*

Activities

FISHING

You won't lack for places to land some whopping brown trout in this region. Fishing season here runs from October to April. Fly-fishing excursions to local rivers and remote backcountry areas, for example, Kahurangi National Park, involve hiking or helicopter trips and give plenty of excitement to visiting anglers. Daily guiding rates are generally around NZ$900 and include lunches, drinks, and 4WD transportation. (Helicopter access is additional.) The best areas to base yourself for trout fishing are: St. Arnaud, Motueka, Murchison, or at one of the dedicated though pricey fly-fishing lodges close to these towns.

Strike Adventure Fishing

FISHING | Zane Mirfin is a very experienced fly-fishing guide, with huge local knowledge. His company takes clients to the best spots throughout Nelson and Marlborough, as well as the West Coast and North Canterbury. ⊠ *207 Hill St., Richmond* ☎ *03/544–2100* ⊕ *www. strikeadventure.com* ➴ *From NZ$900 per day* ➲ *2-day minimum.*

Abel Tasman National Park

77 km (48 miles) northwest of Motueka, 110 km (69 miles) northwest of Nelson.

Abel Tasman National Park is a stunning yet accessible swath of idyllic golden beaches and estuaries backed by a hinterland of native beech forests, granite gorges, and waterfalls. Unlike many of New Zealand's national parks, Abel Tasman has few serious challenges in its climate or terrain, making it a perfect place for a hiking, kayaking, or just cruising day-trip.

GETTING HERE AND AROUND

From Motueka, the drive to the two southern entry points of Abel Tasman National Park is about 20 minutes. Tour boats leave from Kaiteriteri and Marahau—turn hard right off State Highway 60 just after the little townships of Riwaka to reach Kaiteriteri. Keep left at the same intersection to reach Marahau, but then take an immediate right for a road that leads over the Marahau Hill to Marahau. This is where the popular Abel Tasman Coast Track begins, although you can also get access to the track via water taxis at Kaiteriteri. ScenicNZ coaches service Abel Tasman National Park from Nelson and Motueka to Kaiteriteri and Marahau, the southern entry points. Golden Bay Coachlines travels to Totaranui, the Golden Bay entry point to the park. Many tour operators provide transfers as well.

Four companies provide boat transport to the coastal areas of the park, offering day cruises, cruise/walk/kayak combos, and water taxi services for hikers and kayakers. These are Wilsons Abel Tasman, Abel Tasman Sea Shuttles, Marahau Water Taxis, and Abel Tasman Aqua Taxi.

Abel Tasman National Park information is available from the Motueka i-SITE Visitor Centre in Motueka.

BOAT TRANSPORTATION Abel Tasman Aqua Taxi. ✉ 275 Sandy Bay Rd., Marahau ☎ 0800/278–282, New Zealand only; ☎ 03/527–8083 elsewhere ⊕ www.aquataxi.co.nz. **Abel Tasman Sea Shuttles.** ✉ *Kaiteriteri Beach, Abel Tasman National Park* ☎ *03/527–8688, 0800/732–748 New Zealand only* ⊕ *www.abeltasman-seashuttles.co.nz.* **Marahau Water Taxis.** ✉ *8 Franklin St., Marahau, Abel Tasman National Park* ☎ *03/527–8176, 0800/808–018 New Zealand only* ⊕ *www.marahau-watertaxis.co.nz.* **Wilsons Abel Tasman.** ✉ *409 High St., Abel Tasman National Park* ☎ *03/528–2027, 0800/223–582 New Zealand only* ⊕ *www.abeltasman.co.nz.*

VISITOR INFORMATION

CONTACTS Abel Tasman Centre. ✉ *229 Sandy Bay–Marahau Beach Rd., Marahau, Abel Tasman National Park* ☎ *03/527–8176* ⊕ *www.abeltasmancentre.co.nz.* **Motueka i-SITE Visitor Centre.** ✉ *20 Wallace St., Motueka* ☎ *03/528–6543* ⊕ *www.nelsontasman.nz.*

⊙ Sights

★ Abel Tasman National Park

NATIONAL PARK | One of New Zealand's most easily accessible parks is also one of the most visited, thanks to its golden sand beaches, sculptured granite headlands, and forest-lined tidal inlets and islands. Unlike other South Island parks, Abel Tasman has few extremes in weather, and its coastal track, one of the Great Walks, is an ideal place to explore without the need of serious technical equipment or experience. Day and multiday trips, walking, sea-kayaking, sailing, scenic cruises, and combos of all of these are popular ways to explore the area. Keep in mind in the peak summer holiday season (Christmas to late January) this area is very busy, and you will rarely be on that dream beach alone. Any time of the year, however, is perfectly suitable for an Abel Tasman trip. The small settlements of Kaiteriteri and Marahau are the main gateways to the

Planning Your Trip to Abel Tasman

Best Time to Go

Anytime, but be wary during the peak summer holiday period from Christmas to mid-January, when the locals flock here in great numbers. Most people prefer to visit in summer, November through April, but don't let winter put you off, especially if you prefer your solitude. Though colder, winter weather can be very settled and sunny.

Best Activities

Cruise or Water Taxi. In midsummer the coastline buzzes with little water taxis and bigger cruising catamarans delivering people to various parts of the track, picking up those who have walked or kayaked a section or two, and dropping off supplies and even kayaks. If you just want to sit back and enjoy the scenery, join a cruise up the coast and back.

Kayak. Sea kayaking is popular, and several companies offer packages, often combining paddling and walking. These can be from half-day to multiday trips, self- or fully guided and catered, with optional accommodations arranged. Water taxis can also be arranged to deliver your packs to your next stopover point. It's a pleasant, possibly invigorating trip,
especially if the wind is going your way.

Sail. Almost without fail a healthy sea breeze comes up along the coast every summer afternoon. With this in mind catch a sailboat cruise out of Kaiteriteri in the morning. It's a slow gentle way to interact with the park. Then hang on as the skipper hooks the boat into that sea breeze, behind a fully set spinnaker, on the way home.

Walk. The entire 60 km (37 miles) Abel Tasman Coast Track, from Wainui Bay in the north to Marahau in the south, can be walked in three to five days, depending on your pace and how many swims you want along the way. This designated Great Walk is well formed and easy to follow. Alternatively you can walk short sections by arranging a drop-off and pickup by water taxi. Bark Bay to Torrent Bay and Awaroa to Torrent Bay are ideal for this. A few tidal crossings along the track can only be traversed at mid- to low tides. Each of these has a longer all-tide alternative, but plan ahead and remember to allow for this if you are meeting a water taxi. The park's inland tracks explore more rugged, forest-covered areas—best tackled by more experienced hikers.

national park, both at the southern end and 20- to 40-minutes' drive from Motueka. Stop first at the Nelson or Motueka i-SITE Visitor Centre for maps and information. If you're planning to stop overnight at any of the Department of Conservation's campsites or huts along the Abel Tasman Coast Track, you need to book ahead. You can do this online or at the Nelson or Motueka i-SITE. It pays to book well ahead, especially in summer. Water taxis service the coastline, and
they drop-off or pick-up at many points along the way. At the northern end of the park, a road leads from Golden Bay through the park to Totaranui, where there is a large Department of Conservation campground and long, beautiful beach. This is a popular start/finish point for those walking the Abel Tasman Coast Track. ✉ *Abel Tasman National Park* ⊕ *www.doc.govt.nz.*

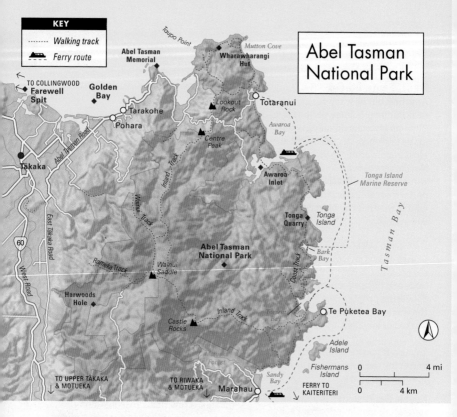

Abel Tasman National Park

KEY
- - - - - - *Walking track*
- *Ferry route*

TO COLLINGWOOD
Farewell Spit
Golden Bay
Taupo Point
Abel Tasman Memorial
Mutton Cove
Wharawharangi Hut
Tarakohe
Pohara
Lookout Rock
Totaranui
Takaka
Abel Tasman Road
Centre Peak
Awaroa Bay
Inland Track
Wainui Track
Awaroa Inlet
Tonga Island Marine Reserve
East Takaka Road
60
West Road
Tonga Quarry
Tonga Island
Rameka Track
Wainui Saddle
Abel Tasman National Park
Bark Bay
Coast Track
Tasman Bay
Harwoods Hole
Inland Track
Te Puketea Bay
Castle Rocks
Adele Island
Forest
Fishermans Island
TO UPPER TAKAKA & MOTUEKA
TO RIWAKA & MOTUEKA
Marahau
Sandy Bay
FERRY TO KAITERITERI
0   4 mi
0   4 km

🏖 Beaches

Kaiteriteri Beach

BEACH | The approach to Kaiteriteri Beach, through orchards then forest-lined coast, is lovely, and the beach is one of the area's prettiest, with its curve of golden sand, rocky islets offshore, and deep clear water. This place is packed in midsummer, but once the four-week post-Christmas rush is over, the area returns to its usual less-frenzied pace. Many water-taxi and scenic cruises leave from here for Abel Tasman National Park. The Great Taste cycle trail, which starts in Nelson, ends here, at the Kaiteriteri Mountain Bike Park. There is a popular campground and a few cafés in the village, although all prune their hours or close in winter. A number of private vacation homes are also located here. **Amenities:** food and drink; parking (free);

toilets. **Best for:** swimming; walking. ✉ *Kaiteriteri–Sandy Bay Rd., Motueka.*

🛏 Hotels

★ Abel Tasman Lodge

$$ | **HOTEL** | Spacious chalets and studios, with native gardens between them, are nestled between Abel Tasman National Park and Marahau Beach. **Pros:** stylish, homey accommodations overlook the hills of Abel Tasman National Park; close to everything in Marahau; travelers share tales in the communal kitchen. **Cons:** studios don't have kitchen facilities; no breakfast in the room rate; need to remember to stock up with groceries before getting here. $ *Rooms from: NZ$200* ✉ *295 Sandy Bay–Marahau Rd., Marahau* ☎ *03/527–8250* ⊕ *www. abeltasmanlodge.co.nz* ⦿ *No Meals* ➭ *12 rooms.*

One-Day Itinerary in Abel Tasman

Try a walking–boat trip combo on the beautiful coastal track. Pack a picnic, your sunblock, and walking shoes and, if leaving from Nelson, hit the road by 8 am. Most operators will pick you up from accommodations; if you're driving, there's parking available at Kaiteriteri and Marahau beaches, the departure points for boat tours and water taxis. The drive across to the park takes around 80 minutes from Nelson and around 30 minutes from Motueka.

Midmorning, catch a big, modern catamaran or small, fast-water taxi along the coast to Bark Bay. On the way, if you've left from Kaiteriteri, you will pass Split Apple Rock, a giant granite marble in the sea that looks just like ... a giant split apple. Farther up the coast you'll pass sandy beaches like Apple Tree Bay and Coquille Bay before cruising past the birdlife sanctuary of Adele Island. Then, the boat hits open water for a short stretch before rounding Pitt Head and calling into Anchorage, a beautiful sheltered bay with a Department of Conservation (DOC) hut and campsite that looks across to neighboring Torrent Bay, with its

few private vacation homes. Your boat will most likely drop off and pick up walkers, kayakers, and supplies here, then continue to Bark Bay, a little farther up the coast. Here is where you disembark. You'll walk off the boat ramp onto the beach and be shown where to join the Abel Tasman Coastal Track for your afternoon's walk back to Anchorage.

By now you'll be ready for lunch. There are few more idyllic spots than the forest-lined beach and estuary of Bark Bay for a picnic. From here it's an easy and scenic three-hour walk to Torrent Bay. The track climbs steeply at first, before ambling around several hillsides with pleasant outlooks through gaps in the trees. In summer, you'll meet plenty of other walkers. Follow the track as it descends to Torrent Bay, then continue on to Anchorage, which you can now see across the bay. Depending on the tide, you can either cross the estuary or walk around the all-tide track to Anchorage. Pass through the DOC campground and relax on the beach until your boat arrives to return you to Kaiteriteri or Marahau, all in good time for a well-earned sundowner.

Kimi Ora Eco Resort

$$$ | RESORT | The cozy wood walls and simple furnishings of the guest quarters are part of the philosophy here: Kimi Ora means "seek health" in Māori, and this aims to be an environmentally friendly, health-oriented resort. **Pros:** bordered by a mix of exotic forest and regenerating native bush; geared toward healthy living; all the rooms have distant sea views. **Cons:** healthy lifestyle isn't for everyone; native birdsong will wake you early; 10-minute walk to Kaiteriteri Beach. $ *Rooms from: NZ$205* ✉ *Martins*

Farm Rd., Kaiteriteri ☎ *03/527–8027, 0508/5464–672* ⊕ *www.kimiora.com* ⮑ *22 units* ❍❙ *Free Breakfast.*

 Activities

HIKING
Abel Tasman Coast Track

HIKING & WALKING | One of the most popular multiday hikes in any New Zealand national park is the three- to five-day Abel Tasman Coast Track. From beach to golden beach, over gentle forest-covered

Overnight in Abel Tasman

Plan ahead if you want to stay in the park overnight, at either a Department of Conservation (DOC) campground or hut, like those at Anchorage, a four-hour, 12.4-km (7-mile) walk from the start of the track at Marahau. These huts and campsites are on the Abel Tasman Coast Track, which is a part of the national Great Walks system. Tickets (NZ$75 per night for huts and NZ$30 per night for campsites, or NZ$32 and NZ$15, respectively, for New Zealanders) must be bought beforehand, either at the Nelson or Motueka i-SITE Visitor Centre, DOC visitor centers throughout the country, or on the DOC website (*booking.doc.govt.nz*). Huts are basic, with cooking, shower and toilet facilities, filtered water, and

sleeping bunks. There are four huts and 18 campsites (some accessible by sea, for kayakers) plus Totaranui Campground. You will need to bring all your food (water taxis can be arranged to deliver fresh supplies, at a cost). You will also be expected to pack out all your rubbish. There are more salubrious park accommodations, like the lodges at Awaroa and Torrent bays, should comfort be your thing. From Torrent Bay, near Anchorage, there's a lovely short walk from the bridge over the Torrent River inland a short distance to Cleopatra's Pool. This rugged rock pool sits in between huge granite boulders and is surrounded by bush. But it's a frosty swim, even in summer.

hills and across tidal inlets, this is stellar hiking. One of the premier-rated Great Walks, and traversed year-round, the track is popular because of its relatively easy terrain, short distances between huts and campsites, and the stunning landscapes. Water taxis can be booked to drop off and pick up hikers from several points along the track, allowing flexible options for walks of anything from one hour to five days. There are four huts and 18 campsites, and spaces in both must be booked year-round. Bookings can be made online, through DOC visitor centers anywhere, and i-SITES in the Nelson region. ⊠ *Abel Tasman Coast Track, Abel Tasman National Park* ☎ *03/546–7393 Nelson i-SITE Visitor Centre, 03/546–8210 DOC Great Walk Bookings Helpdesk* ⊕ *www.doc.govt.nz.*

MULTISPORT ADVENTURES AND TOURS

Wilsons Abel Tasman

HIKING & WALKING | Pioneer operator of excursions to this beautiful park, the Wilson family team offer trips from three hours to five days. Choose hiking (guided and self-guided), guided sea kayaking, a Vista cruise, or just water-taxi service. You can also stay overnight at the family's stylish beachfront lodges in the national park, Torrent Bay Lodge, and Meadowbank homestead at Awaroa. Departures are everyday from Kaiteriteri, with bus connections to Nelson. ⊠ *409 High St., Motueka* ☎ *03/528–2027, 0800/223–582 New Zealand only* ⊕ *www.abeltasman. co.nz* ⊠ *From NZ$69.*

SAILING AND KAYAKING

Abel Tasman Sailing Adventures

SAILING | If you'd like a unique day in the park without breaking a sweat, call up these sailing gurus. Their large

Did You Know?

Abel Tasman National Park is New Zealand's smallest, and arguably most popular, national park. The forest-lined golden sand beaches, estuaries, islands, and fascinating, weathered granite rock are the big attractions.

catamarans set sail daily from Kaiteriteri. Along the way you might stop for a photo at Split Apple Rock, stop for a swim at a golden sand beach or to check out the seals around Motuareronui/Adele Island. The most popular trip is a full-day sail that includes lunch. You can also arrange overnight trips, walking–sailing combos, and exclusive charters. ✉ *5 Kaiteriteri-Sandy Bay Rd., Kaiteriteri* ☎ *03/527–8375, 0800/467–245 New Zealand only* ⊕ *www.sailingadventures.co.nz* ✈ *Short sails from NZ$85 ranging up to NZ$2400 daily charters.*

Kaiteriteri Kayak

KAYAKING | One of the long-standing operators here offers the whole gamut of guided half-day, full-day, and multiday kayak trips, plus walk–kayak combos and kayak rentals. They work with partner company Sea Shuttle Cruises to get you quickly into the best spots along this incredible coast—for example, to Tonga Island Marine Reserve, a trip that encompasses golden beaches, seals for company, a sheltered lagoon, and amazing rock formations. ✉ *3 Kaiteriteri-Sandy Bay Rd., Kaiteriteri, Abel Tasman National Park* ☎ *03/527–8383, 0800/252–925 New Zealand only* ⊕ *www.abeltasman.co.nz* ✈ *From NZ$90.*

The Sea Kayak Company

KAYAKING | Family owned and operated, this smaller company's guided kayaking trips include stops on beaches and campsites that simply can't be reached by hikers. Popular options include the Ab-Fab Marine Reserve one-day paddle and walk and a two-day More than Beaches tour. All multiday tours are fully catered and and fully equipped. Reservations are recommended. They'll also rent kayaks and gear for independent travel and give you a heap of advice to help make your trip a happy and safe one. ✉ *506 High St., Motueka* ☎ *03/528–7251,* ⊕ *www.seakayaknz.co.nz* ✈ *From NZ$85.*

Golden Bay and Tākaka

55 km (35 miles) northwest of Motueka, 110 km (70 miles) west of Nelson.

The gorgeous stretch of coastline that begins at Separation Point, in Abel Tasman National Park, and runs northwest past Tākaka to Farewell Spit is known as Golden Bay, named for the gold discovered there in the 1850s. It's a 40-km (25-mile) crescent of beaches, farms, and orchards. Alternating sandy and rocky shores curve up to the sands of Farewell Spit, the arcing prong that encloses the bay. A 19th-century lighthouse station near its tip, there to warn shipping of the low-lying sandy spit, is the only man-made intrusion. Dutch navigator Abel Tasman anchored briefly in Golden Bay a few days before Christmas 1642. His visit ended abruptly when four of his crew were killed in an altercation with local Māori iwi (tribe), Ngāti Tūmatakōkiri. Tasman named the place Moordenaers Baij, or Murderers' Bay, and sailed away without ever setting foot on New Zealand soil. Today, a relaxed crew of approximately 5,000 locals firmly believe they live in paradise, and a huge annual influx of summertime vacationers agrees with them. The only road to Golden Bay climbs over the steep Tākaka Hill from Motueka, the longest stretch of hill road in the country. You need to be determined to get here; it's not a place you pass on the way to somewhere else.

The Golden Bay lifestyle has for some years been considered "alternative"—a hideout for hippies, musicians, and artists. It's also the center of a rich dairy farming area, and its warm, sheltered climate nurtures crops such as citrus, avocados, and kiwifruit that struggle on the colder, Nelson side of "The Hill."

GETTING HERE AND AROUND

Golden Bay Air flies scheduled flights from Wellington to Tākaka and charters to Karamea. The company also offers shuttle connections to both ends of the Heaphy Track (a Great Walk) and Abel Tasman National Park.

The road into Golden Bay, over the Tākaka Hill on State Highway 60, rises 2,500 feet before plunging again to sea level to the tiny township of Tākaka, a jumping-off point for Farewell Spit, Kahurangi National Park, and the Heaphy Track. This road is a 40-minute climb of twisting corners, steep drop-offs, and occasional bays. Don't be tempted to check the views while you're driving; wait until you reach Bob's Lookout, on the Nelson side of the hill, and Harwood Lookout, on the Tākaka side, for safe viewing.

AIRLINE CONTACTS Golden Bay Air.
☎ 03/525–8725, 0800/588–885 New Zealand only ⊕ www.goldenbayair.co.nz.

BUS CONTACTS Golden Bay Coachlines.
✉ 98 Commercial St., Tākaka ☎ 03/525–8352 ⊕ www.goldenbaycoachlines.co.nz.

VISITOR INFORMATION
CONTACTS Golden Bay Visitor Centre.
✉ 16 Willow St., Tākaka ☎ 03/525–9136 ⊕ www.goldenbaynz.co.nz.

Sights

Golden Bay begs to be explored, so if you take the trouble to cross the Tākaka Hill into this special area, plan to stay at least two nights, or you'll spend your whole time driving and none enjoying the rewards of your travels. Golden Bay Coachlines runs daily services to Tākaka, the Heaphy Track, and Totaranui (check times in winter).

Collingwood
TOWN | After winding past several small farming districts and close to beach communities such as Paton's Rock, Onekaka, and Tukurua, State Highway 60 ends at Collingwood, a small and picturesque seaside village at the mouth of the giant Aorere River, 26 km (16 miles) west of Tākaka. The earliest European settlers came here in the 1840s to build small ships from the timber lining the beaches and to farm the fertile river plain that spills out of the surrounding mountains. In the late-1850s, gold was discovered nearby and Collingwood became a thriving port-of-entry town; at one time it was even under consideration to be the country's capital. Collingwood is a bit out on a limb from the main roads, but nevertheless has much to offer. It's the northern access point for the Heaphy Track Great Walk and the main base for trips to internationally recognized bird-watching site Farewell Spit and to the wild, remote coastline of the northernmost West Coast, notably Wharariki Beach. The town's rich heritage is well documented, in both the small Collingwood Museum and the neighboring Aorere Centre.

Totaranui
TOWN | From Tākaka, the coast road heading northeast leads to Totaranui, the northern entry for Abel Tasman National Park. This scenic road passes through Pohara Beach, which has a few cafés and a holiday park, before winding around to Wainui Bay with its alternative Tūi community (a residential community that welcomes visitors) and cascading Wainui Falls (a 75-minute return walk from the road). From Wainui Bay, the road over the Totaranui Hill is a gravel surface. Take it slowly: it's a gorgeous drive through dense native bush to the coast. Totaranui Beach is a long golden-sand beach that is safe for swimming. This area can also be reached by scheduled boat services from Kaiteriteri and Marahau, on the Motueka side of the Tākaka Hill. It's a slice of pure beach bliss, and there's an unpowered campground with basic facilities. There's generally a wait-list to camp here for the first few weeks after Christmas, large though it is. Otherwise, you should be fine—however, reservations are required no matter what time of year. ⊕ www.doc.govt.nz.

Waikoropupu Springs

BODY OF WATER | Six kilometers (4 miles) west of Tākaka you'll find the largest cold-water spring system in the southern hemisphere, the Main Springs, likened to a fresh-water equivalent of a coral reef because of its superb variety of aquatic vegetation. The water here is among the clearest water ever measured, anywhere in the world. Swimming or touching the water is not allowed, to prevent the introduction of weeds and damage to the delicate flora within the springs, so leave your wetsuits and dive gear in the car. Instead, take a leisurely stroll around the Scenic Reserve on the 40-minute, top-quality walk to the Main Springs, Dancing Sand Spring, and Fish Creek Springs. Go quietly—the better to spot *tūī*, bellbirds, wood pigeons, and other birdlife. The turnoff from State Highway 60 to Pupu Springs Road is signposted on the western side of the Tākaka River bridge. Pick a sunny day when the Springs are fully illuminated. ⊠ *Pupu Springs Rd., Tākaka* ⊕ *www.doc.govt.nz.*

🏖 Beaches

Golden Bay has miles of swimming beaches and small bays. Popular with families for its safe, shallow water is Ligar Bay, while Tata Beach is deeper—these are two of the best spots near Tākaka. This area has a dramatic tidal range so it pays to pick your times.

Wharariki Beach

BEACH | A must-see for its dramatic seascapes is Wharariki Beach, out beyond the road to Farewell Spit. To get here, drive past Collingwood to Pakawau and follow the signs. Go as far as the road will take you, and then walk over farmland on a well-defined trail for 20 minutes. Allow at least an hour for the return circuit, along the beach and back via another well-marked track along the Farmpark. Be wary though: it's too rough for swimming and very easy to get

The Grove

The Grove Scenic Reserve is a small patch of native forest at Rocklands that escaped development when the area was cleared for farming. It's an enchanting collection of giant *rata* tree (noteworthy for its dark red wood), elegant *nikau* palms, and trailing vines that grow between and over gnarly limestone outcrops and gulches. In early summer, the rata wear a cloak of bright scarlet flowers. Heading toward Pohara from Tākaka, turn right off Abel Tasman Drive at Clifton and follow the signs. The lookout over the Tākaka Valley at the top is worth the excursion alone.

caught by the incoming tide. Remember, this dramatic coast is quite remote, with few people (certainly no lifeguards) and tides change very quickly. Don't be one of those who gets trapped by the sea walking out to the offshore rocks. Also, among the massive sand dunes you're likely to come across fur seals and their pups. Keep at least a 30-foot distance, as they can move quickly and do bite, and never get between a seal and the sea. It can be very windy here, at which times the sand will whip you like in a Sahara storm. But don't let any of that put you off this inspiring place. ■**TIP→ Be sure to bring drinking water; there's none available anywhere at the beach. Amenities:** none. **Best for:** solitude; walking. ⊠ *Tākaka* ⊹ *Drive past Collingwood to Pakawau and follow signs.*

🍽 Restaurants

The Brigand

$$$ | NEW ZEALAND | This bar and café is located in a lovely old house on Tākaka's main street and has a sunny courtyard, cool handmade furniture, plenty of indoor seating, and roaring fires (indoor and out) for cozy nights. The menu consistently provides New Zealand classics, from light snacks and daily specials to full dinners. **Known for:** sticky pork spare ribs; sea-run salmon; nice garden. [$] *Average main: NZ$29* ✉ *90 Commercial St., Tākaka* ☎ *03/525–9636* 🌐 *www.thebrigand.nz.*

Courthouse Cafe

$$ | **NEW ZEALAND** | In the lovely old former Collingwood Courthouse, on the main crossroads into town, this laid-back and popular café makes good use of local produce. Their big breakfast and eggs Benedict will set you up for a trip to the beach or Farewell Spit or Heaphy Track. **Known for:** house-made pies; lots of gluten-free and vegan options; breakfast tortillas. [$] *Average main: NZ$18* ✉ *At Gibbs and Elizabeth Sts., Collingwood* ☎ *03/524–8194* 🌐 *www.thecourthouse-cafecollingwood.com* ⏲ *No dinner.*

★ Mussel Inn

$$$ | **NEW ZEALAND** | **FAMILY** | Swing by the Mussel Inn for a quintessential slice of Golden Bay life: music, craft beer, and darn good pub food. Locals come for the live music (most evenings in summer), mussel chowder, steamed mussels, or goat curry, washed down with house-brewed beer and ciders. **Known for:** live music; craft beers and ciders; rustic, country ambience. [$] *Average main: NZ$27* ✉ *1259 Tākaka-Collingwood Hwy., Onekaka* ☎ *03/525–9241* 🌐 *www.musse-linn.co.nz* ⏲ *Closed Aug.*

Wholemeal Cafe

$$$ | **CAFÉ** | Set in the old Tākaka movie theater, this place is synonymous with the alternative feel that is Golden Bay. The breakfast and lunch menus are substantial and wholesome, or you can catch an early dinner on Friday and Saturday when they are open until 8 pm. **Known for:** coffee sourced direct from high-altitude farmers in Timor Leste; funky vibe; amazing baked goods. [$] *Average main: NZ$21* ✉ *60 Commercial St., Tākaka* ☎ *03/525–9426* 🌐 *www.wholemealcafe.co.nz* ⏲ *No dinner Sun.–Thurs.*

Hotels

Adrift In Golden Bay

$$$$ | **HOTEL** | Here, a short walk across soft grass from your luxurious, fully self-contained villa or studio unit gets you to your own quiet beach. **Pros:** sundecks out front and private rear courtyards; Jacuzzi-style hot tubs; calm, thoughtful atmosphere. **Cons:** expensive; minimum night stays enforced (up to four nights in peak summer); isolated location. [$] *Rooms from: NZ$529* ✉ *52 Tukurua Rd., 18 km (11 miles) north of Tākaka* ☎ *03/525–8353* 🌐 *www.adrift.co.nz* ⏲ *Closed July* 🍴 *Free Breakfast* ☞ *No children under 12* 🛏 *6 units.*

Pohara Top 10 Holiday Park

$ | **MOTEL** | Well-appointed cabins and motel units, with various bedding configurations and some with full kitchens, are set on 5 beachfront acres with plenty of trees for shelter. **Pros:** helpful, professional hosts; beachfront property; good casual dining options nearby. **Cons:** might be lots of kids making noise; some units have shared bathroom facilities; cabins are quite small. [$] *Rooms from: NZ$85* ✉ *809 Abel Tasman Dr., Pohara* ☎ *03/525–9500, 0800/764–272 New Zealand only* 🌐 *www.poharabeach.com* 🍴 *No Meals* 🛏 *24 units.*

Twin Waters Lodge

$$ | **B&B/INN** | A small but stunning lodge nestled on a small peninsula beside the Pakawau Estuary, Twin Waters overlooks the surrounding hills and wetlands. **Pros:** good location to explore Farewell Spit and Wharariki Beach; interesting tidal estuary out the door; thoughtful and friendly hosts. **Cons:** probably not the best spot as sea levels rise; limited evening dining options in shoulder seasons; remote from town and shops. [$] *Rooms from: NZ$200* ✉ *30 Totara Ave., Pakawau, 9 km (5½ miles) past*

*Collingwood on road to Farewell Spit,
Collingwood ☎ 03/524–8014 ⊕ www.
twinwaters.co.nz ⊗ Closed June–mid-
Oct. ⦿ Free Breakfast ⇨ 4 rooms.*

Activities

FISHING
Anatoki Salmon
FISHING | FAMILY | At this salmon farm,
on the banks of the Anatoki River, you
can fish for salmon then have your catch
prepared for your lunch while you wait.
Or they will smoke it for you or package it to take away and prepare at your
leisure. Entry is free; just pay for what
you catch. Fishing gear is provided, and
experience is not necessary. You can
also feed eels here, and there's a petting
farm for kids—and a café to round off the
day. ✉ *230 McCallum Rd., Anatoki Valley
☎ 03/525–7251, 0800/262–865 New Zealand only ⊕ www.anatokisalmon.co.nz
⊠ Salmon NZ$30 per kg.*

HORSE TREKKING
Cape Farewell Horse Treks
HORSEBACK RIDING | FAMILY | Saddle up at
Cape Farewell, and ride off into the sunset or to the beach. This outfit provides
some of the best horse trekking in the
country, on possibly the most spectacular
beaches. For the best views, ride the
Old Man Range trek, or try the Puponga
Beach ride for something more tranquil;
it's also suitable for kids age five and up.
If you're into wild beach gallops then join
the Wharariki Beach Trek. ✉ *102 Wharariki
Rd., Puponga ☎ 03/524–8031 ⊕ www.
horsetreksnz.co.nz ⊠ From NZ$80.*

Farewell Spit

*30 km (19 miles) north of Collingwood,
which is 23 km (14 miles) north of Tākaka.*

A 35-km (22-mile) sandspit that expands
tenfold when the tide goes out, Farewell
Spit is the home of tens of thousands of
seabirds, many of them migrants from
the northern hemisphere, and is an internationally recognized bird sanctuary. The
landscape is wild and can be a hostile
environment when conditions turn. The
'Triangle Walk' (allow 1½ hrs) from the
base of the Spit goes from the parking
lot along the inner spit before crossing
over to the outer beach and returning via
Triangle Flat. Public access along the spit
is restricted to only the first 4 km (2½
miles).

GETTING HERE AND AROUND
The nearest town to Farewell Spit is
Collingwood, 2½ hours from Nelson at
the end of State Highway 60. The road
continues 30 km (19 miles) from Collingwood to Puponga Farm Park, where
the public road ends at the base of the
Spit. Golden Bay Coachlines runs a daily
service from Nelson to Tākaka, which
includes a connection 23 km (14 miles)
farther to Collingwood. Golden Bay Air
flies from Wellington to Tākaka. If you fly,
rental vehicles can be hired in Tākaka.

Access onto the spit itself is only
possible with the licensed tour operator
Farewell Spit Eco Tours, based in Collingwood. Tours run daily, times depending
on the tides.

TOURS
Farewell Spit Eco Tours
SPECIAL-INTEREST TOURS | This is one
of the premier bird-watching tours of
New Zealand, and, even if you're not an
avid bird-watcher, traversing this vast,
windblown, sandy landscape is a must.
(Sliding down the massive sand dunes
is optional). Most popular is the 6½-hour
Eco Tour, driving all-terrain vehicles on
the sand to a lighthouse near the tip of
the spit. The Gannet Tour travels farther
to a hardy gannet colony, or there's the
two-hour Wader Watch Tour. A shorter,
4½-hour Eco Tour onto the spit is also
offered. This company has been running
tours for generations and is the only one
licensed to travel on the spit (which is

closed to public access). Reservations are essential. Times vary with the tides. ✉ *6 Tasman St., Collingwood* ☎ *03/524–8257, 0800/808–257 New Zealand only* ⊕ *www.farewellspit.com* 🗐 *From NZ$155.*

Kahurangi National Park

35 km (21 miles) west of Tākaka.

New Zealand's second-largest national park, Kahurangi is 1.2 million acres of ancient granite and marbled mountains with fluted rock forms, arches, shafts, and sinkholes (featured in the Lord of the Rings films), remote river gorges, subalpine tops, beech forests, and coastal rain forests, plus designated wilderness areas where no development or helicopter access is allowed. There are more than 563 km (350 miles) of hiking trails of various levels of difficulty, including the longest Great Walk, the Heaphy Track. Beneath the park are the deepest and longest cave systems in the southern hemisphere. The Visitor Centre (*www.goldenbaynz.co.nz*) provides local trail maps.

GETTING HERE AND AROUND

There are two main entry points to the park from Tākaka. One is at the northern end of the Heaphy Track, south of Collingwood. Most people walk the four- to five-day trail one-way and arrange a bus pickup or drop-off. The second entry point is up the Cobb Valley: turn left at Upper Tākaka, at the base of the Tākaka Hill on its western side. The Cobb Valley road ends approximately 32 km (20 miles) farther in. You'll find camping areas and short walks, plus the starting points to several park hiking trails in this valley. Golden Bay Coachlines also runs daily connections to the northern end of the Heaphy Track in summer.

◉ Sights

★ Kahurangi National Park

NATIONAL PARK | Kahurangi is a vast wilderness of marbled karst mountains; glaciated landforms; alpine tablelands; rivers; alpine tarns; and beech, podocarp, and coastal rain forests. Underground are the country's longest, deepest, and oldest cave systems. Multiday hikes, short walks, caving, extreme rafting, fly-fishing, and hunting are what people like to do here. Kahurangi National Park spans 1.1 million acres, much of it untamed, yet crisscrossed by 570 km (353 miles) of hiking trails of various levels. Most well known is the four- to five-day Heaphy Track, one of New Zealand's Great Walks. Probably the most popular road access from Nelson is the steep, slightly scary climb to Flora Carpark on Mt. Arthur, and from Golden Bay its into the Cobb Valley. The main West Coast access is through Karamea; this is also the southwestern entry to the Heaphy Track. Helicopters regularly transport fishing fans to secret river spots, though large areas of the park are designated wilderness, where no development or helicopter transport is permitted. ⊕ *www.doc.govt.nz/parks-and-recreation/places-to-go/nelson-tasman/places/kahurangi-national-park.*

Oparara Cave System

CAVE | The magical rain forests and sculpted landforms here are amid the Honeycomb Hill Caves Specially Protected Area that's within Kahurangi National Park. Spectacular features at Oparara include a series of huge limestone arches (including the largest in the southern hemisphere, at 470 feet), passages, and caverns. Several short walks explore the caves, which are about a 45-minute drive northeast of Karamea. The Oparara Valley Project Trust, a community project, has enhanced visitor facilities and offers guided tours that can include both walks and kayaking explorations. Also in this

Planning Your Trip to Kahurangi

Best Time to Go

Kahurangi can be visited any time of the year, although snow in winter will inhibit access to the higher areas like Mt. Arthur and the Mt. Owen massif. The Heaphy Track is generally passable year-round. It's particularly popular with walkers in summer, and mountain bikers are permitted on the track in winter (May to September).

Best Activities

Caving and Cave Diving. There is a spectacular network of caves beneath the park, in particular under "the mountains with plumbing," as Mt. Arthur and Mt. Owen are known. New passages are still being discovered, and the cave systems at the northern end of Kahurangi join up with those under Abel Tasman. Local guides are essential if you want to explore these. The Pearce and Riwaka rivers, on the eastern side of Mt. Arthur, are both well-known cave-diving spots with well-defined resurgence caves. The Riwaka resurgence is popular with scuba enthusiasts. A local guide is essential.

Helicopter or Plane Flights. In some areas of the vast Kahurangi there's absolutely no development permitted, and the only way to get there is to walk. In other areas, however, helicopters can be chartered to fly hikers and rafters to remote rivers and trails, to get trout fishermen to favored spots, and for general sightseeing. A helicopter flight to Lord of the Rings film locations on spectacular Mt. Owen and Mt. Olympus has also become popular.

Hiking. The four- to five-day Heaphy Track is one of the country's Great Walks, traversing tussock-covered tablelands and remote, wild West Coast beaches in the northwest corner of the park, between Collingwood and Karamea. Other challenging and less-known walks are available; while shorter, easier and popular tracks leave from the Flora Carpark (accessed from Motueka and Nelson) and the Cobb Valley (south of Tākaka).

White-Water Rafting and Kayaking. The Grade V Karamea River offers some of the country's most remote white-water rafting and kayaking. Access is generally by helicopter, and rafting trips can last up to a week, thus involving overnight camping. There is also great white water on the Buller River near Murchison, which runs along part of the park's southern boundary. Local knowledge is essential on these trips so use a local guiding company of good repute.

cave system is Honeycomb Hill, featuring underground passages of more than 13 km (8 miles) that contain the largest collection of subfossil bird bones found in New Zealand; many of them are extinct, including nine moa species and the giant New Zealand eagle. The caves are protected, and access is by guided tour only. ✉ *McCullums Mill Rd., Karamea* ☎ *03/782–6652* ⊕ *www.oparara.co.nz* 🎫 *Guided tours from NZ$95.*

🏃 Activities

HIKING

Bush & Beyond Guided Walks

HIKING & WALKING | Walk with the locals on guided day walks or multiday hikes throughout Kahurangi National Park. Trips are tailored to your level of fitness and interests. They can be self-catering (still guided) or fully catered, where your accommodations, food, and transfers

There are numerous hiking trails through the vast tracts of forest, deep river valleys, tussock tablelands, and mountain ridges of Kahurangi National Park.

are all taken care of. These guys operate year-round and know the Kahurangi area and beyond. They are also ardent conservationists, volunteering with predator pest control groups aimed to restore the wildlife in the park. ☎ 03/543–3742, 021/0270–8209 ⊕ www.heaphytrackguidedwalks.co.nz ✉ Multi-day trips from NZ$1150.

Heaphy Track

HIKING & WALKING | The 78-km (49-mile), five-day Heaphy Track is a Great Walk, one of New Zealand's premier multiday trails. It traverses a grand landscape—of beech, rata, nikau, and coastal rain forests along with tussock-covered table lands—as it crosses Kahurangi National Park from Golden Bay to the West Coast. The track can be approached from Karamea or Collingwood. Kiwi are often heard at night. There are seven huts and nine campsites, and spots in both must be booked year-round. Bookings can be made online or through Department of Conservation offices or the Nelson,

Motueka, or Golden Bay i-SITE Visitor Centre. Each end of this track is a drive of several hours apart; shuttle transport (by coach or air) can be arranged. Mountain bikers are permitted on the track in winter (from May 1 to November 30). Several companies offer guided options. ✉ Kahurangi National Park ☎ 03/546–8210 Great Walks Help Desk, Nelson DOC office ⊕ www.doc.govt.nz ✉ Huts from NZ$56 per night.

Kahurangi Guided Walks

HIKING & WALKING | If you'd like some expert company on hikes around the national park, these specialists run one-day treks on the best routes, as well as the full five-day Heaphy Track hike. These folks also offer guided walks in Abel Tasman National Park and around Golden Bay. ☎ 03/391–4120 ⊕ www.kahurangi-walks.co.nz ✉ Day walks from NZ$250 per person.

Nelson Lakes National Park

100 km (62 miles) south of Nelson.

Spread around mountains and two spectacular glacial lakes, Rotoroa and Rotoiti, Nelson Lakes National Park also extends to high alpine passes and rocky peaks, clear-running rivers, and bush-lined trails. The native beech forests pour down to the lakeshore. On cloudy days, mist swirls through the trees, wetting the draping mosses. On sunny days, the intense green shines through, and the birdsong resounds. Lake Rotoiti is also one site of the Rotoiti Nature Recovery Project, through which long-term intensive pest control has helped the recovery of some native birds and the reintroduction of others, including great spotted kiwi.

GETTING HERE AND AROUND

It's a 100-km (65-mile) drive south from Nelson to St. Arnaud, the hub of the park. Head south on State Highway 6; at Wai-iti, just south of Wakefield, veer left off the highway and follow the Golden Downs Road through to St. Arnaud. If coming up from the West Coast, pass through Murchison then after 35 km (21 miles), turn right at Kawatiri Junction. It's a further 30 minutes from here to St. Arnaud. From the East Coast, drive up the Wairau Valley from Blenheim, heading left (west) off State Highway 6 at Renwick.

Shuttle transport to the park is available through Nelson Lakes Shuttles; they will deliver to most track terminus points and the main stops as well. They can also link you between the various local national parks and track entry points.

BUS CONTACTS Nelson Lakes Shuttles.
☎ *03/540–2042* ⊕ *www.nelsonlakesshuttles.co.nz.*

VISITOR INFORMATION
CONTACTS DOC Nelson Lakes Visitor Centre. ✉ *View Rd., St. Arnaud* ☎ *03/521–1806* ⊕ *www.doc.govt.nz.*

 Sights

Nelson Lakes National Park

NATIONAL PARK | Snow-covered peaks and alpine passes sit between two deep brooding, forest-surrounded lakes. Dense native forest, swampy wetlands, and tumbling rivers line the valleys, and birdlife join in a resounding dawn chorus. It's an exhilarating environment. Two stunningly scenic glacial-formed lakes, Rotoroa and Rotoiti, are the central focus of Nelson Lakes National Park. Also in the park are rocky peaks and tussock-covered tops, glacier-gouged river valleys, and bush-lined trails. Native beech forest pours down to the lakeshores. On cloudy days, mist swirls through the trees, wetting the draping mosses. On sunny days, the intense greens shine through and the birds' chorus resounds. Of the two lakes, Rotoroa is less developed, with just a few fishing cottages and a campsite on its northern shore. The village of St. Arnaud, at the northern end of Lake Rotoiti, is the main gateway to the park. An accommodation lodge, a handful of B&Bs, a general store, a café, the Department of Conservation (DOC) Nelson Lakes Visitor Centre, and a host of private vacation homes are located here. Each year, in late February or early March, the Antique and Classic Boat Show is held at Lake Rotoiti with close to 200 antique vessels congregating for several days of boat racing and boat talk. The visitor center is particularly good, with information on the area's geology, ecology, and human history. Maps, details, and advice on the hiking trails are available, and a mountain weather forecast is issued daily. The DOC also administers two excellent campgrounds near the lake frontage. Bookings for these, at Kerr Bay and West Bay, can

Planning Your Trip to Nelson Lakes

Best Time to Go

Summer is the most popular time of year to visit as the weather is warm (for an alpine region), the lakes are swimmable (barely), and, for climbers, the high-alpine passes are usually free of snow and avalanche risk. Voracious sand flies, however, are a problem at any time. Bring your repellent.

Best Activities

Climbing. Experienced alpinists enjoy the challenges of the high passes and summit ridgelines that lead to the highest peaks of the park. Experience is vital; some of this climbing is technical and subject to severe and changeable weather.

Kayaking. Both Rotoroa and Rotoiti are excellent places to kayak. Although both lakes can attract high winds, summer conditions are usually favorable. Pick your day, pack a lunch, and leave from the jetty at the head of either lake. At St. Arnaud in summer, kayaks can be rented from the Rotoiti lakeshore. Pull up to a quiet stretch of pebble beach, where all you will hear are the birds and the breeze singing through the trees. Don't forget your sand fly repellent.

Skiing. In winter, a small club ski field welcomes visitors. Rainbow Ski Area is an hour's drive from St. Arnaud. It has basic facilities (rope tows and a café) and access is via a steepish mountain road (open June to October). You can also rent skis at Rainbow.

Walking. The park is laced with walking trails that center on the two lakes and range from easy 30-minute wanders to serious multiday treks deep into the mountains. In summer, the longer walks are usually passable, although a cold snap can bring snow at any time to the passes between valleys. Day walks include the climb Mt. Robert on the zigzagging Pinchgut Track, the climb to Parachute Rocks, and the lakeside walk around Rotoiti. Popular longer hikes are overnight to Lake Angelus Hut (often crowded in summer) and the three- to four-day Travers-Sabine circuit, which leads up the Travers, crosses an alpine pass, and returns down the Sabine. You camp or stay in park huts along the way.

Water Taxis. During summer, water taxis work on both lakes. They save a half-day walk at the start of some longer trails, such as the Travers/Sabine circuit, and give non-walkers quick access into the park. Remember to take everything you need with you as there are no shops, cafés, or amenities away from St. Arnaud.

be made online or at the visitor center. 🌐 *www.doc.govt.nz.*

Hotels

Alpine Lodge

$$ | HOTEL | This might be a European alpine-inspired lodge, but the view out the window is all Kiwi—wetlands, forest, and mountains. **Pros:** varied, wholesome menu selection; nice backcountry lodge ambience; the bushwalks are beautiful. **Cons:** restaurant closed July through October; bring repellent for the sand flies; a bit of a long walk to some rooms. *[$] Rooms from: NZ$185 ✉ Main Rd., St. Arnaud ☎ 03/521–1869 🌐 www.alpinelodge.co.nz 🍴 No Meals 🛏 32 rooms.*

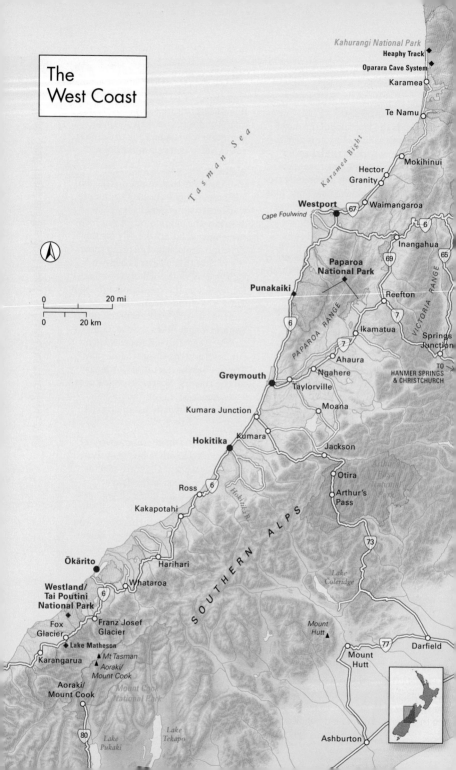

🏃 Activities

Nelson Lakes has a number of half-, full-, and multiday trails that leave from the area around St. Aranud. The **Lake Rotoiti Circuit** gets you around the lake in a 7- to 10-hour walk, but it can be broken up by using a water taxi or staying in Lakehead Hut at the head of the lake. The rather steep **Mt. Robert Track** zigzags up the face of Mt. Robert, giving you a superb view back across Lake Rotoiti toward St. Arnaud village. The return walk (fitness and good weather required) can be done in a loop by descending a marked track down Mt. Robert's eastern slopes to meet up with the Lake Rotoiti Circuit Track. Other tracks lead off these into the higher and more remote mountain areas and river valleys. Hut accommodations are available on a first-come, first-served basis. Backcountry experience (or traveling with someone who has this) and quality outdoor equipment are necessary on these longer tracks. Walkers on the Te Araroa Trail (which travels the length of New Zealand) tend to crowd into the huts here in late summer.

Murchison

125 km (78 miles) south of Nelson, 63 km (40 miles) west of Lake Rotoiti.

Surrounded by high mountains and roaring rivers, this small town is in some big country. With Nelson Lakes National Park to the east, Kahurangi National Park to the north, and the Matakitaki, Buller, Matiri, and Mangles rivers all converging on its doorstep, Murchison has gained the reputation as New Zealand's "white-water capital," and it boasts the most-kayaked stretches of white water in the southern hemisphere. There are 13 rivers within 20 km (12½ miles) of town and white-water kayakers and rafters turn up every year to enjoy the sport these rivers offer. In particular, the first weekend in March brings more than 500 devotees to Murchison for Bullerfest, a churning gathering of white-water junkies. These local rivers are also teeming with trout and fly-fishing enthusiasts from all over the world who converge to test their skills in one of the world's top fishing regions. Murchison residents still consider their landmark historic event "the earthquake," a major quake that hit in June 1929. The epicenter was just offshore at Kahurangi Point, but most of the fatalities centered around Murchison, and the quake drastically altered the landscape. A second in 1968 (centered on nearby Inangahua) also rearranged the landscape considerably but was less destructive in loss of life. Although most operators now accept credit cards, the only ATM in town (outside 4 Square) accepts New Zealand cards and only a few overseas cards, so if yours is from elsewhere, it's advisable to have some cash on you.

If you're driving to the West Coast from Nelson or Motueka, State Highway 6 passes through Murchison before turning right, crossing the Buller River 12 km (7 miles) farther south, then heading through the Buller Gorge toward the West Coast. This twisting, narrow road follows the mighty Buller as it carves a deep gorge below the jagged, earthquake-rocked mountain bluffs. Not far from here is New Zealand's longest swaying footbridge, the Buller Gorge Swing Bridge, and the departure point for the Buller Canyon Jet, should you want to ride a few rapids. The upper gorge is tight and hilly, but once past the township of Inangahua, the lower gorge is easier to navigate. This is all forested country, so you'll have to use your imagination to reconstruct the days when places such as Lyell, 34 km (21 miles) west of Murchison, were bustling gold-mining towns. There's now only a peaceful, Department of Conservation campsite at Lyell, also the trailhead for The Old Ghost Road and a multiday mountain biking and walking route to the West Coast. As you drive, you'll pass high forest-clad mountains, narrow single-lane bridges, and the village of Inangahua.

GETTING HERE AND AROUND

Although it's 100 km (62 miles) from the nearest town, Murchison is easy to access by road, sitting right on State Highway 6. It's a 1¾-hour drive south of Nelson, 4¼ hours north of Christchurch, and 1½ hours east of Westport (without scenic stops). It is also one of only a couple of comfort and fuel stops on these long stretches so if you are only passing through, take advantage of its conveniences.

InterCity buses pass through daily on its services between Nelson and Christchurch and Nelson and the West Coast.

VISITOR INFORMATION

CONTACTS Murchison Information Centre. ✉ *47 Waller St., Murchison* ☎ *03/523–9350* 🌐 *www.visitmurchison.nz.*

Sights

Murchison District Museum

HISTORY MUSEUM | For a small-town operation this local, community-run museum has a lot to look at. The rustic little building features an exhibit and memorial for the 1929 earthquake here, in which 17 locals died and many more were made homeless. There's also a good collection of farming and agricultural machinery from the town's colonial era, plus displays on the region's gold and coal mining history. The museum is run by a few volunteers who make a valiant attempt to open regularly. ✉ *60 Fairfax St., Murchison* ☎ *03/523–9392.*

The Natural Flames

OTHER ATTRACTION | There are few places in the world where you can find a natural gas flame, but this is one. In an ancient forest setting near Murchison, there's been one quietly glowing since the 1920s, and this tour company has sole access rights. The four-hour tour involves a short, scenic drive, education about local oil drilling and farming, a one-hour backcountry walk (you might get wet feet) through farmland and forest to the flames, and a hot brew and pikelets cooked up on the natural fire. Tour groups are restricted to ten people. Booking ahead is essential. ✉ *47 Waller St., Murchison* ☎ *0800/687–244 New Zealand only* 🌐 *www.naturalflames.co.nz* 🎟 *NZ$105.*

Restaurants

Murchison has a selection of casual cafés serving fresh, wholesome fare, just what you need after a day playing in white water.

Beechwoods Cafe

$$ | **CAFÉ** | Lots of wholesome breakfast and lunch options, hot snacks, and sweet treats are offered here. Some popular choices include the snapper (fish) sandwich, Beechwood burgers, and real fruit ice cream. **Known for:** nice selection of to-go foods; popular stop for bus passengers so gets crowded; classic highway café. [$] *Average main: NZ$16* ✉ *32 Waller St., Murchison* ☎ *03/523–9571.*

Rivers Café

$$$ | **CAFÉ** | Good food and good coffee is served every day in a welcoming, rustic setting. It's hard to find, tucked around a corner, so it's mostly frequented by locals and those in the know. **Known for:** lamb shank; family-friendly atmosphere; big helpings. [$] *Average main: NZ$23* ✉ *51 Fairfax St., Murchison* ☎ *03/523–9009* 🌐 *www.visitmurchison.nz/rivers-cafe.html.*

Hotels

★ Murchison Lodge

$$$ | **B&B/INN** | Tucked on a quiet side street, these comfortably countrified guest rooms, with strong colors and lots of wood in a beautiful old villa, are within easy walking distance of the mighty

Buller River. **Pros:** incredible breakfast included; private access to the Buller River through a grassy field; welcoming hosts. **Cons:** lounge (albeit beautiful) is shared with other guests; a few stairs to climb; bathrooms on the small side. [$] *Rooms from: NZ$230* ✉ *15 Grey St., Murchison* ☎ *03/523–9196* 🌐 *www.murchisonlodge.co.nz* 🕒 *Closed July and Aug.; exact dates vary* 🍴 *Free Breakfast* ☞ *No children under 12* 🛏 *6 rooms.*

Owen River Lodge

$$$$ | HOTEL | One of the classiest of several fully inclusive luxury fly-fishing lodges in this region, Owen River has six beautifully appointed cottages overlooking the Owen River Valley. **Pros:** beautiful views; large garden; fully equipped tackle room and fly-making table. **Cons:** quite remote; the last mile or two to the lodge is not paved but is easy enough to drive; if you're not into fishing, you might feel out of it. [$] *Rooms from: NZ$895* ✉ *173 Owen Valley East Rd., 15 min north of Murchison, Murchison* ☎ *03/523–9075* 🌐 *www.owenriverlodge.co.nz* 🕒 *Closed May–Sept.* 🛏 *6 suites* 🍴 *All-Inclusive.*

Activities

Murchison's claim as a white-water destination is not to be ignored. This region has some of the best white water anywhere.

BOATING AND RAFTING

Buller Gorge

BOATING | Buller Gorge is a bit of an oddity. In what is seemingly the middle of nowhere you can cross what is reportedly New Zealand's longest swing bridge. Then, instead of returning on foot, for an additional fee, you can zip line back across the river. Jet boat trips through the gorge also leave from here; the 40-minute rides depart hourly throughout the summer, 10 to 4, and by arrangement in winter. You can also try your luck panning for gold or simply read about the massive earthquakes that shook the land around here in 1929 and 1968. ✉ *Upper Buller Gorge, State Hwy. 6, Murchison* ☎ *0800/285–537 New Zealand only, 03/523–9809* 🌐 *www.bullergorge.co.nz* 🎟 *Swing bridge toll NZ$10, zip line NZ$40, jet boat trips NZ$125.*

★ **Ultimate Descents New Zealand**

WHITE-WATER RAFTING | FAMILY | Highly experienced guides run rafting trips on the Maruia (Grade III), Clarence (Grade II), Buller (Grade II–IV), Mokihinui (Grade IV), and Karamea (Grade V) rivers. All half-day and day trips include a light snack, and the multiday trips are fully catered. They also run family trips, day trips on a gentle section of the Buller, and overnights on the Maruia River. They've been doing this for years and know the water well. ✉ *38 Waller St., Murchison* ☎ *03/523–9899, 0800/748–377 New Zealand only* 🌐 *www.rivers.co.nz* 🎟 *From NZ$160.*

Wild Rivers Rafting

WHITE-WATER RAFTING | Qualified guides introduce even first-time rafters to one of the premium white-water rafting experiences in the country, the legendary "Earthquake Rapids" on the Buller River. These are Grade III and IV rapids. The 25-foot cliff jump into the river is optional. River time is two hours; allow four hours total. Pickup is at the Iron Bridge on State Highway 6, 37 km (23 miles) from Murchison. ✉ *Iron Bridge, Upper Buller Gorge Rd., State Hwy. 6, Murchison* ☎ *0508/467–238 in New Zealand, 022/698–1244, 03/789–0213* 🌐 *www.wildriversrafting.co.nz* 🎟 *NZ$160 for 4-hr trip.*

Westport

230 km (144 miles) southeast of Nelson.

One of New Zealand's oldest ports sits at the mouth of the mighty Buller River. Once a boomtown for two separate gold rushes, it's now a quiet little hub (population 4,660) for the local farming and coal industries, plus the rapidly expanding adventure-tourism niche. It's an interesting place to stop before heading south toward Punakaiki and the glaciers or north to remote Karamea and the Heaphy Track; the best of Westport is out of town, either on the coast or up the rivers. The classic sights of the Westport region are breaking white-capped waves, blue sea, seals, rocky outcrops, and acres of flax and wetlands. In the town itself, several striking art deco buildings line the main street. Stop by the little Coaltown Museum at the i-SITE Visitor Centre on Palmerston Street to learn about the town's coal mining history. Or treat yourself to a drive to the Denniston Plateau, 18 km (11 miles) northeast of town and high on a mountain plateau. Information panels and actual machinery detail life in this lonely outpost from the late 1800s through the early 1900s. Carving a living from the rich seams of coal in the surrounding tussock-covered hills, the miners and their families had to struggle with wild weather, isolation, and primitive conditions. A popular historical novel about these coal mining pioneers and their families, *The Denniston Rose,* by New Zealand writer Jenny Pattrick, details the area and the harsh colonial lifestyle.

The Westport i-SITE Visitor Centre can also provide information on Karamea township and Kahurangi National Park.

GETTING HERE AND AROUND

It's a 3-hour drive to Westport from Nelson to the north, or a 1½-hour drive south to Greymouth. Either way you'll pass along incredibly scenic coastlines or river gorges surrounded by thick native bush and high ranges. InterCity buses travel to Westport daily, en route between Nelson and the glaciers.

TOURS

OutWest Tours

GUIDED TOURS | Four-wheel drive tours take you through private farmland and forest, with interesting limestone landscapes, rivers and waterfalls, historic mining trails, and local characters to meet along the way. They'll also take you onto the Denniston Plateau and explain the history of the mining village that struggled to survive on this remote, mist-clad mountain. ☎ *027/641–8267, 0800/688–937 New Zealand only* ⊕ *www.outwest.co.nz* ✉ *From NZ$140.*

Underworld Adventures

ADVENTURE TOURS | Near the small town of Charleston, you'll find several gentle adventures leading into the nearby rain forest and then beneath it. Ride an open-sided bush-train through the forest, take a cave walk into a limestone mountain in the Nile Valley (the glow-worm grotto is the highlight), and drift slowly by raft through the glowworm caves before breaking out to the river. For a bigger challenge, try the full-day caving adventure; it includes a 154-foot abseil (rappel), then crawling, swimming, and climbing your way back to the surface. The guides are great. Reservations are essential. ⊠ *Charleston Hotel, State Hwy. 6, Charleston* ☎ *03/788–8168* ⊕ *www. caverafting.com* ✉ *Train ride NZ$25, activities from NZ$155.*

VISITOR INFORMATION

CONTACTS Westport i-SITE Visitor Centre and Coaltown Museum. ⊠ *123 Palmerston St., Westport* ☎ *03/789–6658* ⊕ *www. westport.nz.*

 Sights

Coaltown Museum

HISTORY MUSEUM | Westport is a town based around coal, and the stories, challenges, and hardships of mining on (and under) the high plateau behind the town are related in this interactive museum. Hogging the limelight is the 8-ton coal wagon, perched on the 45-degree angle just as it would have been when descending the famous incline, off the Denniston Plateau. Museum entry is through the Westport i-SITE Visitor

Centre. ✉ *123 Palmerston St., Westport* ☎ *03/789–6658* 🎫 *NZ$10.*

🍴 Restaurants

Denniston Dog

$$$ | **CAFÉ** | **FAMILY** | This old bank building is loaded with local character in its current guise as a cheerful pub and gathering spot. If the coal-mining heritage of this town interests you, you will enjoy the memorabilia and photos on display. **Known for:** stone-grilled meats and seafood; traditional New Zealand food; big breakfasts. [$] *Average main: NZ$28* ✉ *18 Wakefield St., Westport* ☎ *03/789–5030* 🌐 *www.dennistondog.co.nz.*

PortSide Bistro & Bar

$$$ | **MODERN NEW ZEALAND** | There's a huge range of fare on the menu here, be it for breakfast, lunch, or dinner. Breakfasts are served until 3 pm, and coffee and cake are always ready on the go. **Known for:** local atmosphere; fresh market fish, delivered directly from the boats; bistro burgers. [$] *Average main: NZ$30* ✉ *13 Cobden St., Westport* ☎ *03/789–7133* 🌐 *www.portsidebistro.co.nz* 🕒 *Closed Mon.*

🛏 Hotels

Archer House

$$$ | **B&B/INN** | Rooms are spacious, linens are fine, and the art collection is impressive at this villa that was built in the late 1800s. **Pros:** gracious old home with beautiful garden; short walk to Westport restaurants; sunny conservatory for coffee. **Cons:** decor not for everyone; patchy Wi-Fi; no modern heating. [$] *Rooms from: NZ$260* ✉ *75 Queen St., Westport* ☎ *03/789–8778, 0800/789–877 New Zealand only* 🌐 *www.archerhouse.co.nz* 🔑 *3 rooms* 🍴 *Free Breakfast.*

Steeples Cottage and Studio

$ | **B&B/INN** | Perched on the cliff overlooking the Steeples rocks offshore, this self-contained cottage (with sea views) along with a studio are great value. **Pros:** stunning coast views; safe swimming at nearby beach; charming, helpful hosts. **Cons:** can be hard to find; out of town so need to stock up before you go; parking can be a bit tight. [$] *Rooms from: NZ$110* ✉ *48 Lighthouse Rd., Cape Foulwind, Westport* ☎ *03/789–7884, 029/274–6035* 🌐 *www.steeplescottage.co.nz* 🍴 *Free Breakfast* 🔑 *4 rooms.*

Punakaiki and Paparoa National Park

269 km (168 miles) southwest of Nelson.

Paparoa National Park extends from the mountainous inland Paparoa Range to the coast. With steep bluffs, limestone basins, canyons, caves, and fluted rock, it's a formidable yet fascinating environment. The cliffs, flood-prone rivers, dense rain forest, and extensive cave systems in this park draw hikers, cavers, and, of course, photographers. The major track entry points—Bullock Creek, Fox River, and Pororari River on the coast and Blackball township on the eastern side of the park—open onto an otherworldly zone of jungle green, striking *nikau* palms, rain forest, beech forest, and rushing streams. A purpose-built Great Walk, the Paparoa Track, is a two- or three-day walk or bike ride that crosses the park from east to west. Along the Punakaikai coastal road there is much to do, like day hikes into the park, canoeing on the Pororari River, coastal tracks to collapsed sea caverns, horse-and-wagon treks, and entry-level cave experiences. Call the Paparoa National Park i-SITE Visitors Centre for maps and information.

One of the stars of the West Coast is the walk to the Pancake Rocks and Blowholes, one of New Zealand's most popular short walks. The huge swells that batter this coast have eroded the limestone cliffs, carving them into fantastical

Paparoa National Park's eroded coastline includes the amazing Pancake Rocks.

shapes. A paved walkway leads you past the curious pancake-stacked rocks and through the windswept cover of tenacious New Zealand flax and nikau palms to the most dramatic viewpoints, including the broiling cauldron called the Surge Pool (once a sea cavern before the roof collapsed) and the pumping fissure of the Chimney Pot. In the right conditions, particularly a high tide combined with a surging sea, these blowholes can spout a thundering geyser of spray. To add to the drama, New Zealand's highest mountain, Aoraki/Mt. Cook, is sometimes visible across the sea to the south. To reach the rocks from the highway, cross the road from the visitor center and follow the clearly signed, easy 20-minute walk. Keep turning left along the path so you don't miss the best bits out around the Surge Pool. Look for white-fronted terns, which nest on the spray-soaked rock stacks here.

GETTING HERE AND AROUND

At first glance, Punakaiki looks like nothing more than a small cluster of beach houses and shops—a blip on the radar without even a gas station or ATM. It's worth stopping, though, for its famous Pancake Rocks—a maze of limestone stacked high above the sea and an easy walk from the road. Punakaiki is also the main entry point to the Paparoa National Park tracks and river activities. Punakaiki is roughly halfway along the coast between Greymouth and Westport on State Highway 6, 40 minutes north of Greymouth and 50 minutes south of Westport. The road is winding and steep in places, with high drop-offs to the coast on the stretch north of Punakaiki. Inter-City buses pass through daily. Accommodations range from a holiday park to vacation homes, B&Bs, and a resort-style hotel.

If you have a spare half-hour, follow the Truman Track, 3 km (2 miles) north of the village down to the coast. It's a delightful walk through native bush to a dramatic coastal bay. There's also easy access to the coast from the beach in front of the Punakaiki Resort just south of the Pancake Rocks.

The Paparoa National Park i-SITE Visitors Centre, across the road from the track to the Pancake Rocks, is a handy place to learn more about the rock formations and the park.

VISITOR INFORMATION

CONTACTS Paparoa National Park i-SITE Visitors Centre. ✉ *4294 Main Rd., State Hwy. 6, Punakaiki* ☎ *03/731–1895* 🌐 *www.doc.govt.nz.*

🍴 Restaurants

Eating options are limited in tiny Punakaiki, with just a pub and couple of daytime cafés open to the public. The oceanfront restaurant at Punakaiki Resort is a slightly higher-priced option. If you decide to stay in a self-catering unit, you'll need to bring in all your food, as there are no general stores in town.

Pancake Rocks Cafe

$$$ | **CAFÉ** | A little café open daily, Pancake Rocks serves a full breakfast, lunch, and (in summer) dinner menu. This place is famous for it all-day pancake stacks and gourmet stone-oven pizzas, the cabinet food is delicious too. **Known for:** stone-oven pizzas; pancake stack with maple syrup and bacon; quirky decor. [$] *Average main: NZ$21* ✉ *Coast Rd., Punakaiki* ☎ *03/731–1122* 🌐 *www.pancakerockscafe.com.*

🛏 Hotels

Although tiny, Punakaiki is a popular tourist spot, and, therefore, has some good accommodations available, including a sizable hotel and self-catering cottages with friendly hosts.

Hydrangea Cottages

$$ | **APARTMENT** | You'll be lulled by the constant roar of the ocean in these secluded, stylish, and spacious apartments with recycled native timbers and contemporary furniture; there's also a rustic studio cottage (Rimu), a larger cottage with sea views and a bath on the deck, a seaside house (Takutai) for larger groups, and a quaint cottage for couples (The Stables Hut) near the lagoon and among the bush. **Pros:** close to Pancake Rocks; ocean views; relaxing atmosphere. **Cons:** turns onto a main road that's very busy, especially in summer; steep driveway; native birds pūkeko and weka will grab scraps off the decks if you're not careful. [$] *Rooms from: NZ$140* ✉ *4244 State Hwy. 6, Punakaiki* ✣ *Between Punakaiki Lagoon and Pancake Rocks* ☎ *03/731–1839* 🌐 *www.pancake-rocks.co.nz* 🍴 *No Meals* 🛏 *6 cottages.*

Punakaiki Resort

$$$ | **HOTEL** | The modern beach house design at this resort blends well with the dynamic coastal site; the front steps almost reach to the beach. **Pros:** restaurant dinner menu is very good; prime seafront location; spectacular views from rooms and oceanfront restaurant and bar. **Cons:** not all rooms have a balcony; guest rooms quite basic; traffic noise in some units. [$] *Rooms from: NZ$300* ✉ *State Hwy. 6, 1 km (½ mile) south of Pancake Rocks, Punakaiki* ☎ *03/731–1168, 0800/706–707 New Zealand only* 🌐 *www.punakaiki-resort.co.nz* 🛏 *61 rooms* 🍴 *No Meals.*

🏃 Activities

★ Punakaiki Canoes

CANOEING & ROWING | **FAMILY** | The essence of this region is best understood by a paddle up the Pororari River, on the northern edge of Punakaiki. Glide the dark yet clear waters between sheer limestone cliffs, nikau palms, and giant rata trees. Pretend you're in the movies—The Hobbit cliff scenes were actually filmed here. Or head to the estuary, where the water opens out into a more playful area. These trips are suitable for all abilities and ages but are dependent on the weather and the river level. All gear is provided. ✉ *State Hwy. 6, by Pororari Bridge, Punakaiki* ☎ *03/731–1870* ⊕ *www.river-kayaking.co.nz* ⬚ *From NZ$45.*

Golden Sands Horse and Wagon Tours
HORSEBACK RIDING | Travel in the footsteps of the pioneers down unspoiled Barrytown Beach. The pace is relaxed with plenty of time for exploring, including jade collecting (Barrytown Beach is the premier jade-hunting beach in all New Zealand), making damper bread, and boiling the billy over an open fire. There are great opportunities for wildlife spotting and photography. ✉ *3456 Coast Rd., Punakaiki* ⬥ *Barrytown* ☎ *03/731–1136* ⊕ *www.wagontours.co.nz* ⬚ *From NZ$60.*

Greymouth

44 km (28 miles) south of Punakaiki, 258 km (160 miles) west of Christchurch.

The town of Greymouth sits, as the name suggests, at the mouth of the Grey River. But gold and green (as in *pounamu*, or jade) were initially the colors of note around this settlement, thanks to its strong mining history. It's the biggest town on the West Coast, and today many travelers arrive here on the TranzAlpine train from Christchurch. Instead of being captivated by the area's stunning coastal drives, train-goers will enjoy a breathtaking ride on viaducts high above riverbeds, beneath steep peaks, and through dripping rain forest. If you're arriving and returning by train, take an extra day or two for a trip up to Punakaiki or down to the glaciers, to grasp the scope of the landscape in these parts.

The pounamu (greenstone, New Zealand jade) found here is highly prized by Māori. This is all Ngai Tahu iwi (tribe) area, and as part of the 1997 Ngai Tahu Settlement between the tribe and the Crown,

the government recognized Ngai Tahu as having sole rights to collect and sell the precious pounamu in its natural form. If you want the authentic product, when buying greenstone on the West Coast, make sure it is local greenstone and not imported jade. All genuine greenstone found by iwi in local waters is identified with a unique traceability code.

GETTING HERE AND AROUND
Drive from Nelson or Westport in the north, from the glaciers to the south, or from Christchurch in the east, over Arthur's Pass. Be on your guard around Greymouth and Hokitika as there are a number of one-way bridges and unalarmed rail crossings. InterCity buses arrive in Greymouth daily.

The TranzAlpine train departs Christchurch daily at 8:15 am and arrives in Greymouth at 1:05 pm; the return train departs Greymouth at 2:05 pm and arrives at Christchurch at 6:31 pm. One-way fare options range from NZ$89 to NZ$219.

BUS DEPOT Greymouth InterCity. ✉ *Railway Station, 164 Mackay St., Greymouth* ⊕ *www.intercity.co.nz.*

TRAIN CONTACTS TranzAlpine Express. ☎ *04/495–0775, 0800/872–467 New Zealand only* ⊕ *www.greatjourneysofnz.co.nz/tranzalpine.*

VISITOR INFORMATION
CONTACTS Greymouth i-SITE Visitor Centre. ✉ *Old Railway Station, 164 Mackay St., Greymouth* ☎ *03/768–7080; 0800/473–966* ⊕ *www.westcoasttravel.co.nz.*

 Sights

Shantytown Heritage Park
MUSEUM VILLAGE | **FAMILY** | A hands-on reenactment of an 1880s mining town, Shantytown will show you it was all about steam in those days. Most of the buildings are reproductions, including a jail, a blacksmith shop, a railway station,

and Chinatown. Gold-digging displays include a giant water cannon for blasting the gold-bearing rock and soil from the hillside, water races, and a stamper battery—powered by a 30-foot waterwheel—for crushing the ore. You can pan for gold, ride an old bush tramline, take a break in the café, or share a picnic on the lawns and then go back for more. ✉ *310 Rutherglen Rd., Greymouth* ☎ *03/762–6634, 0800/742–689 New Zealand only* 🌐 *www.shantytown.co.nz* 🎫 *NZ$35.50, train ride included.*

🍴 Restaurants

DP1 Cafe

$$ | **CAFÉ** | Homey hospitality and a great vibe in this colorful, retro-style spot comes with house-cooked breakfasts (scrambled eggs are as good as you'll find anywhere), lunches, and baked goods. Plus, the outlook over the Grey River is terrific. **Known for:** tasty coffee and breakfasts; local art on display; hip, funky vibe. [$] *Average main: NZ$17* ✉ *104–108 Mawhera Quay, Greymouth* ☎ *03/768–4005* 🌐 *www.facebook.com/dp1cafe* 🕒 *No dinner.*

★ Monteiths Brewing Company

$$$ | **MODERN NEW ZEALAND** | They started brewing beer on the West Coast right here in 1868, and now the modern version of the brewery offers a full restaurant, a brewing museum, brewery tours and, of course, lots of fresh brews. The restaurant serves standard Kiwi fare, along with tapas and platters to match the beers. **Known for:** great local brews; historic brewery tours; antipasto platters. [$] *Average main: NZ$23* ✉ *60 Herbert St., Greymouth* ☎ *03/768–4149* 🌐 *www.thebrewery.co.nz.*

Speight's Ale House

$$$ | **NEW ZEALAND** | The bistro-style menu here includes the signature whitebait (seasonal September through to November) and blue cod, along with the usual steaks, lamb, salmon, and mussels. In addition, the ales of the famous southern brand, Speight's, flow in the stylishly restored interior with shiny, bold copper vents contrasting against the wood and brick decor. **Known for:** historic building convenient to the railway station; only local restaurant with a dedicated outdoor dining area; pot pies. [$] *Average main: NZ$30* ✉ *130 Mawhera Quay, Greymouth* ☎ *03/768–0667* 🌐 *www.speightsalehousegreymouth.co.nz.*

Stationhouse Café

$$$ | **ECLECTIC** | The café is in an old railway house with a superb view across Lake Brunner and the forests and wetlands beyond. Lunch options include chowders, salads, homemade pies with mashed potatoes and peas, blue cod, and chips. **Known for:** family-friendly atmosphere; handy stop for train travelers; whitebait fritters (in season). [$] *Average main: NZ$28* ✉ *40 Koe St., Moana* ☎ *03/738–0158* 🌐 *www.lakebrunner.net* 🕒 *Sometimes closed for dinner in winter.*

🛏 Hotels

★ Breakers Boutique Accommodation

$$$ | **B&B/INN** | At this welcoming B&B between Greymouth and Punakaiki, two rooms in the main house and two suites in the garden overlook spectacular coastline and native bush surroundings, and hosts Jan and Stephen will tell you about the local mountain biking and mining. **Pros:** brilliantly friendly and helpful hosts; scenic coastal views; dinner by arrangement to save a late drive into Greymouth. **Cons:** by the main road; 15-minute drive from Greymouth; can get cold at night. [$] *Rooms from: NZ$295* ✉ *1367 State Hwy. 6, 14 km (9 miles) north of Greymouth* ☎ *03/762–7743* 🌐 *www.breakers.co.nz* 🍽 *Free Breakfast* 🛏 *4 rooms.*

Shopping

Left Bank Art Gallery

ART GALLERIES | This is a top spot to see and purchase a range of artworks, including contemporary pounamu (greenstone or jade) carvings. Housed in the old Greymouth branch of the Bank of New Zealand, this progressive little gallery supports local artists and holds regularly changing exhibitions. Displays in the old vault include a collection of older pounamu artworks. ⊠ *1 Tainui St., Greymouth* ☎ *03/768–0038* ⊕ *www. leftbankarts.com.*

Shades of Jade

JEWELRY & WATCHES | Come here to find quality greenstone sourced from West Coast rivers from Punakaiki to Haast. Be sure to check out the unique flower jade, with gold or white markings found in rivers close to Greymouth. Pendants, sculptures, and a variety of jade types are on display. The gallery's principal carver, Jeremy Dalzell, can often be seen at work here. ⊠ *22 Tainui St., Greymouth* ☎ *03/768–0794* ⊕ *www.shadesofjade. co.nz.*

Activities

On Yer Bike!

ADVENTURE TOURS | FAMILY | If it's raining, your outdoor options just got a lot more exciting. On Yer Bike! makes the most of rain and mud with some wild fun. The two-hour Forest and Waterfall tour and the one-hour Enchanted Forest tour will both take you through beautiful native forest, streams, mud, and puddles on an easy-to-ride 4WD buggy. It's not all mud and action if your preference is to take in the bush and scenery, as this outfit has options for everyone. ⊠ *511 State Hwy. 6, Greymouth* ✛ *5 km (3 miles) north of Greymouth* ☎ *03/762–7438, 0800/669– 372 New Zealand only* ⊕ *www.onyerbike. co.nz* ⊠ *From NZ$110.*

Hokitika

41 km (26 miles) south of Greymouth.

Hokitika ("Hoki" to locals) is one of the larger towns along the West Coast, nestled between the pounding ocean and farms and bush-covered hills. It's a place of simple pleasures: scouting the craft galleries, taking a bushwalk, enjoying the seafood, and looking for evocatively shaped driftwood on the often stormy beach. Hokitika is central enough to take a day trip to Punakaiki or Arthur's Pass. During the height of the 1860s gold rushes, Hokitika was New Zealand's busiest port and had more than 100 hotels. Pick up a Hokitika Heritage Walk brochure (NZ50¢) from the i-SITE Visitor Centre and explore this rich heritage, along with more recent colonial history. Start with a walk along the Quayside Heritage Area at the southern end of Tancred and Revell streets, and walk along to Sunset Point Lookout. See the old Custom House and river mouth; on a clear day you'll see Aoraki/Mt. Cook across the sea. West Coast rivers are the source of pounamu (greenstone or New Zealand jade), which has long been a precious resource for the South Island Māori people, Ngai Tahu. Hokitika is recognized as the center for artists and carvers who create stunning jewelry, from pounamu and other material. The town is filled with studios and galleries where you can watch the artists at work and perhaps take home something special. Wood carvings, pottery, textiles, and photography are also showcased in the galleries, mostly found along Tancred and Weld streets.

The annual **Wildfoods Festival** celebrates bush tucker (food from the bush) from the West Coast's natural food sources. Bite into such delectables as *huhu* grubs, grasshoppers, beetles, whitebait patties (far more mainstream), and wild pork (as in from pigs running wild in the bush, not farmed—or angry), and follow it all with gorse wine, elderflower champagne, or Monteith's bitter beer. It's usually held in the second weekend of March. Book well ahead, as there's a cap of 10,000 participants, and it usually sells out.

GETTING HERE AND AROUND

There are daily flights to Hokitika from Christchurch with Air New Zealand. Arrive by road from Christchurch or Greymouth to the north or from the glaciers to the south (via State Highway 6). Either way you will enjoy a spectacular drive through mountainous country, national parks, and scenic reserves. InterCity buses arrive in Hokitika daily and stop in front of the National Kiwi Center on Tancred Street.

VISITOR INFORMATION

CONTACTS Hokitika i-SITE Visitor Centre. ✉ *36 Weld St., Hokitika* ☎ *03/755–6166* 🌐 *www.hokitikainfo.co.nz.*

👁 Sights

Waewae Pounamu

OTHER ATTRACTION | Ngati Waewae is the iwi (tribe) of this area, a subtribe of the South Island Ngai Tahu. The iwi owns and carves all the pounamu (greenstone) at this center. The artists will reveal how every stone has a story. If you buy a piece, they will give you its unique code, which you can use to trace the story of your stone on the center's website. ✉ *39 Weld St., Hokitika* ☎ *03/755–8304* 🌐 *www.waewaepounamu.co.nz.*

West Coast Treetop Walk and Cafe

FOREST | You can wander the tops of the ancient trees in the West Coast rain forest on this 1,500-foot long, 65-foot-high walkway through the canopy. You can go even higher on the Hokitika Tower, 130 feet above the forest floor. Views extend over the rain forest to dark, glacial Lake Mahinapua and beyond to the Southern Alps. The walkway is fully wheelchair-accessible. A café and gift shop are also on site. ✉ *1128 Woodstock Rimu Rd., Hokitika* ☎ *03/755–5052,* 🌐 *www.treetopsnz.com* 🎟 *NZ$32.*

🍴 Restaurants

Stations Inn—Waterwheel Restaurant and Bar

$$$$ | **NEW ZEALAND** | Experience quality, classic New Zealand fare in a setting with grand views of the Southern Alps and Tasman Sea. Whether it's meat, fish, shellfish, or vegetables, this place delivers, and also matches its food with the local West Coast brew, Monteith's. **Known for:** excellent beef and lamb dishes; special occasion dining; stunning views. [$] *Average main: NZ$34* ✉ *Blue Spur Rd., Hokitika* ☎ *03/755–5499* 🌐 *www.stationsinnhokitika.co.nz* 🕒 *Closed Sun. and Mon. No lunch.*

Stella Cafe and Cheesery

$$ | **CAFÉ** | At this quirky café and delicatessen, the honey comes directly from the in-house beehive. A breakfast menu, baked goods (try the cheese scones), and lunch dishes that change with the seasons are on offer. **Known for:** in-house beehive; wholesome to-go food; cheese tasting menus. [$] *Average main: NZ$15* ✉ *84 Revell St., Hokitika* ☎ *03/755–5432* 🌐 *https://www.facebook.com/StellaCafeHokitika.*

★ **Theatre Royal Hotel Kumara**

$$$ | **MODERN NEW ZEALAND** | The owners spent years restoring this old pub, and now the place hums with activity and tasty food. Locally cured bacon, venison patties, wild (bush) pork sliders, house-made pies, and salads all vie for attention on the breakfast/brunch/lunch menus. **Known for:** classic miner's breakfast; the community's local pub; history (ambience) meets modernity (food). [$] *Average main: NZ$30* ✉ *81 Seddon St., Kumara, Hokitika* ☎ *03/736–9277* 🌐 *www.theatreroyalhotel.co.nz.*

Hotels

Rimu Lodge

$$$$ | B&B/INN | This two-story luxury lodge sits in the country, high above the Hokitika River valley. **Pros:** warm hosts who make a great breakfast; bird-watchers' delight; good local walks and heritage walks nearby. **Cons:** 10 minutes out of town and away from shops; bit hard to find at night; cave wetas (crickets) in house might not be for everyone (although they are harmless). $ *Rooms from: NZ$345* ⊠ *33 Seddons Terrace Rd., Rimu* ☎ *03/755–5255* ⊕ *www.rimulodge. co.nz* ❯○❮ *Free Breakfast* ⇆ *4 rooms.*

Shining Star

$$ | HOTEL | FAMILY | These stylish ocean-front wooden cabins, chalets, and motels are as close to the beach as you'll get. **Pros:** pet animals and playground to amuse kids; faces wild surf beach; very peaceful. **Cons:** long walk to restaurants; on the edge of town; need to book well ahead in summer. $ *Rooms from: NZ$180* ⊠ *16 Richards Dr., Hokitika* ☎ *0800/744–646 New Zealand only, 03/755–8921* ⊕ *www.accommodation-westcoast.co.nz* ⇆ *23 suites* ❯○❮ *No Meals.*

Teichelmann's Bed & Breakfast

$$$ | B&B/INN | At this friendly, traditional B&B in the center of town, accommodation is in five rooms in the house (upstairs and downstairs) and in a cute, stand-alone cottage set in a delightful "miner's garden" behind the house. **Pros:** one of the West Coast's most historic accommodations; location right in town; gracious hosts who are history buffs. **Cons:** some rooms have a shared bathroom; smallish en suites in some rooms; no ocean or mountain views. $ *Rooms from: NZ$260* ⊠ *20 Hamilton St., Hokitika* ☎ *03/755–8232* ⊕ *www.teichelmanns. nz* ❯○❮ *Free Breakfast* ⇆ *6 rooms.*

Shopping

Traditional Jade

CRAFTS | This small family business creates carvings and sculptures and has a collection of raw jade for you to admire. Visit in the mornings for the best chance of seeing one of the family artists at work. ⊠ *2 Tancred St., Hokitika* ☎ *03/755–5233* ⊕ *www.traditionaljade. co.nz.*

Activities

BIKING

★ West Coast Wilderness Trail

BIKING | Hokitika is at about the halfway point of the West Coast Wilderness Trail, one of the Nga Haerenga, New Zealand Cycle Trails. This three-to-four-day purpose-built trail explores the mountains, rivers, rural countryside, and mining history here, and this local company is your best friend to help you with logistics so that you can simply enjoy yourself. They'll rent you bikes, shuttle you to wherever you need, deliver your luggage to your accommodations, and organize day trips that focus on the best trail sections. ⊠ *216 Revell St., Hokitika* ☎ *021/263–3299* ⊕ *wildernesstrailshuttle.co.nz* ⊟ *Shuttle NZ$30, Bag tansfer NZ$18, Bike delivery or transfer NZ$15.*

Ōkārito

128 km (80 miles) south of Hokitika, 27 km (17 miles) north of Franz Josef.

Back in 1866, Ōkārito was a thriving town of more than 1,200 people, with three theaters and 25 hotels. People came for the gold, and, for many years, there was a working port inside the bar at the entrance to the lagoon. Things have changed dramatically, and Ōkārito is now known for its natural values. A tiny settlement remains, but most people just visit to kayak or cruise on the lagoon, watch the birds, walk the short forest

The Southern Alps are reflected in Lake Matheson's calm waters in Westland/Tai Poutini National Park.

and coastal trails, or head out at night for a kiwi-spotting expedition.

Sights

Ōkārito Lagoon

BODY OF WATER | Don't miss a visit to beautiful, coastal Ōkārito Lagoon, just a 13-km (8-mile) detour off the highway, 15 km (9.3 miles) north of Franz Josef township. An immense, forest-fringed, coastal lagoon, nestled in scenic splendor beneath the Southern Alps, Ōkārito is arguably one of the largest, most pristine wetlands remaining in New Zealand. It is home to thousands of sea and wading birds and is backed by the Ōkārito Kiwi Sanctuary, 27,000 acres of lowland forest and home of the rowi, a rare species of kiwi. ⊠ *Ōkārito* ✛ *128 km (80 miles) south of Hokitika.*

Activities

Ōkārito Boat Tours

BOAT TOURS | Your open air, shallow-draft boat glides across the lagoon, nosing into narrow channels lined with ancient rain forest. Watch the feeding birds, possibly a white heron visiting from its nearby breeding colony, or a godwit, one of thousands that fly here each summer from Arctic Siberia. Look up to the majestic backdrop of Aoraki/Mt. Cook and Franz Josef Glacier. Your host Swade runs three daily tours. Trips leave from Ōkārito Wharf; booking ahead is recommended. ⊠ *31 Wharf St., Ōkārito* ☎ *03/753–4223* ⊕ *okaritoboattours.co.nz* ✉ *From NZ$85.*

Ōkārito Kiwi Tours

GUIDED TOURS | Rowi, or Ōkārito brown kiwi, live only in this forest and this company holds the only license to guide people to them in their natural habitat. You'll walk softly through the bush, listening for their scuffles and calls before most likely catching a glimpse. They say there's a 98% chance of seeing one on a night tour; all you need is patience and warm, quiet clothes (no nylon windbreakers). Tours last three to five hours, depending on how shy the kiwi are. ⊠ *53 The*

Strand, Ōkārito ☎ 03/753–4330 ⊕ *www. okaritokiwitours.co.nz* ✉ *NZ$75.*

Ōkārito Kayaks

BOAT TOURS | Explore the largest and possibly least modified coastal wetland in New Zealand by kayak, either on a guided tour or by paddling independently. The lagoon is renowned for its birdlife; plucky godwits and other migrants fly here all the way from Siberia each spring (and back in autumn). It's also a great spot to see white herons, who fly here to feed from their sole New Zealand nesting ground in the Waitangiroto River nearby. Enjoy the views—dense rain forest backed by the Southern Alps. ✉ *1 The Strand* ☎ *03/753–4014* ⊕ *www.okarito. co.nz* ✉ *From NZ$60.*

Westland/Tai Poutini National Park

North end of the park is 146 km (91 miles) south of Hokitika.

Westland/Tai Poutini is a place of extremes, from the highest mountains to most ancient rain forest, and certainly extreme precipitation.

Try to allow more than a day in the region to increase your chance of clear weather. Otherwise, put your rain gear on and get out in it: walking in the rain forest, or in those massive glacial valleys with waterfalls roaring down the sheer sides, is a special experience. Annual rainfall here ranges from more than 120 inches at the coast to an incredible 16 feet on the alpine summits. Huge volumes of snow are dumped each year, feeding the 140 glaciers. The snow is compressed into ice on the névé, or head, of the glaciers (New Zealanders say "glassy-urs"), then moves steadily downhill under its own weight. The best-known and most visited glaciers are Franz Josef and Fox. If, however, you're driving through on a cloudy or wet day—quite likely—you will get no

idea of the size of the mountain ranges looming beside you. The main stopping places are townships near these glaciers, named simply Fox Glacier and Franz Josef, the latter more substantial. Both towns have solid tourist infrastructures. The summer tourist rush means you should make reservations well in advance for lodgings and restaurants, or plan to travel in the shoulder seasons. In winter, some places close so be sure to check ahead.

GETTING HERE AND AROUND
State Highway 6 passes through this region and is the only road access in and out. Drive in from Hokitika in the north or Wanaka and Haast to the south. There are only a few fuel stops between Hokitika and Haast so plan ahead. InterCity buses travel daily from the north and the south, stopping at both glacier villages.

BUS DEPOTS Fox Glacier. ✉ *Northbound: Fox Glacier Guiding, Main Rd.; Southbound: opposite Fox Glacier Guiding, Main Rd., Westland National Park.* **Franz Josef.** ✉ *Franz Josef Bus Stop, Main Rd.; Franz Josef YHA, 2–4 Cron St., Westland National Park.*

VISITOR INFORMATION
CONTACTS Westland/Tai Poutini National Park Visitor Centre. ✉ *69 Cron St., Franz Josef* ☎ *03/752–0360* ⊕ *www.doc.govt. nz.*

 Sights

Glacier Hot Pools
HOT SPRING | After your day touring and hiking, fall into these pools nestled in a bewitching area of rain forest right in Franz Josef village. The three public pools range from family-friendly to completely relaxing. There is also a massage therapy room, as well as three private hot tubs with their own shower, changing areas, and towels. This is a great stop if the weather just won't cooperate, but the compact complex may fill up on such days. ✉ *63 Cron St., Franz Josef*

☎ 03/752–0161, 0800/044–044 New Zealand only ⊕ www.glacierhotpools.co.nz ✉ Pools from NZ$29.

★ **West Coast Wildlife Centre**

WILDLIFE REFUGE | FAMILY | Here you can see firsthand the Department of Conservation's successful breeding program of the rare kiwi species, the rowi. You can see a few rowi in the Nocturnal House, but by far the best option is to witness the incubation and rearing program in the Kiwi Backstage Tour. If your timing is lucky, perhaps you'll see a hatching chick. Other displays here include the West Coast storytelling hut, where you can learn from the "old-timers" and undertake a quite lifelike glacial exploration. ✉ At Cron and Cowan Sts., Franz Josef ☎ 03/752–0600 ⊕ www.wildkiwi.co.nz ✉ From NZ$34.

Westland/Tai Poutini National Park

NATIONAL PARK | The glaciers are the main attractions here, yet there are many other beautiful places to explore in this magnificent national park and World Heritage region, which encompasses everything from New Zealand's highest mountains to glaciers, rain forests, hidden lakes, and coastal wetlands. Scenic drives and a couple of walks in the glacial valleys bring you to viewpoints within 500 feet or so of the glaciers. Alternatively, from Fox township, drive about 4 km (2½ miles) toward the coast on Cook Flat Road for a roadside view of Fox Glacier (weather permitting). Because of glacial recession access onto the actual glaciers is no longer possible by foot, but by helicopter only. There are many guided heli–hike options, as well as scenic flights for both glaciers. Flights are generally best early in the morning, when visibility tends to be clearest. Summer may be warmer, but there is more rain and fog that can scuttle flightseeing and hiking plans. In winter, there are fewer people, and the skies are clearer, which means fewer canceled flights and more spectacular views. In fact, winter in this area can be

a lot warmer than the snow resort towns east of the Southern Alps. Note that the glaciers are currently receding fast, and with less ice to bind their rocks, the mountains and valleys are increasingly prone to slips and landslides. Accordingly, access roads and trails change regularly for safety reasons; do check with the Department of Conservation (DOC) or i-SITE Visitor Informtion Centre about current conditions, and be sure to heed all DOC warning signs. Away from the ice, just a five-minute drive west of Fox Glacier township is the walk around Lake Matheson, leading to one of the country's most famous views. A trail winds by the lakeshore to where (weather permitting) the snowcapped peaks of Aoraki/Mt. Cook and Mt. Tasman are reflected in the water. It's an easy 2.6-km (1-mile) walk right around the lake. The best times to visit are sunrise and sunset, when the mirror-like reflections are less likely to be fractured by the wind. Other beautiful park walks are on the coast; at Gillespies Beach (coastal wetlands and forests and wild surf), and at Ōkārito, where your choices are the wetland boardwalk (20 minutes), Ōkārito Trig for an amazing viewpoint of Ōkārito Lagoon and Aoraki/Mt. Cook (1½ hour round-trip), and the Three Mile Pack Track, where you can return along the beach if you get the tide right. ✉ Fox Glacier Hwy., Westland National Park ⊕ www.doc.govt.nz.

🍴 Restaurants

There are several dining options in the glacier villages (Franz Josef and Fox). Remember, these places shut early in winter, so get in soon after the sun goes down.

★ **The Alice May**

$$$ | NEW ZEALAND | One of those cozy, buzzing places so prevalent on the West Coast, The Alice May serves country fare that is good and plentiful, with a welcome range of light meals (fish-and-chips, curries, venison burgers) and

Did You Know?

Glacier guides have to check paths through the ice every day on Fox and Franz Josef glaciers because the glaciers' movement changes the terrain overnight.

more substantial main courses (slow roasted pork belly, beef cheeks, and good vegetarian options). The wine and beer lists are stacked with mainstream NZ favorites. **Known for:** full of character and ambience; interesting à la carte menu; great service even when packed. [$] *Average main: NZ$28* ✉ *30 Cron St., Franz Josef* ☎ *03/752–0740.*

Blue Ice Café

$$$$ | **NEW ZEALAND** | Head here for quality New Zealand dishes and a bar that can carry you to the wee small hours of the morning. This place can become a late-night party spot during the tourist season. **Known for:** party hotspot; lamb shanks; huge salads. [$] *Average main: NZ$32* ✉ *5 Main Rd., Franz Josef* ☎ *03/752–0707* ⏲ *No lunch May–Oct.*

Café Neve

$$$ | **NEW ZEALAND** | This standout along Fox Glacier's main street sparks up no-nonsense options with fresh local flavors, such as the Neve pizza topped with mozzarella, ham, bacon, pepperoni, tomatoes, and pineapple. From breakfast and on to lunch and dinner, the menu is big and varied, taking you through eggs Benedict, BLT sandwiches, soups and chowders, burgers, chicken, pizzas, and rib-eye steak—just what you need after a day exploring or driving. **Known for:** New Zealand–focused wine list; varied menu of NZ classics; veranda dining to watch the tourists. [$] *Average main: NZ$22* ✉ *37 Main Rd., Fox Glacier* ☎ *03/751–0110.*

★ Matheson Cafe

$$$$ | **CAFÉ** | The food at this all-day café is great (a huge breakfast menu, burgers at lunch, beef rib eye, and lamb cutlets for dinner) but the scenery steals the show. If the weather plays ball you'll be able to enjoy a memorably stunning view: an amphitheater of mountains (Aoraki/Mt. Cook and Mt. Tasman) and, in the foreground, tall *kahikatea* forest. **Known for:** outside seating; incredible view (weather permitting); classy evening menu worthy of special-occasion dining. [$] *Average main: NZ$32* ✉ *1 Lake Matheson Rd., Fox Glacier* ☎ *03/751–0878* 🌐 *www.lakematheson.com* ⏲ *No dinner Apr.–Oct.*

Hotels

As major tourist destinations both Fox and Franz Josef townships, and nearby areas, are well serviced with campsites, backpacker motels, B&Bs, hotels, and lodge accommodations.

58 On Cron Motel

$$$ | **MOTEL** | Cook for yourself if you wish at this modern motel-style accommodation that offers great value, with well-appointed studios and apartments, excellent facilities, and a sunny environment. **Pros:** location close to attractions and cafés but off the noisy main road; parking is right outside your door; property is well-managed. **Cons:** slow Wi-Fi; birdsong might wake you early; the units are a bit crowded and on the small side. [$] *Rooms from: NZ$220* ✉ *58 Cron St., Franz Josef* ☎ *03/752–0627, 0800/662–766 New Zealand only* 🌐 *58oncron.co.nz* 🛏 *16 rooms* 🍴 *No Meals.*

Glenfern Villas

$$$ | **APARTMENT** | **FAMILY** | A short drive north of Franz Josef village, these stylish, well-equipped one- and two-bedroom villas are in a quiet rural location away from the tourist bustle and helicopters. **Pros:** villas are luxuriously appointed and very well-equipped; home-away-from-home in size and feel; rural and mountain views. **Cons:** a bit out of town for handy shopping or dining; some road noise from the highway; not all villas face the mountains. [$] *Rooms from: NZ$260* ✉ *2761 State Hwy. 6, Franz Josef* ✣ *3½ km (2 miles) north of Franz Josef village* ☎ *03/752–0054, 0800/453–633 New Zealand only* 🌐 *www.glenfern.co.nz* 🍴 *No Meals* 🛏 *18 suites.*

Te Waonui Forest Retreat

$$$$ | **HOTEL** | Here you'll feel ensconsed not only in luxury but also the rain forest,

as the hotel has been built to fit in and not intrude on the trees—from concrete jungle to real jungle, as their mantra states. **Pros:** walking distance to village; quiet atmosphere; surrounded by rain forest. **Cons:** no room-only rate; subdued guest room lighting for ambience makes reading difficult; closed for winter. [$] *Rooms from: NZ$827* ✉ *3 Wallace St., Franz Josef* ☎ *03/752–0555* 🌐 *www.tewaonui.co.nz* 🕒 *Closed May–Aug.* 🍴 *Free Breakfast* 🛏 *100 rooms.*

Westwood Lodge

$$$ | B&B/INN | For unpretentious luxury near the glaciers, turn to this spacious, modern lodge-style B&B just a few minutes' drive from Franz Josef village. **Pros:** some private decks with mountain views; large dining and lounge conservatory area with pool table; alpine gardens. **Cons:** in-house labradoodles won't be for everyone; a bit away from town and its restaurants; on the pricey side. [$] *Rooms from: NZ$300* ✉ *2919 Franz Josef Hwy, Franz Josef* ☎ *03/752–0112, 0800/200–209 New Zealand only* 🌐 *www.westwoodlodge.co.nz* 🍴 *Free Breakfast* 🛏 *9 rooms.*

★ Wilderness Lodge Lake Moeraki

$$$$ | HOTEL | Located alongside Lake Moeraki and surrounded by World Heritage Park, this lodge is a stunning place to relax and learn about New Zealand nature. **Pros:** a top eco-experience; pure luxury, in both facilities and specialist knowledge; guides have licenses to visit hidden tawaki (rare penguin) sites. **Cons:** lunch not included in all-inclusive plan; minimum two-night stay in high season; remote location. [$] *Rooms from: NZ$650* ✉ *State Hwy. 6, Westland National Park* ✥ *90 km (56 miles) south of Fox Glacier, 30 km (19 miles) north of Haast* ☎ *03/750–0881* 🌐 *www.wildernesslodge.co.nz* 🕒 *Closed June and July* 🍴 *All-Inclusive* ☞ *Rates also include 2 short guided activities daily* 🛏 *28 rooms.*

Activities

BIRD-WATCHING

★ White Heron Sanctuary Tours

BIRD WATCHING | FAMILY | For over 35 years, the local Arnold family has taken exclusive tours to the rare (in New Zealand) kotuku (white heron) colony, hidden in the wetlands and rain forest of Waitangiroto Nature Reserve and reached by a gentle jet boat trip along the Waitangiroto River. You'll see other wetland birds and walk a boardwalk through the rain forest to the hide, just yards from the colony. Trips last 2½ hours and run four times daily, from mid-September to early March. In winter, they offer a gorgeous Rainforest Nature Tour. Reservations are essential. ✉ *7857 State Hwy. 6, Whataroa* ☎ *03/753–4120, 0800/523–456 NZ only* 🌐 *www.whiteherontours.co.nz* 🎟 *From NZ$150.*

GLACIER TOURS

The walks to the Fox Glacier viewpoint and Franz Josef Glacier viewpoint are the easiest and cheapest ways to see the ice of a glacier. Landing on a glacier by helicopter and perhaps joining a guided walk on the ice is unforgettable. All the helicopter companies listed here offer similar tours and prices, as well as similarly stunning spectacles.

Fox and Franz Heliservices

AIR EXCURSIONS | This company has been operating since 1986. If your time is limited, try a 20-minute spin with a landing on either Fox or Franz Josef glacier. Longer flights also include glacier landings, exploring close to Mt. Aoraki/Mt. Cook and Mt. Tasman, and, weather permitting, across the Main Divide. Departures are from both Franz Josef and Fox Glacier townships. ✉ *Alpine Adventure Centre, 29 Main Rd., Fox Glacier* ☎ *03/752–0793, 0800/800–793 New Zealand only* 🌐 *www.heliservices.nz* 🎟 *From NZ$185.*

★ Fox Glacier Guiding

MOUNTAIN CLIMBING | FAMILY | This pioneering guiding company offers glacier heli-hikes and climbs to suit all fitness levels. They start from the most popular four-hour round-trip, where your guide will escort you from your helicopter high on the glacier, fit you with crampons, and then show you the amazing crevices and tunnels. There's also an Extreme Fox all-day heli-hike, and a heli–ice climbing trip, plus an amazing daylong heli trip and guided climb of Chancellor Dome, located high above the glacier, with the option to stay overnight in a historic alpine hut. Reservations are recommended for all trips, which are highly weather dependent. ⊠ *Fox Glacier Guiding Bldg., 44 Main Rd., Fox Glacier* ☎ *03/751–0825, 0800/111–600 New Zealand only* ⊕ *www. foxguides.co.nz* 🔁 *From NZ$450.*

Franz Josef Glacier Guides

MOUNTAIN CLIMBING | With these guides, you'll be helicoptered high up onto the Franz Josef glacier and guided on an amazing icy adventure, either a glacier walk (three hours) or ice climb (up to eight hours). The company also offers a guided glacier valley walk up the canyon-like floor where the glacier once ground its icy way before retreating. You won't get to stand on the ice on this trip, but you'll learn about its awesome power. Booking ahead is essential for all tours, which are highly weather dependent. ⊠ *Glacier Base, 63 Cron St., Franz Josef* ☎ *03/752–0763, 0800/484–337 New Zealand only* ⊕ *www.franzjosefglacier. com* 🔁 *Heli-hike from NZ$485.*

Glacier Country Scenic Flights

AIR EXCURSIONS | Scenic flights leave from alongside the Whataroa River, just a 30-minute drive north of Franz Josef township. The advantage is you get to see more mountains en route to the glaciers, and the weather can be more settled in the open valley, away from the glaciers. This company will also book heli-hikes for you with the local companies. ⊠ *Main Rd., Whataroa* ☎ *03/753–4096, 0800/423–463 New Zealand only* ⊕ *glacieradventures.co.nz* 🔁 *From NZ$195.*

Mountain Helicopters

AIR EXCURSIONS | Fly out of Fox Glacier on a quick but dramatic helicopter flight. Smaller choppers mean that everyone gets a window seat, and the experience is more intimate than it can be with the bigger operators. Options range from 10-, 20-, and 30-minute flights, taking in glacier, mountain, and rain-forest scenery, plus a 40-minute flight that includes a quick snow landing. Reservations are required, and all trips are weather dependent. ⊠ *Next to Snakebite Restaurant, State Hwy. 6, Franz Josef* ☎ *03/751–0045, 0800/369–423 New Zealand only* ⊕ *www.mountainhelicopters. co.nz* 🔁 *From NZ$99.*

KAYAKING AND RAFTING

Franz Josef Wilderness Tours

KAYAKING | **FAMILY** | Glacial Lake Mapourika is (usually) mirror-still, reflecting its rain forest and mountain surroundings. Kayaking is the way to explore it, and you'll navigate your kayak into an estuary that backs onto protected forest where rare Rowi kiwi live—on a sunset paddle you might hear them calling. Lots of options are offered: kayak-only trips, kayak-and-walk combos, paddleboarding, and even combinations with skydiving and glacier heli-hikes. You can also take their fully covered boats for a scenic cruise or fish for brown trout and salmon (in season) out on the lake. Book the barbecue tour to make an evening of it. Reservations are essential. ■ **TIP→ The best views are likely to be in winter, when the weather is clearer and calmer.** ⊠ *Glacier Hot Pools Building, 63 Cron St., Franz Josef* ☎ *03/752–0230, 0800/423–262 South Island only* ⊕ *www.frqanzjoseftours.co.nz* 🔁 *From NZ$85.*

CHRISTCHURCH AND CANTERBURY

Updated by
Gerard Hindmarsh

 Sights
★★★★☆

 Restaurants
★★★★☆

 Hotels
★★★☆☆

 Shopping
★★☆☆☆

 Nightlife
★★★☆☆

WELCOME TO CHRISTCHURCH AND CANTERBURY

TOP REASONS TO GO

★ **The Arts:** Christchurch's galleries, museums, and cultural activities highlight the city's heritage and its bright future; thought-provoking art projects are dotted around the city.

★ **The Great Outdoors:** You don't have to go far to be among mountains, forests, rivers, and beaches. There is an abundance of places to hike, trek, cycle, mountain-bike, boat, and ski, and it's easy to hire any gear you need.

★ **Parks and Gardens:** The Botanic Gardens and Hagley Park are Christchurch's green living rooms. Riverside promenades and landscaped squares line the city center. In spring and summer, several public and private gardens are open for viewing.

★ **Superb Skiing:** Christchurch has 12 ski areas all within a few hours' drive. The season usually runs from June until early October.

★ **Fantastic Festivals:** Festivals celebrate the arts, music, seasons, heritage, wine, and food.

1 Christchurch. New Zealand's second largest and newest city, Christchurch has survived two major earthquakes to become a place filled with art, adventure, and unbridled optimism.

2 Arthur's Pass National Park. In the heart of the Southern Alps, this national park offers richly diverse landscapes, from beech forests and snowcapped mountains to dense rain forests and beautiful wildflower fields.

3 Lyttelton. This small, quiet town was where many settlers first arrived in Canterbury and today attracts artists.

4 Akaroa and the Banks Peninsula. The fishing village of Akaroa and its surrounding coastline is a lovely day trip from Christchurch.

5 Waipara Valley. This low-key valley is filled with excellent wineries.

6 Hanmer Springs. This spa town still offers hot springs for soaking as well as plenty of outdoor adventures.

7 Methven. One hour from Canterbury, this is a great base for skiing in the area.

8 Geraldine. This charming town makes a great stop while traveling to Aoraki/Mt. Cook.

With its vast food basket, abundant pure water, and natural resources, Canterbury could be its own country. The expansive coast, fertile plains, and snow-lined Alps not only define the region's beauty, they also sustain a thriving agricultural industry.

The province is served by a major international airport, several ports, and an excellent road network. The dynamic city of Christchurch (Otautahi in Māori) with its growing immigrant population, has become known as the southern gateway to Antarctica and has a keen arts community and a vibrant culinary scene.

Captain Cook sailed right past the Canterbury coast in 1770 and thought Banks Peninsula was an island. The Māori knew better: they were already well established (by nearly 600 years) around Te Waihora and Waiwera—lakes Ellesmere and Forsyth today. In 1848, the English were back to colonize the land. John Robert Godley had been sent by the Canterbury Association to prepare for the arrival of settlers for a planned Church of England community. That year, four settler ships arrived bearing roughly 800 pioneers, and their new town was named for Godley's college at Oxford.

Built in a Gothic Revival style of dark gray stone, civic buildings such as the Arts Center (originally Canterbury University) and Canterbury Museum give the city an English quality. This style, plus elements such as punting and cricket, often pegs Christchurch as a little slice of England. Though the city may have a conservative exterior, it has been a nursery for social change. It was here that Kate Sheppard began organizing a campaign that led to New Zealand being the first country in the world to grant women the vote.

Beyond Christchurch the wide-open Canterbury Plains sweep to the north, west, and south of the city. This is some of New Zealand's finest pastureland, and the higher reaches are sheep stations where life and lore mingle in the South Island's cowboy country. This is where young Samuel Butler dreamed up the satirical *Erewhon*—the word is an anagram of *nowhere*. But the towns here are no longer considered the back of beyond; communities such as Hanmer Springs, Akaroa, and Geraldine are now favorite day-trip destinations. Arthur's Pass is probably the best place for a one-day-wonder experience of the Southern Alps while the Waipara Valley is now an established vineyard area, highly regarded for its pinot noir, chardonnay, and aromatics.

Canterbury is the South Island's largest geographical region, with a natural boundary formed by the Main Divide (the peaks of the Southern Alps) in the west and stretching from Kaikoura in the north down to the Waitaki River in the south. The region's main city is Christchurch, and the area also includes Banks Peninsula, the Waipara wine country, the ski town of Methven, and the alpine resort town of Hanmer Springs, north and west of the city. Arthur's Pass National Park is a few hours northwest of Christchurch by car or train and a great mountain day trip from the city.

MAJOR REGIONS

Christchurch. The city spreads out from the Port Hills, with stand-out contemporary buildings sitting alongside restored heritage properties.

Greater Christchurch. To the south, there's the Air Force Museum of New Zealand. To the west, Christchurch's leafy suburbs are reminders of a genteel history like the Mona Vale Gardens & Homestead and the International Antarctic Centre. To the east, exciting projects like the Otakaro Avon River Corridor are meant to regenerate the area following severe earthquake damage in 2011. It's also where you'll find the Christchurch Gondola, Ferrymead Heritage Park, and the Riccarton House and Bush.

Lyttelton and Akaroa and the Banks Peninsula. East of the city, you can explore the wonderful coastline of the Banks Peninsula. Its two harbors, Lyttelton and Akaroa, were formed from the remnants of two ancient volcanoes; their steep grassy walls drop dramatically to the sea.

Canterbury. Looking north, consider stopping in Waipara and its wineries if you're en route to or from Kaikoura or Hanmer Springs. Hanmer Springs' thermal baths are good for a relaxing soak, or you can ride the white water on the river, ski, or mountain bike. Head south or west of town into the Canterbury Plains countryside, and you can ski at Mt. Hutt (in winter) or drive the scenic inland highway to Geraldine and Timaru. Where once only sheep and cattle grazed, you're now just as likely to spot alpacas, deer, and ostriches. If you're heading to the West Coast by road or rail, then Arthur's Pass is worth investigating. You should set an entire day aside for any of these side trips, or, better still, stay overnight.

Planning

Getting Here and Around

AIR

Direct flights arrive into Christchurch from the major New Zealand cities, the larger Australian cities, Singapore, China, and the Pacific Islands. There are no direct flights from North America, but easy daily connections can be found through Auckland. Air New Zealand connects Christchurch to most New Zealand centers. Jetstar has flights to all New Zealand's main centers and several regional centers. For access to the Chatham Islands there's Air Chathams. Air New Zealand, Qantas, Jetstar, Virgin Australia, and Emirates fly direct from Australia. A private jet terminal is operated by Garden City Aviation at Christchurch Airport, with charter helicopters connecting to high country and remote lodges.

AIRPORTS Christchurch International Airport. ✉ 30 Durey Rd., Harewood ☎ 03/353–7777 ⊕ www.christchurchairport.co.nz.

AIRLINES Air New Zealand. ☎ 0800/737–000 NZ only ⊕ www.airnewzealand.co.nz. **Jetstar.** ☎ 0800/800-995 ⊕ www.jetstar.com. **Virgin Australia.** ☎ 0800/670-000 ⊕ www.virginaustralia.com.

BUS

InterCity bus service connects Christchurch with major towns and cities on the South Island.

CONTACTS Great Journeys of NZ. ☎ 0800/872–467 ⊕ www.greatjourneysofnz.co.nz. **InterCity Coachlines.** ☎ 03/365–1113 ⊕ www.intercity.co.nz. **Interislander.** ☎ 0800/802–802 ⊕ www.greatjourneysofnz.co.nz/interislander.

Christchurch Earthquakes

The first earthquake was early in the morning of September 4, 2010, magnitude 7.1, centered beneath farmland on the Canterbury Plains. It caused considerable damage in the city but no loss of life. Collectively, Cantabrians believed they had been spared. But not so. At lunchtime, on February 22, 2011, a magnitude 6.3 aftershock, centered almost directly beneath the city, caused massive damage, injured several thousand people, and resulted in the loss of 185 lives. Many of the city's heritage buildings crumbled, suburban streets were swamped with liquefaction (a black silty deposit shaken up from underground gravels), and even modern, inner-city buildings rocked and rolled on their foundations as the earth heaved. The central business district was cordoned off for more than two years afterward and more than half of the buildings there had to be demolished. The Canterbury Earthquake National Memorial on the banks of the Avon River is a now place to reflect on the events that changed Canterbury forever. It combines a riverside garden on the north bank and a memorial wall on the south bank, designed by Slovenian architect Grega Vezjak.

Christchurch is now focused on the future, with much of the central city rebuilt or nearing completion. It is achieving international acclaim for creative and clever urban design, evidenced by inspiring street art, cycle- and pedestrian-friendly streets, world-class hospitality and shopping precincts, and a "cardboard" cathedral awarded the world's top architecture prize. The city's focal point is the Avon/Otakaro River, and an attractive promenade now follows the river through the city, lined with gardens, artworks, access points to the water, seating, and restaurants.

CAR

Outside the city the best way to explore the region is by car. Roads across the Canterbury Plains tend to be straight and flat with good signage and low traffic volume. State Highway 1 runs the length of the region's coast, linking all the major towns. State Highway 72 follows the contours of the hills, farther inland, beneath the Alps. State Highway 7 leaves the main road at Waipara and heads inland to Hanmer Springs before heading north to Nelson, and State Highway 73 heads west across the plains before leaping into the Southern Alps on its way to the West Coast.

TRAIN

The Coastal Pacific train runs from Christchurch to Blenheim and Picton at the top of the South Island and connects with the Interislander Ferry to the North Island. The TranzAlpine train is one of the Great Train Journeys of the World and departs Christchurch daily. Christchurch has a good metropolitan bus service.

Hotels

There's an extraordinary array of lodging in Christchurch to suit all tastes and budgets—from backpacker lodges to gorgeous boutique B&Bs, from modern multilevel contemporary hotels within the city center to plenty of motels heading out west and toward the airport. The more substantial lodges tend to be out in the hinterland. Many accommodations do not include breakfast in their room rates. Reservations are most necessary in summer, on public holidays, during rugby tests, and at festival times.

Outside Christchurch, it can be hard to find a place to stay in summer, especially over the holidays. If you're planning on going to Akaroa, Hanmer Springs, or Waipara during peak season, be sure to reserve well in advance. Bookings can also be heavy in winter around the ski areas and during school holidays.

Restaurant and hotel reviews have been shortened. For full information, visit Fodors.com. Restaurant prices are the average cost of a main course at dinner or, if dinner is not served, at lunch. Hotel prices are the lowest cost of a standard double room in high season.

WHAT IT COSTS in New Zealand Dollars

$	$$	$$$	$$$$
RESTAURANTS			
under NZ$15	NZ$15–NZ$20	NZ$21–NZ$30	over NZ$30
HOTELS			
under NZ$125	NZ$125–NZ$200	NZ$201–NZ$300	over NZ$300

Planning Your Time

Take at least four days to explore the Canterbury region. A full day in the city only skims the surface. An overnight trip to Hanmer, Arthur's Pass, or Akaroa gives you a taste of the hinterland. Waipara and Hanmer Springs can be visited when heading north to Kaikoura or Nelson. Arthur's Pass is on the main road to the West Coast, and Geraldine is on the main route south to Dunedin and Queenstown.

FESTIVALS
Christchurch Arts Festival
ARTS FESTIVALS | In odd-numbered years, the city hosts a late-winter, month-long arts festival, featuring everything from

dance and theater to comedy, visual art, and cabaret. ⊕ *www.artsfestival.co.nz.*

Restaurants

Christchurch has an exciting foodie scene, and many new restaurants, cafés, and bars have opened in recent years. Restaurants are usually open every day; if they do close, it's either Sunday or Monday. Outside Christchurch, restaurants are more likely to close on Monday and Tuesday and during the winter.

The Waipara Valley wine region is seeing a surge in exotic food production. North Canterbury is now a key producer in the country's fledgling black truffle industry. Locally sourced saffron, hazelnuts, *manuka* (an indigenous kind of tea tree) honey, horopito (pepper tree), and olive oil are also making their way onto area menus.

Visitor Information

The Christchurch Visitor Information Centre is open daily from 9:30 to 4 (later in summer) and is located in the Arts Center on Worcester Boulevard. The knowledgeable and friendly staff can help you learn about possible activities and book everything from lodging to bike rentals. Here you will also find the Department of Conservation's (DOC's) visitor center, with information and bookings for all of New Zealand's national parks and Great Walks. *Cityscape,* a local magazine and website with events listings and reviews, is also worth a browse (*www.cityscape-christchurch.co.nz*).

CONTACTS ChristchurchNZ. ✉ *28 Worcester Blvd.* ☎ *03/379–4082* ⊕ *www.christchurchnz.com/city-events* Ⓜ *Christchurch.* **Christchurch Visitor Information Centre.** ✉ *Old Boys High Bldg., Arts Center, 28 Worcester Blvd., Christchurch* ☎ *03/379–9629* ⊕ *www. christchurchnz.com.*

When to Go

Christchurch is a city of four distinct seasons and generally low rainfall. Spring brings cherry blossoms and daffodils while summer days are often hot and windy. Winter's weather is crisp and cool, but this is the perfect time to come for skiing and snowboarding. From late June through early October you can be assured of snow at Mt. Hutt (remember seasons are switched from the northern hemisphere). Snow on the ground in Christchurch is a rarity.

November's New Zealand Cup and Show Week is a wacky time, when locals kick their heels up at Riccarton Park and Addington Raceway for horse racing and the country's largest agricultural and pastoral show where "country comes to town." If you've organized your accommodation well in advance it can be good fun but very busy. Wine and beer festivals follow in the summer and the Garden City Summer Times festival runs from New Year's until late February, while mid-January brings the World Buskers Festival; the Electric Avenue Music Festival is in February. In winter, the Christchurch Arts Festival is held biennially. Every second July, the Botanic Gardens and the Arts Centre are lit up with an interactive lighting and projection event called Botanic D'Lights, which coincides with Matariki or Māori New Year.

Christchurch

Earthquakes aside, the face of Christchurch (pop. 383,200) is changing, fueled by both New Zealand residents drawn from other centers as well as immigrants attracted by rebuilding opportunities. The Māori community, although still below the national average in size, is growing. Ngai Tahu, the main South Island Māori tribe, settled Treaty of Waitangi claims in 1997 and has invested in many high-profile property and tourism ventures. There is a growing Asian population, reflected in the number of restaurants and stores catering to their preferences. Christchurch's population is rising, the arts scene is flourishing, and the city continues to attract cutting-edge technology companies.

Christchurch is also the forward supply depot for the main U.S. Antarctic base at McMurdo Sound, and if you come in by plane in summer, you are likely to see the giant U.S. Air Force transport planes of Operation Deep Freeze parked on the tarmac at Christchurch International Airport.

GETTING HERE AND AROUND

The inner city is compact and easiest to explore on foot or by bicycle; the central sights can be reached during an afternoon's walk. Beyond this core are a number of special-interest museums and activities, about 20 minutes away by car.

Outside the central city, the best way to get around is to use the network of buses. A state-of-the-art indoor Bus Interchange is located on the corner of Lichfield and Colombo Streets. Maps and timetables are clearly displayed on real-time arrival information screens.

Metro, the city's main municipal bus line, has a great website that helps plan your route. Once in Christchurch you can purchase a Metrocard at the Bus Interchange or a Metro Agent (their website provides a list); a Metrocard is a preloaded card that will give cheaper fares. You can also top-up these cards once you've used the initial funds. ■TIP→ Free shuttle buses depart from the main terminal for a number of tourist attractions, including Orana Park and the Gondola.

BUS Christchurch Bus Interchange.
✉ Corner of Lichfield and Colombo Sts., Christchurch ☎ 03/366–8855 ⊕ www.metroinfo.co.nz.

TRAIN Christchurch Railway Station.
✉ Troup Dr., Addington ☎ 03/341–2588.

TOURS

BICYCLE TOURS

Christchurch Segway Tours

GUIDED TOURS | Informative and fun Segway tours with a knowledgeable local guide are popular with visitors to Christchurch. You can book a two-hour guided tour with three different route options. Full training and helmets are provided. Tours meet in South Hagley Park off Hagley Avenue. ⊠ *Hagley Ave., Christchurch* ☎ *027/542–1887* ⊕ *www. urbanwheels.co.nz* ☞ *From NZ$109.*

SIGHTSEEING TOURS

Soaring Kiwi Tours

BUS TOURS | Hop-on, hop-off Christchurch City tours depart from outside the Canterbury Museum aboard classic London double-decker buses, with open tops in summer. One-hour tours of the central city (red loop) with an expert guide are offered, as is a two-hour circumnavigation of the outer suburbs (blue loop) on the Discover Christchurch tour, which includes Sumner Beach and the Port Hills. There are regular departures from 10 am until 2 pm daily. The same company runs Hassle-free Tours with four-wheel-drives to the Canterbury high country, including guided Lord of the Rings tours, alpine safaris, and jet boat river tours, all with regular departures and hotel pick-ups in Christchurch. Private and specialized tours can also be arranged. ⊠ *Rolleston Ave., Christchurch* ☎ *03/385–5775* ⊕ *www.soaringkiwi.co.nz* ☞ *From NZ$35.*

Wildsouth Discovery

GUIDED TOURS | Small, stylish, and customized tours are offered by this Christchurch couple who have lots of experience in hospitality and tourism. They'll take you off-the-beaten-track, where you'll discover little-known secrets not crowded with tourists. With picnics loaded in the trunk you won't go hungry, and they might even take you to their own vacation home for wine and cheese. Paula and Brian run day tours from Christchurch and multiday itineraries exploring the South Island, or they can make a bespoke itinerary just for you and your interests. Tours are best suited to just one or two couples traveling together, but groups up to 10 can be accommodated. ⊠ *Christchurch* ☎ *03/332–3665, 027/436-3068* ⊕ *www.wildsouth.com* ☞ *Tours from NZ$690.*

WALKING TOURS

Botanic Gardens Tour

GUIDED TOURS | Take the hard work out of walking around the 52-acre Botanic Gardens on this hop-on, hop-off tour. The vehicles are environmentally powered (electric and solar) and a ticket lasts two days. You can buy tickets online or over the phone. The full circuit with commentary from an expert guide takes approximately 50 minutes. ⊠ *9 Rolleston Ave., Christchurch* ⊕ *www.christchurchattractions.nz* ☞ *From NZ$20* ⊗ *Christmas Day.*

Canterbury Horticultural Society—Garden Tours

GUIDED TOURS | The Canterbury Horticultural Society began with the colonization of Canterbury in the 1850s and continues to provide inspiration to gardeners throughout the region today. The society runs seasonal tours of gardens and is happy to have nonmembers join in. Their Ramblers walks start at 9:45 am every second and fourth Tuesday of the month. Check the website for details of upcoming dates and for a list of gardens that are open to view. ⊠ *The Kiosk, Botanic Gardens, Christchurch* ☎ *03/366–6937* ⊕ *www. chsgardens.co.nz* ☞ *Free.*

Sights

Although the Christchurch Art Gallery—Te Puna O Waiwhetu is the city's visual arts mother ship, there are many smaller galleries and plenty of street art to check out. For more information, check the Canterbury Art Trails website (*www. arttrails.nz/canterbury/index.htm*).

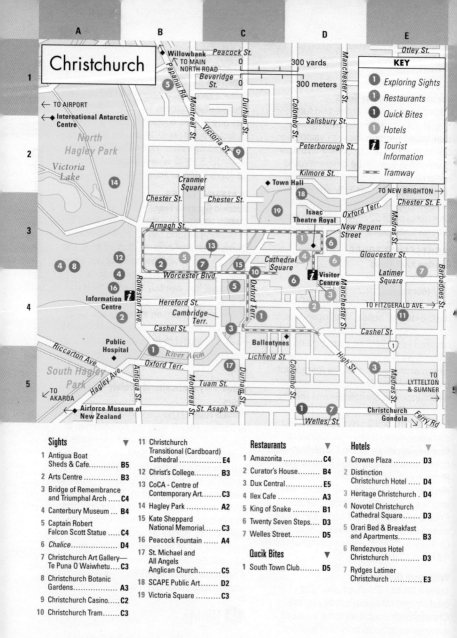

Christchurch

KEY

- **1** Exploring Sights
- **1** Restaurants
- **1** Quick Bites
- **1** Hotels
- **i** Tourist Information
- Tramway

Sights ▼

1 Antigua Boat Sheds & Cafe............ **B5**
2 Arts Centre **B3**
3 Bridge of Remembrance and Triumphal Arch **C4**
4 Canterbury Museum ... **B4**
5 Captain Robert Falcon Scott Statue **C4**
6 Chalice.................... **D4**
7 Christchurch Art Gallery— Te Puna O Waiwhetu... **C3**
8 Christchurch Botanic Gardens................. **A3**
9 Christchurch Casino..... **C2**
10 Christchurch Tram....... **C3**
11 Christchurch Transitional (Cardboard) Cathedral **E4**
12 Christ's College.......... **B3**
13 CoCA - Centre of Contemporary Art....... **C3**
14 Hagley Park **A2**
15 Kate Sheppard National Memorial....... **C3**
16 Peacock Fountain **A4**
17 St. Michael and All Angels Anglican Church.......... **C5**
18 SCAPE Public Art **D2**
19 Victoria Square **C3**

Restaurants ▼

1 Amazonita **C4**
2 Curator's House......... **B4**
3 Dux Central............... **E5**
4 Ilex Cafe **A3**
5 King of Snake **B1**
6 Twenty Seven Steps.... **D3**
7 Welles Street............. **D5**

Qucik Bites ▼

1 South Town Club........ **D5**

Hotels ▼

1 Crowne Plaza **D3**
2 Distinction Christchurch Hotel **D4**
3 Heritage Christchurch . **D4**
4 Novotel Christchurch Cathedral Square........ **D3**
5 Orari Bed & Breakfast and Apartments.......... **B3**
6 Rendezvous Hotel Christchurch **D3**
7 Rydges Latimer Christchurch **E3**

Antigua Boat Sheds & Cafe

MARINA/PIER | **FAMILY** | Built for the Christchurch Boating Club in 1882, this green-and-white wooden structure is the last shed standing of a half dozen that once lined the Avon. On sunny days, punts, canoes, and paddleboats take to the river paddled by visitors and families alike. Join them by renting a boat and taking a champagne picnic into the Botanic Gardens or farther up into the woodlands of Hagley Park. After exploring the waterway you can rent a bike for more action or rest a while at the boat shed's licensed café (open for breakfast and lunch) with a deck overlooking the Avon. ✉ *2 Cambridge Terr., Christchurch* ☎ *03/366–5885 boat shed, 03/366–6768 café* ⊕ *www.boatsheds.co.nz* ⊠ *From NZ$15 per hr.*

★ Arts Centre

NOTABLE BUILDING | After major restoration, a large section of the historic Arts Centre, once a popular cultural venue, has reopened with galleries, theaters, boutique shopping, and dining. Further careful restoration and strengthening is still underway on this fine collection of 23 Gothic Revival stone buildings that were originally built as Canterbury's University. ✉ *Worcester Blvd. between Montreal St. and Rolleston Ave., Christchurch* ☎ *3/366–0089* ⊕ *www.artscentre.org.nz.*

Bridge of Remembrance and Triumphal Arch

MONUMENT | Arching over Cashel Street, this Oamaru limestone memorial arch and Avon River bridge was built in memory of the soldiers who crossed the river here from King Edward Barracks on their way to the battlefields of Europe during World War I. ✉ *76 Cashel St. at Avon River, Christchurch.*

★ Canterbury Museum

HISTORY MUSEUM | **FAMILY** | When this museum was founded in 1867, its trading power with national and international museums was in moa bones (these Jurassic birds roamed the plains of Canterbury and are believed to have been hunted to extinction by early Māori). The museum still houses one of the largest collections of artifacts from the moa hunting period. You'll also find an interactive natural-history center, called Discovery, where kids can dig for fossils. The Hall of Antarctic Discovery charts the links between the city and Antarctica, from the days when Captain Cook skirted the continent in a small wooden ship. Among the 20th-century explorers celebrated here are the Norwegian Roald Amundsen, who was first to visit the South Pole, and Captain Robert Falcon Scott, who died returning from the continent. *Fred & Myrtle's Paua Shell House* tells the story of an iconic Kiwi couple and recreates their *paua* (abalone) shell–covered living room which was originally in Bluff. The café looks out over the Botanic Gardens. ✉ *11 Rolleston Ave., Christchurch* ☎ *03/366–5000* ⊕ *www. canterburymuseum.com* ⊠ *Free admission, donations appreciated; Discovery, NZ$2.*

Captain Robert Falcon Scott Statue

PUBLIC ART | The captain known as Scott of the Antarctic (1868–1912), who stayed in Christchurch while preparing for his two Antarctic expeditions, is memorialized by this unfinished white marble statue sculpted by his widow, Kathleen. It's inscribed "Do not regret this journey, which shows that Englishmen can endure hardships, help one another and meet death with as great fortitude as ever in the past." Scott wrote these words in his diary as he and his party lay dying in a blizzard on their return journey from the South Pole—a story of endurance taught to all New Zealand schoolkids. Scott's marble statue was toppled and broken in the earthquakes, but has now been restored. ✉ *Worcester Blvd. and Oxford Terr., Christchurch.*

Chalice

PUBLIC ART | **FAMILY** | An artwork created by internationally acclaimed Christchurch sculptor Neil Dawson, this giant steel vessel was installed in Cathedral Square in 2001 to celebrate the 150th anniversary of the founding of Christchurch and Canterbury. It survived the earthquakes and is now a major city landmark. ⊠ *Cathedral Sq., Christchurch* ⊕ *www. ccc.govt.nz.*

★ Christchurch Art Gallery—Te Puna O Waiwhetu

ART MUSEUM | The city's stunning art gallery wows visitors as much for its architecture as for its artwork. Its tall, wavy glass facade was inspired by Christchurch's Avon River and the shape of the native koru fern. The museum's Māori name refers to an artesian spring on site and means "the wellspring of star-reflecting waters." Free guided tours, entertaining events, and family activities make the gallery a must-see. Shop for a great selection of gifts, or relax at the brasserie and café. Check the website for updates on the gallery program. ⊠ *Worcester Blvd. and Montreal St., Christchurch* ☎ *03/941–7300* ⊕ *www. christchurchartgallery.org.nz* ⊠ *Free.*

Christchurch Botanic Gardens

GARDEN | FAMILY | One of the largest city parks in the world, these superb gardens are known for the magnificent trees planted here in the 19th century. Pick up the Historic Tree Walk brochure from the information center for a self-guided Who's Who tour of the tree world. Spend time in the conservatories and the award-winning Visitor Centre and Ilex Cafe to discover tropical plants, cacti, and ferns on days when you'd rather not be outside. Go to the New Zealand plants area at any time of the year; the modern and heritage rose gardens are also quite lovely. ⊠ *City Centre, Rolleston Ave., Christchurch* ☎ *03/941–7590* ⊠ *Free.*

Christchurch Casino

CASINO | When all else has closed, make your way to the Christchurch Casino for blackjack, American roulette, baccarat, and gaming machines; it's open until 2 am over the weekend and until midnight

Monday to Thursday. There are four restaurant and bar areas in the casino including The Cafe, Valley Bar, and the Monza Sports Bar. The latter has TV monitors at every vantage point plus one huge screen for watching live sports. The casino is strict on its dress code; if you're unsure of what to wear, check their website for details. ■TIP→ **Free shuttles go to and from some local hotels and motels daily from 6 pm to 2 am—book through the casino reception.** ⊠ *30 Victoria St., Christchurch* ☎ *03/365–9999* ⊕ *www. chchcasino.co.nz.*

★ Christchurch Tram

TRANSPORTATION | FAMILY | There's something nostalgic and reassuring about the *ding-ding* of these heritage trams. All-day tickets allow you to hop on and off and explore the inner city with fascinating commentary by the conductors. The Tramway Restaurant departs daily at 7 pm (bookings are essential). The Tramway ticket office is in Cathedral Junction, but you can buy tickets at other places en route and onboard. Tickets can also be bought in a combination pass that includes the Punting, Gondola, and the Botanic Gardens Tour. ⊠ *Cathedral Junction, Christchurch* ☎ *03/366–7830* ⊕ *www.christchurchattractions.nz* ⊠ *NZ$25.*

★ Christchurch Transitional (Cardboard) Cathedral

NOTABLE BUILDING | After the famed Christchurch Cathedral was severely damaged from the 2010–11 earthquakes, the Anglican church's Transitional Cathedral opened to help fill a little of the enormous gap left by the loss. Locals call it the Cardboard Cathedral because it is built largely from 98 cardboard tubes, covered in plastic. It can seat 700 and is the largest "emergency structure" to be designed by award-winning Japanese architect Shigeru Ban, who gifted the design (right down to its unusual chairs) to Christchurch. The large triangular window at the front contains images from

Did You Know?

Hagley Park includes, among other things, the botanic gardens, a hospital, 11 rugby fields, 13 soccer fields, a world-class cricket oval, a polo ground, tennis courts, croquet lawns, a golf course, and a small lake—and there's plenty of space for the city's many festivals.

Christchurch Cathedral's original rose window. Built to last at least 50 years, it has been named by *Architectural Digest* magazine as one of the world's 10 daring buildings. The striking venue is also used for functions and community events outside of church hours. ⊠ *234 Hereford St., Christchurch* ⊕ *www.cardboardcathedral.org.nz.*

Christ's College

COLLEGE | FAMILY | Founded in 1850, Christ's College is New Zealand's most well-known private school for boys. It is housed in a magnificent precinct of buildings designed by the city's leading architects over a period of 165 years. Set around an open quadrangle neighboring Hagley Park and the Botanic Gardens, the school's many heritage buildings are undergoing extensive repair and strengthening following the earthquakes. Guided tours of the school are available during summer from mid-October to late April, at 10 am for 80 minutes on Monday, Wednesday, and Friday. ⊠ *Rolleston Ave., Christchurch* ⊕ *www.christscollege. com* ⊠ *NZ$10.*

★ CoCA—Centre of Contemporary Art

ARTS CENTER | Christchurch's leading contemporary art home was built in 1968 and has since been restored and remodeled as a modern and stylish gallery space. Formed in 1880 as the Canterbury Society of Arts, CoCA is a not-for-profit art gallery run by a trust whose members include several of New Zealand's leading contemporary artists. The gallery commissions, produces, and collaborates with top artists to present an ever-changing set of exhibitions ⊠ *66 Gloucester St., Christchurch* ☎ *03/366–7261* ⊕ *www. coca.org.nz.*

Hagley Park

CITY PARK | FAMILY | Hagley Park was developed by European settlers in the mid-1800s with imported plants given trial runs in what would become the Botanic Gardens. Now the 407-acre park includes a golf course, sports fields, world-class cricket oval, netball and tennis courts, cycling paths, walking and jogging tracks, and a 17-station fitness circuit. In spring, you'll be treated to a magnificent blossom display from the flowering cherry trees and a host of golden daffodils. You can access the park from most of its perimeter. The Botanic Gardens are near the middle, closest to the city center. Every Saturday morning at 8 am, hundreds join in the Hagley Parkrun, a free timed 5,000-meter (3-mile) run. ⊠ *8 Riccarton Ave., Christchurch* ⊕ *www.ccc.govt.nz.*

Kate Sheppard National Memorial

PUBLIC ART | This bronze memorial wall, unveiled in 1993, commemorates 100 years of votes for women. New Zealand was the first country in the world to grant all women the vote, and Christchurch resident Kate Sheppard played a key role in petitioning Parliament for this essential right. The vote for all women over 21, including Māori women, was granted on September 19, 1893; the work of Sheppard and other activists is celebrated each year on that date at the memorial. The women featured on the memorial are (left to right) Helen Nicol, Kate Sheppard, Ada Wells, Harriet Morison, Meri Te Tai Mangakahia, and Amey Daldy. ⊠ *Oxford Terr. and Worcester Blvd., Christchurch.*

Peacock Fountain

FOUNTAIN | This colorful sight at the entrance to the Botanic Gardens is a fine and rare example of Edwardian ornamental cast ironwork, set in a large circular pool. It was made in Shropshire, England, funded by a bequest to the city from politician and philanthropist John Peacock in 1911. ⊠ *Rolleston Ave, Christchurch.*

SCAPE Public Art

PUBLIC ART | SCAPE public art installs free-to-view contemporary art all year round in Christchurch, with a focus on its Public Art Annual Seasons between September and November. The works, many of which are now permanent, are urban and alternative arts such as conceptual architecture, sculpture, and city murals. Check the website for details. 🌐 *www.scapepublicart.org.nz.*

St. Michael and All Angels Anglican Church

NOTABLE BUILDING | The bell in this church's belfry came out with the Canterbury Pilgrims on one of the first four ships and was rung hourly to indicate time for early settlers; it is still rung every day. The original building was the first church to be built in Christchurch. The current white-timber church was built in 1872, entirely of matai, a native black pine, and has 26 English-made stained-glass windows dating back as far as 1858. It's one of the largest timber Victorian Gothic churches in Australasia. The building stood up to the 2010–11 earthquakes, apart from its 1872 Bevington pipe organ, which was badly damaged but has been beautifully restored. ✉ *At Oxford Terr. and Durham St., Christchurch* ☎ *03/379–5236* 🌐 *wwwchchstmichaels.org.nz.*

Victoria Square

PLAZA/SQUARE | **FAMILY** | This central square was named for Queen Victoria in her jubilee year and has recently been restored, keeping its character and heritage. A *poupou,* a tall, carved, wood column in the square, acknowledges the site's history as a significant trading point between Māori and the European settlers. It is home to Christchurch's oldest iron bridge, a floral clock, two fountains, and statues of Queen Victoria and Captain Cook. ✉ *Armagh and Colombo Sts., Christchurch.*

🍴 Restaurants

Cuisine hubs are now dotted throughout the central city, in areas like The Terrace, High Street, Lichfield Street, and New Regent Street. St. Asaph Street hosts an array of international cuisines. You can kick on into the night here, too, with live music and dancing. Victoria Street, near the city center, is packed with easygoing bars, top restaurants, and cafés. Papanui Road, starting across Bealey Avenue from Victoria Street and going all the way up to Merivale Mall, has several popular bars, cafés, and restaurants, while Addington also has a lively café and restaurant scene, plus bars and live music along Lincoln Road.

Amazonita

$$$$ | **MEDITERRANEAN** | Set in the heart of Christchuch's dining haven, The Terrace, this rain-forest-inspired restaurant combines delicious food with friendly service. Behind the busy bar is an opulent dining area with an open kitchen where you can watch the talented chefs create Mediterranean-style dishes. **Known for:** chefs willing to cook to order if you have special requirements; wood-fired grill; impressive interior design. [$] *Average main: NZ$34* ✉ *126 Oxford Terr., Christchurch* ☎ *03/377–4144* 🌐 *www.amazonita.co.nz.*

Curator's House

$$$$ | **SPANISH** | Here you can dine in a 1920s Tudor-style house, looking out on the Botanic Gardens and the Peacock Fountain, or take a garden table and be part of it. The menu has tapas selections and a good variety of seafood, with owner–chef Javier Garcia producing authentic Spanish cuisine evoking an old-world atmosphere. **Known for:** impressive kitchen garden supplying herbs and vegetables all year-round; alfresco dining in summer, and cozy fireside dining in winter; excellent paella. [$] *Average main: NZ$39* ✉ *7 Rolleston Ave., Christchurch* ☎ *03/379–2252* 🌐 *www.curatorshouse.co.nz.*

★ Dux Central

$$$ | **MODERN NEW ZEALAND** | **FAMILY** | This restaurant's laneway setting and beautifully restored two-level building gives it a London pub feel. With food and drinks to suit all tastes, it's a popular hangout for locals day and night. **Known for:** DJs and live bands late night; nearly 200 beers, including their own brews, and an extensive wine list; great options for vegans, seafood lovers, and meat-eaters alike. $ *Average main: NZ$25* ⊠ *10 Poplar St., Christchurch* ☎ *03/366–6919* ⊕ *www. duxdine.co.nz.*

Ilex Cafe

$$ | CAFÉ | One of the city's most beautiful pieces of architecture also houses one its most popular cafés. Christchurch Botanic Gardens's rare plants and nurseries sit alongside a busy dining room in this modern take on a glass conservatory. **Known for:** clever kids' menu; fresh produce from local suppliers and the kitchen garden; creative brunch fare. $ *Average main: NZ$20* ⊠ *Christchurch Botanic Gardens, Armagh St., Christchurch* ⊹ *Entrance off Armagh St., walk across bridge from parking lot* ☎ *03/941–5556* ⊕ *www. goodcompany.nz/ilex.*

★ King of Snake

$$$$ | ASIAN | Don't be fooled by the unassuming alleyway outside: this chic restaurant and bar delivers fine Asian fusion cuisine on all levels. It's hard to recommend particular dishes because they are all exquisitely prepared and taste so good, served in a striking, seductive setting. **Known for:** delicious snack menu at the bar; exotic dishes designed to share; signature King of Snake cocktail with potent kick of chili and ginger. $ *Average main: NZ$35* ⊠ *145 Victoria St., Christchurch* ☎ *03/365–7363* ⊕ *www. kingofsnake.co.nz* ⊗ *No lunch weekends.*

★ Twenty Seven Steps

$$$$ | BISTRO | It's worth the climb 27 steps to this stylish European bistro, consistently rated one of New Zealand's best and situated on New Regent Street's heritage row. The welcoming staff delivers stand-out dishes (including several excellent vegan options) made with a wide variety of fresh local produce, including Canterbury beef, lamb, Te Tapu venison, and Akaroa salmon. **Known for:** top local wines and beers in a cute

little bar; contemporary bistro style in a beautiful heritage space; stellar service from the owners and staff, who really know their food. $ *Average main: NZ$35* ⊠ *16 New Regent St., Christchurch* ☎ *03/366–2727* ⊕ *www.twentyseven-steps.co.nz* ⊗ *No lunch.*

Welles Street

$$$ | MODERN NEW ZEALAND | FAMILY | This inner-city pub anchors the emerging South Town neighborhood of the Central Business District, and this big indoor–outdoor space has plenty of atmosphere. Menu items range from contemporary pub food to Mediterranean cuisine, all made using local produce. **Known for:** outdoor seating year-round; amazing free-range rotisserie chicken; 18 beers on tap and massive wine list. $ *Average main: NZ$23* ⊠ *44 Welles St., Christchurch* ☎ *03/366–0172* ⊕ *www.wellesstreet. co.nz.*

☕ Coffee and Quick Bites

South Town Club

$$ | CAFÉ | A great place to get a coffee fix, this hip café is styled with a utilitarian look based on a distinctive red-and-white grid pattern. Careful attention to detail is evident on the food side, too, with simple house-made, organic, and locally sourced breakfast and lunch dishes. **Known for:** jack's eggs omelet for breakfast, miso-glazed mushroom dish for lunch; great coffee and can't-miss milkshakes; trendy ex-garage location on Christchurch's coolest street. $ *Average main: NZ$16* ⊠ *10 Welles St., Christchurch* ☎ *03/365–0445* ⊕ *www.southtownclub.co.nz* ⊗ *No dinner.*

🛏 Hotels

Staying in the central city is a good choice, with most hotels either relatively new or recently refurbished. All the city sights, shopping, restaurants, and bars are within easy walking distance of central city hotels. There are also some lovely boutique B&Bs that offer more personal accommodation around the arts district.

Crowne Plaza

$$ | **HOTEL** | **FAMILY** | As Christchurch's tallest central city building (once an office tower), this is a prime location with spectacular views overlooking historic Victoria Square and the Avon River. **Pros:** luxurious tiled bathrooms; latest technology including smart TVs with device mirroring; three in-house dining options. **Cons:** long-term building work surrounds the hotel site; large tour groups can often take over the lobby; rooms are compact. [$] *Rooms from: NZ$190* ✉ *764 Colombo St., Christchurch* ☎ *03/741–2800* 🌐 *www.christchurch.crowneplaza.com* 🍴 *No Meals* 🛏 *204 rooms.*

Distinction Christchurch Hotel

$$$ | **HOTEL** | **FAMILY** | This 11-floor, upscale, New Zealand-owned and operated hotel is a post-earthquake renovation with a contemporary design. **Pros:** valet parking at reasonable rates; great soaking bathtubs; plush slippers, toothbrush, and bathrobes. **Cons:** conference hotel, so can be busy; room lighting needs dimmer options; overlooks the earthquake-damaged Christchurch Cathedral. [$] *Rooms from: NZ$245* ✉ *14 Cathedral Sq., Christchurch* ☎ *03/377–7000* 🌐 *www.distinctionhotels.co.nz* 🍴 *No Meals* 🛏 *179 rooms.*

Heritage Christchurch

$$$$ | **HOTEL** | Inside the beautifully restored Old Government Building built in 1913, with its sweeping central staircase and high ceilings, the Heritage has suites in an Italian High Renaissance Palazzo style complete with stained-glass windows and dark-wood paneling. **Pros:** extremely comfortable beds; self-contained with kitchen and laundry; decent spa and lap pool. **Cons:** O.G.B. bar is always busy and can be noisy outside, especially in summer; short-term parking can be difficult; Christchurch Cathedral and the square surrounding are under long-term restoration. [$] *Rooms from: NZ$330* ✉ *28–30 Cathedral Sq., Christchurch* ☎ *03/983–4800, 0800/368–888* 🌐 *www.heritagehotels.co.nz/christchurch* 🍴 *No Meals* 🛏 *42 suites.*

Novotel Christchurch Cathedral Square

$$$ | **HOTEL** | From the moment you walk in to the futuristic lobby you will receive a warm welcome from staff who know the city well and can help with directions and recommendations. **Pros:** comfortable contemporary bar open 'til late; right in the heart of the city; stunning views of the Southern Alps from executive rooms. **Cons:** quake-damaged Cathedral is right next door, and building work surrounds it; bathroom sink is set outside the bathroom door in the living areas; valet parking is expensive (better to use public lot nearby). [$] *Rooms from: NZ$223* ✉ *52 Cathedral Sq., Christchurch* ☎ *03/372–2111* 🌐 *www.all.accor.com* 🍴 *No Meals* 🛏 *154 rooms.*

★ Orari Bed & Breakfast and Apartments

$$ | **B&B/INN** | Hidden behind an ivy-clad wall and pretty gardens, this lovely heritage villa boasts modern, spacious rooms. **Pros:** extremely helpful and friendly hosts; no need for a car with so much nearby; the apartments are ideal for longer stays and for larger families. **Cons:** you will need to book well ahead to get a room in peak summer season; two of the rooms have separate bathrooms that are not ensuite; some uneven, squeaky floorboards. [$] *Rooms from: NZ$180* ✉ *42 Gloucester St., Christchurch* ☎ *03/365–6569, 0800/267–274 New Zealand only* 🌐 *www.orari.co.nz* 🍴 *Free Breakfast* 🛏 *15 rooms.*

Rendezvous Hotel Christchurch

$$ | **HOTEL** | **FAMILY** | Hard to miss, this city landmark has expansive central city, Port Hills, and mountain views. **Pros:** small well-equipped gym and sauna; valet parking in a clever car-stacker inside the

building; across the road from the Isaac Theatre Royal and New Regent Street. **Cons:** at busy times there can be a long wait for the elevators; some rooms are on the small side and corridors are narrow; pillow and blanket choice is limited. ⓢ *Rooms from: NZ$194* ✉ *166 Gloucester St., Christchurch* ☏ *03/943–3888* ⊕ *www.tfehotels.com* ⦿ *No Meals* ⇨ *171 rooms.*

Rydges Latimer Christchurch

$$$ | HOTEL | FAMILY | Set on leafy Latimer Square, this newly built low-rise hotel is just a few minutes' walk from the central city, but far enough away to be quiet and relaxed. **Pros:** excellent in-house dining options; free Wi-Fi throughout the hotel; free parking on-site. **Cons:** just a little too far to walk into the central city on cold days; big conference hotel often busy with large groups; traffic on the one-way roads surrounding the hotel. ⓢ *Rooms from: NZ$225* ✉ *30 Latimer Sq., Christchurch* ☏ *0800/176–176 NZ only* ⊕ *www.rydges.com* ⦿ *No Meals* ⇨ *175 rooms.*

 Nightlife

BARS AND PUBS

Boo Radley's Food and Liquor

LIVE MUSIC | Hip music and top-notch craft beers go nicely together in this cozy southern USA–themed bar. Add great food and a heady cocktail list for a memorable night out. There's a good sharing plate selection, a huge range of bourbons, and excellent craft beers and wines. Don't expect to talk too much when the live music starts, as it can get pretty loud here. Open-mike comedy nights are fun, too. ✉ *Level 1, 98 Victoria St., Christchurch* ☏ *03/366–9906* ⊕ *www.booradleys.co.nz.*

Fat Eddie's

LIVE MUSIC | Christchurch's most popular jazz club is in a prime position on the corner of Oxford Terrace and Hereford Street. It boasts a big dance floor and top local and visiting artists every night of the week, from 6:30 pm and until late on weekends. This place is packed from around 9 pm later in the week, so it's worth coming early to get a booth and some of their tasty pizzas and New Orleans–inspired snacks. Make the most of the big beer selection, too. ✉ *Level 1, Corner of Hereford St. and Oxford Terr., Christchurch* ☏ *03/595–5332* ⊕ *www. fateddiesbar.co.nz.*

The Last Word

WINE BARS | Time for a wee dram anyone? Far from being a den for older whisky drinkers, The Last Word is, just as its name suggests, the ultimate place to go if you are an up-and-coming discerning drinker looking for something different. Christchurch's character-filled heritage row, New Regent Street, is the perfect location for this intimate whisky-and-cocktail lounge. There are dozens of hand-picked whiskies to choose from and some excellent cocktails, local wines, and beers on the menu, too. ✉ *31 New Regent St, Christchurch* ☏ *022/094–7445* ⊕ *www.lastword.co.nz.*

O.G.B. Bar and Cocktail Lounge

WINE BARS | Located in a charming neo-Renaissance building that overlooks Cathedral Square, this popular speakeasy-style bar relives a timeless yet bygone era of the inner city. Guests can dine al fresco while watching the trams and passersby, or, they can head for the opulent and dimly lit cocktail lounge, The Parlour. ✉ *28 Cathedral Sq., Christchurch* ☏ *03/377–4336* ⊕ *www.ogb.co.nz.*

Performing Arts

Christchurch has a strong arts scene, with impressive orchestras, choirs, and theaters. The Isaac Theatre Royal has been restored to its former glory, adding a grand venue for performances and film. Christchurch Town Hall recently underwent a major restoration project and is now the permanent home of the Christchurch Symphony Orchestra. To find out what's on when you're visiting, check out *www.christchurchnz.com* and *eventfinda.co.nz*. *Cityscape* magazine also has an excellent website and app (*www.cityscape-christchurch.co.nz*) with information about the city's events. Tickets for many performance venues and concerts are sold through Ticketek (*www.ticketek.co.nz*).

MUSIC

Christchurch Town Hall

CONCERTS | The Christchurch Town Hall underwent a NZ$167 million restoration after being damaged in the earthquakes. It opened in stages with the main auditorium, foyer and function rooms in February 2019, followed by the James Hay Theatre and facilities for the Christchurch Symphony Orchestra later that year. With superb acoustics, the 2,500-seat auditorium is recognized as one of finest concert halls in the world. ⊠ *86 Kilmore St, Christchurch.*

THEATER

★ Isaac Theatre Royal

THEATER | The grand lady of Christchurch's theater scene, dating back to 1908, was fully restored in 2014. This opulent setting, complete with an intricate painted ceiling dome and marble staircase, hosts some of New Zealand's best touring shows including ballet and music. It is also home to a giant screen for the New Zealand International Film Festival, held every July. Get dressed up and enjoy the glamour of a bygone era in the comfort of today's plushest seating. There are stylish bars on every level for a drink before the show or during intermission. ⊠ *145 Gloucester St., Christchurch* ☎ *03/366– 6326* ⊕ *www.isaactheatreroyal.co.nz.*

🛍 Shopping

SHOPPING STREETS AND CENTERS

ANZ Centre

SHOPPING CENTER | This retail precinct in the lower levels of a big bank building offers standout local designer brands, including Macpac, Partridge Jewellers, Superette, Glassons, Hallensteins Brothers, the North Face, Platypus, and Merchant. There's also a Mecca Maxima cosmetics store and an ANZ bank, along with eight levels of parking. ⊠ *Junction of Colombo, High, and Cashel Sts., Christchurch* ⊕ *www.anzcentre.co.nz.*

★ Ballantynes

DEPARTMENT STORE | Established in 1854 as New Zealand's first department store, Ballantynes is an institution in the South Island. Far from allowing its traditions to slow it down, it has morphed into a world-class shopping experience with some of the best New Zealand and international designer brand names all under one roof. Allow plenty of time to browse the racks and shelves, where you will find everything from the latest trends, from designer concept-store items to New Zealand gifts and wine, to the very best crystal and china. When you need a break there are two cafés and a wine bar. They also have a store at the departure lounge of Christchurch Airport, where you can pick up your purchases and take advantage of tax-exempt shopping. ⊠ *Cashel Street Mall, Cashel St., Christchurch* ☎ *03/379–7400* ⊕ *www. ballantynes.co.nz.*

The Crossing

SHOPPING CENTER | Dubbed Christchurch's new retail heart, the Crossing is an artfully designed precinct boasting top international and local brands. Walking through the outdoor courtyards and laneways lined with impressive contemporary sculptures, you will find designer clothes and shoes, along with a florist, cafés, beauty salons, a bakery, and even a gourmet supermarket. ✉ *166 Cashel St., Christchurch* ☎ *027/506–8149* ⊕ *www. thecrossing.co.nz.*

SPECIALTY STORES
Kathmandu
SPORTING GOODS | This store in Cashel Mall sells a colorful range of outdoor clothing, backpacks, accessories, and tents. This chain is found throughout New Zealand and has particularly good markdowns at sale times. It has several stores throughout the city and a clearance outlet at 119 Riccarton Road. ✉ *Cashel Mall, Cnr Cashel and Colombo Sts., Christchurch* ☎ *03/943-7846* ⊕ *www.kathmandu.co.nz.*

★ Scorpio Bookshop
BOOKS | This independent bookstore started in the early 1970s and has gathered a cult following over the years. The shop stocks a wide range of fiction, cooking, and history books as well as design studies, philosophy tomes, and travelogues. It's a great place to spend a few hours browsing. ✉ *Five Lanes, 120 Hereford St., Christchurch* ☎ *03/379–2882* ⊕ *www. scorpiobooks.co.nz.*

 Activities

BALLOONING
★ Ballooning Canterbury
BALLOONING | Here's an activity worth getting up early for: Ballooning Canterbury picks you up from most central city accommodations. Your pilot will brief you on what to expect on your sunrise flight, before asking for your assistance to help set up the mighty balloon. Photo opportunities of the beautiful Canterbury Plains are endless during the one-hour flight, with stunning views out to the Pacific Ocean and around to the Southern Alps as well. Inflight photos are taken and supplied free to all passengers. Upon landing, you're treated to champagne or fruit juice. It's very weather-dependent so don't leave it to the last minute to organize. You must be at least 4½ feet

tall to ride. ✉ *2136 Bealey Rd., Darfield* ☎ *0508/422–556* ⊕ *www.ballooningcanterbury.com* ✉ *NZ$395 per person.*

BIKING
Christchurch's relative flatness makes for easy biking, and the city has cultivated excellent resources for cyclists. A network of well-marked and well-designed Major Cycle Routes connects the central city with local attractions. The award-winning Uni-Cycle runs 3½ miles from the city center through Hagley Park and leafy suburbs to the University of Canterbury. Other popular cycle trails include the Rail Trail at Little River and the spectacular trails around the Port Hills.

You can pick up a route map from the city council or visit their cycling website (*www.ccc.govt.nz/cycling-maps*), which shows cycleways and recreational routes.

★ Christchurch Adventure Park
BIKING | Christchurch's Port Hills are home to New Zealand's longest chairlift as well as the country's longest and highest zip line; both are found within the 900-acre Christchurch Adventure Park. Just 17 minutes by bike from the central city, you can be on the downhill mountain biking trails via chairlifts (for you and your bike) or experiencing dual zip line tours and incredible sightseeing. Bikes and protective gear are available for rent. There's an excellent café here, too. ✉ *225 Worsleys Rd., Christchurch* ☎ *0508/247–478* ⊕ *www.christchurchadventurepark.com* ✉ *NZ$20 chairlift; NZ$130 zip line.*

City Cycle Hire
BIKING | FAMILY | Here you can rent mountain and touring bikes for half-day, full-day, or multiday excursions. Rentals include helmets, locks, and cycle map; and they'll deliver your bike to your accommodation. ✉ *18 Settlers Crescent, Unit 62, Ferrymead* ☎ *03/377–5952, 0800/343–848 NZ only* ⊕ *www.cycle-hire-tours.co.nz* ✉ *From NZ$25 half day, NZ$35 full day.*

Cyclone Cycles

BIKING | Cycles can be rented from Cyclone Cycles for a flat fee of NZ$45 per rental bike. Special rates are available for groups or longer periods. Book online. ✉ *245 Colombo St., Christchurch* ☎ *03/332–9588* ⊕ *www.cyclone.net.nz.*

Mountain Bike Adventure Company

BIKING | The Mountain Bike Adventure Company offers a NZ$70 package including a ride up on the Christchurch Gondola to the summit station. Then there's the choice of either an off-road mountain-bike trail or a scenic-road route down to the beach and back to the Gondola base—cycle distance is approximately 16 km (10 miles). ✉ *Christchurch* ☎ *03/377–5952, 0800/424–534 NZ only* ⊕ *www.cycle-hire-tours.co.nz.*

BOATING

Punting on the Avon

BOATING | Sit back and enjoy the changing face of the central city from water level, framed by weeping willows, tranquil parks, and ornate bridges. Replicating English punting at Oxford and Cambridge, the skilled drivers even dress up in Edwardian attire. Guided tours leaving from the Antigua Boat Sheds go through the Botanic Gardens, while departures from near Worcester Street Bridge go through the revitalized Avon River Precinct. Tours are offered daily from 9 to 6 in summer and from 10 to 4 the rest of the year. Private 45-minute charters can be arranged. ✉ *2 Cambridge Terr., Christchurch* ☎ *03/366–0337* ⊕ *www. christchurchattractions.nz* 🚤 *From NZ$30 for 30 minutes.*

HIKING

Godley Head—Taylors Mistake Walkway

HIKING & WALKING | To reach this scenic trail take the coast road through Sumner then take a left turn at the summit intersection. The road climbs and winds for several kilometers before breaking out above Lyttelton Harbour with startling views to the hills of Banks Peninsula.

You'll see some of the World War II coastal defense battery built in 1939, rated one of the country's significant defense-heritage sites. There's also a 1½-hour walking trail from here back to Taylors Mistake near Sumner (although you'll need to arrange a pickup at the other end, or plan on a three-hour round-trip). The Godley Head lookout is particularly exciting in a strong southerly wind. ⊕ *www.ccc.govt. nz.*

Port Hills Walks

HIKING & WALKING | **FAMILY** | Christchurch's Port Hills are worth climbing for spectacular views of the city, the Southern Alps, and the Banks Peninsula. This is the route the first settlers took when they arrived at the port of Lyttelton. Well-marked trails include the Bridle Path, Rapaki Track, and the Bowenvale-Sugarloaf Circuit. ⊕ *www. christchurchnz.com.*

RUGBY

Canterbury fans are as rugby-mad as the rest of the country. In fact, the first match ever played in New Zealand took place in 1862 in central Christchurch's Cranmer Square. This is the home of the Crusaders, and the breeding ground for many famous All Blacks. Every Saturday in winter you can catch little All-Blacks-in-the-making playing games in Hagley Park and suburban parks.

Christchurch Stadium

RUGBY | Canterbury's professional rugby union team, the Crusaders, have won the most titles in the history of the Super Rugby competition, played between teams from South Africa, Australia, and New Zealand. So they're not a bad team to watch if you get the chance to cheer them on at their home turf. The season goes from February through September. ✉ *95 Jack Hinton Dr., Addington* ☎ *03/379–1765* ⊕ *crusaders.co.nz.*

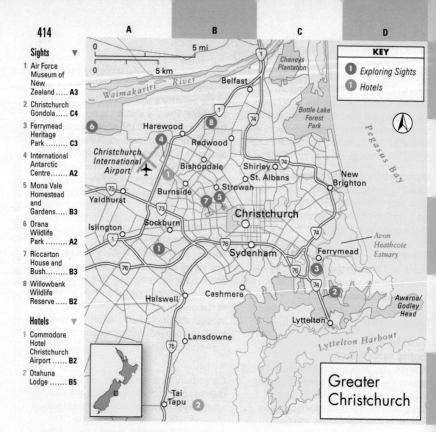

Greater
Christchurch

Greater Christchurch

Some of Christchurch's most popular attractions lie around the outskirts of the city. To the southeast, the Christchurch Gondola takes passengers from a terminal in the Heathcote Valley to the top of an extinct volcano, at the top of the Port Hills. Just beyond the airport at Harewood can be found Orana Wildlife Park, New Zealand's only open-range zoo, while the nearby International Antarctic Centre showcases the frozen continent. The national museum for the Royal New Zealand Air Force can be found at Wigram.

◉ Sights

Air Force Museum of New Zealand

HISTORY MUSEUM | FAMILY | Starting in 1916, New Zealand pilots learned how to fly at Wigram Airfield. The Air Force's old hangars plus a state-of-the-art aircraft hall now hold exhibits on aviation history, including the Royal New Zealand Air Force, flight simulators, and 30 classic aircraft. Take the behind-the-scenes guided tour to see aircraft restoration projects in action in other hangars. ✉ 45 Harvard Ave., Wigram ✛ By bus, take No. 5, 81, or Metro Star and walk from Main South Rd., just south of Sockburn Overbridge ☎ 03/343–9532 ⊕ www.airforcemuseum.co.nz ⊠ Free.

★ **Christchurch Gondola**

VIEWPOINT | FAMILY | For one of the best vantage points to view Christchurch, the Canterbury Plains, and Lyttelton Harbour head to Christchurch Gondola. At the top, you can journey through the Time Tunnel to experience the history and geological evolution of the Canterbury region. Afterward, sit with a glass of local wine at the Red Rock Café. Ride the gondola with your back to the Port Hills for the best views of the Southern Alps. The adventurous can walk or mountain-bike back down (your bike can be transported to the top); it's steep in parts so watch yourself. If you don't have a car, hop on a No. 28 bus from the city center or take a Gondola shuttle from the i-SITE next to the Canterbury Museum. ⊠ *10 Bridle Path Rd., Heathcote* ☎ *03/384–0310* ⊕ *www.christchurchattractions.nz* ⊠ *NZ$30.*

Ferrymead Heritage Park

MUSEUM VILLAGE | FAMILY | Ferrymead is the site of the country's first railway (built in 1863) and is now home to a replica Edwardian township and museum area. While exploring the shops and cottages, you can taste homemade scones or an old-fashioned lamington (chocolate-covered sponge cake dipped in coconut). You can watch an old-time movie at the Arcadia; see some knees-up dancing; or check out displays of fire engines, farming tools, and printing equipment. The park is home to 19 societies, particularly train and tram enthusiasts, who maintain their collections here, so trams and trains run on weekends and public holidays. A steam train operates on the second Sunday of each month. ⊠ *50 Ferrymead Park Dr., Harewood* ☎ *03/384–1970* ⊕ *www. ferrymead.org.nz* ⊠ *NZ$12.50; tram tickets NZ$5.50; train tickets NZ$5.*

International Antarctic Centre

SCIENCE MUSEUM | FAMILY | Ever since Captain Robert Falcon Scott wintered his dogs at nearby Quail Island in preparation

for his ill-fated South Pole expedition of 1912, Christchurch has maintained a close connection with the frozen continent. You can experience a small taste of the modern polar experience here. Bundle up in extra clothing and brave a simulated storm with temperatures of minus 25 degrees Fahrenheit for a few minutes. Or take a ride on the Hägglund vehicle used to get around the ice. The 4D extreme theater show of life at New Zealand's Scott Base is superb, and the Penguin Encounter lets you get up close with some blue penguins, the smallest penguin species. ⊠ *38 Orchard Rd., Harewood* ☎ *03/357–0519* ⊕ *www.iceberg. co.nz* ⊠ *NZ$49.*

★ **Mona Vale Homestead and Gardens**

HISTORIC HOME | Visit this beautifully restored Arts & Crafts movement home, enjoy tea or lunch in the Mona Vale Pantry, and stroll or punt along the Avon River and through the well-tended perennial gardens. Built in 1899, the house and 13½-acre gardens were almost lost to the city in the 1960s when the estate was in danger of being subdivided. A public campaign saw the homestead "sold" to individual Christchurch residents for NZ$10 per square foot. To get here, you can catch a 29 City–Airport via Fendalton bus and get off a short stroll from the entrance. ⊠ *40 Mona Vale Ave., Fendalton* ✛ *2 km (1 mile) from city center* ☎ *03/341–7450* ⊕ *www.monavale. nz* ⊠ *Free.*

Orana Wildlife Park

ZOO | FAMILY | New Zealand's only open-range zoo is now home to its only Great Ape Center for gorillas and orangutans, making it the place to come to glimpse these endangered animals. You will also see both native (kiwi birds and tuatara reptiles) and exotic (tigers, wild dogs, cheetah, zebras, and white rhinos) animals. Orana is world-renowned for its conservation work and breeding programs for endangered native and exotic

Youngsters press in close to see penguins at the International Antarctic Centre.

species. Check out the different animal feeding times; hand-feeding the giraffes is a real highlight, and even small kids manage with a bit of help. For a seriously close-up view of the lions being fed, join the Lion Encounter, where you can watch from inside a specially modified vehicle. A zebra-striped Safari Shuttle with commentary loops around the park, or you can join a guided walk. It's about a 15-minute drive from Christchurch airport; there's also a door-to-door shuttle for an additional cost. ✉ *Orana Park, 793 McLeans Island Rd., Harewood* ☎ *03/359-7109* ⊕ *www.oranawildlifepark.co.nz* 🖃 *NZ$36.50.*

★ Riccarton House and Bush

HISTORIC HOME | The Deans, a Scottish family, beat even the Canterbury Association settlers to this region. Riccarton Bush, their home, is now run by a trust. You can view the small wooden cottage (built 1843) that was their first house. The larger Victorian–Edwardian wooden house, built between 1856 and 1900, now houses a café called Local. Guided heritage tours are available; check the website for details. You can also amble through the last remnant of the original native floodplain forest still standing in Christchurch, with its 600-year-old kahikatea trees. ■**TIP→ The Christchurch Farmers' Market is held in the grounds of Riccarton House each Saturday morning from 9 to 1, and there are guided house tours at 11 am and 2 pm Sunday through Friday.** ✉ *16 Kahu Rd., Riccarton* ☎ *03/341-1018* ⊕ *www.riccartonhouse.co.nz* 🖃 *$18 includes guided house tour; free entry to gardens and bush.*

Willowbank Wildlife Reserve

ZOO | FAMILY | In addition to familiar farm animals and other zoo regulars, Willowbank has a section devoted to New Zealand's unique wildlife, from the national symbol, the kiwi, to the tuatara—the world's only living dinosaur. There's the cheeky mountain parrot, kea; the bush parrot, kaka; and the very rare but majestic takahe. To have all five of these iconic creatures in one place is a rarity. Willowbank is also home to Ko

Tane, a fun, interactive Māori cultural experience followed by a traditional meal with a *hāngi* main course. You'll be greeted with a *powhiri,* a welcome ceremony, and you can try your hand at swinging the *poi,* flaxen balls on long strings used in traditional Māori dances (it's not as easy as it looks), or the famous *haka* (ceremonial dance). ✉ *60 Hussey Rd., Harewood* ☎ *03/359–6226* 🌐 *www.willowbank.co.nz* 🎫 *NZ$32.50; guided tour, Ko Tane, and dinner, NZ$165.*

Beaches

New Brighton Beach

BEACH | Popular with surfers, this beach has a pier that goes well out into the surf. It's a great place to stroll when the sea is calm but even better when it's rough. Yellow Line buses travel here. **Amenities:** food and drink. **Best for:** surfing; walking. ✉ *Christchurch* ✣ *8 km (5 miles) east of city center.*

Sumner Beach

BEACH | This is a popular swimming and surfing spot. The sandy beach and the beach promenade are great for walking, and there are some excellent ice-cream parlors nearby. You can catch a Purple Line bus if you don't have a car. **Amenities:** food and drink; lifeguards. **Best for:** swimming; walking. ✉ *Christchurch* ✣ *12 km (7 miles) southeast of city center.*

Taylor's Mistake

BEACH | Experienced surfers prefer Taylor's Mistake to Sumner Beach because the waves are often higher. This area is also popular for hikers, bikers, and runners thanks to the spectacular cliff-top views. You can catch the Purple Line bus to Sumner and then walk the Flower Track in Scarborough down to the beach. If you're lucky, you'll see tiny, rare Hector's dolphins playing off Sumner Head on your way out. **Amenities:** none. **Best for:** surfing. ✉ *Christchurch* ✣ *16 km (10 miles) southeast of city center.*

Hotels

Commodore Hotel Christchurch Airport

$$$ | **HOTEL** | **FAMILY** | Just minutes from the airport and 10 minutes from central Christchurch, this family-owned, resort-style accommodation includes a heated indoor pool, sauna, spa, fitness center, and tennis court. **Pros:** plenty of outdoor space and gardens; free 24-hour shuttle service to and from the airport; free Wi-Fi throughout the hotel. **Cons:** no other amenities nearby; there can be big functions here, keeping the lobby and the car park full; longish walk to get from one end of the property to the other. [$] *Rooms from: NZ$228* ✉ *449 Memorial Ave., Christchurch* ☎ *03/358–8129* 🌐 *www.commodorehotel.co.nz* 🍴 *No Meals* 🛏 *157 rooms.*

Otahuna Lodge

$$$$ | **HOTEL** | Just 20 minutes from Christchurch and almost hidden by glorious century-old gardens is one of New Zealand's most important historic homes, now an award-winning luxury retreat. **Pros:** exceptional hosts with special touches at every turn; memorable five-course degustation dinner included; lots of fresh homegrown fruits and vegetables and cooking classes are available. **Cons:** TV only available by request; not for the budget-minded; you will need a car if you want to visit the city. [$] *Rooms from: NZ$2680* ✉ *224 Rhodes Rd., 17 km (10 miles) from Christchurch, Tai Tapu* ☎ *03/329–6333* 🌐 *www.otahuna.co.nz* 🍴 *All-Inclusive* 🛏 *7 suites.*

Shopping

SHOPPING STREETS AND CENTERS

The Colombo

SHOPPING CENTER | A new take on a neighborhood mall, this haven for food and fashion fans includes a stylish mix of designer clothes, eats, and gifts along with an arthouse cinema. Shops to spend time browsing include Bolt of Cloth for homewares, Annah Stretton for designer frocks, and the Beer Library, which has the region's largest craft beer selection. It's located just outside the central city, in Sydenham. ✉ *363 Colombo St., Christchurch* ☎ *03/365–5091* ⊕ *www.thecolombo.co.nz.*

The Tannery

SHOPPING CENTER | It is one of those unlikely projects that would probably never have gotten off the ground in Christchurch before the earthquakes: turning an old former industrial tannery on the banks of the Heathcote River into a Victorian shopping mall. Not only that but the developer had each brick removed, cleaned, then put back once the buildings were reinforced. The Tannery's now an interesting place to head, with quirky shops, fashion, deluxe cinemas, and a fabulous cake shop and deli. Try Mitchelli's Cafe Rinato for tasty food in a friendly atmosphere or The Brewery for craft beers and superb wood-fired pizza. ✉ *3 Garlands Rd., Christchurch* ⊕ *www.thetannery.co.nz.*

SPECIALTY SHOPS

de Spa Chocolatier

CHOCOLATE | The delicious sweets at de Spa Chocolatier's pair Belgian chocolate with Kiwi ingredients and fruit fillings (among other delectable things). Here you can watch the chocolatiers at work through a glass-walled kitchen, and they conduct factory tours. They also make a special line of sugar-free chocolate. The factory and showroom are on the way to Ferrymead Heritage Park and Sumner. ✉ *1013 Ferry Rd., Ferrymead* ☎ *03/384–5285* ⊕ *www.despa.co.nz.*

Dunsandel Store

FOOD | **FAMILY** | If you've left Christchurch a bit late for breakfast, about 30 minutes south in the Selwyn district, stop at the Dunsandel Store. It's a fascinating mix of local store, deli, and café with excellent food. The cabinets are stuffed with tasty

sandwiches and baked goods. They have a good range of breakfasts and all-day treats made from mostly local and organic produce. There are tables indoors and out, surrounded by a courtyard full of fruit trees and vegetables. ✉ *7 Kanes Rd., Dunsandel* ☎ *03/325–4037* ⊕ *www.dunsandelstore.co.nz.*

Macpac

SPORTING GOODS | Founded in Christchurch in 1973, Macpac sells good-quality outdoor (and merino) clothing, backpacks, accessories, sleeping bags, and tents. The store is now found at locations across New Zealand, with four outlets in Christchurch including the central city flagship store. It also frequently has great sale prices, but if you're not here at the right time, you can hunt for a bargain in its biggest clearance area—upstairs at Tower Junction off Mandeville Street, Riccarton. ✉ *Tower Junction, 1/7a Mandeville St., Christchurch* ☎ *03/371–9342* ⊕ *www.macpac.co.nz.*

Untouched World

MIXED CLOTHING | New Zealand's leading sustainable lifestyle fashion brand was established in Christchurch and has a real designer edge. The stylish lifestyle clothing is easy on the Earth too, with signature fabrics including organic cotton, Ecopossum (a mixture of possum fur and merino wool), and Mountainsilk (silky-fine machine-washable organic merino). Their flagship store has a licensed café, Untouched World Kitchen, serving fresh food, organic and free range when possible, in its native garden environment. ✉ *155 Roydvale Ave., Burnside* ☎ *03/357–9399* ⊕ *www.untouchedworld.com.*

Lyttelton

12 km (7½ miles) east of Christchurch.

Lyttelton, a sleepy port town, was the arrival point for many of the early Canterbury settlers. The Canterbury Pilgrims' landing place is marked by a rock near the road entrance to the port. A mix of renovated wooden villas and contemporary homes now rises halfway up what was once a volcanic crater. Today, although only a 20-minute drive from Christchurch, Lyttelton has developed its own distinctive quality, with a funky, hipster vibe created by a strong-knit local community that was attracted here by the wonderful harbor views and abundant creative energy. Saturday is a good day to come, with a farmers' market from 10 to 1, then you can explore the boutique shops known for handmade crafts, gourmet foods, and art. Governors Bay and farther 'round to Diamond Harbour makes a nice half-day drive from the city.

GETTING HERE AND AROUND

Lyttelton can be reached by driving down Ferry Road from Christchurch, heading toward Sumner, and then taking the road tunnel. Another scenic route is to follow the main street, Colombo, east out of the city, up the Port Hills, and over Dyers Pass to Governors Bay. Then turn left and head back along the harbor edge to Lyttelton. If you don't have a car, you can catch Bus 28 from Christchurch.

Lyttelton stretches along a terrace above the port. Norwich Quay runs along the waterfront, but the main street, London Street, runs parallel a block higher up the hill. London Street joins the road back over to Sumner, and in the other direction back past the tunnel entrance along Simeon Quay toward Governors Bay. Visit the Lyttelton Harbor Information Center at 20 Oxford Street for maps and brochures.

VISITOR INFORMATION

CONTACTS Lyttelton Harbour Information Centre. ✉ *20 Oxford St., Lyttelton* ☎ *03/328–9093* ⊕ *www.lytteltonharbour.info.*

Sights

Diamond Harbour

TOWN | Diamond Harbour is the largest township on the far side of Lyttelton Harbour. You can drive to Diamond Harbour (around 40 minutes from Christchurch) or take a 10-minute journey on the Black Diamond ferry from Jetty B at Norwich Quay. Sailings are frequent. There's a small farmers' market once every two weeks over summer, excellent cafés and restaurants, some great walks, and the beautiful Charteris Bay Golf Club. ✉ *"B" Jetty, 17 Norwich Quay, Lyttelton* ☎ *03/328–9078, 0800/436–574* ⊕ *www.diamondharbour.info* 🎫 *NZ$13.40 round-trip.*

★ Ohinetahi

GARDEN | Sir Miles Warren is one of New Zealand's foremost architects with a pedigree as large as his garden. Ohinetahi, which is also the Māori name for the area, features not only his large, stone, colonial villa, but also his immaculate garden—considered one of the best formal gardens in the country. Blending Sir Miles's eye for detail and design with a stunning situation, this garden maximizes the use of "garden rooms"—the red room being particularly memorable—hedging, and color. Over 30 sculptures now complement the layout. ✉ *31 Governors Bay-Teddington Rd., Lyttelton* ☎ *03/329–9852* ⊕ *www.ohinetahi.co.nz* 🎫 *NZ$15* ⊙ *Closed Apr.–Aug.*

Quail Island

ISLAND | Located in Lyttelton Harbour, Quail Island was used by the early European settlers as a quarantine zone and leper colony and was named after the now-extinct native quail. It was once

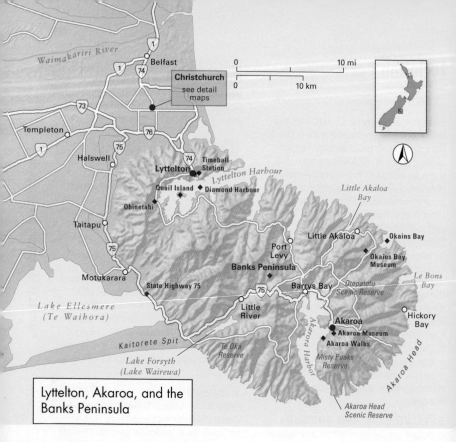

Lyttelton, Akaroa, and the
Banks Peninsula

a significant area for collecting birds' eggs by local Māori. These days, Quail Island, also known as Otamahua, is being restored as an ecological reserve, and is home to many native birds including kingfisher, fantail, silvereye (a small bird common in New Zealand), and various seabirds. The *Black Cat* ferry from Lyttelton can zip you out here for a hike or a picnic. ⊠ *"B" Jetty, 17 Norwich Quay, Lyttelton* ☎ *03/328–9078* ⊕ *www.blackcat. co.nz* ⊠ *NZ$30.*

Timeball Station

HISTORIC SIGHT | After Timeball Station was almost totally demolished in the Christchurch earthquakes, the New Zealand Historic Places Trust committed to rebuilding its tower, which is a prominent landmark overlooking the port of Lyttelton. This piece of maritime history is one of only five remaining timeball stations known to be in working order in the world, and it holds a special place in the hearts of Canterbury's people. Built in the 1870s, the ball would drop from its mast as an exact time signal for ships. After the castle-like structure was destroyed over the course of the 2010 and 2011 earthquakes, much of the building was retrieved and stored for its restoration. ⊠ *2 Reserve Terr., Lyttelton* ⊕ *www.historicplaces.org.nz.*

Restaurants

Civil and Naval

$$ | **TAPAS** | This cozy haunt is packed with locals who come for the tasty tapas-style food, produced in a tiny kitchen, and the excellent cocktails. There's an eclectic selection of international and New Zealand wines, spirits, and craft beers. **Known for:** beautifully executed and affordable food; green courtyard on sunny days and cozy log fires in winter; inventive cocktails created by a master barman. $\boxed{\$}$ *Average main: NZ$16* ⊠ *16 London St., Lyttelton* ☎ *03/328–7206* ⊕ *www.civilandnaval.nz.*

Super

$$$ | ASIAN FUSION | This eatery's clever take on Asian fusion has won rave reviews from locals thanks to its selection of carefully crafted dishes that are perfect for sharing. It's set in the beautiful Old Royal Hotel Building on the waterfront, and the atmosphere is stylish and relaxed. **Known for:** intriguing desserts; tasty *okonomiyaka* (Japanese pancakes with a twist); locally sourced, organic produce with lots of vegan options. $\boxed{\$}$ *Average main: NZ$22* ⊠ *5 Norwich Quay, Lyttelton* ☎ *021/0862–2632* ⊕ *www.super.restaurant.*

Coffee and Quick Bites

Lyttelton Coffee Company

$$ | CAFÉ | Well-known for its excellent coffee available in many Christchurch cafés, this is the home of the legendary roastery and plenty of hearty fare to match. Great service and an arty atmosphere mean this heritage building is buzzing from early morning until late afternoon every day. **Known for:** freshly baked muffins big enough for two; some of the best coffee in the region; outdoor deck with fabulous views over the harbor. $\boxed{\$}$ *Average main: $17* ⊠ *29 London St., Lyttelton* ☎ ⊙ *No dinner.*

🍸 Nightlife

Wunderbar

BARS | Not your average bar, this Lyttelton institution prides itself on being different, some would even call it weird. Dolls' heads as lamp shades, a supersize Madonna, and 1950s newspapers on the bathroom walls give you an idea of the fun to be had here. There's live music just about every night. Pool and foosball tables will also keep you entertained as will the great views over Lyttelton port. ⊠ *19 London St., Lyttelton* ☎ *03/328–8818* ⊕ *www.wunderbar.co.nz.*

🏃 Activities

HIKING
Bridle Path

HIKING & WALKING | Quail Island is a good option, but if you'd rather stay on the mainland, you could instead follow in the trail of the early settlers by taking the Bridle Path. The steep zigzag track goes from Cunningham Street up to the crater rim. You can walk to the Gondola Summit Station, a few minutes' farther, to see the Canterbury Plains from the site of the memorial to the pioneer women, or walk down the rest of the trail to finish near the Christchurch Gondola base station. A No. 28 bus will take you to Lyttelton, and the same bus will pick you up on the other side. Allow 1½ hours for the walk—some of which is quite steep. ⊠ *Bridal Path at Cunningham Terr., Lyttelton.*

Akaroa and the Banks Peninsula

86 km (53 miles) east of Christchurch.

Sheep graze almost to the water's edge in the many small bays indenting the coastline of the Banks Peninsula, the nub that juts into the Pacific east of Christchurch. On the southern side of the peninsula, in a harbor created when the crater wall of an extinct volcano collapsed into the sea, nestles the fishing village of Akaroa (Māori for "long harbor"). The port is a favorite day trip for Christchurch residents on Sunday drives, and on weekends and over the summer holidays (December to February) it can be extremely busy, especially if a cruise ship is in. If you're planning to stay the night during the busy times (summer and weekends), book a room and dinner before you leave Christchurch.

Although Akaroa was chosen as the site for a French colony in 1838, the first French settlers arrived in 1840 only to find that the British had already established sovereignty over New Zealand by the Treaty of Waitangi. Less than 10 years later, the French abandoned their attempt at colonization, but the settlers remained and gradually intermarried with the local English community. Apart from the *rue* (street) names, a few family surnames, and architectural touches, there is little sign of a French connection anymore, but the village has splendid surroundings. A day trip from Christchurch will get you to and from Akaroa, including a drive along the Summit Road on the edge of the former volcanic dome, but take an overnight trip if you want to explore the peninsula bays as well as the town. It's an easy drive most of the way, but the last hill over to Akaroa is narrow and winding with few passing areas. By the time you've taken a harbor cruise, driven around a few bays, and stopped for a meal, you'll be right in the mood to kick back overnight in this quiet spot.

GETTING HERE AND AROUND

The main route to Akaroa is State Highway 75, which leaves the southwest corner of Christchurch as Lincoln Road. The 82-km (50-mile) drive takes about 90 minutes. You can also head out through Lyttelton and Teddington, then over the hill to Little River for a really scenic but slightly longer trip.

If you'd rather not drive, the Akaroa Shuttle has a daily service between Christchurch and Akaroa from October to April for NZ$56 per person round-trip or NZ$36 one-way. Direct shuttles run from Rolleston Avenue in Christchurch and from outside the Akaroa Adventure Centre, and there is also a free pickup service from central city hotels.

BUS CONTACTS Akaroa Shuttle. ✉ *47a Riccarton Rd., Riccarton* ☎ *0800/500–929 NZ only* ⊕ *www.akaroashuttle.co.nz.*

TOURS

Akaroa Harbour is home to the world's smallest and rarest dolphins. The Akaroa Marine Reserve is a fully protected area, similar to a national park. White-flippered blue penguins, the smallest penguins in the world, also frequent the harbor. To get up close to the wildlife, you can take a swimming-with-dolphins tour, hire a kayak, or book a scenic nature safari to see the penguin colony.

VISITOR INFORMATION

CONTACTS Akaroa i-SITE Information Centre. ✉ *61 Beach Rd., Akaroa* ☎ *03/304–7784* ⊕ *www.visitakaroa.com.*

 ## Sights

Akaroa Museum

HISTORY MUSEUM | The focus of historic interest is the Akaroa Museum, which has a display of Māori *pounamu* (greenstone) as well as alternating exhibits on the area's multicultural past. The peninsula supported a significant Māori population, and the collections and displays tell some of the exciting stories of Kai Tahu, the people of the land. The building is currently being strengthened for earthquakes, but the museum is still open. The Old Courthouse, the old Custom House, and Langlois-Eteveneaux House, the two-room cottage of an early French settler, are also part of the museum. ✉ *71 Rue Lavaud at Rue Balguerie, Akaroa* ☎ *03/304–1013* ⊕ *www.akaroamuseum.org.nz* ✉ *Free.*

Akaroa Walks

TRAIL | Take the village walk, where you amble along the narrow streets past old-fashioned little cottages and historic buildings that reflect the area's multicultural background. If you are feeling more ambitious try the country walks on routes ranging from two hours to all day. For hikers, there are also 20 km (12½ miles) of well-mapped tracks from summit to sea level. Start at the Akaroa i-SITE Information Centre and choose from a range of free brochures and maps to enhance your experience. ✉ *74a Rue Lavaud, Akaroa* 🌐 *www.visitakaroa.com.*

Okains Bay

BEACH | The contrast of the rim of the old volcanic cone and the coves below is striking—and when you drop into one of the coves, you'll probably feel like you've found your own little corner of the world. One of the easiest bays to access is Okains Bay. Take the Summit Road at Hilltop if approaching from Christchurch or Ngaio Point Road behind Duvauchelle if approaching from Akaroa. It's about 24 km (15 miles) from Akaroa and takes about a half hour to drive. The small settlement lies at the bottom of Okains Bay Road, which ends at a beach sheltered by tall headlands. ✉ *Okains Bay, Akaroa.*

Okains Bay Museum

HISTORY MUSEUM | This collection of buildings contains 20,000 Māori and 19th-century colonial artifacts, including *waka* (canoes) used in Waitangi Day celebrations and displays such as a smithy and print shop. There are also a *wharenui* (Māori meetinghouse), colonial homes, including a *totara* slab cottage, and a saddlery and harness shop. If you happen to be in the area on Waitangi Day (February 6), New Zealand's national day, the museum marks it in style. ✉ *1146 Okains Bay Rd., Okains Bay* ☎ *03/304–8611* 🌐 *www.okainsbaymuseum.co.nz* 🎫 *NZ$10.*

State Highway 75

SCENIC DRIVE | State Highway 75 leads from Christchurch out onto the peninsula, curving along the southern portion past Lake Ellesmere. There are interesting stops on your way out to Akaroa. The small town of Little River used to be the end of the line for a now-defunct railway that ran from Christchurch; the route is now a walkway and bicycle trail. The old, wooden train station houses a crafts gallery and information office, and a café is next door in the grocery store. Look out for SiloStay, where grain silos have been cleverly transformed into eco-accommodation units called Silococoons. When you reach Hilltop, pause for your first glimpse of Akaroa Harbour; on a sunny day it's magnificent. (At Hilltop the highway crosses the Summit Road, the other major route through the peninsula.) ✉ *State Hwy. 75, Christchurch* 🌐 *www.visitakaroa.com.*

🍴 Restaurants

Bully Hayes Restaurant & Bar

$$$$ | **NEW ZEALAND** | Named after a notorious American pirate, this modern restaurant occupies a great site overlooking the yachts moored in the harbor. New Zealand cuisine is highlighted, and there are light and full-size main courses for breakfast, lunch, and dinner all year round. **Known for:** home-cured Akaroa salmon gravlax; spectacular views of Akaroa harbor; craft beers and a great wine list. [$] *Average main: NZ$34* ✉ *57 Beach Rd., Akaroa* ☎ *03/304–7533* 🌐 *www.bullyhayes.co.nz.*

Murphy's on the Corner

$ | **CAFÉ** | Acclaimed around the country as having some of the best fish-and-chips available, this takeout-style eatery often has queues out the door. The deep-fried fish is served with a big side of perfectly cooked chips and a big chunk of lemon, or try the ciabatta fish sandwich from the wharfside caravan. **Known for:** Akaroa salmon cooked to perfection; Murphy himself spending most days filleting his morning catch; classic and delicious fish-and-chips. [$] *Average main: NZ$14* ✉ *7 Church St., Akaroa* ☎ *03/304–8887.*

The Trading Rooms Restaurant & Bar

$$$$ | **NEW ZEALAND** | European spins on local produce, meat, and seafood, along with a seaside location, make for sought-after reservations here. Dark wooden floors, white tablecloths, and leather chairs lend a seaside chic quality, and, on a nice day, you can sit outside. **Known for:** signature dish of Canterbury lamb; excellent seafood, particularly Akaroa salmon and grouper; boutique Banks Peninsula wines. Ⓢ *Average main: NZ$32* ✉ *71 Beach Rd., Akaroa* ☎ *03/304–7656* ⊕ *www.thetradingrooms. co.nz* ⊘ *Closed every June but may vary; check website.*

 Hotels

Annandale Villas

$$$$ | **ALL-INCLUSIVE** | **FAMILY** | This gem set on a private farm at Pigeon Bay is made up of four secluded villas, including an ultramodern waterfront home and a magnificent Victorian homestead surrounded by expansive heritage gardens with an impressive pool and spa facilities. **Pros:** working farm and garden you can explore; amazing views amid complete privacy; superb farm-to-table cuisine. **Cons:** rather difficult to get to; expensive; minimum two-night stay. Ⓢ *Rooms from: NZ$1200* ✉ *130 Wharf Rd., Pigeon Bay, Akaroa* ☎ *03/304–6841* ⊕ *www.annandale.com* ⦿ *All-Inclusive* ⇄ *12 rooms.*

The Giant's House

$$$$ | **B&B/INN** | Named so because it looked like a giant's house to a visiting child, this grand old 1880 villa is full of art in unexpected places, all thanks to the long tenure of its mixed-media artist owner Josie Martin. **Pros:** contemporary art gallery; fabulous, crazy mosaic artwork; pleasant garden and leafy outlook. **Cons:** garden tour visitors wander through in the afternoon; very steep driveway; mosaic paths can be slippery after rain. Ⓢ *Rooms from: NZ$400* ✉ *70 Rue Balguerie, Akaroa* ☎ *03/304–7501* ⊕ *www. thegiantshouse.co.nz* ⇄ *3 rooms* ⦿ *Free Breakfast.*

Oinako Bed and Breakfast

$$$$ | **B&B/INN** | Surrounded by a tranquil garden, just a two-minute walk from town and a few steps from Akaroa

Harbour, this character Victorian manor house has its original, ornate plaster ceilings and marble fireplaces. **Pros:** beautifully restored homestead; tea, coffee, wine, cookies, feather pillows, and duvets add a luxurious touch; old-fashioned leafy garden overlooking the harbor. **Cons:** no fridges in rooms; no televisions in rooms; no desks or chairs in rooms, but they can be provided on request. Ⓢ *Rooms from: NZ$325* ✉ *99 Beach Rd., Akaroa* ☎ *03/304–8787* ⊕ *www.oinako.co.nz* ⊘ *Closed June–Aug.* ⦿ *Free Breakfast* ⇄ *6 rooms.*

Activities

Akaroa Dolphins

WILDLIFE-WATCHING | **FAMILY** | On these nature cruises around Akaroa Harbour, you'll have a 98 percent chance of spotting the Hector's dolphin, the word's smallest and one of its rarest. Cruises last around two hours and depart three times daily in summer, and once a day in winter for two hours, from the main wharf. Informed guides give you insight into the marine life found here, and a beverage and home-baked snacks are also included as part of the ticket price. ✉ *65 Beach Rd., Akaroa* ☎ *03/304–7866* ⊕ *www.akaroadolphins.co.nz* ✍ *NZ$92.*

Banks Track

HIKING & WALKING | **FAMILY** | The 35-km (22-mile) Banks Track crosses spectacular coastal terrain. From Akaroa hike over headlands and past several bays, waterfalls, and seal and penguin colonies, and you might even see Hector's dolphins at sea. Two-day and three-day self-guided hikes are available from October to April. The tracks follow the same route, so if you're a novice hiker or have plenty of time, take the longer option. You will stay overnight in cozy cabins with fully equipped kitchens and a bath under the stars. Rates include lodging, transport from Akaroa to the first hut, landowners' fees, and a booklet describing the features of the trail. No fear of overcrowding

Canterbury

here—the track is limited to up to only 16 people at a time. ⊠ *Banks Track, Southeast Banks Peninsula, Akaroa* ☎ *03/304–7612* ⊕ *www.bankstrack.co.nz* ⊠ *NZ$370* ⊗ *Closed May–Sept.*

Black Cat **Cruises**

SAILING | The *Black Cat* catamaran runs Akaroa Harbour Nature Cruises and two different Swimming with Dolphins trips. On the Nature Cruise, you'll pull in beside huge volcanic cliffs and caves and bob around in the harbor entrance while tiny Hector's dolphins—an endangered and adorable species of dolphin with rounded dorsal fins that look like Mickey Mouse ears stuck on their backs—play in the wake of the boat. Trips leave daily and cost NZ$79. Or take your swimsuit and get in the water for the Swimming with Dolphins cruise. Dolphin-swim trips cost NZ$160 (NZ$89 to watch). Wetsuits

are provided, and advance reservations are essential. ⊠ *Main Wharf, Akaroa* ☎ *03/304–7641, 0800/436–574* ⊕ *www.blackcat.co.nz* ⊠ *Swimming with Dolphins $95* ⊗ *Swimming with Dolphins not available in winter.*

Pohatu Penguins Nature & Sea Kayaking Safaris

KAYAKING | Pohatu Marine Reserve is a key breeding area for the little penguin (*korora*), which is endemic to the Canterbury region. The best time for viewing is during the breeding season, September to January. You may also see the yellow-eyed penguin (*hoiho*), which also breed in the bay. Options range from day and evening penguin or nature tours (from NZ$75 per person) and 4WD sea-kayaking safari trips (from NZ$95). Prices include a scenic drive to Pohatu with photo stops along the way. There are several other tour options, as well as an accommodation package featuring a stay at a self-catering cottage inside the penguin colony—a rare opportunity—(from NZ$150 per person for 24-hour stay). All trips leave from Akaroa. ⊠ *Wildside Booking Office, Unit 2, 8 Rue Balguerie, Akaroa* ☎ *03/304–8542, 021/246–9556* ⊕ *www.pohatu.co.nz.*

Arthur's Pass National Park

148 km (92 miles) northwest of Christchurch.

Established in 1929, Arthur's Pass was the South Island's first national park. Follow in the footsteps of ancient Māori hunters, 1860s gold rushers, and 1990s road workers who constructed the 1,444-foot Otira Viaduct. Each of the many twists and turns reveals another photo op: waterfalls, fields of wildflowers, dizzying drops. And it's all easily accessible from Christchurch.

GETTING HERE AND AROUND
For any confident driver the road through Arthur's Pass is a glorious drive—paved all the way, but with a few steep, gnarly sections in the middle. The train and bus tours are also good options, but you lose the flexibility to stop and do a walk or follow a waterfall trail or to just admire the breathtaking scenery.

To drive here from Christchurch, head out on the West Coast Road—well signposted from town. The turnoff is near the airport. This being the only road over the Alps within 100 km (62 miles), you can't go wrong. The road heads out through the small town of Springfield, and then travels up toward Porter's Pass and Cass before hitting the real stuff at Arthur's Pass.

Information on the park is available on the Department of Conservation's (DOC's) website and at the DOC-run Arthur's Pass Visitor Center. The Arthur's Pass Mountaineering site is another good source for information on local mountaineering conditions.

VISITOR INFORMATION
CONTACTS Arthur's Pass Mountaineering. ⊕ *www.arthurspass.com.* **Department of Conservation Arthur's Pass Visitor Centre.** ⊠ *104 West Coast Rd., Arthur's Pass* ☎ *03/318–9211* ⊕ *www.doc.govt.nz.*

Sights

Arthur's Pass National Park
NATIONAL PARK | This spectacular alpine region is a favorite hiking destination. Initially hacked through as a direct route to the West Coast gold fields in 1865, the road over Arthur's Pass was a tortuous, dangerous track. When the railway arrived, in 1923, the pass's skiing and hiking opportunities came to the fore, and the TranzAlpine train service now offers a supreme way to see this rugged area without getting your shoes dirty. On the way to the pass, along State Highway 73 from Christchurch, you'll pass the Castle Hill Conservation Area, which is filled with interesting rock formations. Nearby Craigieburn Conservation Park has wonderful beech and fern forests and some great mountain-biking trails—take the road leading to Broken River Ski Field. Above the tree line you'll find ski slopes and, between November and March, masses of wildflowers, including giant buttercups. Around the summit you'll also have a good chance of seeing kea, the South Island's particularly intelligent and curious mountain parrots. Arthur's Pass Village, at 2,395 feet, is a true alpine village, so pack a jacket even in summer. A couple of restaurants and a store provide basic food supplies, and there are several places to stay, including an excellent wilderness lodge near Bealey. There's also a Department of Conservation visitor center to help with enjoying the vast selection of mountains

Planning Your Trip to Arthur's Pass

Best Time to Go

November through March brings gorgeous wildflowers to the park. Ski at Temple Basin from late June to early October. Remember: with mountain peaks up to 6,562 feet. the weather in the park can change for the worse *anytime* at this altitude.

Best Ways to Explore

By car. Driving offers the flexibility to stop for hikes and sightseeing when you please. The road, extensively revamped in the 1990s, is a feat of engineering, particularly the Otira Viaduct. Five thousand cubic meters (176,573 cubic feet) of concrete were used to create the viaduct on a steep unstable foundation in an area prone to flash floods, slips, and earthquakes. As you navigate the turns, spare some thoughts for the men who spent backbreaking years creating it.

By foot. Everything from 10-minute strolls to multiday hikes are available in the park. We recommend the Punchbowl Falls Track (one-hour round-trip from Arthur's Pass Village) and Dobson Nature Walk (30-minute round-trip), which follows a lovely loop at the summit of Arthur's Pass. Marvel at brilliantly colored alpine lichen splashed across boulders and cliff faces. Kea, wrybill (with bent beaks), and green bellbirds populate the park. Lucky visitors will spot the roroa—or great-spotted kiwi—that roam the steep terrain.

By mountain climbing. There are plenty of ways up the peaks of Arthur's Pass. Mountain climbing in the area is prone to changeable weather, and many routes involve river crossings, so check in with the Department of Conservation before any endeavor and make sure you are well-equipped and up to the challenge.

By train. Take to the tracks and relax on board the TranzAlpine Scenic Journey. It takes you from Christchurch ("ChCh" to locals) to Greymouth in 4½ hours, through 16 tunnels and over 5 viaducts. The train has an open-air observation carriage, which provides breathtaking views of the plains, gorges, valleys, and beech forests.

and rivers in the area. Both the Devil's Punchbowl and Bridal Veil Falls are worth the short walk. The tracks are in good condition, and, although they're a bit steep and rocky in places, no serious hiking experience is required. ☎ *03/318–9211* 🌐 *www.doc.govt.nz.*

🍴 Restaurants

The Wobbly Kea Café and Bar

$$$ | **NEW ZEALAND** | This pleasant place in the heart of the alpine village is named for the cheeky mountain parrots that circle above it day after day. Open daily from 10 am to 8 pm, the cafe offers a wide menu that includes great pizza, bratwurst bangers and mash, and the fresh beer-battered fish. **Known for:** classic pub atmosphere; bratwurst bangers and mash; great breakfasts. [$] *Average main: NZ$25* ✉ *108 Main Rd., Arthur's Pass* ☎ *03/318–9101* 🌐 *www.wobblykea.co.nz.*

🛏 Hotels

★ Arthur's Pass Wilderness Lodge

$$$$ | **B&B/INN** | Surrounded by spectacular peaks, beech forests, and serene lakes, this sophisticated back-to-nature lodge shares 4,000 acres with its own

Did You Know?

Arthur's Pass National Park forms the South Island's "backbone" between Canterbury and the West Coast. The park is a study in contrasts, with dry beech forests to the east and dense rain forests to the west.

high-country merino sheep station and nature reserve in a valley called Te Ko Awa a Aniwaniwa (Valley of the Mother of Rainbows). **Pros:** rates include breakfast, dinner, and guided activities; on alternate days, you can muster sheep with border collies and help blade-shear sheep the old-fashioned way; great wine and food with a view. **Cons:** closed in the off-season; quite remote if you like shopping; surcharge on New Zealand holidays. $ *Rooms from: NZ$450 per person* ✉ *State Hwy. 73, 16 km (10 miles) east of Arthurs Pass Village on State Hwy. 73, Arthur's Pass* ✛ *140 km (87 miles) west of Christchurch, 110 km (68 miles) east of Greymouth* ☎ *03/318–9246* ⊕ *www.wildernesslodge.co.nz* ⊗ *Closed June and July* ⦿ *All-Inclusive* ⊋ *24 rooms.*

🏃 Activities

HIKING AND WALKING

There are plenty of half- and full-day hikes and 10 backcountry trails with overnight huts for backpacking. A popular walk near Arthur's Pass Village is the short Punchbowl Falls Track, which passes through diverse subalpine forest to a 450-foot-high waterfall. It takes roughly one hour to do the track. For a full-day hike, trails leading to the summits of various mountains are all along State Highway 73. Be prepared for highly changeable weather conditions. Two of the most popular and challenging overnight treks are the Cass/Lagoon Saddle trip and the Avalanche-Crow route over Avalanche Peak. For these, you'll need an experienced leader and full gear. The Department of Conservation Visitor Centre has up-to-date information on weather and trail conditions. Before you go into the outdoors, tell someone your plans, and leave a date to raise the alarm if you haven't returned.

Waipara Valley

65 km (40 miles) north of Christchurch.

Once known for its hot, dry summers and sheep farms, the Waipara Valley is now an established vineyard area. The local riesling, chardonnay, and pinot noir are particularly good. Sheltered from the cool easterly wind by the Teviotdale Hills, the valley records hotter temperatures than the rest of Canterbury, and warm dry autumns ensure a longer time for the grapes to mature. Winemakers also appreciate the area's limestone soil for growing pinots—pinot noir, pinot gris, and pinotage. The valley's 26 wineries and 80 vineyards produce around 100,000 cases of wine a year.

GETTING HERE AND AROUND

To reach Waipara from Christchurch, take State Highway 1 north. Waipara's about 45 minutes away, north of Amberley, where State Highway 7 turns left off the main road. You can head from here to Hanmer Springs and Nelson on State Highway 7 and other northern towns along State Highway 1. The Hanmer Connection runs a daily service between Hanmer Springs and Christchurch, stopping in Waipara and elsewhere en route in the Waipara Valley. You can also join a wine tour from Christchurch.

CONTACTS Hanmer Connection. ✉ *Canterbury Museum, 47 Riccarton Rd., Christchurch* ☎ *0800/242–663, 03/382–2952, 03/382–2952* ⊕ *www.hanmerconnection.co.nz.*

👁 Sights

Pick up a copy of the *North Canterbury Food and Wine Trail* guide and map from the Christchurch i-SITE Visitor Centre or visit the website (*www.foodandwinetrail.co.nz*) to locate all the wineries, eateries, and activities in the region. Waipara's wines are celebrated each year at the North Canterbury Wine and Food Festival

Did You Know?

In the Waipara region of North Canterbury, the cool and dry atmosphere makes for some outstanding chardonnays and pinot noirs.

held in March under the oaks of the local Glenmark Domain. The leafy tree-lined gardens are filled with music, local produce like cheese, nuts, and breads, and, of course, plenty of wine from dozens of local vineyards.

★ Black Estate

WINERY | With its distinctive black barn tasting room and restaurant on the warm, sunny slopes of the Omihi Hills, this family-run vineyard has become a local landmark. The award-winning architecture perfectly complements the acclaimed pinot noir, chardonnay, and riesling vintages hand-harvested and made on site. Add to this a delicious lunch and tasting menu, focusing on the best local produce and superb service to match the wine. While you dine and sip, enjoy a beautiful view overlooking the vineyards and west to the Main Divide. ✉ *614 Omihi Rd., Waipara Valley, Amberley* ☎ *03/314–6085* ⊕ *www.blackestate. co.nz* ✑ *Tour and tasting from NZ$95.*

Hurunui Hotel

HOTEL | Built from limestone blocks, the Hurunui Hotel, New Zealand's oldest continually licensed hotel (since 1860), refreshed weary drovers bringing sheep down from Marlborough; it's still a great place to rest yourself with a beverage. There are seven quaint rooms in this stagecoach-style hotel, and the restaurant with its old-fashioned pub serves à la carte dinners including a succulent fillet steak. You can dine in the pub, where there is a roaring fire in winter, or outside in the tree-lined beer garden. ✉ *State Hwy. 7, about 20-min drive from Waipara turnoff, 1224 Karaka Rd., Hurunui* ☎ *03/314–2207* ⊕ *www.hurunuihotel. co.nz.*

Pegasus Bay

WINERY | Family-run Pegasus Bay has one of the region's best reputations for wine and food, and the helicopters lined up on the lawn at lunchtime will confirm that. Taste the award-winning rieslings, chardonnay, and pinot noir while you look through a window at floor-to-ceiling stacks of oak aging casks. It has been ranked among the top five wine producers nationally by Robert Parker's buyer's guide, and it's been named Best Winery Restaurant in New Zealand by *Cuisine* magazine nine times. In good weather, dine outdoors in the garden, or picnic in a natural amphitheater by a small man-made lake. It's best to book ahead if visiting for a meal or large group tastings. ✉ *263 Stockgrove Rd., Waipara* ☎ *03/314–6869* ⊕ *www.pegasusbay. com* ✉ *Tastings from NZ$10* ⊗ *Closed weekdays Mar.–Nov.*

Torlesse Wines

WINERY | Kym and Ben Rayner are consummate winemakers, and Kym is one of the pioneers of Waipara winemaking. At Torlesse Wines they use grapes from several vineyards around Waipara and farther afield, and riesling is their biggest seller. Sauvignon blanc, gewürztraminer, chardonnay, pinot gris, pinot noir, and rosé are also produced, as are the Omihi Road reserve wines and Old Reserve port, made in the same barrels since 1992. While you're here you can also check out the local arts and crafts for sale. ✉ *10 Loffhagen Dr., off State Hwy. 1, Waipara* ☎ *03/314–6929* ⊕ *www. torlesse.co.nz.*

Waipara Hills

WINERY | The huge, cathedral-like European castle rock-and-timber building at Waipara Hills, although just more than 20 years old, looks somewhat medieval. The Waipara Hills riesling, pinot gris, rosé, and pinot noir are all worth trying. The label uses grapes from Marlborough, Otago, and Waipara so there's a lot happening in a bottle. The café in the Cloisters, the high ceiling–medieval style section of the building, is open for lunch and afternoon coffee. There's a cellar door across the entrance hall for tastings. ✉ *780 Glasnevin Rd. (part of State Hwy. 1), Waipara* ☎ *03/314–6900* ⊕ *www. waiparahills.co.nz.*

Coffee and Quick Bites

Little Vintage Espresso
$$ | **CAFÉ** | **FAMILY** | Tucked away down a side street off the main road, this cute little café with a red door is packed with country locals and is fast becoming a popular visitor stop, too. Besides the great coffee, there's also an excellent selection of well-priced baked goods, including delicious muffins, and a tasty brunch menu to suit all appetites. **Known for:** delicious gluten-free cakes and slices; power-packed salads; cinnamon scrolls. [$] *Average main: NZ$15* ✉ *20 Markham St., Amberley* ☎ *03/314–9580* ⏲ *Closed Sun.*

Hotels

Black Estate B&B
$$$$ | **B&B/INN** | The highly rated accommodations located right at Black Estate's award-winning winery–restaurant is a perfect escape for couples. **Pros:** gorgeous decor and architecture; sunny terrace with vast vineyard and mountain views; exceptionally knowledgeable and friendly hosts. **Cons:** need to book well ahead; only room for two people; apartment is downstairs below the winery, which is busy most days until 5 pm. [$] *Rooms from: NZ$320* ✉ *614 Omihi Rd., Waipara* ☎ *03/314–6085* 🌐 *www.blackestate.co.nz* 🍴 *Free Breakfast* 🛏 *1 room.*

Greystone PurePod
$$$$ | **HOTEL** | Set high above the award-winning, organic Greystone Vineyard, you will find a beautiful setting for a private lodging experience under the stars with glass floors, walls, and ceilings. **Pros:** optional guided tour of the vineyard and winery that includes tasting and lunch; complete immersion in nature; dinner and breakfast packages available. **Cons:** can get pretty hot in summer, so remember to pull the shades down; no power plugs or Wi-Fi (USB device charger available); ½-mile walk from the parking lot with no lighting. [$] *Rooms from: NZ$590* ✉ *376 Omihi Rd., Waipara* ☎ 🌐 *www.purepods.com* 🍴 *No Meals* 🛏 *1 room.*

Old Glenmark Vicarage
$$$ | **B&B/INN** | Once a real vicarage, Old Glenmark is now a funky barn lodging—with lots of rough-sawn timber and colonial trimmings—that's suitable for families and makes a very comfortable base while touring the area. **Pros:** large well-equipped kitchen and barbecue area for self-catering; central to most Waipara wineries and restaurants; on-site boutique vineyard and vegetable garden. **Cons:** rustic style may be too eclectic for some; close to busy State Highway 1; popular in summer. [$] *Rooms from: NZ$250* ✉ *161 Church Rd., Waipara* ☎ *03/314–6775* 🌐 *www.glenmarkvicarage.co.nz* 🍴 *No Meals* 🛏 *3 rooms.*

Waipara Sleepers
$ | **B&B/INN** | Wake up to fresh-baked bread and newly laid eggs (when chickens are laying) at this basic-but-rather-quirky backpacker lodge housed in old railway carriages and huts. **Pros:** good stop for anyone cycle-touring; complete with all the sounds and smells of the country; very rustic and rural. **Cons:** cramped parking if it's busy; often cold at night; some of the accommodations and services are quite basic. [$] *Rooms from: NZ$60* ✉ *10–12 Glenmark Dr., Waipara* ☎ *022/573–7101* 🌐 *www.waiparasleepers.co.nz* 🍴 *No Meals* 🛏 *6 rooms.*

Activities

Mt. Cass Walkway
HIKING & WALKING | Here's a moderately strenuous way to wear off some of those wine- and lunch-induced calories. This three-hour round-trip climb up Mt. Cass produces a spectacular view over the limestone formations and vineyards of the Waipara Valley. As it crosses through working farmland on the Tiromoana Station, be careful to leave gates and

marker posts as you find them. Use the stiles provided for crossing fence lines, and wear strong walking shoes. The track is closed each year in spring while the sheep are lambing. ⊠ *Mt. Cass Rd., Waipara* ✢ *Track starts 3.3 km (2 miles) from State Highway 1* ⊕ *www.visithurunui.co.nz.*

Hanmer Springs

134 km (84 miles) northwest of Christchurch.

People used to come to Hanmer Springs to chill out with quiet soaks in the hot pools and to take gentle forest walks, but things have been changing fast. The number of boutique stores and restaurants has tripled, and an increasing number of off-road and backcountry activities are turning Hanmer Springs into Canterbury's adventure-sports hub. It is also a spa town in the true sense of the word, with relaxing and indulgent spa facilities available at the Hanmer Springs Thermal Pools and Spa and in the village. On holidays and weekends, the springs can be busy. The Amuri Ski Field, a small ski area in the mountains behind town, attracts a dedicated following of local skiers in winter. Mountain biking is especially big, and Hanmer Springs is now the end point for several long-distance mountain-bike and endurance races through the backcountry. During the summer months, Hanmer Springs is also the southern terminus of the drive along the Acheron Road through the Molesworth Station, which runs through from the Awatere Valley in Marlborough. This backcountry trail is open for only a few months a year and is a solid six-hour drive on an unpaved road through some spectacular country. Go to the Department of Conservation website and search for Molesworth for more information.

GETTING HERE AND AROUND

The Hanmer Connection runs a daily service between Hanmer Springs and Christchurch. Service goes through Waipara on the way. By car, take State Highway 1 north out of Christchurch. About 45 minutes north, State Highway 7 turns left off the main highway toward Nelson. From here, drive through the small town of Culverden and the foothills for another 45 minutes on State Highway 7, before turning onto Highway 7A toward Hanmer Springs (this is well signposted).

Navigation around Hanmer Springs is easy, as it's a really small place. The main road into town, Amuri Drive, is a wide tree-lined road, with the thermal resort and visitor center opening off it. Conical Hill Road carries on up the hill and has most of the stores and cafés along its lower portion. Jacks Pass Road to the left and Jollies Pass Road to the right lead to the great outdoors and many of the adventure activities.

BUS Hanmer Connection. ⊠ *Hanmer Springs* ☎ *0800/242–663 NZ only, 03/382–2952* ⊕ *www.hanmerconnection.co.nz.*

VISITOR INFORMATION

CONTACTS Department of Conservation. ⊕ *www.doc.govt.nz.* **Hurunui i-SITE Visitor Centre.** ⊠ *40 Amuri Ave., Hanmer Springs* ☎ *03/315–0020, 0800/442–663 New Zealand only* ⊕ *www.visithurunui.co.nz.*

 # Sights

Hanmer Springs Thermal Pools & Spa

HOT SPRING | FAMILY | The Hanmer Springs Thermal Pools & Spa consists of 22 outdoor thermal pools of varying temperatures, including a heated freshwater pool with lazy river, a family activity pool, and three waterslides. There are also six private mineral-rich thermal pools, as well as adults-only aquatherapy pools, private sauna, and steam rooms. Massage and beauty treatments are available at the on-site spa. The Tea Kiosk Cafe and Grill, a beautifully renovated 1904 building, has bar facilities, and there's a picnic area, too. The heated changing rooms are a real treat. ✉ *42 Amuri Ave., Hanmer Springs* ☎ *03/315–0000, 0800/442–663 New Zealand only* ⊕ *www.hanmer-springs.co.nz* ⊠ *From NZ$35.*

Jacks Pass

SCENIC DRIVE | The scenic gravel drive along Jacks Pass, to the north of the village, crosses the lower slopes of Mt. Isobel before dropping into the upper Clarence River valley, an alpine area 15 minutes from Hanmer Springs. This is the beginning of some serious backcountry. The tiny stream trickling past the road at the end of the pass eventually reaches the coast north of Kaikoura at the rough and rumbling Clarence River—a favorite for rafters and kayakers. This is also the southern end of the Acheron Road through the Molesworth Station and the 4WD Rainbow Road through to St. Arnaud and the Nelson Lakes. There's restricted access at certain times of the year, and the roads can be impassable during winter, so before you go, check with the Hanmer Springs i-SITE Visitor Centre.

🍴 Restaurants

No. 31 Restaurant & Bar

$$$$ | MODERN NEW ZEALAND | In a renovated villa on the main road into Hanmer, No. 31 serves exceptional food. Its well-established local chef specializes in modern New Zealand cuisine, using the best local produce, offered with a selection of wines from the Waipara–Hanmer area. **Known for:** romantic atmosphere; award-winning beef, lamb, and venison dishes; great craft beer selection. $ *Average main: NZ$39.50* ✉ *31 Amuri Ave., Hanmer Springs* ☎ *03/315–7031* ⊗ *Closed Mon. and 2 wks in winter (dates vary).*

Powerhouse Cafe and Restaurant

$$$ | CAFÉ | Now a popular café for locals, the Powerhouse building used to contain a small hydroelectric generator that supplied power to the old Queen Mary Hospital and a few streetlights. Today, it opens at 8 am offering a great brunch menu to suit all tastes with local and free-range ingredients used in dishes that are all house-made. **Known for:** wonderful fresh salads for lunch; hearty high-country breakfasts; lots of gluten-free options. $ *Average main: NZ$21.50* ✉ *8 Jacks Pass Rd., Hanmer Springs* ☎ *03/315–5252* ⊕ *www.power-housecafe.co.nz* ⊗ *No dinner Sun.–Fri.*

Hotels

Braemar Lodge & Spa

$$$ | HOTEL | Part lodge, part boutique hotel, these slick accommodations were built around all that remained of the original Braemar Lodge—an impressive two-story-high river stone fireplace. **Pros:** large rooms with great views; on-site day spa; packages available with outdoor activities included. **Cons:** access is by several kilometers of gravel road with a steep but paved driveway; 10-minute drive from Hanmer; some parts need an upgrade. $ *Rooms from: NZ$254* ✉ *283 Medway Rd., Hanmer Springs* ☎ *03/315–7555* ⊕ *www.braemarlodge.co.nz* ❍ *Free Breakfast* ⤴ *24 suites.*

Hanmer Springs Hotel

$$$ | HOTEL | Set in beautifully landscaped gardens, this hotel is across the road from the thermal pools, and staying here will remind you of the grand, genteel era in which it was built. **Pros:** very comfortable beds; lovely old Spanish Mission–style building; in the middle of town within easy walk of most things. **Cons:** renovations underway, but some rooms still need upgrades; during New Zealand school holidays it can get busy; no elevator. $ *Rooms from: NZ$238* ✉ *1 Conical Hill Rd., Hanmer Springs* ☎ *03/975–1010*

The central Canterbury Plains area is the premier hot-air ballooning spot.

🌐 *www.cpghotels.com/hanmersprings* 🍴 *No Meals* 🛏 *65 rooms.*

Settlers Motel

$$ | **HOTEL** | This property has peaceful apartments and studios set off Amuri Avenue, the main street into Hanmer. **Pros:** flexible check-in and check-out times; quiet, friendly, motel-style establishment; short walk to town. **Cons:** reservations are essential over weekends and holiday periods; units all open onto central courtyard and parking lot; popular with families and can be busy. [$] *Rooms from: NZ$200* ✉ *6 Leamington St., Hanmer Springs* ☎ *03/315–7343, 0800/587–873* 🌐 *www.settlershanmer.co.nz* 🍴 *No Meals* 🛏 *14 rooms.*

Tussock Peak Motor Lodge

$$ | **B&B/INN** | **FAMILY** | Adjacent to the thermal pools, this stylish, eco-friendly, 14-unit complex offers a choice of spacious one- and two-bedroom units. **Pros:** excellent power steam showers; Netflix on demand with smart TVs in every room; free Wi-Fi. **Cons:** no air-conditioning in summer; can be busy with lots of families during New Zealand school holidays; basic kitchen facilities in units. [$] *Rooms from: NZ$175* ✉ *25 Amuri Ave., Hanmer Springs* ✥ *Corner Amuri Ave and Leamington St.* ☎ *03/315–5191* 🌐 *www.tussockpeak.co.nz* 🍴 *No Meals* 🛏 *14 units.*

🍸 Nightlife

Saints Pizzeria and Bar

BARS | The eclectic Saints Pizzeria and Bar is probably the closest thing to a nightclub in Hanmer Springs. It's open until 1 am Friday and Saturday, but it closes around 11 other nights. It has a dance floor and pool table and features a DJ some Saturday nights. It serves brunch and lunch, too, but not always during the week when it's quiet. Service can be a bit slow if it's really busy, but the wait is usually worth it. ✉ *6 Jacks Pass Rd., Hanmer Springs* ☎ *03/315–5262* 🌐 *www.saintshanmer.co.nz.*

⚡ Activities

ADVENTURE SPORTS

Hanmer Springs Adventure Centre

FOUR-WHEELING | Hanmer Springs Adventure Centre runs quad-bike tours, clay-bird shooting, mountain biking, and archery in the backcountry behind Hanmer Springs. Quad-bike tours leave at 10, 1:30, and 4 each day, bouncing through some spectacular hill country, native bush, river crossings, hill climbs, and stunning scenery over their 15,000-acre Woodbank Station. For something a little more leisurely, try their Wine Trail tour. ✉ *20 Conical Hill Rd., Hanmer Springs* ☎ *03/315–7233, 0800/368–7386 New Zealand only* ⊕ *www.hanmeradventure. co.nz* 🎟 *From NZ$139.*

Hanmer Springs Attractions

LOCAL SPORTS | **FAMILY** | This high-energy adventure company offers it all, including 115-foot bungy jumps off the 19th-century Ferry Bridge. You can also choose to raft or ride on a jet boat through the scenic gorge or let the kids do a quad-bike safari. Try clay-bird shooting or paintball, or just peer off the 100-foot balcony and watch the bungy jumpers and jet boats in the canyon below. ✉ *839 Hanmer Springs Rd., Hanmer Springs* ☎ *03/315–7046, 0800/661–538 New Zealand only* ⊕ *www.hanmerspringsattractions.nz* 🎟 *NZ$169; jet boat NZ$125.*

Methven

97 km (60 miles) southwest of Christchurch.

Methven's main claim to fame is as a ski town. It's a one-hour drive from Christchurch and the closest town to Mt. Hutt, which has New Zealand's longest ski season from June to October. You can't stay on the mountain, so Methven is après-ski central. It's also a great base to stay if you are skiing at the five boutique club fields within the region. The small boutique ski club fields are also open to the public—the accommodation is members-only during peak season but you can stay in Methven and go to these club fields for the day. They have basic facilities and are suited to more experienced skiers. Tow prices are cheaper if you are a member. An hour away is Canterbury's other major ski area, Porters. Some of New Zealand's best heli-skiing is available from Methven, too. In late September, the famous Peak to Pub race challenges competitors to skiing, biking, and running across snow, dirt, and pavement from the top of the mountain to the famous Blue Pub. If you are here in summer, you will get a feel for the area's strong mountain bike culture. There's a range of established mountain bike trails and many more in the works, while uncrowded country roads provide great flat riding for road cyclists. You can also enjoy horseback riding, hiking, salmon fishing, jet boating, tandem skydiving, and hot-air ballooning.

GETTING HERE AND AROUND

The best way to get to Methven by car is the quiet Scenic Highway 72, which you can join near Darfield, or via Hororata (but be wary of icy spots in the shade and hidden speed cameras on these straight roads). You could also travel down the busy State Highway 1 to Rakaia and take Thompson's Track (clearly signposted and paved) to Methven. Or join it from the north at Amberley, passing through Oxford and Sheffield. This stretch of highway, known as the Inland Scenic Route, makes a nice day drive from Christchurch, taking in the upper Rakaia and Rangitata River gorges, the small towns of Darfield, Methven, and Geraldine; scenic views of the Southern Alps; and the wide-open farmlands of the plains.

There are plenty of buses from Christchurch to Methven and Mt. Hutt in ski season, but the options drop off in summer. Mt. Hutt Ski Bus runs daily in winter, and Methven Travel runs a daily bus in winter and four times a week in summer.

BUS Methven Travel. ✉ *160 Main St., Methven* ☎ *03/302–8106, 0800/684–888* 🌐 *www.methventravel.co.nz.* **Snowman Shuttles.** ☎ *03/337–5750, 0800/766–928 NZ only* 🌐 *www.snowmanshuttles.co.nz.*

VISITOR INFORMATION

CONTACTS Methven i-SITE Visitor Centre. ✉ *160 Main St., Methven* ☎ *03/302–8955* 🌐 *www.methvenmthutt.co.nz.*

Sights

New Zealand Alpine and Agriculture Encounter

OTHER ATTRACTION | FAMILY | This purpose-built attraction brings to life the stories of the mountains, plains, and people who live there with multimedia and interactive displays. Get on board a huge combine harvester, operate a digger, explore a snow cave, view a ski film, and learn about Mid-Canterbury's dairying and seed growing. ✉ *Methven Heritage Centre, 160 Main St., Methven* ☎ *03/302–9666* 🌐 *www.methvenheritagecentre.co.nz* 🎫 *NZ$12.50.*

Restaurants

Methven isn't a culinary hotbed, but it has several good casual places and is known for its two famous watering holes: the **Blue Pub** and the **Brown Pub** on opposite corners in the middle of town. Both have reasonably priced bistro-style meals and a courtyard where you can sit and have a beer. For a quintessential New Zealand café experience head to **Cafe Primo e Secundo** set in a retro-vintage shop on MacMillan Street, where you'll find treasures along with their legendary bacon-and-egg sandwiches and excellent coffee. Grab a granola breakfast here and a muffin for later.

Hotels

Alpenhorn Chalet

$ | B&B/INN | FAMILY | This wonderfully pleasant backpacker lodge is in a wooden 1900s villa that's very typical of the small-town Victorian architecture in New Zealand at the time. **Pros:** superb free espresso coffee; homey feel is far removed from the usual backpacker-hostel vibe; wonderful conservatory garden. **Cons:** no credit cards; short walk from the center of Methven; spa open in winter only. [$] *Rooms from: NZ$60* ✉ *44 Allen St., Methven* ☎ *03/302–8779* 🌐 *www.alpenhorn.co.nz* 🍴 *No Meals* 🛏 *5 rooms.*

Brinkley Resort

$$ | RESORT | FAMILY | These affordable one- and two-bedroom apartment-style units are just a two-minute walk from the center of town, surrounded by landscaped gardens. **Pros:** 12 ski areas within easy range, including Mt. Hutt; tennis court, hot tub, children's playground, and putting green; plenty of off-street parking and a helipad. **Cons:** convention center on site, so sometimes it can be busy; some rooms are compact; rooms overlooking the parking lot are noisy. [$] *Rooms from: NZ$145* ✉ *43 Barkers Rd., Methven* ☎ *03/302–8855* 🌐 *www.brinkleyresort.co.nz* 🍴 *No Meals* 🛏 *80 rooms.*

Central Luxury Apartments

$$$ | APARTMENT | FAMILY | These modern apartments just off the main street of Methven offer all the amenities, and they're built to display the best of the Southern Alps' views. **Pros:** drying room downstairs for the skis and ski gear and laundry in each apartment; very quiet; good parking. **Cons:** Wi-Fi connections are intermittent and patchy; overpriced for amenities provided; style is neutral with minimal decoration. [$] *Rooms from: NZ$240* ✉ *7 Methven Chertsey Rd., Methven* ☎ *03/302–8829, 0800/128–829 New Zealand only* 🌐 *www.centralapartmentsmethven.co.nz* 🍴 *No Meals* 🛏 *6 apartments.*

Methven Motels and Apartments

$$ | **B&B/INN** | **FAMILY** | This modern accommodation complex has both motel rooms and apartments for small or large groups. **Pros:** upstairs rooms have views of Mt. Hutt; drying cupboard for ski clothing and short-term gear storage; electric blankets. **Cons:** free Wi-Fi only if you book directly with the hotel; road outside can be busy; TVs could do with an upgrade. [$] *Rooms from: NZ$148* ✉ *197 Main St., Methven* ☎ *03/302–9200* 🌐 *www.methvenmotels.co.nz* 🍴 *No Meals* 🛏 *8 units.*

Mt. Hutt Lodge

$$ | **B&B/INN** | If you've come south for the views and outdoor activities then the Mt. Hutt Lodge delivers with its laid-back atmosphere. **Pros:** restaurant on site with beef steak specialty; close to great fishing spots, skiing, golf, and hiking; amazing views of the mountain. **Cons:** 15-minute drive from Methven, so you'll need a car to get here; building is very 1970s and needs an upgrade; no washer in room, but there's a communal laundry. [$] *Rooms from: NZ$150* ✉ *45 Zig Zag Rd., Methven* ☎ *03/318–6898* 🌐 *www.mthuttlodge.co.nz* 🍴 *No Meals* 🛏 *14 rooms.*

Terrace Downs

$$$$ | **HOTEL** | Considered a top golf resort in New Zealand, Terrace Downs is a good place to base yourself for a vacation away from the crowds. **Pros:** kid's club and babysitting available; 18-hole championship golf course; day spa and extended list of on- and off-site activities. **Cons:** high winds in this exposed area; you'll need two nights if you want to really appreciate the surroundings and venue; the hotel has been through a series of management changes, and service can be varied. [$] *Rooms from: NZ$430* ✉ *623 Coleridge Rd., Rakaia Gorge* ☎ *03/318–6943* 🌐 *www.terracedowns.co.nz* 🍴 *No Meals* 🛏 *19 villas.*

Nightlife

Black Beech Wine Bar

WINE BARS | This sophisticated meeting place in Oxford offers a vast selection of wines and craft beers served alongside excellent gourmet pizzas and live music. ✉ *46 Main St., Unit 1, Oxford* ☎ *03/312–3338* 🌐 *www.blackbeechbar.com.*

Activities

BOATING

Discovery Jet

BOATING | **FAMILY** | Zoom along the glacier-fed Rakaia River with Discovery Jet as you journey through the deep canyon and braided courses of the river. The Rakaia's jewel-like aqua water contrasts wonderfully with the white limestone cliffs and views of Mt. Hutt ski field. Fishing and scenic tours are options, or catch a ride up to the Rakaia Gorge Walkway. Tours vary from 15 to 45 minutes and are suitable for all ages. ✉ *Terrace Downs Resort, Coleridge Rd., Rakaia Gorge* ☎ *0800/538–2628 New Zealand only, 021/538–386* 🌐 *www.discoveryjet.co.nz* 🎟 *From NZ$45 for 15 mins.*

HIKING

Mt. Somers Track

HIKING & WALKING | One of New Zealand's top 10 walkways, the Mt. Somers Track is a great way to get a taste of the subalpine New Zealand bush. Start at the Mt. Somers–Woolshed Creek end and hike downhill to the Staveley end and Sharplin Falls. The 16-km (10-mile) walk will take one to two days, and there are two huts to stay in along the way—or do it in reverse. Call the Staveley Village Store (*03/303–0859*), which also has a great café, before you start your trip for information on transport to the end of the trail; there are a number of small guiding companies. There are excellent self-contained accommodations at Red Cottages Staveley, too. 🌐 *www.doc.govt.nz.*

The Chatham Islands

Although officially part of New Zealand, the Chatham Islands, approximately 800 km (500 miles) east of the South Island, are a land apart. Bearing the full force of the open Southern Ocean, the islands are wild and weather-beaten. The air has a salty taste to it, the colors of the landscapes are muted by salt spray, and the vegetation is stunted and gnarly. Many unusual plants and birds are about—including the extremely rare black robin—and the empty beaches invite fishing and diving (although the presence of great white sharks makes the latter unadvised).

Locals here refer to the mainland as New Zealand, as though it were an entirely separate country. Just 2 of the 10 islands are inhabited—the main island and tiny, neighboring Pitt Island, which is well known for its extensive conservation programs. Most of the 600 residents are either farmers or fishermen, but tourism is increasing. The Chathams were first settled by the Moriori, a race of Polynesian descent, about 800–1,000 years ago, although there are now no full-blooded Moriori left. Māori and Europeans followed, and conflicts broke out between the separate populations throughout the 1800s. By the end of the 19th century, however, tensions had died down after the Native Land Court intervened in key disputes, and the new settlers established the strong maritime culture that still prevails on the islands.

When booking to fly to the Chathams, it's imperative that you make lodging reservations in advance. There is only one round-trip flight a week from Christchurch on Tuesday, but you can return earlier through Auckland or Wellington, and **Air Chathams** (09/257–0261; www.airchathams. co.nz) is the only carrier. The islands are 45 minutes ahead of NZ time and, therefore, the first place on Earth to see the sun each day. Check out the Air Chathams website for more details on the islands, their natural history, accommodation, and activities. Allow at least three days to visit—you'll rarely get the chance to visit anywhere this remote. And don't forget to try the crayfish and blue cod.

Rakaia Gorge Walkway

HIKING & WALKING | Leaving from just below the Rakaia River gorge bridge, the Rakaia Gorge Walkway provides upstream access to the northern bank of the river and offers easy walking, taking in some beautiful scenery. You can also take a jet boat upriver and walk back— just name your distance. ⊠ *State Hwy. 72, Methven* ⊕ *www.methvenmthutt. co.nz.*

MULTISPORT OUTFITTERS
Big Al's Snowsports

BIKING | In summer, Big Al's Snowsports turns into a cycling center for those keen to don Lycra and head to the trails. Al and his team have decades of experience and really know what they're talking about with trail maps and the best riding tips for the region. You can rent full-suspension cross-country bikes and 29r xc hardtails from them, too. ⊠ *The Square, Methven* ☎ *03/302–8003* ⊕ *www.bigals. co.nz* ✉ *Ski rental NZ$39 per day; bike rental from NZ$15 per hr.*

SKIING
Methven Heliski

SKIING & SNOWBOARDING | Methven has access to some of New Zealand's best backcountry helicopter-accessed terrain and hundreds of square miles of pristine snow. You don't have to be an advanced skier or snowboarder to enjoy it—there is something for every range of ability here, including long runs in deep powder, gentle glaciers, plus a fabulous day out soaring over the Alps with a friendly team. Methven Heliski is located at Glen-falloch Station, and there are excellent accommodations available here, too, with superb meals and drinks included. They fly every fine day from July 1 through September 30. ⊠ *114 Main St., Methven* ☎ *03/302–8108* ⊕ *www.methvenheli. co.nz* ⊠ *NZ$1150 per person for full day.*

Mt. Hutt Ski Area

SKIING & SNOWBOARDING | **FAMILY** | The views across the Canterbury Plains are amazing from this high-country ski area. It has one of the longest vertical drops on the South Island and a complete terrain mix for all skiers and boarders. A great family ski spot, there is a beginner's area, with a 140-meter-long enclosed Magic Carpet, and modern chairlifts. For advanced skiers and snowboarders there's plenty of off-piste action, too. ⊠ *Mt. Hutt Ski Area, Methven* ☎ *03/308–5074, 0800/697-547* ⊕ *www.mthutt.co.nz* ⊠ *From NZ$102.*

Porters

SKIING & SNOWBOARDING | **FAMILY** | Take the drive from Methven along the Great Alpine Highway to the Porters ski area, with some spectacular views along the way. The access road is one of the short-est and least intimidating in the region, too. There are excellent learner facilities here, as well as a terrain park for board-ers. An Easyrider chairlift connects the base with the upper mountain. Two of New Zealand's legendary runs are here—Bluff Face and Big Mama. If you need a break, the café has great views over the Torlesse Range. ⊠ *Access Rd., Porters Ski Area, Methven* ☎ *03/318–4731* ⊕ *www.skiporters.co.nz* ⊠ *From NZ$99.*

Geraldine

138 km (85½ miles) southwest of Christchurch.

For years, this lovely town has been a favorite stop on the road to Aoraki/Mt. Cook. These days, it's becoming a magnet in southern Canterbury for art mavens and foodies.

GETTING HERE AND AROUND

State Highway 1 is the fastest route here from Christchurch; just after crossing the Rangitata River, turn inland for about 10 minutes on State Highway 79. State Highway 72—known as the Inland Scenic Route—gives you closer views of the mountains and river gorges but takes a bit longer. The rolling downs around Geraldine are especially breathtaking in the late afternoon, when the sun turns them golden.

Geraldine is three hours from Christchurch by bus and even faster by car. It is served by InterCity buses.

BUS CONTACTS InterCity Coachlines.
☎ *03/365–1113* ⊕ *www.intercity.co.nz.*

 Sights

You know you're in small-town New Zealand when the biggest store on the main street is the rural merchandiser. Luckily, along Geraldine's main drag, Talbot Street, you'll find other stores and galleries to browse as well. Or stop in at Barker's of Geraldine for their legendary fruit preserves and Talbot Forest Cheese for some delicious locally made cheeses, ice creams, fudge, and other tasty delights. Head farther to the Rangitata Valley and visit Peel Forest, the ancient podocarp remnant of the vast forest expanse that once covered much of Mid- and South Canterbury. The area is now a haven for birdlife, and there are many trails for hikers and bikers.

Geraldine Vintage Car and Machinery Museum

OTHER MUSEUM | At the Geraldine Vintage Car and Machinery Museum, there's some good rural stuff with more than 100 tractors (some dating back to 1912) and other farm machinery sharing space with vintage cars. ✉ *178 Talbot St., Geraldine* ☎ *03/693–8756* 🎟 *NZ$15.*

Hotels

Peel Forest Lodge

$$$$ | **B&B/INN** | Tucked in among giant kahikatea trees and native forest, and overlooking Little Mt. Peel (which isn't so little), this comfortable log lodge provides a haven of peace and quiet. **Pros:** big schist fireplace in the lounge; café and bar just down the road at Peel Forest village; full kitchen for your use. **Cons:** can sometimes be booked out for weddings; you will need a car to get here; a few trophy heads on the walls, which might not be for everyone. [$] *Rooms from: NZ$430* ✉ *96 Brake Rd., off Dennistoun Rd., Peel Forest, Geraldine* ✣ *Don't drive into Peel Forest Estate, take a right at their gate and continue another mile or so along gravel road* ☎ *03/696–3703* 🌐 *www.peelforestlodge.co.nz* 🍴 *No Meals* 🛏 *4 rooms.*

Shopping

Barker's

FOOD | For foodie treats, stop by Barker's to try fruit chutneys, fruit syrups, sauces, spreads, and tasty jams. They do good gift boxes, and they ship overseas, too. ✉ *71 Talbot St., Geraldine* ☎ *0508/227–537 NZ only, 03/693–9727* 🌐 *www.barkers.co.nz.*

Louk NZ Clothing

MIXED CLOTHING | Stop off at Louk NZ Clothing for a big range of designer merino wear and cool outdoor gear, for both males and females. They also have the biggest Swazi range (another hip outdoor label) on the South Island, as well as the most extensive range of socks you'll find anywhere. They're in the old post office on the main street. ✉ *Old Post Office, 47 Talbot St., Geraldine* ☎ *03/693–9070* 🌐 *www.louknzclothing.co.nz.*

The Tin Shed

SOUVENIRS | Looking more like a shearing shed than a store, The Tin Shed is exactly that. Surrounded by farmland and animals, it is an authentic piece of rural New Zealand architecture being put to good use. Inside is a selection of lifestyle and handmade clothing. There's a good range of merino and possum-fur knits and shawls, knitwear, thermals, oilskins, sheepskin footwear, and locally produced skin-care items. This is a great spot to stock up with gifts before leaving the country, and they can arrange shipping. Watch the turn-in off the main road as traffic moves fast here. ✉ *809 State Hwy. 79, Geraldine* ☎ *03/693–9416, 0508/504-006* 🌐 *www.thetinshed.co.nz.*

Activities

Rangitata Rafts

WHITE-WATER RAFTING | Rangitata Rafts runs white-water rafting trips on the Grade V Rangitata River starting at 11:30 most days from October through May. The river grades build as you drop lower so if you can't face the Grade V section (the last part of the trip), you can walk around with the photographer then rejoin the raft. Rates include an early lunch, hot showers, spectacular scenery, a barbecue, and 2½ hours of rafting. Reservations are essential. They also do a more gentle Grade II trip that's suitable for anyone eight years or older; it's good fun and a nice introduction to white-water rafting. Nonrafters can relax at the lodge. ✉ *53 Waikari Rd., Peel Forest* ☎ *03/696–3534, 0800/251–251 New Zealand only* 🌐 *www.rafts.co.nz* 🎟 *From NZ$219* 🕒 *Closed June–Sept.*

Chapter 11

THE SOUTHERN ALPS AND FIORDLAND

11

Updated by
Gerard Hindmarsh

☉ Sights	🍴 Restaurants	🛏 Hotels	🛍 Shopping	🍸 Nightlife
★★★★★	★★★☆☆	★★★☆☆	★★☆☆☆	★★☆☆☆

WELCOME TO THE SOUTHERN ALPS AND FIORDLAND

TOP REASONS TO GO

★ **Adventure Sports:** Jump, fly, splash, jet boat, or swing; your inner daredevil will find its voice in Queenstown's multitude of adventurous activities.

★ **Stargazing:** Everything is clearer here. Filmmakers comment on the quality of the light, and you will see an extraordinary number of stars. This is where the world's largest International Dark Sky Reserve was declared in 2012.

★ **Fly-Fishing:** The crystal-clear lakes and rivers of the Southern Alps are some of the world's best fly-fishing spots.

★ **Hiking:** Tramping doesn't get any better than the Milford, the Kepler, the Routeburn, and the Hollyford tracks. Because trail traffic is carefully managed, you'll feel wonderfully alone in the wilderness.

★ **Scenery:** The landscape here is breathtaking: peaks, fjords, lakes, forest, and tussock lands lie in close proximity. A scenic flight to take it all in is money well spent.

1 Mackenzie Country and Lake Tekapo. The country's highest lake and some of the world's best star-gazing.

2 Aoraki/Mount Cook National Park. New Zealand's tallest mountain at the center of a park filled with hikers and mountain climbers.

3 Twizel. A service town that's a good base for visiting Aoraki and Mount Cook.

4 Mount Aspiring National Park. The country's third-largest national park, full of geological wonders.

5 Wanaka. A quieter alternative to Queenstown and a good base for Mt. Aspiring.

6 Queenstown. The extreme sports capital of the world.

7 Arrowtown. A quaint village with a glimpse into the region's gold rush history.

8 Te Anau and Fiordland National Park. A good base for Fiordland.

9 Milford Sound. The most popular part of Fiordland, with dramatic views of breathtaking fjords.

10 Lake Manapouri and Doubtful Sound. A lovely lake with access to less traveled but still beautiful fjords.

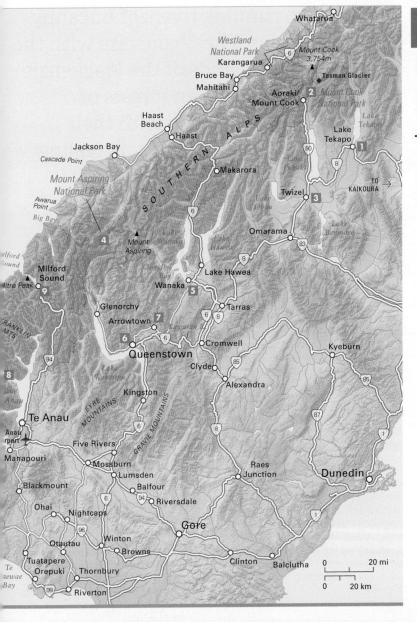

Whararoa

Westland
National Park

Mount Cook
3,754m

Karangarua

Bruce Bay

Mahitahi

Aoraki/
Mount Cook

Tasman Glacier

Mount Cook
National Park

2

Haast
Beach

SOUTHERN

Haast

Lake
Tekapo

Jackson Bay

Lake
Tekapo

1

Cascade Point

ALPS

Mount Aspiring
National Park

Makarora

Lake
Pukaki

Awarua
Point

Big Bay

80

Twizel

3

TO
KAIKOURA

8

4

Mount
Aspiring

Lake
Wanaka

Lake
Hawea

Omarama

Lake
Benmore

6

83

ilford
Sound

Milford
Sound

itre Peak

9

Otendin

Lake Hawea

Wanaka

5

8

Glenorchy

Arrowtown

7

Tarras

6

8

FRANKLIN
MTS

Kawarau R.

6

Cromwell

Kyeburn

6

Queenstown

Clyde

85

85

8

Lake
Anau

94

Lake
Wakatipu

Alexandra

Kingston

EYRE
MOUNTAINS

87

Te Anau

GRAVIE MOUNTAINS

8

1

Anau
rport

Five Rivers

Manapouri

Mossburn

Raes
Junction

Dunedin

Lumsden

Blackmount

Balfour

6

Ohai

Nightcaps

94

Riversdale

1

96

Otautau

Winton

Gore

Tuatapere

Browns

Orepuki

Thornbury

Clinton

Balclutha

Te
ewae
Bay

99

Riverton

0   20 mi

0   20 km

There are hundreds of glaciers locked in the Southern Alps, slowly grinding their way down to lower altitudes and melting into running rivers of uncanny blue-green hues. These conspire with the vast brown grasslands of the Mackenzie Basin and ancient green forests of Fiordland to humble you with their imposing presence, leaving you feeling very small and temporary. Nothing is permanent though—the freeze-thaw cycle constantly refreshes this mighty landscape making it feel absolutely *alive*.

Aoraki, or Mt. Cook, at 12,217 feet, is New Zealand's highest mountain, and 20 other peaks in this alpine chain are higher than 10,000 feet. Aoraki/Mount Cook National Park is part of a UNESCO World Heritage Area, and the alpine region around it contains the Tasman Glacier, at 27 km (17 miles), New Zealand's longest.

The Southern Alps region is great for hiking. Terrain varies from high alpine tundra to snow-covered peaks, heavily forested mountains, and wide, braided river valleys. A good network of trails and marked routes weave throughout the mountains, but be well informed before venturing into them. Always make your intentions known: go to the Adventure Smart website for details (*www.adven-turesmart.org.nz*); Aoraki/Mt. Cook is the only Department of Conservation (DOC) office where you still sign your intentions in person.

There are many easier options for exploring the foothills and less arduous parts of the Southern Alps. On the southwest corner of the island, glaciers over millennia have cut the Alps into stone walls dropping into fjords, and walking trails take you into the heart of the wild Fiordland National Park. The Milford Track is the best known—it has been called the finest walk in the world since a headline to that effect appeared in the London *Spectator* in 1908. If you're not keen on walking to Milford Sound, hop on a boat and take in the sights from on deck. Most river valleys with road access have well-marked walking trails leading to scenic waterfalls, gorges, and lookout points.

Floods of tourists have come to see the otherworldly landscape used in shooting The Hobbit and Lord of the Rings film trilogies, and Hollywood directors have been drawn to the area for the magnificent backdrops that depicted Tolkien's Middle-earth. The vastness of the region keeps it from feeling crowded, even with all the new visitors. Queenstown, often billed as an adventure-sports hot spot, is perhaps the best-known destination in the Southern Lakes district. It and the nearby town of Wanaka are steeped in gold-rush history and surrounded by stunning mountain scenery.

GETTING ORIENTED

The Southern Alps start in the northern end of the South Island around Kaikoura and stretch through the provinces of Canterbury, inland Otago, Westland, and Southland. These are serious mountains, with jagged 9,000-feet-plus peaks. The Mt. Cook area is the heart of Kiwi mountaineering. These majestic formations take center stage, and amazing landscapes unfurl at their feet—green rivers braided with white stone banks, acres of lupines, and lakes hued with indescribable blues. From Lake Tekapo, you finally come to "rest" at the adventure-friendly cities of Queenstown and Wanaka, historic Arrowtown, and the truly restful aura of the Otago vineyards. To the west, magnificent Milford Sound dominates Fiordland.

MAJOR REGIONS

The Southern Alps. In Aoraki/Mount Cook National Park, activities naturally revolve around the mountain—climbing, hiking, skiing, and scenic flights. But as you travel down into the foothills and valleys, the choices for adventure multiply. Stargaze at Lake Tekapo in Mackenzie Country, or explore Mount Aspiring National Park. Places like Twizel and Wanaka make good bases for these outdoor activities. Enjoy the miles of hills and farmland as you travel through Lindis Pass; soon the uninhabited country will give way to the bustle of Queenstown, which provides dozens of ways to get your adrenaline pumping. A handful of notable vineyards calms the nerves post-extreme-sport

experience while Arrowtown will give you an intriguing glimpse into the area's history.

Fiordland. On the southwest of the South Island, this is a majestic wilderness of rocks, ice, and beech forest, where glaciers have carved mile-deep notches into the coast. Most of this terrain is officially designated Fiordland National Park, and in conjunction with South Westland National Park, is a designated UNESCO Te Waipounamu World Heritage Area. Parts of the park are so remote that they have never been explored, and visitor activities are mostly confined to a few of the sounds and the walking trails. Te Anau serves as the base, with lodgings, a supermarket, cafés/restaurants, and sports outfitters. The most accessible scenic highlight of this area—and perhaps of the whole country—is Milford Sound, where trees cling to tremendous rock faces that plunge into the sea, and rare species of coral wait just below the water's surface. Doubtful Sound is also a beautiful area and is actually closer to Te Anau than Milford but involves crossing Lake Manapouri and an alpine pass to get there.

Planning

Getting Here and Around

AIR

Air New Zealand flies from Auckland, Wellington, and Christchurch into Queenstown, the main hub. Jetstar flies in from Auckland. Air NZ, Jetstar, Virgin Australia, and Qantas provide trans-Tasman flights (Brisbane, Sydney, and Melbourne). Tourist enterprises operate helicopters and fixed-wing planes, which buzz between Queenstown, Wanaka, Milford Sound, Franz Josef, Fox Glacier, and Mt. Cook. You can do fly-cruise-fly packages from Queenstown to Milford, although the flight from Wanaka to Milford is the most spectacular.

BUS

It may take a full day, but you can take buses to and from the major towns in the Southern Alps and Fiordland area. InterCity operates a daily bus service between Christchurch and Queenstown down the South Island's eastern flank via Dunedin or the longer, more scenic route via Mount Cook Village, with a one-hour stop at the Hermitage Hotel for lunch. Their coaches also make daily trips from the Franz Josef and Fox glaciers through Wanaka to Queenstown. InterCity also has a daily bus round-trip route from Queenstown and Te Anau to Milford Sound. Alpine ConneXions sends buses between Wanaka and Queenstown twice a day. They also run to Cardrona, Clyde, Cromwell, Dunedin, Ranfurly, Alexandra, and pickup and drop-off at various walking tracks and rail trails.

CONTACTS Ritchies Transport. ☎ 03/443–9120 ⊕ www.ritchies.co.nz. **InterCity Coachlines.** ☎ 03/442–4922 ⊕ www. intercity.co.nz.

CAR

Exploring is best done by car on the state highways that weave through the vast mountain ranges, skirting several major lakes and rivers. Be prepared for rugged, quickly changing terrain, ice in winter, and frequent downpours, particularly around Milford Sound. Rental-car companies may discourage driving on some of the smaller, unpaved roads, so it is best to avoid them. That said, an ideal way to see the Alps is to "tiki-tour" (wander around) by car, as the main network of roads is paved and easy to negotiate.

Hotels

Lodgings in the Southern Alps and Fiordland milk the fantastic views for all they're worth. You can almost always find a room that looks out on a lake, river, or rugged mountain range. Queenstown and Wanaka are busy in summer (January through March) and winter (July through September), so you should reserve in advance. Luxury options are plentiful in Queenstown, and costs are correspondingly high. Other towns, such as Aoraki/Mount Cook Village, have extremely limited options, so you should plan ahead there, too. Air-conditioning is rare because it's rarely needed. Heating, though, is standard, and essential in winter.

Restaurant and hotel reviews have been shortened. For full information, visit Fodors.com. Restaurant prices are the average cost of a main course at dinner or, if dinner is not served, at lunch. Hotel prices are the lowest cost of a standard double room in high season.

WHAT IT COSTS in New Zealand Dollars			
$	$$	$$$	$$$$
RESTAURANTS			
under NZ$15	NZ$15– NZ$20	NZ$21– NZ$30	over NZ$30
HOTELS			
under NZ$125	NZ$125– NZ$200	NZ$201– NZ$300	over NZ$300

Planning Your Time

Give yourself two to three days to explore the Aoraki/Mount Cook area; two days is a good idea at Mt. Cook in case the namesake peak is hiding behind clouds, and you'll want to allow for an evening at the space observatory in Tekapo. Once you head south you can use Queenstown or Wanaka as a base from which to visit Mount Aspiring National Park, wine country, and take on some exciting adrenaline-fueled activities around Queenstown—three days should be sufficient to pack it all in. Then head to Te Anau, which is a perfect base for seeing Fiordland National Park. An overnight on Milford or Doubtful Sound is recommended for unwinding and reflecting after the road-tripping, bungy jumping excitement of the past week.

Restaurants

Queenstown, as the main regional resort, has the widest range of restaurants. Throughout the area, menus focus on local produce, seafood, lamb, and venison. Wine lists often highlight South Island wines, especially those from Central Otago and Gibbston Valley. Cafés and restaurants driven by the summer tourist trade shorten their hours in winter. Dress standards are generally relaxed, with jeans or khakis acceptable almost everywhere. At high-end places, particularly in Queenstown, you'll need to reserve a table at least a day in advance.

Outside of Queenstown and Wanaka dining options can be limited. In summer, meals of some sort are available almost everywhere, but outside the high season, there are fewer options in the smaller settlements, and they don't tend to stay open late.

Visitor Information

The regional visitor bureaus are open daily year-round, with slightly longer hours in summer. These local tourism organizations have helpful websites, including Destination Fiordland, Destination Queenstown, and Aoraki/Mount Cook Mackenzie Region Tourism.

CONTACTS Aoraki/Mount Cook Mackenzie Region Tourism. ⊕ *www.mackenzienz. com.* **Destination Fiordland.** ⊕ *www. fiordland.org.nz.* **Destination Queenstown.** ⊕ *www.queenstownnz.co.nz.*

When to Go

Although the Southern Alps and Fiordland have four distinct seasons, it's not unusual for the mountains to get snow even in summer. If you're traveling in winter, check the weather forecasts and road conditions regularly. The road into Milford Sound can close for days at a time because of snow or avalanche risk, and you must carry chains.

For winter sports, from July through September you can be assured of snow around Queenstown and Wanaka, where the ski scene is ushered in by the Queenstown Winter Festival. In the height of summer—from January to March—both resort towns have a lot of Kiwi vacationers. If you're planning on hiking one of the major trails, such as the Milford Track, summer and early autumn are the best times, but you'll need to book well ahead.

Mackenzie Country and Lake Tekapo

227 km (141 miles) west of Christchurch.

You will know you have reached the Mackenzie Country after you cross Burkes Pass and the woodland is suddenly replaced by high-country tussock grassland, which is full of lupines in the summer months. The area is named for James ("Jock") McKenzie, one of the most intriguing and enigmatic figures in New Zealand history. McKenzie was a Scot who may or may not have stolen the thousand sheep found with him in these secluded upland pastures in 1855. Arrested, tried, and convicted, he made several escapes from jail before he was granted a pardon nine months after his trial—and disappeared from the pages of history. Regardless of his innocence or guilt, McKenzie was a master bushman and herdsman. A commemorative

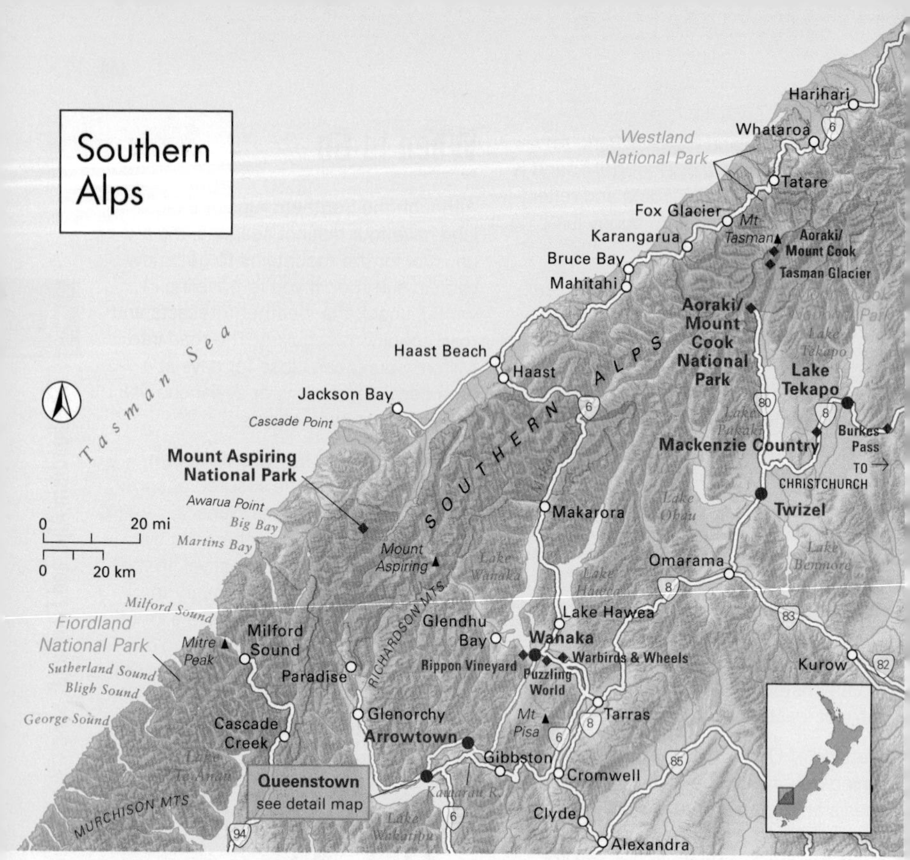
Southern Alps
Harihari
Whataroa
Westland National Park
Tatare
Fox Glacier
Mt Tasman
Karangarua
Aoraki/ Mount Cook
Tasman Glacier
Bruce Bay
Mahitahi
Aoraki/ Mount Cook National Park
Tasman Sea
Haast Beach
Haast
SOUTHERN ALPS
Lake Tekapo
Jackson Bay
Cascade Point
Lake Pukaki
Burkes Pass
Mackenzie Country
Mount Aspiring National Park
TO CHRISTCHURCH
Awarua Point
Big Bay
Martins Bay
Makarora
Lake Ohau
Twizel
0 20 mi
0 20 km
Mount Aspiring
Lake Wanaka
Lake Hawea
Omarama
Lake Benmore
Milford Sound
Fiordland National Park
RICHARDSON MTS
Glendhu Bay
Wanaka
Mitre Peak
Sutherland Sound
Bligh Sound
Paradise
Rippon Vineyard
Warbirds & Wheels
Puzzling World
Kurow
George Sound
Glenorchy
Mt Pisa
Tarras
Cascade Creek
Arrowtown
Gibbston
Cromwell
Lake Te Anau
Queenstown see detail map
Kawarau R.
MURCHISON MTS
Lake Wakatipu
Clyde
Alexandra

obelisk marks Mackenzie Pass, 30 km (18 miles) off the main highway if you turn off at Burkes Pass.

GETTING HERE AND AROUND

From Christchurch take Highway 1 south. At the tiny town of Rangitata turn right onto Highway 79 to Lake Tekapo. Bus companies that serve Lake Tekapo include InterCity Coach, The Cook Connection (summer only), and several tour operators. Check 🌐 *www.mtcooknz.com* for a complete list.

VISITOR INFORMATION

CONTACTS Lake Tekapo New Zealand. 🌐 *www.laketekaponz.co.nz*. **Tekapo Springs Information Centre.** ✉ *State Hwy. 8, Village Center* ☎ *03/680–6579* 🌐 *www.mackenzienz.com.*

Sights

Bullock Wagon Trail

TRAIL | This 268-km (167-mile) heritage highway, which stretches from Timaru to Twizel via Mt. Cook, recognizes the long, arduous journeys early settlers in the region made by bullock wagon. Leaving the Canterbury Plains at Geraldine or Pleasant Point (depending on whether you are coming directly from Christchurch or through from Timaru), the highways join at Fairlie and quickly climb toward the first of the alpine passes—Burkes Pass—along the Bullock Wagon Trail. The Burkes Pass monument marks the division between the high and low country, and from there the country immediately takes on the dried look of high-country tussock lands. To learn more about the trail and the history of the region, stop in at one of two information centers along the way.

Church of the Good Shepherd

CHURCH | On the east side of the township, the tiny Church of the Good Shepherd is one of the most photographed buildings in New Zealand. This beautifully simple stone interdenominational church has sat on the shore of Lake Tekapo since 1935. There's no need for stained glass as the view through the window is the lake's brilliant blue. A victim of its own popularity, the church has restricted parking and no longer allows photography inside the building. Right next to the church is a lovely bronze statue dedicated to the working sheep dogs of the area. ✉ *Pioneer Dr., Lake Tekapo* ☎ *03/685–8389* 🌐 *www.churchofthegoodshepherd.org.nz.*

Dark Sky Project

OBSERVATORY | **FAMILY** | If you're extremely lucky, you'll see the southern lights in this area. Even if you don't, you're still at one of the best stargazing sites in the world. Dark Sky Project operates from the Mt. John Observatory and studies the skies above Lake Tekapo. The glass-enclosed Astro Café has ham-off-the-bone sandwiches, telescopes, and dizzying views. Stargazing trips leave from the town office in the evening, and reservations are essential. Dark Sky Project also offers a shorter 75-minute tour of the Cowan's Observatory, which is more suitable for those with younger children. ✉ *Godley Peaks Rd., Lake Tekapo* ☎ *03/680–6960* 🌐 *www.darkskyproject.co.nz* 🎟 *From NZ$99.*

Lake Tekapo

TOWN | The long, narrow expanse of Lake Tekapo anchors the area. Its extraordinary milky-turquoise color comes from rock flour, rock ground by glacial action and held in a soupy suspension. Tekapo, the country's highest large lake, has good fly-fishing in its waters and in the surrounding rivers and canals. As you drive into the small town, you'll notice a knot of restaurants with tour buses parked outside. It's a rather off-putting image, but it's relatively easy to keep the township at your back and your eyes on the lake and mountains. If you're not planning to stay at Mt. Cook, then Tekapo is the best place in the Mackenzie Basin to stop for the night. And once the buses have passed through for the day, it's a quiet spot—at least until the hordes of Cantabrians arrive for the summer break. A pleasant lakefront recreation area separates the town retail area from the lakeshore. ✉ *Lake Tekapo*

Tekapo Springs

HOT SPRING | **FAMILY** | If you've taken advantage of the walks around Tekapo then you'll really appreciate this complex with its beautiful views. There's a day spa, sauna, steam room, three hot pools, and a traditional plunge pool at lake temperature. In winter, there's a skating rink and tube park. ✉ *6 Lakeside Dr., Lake Tekapo* ☎ *03/680–6550* 🌐 *www.tekaposprings.co.nz* 🎟 *From NZ$27.*

🍴 Restaurants

Kohan Japanese Restaurant

$$$ | **JAPANESE** | **FAMILY** | For nearly 30 years, Masato Itoh has run the only Japanese restaurant in town, combining fresh local ingredients with imported spices and seasoning to produce a traditional Japanese menu. The food is a refreshing change from the more traditional offerings in town; any salmon dish is a winner, but the Bento Box is an especially good value. **Known for:** lots of locals; great lake views; big crowds. [$] *Average main: NZ$25* ✉ *State Hwy. 8, Village Center* ☎ *03/680–6688* 🌐 *www.kohannz.com* 🕒 *No dinner Sun.*

🛏 Hotels

The Chalet

$$$ | **HOTEL** | The Chalet's six fully self-contained apartments stretch beside the turquoise waters of Lake Tekapo, with units ranging from studio size to a two-bedroom cottage apartment. **Pros:** extremely comfortable rooms; superb views; host is an experienced local guide. **Cons:** garden rooms lack lake views; it's difficult to book a single night stay; subtle clown theme not for everyone. $ *Rooms from: NZ$230* ⊠ *14 Pioneer Dr., Lake Tekapo* ☎ *03/680–6774* ⊕ *www.thechalet. co.nz* ❤ *No Meals* ⇶ *7 units.*

★ Lake Tekapo Lodge

$$$$ | **B&B/INN** | The large picture windows offer spectacular lake views, providing a blend of natural beauty and modern sophistication to this quiet and luxurious property; they don't allow children. **Pros:** wonderful personal attention; the most luxurious stay in Lake Tekapo; dinner available by arrangement. **Cons:** some buildings in the foreground of lake and mountain views; book well in advance; no pool. $ *Rooms from: NZ$450* ⊠ *25 Aorangi Cres., Lake Tekapo* ☎ *03/680– 6566* ⊕ *laketekapolodge.co.nz* ❤ *Free Breakfast* ☞ *No children allowed* ⇶ *3 rooms.*

Lake Tekapo Village Motel

$$$ | **HOTEL** | **FAMILY** | A nice midrange alternative with good family-style facilities, this resort is in the center of town. **Pros:** right next to restaurants; huge bathrooms; good value. **Cons:** adjoins backpacker accommodation; many rooms face parking lot; lake views obstructed by buildings in front. $ *Rooms from: NZ$255* ⊠ *Village Centre, State Hwy. 8, Lake Tekapo* ☎ *03/680–6808, 0800/118– 666* ⊕ *www.laketekapo.com* ❤ *No Meals* ⇶ *19 rooms.*

 Activities

If you're not up for tourist adventures on a particular day, a nice walk around Tekapo may suffice. This will lead you to spectacular views, and there's always the hot pools at Tekapo Springs to relax in afterward.

HIKING

Domain to Mt. John Lookout Track

HIKING & WALKING | Pick up a walking-trail map at the Tekapo Information Centre and take off to hike the Domain to Mt. John Lookout Track. In a couple of hours you can be well above the township, enjoying extensive views of the Mackenzie Basin, Southern Alps, and Lake Tekapo.

Aoraki/Mount Cook National Park

99 km (62 miles) from Lake Tekapo.

If you think you've experienced all the grandeur New Zealand has to offer, just wait until you visit Aoraki/Mount Cook National Park. A few things about Aoraki/ Mt. Cook: it's dually named with Māori and Anglo titles. Second, you may never see New Zealand's tallest mountain, as weather can descend quickly and shroud the peaks for days. Plan to stay in the park overnight in case your arrival coincides with curtains of clouds. Note that shopping in Aoraki/Mount Cook Village is very limited. If you don't intend to eat every meal in a restaurant, purchase food and necessary supplies in Twizel or Lake Tekapo. The ice cornices and granite faces are in the realm of serious mountain climbers. Nonclimbers can still get a strong sense of the place with hikes, scenic flights, glacier ski trips, and a visit to the excellent Sir Edmund Hillary Alpine Centre at the Hermitage Hotel. And, finally, be prepared to be awed by these majestic peaks, the stunning immensity of Tasman Glacier, and the fast-growing iceberg-studded Lake Tasman.

WHEN TO GO

For driving to and hiking in the park unhampered by bad weather, visit in the summer. Book accommodations and activities well in advance for November to March. If your trip revolves around

Did You Know?

New Zealand's Southern Alps are young by geological standards. In fact, they're still growing. Due to collidiing tectonic plates, the mountains shoot up at a rate of about ¼ inch per year.

heli-skiing or snowboarding, then winter is a wonderland here, albeit a somewhat inaccessible one during snow storms.

GETTING HERE AND AROUND

The 330-km (205-mile) drive from Christchurch straight through to Aoraki/Mount Cook Village takes four hours. Take Highway 1 south out of Christchurch. At the tiny town of Rangitata turn right onto Highway 79 to Lake Tekapo. Pass through Lake Tekapo and look on the right for Highway 80 to Aoraki/Mount Cook Village. InterCity buses make daily stops at Mount Cook Village. The village itself is small and manageable on foot.

BUS COMPANY InterCity Coachlines.
✉ *Cnr. Lichfield and Colombo Sts., Lichfield St, Christchurch, Regional Platform, outside Bus Exchange* ☎ *03/365–1113* ⊕ *www.intercity.co.nz.*

TOURS
Glacier Explorers
SPECIAL-INTEREST TOURS | Take a spectacular, almost surreal, boat trip on the terminal lake of New Zealand's largest and longest glacier, the Tasman Glacier. The lake only formed in the mid-1980s, and every now and then icebergs calve and increase its size. It's the only place in the country where you can do a trip like this. The season starts once the lake has thawed, but generally runs from mid-September to late May. It's a good idea to book ahead, and bring a warm jacket. The trip starts with a 15-minute walk to the lake. ✉ *Terrace Road, Aoraki/Mount Cook* ☎ *03/435–1809, 0800/686–800* ⊕ *www. glacierexplorers.com* ✉ *NZ$129.*

VISITOR INFORMATION
CONTACTS Aoraki/Mount Cook National Park Visitor Centre. ✉ *Aoraki/Mount Cook Village, 1 Larch Grove, Aoraki/Mount Cook* ☎ *03/435–1186* ⊕ *www.doc.govt. nz.*

Sights

★ **Aoraki/Mount Cook National Park**
MOUNTAIN | Aoraki/Mt. Cook is New Zealand's highest peak at approximately 12,218 feet. There are 22 peaks over 10,000 feet in Aoraki/Mount Cook National Park. According to Māori legend, Aoraki was one of three sons of Rakinui, the sky father. Their canoe caught on a reef and froze, forming the South Island. South Island's oldest name to local Māori is Te Waka O Aoraki (Aoraki's canoe) and the highest peak is their ancestor Aoraki, frozen by the south wind, and turned to stone. The officially recognized names of this mountain and the national park were changed to their original Māori names of Aoraki (Aorangi to North Island Māori) as part of a 1998 settlement between the government and the major South Island Māori tribe, Ngai Tahu. The Māori and Anglo names are used interchangeably or together. The 273-square-mile national park surrounds tiny Aoraki/Mount Cook Village, which consists of a visitor center, an airfield, a pub, a little school, and a range of accommodation providers. Walking is always an option, and in winter there's heli-skiing. If the weather is clear, a scenic flight can be the highlight of your stay in New Zealand. Contact the Aoraki/Mount Cook National Park Visitor Centre or the Metservice weather website to check conditions before setting out on an unguided excursion. Hiking trails radiate from the visitor center, providing everything from easy walking paths to full-day challenges. Be sure to fill your car's gas tank and purchase essentials before leaving Twizel or Tekapo as services are very limited in the village. For a unique hands-on educational experience take a half-hour hike to the fast-growing 7-km (4.3-mile) Terminus Lake of the Tasman Glacier. Fed by the retreating glacier and the Murchison River, the lake was formed only in the past couple of decades. From Terminus Lake, you can examine up close the terminal face of the

Did You Know?

Practice makes perfect at Aoraki/Mt. Cook. Sir Edmund Hillary honed his climbing skills here to prepare for his historic ascent of Mt. Everest.

Safety in the High Country

The Fiordland region's remoteness and changeable weather make it necessary to take some sensible precautions. So, before you head out on that trek or boat trip, keep the following in mind:

Be sure to wear the right protective clothing: sturdy hiking boots, a thoroughly waterproof jacket, and a warm layer such as a fleece or wool pullover. Weather in this region, especially at high altitude, can change dramatically in a short time.

Watch out for sunburn—take sunscreen and a hat with you. Also bring bug repellent for sand flies, which are impossible to avoid in this region unless you're traveling offshore by boat.

If you're heading off without a guide for more than an hour or two, let someone know where and when you're going and when you've returned. See the Adventure Smart website for advice (*www.adventuresmart.nz*). DOC visitor centers issue regular weather and trail updates.

Use extreme caution when crossing rivers. Especially after rain, mountain runoff can quickly turn a gentle stream into an angry torrent, and drowning is a major hazard. If you do get trapped on one side of a quickly rising river, wait for the water to recede rather than risk crossing.

For longer treks into serious country always carry a map and compass, first-aid gear, bottled water, high-energy foods, warm clothes and tent, and a mountain radio or EPIRB (locator beacon—these can be rented locally). Cell phones don't work in the mountains.

glacier, which is 3 km (2 miles) wide. A trip with Glacier Explorers takes you by boat to explore some of the large floating icebergs that have calved (fallen away) from the glacier. It's an eerie experience skimming across the milky-white water and closing in on icebergs. From the airfield at Mount Cook Village, helicopters and fixed-wing aircraft make spectacular scenic flights across the Southern Alps. One of the most exciting is the one-hour trip aboard the ski planes that touch down on the Tasman Glacier after a gorgeous scenic flight. The 10-minute stop on the glacier doesn't allow time for much more than a snapshot, but the sensation is tremendous. The moving tongue of ice beneath your feet—one of the largest glaciers outside the Himalayas—is 27 km (17 miles) long and up to 2,000 feet thick in places. The intensity of light on the glacier can be dazzling, and sunglasses are a must. ✉ *Aoraki/Mount Cook.*

🍴 Restaurants

The Old Mountaineers Cafe, Bar & Restaurant

$$$ | **CAFÉ** | This cozy, very personable café–restaurant has big picture windows for grand views of the Alps and all sorts of interesting mountaineering memorabilia and photos to peruse inside. The meals are flavorful, hearty, and wholesome, and they source a lot of organic produce, including organic wines and coffee (if you take it with milk, that's organic, too). **Known for:** huge Mountaineers' Breakfast served all day; organic produce; spectacular views. [$] *Average main: NZ$25* ✉ *3 Larch Grove, Aoraki/Mount Cook* ☎ *03/435–1890, 027/434–2277* 🌐 *www.mtcook.com.*

🛏️ Hotels

Aoraki Alpine Lodge

$$ | **HOTEL** | **FAMILY** | This lodge, run by a young local family, has twin, triple, and family rooms, all with private bathrooms and two have kitchenettes. **Pros:** bikes for rent; great guest lounge with fireplace; nice views from rooms. **Cons:** thin walls; not many meal options, so be prepared to buy groceries and cook; lots of stairs to climb. ⓢ *Rooms from: NZ$179* ✉ *111 Bowen Dr., Aoraki/Mount Cook* ☎ *03/435–1860* ⊕ *www.aorakialpinelodge.co.nz* ⍟ *No Meals* ⇲ *16 rooms.*

Aoraki Court Motel

$$$$ | **HOTEL** | **FAMILY** | Being fully self-catering is a huge plus with the lack of shopping in Mount Cook Village, and Aoraki Court Motel has 25 modern studio or two-bedroom units, all of which have kitchenettes. **Pros:** removed from the hordes of bus groups; option to cook your own meals; great walks right out the door. **Cons:** books up months in advance; expensive for what you get; free Wi-Fi is patchy due to the remote location. ⓢ *Rooms from: NZ$375* ✉ *26 Bowen Dr., Aoraki/Mount Cook* ☎ *03/435–1111* ⊕ *www.aorakicourt.co.nz* ⍟ *No Meals* ⇲ *25 rooms.*

Hermitage Hotel

$$$$ | **HOTEL** | Famed for its stupendous mountain vistas from most rooms (there are floor-to-ceiling windows), the Hermitage is also home to the Sir Edmund Hillary Alpine Centre, a tribute to one of the most famous New Zealanders. **Pros:** excellent in-house dining; unbeatable mountain views; most local activities are operated by the hotel. **Cons:** lots of tour groups in summer; no gym, pool, or spa; sprawling layout. ⓢ *Rooms from: NZ$310* ✉ *89 Terrace Rd., Aoraki/Mount Cook* ☎ *03/435–1809* ⊕ *www.hermitage.co.nz* ⍟ *No Meals* ⇲ *183 rooms.*

🏃 Activities

You don't want to miss the chance to see Sir Edmund Hillary's playground or the backdrop of Lord of the Rings. Climbing the icy slopes yourself will provide a day full of exercise and an unforgettable experience.

CLIMBING AND MOUNTAINEERING

Alpine Guides Ltd.

MOUNTAIN CLIMBING | Alpine Guides is NZ's longest-established mountain- and ski-guiding company. In summer, they offer guided ascents and climbing instruction—trips are 6–10 days. In winter, they have two heli-ski operations at Mount Cook and Methven, Ski the Tasman, and ski touring. Heli-hikes and day out rock climbing offered too. ✉ *81 Bowen Dr., Aoraki/Mount Cook* ☎ *03/435–1834* ⊕ *www.alpineguides. co.nz* ☜ *Rock climbing from NZ$180. Ascents from NZ$1425.*

FLIGHTSEEING

Flightseeing gives you an unparalleled view of the mountains, with the added thrill of landing on a glacier for a short walk. The light can be intensely bright in such dazzlingly white surroundings, so be sure to bring sunglasses. Generally, the best time for flights is early morning.

Air Safaris

AIR EXCURSIONS | Take a breathtaking 50-minute scenic flight over the two longest glaciers in New Zealand, the Tasman and the Murchison, as well as the Fox and Franz Josef glaciers. You'll pass high-country sheep farms and see Aoraki/Mt. Cook and the rain forests on the west side of the Main Divide. There are three helicopter charter options, too. ✉ *253 Tekapo-Twizel Rd., Tekapo* ☎ *03/680–6880* ⊕ *www.airsafaris.co.nz* ☜ *Flights NZ$395 per person; helicopter from NZ$295 per person.*

Helicopter Line

AIR EXCURSIONS | The Helicopter Line runs flights from 20 to 55 minutes, all of which include a remote landing, from Glentanner Park, about 20 km (12 miles) toward Pukaki from the Hermitage. You can land on the glaciers or high ski slopes, depending on the weather. ⊠ *Glentanner Park, State Hwy. 80, Aoraki/Mount Cook* ☎ *03/435–1801* ⊕ *www.helicopter.co.nz* ✆ *From NZ$270 per person.*

Mount Cook Ski Planes & Helicopters

AIR EXCURSIONS | Choose between a ski plane or helicopter; it's the way to go for a bird's-eye view of the stunning Mt. Cook. Flightseeing options include a 25-minute flight up the Tasman Glacier or a 45-minute flight with a glacier landing. Other options include the Mt Cook 360 and Grand Circle tour. ⊠ *Mount Cook Airport, State Hwy. 80, Aoraki/Mount Cook* ☎ *03/430–8026, 0800/800–702* ⊕ *www.mtcookskiplanes.com* ✆ *From NZ$249 per person.*

HIKING

The hiking trails spooling out from the visitor center range in difficulty and length, from the 10-minute Bowen Track to the 5½-hour climb to the 4,818-foot summit of Mt. Sebastopol. Several tracks can be done in running shoes and don't require hiking experience; the rest of the park's trails require some hiking experience, and the higher routes require serious mountaineering experience. The Mueller Hut route is a popular climb, taking three to four hours; a 28-bunk hut provides overnight accommodation (book and pay at the visitor center). The rewarding Hooker Valley walk, a four-hour round-trip, will take you across three swingbridges to the Hooker Glacier terminus lake, and the Tasman Glacier Lake walk gives an intimate view of New Zealand's longest glacier.

Twizel

65 km (40 miles) from Lake Tekapo, 40 km (25 miles) from Aoraki/Mt. Cook.

A service town to its core, Twizel was built in 1968 as a base for workers constructing a major hydroelectric power plant. When the hydroelectric scheme wrapped up, the residents fought to keep their town intact. Now it's a handy place for tourist overflow in the Aoraki/Mt. Cook area. There's good fishing to be done in its rivers and those hydro canals (a world record 42-pound brown trout was landed there in 2016). Birders should check with the visitor center about tours to the *kakī* aviary to see these striking endangered red-legged birds.

Twizel is close to five good-size boating and leisure lakes and has a couple of good places to eat. Having already passed Tekapo and Pukaki, you'll find Lake Ruataniwha a little tame. Lake Ohau is off the main road, but is another high-country fishing gem. A ski slope, Ohau Snow Fields, opens in July each winter, and a number of walks are in the nearby Ohau Forest Range.

GETTING HERE AND AROUND

Twizel is on State Highway 8. If you're driving south from Christchurch on Highway 1, turn onto Highway 8 at Fairlie. If you're coming north from Queenstown, follow Highway 6 to Cromwell, then turn onto Highway 8 and continue over the Lindis Pass to Twizel. InterCity Coachlines serve Twizel.

BUS INFORMATION InterCity Coachlines. ☎ *03/365–1113* ⊕ *www.intercity.co.nz.*

 **Restaurants**

Poppies Cafe

$$$$ | **CAFÉ** | **FAMILY** | Set in an extensive garden, Poppies has for years been a great place to eat, drink, socialize, and bask in the sun. Meat, seafood, pizza, and pasta are complemented by organic produce from the on-site vegetable garden along with fresh-baked bread and pizzas. **Known for:** lovely wine list; popularity with locals; summer alfresco dining. $ *Average main: NZ$32* ⊠ *1 Ben-more Pl., Twizel* ☎ *03/435–0848* ⊕ *www. poppiescafe.com.*

 ## Hotels

MacKenzie Country Hotel
$$ | HOTEL | Filled mainly by busloads of package tourists, the stone-and-timber buildings have comfortable rooms, and large lounges complete with welcoming fires, that make quite an impression in this otherwise nondescript town. **Pros:** comfortable rooms; reasonably priced; great location. **Cons:** tired decor; food isn't great; can be noisy. $ *Rooms from: NZ$170* ⊠ *2 Wairepo Rd., Twizel* ☎ *03/435–0869, 0800/500–869* ⊕ *www. mackenzie.co.nz* ⊙ *No Meals* ⊃ *108 rooms.*

Matuka Lodge
$$$$ | B&B/INN | This lodge is ideal for any-one wanting to enjoy the hikes and activ-ities of the Mt. Cook area; it's particularly nice for fly fishermen. **Pros:** incredible night sky; endearing hosts; rooms have verandas with mountain views. **Cons:** you have to drive to the nearest restaurant; 50-minute drive to Mt. Cook; books up quickly. $ *Rooms from: NZ$450* ⊠ *395 Glen Lyon Rd., Twizel* ☎ *03/435–0144* ⊕ *www.matukaluxurylodge.com* ⊙ *Closed June and July* ⊙ *Free Break-fast* ⊃ *4 rooms.*

Mount Aspiring National Park

Roads only skirt the edge of this huge park, which compels you to hike, boat, and fly to see it. Only a winged, hoofed supercreature could possibly see the majority of Aspiring's wilderness.

Daunting yet tantalizing: that's the magic draw of this unspoiled landscape.

At 878,566 acres, Mount Aspiring is the country's third-largest national park. The park's namesake mountain is only one of the numerous geological wonders. The area has yielded much *pounamu* or greenstone, and the famous Otago schist is featured in the architecture of the gate-way communities. One unusual stretch of peaks is known as the Red Hills, where the toxic minerals in the soil ren-dered the landscape barren (and a deep rusty red). Most of the park is marked by beech forest and wildflower-filled valleys, with snow tussock grasslands and alpine herb fields above the snowline. The park is home to the famous Routeburn Track, a three-day Great Walk, and dozens of shorter hikes. Gateway communities include lively Wanaka, which offers a multitude of choices for lodging, dining, shopping, and those rewarding posthike pints.

GETTING HERE AND AROUND
Gateway communities to the park are Wanaka, Makarora, Queenstown, Glenorchy, and Te Anau. These towns are all served by bus companies, and you can fly into Wanaka, Queenstown, and Te Anau. Major thoroughfares lead to them, and driving to any of these locations is a treat—the scenery in this part of the country is dramatic and roadside attractions include gorgeous vineyards, fresh-fruit stands, mountain passes, and white-water rivers. If you're en route to Wanaka from Queenstown you can stop and bungy jump, too.

For maps, information on local walks, and information on the three campgrounds and 20 backcountry huts in the park, con-tact or visit the Mount Aspiring National Park Office. Many tours to the park also leave from Wanaka.

VISITOR INFORMATION
**CONTACTS Mount Aspiring National Park
Office.** ⊠ *1 Ballantyne Rd., Wanaka*
☎ *027/269–6871* ⊕ *www.doc.govt.nz.*

 Activities

Siberia Experience
SKYDIVING | Siberia Experience has one
of the area's best adventure packages.
The journey begins with a funky little
yellow plane in a paddock-cum-airstrip.
After a breathtaking 25-minute journey
from Makarora, the pilot drops you off in
the pristine wilderness of Mount Aspiring
National Park's Siberia Valley and points
you to a trailhead. From there, embark
on a magnificent three-hour hike on a
well-marked, relatively easy trail. Finally,
a jet boat meets you at the Wilkin River
and returns you to Makarora. There is a
hut out there if you'd like to arrange overnight stays. ⊠ *5944 Haast Pass-Maka-
rora Rd., Makarora* ☎ *0800/345–666,
03/443–4385* ⊕ *www.siberiaexperience.
co.nz* ⊠ *NZ$415.*

Wanaka

*70 km (44 miles) northeast of Queens-
town, 140 km (87 miles) southwest of
Twizel.*

On the southern shore of Lake Wanaka,
with some of New Zealand's most striking mountains behind it, Wanaka is the
welcome mat for Mount Aspiring National Park. It has labeled itself the world's
first "Lifestyle Reserve" and is a favorite
of Kiwis on vacation, a smaller, quieter
alternative to Queenstown. The region
has two ski resorts, numerous trekking
and river-sports opportunities, and if you
arrive on a rainy day, you can hit a couple
of unusual cultural attractions. These
good points have not gone unnoticed,
and Wanaka is one of the fastest-growing
towns in New Zealand, with new housing
popping up in record time.

GETTING HERE AND AROUND
If you're coming from Queenstown, you
have two choices for getting to Wanaka:
go over the Crown Range for stunning
views (not recommended in snow) or
take the winding road along the Kawarau
River through wine and fruit country.
From Christchurch, drive south through
Geraldine and Twizel. Once in Wanaka it's
easy to park and walk around town, and
a taxi service can get you back to your
accommodations if you take advantage
of the nightlife. A short but pleasant drive
to the western side of the lake brings you
to Glendhu Bay. With nothing here but a
campground and fabulous mountain and
lake views, the real beauty in this drive
lies in the unspoiled calm and surreal
quiet (except in midsummer, when it is
packed full of vacationing locals). This
road also leads to the Aspiring region
and the Treble Cone ski area. Several bus
companies serve Wanaka.

BUS COMPANIES Ritches Transport.
☎ *03/4414471* ⊕ *www.ritchies.co.nz.*

TOURS
Deep Canyon
GUIDED TOURS | With the steep rugged
waterways of the Matukituki and Wilkin
valleys within easy reach, Wanaka is a
key spot in the country for canyoning.
Deep Canyon leads expeditions down
the Niger Stream, Wai Rata Canyon, the
Leaping Burn, and others. No experience
is necessary, but the minimum age is 12.
⊠ *100 Ardmore St., Wanaka* ☎ *03/443–
7922* ⊕ *www.deepcanyon.co.nz* ⊠ *From
NZ$260.*

Eco Wanaka
GUIDED TOURS | Visit the lake that's on
top of an island that's on top of the lake.
Wordplay aside, this is a journey to the
Mou Waho Island Nature Reserve in the
middle of Lake Wanaka; a guided nature
walk to the summit reveals the lake on
top and hopefully you'll hear or catch a
glimpse of rare native birds along the
way. On every trip, guests plant a native
tree. The guides are all locals, incredibly

knowledgeable, and guide walks all over this World Heritage Area, including the Rob Roy Glacier. ✉ *Lake Wanaka i-SITE, 103 Ardmore St., Wanaka* 🕿 *03/443–2869* 🌐 *www.ecowanaka.co.nz* 🎫 *From NZ$245.*

VISITOR INFORMATION

CONTACTS Lake Wanaka i-SITE Visitor Information Centre. ✉ *103 Ardmore St., Wanaka* 🕿 *03/443–1233* 🌐 *www.lake-wanaka.co.nz.*

Sights

Cardrona Distillery

DISTILLERY | Although it will be several years (around 2025) before their first batch of 10-year old single malt whisky is ready, Cardrona Distillery has released its three- and five-year-old batches, and a lovely range of spirits is ready to go, including vodka and gin. The setting, tucked away high in the Cardrona Valley, is beautiful, and they offer tours departing hourly 10–3 every day. **◼TIP➜ Book tours in advance if you're visiting during the holidays or long weekends.** ✉ *2125 Cardrona Valley Rd., Wanaka* 🕿 *03/443–1393* 🌐 *www.cardronadistillery.com* 🎫 *Tours NZ$25.*

Crossfire

OTHER ATTRACTION | **FAMILY** | At this excellent facility, you can have a hand at clay-bird or rifle shooting, archery, or get a basket of golf balls and swing away. It's fun for experts, and you get full instruction if you're a novice. There's an activity for everyone including the kids at the minigolf course. Largely undercover, this is a great option if the weather's misbehaving. ✉ *9 Mt. Barker Rd., opposite Wanaka Airport, Wanaka* 🕿 *03/443–5995* 🌐 *www.crossfirewanaka.co.nz* 🎫 *From NZ$13.*

Puzzling World

AMUSEMENT PARK/CARNIVAL | **FAMILY** | The cartoon-like houses built at funny angles with the Leaning Tower of Wanaka is just the start. Turn off here for a number of puzzling life-size brainteasers, including the amazing Tumbling Towers, Hologram Halls, and Tilted House, which is on a 15-degree angle (is the water really running uphill?). There's a 3D Great Maze to get lost in and a Sculptillusion gallery. For a break, head to the café, take on the puzzle of your choice, order a cup of coffee, and work yourself into a puzzled frenzy. ✉ *Hwy. 84, 188 Wanaka Luggate Hwy., Wanaka* 🕿 *03/443–7489* 🌐 *www.puzzlingworld.co.nz* 🎫 *NZ$25.*

Rippon Vineyard

WINERY | Lying spectacularly by the shores of Lake Wanaka, Rippon is one of the most photographed vineyards in the country. The vineyard's portfolio includes riesling, gewürztraminer, sauvignon blanc, and fine pinot noir. Head west from Wanaka along the lake on Mt. Aspiring Road for 4 km (2½ miles). ✉ *246 Mt. Aspiring Rd., Wanaka* 🕿 *03/443–8084* 🌐 *www.rippon.co.nz.*

Wanaka National Transport and Toy Museum

CHILDREN'S MUSEUM | **FAMILY** | Lying somewhere between a treasure trove and a junkyard, this compelling and slightly disorienting museum covers a full century of memories. One man's hoard featuring hundreds of vehicles, from cars and motorcycles to fire engines and aircraft, is almost overwhelming in its abundance. It can feel like there is just *too much stuff*. The toy collection is also enormous and includes display cabinets overflowing with Star Wars collectibles and many other well-known brands. ✉ *891 State Hwy. 6, Wanaka* ✈ *Beside Wanaka Airport* 🕿 *03/443–8765* 🌐 *www.nttmuseumwanaka.co.nz* 🎫 *NZ$20.*

Warbirds & Wheels

OTHER MUSEUM | There are around 30 privately owned classic cars on display here. Their 1934 Duesenberg is the star of the show, with Packards, Lincolns, and Fords among the mix. You may have heard of the NZ Fighter Pilots Museum—it's long gone but you can still see some of the planes here, including a WWI SE5A, Hawker Hurricane, Vampire, and Strikemaster. This is also home of New Zealand's largest contemporary touring art collection; at least half the collection stays here, including a fine collection of Grahame Sydney lithographs. There's also a retro diner serving breakfast and lunch daily. ✉ *11 Lloyd Dunn Ave., Wanaka Airport, Wanaka* ☎ *03/443–7010* 🌐 *www.warbirdsandwheels.com* 🎫 *NZ$20* 🕒 *Closed weekends.*

🍴 Restaurants

★ Bistro Gentil

$$$$ | **FRENCH** | Indulge with a modern fine French meal at this trendy bistro with lake and mountain views on the outskirts of Wanaka. The menu changes regularly, but the local Cardrona merino lamb is always there in one form or another, accompanied by heirloom vegetables and herbs from the kitchen garden. **Known for:** multicourse tasting menus; provincial olive oils; self-dispensed wine tastings. [$] *Average main: NZ$38* ✉ *76a Golf Course Rd., Wanaka* ☎ *03/443–2299* 🌐 *www.bistrogentil.co.nz* 🕒 *Closed Sun. and Mon.*

Kai Whakapai

$$$ | **ECLECTIC** | Just across the road from the lake, this is a great place to sit shoulder to shoulder with the locals for breakfast outside on a crisp sunny morning. The cafe's Māori name means "food made good," and the menu ranges from simple breakfast and lunch choices (coffee and croissants, salads, nachos, and kebabs) to beef ribs and rump roast for dinner. **Known for:** live music; local beers on tap; bustling crowds. [$] *Average main: NZ$22* ✉ *121 Ardmore St., Wanaka* ☎ *03/443–7795.*

Relishes Café

$$$$ | **NEW ZEALAND** | You could hit this lakeside spot for every meal of the day, starting with the bacon or salmon eggs Benedict or something house-made and delicious like their cinnamon sticky buns. The café focuses on local, seasonal fare (and caters to all dietary needs), and guests can expect good service and great coffee; check the blackboard at lunch and dinner for ever-changing specials like their pan-roasted Te Mana lamb with crispy potato gnocchi and vegetables, pecorino, and lemon gremolata. **Known for:** lake views; best coffee in town; local pinot of the week. [$] *Average main: NZ$32* ✉ *99 Ardmore St., Wanaka* ☎ *03/443–9018* 🌐 *www.relishescafe.co.nz.*

🛏 Hotels

Cardrona Hotel

$$ | **HOTEL** | This classic mid-19th-country hotel and pub, 20 minutes from Wanaka on the Crown Range Road, is the Cardrona après-ski spot for mulled wine in front of the outdoor fireplace. **Pros:** crowds leave after dinner; genuinely historic property; hearty dinner and drinks. **Cons:** no air-conditioning; squeaky floorboards; basic rooms. [$] *Rooms from: NZ$155* ✉ *Cardrona Valley Rd., Wanaka* ☎ *03/443–8153* 🌐 *www.cardronahotel.co.nz* 🛏 *17 rooms* 🍽 *No Meals.*

Edgewater

$$$$ | **HOTEL** | On the lakefront in a quiet area away from town, this property is great for a longer stay in Wanaka. **Pros:** spa and sauna; washer/dryer in some rooms; only accommodation in Wanaka on the lakefront. **Cons:** no air-conditioning; ½-hour walk from the middle of town; sprawling property. [$] *Rooms from: NZ$310* ✉ *54 Sargood Dr., Wanaka* ☎ *03/443–0011* 🌐 *www.edgewater.co.nz* 🍽 *No Meals* 🛏 *103 rooms.*

Lakeside Apartments

$$$$ | **APARTMENT** | **FAMILY** | These modern apartments provide nice family-size accommodations in a particularly central location. **Pros:** lovely pool; great location; use of a barbecue. **Cons:** pool area can get noisy; books up quickly; check

out by 10 am is a little early. $ Rooms from: NZ$349 ✉ 9 Lakeside Rd., Wanaka ☎ 03/443–0188 ⊕ www.lakesidewanaka. co.nz ⦿ No Meals ↻ 22 rooms.

★ Waiorau Homestead

$$$ | B&B/INN | From the peaceful rural setting and exceptionally good food to the warmth of the hospitality and finest linen on your bed, this is a memorable place to stay. **Pros:** owner is a fantastic chef; lovely guest lounge; outdoor hot tub. **Cons:** very limited availability; 20-minute drive from Wanaka; one room isn't en suite. $ Rooms from: NZ$270 ✉ 2127B Cardrona Valley Rd., Wanaka ☎ 03/443–2225 ⊕ www.waiorauhomestead.co.nz ↻ 3 rooms ⦿ Free Breakfast.

Wanaka Alpine Lodge

$$$ | B&B/INN | This hosted accommodation is in a purpose-built lodge, and the hosts are so warm and friendly, it always feels like you're staying with friends. **Pros:** freshly baked treats; lovely breakfast; large, modern rooms. **Cons:** some noise; quite far from town; some uphill walking to get to town. $ Rooms from: NZ$269 ✉ 114 Albert Town-Lake Hawea Rd., Wanaka ☎ 03/443–5355 ⊕ www.wanakaalpinelodge.co.nz ↻ 5 rooms ⦿ Free Breakfast ↺ No children under 13.

Wanaka Homestead Lodge and Cottages

$$$ | B&B/INN | The owners used local schist and timber from the farm buildings that once stood here to build their fine solar-powered lakeshore lodge. **Pros:** outdoor fireplace; all rooms have heat pumps which can be used as air-conditioning; hot tub. **Cons:** occasional noise from the road disrupts tranquility; longish walk into town; large communal breakfast table not for everyone. $ Rooms from: NZ$240 ✉ 1 Homestead Close, Wanaka ☎ 03/443–5022 ⊕ www.wanakahomestead.co.nz ↻ 7 rooms ⦿ Free Breakfast.

▼ Nightlife

Cinema Paradiso

FILM | FAMILY | The local institution, three-screen Cinema Paradiso is not your usual movie house—its seating includes couches, recliners, pillows, and even a yellow Morris Minor car or two. During intermission you can snack on homemade ice cream and warm cookies (straight out of the oven) or even have dinner with a glass of wine. Check the local paper or website for film details, and make sure you book ahead. ✉ 72 Brownston St., Wanaka ☎ 03/443–1505 ⊕ www.paradiso.net.nz ⊠ NZ$16.50.

The Cow

WINE BARS | If you want a late bite and a good bottle of wine, pop into The Cow on Post Office Lane for good garlic bread, pizza, and spaghetti. It's a very comfortable place, modeled in local stone and heavy timber, just like the original Cow in nearby Queenstown. In winter, the open fireplace does an incredible job of warming the bones (and the wine). Feel free to add commentary to their restroom chalkboard walls. ✉ Post Office La., 33 Ardmore St., Wanaka ☎ 03/443–4269 ⊕ www.thecowpizza.co.nz.

Lake Bar

PUBS | This bar's in an iconic spot at the top of Ardmore Street. Sit inside or out and soak up the amazing views of the lake and mountains; if you get hungry they turn out pub-style tapas and lunch, as well as dinner with a separate kids' menu. If you just want a pint in the sun, or after dark, the Lake Bar is a great place for visitors and locals alike. ✉ 155 Ardmore St., Wanaka ☎ 03/443–2920 ⊕ www.lakebar.co.nz.

Water Bar

BARS | This is a very popular upscale bar with a deck on the lakefront and an outdoor fire in winter. Head here for late-night entertainment. It has an attractive and hearty food menu, and it often hosts live music acts. ✉ 145 Ardmore St.,

Wanaka ☎ 03/443–4345 ⊕ www.water-barwanaka.co.nz.

 Activities

With the base of Mount Aspiring National Park on Wanaka's doorstep, renting a bicycle isn't such a bad idea. Soon mountains will surround you and then swingbridges will connect you to the trails, where you'll embark on foot.

BIKING

Rent a bicycle and explore along the shores of Lake Wanaka, and out along the Clutha River toward Albert Town. There are many places to rent bikes and get trail maps including **Outside Sports** (*17-23 Dunmore St.*) or **Thunderbikes** (*16 Helwick St.*). Both the Deans Bank Track near Albert Town, a scenic 11½ km (7 miles) intermediate-level loop track, and the Plantation or "Sticky Forest," as locals call it, have good networks of mountain bike trails for all abilities.

FISHING

Locals will tell you that fishing on Lake Wanaka and nearby Lake Hawea is better than at the more famed Taupo area. You won't want to enter that argument, but chances are good you'll catch fish if you have the right guide. Fishing is year-round.

If you're not keen on hiring a guide, you can rent fly-fishing gear and buy your fishing license at **Southern Wild** (*10 Helwick St.*) or **Lakeland Adventures** (*in the Log Cabin, 100 Ardmore St.*).

Telford Fishing and Hunting Services

FISHING | Fishing and hunting guide Gerald Telford will tailor an experience just for you, whether you're in the mood to go fly-fishing, experience a multiday fishing expedition, or go hunting in the wild. Gerald has been doing this for more than 30 years and will show you the very best spots. ✉ *37 Domain Rd., Hāwea Flat, Wanaka* ☎ 027/517–4006 ⊕ www.flyfishhunt.co.nz ✉ From NZ$450.

RAFTING
Fresh Adventures

WHITE-WATER RAFTING | At Fresh Adventures you can do some white-water rafting at a calmer pace down the Hawea River, which is a great trip for families. If you want something more challenging, go for their Clutha trip. Both full-day and half-day trips are available and leave from the visitor center in Wanaka. It's closed May through August. ✉ *Lake Wanaka i-SITE Visitor Centre, 103 Ardmore St., Wanaka* ☎ 021/766–612 ⊕ www.freshadventures.nz ✉ From NZ$150.

SCENIC FLIGHTS

The weather around Wanaka is clear much of the time, which has allowed it to become a scenic-flight base for fixed-wing planes and helicopters. Flights take in Mt. Cook and the West Coast glaciers, the Mt. Aspiring area, Queenstown, and Fiordland.

Aspiring Helicopters

AIR EXCURSIONS | It may be hard to believe the scenery can get any better, but fasten your seat belt and prepare to be enthralled. Aspiring Helicopters does scenic and adventure trips ranging from a 20-minute local flight to a three-hour trip to Milford Sound. If you can, the longer flight to Milford goes via Mt. Aspiring and includes a landing at a high-alpine lake and on a glacier. If you're after the serious wilderness spots to climb, ski, bike, fish, or even get married—they'll take you there, too. ✉ *2211 Wanaka-Mount Aspiring Rd., Wanaka* ☎ 03/443–7152 ⊕ www.aspiringhelicopters.co.nz ✉ From NZ$210 per person.

SKIING

With reliable snow and dry powder, Wanaka has some of the best skiing and snowboarding in New Zealand. Cardrona and Treble Cone are the two biggest winter-sports resorts, and Snow Farm specializes in cross-country skiing. For more information about skiing and snowboarding in the area, check out ⊕ www.lakewanaka.co.nz.

Cardrona Alpine Resort

SKIING & SNOWBOARDING | Cardrona, 34 km (21 miles) southwest of Wanaka, is great for families with its wide open trails, a kids' ski school and activity center, kid- and beginner-friendly lifts, and food outlets. A special "heavy metal" trail pours on the rails and jumps, and there are two half pipes that are well used by international snowboarding teams (American snowboard star Shaun White landed his first back-to-back cork 10-80 in competition on one of them). The season is roughly mid-June–early October. A bonus at Cardrona is the 15 apartments up on the mountain, but you'll need to book early to get in. Daily shuttles are available from Wanaka and Queenstown. ⊠ *Cardrona Valley Rd., Cardrona* ☎ *03/443–7341* ⊕ *www.cardrona.com* 🎫 *1-day lift pass NZ$140.*

Treble Cone

SKIING & SNOWBOARDING | Treble Cone, 19 km (11½ miles) west of Wanaka, is the South Island's largest ski area, with lots of advanced trails and off-piste skiing. You can purchase a single-day lift pass, or if you're planning to ski a few days you can buy a Flexi pass, which makes it a bit cheaper. You can call their Snow Phone to get up-to-date snow reports or check their website. If you're not a skier it's still worth getting a scenic chairlift ride on the home basin chairlift; the view is sensational. ⊠ *Wanaka-Mount Aspiring Rd., Wanaka* ☎ *03/443–1406* ⊕ *www. treblecone.com* 🎫 *Single-day lift pass NZ$140.*

SKYDIVING

Skydive Wanaka

SKYDIVING | Wanaka Airport is a hub for all kinds of aviation adventures. Perhaps the most exciting of these is skydiving. If you've considered skydiving, this is a spectacular place to do it. You can jump from 9,000, 12,000, and 15,000 feet, with photos and video of your jump available for an extra fee. ⊠ *Wanaka Airport,*

14 Mustang La., Wanaka ☎ *03/443–7207* ⊕ *www.skydivewanaka.com* 🎫 *From NZ$279.*

WALKING AND TREKKING

The Mount Aspiring National Park provides serious hiking and mountaineering opportunities, including Wilkins Valley, Makarora River, and Mt. Aspiring tracks and trails.

Diamond Lake Track

HIKING & WALKING | The complete Diamond Lake Track takes three hours and starts 25 km (15½ miles) west of Wanaka, also on the Glendhu Bay–Mt. Aspiring road. The track rises to 2,518 feet at Rocky Peak, passing Diamond Lake along the way. If you've got time for only a short walk, take the one that heads to the lake; it takes only 20 minutes. The Diamond Lake area is also popular with mountain bikers and rock climbers. ⊠ *Matukituki Valley Rd., Wanaka* ☎ *03/443–7660* ⊕ *www.doc.govt.nz.*

Lake Wanaka Outlet Track

HIKING & WALKING | FAMILY | You get maximum views for minimal challenge on one of the prettiest local trails, which meanders along the Clutha River from the Lake Wanaka Outlet to Albert Town. This is a kid-friendly route; it's also fly-fisherman-, bicyclist-, and picnicker-friendly. It takes about an hour one way. ⊠ *Outlet Track, Wanaka.*

Mt. Iron

HIKING & WALKING | If you have time for only one walk, Mt. Iron, rising 780 feet above the lake, is relatively short and rewarding. The access track begins 2 km (1 mile) from Wanaka, and the walk to the top takes 45 minutes. You can descend on the alternative route down the steep eastern face. ⊠ *124 Wanaka-Luggate Hwy., Wanaka.*

Queenstown

111 km (68 miles) southeast of Wanaka, 481 km (300 miles) southwest of Christchurch.

Set on the edge of the glacial Lake Wakatipu, with stunning views of the sawtooth peaks of the Remarkables mountain range, Queenstown is the most popular tourist stop on the South Island. Once prized by the Māori as a source of greenstone, the town boomed when gold was discovered in the Shotover River during the 1860s; the Shotover quickly became famous as "the richest river in the world." By the 1950s, Queenstown had become the center of a substantial farming area, and with ready access to mountains, lakes, and rivers, the town has since become the adventure capital of New Zealand. Today, New Zealanders' penchant for bizarre adventure sports culminates in Queenstown; it was here that the sport of leaping off a bridge with a giant rubber band wrapped around the ankles—bungy jumping—took root as a commercial enterprise. On a short walk along Shotover and Camp streets you can sign up for anything from white-water rafting and jet boating to heli-skiing, parachuting, and ATV adventures. Queenstown unabashedly caters to adrenaline junkies, so height, G-force, and thrill factor are emphasized. Want to go on a nice rope swing? Queenstown has the world's biggest—120 meters (394 feet) long—in the Nevis Canyon; the ride is 120 kph (75 mph). In late June, the Queenstown Winter Festival brings the winter-sport frenzy to a climax, with musical performers, ski-slope antics and races, and serious partying.

If you're not an extreme adventure enthusiast, you might recoil a bit and view the city with a cynical eye. Luckily there's a side to Queenstown that doesn't run on pure adrenaline: a large network of peaceful walks and several world-class golf courses. In addition, you can always find a nice café, have wine by the lake, and sample the cuisine.

GETTING HERE AND AROUND

Highway 6 enters Queenstown from the West Coast; driving time for the 400-km (250-mile) journey from Franz Josef is eight hours. It takes approximately 1½ hours to drive between Queenstown and Wanaka; the drive between Queenstown and Te Anau generally lasts a little over two hours. Bus and airplane service are also available between Christchurch and Queenstown. The town is small and fun for seeing on foot. If you're out and about at night, there are several taxi services available.

AIRPORTS Queenstown Airport. ✉ *Sir Henry Wigley Dr., Queenstown* ☎ *03/450–9031* ⊕ *www.queenstownairport.com.*

AIRPORT TRANSFERS Super Shuttle Queenstown. ☎ *09/522–5100, 0800/748–885 toll-free in NZ* ⊕ *www.supershuttle. co.nz.*

BUS CONTACTS Frankton Terminus. ✉ *Kawarau Rd., Frankton.* **InterCity Coachlines.** ☎ *03/442–4922 for Queenstown services* ⊕ *www.intercity.co.nz.* **The Station—Queenstown.** ✉ *At Camp and Shotover Sts., Queenstown.*

RENTAL CARS Apex. ✉ *26 Shotover St., Queenstown* ☎ *03/442–8040* ⊕ *www.apexrentals.co.nz.* **Avis.** ✉ *Terminal Bldg., Queenstown Airport, Queenstown* ☎ *03/442–3808* ⊕ *www.avis.co.nz.* **GO Rentals.** ✉ *Queenstown Airport., Queenstown* ☎ *03/441–4340* ⊕ *www.gorentals. co.nz.*

TOURS

Milford Sound Scenic Flights

AIR EXCURSIONS | The operator runs small Cessna aircraft to Mt. Cook, Mt. Aspiring, and Milford Sound. They also do private charters to create an itinerary of your choice. ✉ *39 Lucas Pl., Frankton* ☎ *0800/207–206* ⊕ *www.milfordflights. co.nz* ✉ *From NZ$225.*

Nomad Safaris

DRIVING TOURS | Nomad Safaris runs half-day 4WD and quad-bike trips to the old gold-rush settlements (or their remains), Skippers Canyon, and Macetown. Try your hand at gold panning—they don't plant gold so any success or disappointment is genuine. Another off-roading trip takes you to see some of the areas filmed for the Lord of the Rings trilogy, and there's also the option of booking an e-bike tour of Queenstown vineyards or guided half- and full-day tours along the Routeburn Track. All tours include tea/coffee stops. ✉ *37 Shotover St., Queenstown* ☎ *03/442–6699, 0800/688–222* ⊕ *www.nomadsafaris.co.nz* ✉ *From NZ$195.*

Queenstown Heritage Tours

GUIDED TOURS | Take a historical tour to Skippers Canyon in Queenstown Heritage's comfortable air-conditioned vehicles with delicious snacks; one of the highlights is the outdoor picnic prepared while you stroll through the restored Skippers Schoolhouse. They also run separate wine-lovers tours in Gibbston Valley in the afternoon. If you book both as a combo it's cheaper and includes lunch and tastings at three wineries. ✉ *174 Glenda Dr., Unit 10, Queenstown* ☎ *03/409–0949* ⊕ *www.queenstown-heritage.co.nz* ✉ *From NZ$180.*

Real Journeys

SPECIAL-INTEREST TOURS | For a wide choice of fly-drive-cruise tour options to Milford and Doubtful sounds from Queenstown, Te Anau, and Milford, check out Real Journeys. ■**TIP**➔ **Do the overnight cruise if you really want to experience both sounds at their best: early in the morning and in the evening.** The Doubtful Sound cruise is longer and more remote. The boat's engines are cut for a few moments of silence, and what a moment it is—makes you realize how little true silence most of us have in our lives. The food's superb, too, and is all-inclusive. ✉ *Steamer Wharf, Beach St.,* *Queenstown* ☎ *0800/656–501 within NZ, 03/442–7500* ⊕ *www.realjourneys.co.nz.*

VISITOR INFORMATION

CONTACTS Queenstown i-SITE Visitor Information Centre. ✉ *Clocktower Bldg., 22 Shotover St. at Camp St., Queenstown* ☎ *03/442–4100* ⊕ *www.queenstownsite.com.*

 Sights

The vineyards across Central Otago and into the Queenstown and Wanaka areas constitute the world's southernmost, and the country's highest, wine region and are particularly noted for producing outstanding pinot noir. Specifically, Bannockburn, Gibbston Valley, and Lowburn are home to big plantings. There are nearly 100 wineries in the region with more than 4,830 acres planted in vines.

Amisfield Winery & Bistro

WINERY | Step into this expansive winery and bistro and enjoy stunning lake and mountain views. Both the wines and the restaurant have earned accolades over the years. Go for a memorable Trust the Chef lunch or dinner. Wine-tastings are available at the cellar door; the pinot noir, aromatic whites such as riesling and pinot gris, and the *méthode traditionelle* are all worth sampling. ✉ *10 Lake Hayes Rd., Queenstown* ☎ *03/442–0556* ⊕ *www.amisfield.co.nz* ✉ *Tasting NZ$10, refunded with purchase of bottle.*

Chard Farm

WINERY | The Chard Farm vineyard perches on a rare flat spot on the edge of the Kawarau Gorge, not far from Gibbston Valley and opposite AJ Hackett Bungy. Its location and access road are beautiful, and you'll find an excellent portfolio of wines to taste including pinot noir, chardonnay, gewürztraminer, pinot grigio, and riesling. ✉ *205 Chard Rd., Queenstown* ☎ *03/442–6110* ⊕ *www.chardfarm.co.nz.*

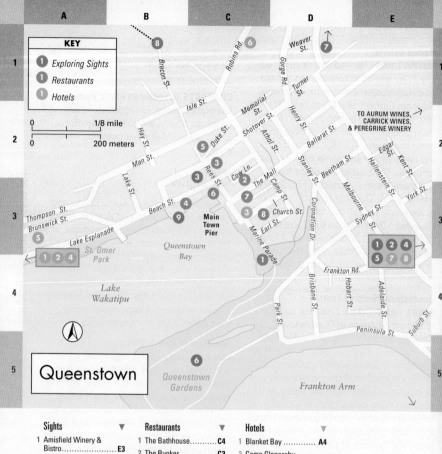

Queenstown

Sights ▼

1 Amisfield Winery & Bistro **E3**
2 Chard Farm **E3**
3 Fear Factory **C2**
4 Gibbston Valley Wines **E3**
5 Mt. Difficulty **E3**
6 Queenstown Gardens ... **C5**
7 Skippers Canyon **D1**
8 Skyline Gondola **B1**
9 T.S.S. EARNSLAW **B3**

Restaurants ▼

1 The Bathhouse **C4**
2 The Bunker **C3**
3 Fergburger **C2**
4 Ivy & Lola's Kitchen & Bar **B3**
5 Jervois Steak House **C2**
6 Vudu Cafe **C3**
7 Winnie's **C3**
8 Yonder **C3**

Hotels ▼

1 Blanket Bay **A4**
2 Camp Glenorchy Eco Retreat **A4**
3 Eichardt's Private Hotel **C3**
4 Heritage Queenstown **A4**
5 QT Queenstown **A3**
6 Queenstown Park Boutique Hotel **C1**
7 The Rees **E4**
8 The Sherwood **E4**

Fear Factory

OTHER ATTRACTION | A scary addition to the adventure scene in Queenstown, Fear Factory challenges you to walk through their haunted house in the center of town. Not for kids—thousands of people have chickened out (just yell "chicken," and you don't have to continue). It's best to do this half-hour activity with friends. Those under 15 must be accompanied by an adult. ⊠ *54 Shotover St., Queenstown* ⊕ *www.fearfactory.co.nz* ⊠ *NZ$30.*

★ **Gibbston Valley Wines**

WINERY | The wine-making industry in Central Otago began with the vines that were first planted here. The best-known vineyard in Central Otago, Gibbston Valley Wines is a beautiful spot for lunch and wine tasting. There are cheese platters and tasty sandwiches through to a full à la carte menu with wine recommendations. You can even taste wines in a cool, barrel-lined cave with cave tours on the hour. If you can't get out to the winery, Gibbston Valley also has a café in Arrowtown, where you'll get hint of what you've missed. ⊠ *1820 State Hwy. 6, Gibbston* ✛ *20-min drive east of Queenstown on State Hwy. 6* ☎ *03/442–6910* ⊕ *www.gibbstonvalley.com* ⊠ *Wine-cave tour and tasting NZ$19.50.*

Mt. Difficulty

WINERY | You could spend a lot of time in the tasting room with the large range of good wines on offer here, or you can keep it simple and grab one of their tasting trays, featuring a selection complete with notes. There are some sweet dessert wines that can only be bought at the cellar door to consider as well. Make sure you stay for lunch. Staffers are friendly and know their stuff, and the view out from Bannockburn is pure Central Otago. ⊠ *73 Felton Rd., Cromwell* ☎ *03/445–3445* ⊕ *www.mtdifficulty.nz* ⊠ *Tastings from NZ$10.*

Queenstown Gardens

GARDEN | The public Queenstown Gardens on the waterfront peninsula are always worth a quiet stroll. A popular picnic spot, it's one of the few places in Queenstown that hasn't changed. There's an easy path to wander along to wear off some of those calories you've consumed during your stay. Rent or bring your own disc and have a toss at the country's first Frisbee golf course. ⊠ *Park St., Queenstown.*

Skippers Canyon

CANYON | One of the enduring attractions in the area is the drive up Skippers Canyon. Harking back to the days when the hills were filled with gold diggers, the Skippers Road was hand carved out of rock, and it reaches into the deep recesses of the Shotover Valley. It's breathtakingly gorgeous, but you could also be breathtakingly scared: there's a good reason that rental car companies don't insure you if you drive on this twisty, narrow, unpaved road fraught with slips and vertical drops. It's usually best to visit this place on a tour. ⊠ *Skippers Rd., Queenstown.*

Skyline Gondola

VIEWPOINT | Get the lay of the land by taking the Skyline Gondola up to the heights of Bob's Peak, 1,425 feet above the lake, for a smashing panoramic view of the town and across the lake to the Remarkables. You can also get there by walking the One Mile Creek Trail. Once there, watch the paragliders jump off the summit for their slow cruise back down to lake level. There is a café and a restaurant with a great buffet at the summit plus a Kiwi *haka*, or Māori song-and-dance show, most evenings. For something a little faster, there's a luge ride, weather permitting. If even that isn't exciting enough, you can bungy jump from the summit terminal. ⊠ *Brecon St., Queenstown* ☎ *03/441–0101* ⊕ *www.skyline. co.nz* ⊠ *From NZ$44.*

★ **T.S.S. Earnslaw**

FARM/RANCH | FAMILY | This lovely old ship is more than 100 years old, and one of the world's few coal-fired steamships still operating. It's in superb condition partly because it's only been on this lake and the water's so pure. T.S.S. (Twin Screw Steamer) *Earnslaw* runs across to Walter Peak and back on a 1½-hour cruise. You can do a stopover at Walter Peak High Country Farm and watch a sheep shearing and farm dog demonstration. But the best trip is to go to the Colonel's Homestead Restaurant for dinner (or lunch); it's an exceptional buffet—make sure you leave room for the sumptuous selection of desserts. The cruise back into Queenstown's particularly beautiful when the sun's going down. ✉ *Steamer Wharf, Beach St., Queenstown* ☎ *03/442–7500, 0800/656–501 NZ only* 🌐 *www.realjourneys.co.nz* 🎫 *Cruises from NZ$70.*

🍴 Restaurants

At first glance Queenstown's little side streets seem full of party bars and pizza joints, but that's because all the really great spots are hidden away or down at Steamer Wharf, which juts out into Lake Wakatipu. Some places aren't easy to find, so ask if you can't find what you're looking for.

The Bathhouse

$$$ | **ECLECTIC** | Built to commemorate the coronation of King George V, this early 1900s bathhouse on the beach now turns out breakfast, lunch, fresh scones, tapas, and dinner from its tiny kitchen. Many people find it by accident as they walk to the Queenstown Gardens, but it's worth seeking out deliberately. **Known for:** some of the best staff in town; unbeatable location; log fire in winter. [$] *Average main: NZ$30* ✉ *38 Marine Parade, Queenstown* ☎ *03/442–5625* 🌐 *www.bathhouse.co.nz.*

The Bunker

$$$$ | **ECLECTIC** | A loungey vibe with log fires, leather armchairs, and an impressive wine list make the Bunker a particularly cozy dining location. Dinner is an all-night affair, especially if you continue with drinks in their upstairs bar; there's even a special Taste of the South degustation menu if you really want to indulge. **Known for:** James Bond-esque vibe; late-night hotspot; excellent wine pairings. [$] *Average main: NZ$42* ✉ *14 Cow La., Queenstown* ☎ *03/441–8030* 🌐 *www.thebunker.co.nz.*

Fergburger

$$ | **BURGER** | A Queenstown institution, the famous Fergburger gets mentioned in media around the world. It began life as a burger bar serving from a hole in the wall and kept growing; now there's a permanent queue stretching outside. **Known for:** long lines at lunch; enormous and legendary burgers; late-night dining. [$] *Average main: NZ$15* ✉ *42 Shotover St., Queenstown* ☎ *03/441–1232* 🌐 *www.fergburger.com.*

Ivy & Lola's Kitchen & Bar

$$$$ | **ECLECTIC** | Feast your eyes on a collection of relics from the 1940s to '60s, right down to the mismatched crockery, and enjoy good food, great service, and a lovely atmosphere. The cuisine here is a delightfully eclectic mix, with flavors from New Zealand and around the world. **Known for:** lakeside dining; excellent lamb of the day; generous portions. [$] *Average main: NZ$34* ✉ *Steamer Wharf, 88 Beech St., Queenstown* ☎ *03/441–8572* 🌐 *www.ivyandlolas.com.*

★ Jervois Steak House

$$$$ | **STEAKHOUSE** | Dine here and find out why New Zealand is so proud of its beef and lamb: you could take it to the next level with the Wagyu beef, but honestly it's hard to beat the standard Jervois fillet, with onion rings on the side and delicious sauces. Steak is the undisputed hero here, but like the great American steak houses on which Jervois models itself, there's fabulous seafood too, and even a quality vegetarian menu. **Known for:** elegant steak-house atmosphere; pricey cuts of beef; extremely knowledgeable staff. [$] *Average main: NZ$48* ✉ *Sofitel Complex, 8 Duke St.,*

Queenstown ☎ *03/442–6263* 🌐 *www.jervoissteakhouse.co.nz.*

Vudu Cafe

$$ | **CAFÉ** | You'll be fighting the locals for a breakfast seat at this Queenstown institution, thanks to its lakefront seating and delicious array of counter food. Eggs Benedict with a classic coffee is probably the most common breakfast order in New Zealand, and this is perhaps the best in the area. **Known for:** healthy options; big breakfast crowds; coffee to go (and enjoy by the lake). [$] *Average main: NZ$20* ✉ *16 Rees St., Queenstown* ☎ *03/441–8370* 🌐 *www.vudu.co.nz* ⏲ *No dinner.*

Winnie's

$$$ | **PIZZA** | This is a long-standing local favorite restaurant and bar, with a winning combination of excellent pizza, pool tables, and beer. At night it becomes a happening spot with DJs and dancing, and it's extremely popular with backpackers. **Known for:** warm winter hideout; late-night parties; retractable roof. [$] *Average main: NZ$28* ✉ *7 The Mall, Mall St., Queenstown* ☎ *03/442–8635* 🌐 *www.winnies.co.nz.*

Yonder

$$$ | **INTERNATIONAL** | In a lovely old cottage in the middle of town, Yonder has outdoor seating in front; a café-style area in the middle; and, finally, a restaurant, bar, and live venue in the rear. The menu is inspired by the countries of origin of the chefs, and it changes to match the seasons and what's fresh. **Known for:** eclectic global menu; bright, welcoming atmosphere; friendly to those with dietary restrictions. [$] *Average main: NZ$26* ✉ *14 Church St., Queenstown* ☎ *03/409–0994* 🌐 *www.yonderqt.co.nz* ⏲ *No dinner Mon. and Tues.*

Hotels

Blanket Bay

$$$$ | **B&B/INN** | Near the end of a long road, this imposing schist lodge is surrounded by thousands of acres of sheep-station land. **Pros:** celebrity hideaway; spectacular property; unbeatable views. **Cons:** dining area outdated; 40-minute drive to Queenstown; very expensive. [$] *Rooms from: NZ$1950* ✉ *4191 Glenorchy-Queenstown Rd., Queenstown* ☎ *03/441–0115* 🌐 *www.blanketbay.com* 🛏 *12 rooms* 🍴 *Free Breakfast.*

★ **Camp Glenorchy Eco Retreat**

$$$ | **B&B/INN** | **FAMILY** | Built to the exacting standards of the Living Building Challenge, Camp Glenorchy is an inspiration to those with an interest in sustainable building and living. **Pros:** beautiful decor, art, and furniture throughout; huge outdoor fireplace; inspirational and educational ethos. **Cons:** shower time is limited to save energy; 45 minutes from Queenstown; eco-living comes with a price tag. [$] *Rooms from: NZ$245* ✉ *34 Oban St., Glenorchy* ☎ *03/409–0401* 🌐 *www.theheadwaters.co.nz* 🛏 *14 rooms* 🍴 *Free Breakfast.*

Eichardt's Private Hotel

$$$$ | **HOTEL** | Patronized by gold miners during the 1860s, Eichardt's is now an elite boutique resort hotel. **Pros:** exceptional house bar; centrally located; great service. **Cons:** can get some noise from neighbors; breakfast restaurant is small and open to public; busy street front, especially at sunset. [$] *Rooms from: NZ$1350* ✉ *2 Marine Parade, Queenstown* ☎ *03/441–0450* 🌐 *www.eichardts.com* 🍴 *Free Breakfast* 🛏 *10 rooms.*

Heritage Queenstown

$$$$ | **HOTEL** | Situated at the bottom of Fernhill, the Heritage is quieter than other local hotels and has panoramic views of the Remarkables and Lake Wakatipu. **Pros:** great service; very comfortable beds; pleasant rooms. **Cons:** some rooms lack views; due for a refurbishment; 10-plus minute walk to downtown. [$] *Rooms from: NZ$340* ✉ *91 Fernhill Rd., Queenstown* ☎ *03/450–1500*

⊕ www.heritagehotels.co.nz ⤬ 175 rooms ⦿ No Meals.

★ QT Queenstown

$$$$ | **HOTEL** | This genuinely fun and quirky hotel with countless small touches ensures a memorable stay. **Pros:** fun and fanciful decor; very close to town; large rooms and bathrooms. **Cons:** no gym; not all rooms offer lake views; limited parking. ⓢ *Rooms from: NZ$485* ✉ *30 Brunswick St., Queenstown* ☎ *03/450–3450* ⊕ *www.qthotelsandresorts.com* ⤬ *69 rooms* ⦿ *No Meals.*

Queenstown Park Boutique Hotel

$$$$ | **HOTEL** | This plush hotel is located in the center of town, and you can walk to the lake, shopping, dining, and tour departure points in just five minutes. **Pros:** amazing hospitality; great location; tasty predinner drinks and canapes. **Cons:** limited parking; street-view rooms can be noisy; no gym or pool. ⓢ *Rooms from: NZ$530* ✉ *21 Robins Rd., Queenstown* ☎ *03/441–8441* ⊕ *www.queenstownparkhotel.co.nz* ⦿ *Free Breakfast* ⤬ *19 rooms.*

The Rees

$$$$ | **HOTEL** | Named for Queenstown's first European settler—who oversaw the birth of the town during the 1860s gold rush—this hotel's accommodations range from rooms and apartments to multibedroom lakeside residences. **Pros:** amazing wine lounge; exceptional restaurant and wine selection; hourly shuttles to town. **Cons:** no pool; quite far from the town center; no air-conditioning. ⓢ *Rooms from: NZ$355* ✉ *377 Frankton Rd., Queenstown* ☎ *03/450–1100* ⊕ *www.therees.co.nz* ⦿ *No Meals* ⤬ *155 rooms.*

The Sherwood

$$ | **HOTEL** | Built on the bones of an older motor inn, this hotel has reinvented itself as an eco-conscious alternative to the standard hotel experience. **Pros:** wonderfully repurposed property; great lake views (on request); focus on relaxation

and recharging. **Cons:** can be noisy when there's live music; rooms are quite dark; far from town center. ⓢ *Rooms from: NZ$200* ✉ *554 Frankton Rd., Queenstown* ☎ *03/450–1090* ⊕ *sherwoodqueenstown.nz* ⤬ *78 rooms* ⦿ *No Meals.*

 Nightlife

After days spent testing limits, visitors cram Queenstown's clubs and bars. They often end up mingling with the friendly locals next to fireplaces and catching up again as they walk between the popular venues, which are all close together. Grab a copy of the free weekly paper, the *Mountain Scene,* or check out the *Source* magazine, a monthly gig guide available in most cafés and bars or on Facebook.

Bardeaux

WINE BARS | In winter, Bardeaux has that upscale mountain-après-ski atmosphere; even in summer there's a fair chance the fire will be roaring. There's a wide selection of whiskey and wine, and they know how to fix you up a cocktail. It's a pleasing bar that's good for a quiet, intimate evening. ✉ *Eureka Arcade off The Mall, Queenstown* ☎ *03/442–8284* ⊕ *www.goodgroup.co.nz.*

Minus 5° Ice Bar

BARS | Ice bars have become popular over the past few years, and it's great fun if you've never tried one—even just for the beautiful ice sculptures. They deck you out in jackets and gloves prior to entering. In summer, it's a good reminder of how close to Antarctica you are, and, in winter, it just adds to the alpine resort experience. It costs NZ$30 to get in, $35 with a cocktail and $40 for two cocktails. ✉ *Steamer Wharf, 88 Beach St., Queenstown* ☎ *03/442–6050* ⊕ *www.minus5icebar.com.*

Searle Lane

BREWPUBS | With its roaring fire, good food, and quirky decor, Searle Lane is a popular Queenstown spot. There's plenty of beer on tap and a good selection of wine by the glass. They do a mean cocktail, too. The food is made for sharing with hearty choices; their specialty is rotisserie chicken, which is seriously good. ⊠ *15 Church St., Queenstown* ☎ *03/441–3934* ⊕ *www.searlelane.co.nz.*

Smiths Craft Beer House

BREWPUBS | This bar offers the best range of New Zealand and international beer in town, including the stand-out local beer, Queenstown's own Altitude Brewing. There's a great pub food menu of burgers and sandwiches and a nice balcony from which to enjoy the hustle and bustle of Queenstown. ⊠ *53 Shotover St., Queenstown* ☎ *03/409–2337.*

The World Bar

BARS | This is a great place for drinks in the sun or inside by the huge open fire on colder days. Later in the evening, it turns into a rowdy venue, particularly on the weekend, with DJs playing most nights and live music Friday and Sunday, plus an acoustic open mic on Sunday nights. The famed cocktails are served in teapots, and you can get good gastro pub food throughout the day and early evening. ⊠ *12 Church St., Queenstown* ☎ *03/450–0008* ⊕ *www.theworldbar. co.nz.*

🏃 Activities

You'll find many people raving about their bungy jumping experience or their jet boat tour from the day before. Any activity you choose around Queenstown will bring you deep into the scenery that you can only ogle from the wharf or roadside viewpoints.

BUNGY JUMPING

AJ Hackett Bungy

SKYDIVING | This is where bungy really took off in New Zealand, at the original jump site: Kawarau Bridge, 20 minutes from Queenstown on State Highway 6. Even if you don't plan on taking the leap it's worth heading there to watch from the viewing decks. There's also a zip ride that's way easier on the nerves but still gives something to write home about. Those who graduate from the 142-foot plunge might like to test themselves on the Nevis Bungy, suspended 440 feet above the Nevis River, or try out what they claim is the world's biggest swing. If you're short on time, there's always the Ledge by the Skyline Gondola where you can also jump or swing. Be sure to check age, height, and weight requirements. ⊠ *The Station, Camp and Shotover Sts., Queenstown* ☎ *0800/286–4958 NZ only, 03/450–1300* ⊕ *www.bungy.co.nz* 🕮 *From NZ$143.50.*

Shotover Canyon Swing

LOCAL SPORTS | For those who think bungy jumping doesn't keep the adrenaline pumping long enough, the Shotover Canyon Swing gives a terrifying jump with an added scenic boost. Choose your jump style—go forward, backward, or tied to a chair—and leave the edge of a cliff 358 feet above the Shotover Canyon. Price includes transfers to/from town, and age, height, and weight requirements apply. ⊠ *34 Shotover St., Queenstown* ☎ *03/442–6990* ⊕ *www.canyonswing. co.nz* 🕮 *NZ$179.*

HIKING

Several scenic walks branch out from town. For a history lesson with your ramble, head to the **Time Walk,** entering through an iron gateway on the Queenstown Hill trail. Narrative panels line the route; it takes about two hours, and you'll feel good when you see the view at the top. The **Ben Lomond Track** takes you to one of the highest peaks in the basin. Take the gondola to the Bob's Peak summit, then follow signs to the saddle and the steep climb to the peak (5,730 feet). You'll need to be reasonably fit, and this can be a full-day walk, so make sure you bring all the necessary supplies.

★ Queenstown Trail

HIKING & WALKING | For a wonderful journey around the Queenstown area, take a look at the trail map (see website)

Jet boats offer a thrillingly wet way to enjoy the Queenstown area's natural beauty.

of this 120-km (74.5-mile) walking and cycling trail and start planning. The trail is well built, and there are plenty of places to hire all the biking equipment you need (also on its website). The trail takes you to Arrowtown and the wineries of Gibbston, past two lakes and three rivers, over some interesting bridges, and always through stunning scenery. You can do it all or just parts of it. Queenstown is the lowest point on the trail so if you want to make it a little easier for yourself, start your trip in Arrowtown. ⊕ *www. queenstowntrail.co.nz.*

HORSE TREKKING
High Country Horses
HORSEBACK RIDING | Glenorchy is already an incredibly peaceful and beautiful place, and it's even better when enjoyed from horseback. High Country Horses offers half-day, full-day, and overnight tours, including a Lord of the Rings filming location tour that wanders through native beech forest where climactic battle scenes from *The Lord of the Rings: The Fellowship of the Ring* were

shot. They cater to all riding abilities and offer transfers from Queenstown. Maximum rider weight applies. Rides start at NZ$175. ⊠ *243 Priory Rd., Glenorchy* ☎ *03/442–9915* ⊕ *www.highcountryhorses.nz.*

Moonlight Stables
HORSEBACK RIDING | Moonlight Stables offers a 1½-hour ride with spectacular views of the mountains and rivers around the Wakatipu–Arrow Basin. Ride across an 800-acre deer farm in Australian stock saddles and western saddles. Both novice and experienced riders are welcome, and private rides can be arranged. Transportation from Queenstown is provided; allow 2½ hours round-trip. ⊠ *69 Morven Ferry Rd., Arrow Junction, Queenstown* ☎ *03/442–1229* ⊕ *www.moonlightstables.co.nz* ⊠ *From NZ$120.*

JET BOAT RIDES
★ Dart River Wilderness Jet
BOATING | FAMILY | With Dart River you can get an unrivaled look at the Te Wai Pounamu World Heritage area and rugged Mount Aspiring National Park,

together one of the most spectacular parts of South Island. Their route includes jet boating on the upper and lower Dart River, along with a bit of walking and a back-road tour of the "Paradise" area. The Funyak (inflatable kayak) option takes you upstream by jet boat, then you paddle gently downstream, exploring braided rivers and the Rockburn Chasm on the way. Start your adventure from their office in Glenorchy, or catch a shuttle bus, departing daily from Queenstown for the 45-minute ride to the boats. Rates include transfer. ⊠ *45 Mull St., Glenorchy* ☎ *0800/327–853 New Zealand only, 03/442–9992* ⊕ *www.dartriver.co.nz* ⊠ *NZ$189.*

Hydro Attack

BOATING | Strap into the F-16–style cockpit of this watercraft styled to look like a shark and fly across and under Lake Wakatipu. This is the world's first commercial operation using the Seabreacher X watercraft, and your expert pilot will tailor your trip to suit your comfort levels, from scenic cruise to wild ride. Riders are restricted by height and weight, and you need to be somewhat flexible to board the craft. It's not recommended if you are subject to seasickness. ⊠ *Lapsley Butson Wharf, Beach St., Queenstown* ☎ *027/477–9074* ⊕ *www.hydroattack. co.nz* ⊠ *NZ$129.*

KJet

BOATING | With the sun sparkling off the lake, wind whistling past, and traveling way faster than you had imagined, this is good holiday fun. KJet takes you 42 km (27 miles) on Lake Wakatipu and down two rivers, the Kawarau and Shotover, with some exciting spins along the way. Boats leave from the Main Town Pier where there's also an interesting underwater observatory. Reservations are recommended. ⊠ *Main Town Pier, Marine Parade, Queenstown* ☎ *03/442–6142* ⊕ *www.kjet.co.nz* ⊠ *NZ$135.*

Shotover Jet

BOATING | Shotover Jet's famous red boats lead high-speed, heart-stopping rides in the Shotover River canyons; it's got exclusive rights to operate in these waters. The boat pirouettes within inches of canyon walls. The boats are based at the Shotover Jet Beach beneath the historic Edith Cavell Bridge, a 10-minute drive from Queenstown. If you don't have transport, a free shuttle makes frequent daily runs. Reservations are essential. ⊠ *Gorge Rd., over Edith Cavell Bridge at Arthur's Point, Queenstown* ☎ *03/442–8570, 0800/746-868 New Zealand only* ⊕ *www.shotoverjet.com* ⊠ *From NZ$129.*

MOTORSPORTS

Highlands Motorsport Park

AUTO RACING | Fulfill your dream of being a race car driver at Highlands. There's a range of activities including go-kart racing, self-drive hot laps, and ride-along hot laps. The Highlands Taxi is a Porsche Cayenne Turbo driven by a professional racer. The first lap is taken slowly, and the driver talks about the facility; the second lap is full speed ahead. There is also a supercar option, if you want to go faster, as well as a range of purpose-built race cars. Located in Cromwell, Highlands Motorsport Park is a 45-minute drive from Queenstown on State Highway 6, and you can call Highlands to arrange a free shuttle from Queenstown. The Highlands National Motorsport Museum is here, too. ⊠ *Corner State Hwy. 6 and Sandflat Rd., Cromwell* ☎ *03/445-4052* ⊕ *www.highlands.co.nz* ⊠ *From NZ$129.*

RAFTING

Rafting is generally an adult thrill, with age restrictions for children. You'll need your swimsuit and a towel, but all other gear, including wet suit, life jacket, helmet, and wet-suit booties, is provided by the rafting companies. Instructors spend quite a bit of time on safety issues and paddling techniques before you launch.

★ Go Orange Rafting

RAFTING | This company runs white-water rafting in the Queenstown area year-round, with trips on the Shotover (Class III–IV) and Kawarau (Class II–III) rivers. You can double the action with either a helicopter or jet boat combo and save on the individual price of both tours. Prices start at NZ$199. ✉ *35 Shotover St., Queenstown* ☎ *03/442–7340* ⊕ *www.goorange.co.nz.*

Serious Fun River Boarding

WATER SPORTS | This is serious—for the adventurous and those with surfing or water experience. You'll get kitted out in a full wet suit, helmet, life jacket, and fins. There's an introduction to river surfing on calm water first. Then grab your bodyboard and prepare to surf the waves of Queenstown's stunning Kawarau River. Where your guide ends up taking you will depend on the conditions, but the Kawarau River has plenty of white water. They'll pick you up from town. ✉ *37 Shotover St., Queenstown* ☎ *03/442–5262* ⊕ *www.riverboarding.co.nz* 🖅 *NZ$235.*

SCENIC FLIGHTS

Over the Top Helicopters

SKYDIVING | Over the Top Helicopters runs a diverse selection of flights in their executive-style helicopters. Options include glacier and alpine ski slope landings and scenic tours above Queenstown, the Remarkables, Fiordland, and Milford and Doubtful sounds. They'll also deliver you to a three-hole mountaintop golf course, dish up a pavlova on a peak, or take you to fly-fishing spots absolutely miles from anywhere. Heli-skiing or ecotours as far away as Stewart Island are also available. ✉ *Blue Hangar, 10 Tex Smith La., Queenstown* ☎ *03/442–2233, 0800/123–359* ⊕ *www.flynz.co.nz* 🖅 *From NZ$240 per person.*

SKIING

Coronet Peak

SKIING & SNOWBOARDING | Queenstown's original ski resort, 20 minutes from town, rocks day and night to a ski and snowboard crowd that returns year after year. Not only is it accessible, but it also has a veritable army of snow cannons to keep the snow topped up. It has a skiable area of 700 acres, a vertical drop of 1,360 feet, a high-speed six-seater, two express quads, and a T-bar, as well as four learner conveyor lifts in the learners' area. The season usually runs June to October. Night skiing is available on Wednesday, Friday, and Saturday night from late June to early September. Ski shuttles depart regularly from Queenstown Snow Centre. ✉ *Coronet Peak Station Rd., Queenstown* ☎ *03/441–1516* ⊕ *www.coronetpeak.co.nz* 🖅 *Day pass from NZ$139.*

The Remarkables

SKIING & SNOWBOARDING | **FAMILY** | Just across the valley, the Remarkables is a higher ski area that's a bit more of a drive but has something to suit all abilities, from seven terrain parks to wide sunny slopes to serious black runs. The vertical drop here is 1,160 feet, and it has a fast-speed six-seater and three quads. It's a great place to take kids, with good vantage points to watch them on the learners' slopes. It's a 45-minute drive from Queenstown, or you can catch the Ski Shuttle from the Queenstown Snow Centre in town. ✉ *The Remarkables Ski Area, Queenstown* ☎ *03/441–1456* ⊕ *www.theremarkables.co.nz* 🖅 *NZ$139.*

SKYDIVING

NZONE Skydive

SKYDIVING | Here's a different way of taking in the view of Queenstown—from a tandem skydive. At 15,000 feet the Earth is already taking on that round from-out-of-space look about it that says you're a long way up. You don't have to jump from that high: there are 12,000- and 9,000-feet options. Either way it's an unforgettable experience, helped by Jumpmasters who make you feel at ease (relatively speaking). Weight restrictions apply. ✉ *35 Shotover St., Queenstown* ☎ *03/442–5867* ⊕ *www.nzoneskydive.co.nz* 🖅 *From NZ$299.*

A former gold-rush town, Arrowtown now only sees gold in the autumn leaves.

ZIP-LINING
Ziptrek Ecotours

ZIP-LINING | Ziptrek is billed as the world's steepest zip line, descending 30 stories in height in six stages. You can zip every which way (upside down if you want) among the trees on the hills above Queenstown. It's a very scenic adventure, and, as each zip line stops at a tree platform, you learn about the ecology of the area. Most of all, it's good fun; but not for anyone who's scared of heights. Not suitable for children under six. ⊠ *45 Camp St., Queenstown* ☎ *03/441–2102, 0800/947–873 New Zealand only* ⊕ *www.ziptrek.com* ✉ *From NZ$99.*

Arrowtown

22 km (14 miles) northeast of Queenstown, 105 km (66 miles) south of Wanaka.

Arrowtown is tucked into a corner at the foot of the steep Crown Range. It's a quaint village that takes pride in the history of the area, with around 70 buildings from the original gold rush, a partially restored Chinese village from the 1880s, and a small but fantastic museum. Jack Tewa, or Māori Jack, as he was known, found gold along the Arrow River in 1861, and when William Fox, an American, was seen selling large quantities of the precious metal in nearby Clyde shortly afterward, the hunt was on. Eventually, a large party of prospectors stumbled on Fox and his team of 40 miners. The secret was out, miners rushed to stake their claims, and Arrowtown was born. On the first gold escort in January 1863 a whopping 12,000 ounces of gold were carried out. At the height of the rush there were more than 30,000 hardy souls in this tiny settlement. After the gold rush ended in 1865, the place became another sleepy rural town until tourism created a second boom.

Each April, when the trees are at their most spectacular, Arrowtown celebrates the Autumn Festival, which includes the New Zealand Gold Panning championships. On a stroll along Buckingham Street, you can stop in the old post and telegraph office, still open for business. Take time to explore some of the lanes and arcades, which are filled with cafés and boutiques, and to drop in to the Jade & Opal Factory shop to see hand-carving done on-site and to Patagonia chocolates to see chocolate being made (the ice cream here is delicious, too).

GETTING HERE AND AROUND

Arrowtown is a 20-minute drive from Queenstown, and you can take a bus there. Exploring the town is easily and enjoyably done on foot. If you'd like to venture out toward the old gold-mining settlement, Macetown, you can walk or bike if you're a hearty sort (it's 16 km [10 miles] and entails 22 river crossings). A great way to explore the region is in a 4WD vehicle. Nomad Safaris provides a number of 4WD tour options. For a beautiful start to the day, go up in a balloon and see Arrowtown and the Wakatipu Basin from the air.

The local bus network, Orbus, is NZ$10 per trip from the airport, NZ$5 for other trips, or NZ$2 per trip with a GoCard. The card costs NZ$5 and has a minimum top up of NZ$10. It's definitely worth getting the card if you plan on riding the bus more than once or twice. Depending on your destination, you may need to switch buses at the Frankton hub.

BUS COMPANIES Orbus Queenstown.
✉ *Queenstown* ☎ *0800/672–8778*
⊕ *www.orc.govt.nz.*

VISITOR INFORMATION

CONTACTS Arrowtown Visitor Information Centre. ✉ *Lakes District Museum, 49 Buckingham St., Arrowtown* ☎ *03/442–1824* ⊕ *www.arrowtown.com.*

 Sights

Chinese Settlement

MUSEUM VILLAGE | FAMILY | In a less-visited part of the town is the former Chinese settlement. Chinese miners were common on the goldfields, brought in to raise a flagging local economy after the gold rush abated, but local prejudice from resident Europeans forced them to live in their own separate enclave. Some of their tiny 19th-century buildings, which have been restored, were built of sod, which endures well in the dry climate; others were built of layered schist stone, with roofs of corrugated iron or tussock thatch. Ah Lum's store (also restored) was built in a style typical of the Canton Delta region of China and operated until 1972. The settlement is a worthwhile part of any day-walk in the area. ✉ *Bush Creek, west end of town, Arrowtown* ✑ *Free.*

★ Lakes District Museum

HISTORY MUSEUM | FAMILY | Don't leave Arrowtown without dropping in to this small but very cleverly constructed museum. It gives a great insight into the history of the area, with artifacts of the gold-rush days and even a whole streetscape underground, complete with Victorian schoolroom, bakery, and blacksmith. There's also an information center, small bookstore, and gallery. You can even rent a pan for NZ$3 and get gold-panning tips to try your luck in the nearby Arrow River. When your patience frays and your hands go icy, keep in mind that a hobby prospector found a 10-ounce nugget in this very river in 2006. (He sold it on eBay for NZ$15,000). ✉ *49 Buckingham St., Arrowtown* ☎ *03/442–1824* ⊕ *www.museumqueenstown.com* ✑ *NZ$10.*

🍴 Restaurants

The Chop Shop Food Merchants

$$$ | INTERNATIONAL | The Chop Shop is tucked away in a back alley, and locals don't want you to know about it for fear

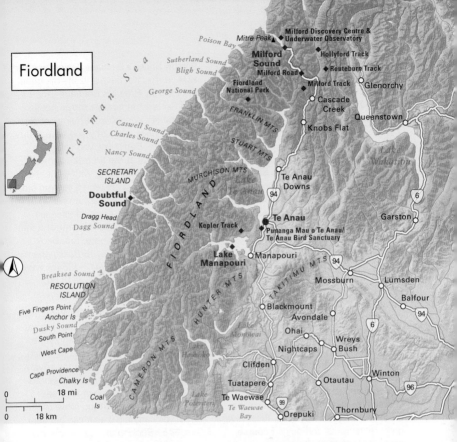

Fiordland

they won't get a seat for themselves. It serves an eclectic mix of international dishes for breakfast and lunch, including some good spicy options. **Known for:** very busy so waits are common; strong coffee; Turkish eggs. $ *Average main: NZ$25* ⊠ *7 Arrow La., Arrowtown* ☎ *03/442–1116.*

★ La Rumbla

$$$ | **TAPAS** | With the owners either cooking in the kitchen or out front making sure this is the best experience it can be, this is one of those rare places that's got all the elements right: food, service, and atmosphere. It's a tapas restaurant, but with generous servings; the food is a mixture of Spanish and all sorts of interesting savory influences. **Known for:** reservations usually necessary; great cocktails; good vegan options. $ *Average main: NZ$30* ⊠ *54 Buckingham St.,* *Arrowtown* ☎ *03/442–0509* ⊕ *www.* *larumbla.co.nz* ⊗ *Closed Mon.*

Patagonia Chocolates

$ | **SOUTH AMERICAN** | **FAMILY** | Owned by a local Argentine couple who missed the desserts of their homeland, Patagonia is the best place around to buy ice cream, chocolates, cakes, and other sweets. They have locations in Queenstown and Wanaka, too. **Known for:** South American confections; chili hot chocolate; specialty chocolates. $ *Average main: NZ$8* ⊠ *31* *Ramshaw La., Arrowtown* ☎ *03/409–* *8636* ⊕ *www.patagoniachocolates.co.nz.*

Provisions of Arrowtown

$$$ | **CAFÉ** | Set in a historic miner's cottage, Provisions gets its name from the range of gourmet preserves they make. The welcoming atmosphere and lovely garden make it a delightful place to have breakfast or lunch. **Known for:** legendary

sticky buns; pretty garden setting; break-fast supplies to go. $ *Average main: NZ$22* ✉ *65 Buckingham St., Arrowtown* ☎ *03/442–0714* ⊕ *www.provisionsofar-rowtown.co.nz.*

 ## Hotels

★ Arrowtown House Boutique Hotel
$$$$ | B&B/INN | Somewhere between a boutique hotel and a bed-and-breakfast, Arrowtown House offers arguably the best service in Arrowtown. **Pros:** great hosts; lovely mountain views; quiet, central location. **Cons:** quite expensive; hard to get a booking in peak season; style is slightly dated. $ *Rooms from: NZ$500* ✉ *10 Caernarvon St., Arrow-town* ☎ *03/441–6008* ⊕ *www.arrow-townhouse.co.nz* �androoms ❮O❯ *Free Breakfast.*

Millbrook Resort
$$$$ | RESORT | A 20-minute drive from Queenstown, this glamorous resort has a special appeal for golfers: a 36-hole course first designed by New Zealand professional Sir Bob Charles. **Pros:** several great restaurants; terrific golf course; plenty of amenities. **Cons:** hotel rooms are dated; sprawling and somewhat impersonal; no air-conditioning. $ *Rooms from: NZ$360* ✉ *1124 Malaghans Rd.,* ☎ *0800/800–604, 03/441–7000* ⊕ *www.millbrook.co.nz* ➦ *160 rooms* ❮O❯ *No Meals.*

 ## Nightlife

The Blue Door
WINE BARS | What goes on behind the Blue Door? Whiskey, wine, and cocktails, served by knowledgeable and chatty (when it's quiet) staff. Sit in a dark corner near the fire, or at the bar. Set in a beautiful old stone building with candles burning around the room, it's the perfect place for a nightcap before walking back to your accommodation. ✉ *18 Bucking-ham St., Arrowtown* ☎ *03/442–0415* ⊕ *www.facebook.com/TheBlueDoorBar.*

Dorothy Brown's Boutique Cinema and Bar
FILM | It may not have a flashy marquee, but Dorothy Brown's Boutique Cinema and Bar is a memorable movie house. The theater doesn't seat many people, but the chairs are cushy and have plenty of legroom. Better yet, you can get a glass of wine at the fireplace bar and bring it with you, along with a cheese-board to nibble from, and if you run out, all screenings have an intermission. The schedule mixes Hollywood releases with art and international films, and they have 3D screenings here, too. Book ahead—it's popular. ✉ *18 Buckingham St., Arrowtown* ☎ *03/442–1964* ⊕ *www.dorothybrowns.com* ✉ *NZ$18.50.*

The Fork and Tap
PUBS | In this cozy historic building there are 20 beers and ciders on tap, a great selection of local Central Otago wine, and a hearty pub-style menu for lunch and dinner. If you're looking for a lively spot to enjoy a beer and share stories after a big day of skiing or sightsee-ing, this is it. Don't sit too close to the fire if you can help it as it can get very hot. ✉ *51 Buckingham St., Arrowtown* ☎ *03/442–1860* ⊕ *www.theforkandtap.co.nz.*

 ## Activities

There are several spectacular walks—**Tobin's Track, Sawpit Gully,** and the **Lake Hayes Walk**—to raise the fitness levels and give you a feeling for where you are. You can get details on all of them from the Lakes District Museum Information Centre. For easier ambles, take the **Arrow River Trail** or the **Bush Creek Trail.** If you want a real challenge, tackle the hike out to the old gold settlement, Macetown. Make sure you take your own picnic: although you might hear the Macetown Bakehouse mentioned, be aware the place is a ghost town now and there are only remnants of the settlement.

You can rent a bike from places like Arrowtown Bike Hire or Queenstown Bike Tours. Grab a map and head to Gibbston Valley for lunch or some wine tasting; the trail is well maintained, and there are several interesting bridges to cross.

There are also three quite distinct golf courses within a 10-minute drive of Arrowtown that offer some of the most scenic golf holes you'll ever play. The most accessible is the Arrowtown Golf Course, but there's also Millbrook and the Hills, which need booking well in advance.

Te Anau

172 km (106 miles) southwest of Queenstown.

Lake Te Anau (tay-*ah*-no), which is 53 km (33 miles) long and up to 10 km (6 miles) wide, is the largest lake in New Zealand after Lake Taupo. The town of Te Anau, on the southern shores, serves as a base for Fiordland National Park. From Te Anau, you can set out on sightseeing trips by bus, boat, or plane to Milford and Doubtful sounds, or take off on one of the park's superb hiking trails. Of these, the most accessible to town is the Kepler Track. The town itself is very quiet and rural, but it does have its attractions and is very picturesque. It's busiest in summer; in winter, some cafés and shops close or reduce their hours.

GETTING HERE AND AROUND
BUS CONTACTS InterCity Coachlines.
☎ *03/442–4922* ⊕ *www.intercity.co.nz.*
Te Anau Bus Station. ⊠ *2 Miro St., Te Anau.*

VISITOR INFORMATION
Fiordland National Park Visitor Centre
⊠ *Lakefront Dr., Te Anau* ☎ *03/249–7924* ⊕ *www.doc.govt.nz.*

◉ Sights

★ Fiordland National Park
NATIONAL PARK | Encompassing more than 3 million acres of wilderness, Fiordland is the country's biggest national park. Nearly a million people visit each year to see playful dolphins and rain forest–coated mountains, but most converge on Milford and Doubtful sounds, the park's stars. Don't worry—the park is massive enough to easily absorb the crowds. The scenery actually quiets them, too: entire boatloads of visitors have been known to just *hush* out on the water. Sand flies and rain (along with your job, breaking news, and the rest of the world) will seem like tiny nuisances when you behold Milford Sound, with Mitre Peak rising along the coast and waterfalls tumbling into the sea. *I see the falls,* said one returning visitor, *and everything just falls away.* ⊕ *www.fiordland.org.nz/about-fiordland/fiordland-national-park.*

Milford Road
SCENIC DRIVE | If there was nothing to see at the end of this road it would still be worth the journey. It's a spectacular route, on one of the highest highways in New Zealand, traveling through mossy beech forests, past waterfalls and grand sweeping valleys. The road is narrow and winding at times, so allow at least 2½ hours. Stop for some great photo ops at Mirror Lakes, Knobs Flat, and Lake Gunn before reaching the Divide, a watershed between rivers flowing both east and west and the starting point for the Routeburn Track. When you reach the Homer Tunnel think of the unemployed workers who began building it as a relief project in 1935 using picks and shovels. Before making the trip, check the transit website (*www.milfordroad.co.nz*) or phone (*0800/444–449*) for avalanche warnings (snow and trees), and, between May and November, come equipped with tire chains, which you can rent in any Te Anau service station. Take care and drive to the conditions, and if you're

Planning Your Trip to Fiordland

Best Time to Go

Spring and summer (October through April) are the best, but busiest, times to go. Still there are many opportunities to commune quietly with the park, such as kayaking, scuba diving, or hiking. Even if you only have time for a cruise, it is still more than worthy of a visit. The drive into Milford in itself is also well worth the trip.

Best Ways to Explore

Cruise the sound. Milford and Doubtful sound cruises run all day and include scenic, nature, and overnight trips. Most of Milford's day trips get you close to a waterfall. Kayak on Milford Sound (guided or not) for eye-level views of New Zealand fur seals, penguins, and dolphins. For high-seas adventure, charter a fishing trip in the Tasman Sea.

Walk the finest walk. New Zealand's most famous walk, the Milford Track, has been called the "Finest Walk in the World." Take the guided walk option if you want to stay warm and dry and have your meals cooked for you; otherwise it requires a bit of gumption and organization—and boat transport from either end—to complete the four-day track. The experience, which includes rain forest, glacial lakes, mountains, and several massive waterfalls, like Sutherland Falls (1,904 feet), is worth the effort. There are other wonderful walks, including the 60-km (37-mile) Kepler Track, which is accessible from Te Anau. Sights along this four-day walk include the Luxmore Cave, beech forests, mountains, and rivers.

Scuba. The thick layer of rainwater, pigmented by forest tannins, that sits atop the sounds' saltwater filters the sunlight and simulates deep-sea darkness. This means creatures of the deep can be found in shallow waters. Scuba divers come here for uncommonly accessible glimpses of spiny sea dragons, sea pens, and black coral. If you don't want to suit up, visit the Milford Discovery Centre & Underwater Observatory.

Drive Milford Road. Most visitors drive to the park themselves, traveling the scenic Milford Road. Places to stop and enjoy short walks include Mirror Lake, which lives up to its name on calm days, and the Avenue of the Disappearing Mountain. And don't drive past the Chasm walk in your haste to get to Milford Sound; it's worth the short walk (20-minutes round-trip).

just not comfortable, you can always take a bus from Te Anau or Queenstown. ■TIP➔ **There have been a number of accidents on this stretch of road caused by overseas drivers, who are unfamiliar with the conditions and are driving too fast or on the wrong side of the road.**

Punanga Manu o Te Anau/Te Anau Bird Sanctuary

WILDLIFE REFUGE | The lakeshore Te Anau Bird Sanctuary gives you the chance to preview some of the wildlife you're likely to encounter when hiking in Fiordland. The center houses one of New Zealand's rare flightless birds, the takahe, which was once thought to be extinct. The lakeside walk to the center makes for a pleasant one-hour stroll. The birds here have either been injured or involved in captive rearing programs. The injured birds are rehabilitated and sent back to the wild if they're strong enough. Entry's free, but if you have a NZ$1 or NZ$2 coin to donate it helps with the upkeep. ✉ *Manapouri Rd., 1 km (½ mile) west of Te Anau* ☎ *03/249–0200* 🎟 *Donation requested.*

Te Anau Glowworm Caves

CAVE | FAMILY | Boats and walkways take you through a maze of caves containing underground whirlpools, waterfalls, and gushing streams. Then you'll reach the inner, quieter part, and, on the cave walls, glowworms shine like constellations in a clear night sky. It's a surreal experience. The caves can only be reached by water. This is a lovely family trip that takes around 2½ hours. Don't miss it if you're going through Te Anau; if you're short on time you can do it in the evening. ✉ *Real Journeys, 85 Lakefront Dr., Te Anau* ☎ *03/249–6000, 0800/656–501* 🌐 *www.realjourneys.co.nz* 🎟 *NZ$99.*

Restaurants

★ Redcliff Café & Bar

$$$$ | NEW ZEALAND | Don't let the modest, homey exterior and laid-back attitude of the staff fool you: this restaurant produces the best meals in Te Anau (it was a favorite hangout spot for the cast and crew of The Lord of the Rings during local filming). The menu is strong on wild game and seafood, and if you stay after dinner, you might get to enjoy live music at the bar. **Known for:** can get booked up so smart to reserve ahead; local venison and hare; lively, cozy, and comfortable atmosphere. [$] *Average main: NZ$36* ✉ *12 Mokonui St., Te Anau* ☎ *03/249–7431* 🌐 *www.theredcliff.co.nz.*

Sandfly Cafe

$$ | CAFÉ | This is the perfect place to load up on coffee and a hearty breakfast before hitting the road to Milford Sound or Queenstown. It's a simple menu, but the house-made counter food is well presented and delicious. **Known for:** outdoor seating; best coffee in town; friendly and fast service. [$] *Average main: NZ$18* ✉ *9 The Lane, Te Anau* ☎ *03/249–9529* 🕒 *No dinner.*

Hotels

Blue Thistle Cottages

$$$ | APARTMENT | A five-minute drive past town on the road to Milford, these four cozy and comfortable cottages make a good base for local exploration and an early start if you're driving to Milford Sound. **Pros:** outdoor seating areas; cottage kitchens have fridges and microwaves; beautiful views. **Cons:** outside of walking distance to Te Anau; a little dated; slow Wi-Fi. [$] *Rooms from: NZ$245* ✉ *168 Te Anau Milford Hwy., Te Anau* ☎ *03/249–8338* 🌐 *www.bluethistle-cottages.com* 🍴 *No Meals* 🛏 *4 cottages.*

Cinema Suites

$$$$ | B&B/INN | This one-of-a-kind, loft-style accommodation sitting above the boutique Fiordland Cinema and Black Dog Bar includes a welcome bottle of wine and tickets to a screening of *Ata Whenua Fiordland Experience* downstairs. **Pros:** quiet; in the heart of everything; full air-conditioning. **Cons:** quite expensive; only one room; requires good mobility. [$] *Rooms from: NZ$400* ✉ *7 The Lane, Te Anau* ☎ *03/249–8551* 🌐 *www.thecinemasuites.co.nz* 🍴 *Free Breakfast* 🛏 *1 room.*

Fiordland Lodge

$$$$ | B&B/INN | A few kilometers out of Te Anau on the road to Milford Sound, glass, stone, and timber blend together to make a stylish place to spend a few days. **Pros:** views are incredible; cabins offer great privacy; outstanding meals. **Cons:** some noise possible between interconnecting rooms; it's 5 km (3 miles) out of town; Wi-Fi slows when busy. [$] *Rooms from: NZ$840* ✉ *472 Te Anau–Milford Hwy., Te Anau* ☎ *03/249–7832* 🌐 *www.fiordlandlodge.co.nz* 🛏 *12 rooms* 🍴 *Free Breakfast.*

Radfords on the Lake

$$$$ | MOTEL | The fabulous lake views and the personal touches make this lakefront motel a great place to stay; it also has spacious, modern rooms and is a few minutes' walk from town. **Pros:** nice barbecue area; incredible service; great location. **Cons:** there's a road between the units and the lake; popular over summer so need to book in early; ground floor faces car park. $ *Rooms from: NZ$334* ✉ *56 Lakefront Dr., Te Anau* ☎ *03/249–9186* ⊕ *www.radfordsonthelake.co.nz* ❍❙ *No Meals* ⇨ *14 rooms.*

Activities

Although Te Anau seems small, its lake serves as a larger and beautiful landmark. Trails around Fiordland reveal the natural blue color of the park's water with looming mountains in the distance.

HIKING

Fiordland National Park Visitor Centre

HIKING & WALKING | Information, transport options, and maps for the plethora of hikes near Te Anau, including the Kepler Track, can be obtained from the Fiordland National Park Visitor Centre. ✉ *Lakefront Dr., Te Anau* ☎ *03/249–7924* ⊕ *www.doc.govt.nz.*

Kepler Track

HIKING & WALKING | The 60-km (37-mile) Kepler Track loops from the south end of Lake Te Anau and takes three to four days to complete. It goes through extensive beech forest, past limestone bluffs, and provides incredible views of the South Fiord and Te Anau Basin. It's a moderate walking trail, but there are a number of hills to climb and a steep zigzag downhill section that takes a couple of hours and can be hard on the knees. It also includes an alpine crossing, and you should beware of high wind gusts while crossing the exposed saddle above the bush line. If you're on a tight schedule, take a day hike to the Luxmore and Moturau huts. Huts cost NZ$65 per person in summer, and you need to book them; check online or call the Great Walks booking office for advice and conditions. ✉ *Te Anau* ☎ *03/249–8514 Great Walks booking* ⊕ *www.doc.govt.nz.*

JET BOATING

Fiordland Jet

BOATING | Fiordland Jet zips you up the Upper Waiau River, where the forest comes down to the river's edge. Once on lovely Lake Manapouri, you'll stop to experience the serene quiet. The company also pairs its jet boat rides with helicopter flights, including an alpine landing in the Kepler Mountain Range. Once you reach Manapouri, you could take off on a floatplane to see Doubtful Sound or Lake Te Anau by air or be whisked back to base by helicopter. You can even combine a jet boat down the Upper Waiau River with a riverside mountainbike ride back to Te Anau along the newly formed Lake2Lake Cycle Trail. ✉ *84 Lakefront Dr., Te Anau* ☎ *0800/253–826 NZ only* ⊕ *www.fjet.nz* ⛴ *From NZ$159.*

KAYAKING

Go Orange Kayaks

CAMPGROUND | If you're an intrepid adventurer at heart, love camping and the great outdoors, and are pretty active, then you'll find Go Orange Kayaks' overnight Doubtful Sound trip an incredibly rewarding experience. It's not for the fainthearted; you can get wet and cold and the sand flies can be bad. But you'll be in a World Heritage Area, and you'll meet some wonderful like-minded people. If you're not keen on the overnight, go sea kayaking for the day in Doubtful or Milford Sound to gain the unique perspective on the fjord that being on the water gives you. Trips operate from September to May, with some differences according to location, so call ahead. They also do one day excursions on Milford Sound ✉ *85 Lake Front Dr., Te Anau* ☎ *03/442–7340, 0800/505–504 NZ only* ⊕ *www.goorange.co.nz* ⛴ *From NZ$139.*

Staying the Night at Fiordland

Overnight cruises are a leisurely, thorough way to experience the sounds. If you choose Doubtful Sound, your tour company will provide a boat across Lake Manapouri and a bus ride to your cruise vessel. Drive to Lake Manapouri, or, for an extra fee, arrange for a coach transfer from Te Anau or Queenstown. Sleeping quarters aboard the vessel range from bunking with three others to a private cabin and bathroom. Dinner and breakfast are included, and you can arrange for a picnic lunch. The park's deepest sound, Doubtful, has three distinct arms and features the 619-meter (2,031-foot) Browne Falls. If you are lucky, you will see Fiordland crested penguins on the rocks or bottlenose dolphins swimming at the bow. Cliffs rise from the sea to 900 meters (2,953 feet), often disappearing in a mist. You can explore the sound in kayaks once you anchor at the evening's mooring. Or you can sit on a viewing deck, sip a beverage from the bar, and take in the sights from your floating hotel. Milford overnight cruises generally leave around 4:30 pm and return around 9 the following morning; Doubtful cruises generally leave around noon and return around noon the next day.

11

The Southern Alps and Fiordland **MILFORD SOUND**

SCENIC FLIGHTS

Fly Fiordland

AIR EXCURSIONS | Fly Fiordland provides a range of scenic flights in its three Cessna fixed-wing aircraft, including to Milford and Doubtful sounds, and on the rare occasion that weather permits, an overfly of the most remote place in New Zealand, Dusky Sound. Prices don't include a cruise in Milford Sound, but you can add this as an option. Prices start at NZ$335. ⊠ 4/52 Town Centre, Te Anau ☎ 0800/359–346 NZ only, 03/249–4352 ⊕ www.flyfiordland.com.

★ Southern Lakes Helicopters

AIR EXCURSIONS | Once you've seen the movie *Ata Whenua* at Fiordland Cinema you'll want to take to the air and see some of this scenery for yourself (or do the flight first and see the movie after). Either way, this helicopter company, privately owned by renowned helicopter pioneer Sir Richard "Hannibal" Hayes, has operated successfully here for more than 35 years. The Southern Lakes pilots have a wealth of knowledge and experience flying in this World Heritage Area and offer a range of airborne services. ⊠ 79 Lakefront Dr., Te Anau ☎ 03/249–7167, 0508/249–7167 ⊕ www.southernlakeshelicopters.co.nz ☎ From NZ$230.

Wings and Water Te Anau

AIR EXCURSIONS | Wings and Water Te Anau operates scenic flights with a floatplane that takes travelers to some of the region's most inaccessible areas, including a 10-minute trip over Lake Te Anau, Lake Manapouri, and the Kepler Track, as well as longer flights over Doubtful, Dusky, and Milford sounds. ⊠ 65 Lakefront Dr., Te Anau ☎ 03/249–7405 ⊕ www.wingsandwater.co.nz ☎ From NZ$150.

Milford Sound

120 km (75 miles) northwest of Te Anau, 290 km (180 miles) west of Queenstown.

Fiordland National Park's most accessible and busiest attraction is Milford Sound; in some ways it's also the most dramatic. Hemmed in by walls of rock that rise straight and sheer from the waterline

up thousands of feet, the 15-km-long (9-mile-long) fjord was carved by a succession of glaciers as they gouged a track to the sea. Its dominant feature is the 5,560-foot pinnacle of Mitre Peak, which is capped with snow for all but the warmest months of the year. Opposite the peak, Bowen Falls tumbles 520 feet before exploding into the fjord. You'll often see seals on rocks soaking up the sun, and dolphins sometimes flirt with the boats. Milford Sound is also spectacularly wet: the average annual rainfall is around 20 feet, and it rains an average of 200 days a year. In addition to a raincoat you'll need insect repellent—the sand flies can be voracious.

GETTING HERE AND AROUND

Highway 94 North out of Te Anau to Milford Sound is only 118 km (73 miles), but between the weather, the views, and the winding, hilly nature of the road, it's best to allow at least 2½ hours to get there safely. Most day tours in Milford Sound offer transport from Te Anau or Queenstown, and InterCity Coachlines runs a daily service from Te Anau. If the weather is clear, there is an airport open to scenic fixed-wing and helicopter landings.

⊙ Sights

Milford Sound does not have a surrounding town. Here you'll fill your days with wondrous exploration. Because of excessive rain, make sure you come prepared with extra clothing and rain gear.

Milford Discovery Centre & Underwater Observatory

AQUARIUM | Even in heavy rain and storms Milford Sound is magical. Rainfall is so excessive that a coat of up to 20 feet of fresh water floats on the surface of the saltwater fjord. Lightly stained with tannins from the plants and soil, it creates a unique underwater environment similar to that found at a much greater depth in the open ocean. Head downstairs at the Milford Underwater Observatory, and you can see rare black coral (that looks white) as well as anemones, starfish, octopus, and any number of fish swimming by. The Discovery Centre and Observatory is operated by Southern Discoveries and is only accessible by boat; you can add it on to most Milford Sound cruises. ⊠ Milford Sound ☎ 03/441–1137, 0800/264–536 NZ only ⊕ www.milforddiscoverycentre.co.nz ⊅ NZ$99 ☞ Admission cost includes cruise and picnic lunch.

❤ Restaurants

Accommodations are scant at Milford Sound; pack your lunch in Te Anau before coming, or preorder the lunch box included on some boat tours. If you're staying overnight, be aware there is no shopping. You can buy dinner at Milford Sound Lodge, whether you are a guest or not.

Discover Milford Information Centre & Cafe

$$ | CAFÉ | Situated at the main public car park, the Discover Milford Information Centre offers coffee, snacks, and counter food. The view out the front window, across Milford Sound to Mitre Peak and the mountains beyond, is amazing. **Known for:** impressive views; only dining option in Milford Sound; high prices for simple food. $ Average main: NZ$16 ⊠ 79 Milford Sound Hwy., Milford Sound ☎ 03/249–7931 ☽ No dinner.

🛏 Hotels

★ Milford Sound Lodge

$$$$ | HOTEL | Just 1 km (½ mile) out of the Milford settlement, on the banks of the Cleddau River, this lodge provides riverside chalets with either one super-king or twin bed, kitchenette, and spectacular mountain and river views. **Pros:** otherworldly views; beautiful chalets; only place to stay in Milford Sound. **Cons:** limited internet; very expensive; shares location with campervans and hostel.

Did You Know?

Mountains comprise two-thirds of the South Island. Rising out of Milford Sound is its largest mountain, the 5,560 foot Mitre Peak.

$ *Rooms from: NZ$495* ⊠ *Milford Sound* ☎ *03/249–8071* ⊕ *www.milfordlodge. com* ❘◎❘ *Free Breakfast* ⤳ *14 chalets.*

Activities

CRUISING

The gorgeous views from the water account for the popularity of cruising here. It's essential to book ahead between mid-December and March. All boats leave from the Milford wharf area. Avoid the midday sailings, as they link with tour buses and are the most crowded. Southern Discoveries and Real Journeys run more than a dozen cruises a day between them, with extra options in summer.

Real Journeys

BOATING | The most satisfying way to experience Milford (or Doubtful) Sound is to do an overnight cruise, giving you time in the fjord when it's at its best—first thing in the morning and early evening. There are two overnight boats: the *Milford Mariner*'s the more luxurious cruise with roomier bunks (with en suites), but the *Milford Wanderer*'s not too far behind. Fewer passengers and shared facilities make it a very friendly boat. An overnight cruise includes a superb dinner and breakfast. If you want to do a day cruise, go for the Nature Cruise over the Scenic Cruise. It's more personal, longer (2½ hours), and it's on a boat with more character and a nature guide who will answer questions. Both trips cruise the full length of Milford Sound to the Tasman Sea and have the same extraordinary views of waterfalls, rain forest, mountains, and wildlife. ⊠ *85 Lakefront Dr., Te Anau* ☎ *03/249–6000, 0800/656–501* ⊕ *www.realjourneys.co.nz* ⤳ *From NZ$510 per person overnight; NZ$89 for day trip* ⊘ *Overnight cruises don't operate through winter (mid-May–Sept.).*

★ Southern Discoveries

BOATING | You can't miss Southern Discoveries' big red boats in Milford Sound. If you're only here for the day the cruise-kayak option is great for getting close to the shore and seeing the edges of the fjord in all its lush detail—right down to its damp, green, earthy smell. It's an easy paddle on calm water so no experience is necessary. Kayaking starts at the Discovery Centre and Underwater Observatory, which is also included in the price and is well worth a visit. ⊠ *Milford Sound Wharf, Milford Sound* ☎ *03/441–1137* ⊕ *www.southerndiscoveries.co.nz* ⤳ *From NZ$71.*

HIKING

Fiordland National Park Visitor Centre

HIKING & WALKING | To hike independently of a tour group for either the Milford, Kepler, or Routeburn Track, call the Great Walks Booking Office at the Fiordland National Park Visitor Centre or book online through the website. Reservations for the coming season can be made starting on the first of July every year. Book well in advance—especially if you plan to go in December or January. Independent walking, without a guide, requires that you bring your own food, utensils, bedding, and other equipment. You stay in clean, basic Department of Conservation huts. ⊠ *Lakefront Dr., Te Anau* ☎ *03/249–8514* ⊕ *www.doc.govt. nz.*

Hollyford Track

HIKING & WALKING | If you're itching to see some coastline during your hike, and you are fit, consider the Hollyford Track. At 56 km (35 miles), it's usually a four-day endeavor, taking you from the Hollyford Road down to Martins Bay by roughly following the Hollyford River. You'll pass a couple of lakes and waterfalls on your way; at the coastline you'll likely spy seals and penguins. Be particularly careful of flooded creek crossings. Make sure you buy your hut tickets, but you can't book in advance. It's a good idea to drop in to the Fiordland National Park Visitor Centre to check on conditions before you head off. ✉ *Lakefront Dr., Te Anau* ☎ *03/249–7924* ⊕ *www.doc.govt.nz.*

★ Milford Track

HIKING & WALKING | If you plan to walk the Milford Track—a rewarding four-day bushwalk through Fiordland National Park—understand that it is one of New Zealand's most popular hikes. The 53½-km (33-mile) track is strictly one-way, and because park authorities control access, you can feel as though you have the wilderness more or less to yourself. The trail ends for the track are remote, both requiring boat access. Independent and guided groups stay in different overnight huts. Guided and unguided walks begin with a 1½-hour ferry ride to Glade Wharf on Lake Te Anau and end with a 20-minute ferry taking you from Sandfly Point over to the Milford Sound wharf. The track's well maintained during the restricted hiking season, which runs from late October to April (because of the risk of avalanche). For seasonal reservations, visit a Department of Conservation office or book online. Make sure you book well in advance. ✉ *Fiordland National Park, Milford Sound* ⊕ *www.greatwalks.co.nz.*

Routeburn Track

HIKING & WALKING | The 33-km (20.5-mile) Routeburn Track, like the Milford Track, is designated one of the country's Great Walks, so you need to book in season. The Routeburn goes between Lake Wakatipu, near Glenorchy, and the road between Milford and Te Anau; it takes about three days to hike. The alpine landscape is stunning, and once you're above the tree line, the sand flies back off. It's a linear track so make sure you organize your transport home. The track's well maintained but be prepared for rain and mud. Tramping out of season is not advised for most people as there's avalanche risk. ⊕ *www.doc.govt.nz.*

Ultimate Hikes

HIKING & WALKING | If you want to do the Milford Track but don't like the idea of hauling a heavy backpack for 34 miles with all your food and gear, then Ultimate Hikes is the rather wonderful alternative. All your meals are provided, you'll have a comfortable bed and hot showers, and you can wash and dry your gear if it rains. They'll organize your transport and provide backpacks. Their Milford Track journey includes a cruise on Milford Sound and transport to and from Queenstown; the Routeburn Track is a bit less expensive. If you're not up for a multiday trek, you can take a single-day "encounter" hike on either the Milford or Routeburn Track. ✉ *The Station, Duke St. entrance, Queenstown* ☎ *03/450–1940, 0800/659–255* ⊕ *www.ultimatehikes. co.nz* ✉ *From NZ$2230 (in multishare accommodation).*

KAYAKING
Rosco's Milford Kayaks

KAYAKING | If you like immersing yourself in nature then sea kayaking's a lovely way to see this extraordinary part of New Zealand and the creatures (seals, penguins, or dolphins if you're lucky) that live here. Rosco's Milford Kayaks leads a number of different guided kayaking options on Milford Sound that can even include a hike along part of the famous Milford Track. You can get picked up and dropped off from Te Anau. ✉ *72 Town Centre, Milford Sound* ☎ *03/249–8500, 0800/476–726 in New Zealand* ⊕ *www. roscosmilfordkayaks.com* ✉ *From NZ$115* ☞ *No children under 14.*

SCENIC FLIGHTS
Glacier Southern Lakes Helicopters

AIR EXCURSIONS | You're in good hands flying with this company, which has highly sought-after helicopter pilots with a wealth of knowledge about the area. Helicopters are easily the best way to see this part of the country, and even a short flight up the Remarkables or over the Skippers Canyon is an incredible experience. Flying to Milford Sound, the West Coast, and Mount Aspiring National Park, landing on a glacier on the way, could be life changing. There's a Middle-earth flight to some of The Lord of the Rings and The Hobbit locations—about as authentic as you can get as one of this company's pilots, Alfie Speight, was the principal aerial photography pilot for the movies. ⌧ *35 Lucas Pl., Queenstown* ☎ *03/442–3016* ⊕ *www.glaciersouthern-lakes.co.nz* 🖃 *From NZ$225 per person.*

Lake Manapouri and Doubtful Sound

Just 20 minutes south of Te Anau, Lake Manapouri has long had the reputation as one of New Zealand's prettiest lakes. The lake, 1,457 feet deep at its deepest, is hemmed by high mountains and studded by many bush-covered islands. Cruises run several times a day to the head of the lake, where you can join a tour of the West Arm hydro station, deep underground. West Arm is also the departure point for those traveling on to Doubtful Sound, a stunning stretch of water, largely untouched by visitors. A connecting bus crosses you over the 2,201-foot Wilmot Pass before dropping steeply down to sea level at Deep Cove, the head of Doubtful Sound.

GETTING HERE AND AROUND

To get to Lake Manapouri, head south of the Te Anau center onto Highway 95 to drive the 20 minutes to Manapouri township. Doubtful Sound is not accessible by car. Book a day trip or overnight tour, and your tour will include a boat ride across Lake Manapouri and a bus ride across Wilmot Pass. You can park you car near the wharf at Pearl Harbour, which is the end of the road. Most tours will have the option to depart on a bus from Te Anau, allowing you to leave your car in town.

 Activities

Fiordland Expeditions

BOAT TOURS | Fiordland Expeditions provides a very Kiwi overnight experience on their two boats, *Tutuko* and *Tutoko II*. With a maximum of 12 passengers, these are relaxed and personal trips and great if you want to do a bit of fishing, kayaking, or just soak up the splendid scenery. There are private or shared cabins, mostly with shared bathroom facilities. All meals (probably some crayfish for dinner), fishing gear, and transfers from Manapouri are included in the price. ⌧ *Deep Cove, Doubtful Sound* ☎ *03/249–9005* ⊕ *www.fiordlandexpeditions.co.nz* 🖃 *From NZ$725.*

★ **Real Journeys**

SPECIAL-INTEREST TOURS | Doubtful Sound is three times as long as Milford Sound, and, because there's no road access, it receives far fewer visitors. The sides of the fjords aren't quite as in-your-face, but they are just as beautiful, and there's a better chance of seeing dolphins and fur seals. Real Journeys runs a range of combined bus and boat trips. Most people take the seven-hour day trip from Lake Manapouri; there are bus connections from Te Anau and Queenstown. Between October and May, the ultimate experience is an overnight on the sound, aboard the *Fiordland Navigator*. Rates include meals and kayaking, and if you're brave enough, you can take a swim in the frigid waters. ⌧ *Lakefront Dr., Te Anau* ☎ *03/249–6000, 0800/656–501* ⊕ *www.realjourneys.co.nz* 🖃 *From NZ$199.*

Chapter 12

OTAGO, INVERCARGILL, AND STEWART ISLAND

Updated by
Gerard Hindmarsh

⊙ **Sights**
★★★★☆

🍴 **Restaurants**
★★★☆☆

🛏 **Hotels**
★★☆☆☆

🛍 **Shopping**
★☆☆☆☆

🎭 **Nightlife**
★★★☆☆

WELCOME TO OTAGO, INVERCARGILL, AND STEWART ISLAND

TOP REASONS TO GO

★ **Local Fare:** Partake in a fresh fillet of blue cod, salty muttonbird prepared the Māori way, succulent Bluff oysters, or a warm cheese roll.

★ **Bird-watching:** See yellow-eyed penguins or an albatross on the peninsula or a kiwi on Stewart Island. Predator-free Ulva Island is the showcase jewel in the crown of Rakiura National Park.

★ **Kiwi Sports:** Rugby puts New Zealand on the world stage, and for many Kiwis it's a passion. Provincial and international teams ruck and maul at Dunedin's Forsyth Barr Stadium.

★ **Pubs and Clubs:** Thanks to the presence of 25,000 university students, Dunedin is full of cafés, funky bars, late-night pubs, and rocking music venues.

★ **The Southern Coastline:** The lower coast of the South Island is breathtakingly wild. Head south along the Catlins section of the Southern Scenic Route for ocean views, diving seabirds, and sandy beaches.

1 Dunedin. A university town, Dunedin is filled with history, a bustling harbor, and creative young academics.

2 Oamaru. This town is well-known for its grand Victorian buildings and nearby penguin colony.

3 Otago Peninsula. This claw-shape jut of land has an albatross colony, a hilltop castle, and some gorgeous scenery.

4 Invercargill. Thanks to its original Scottish immigrants, this small city near the sea comes with plenty of European charm and architecture.

5 Stewart Island. Sparsely inhabited, Stewart Island contains New Zealand's newest national park and some of the world's best bird-watching.

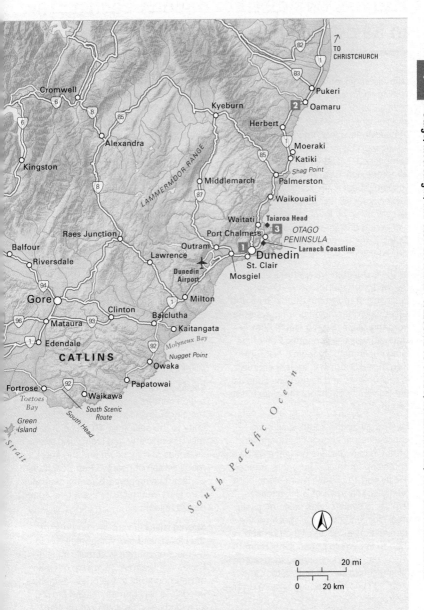

TO
CHRISTCHURCH

82
1

83

Cromwell
6

6

8

85

Kyeburn

Alexandra

Herbert

Pukeri
Oamaru
2

1
Moeraki
Katiki
Shag Point

Kingston

85

Middlemarch

LAMMERMOOR RANGE

87

Palmerston

Waikouaiti

Raes Junction

Waitati
Port Chalmers

Taiaroa Head
3

OTAGO
PENINSULA

Balfour
Riversdale

Outram
Lawrence

Dunedin
Airport

Dunedin
1
St. Clair

Larnach Coastline

Mosgiel

94

Gore

Clinton

Milton

96
Mataura
93

Balclutha

1

Edendale
Kaitangata

CATLINS

92
Molyneux Bay
Nugget Point

Owaka

Fortrose
92
Waikawa
Papatowai

Toetoes
Bay

South Scenic
Route

Green
Island

South Head

Strait

South Pacific Ocean

0   20 mi

0   20 km

Otago Province takes up much of the southeast quadrant of the South Island and has two distinct regions, each a draw in its own right.

Offering spectacular opportunities for wildlife and marine mammal–watching, coastal Otago stretches across moist and verdant hills, its intricate coastline of headlands, inlets, and misty beaches strung with historic settlements. By comparison, inland Otago is stark yet jaw-droppingly beautiful, a drier landscape of spectacular schist outcrops and tussock grasslands, punctuated occasionally by small towns that still exude pioneering character. Draining much of Otago is the mighty Clutha River, the largest-volume waterway in the country.

In 1848, Dunedin was settled, and all the land from the top of the Otago Peninsula south to the Clutha River and sections farther inland were purchased from the Māori. By the mid-1860s, Dunedin was the economic hub of the Otago gold rush. Dunedin's historical wealth and Scottish influence endures in monuments and institutions such as the University of Otago, the oldest in the country.

Invercargill, to the south, was born out of different economic imperatives. After wealthy graziers bought swaths of Southland for their sheep, they needed a local port to bring in more stock from Australia. The town of Bluff, already familiar to sealers, was selected as an ideal location. Invercargill became the administrative center of the port and then to the whole region. Until recent years, the town's economy focused on raising sheep and other livestock and crops; it is now becoming a more diverse metropolis.

Hanging off the bottom of the South Island and separated by 30-km-wide (19-mile-wide) Foveaux Strait, Stewart Island is a world all of its own. Commercial fishing and tourism account for most of the economic activity in the island's only settlement, which soon gives way to bushland that the kiwi bird still haunts. At night, the nocturnal birds can be seen wandering remote beaches. Another late-night show is the aurora australis, the southern hemisphere equivalent of the northern lights, which can light up the sky (the best time to catch a viewing is from March through September).

MAJOR REGIONS

Otago. The country's third largest province comprises the city of Dunedin, along with small towns along with small coastal towns like Oamaru. The region's peninsula is also popular with visitors thanks to its gorgeous scenery.

Southland. New Zealand's southernmost region centers around Stewart Island and the city of Invercargill. Due to its proximity to the sea, "Invers" has been called the "City of Water and Light." The wide flat roads of downtown and the enormous sweep of nearby Oreti Beach were perfect training grounds for homegrown hero Burt Munro (motorcycle land speed record holder).

Stewart Island. If your hand represents the island, your pinky fingernail would be the amount that is actually inhabited. Roads link the main township of Oban at Halfmoon Bay to the other "neighborhoods"—a few homes nestled around adjoining bays. Beaches are pristine;

the sea is crystal green and bountiful. Flowers spill from grounded dories. Beyond town is wilderness teeming with wonderful birds.

Planning

Getting Here and Around

AIR

Most Air New Zealand flights to Dunedin and Invercargill go via Christchurch or come direct from Wellington, while Jetstar connects Dunedin to Auckland. Fog occasionally causes delays, but Christchurch Airport has a slick and modern passenger-friendly terminal with shops and cafés as well as a family entertainment center where the little folks can wear themselves out. Stewart Island flights operate from Invercargill, or you can take a ferry to the island: one local described the choices as "either 60 minutes of fear or 20 minutes of terror," but that's true only on a bad day—both journeys afford breathtaking views.

BUS

InterCity's buses run twice a day between Christchurch and Dunedin, departing at 7:45 am and 2 pm for a trip that takes six hours. A connecting daily InterCity bus continues on from Dunedin to Invercargill; this takes another 3 hours and 15 minutes. On both these routes the company makes an extra run on Sundays. Other bus companies operating in the region include Atomic Travel, Bottom Bus, and Catch-A-Bus.

CAR

The best way to explore the lower South Island is by car, particularly if you want to take your time seeing the Catlins. You cannot ferry your rental car to Stewart Island; there is secure parking in Invercargill and Bluff. Buses serve most places of interest, including daily routes between South Island cities. They go the direct

route between Dunedin and Invercargill on State Highway 1. If you are driving and want to see the Catlins, leave State Highway 1 at Balclutha and take the well-marked Southern Scenic Route.

Planning Your Time

Most people spend a few days in Dunedin and migrate south via State Highway 1. Once you reach Balclutha, you can continue south either by staying on the State Highway heading straight for Invercargill or by going via the Catlins on the Southern Scenic Route. The Catlins route is more demanding but much more scenic. Whichever route you take, by the time you reach the Southland Plains, all roads are wide, flat, and point to Invercargill.

Hotels

Dunedin has a full range of accommodations, from modest hostels to luxury hotels, while Invercargill has more motels than anything else. Local motels generally provide clean rooms with kitchens and TVs. Stewart Island lodging options include camping, hostels, rental houses, hotels, motels, and boutique B&Bs. Throughout the region, air-conditioning is a rarity, but given the temperate climate, this isn't a problem. Heating, on the other hand, is standard in most places.

It's a good idea to make reservations, especially in summer. In Dunedin, rooms can be scarce around special events, such as graduation ceremonies and high-profile rugby games.

Restaurant and hotel reviews have been shortened. For full information, visit Fodors.com. Restaurant prices are the average cost of a main course at dinner or, if dinner is not served, at lunch. Hotel prices are the lowest cost of a standard double room in high season.

12

Otago, Invercargill, and Stewart Island PLANNING

WHAT IT COSTS in New Zealand Dollars

	$	$$	$$$	$$$$
RESTAURANTS				
	under NZ$15	NZ$15–NZ$20	NZ$21–NZ$30	over NZ$30
HOTELS				
	under NZ$125	NZ$125–NZ$200	NZ$201–NZ$300	over NZ$300

Restaurants

Dunedin has the area's highest concentration of good restaurants. Seafood is a big player, in part because of Dunedin's coastal location but also because of its proximity to Bluff, the home of New Zealand's great delicacy, Bluff oysters. Many of the least-expensive options are café-like Asian restaurants; these tend to close early, around 9 pm. Locals don't usually dress up or make reservations for anything other than large groups or the more exclusive establishments.

Invercargill has a more limited selection of mostly moderately priced restaurants. Stewart Island has a reasonable selection considering its location, including some excellent takeaway spots, but in winter some places limit their hours or close entirely.

Visitor Information

Both Dunedin and Invercargill have centrally located i-SITE visitor centers: you can find Dunedin's in The Octagon in the city center and a kiosk branch at the wharf that only opens to greet cruise ships; the Invercargill i-SITE is in the Southland Museum. On Stewart Island check out the Department of Conservation office or the Stewart Island Experience office (in the red building at the ferry wharf).

When to Go

Dunedin gets more visitors in summer, but during the university vacations it's quieter as students head home. Inland Otago remains dry year-round, and you can expect crisp, sunny days in winter, but the coast gets more rain, and Dunedin can have day after day of clouds and showers. Southland in winter isn't any colder, but it is wetter.

It's often said of New Zealand that you may experience all four seasons in one day; on Stewart Island you may experience them all in an hour. In winter, there's a better chance of seeing the aurora australis, but some of the island's walking trails may be closed or just too muddy to walk.

Dunedin

278 km (174 miles) east of Queenstown, 360 km (225 miles) south of Christchurch.

Clinging to the walls of the natural amphitheater at the western end of Otago Harbour, the South Island's second-largest city is enriched with inspiring nearby seascapes and wildlife. Because Dunedin is a university town, floods of students give the city a vitality far greater than its population of 134,100 might suggest. The city's manageable size makes it easy to explore on foot—with the possible exception of Baldwin Street, the world's steepest residential street and home to the annual "gutbuster" race, in which people run up it, and the "Jaffa" race, in which people roll the namesake spherical chocolate candy down it.

Dunedin, the Gaelic name for Edinburgh, was founded in 1848 by settlers of the Free Church of Scotland, a breakaway group from the Presbyterian Church. The city's Scottish roots are still visible: you'll find New Zealand's first legal whisky distillery (now there are nine); a statue of Scottish poet Robert Burns; and more kilts, sporrans, and gillies than you can shake a stick at. The Scottish settlers and local Māori came together in relative peace, but this wasn't true of the European whalers who were here three decades before, as places with names such as Murdering Beach illustrate.

Dunedin has always had a reputation for the eccentric. Wearing no shoes and a big beard here marks a man as bohemian rather than destitute, and the residents wouldn't have it any other way. The University of Otago was the country's first university and has been drawing writers ever since its founding in 1871, most notably Janet Frame and the poet James K. Baxter. Dunedin also has a musical heritage, which blossomed into the "Dunedin Sound" of the 1970s and '80s.

GETTING HERE AND AROUND
AIR
Dunedin Airport lies 20 km (13 miles) south of the city. Both Air New Zealand and Jetstar link Dunedin and Auckland daily; the flight takes just under two hours. Air New Zealand also flies daily from Dunedin to Christchurch and Wellington in around an hour. Internationally, Air New Zealand, Qantas, and Virgin Australia all have connecting flights from Dunedin to Sydney and Brisbane.

AIRPORT CONTACTS Dunedin international Airport. ⊠ *25 Miller Rd., Momona* ☎ *03/486–2879* ⊕ *www.dunedinairport. co.nz.*

BUS
Local buses to Portobello and other towns on the peninsula depart from Stop G Central City Bus Hub on Great King Street.

BUS CONTACTS Central City Bus Hub. ⊠ *Great King St., Dunedin* ☎ *03/474–1699* ⊕ *www.orc.govt.nz.* **GoBus.** ⊠ *1 Transport Pl., Dunedin Central* ☎ *03/477–5577* ⊕ *www.gobus.co.nz.* **InterCity.** ⊠ *331*

Moray Pl., Dunedin Central ☎ *03/477– 8860* ⊕ *www.intercity.co.nz.*

CAR
You can rent a car to explore the region at Dunedin airport on arrival, but confusing one-way roads and twisting hills in the suburbs make driving in Dunedin itself a challenge. Street parking can be limited.

TOURS
City Walks Dunedin
WALKING TOURS | Three separate walks showcasing Dunedin's rich history, architecture, and urban renewal are offered every day except Sunday and depart from the Dunedin i-SITE Visitor Information Centre. The one-hour Vogel Street Walk leaves from Vogel St. Kitchen at 9 am daily. The walk season is mainly October through April, but a reduced winter schedule is offered. ⊠ *Dunedin i-SITE Visitor Centre, 50 The Octagon, Dunedin* ☎ *027/356–9132, 0800/925–571 toll-free* ⊕ *www.citywalks.co.nz* ⊠ *From NZ$30.*

Elm Wildlife Tours
GUIDED TOURS | Passionate and enthusiastic guides lead walks through private conservation areas to penguin, fur seal, and sea lion colonies. A moderate degree of fitness is required to negotiate hilly terrain. ⊠ *19 Irvine Rd., The Cove, Dunedin* ☎ *03/454–4121, 0800/356–563* ⊕ *www.elmwildlifetours.co.nz* ⊠ *From NZ$122.*

Mainland Air Scenic Flights
AIR EXCURSIONS | Scenic flights show off inland mountains and coastal sights as far south as Stewart Island. ⊠ *Dunedin Airport, 3 Airport Dr., Dunedin* ☎ *03/486– 2200, 0800/284–284* ⊕ *www.mainlandair. com* ⊠ *Flights from NZ$225 a person.*

VISITOR INFORMATION
CONTACTS Dunedin i-SITE Visitor Information Centre. ⊠ *50 The Octagon, Dunedin* ☎ *03/474–3300* ⊕ *www.dunedin.govt. nz.* **Dunedin NZ Official Tourist Information.** ⊕ *www.dunedinnz.com.*

The extravagant Dunedin Railway Station is fronted by manicured grounds.

Sights

As you explore Dunedin's city center, do look down. Beneath your feet are bronze plaques embedded in the sidewalks that highlight the city's Victorian history and heritage buildings. Around The Octagon, the thoughts of popular New Zealand writers are captured in bronze pavestones.

Dunedin Botanic Gardens

GARDEN | FAMILY | Relax and enjoy the birdsong of bellbirds, woodpigeon, and *tūī* amid 70 acres of international and native flora at New Zealand's first ever public garden. Some 6,800 plant species thrive on flatlands and hillsides ranging up from Central Dunedin, providing amazing seasonal displays of foliage. Attractions include an aviary, a winter garden hothouse, a comprehensive native plant collection, and the spectacular Rhododendron Dell. Parking at the lower part of the gardens, off Cumberland Street, affords easier access than the Opoho end, which is steeper, but both parts are worth visiting. ✉ *Great King St. N. and Opoho Rd., Dunedin* ☎ *03/477–4000* ⊕ *www.dunedinbotanicgarden.co.nz* 🎫 *Free.*

Dunedin Public Art Gallery

ART MUSEUM | The shell of an original municipal building has been paired with a sweeping, modern, glass facade to house a collection that includes European masters Monet, Turner, and Gainsborough, as well as New Zealand and Otago artists. A special gallery highlights Dunedin native Frances Hodgkins, whose work won acclaim in the 1930s and '40s. Hodgkins's style changed throughout her career, but some of her most distinctive works are postimpressionist watercolors. ✉ *30 The Octagon, Dunedin* ☎ *03/474–3240* ⊕ *www.dunedin.art. museum* 🎫 *Free.*

Dunedin Railway Station

TRAIN/TRAIN STATION | The 1906 Dunedin Railway Station, a cathedral to the power of steam, is a massive bluestone

Otago Central Rail Trail

From Dunedin Railway Station, take the Taieri Gorge Train to Middlemarch (or Pukerangi, 19 km [12 miles] from Middlemarch), one end of the **Otago Central Rail Trail.** This 150-km (93-mile) pleasantly undulating bicycle path follows the old railway line and includes a dizzying wooden viaduct and a 500-foot-long tunnel, with places to eat, sleep, and drink along the way. The only traffic you'll encounter is the occasional flock of daggy (muddy-bottomed) sheep. The ride takes about five days to complete, passing through sheep farms and lovely wee towns such as Ranfurly, an "oasis of art deco," and Alexander, one of the busier hubs in Central Otago on the banks of the paint-green Clutha River. The trail eventually ends in thyme-scented Clyde. The route can be traversed in either direction; Clyde is approximately 80 km (50 miles) from Queenstown. The trail provides a great way to experience the sheep stations, with their puzzling gates and similarly puzzling locks, as well as mud, wind, rivers, pubs, and old gold fields.

structure in Flemish Renaissance style, lavishly decorated with heraldic beasts, nymphs, scrolls, a mosaic floor, and even stained-glass windows of steaming locomotives. This extravagant building, considered one of the best examples of railway architecture in the southern hemisphere, earned its architect, George Troup, a knighthood from the king—and the nickname Gingerbread George from the people of Dunedin because of the detailing on the outside of the building. It was once the busiest station in the country, with up to 100 trains a day coming and going. The station is also home to the **Sports Hall of Fame**, the country's finest sports museum with displays celebrating rugby, cricket, and other athletic pursuits. ✉ *Anzac Ave. at Stuart St., Dunedin* ☎ *03/477–4449 Station, 03/477–7775 Sports Hall of Fame* ⊕ *www.nzhalloffame.co.nz* ✉ *Sports Hall of Fame $6.*

First Church of Otago
CHURCH | On the south side of Moray Place, the church is not vast, but it's still impressive, with a base of Oamaru stone topped by a delicate 200-foot spire. Check out the leaf patterns, dragon, and other carved details around the windows. ✉ *415 Moray Pl., Dunedin* ☎ *03/477–7118* ⊕ *www.firstchurchotago.org* ✉ *Free.*

Milford Galleries Dunedin
ART GALLERY | Milford Galleries, a major fine-art dealer, presents solo and group exhibitions of New Zealand paintings, drawings, sculpture, glasswork, ceramic art, and photography. Among the artists are Neil Frazer (who does large-scale abstract expressionist paintings) and Paul Dibble, one of New Zealand's most acclaimed sculptors. ✉ *18 Dowling St., Dunedin* ☎ *03/477–7727* ⊕ *www.milford-galleries.co.nz* ⊗ *Closed Sun.*

The Octagon
PLAZA/SQUARE | The city's hub is the eight-sided town center, lined with several imposing buildings, and a smattering of market stalls, cafés, and bars with tables spilling onto the pavement. In summer it's a meeting place, and it's also the site for the occasional student demonstration. Dunedin City Council provides free Wi-Fi in this grand arena. A **statue of Robert Burns** sits in front of **St. Paul's Cathedral,** a part-Victorian Gothic, part-modern building with an imposing

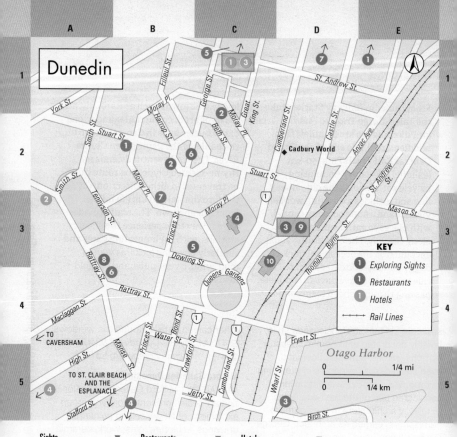

Dunedin

Otago Harbor

0   1/4 mi

0   1/4 km

KEY

1   *Exploring Sights*

1   *Restaurants*

1   *Hotels*

   Rail Lines

← TO
CAVERSHAM

TO ST. CLAIR BEACH
AND THE
ESPLANACLE

♦ Cadbury World

marble staircase leading up to a towering facade of Oamaru stone. On Stuart Street at the corner of Dunbar, check out the late-Victorian **Law Courts.** Their figure of Justice stands with scales in hand but without her customary blindfold (she wears a low helmet instead).

★ Otago Museum

SCIENCE MUSEUM | **FAMILY** | Galleries in an 1877 building are a throwback to Victorian times. The museum's first curator was a zoologist, and many of the original animals collected from 1868 are still on display in Animal Attic, a restored, magnificent, skylighted gallery. Southern Land, Southern People explores the cultural heritage of this region, and other galleries focus on Māori and Pacific Island artifacts, animal and insect specimens, and nautical items, including ship models and a whale skeleton. The Tropical Forest re-creates a humid jungle, complete with live butterflies and other tropical creatures. ⊠ *419 Great King St. N., Dunedin* ☎ *03/474–7474* ⊕ *www.otagomuseum.nz* 🔁 *Free; Discovery World from NZ$10.*

Speight's Brewery Heritage Centre

BREWERY | For a tasty indulgence, head to the Speight's Brewery Heritage Centre for a 90-minute tour of the South's top brewery, which dates back to 1876 on this very same site. Here you can see the various stages of gravity-driven brewing, learn the trade's lingo such as *wort* and *grist,* and taste the results. Speight's makes several traditional beers, the most common being its Gold Medal Ale. The company claims that this is the drink of choice for every "Southern Man," which isn't far from the truth. Watch a video of various Speight's iconic television ads and learn to say the tough Southern way, *Good on ya, mate.* ⊠ *200 Rattray St., Dunedin* ☎ *03/477–7697* ⊕ *www.speights.co.nz* 🔁 *NZ$25* ☞ *Reservations essential.*

Taieri Gorge Railway (*The Inlander*)

TRAIN/TRAIN STATION | **FAMILY** | A route along the now-closed Otago Central Railway (now christened *The Inlander*) runs from Dunedin to Pukerangi and Middlemarch, home of the annual Middlemarch Singles' Ball; each year this very train imports young city gals up to a dance with lonely Otago sheep shearers. The highlight of the trip is the run through the narrow and deep Taieri Gorge, with 10 tunnels and dozens of bridges and viaducts, all of which can be enjoyed from open-air viewing platforms. Also available is a seasonal *Seasider* route from Dunedin up the coast to Palmerston. The train runs every day; check the timetable for its destination. Reservations are essential. Cyclists can connect at Middlemarch to the wonderful Otago Central Rail Trail. ⊠ *Dunedin Railway Station, Dunedin* ☎ *03/477–4449* ⊕ *www.dunedinrailways.co.nz* 🔁 *From NZ$91.*

Toitū Otago Settlers Museum

HISTORY MUSEUM | Documents, works of art, technological items, and forms of transport tell the stories of all Otago settlers, from Māori and early European and Chinese to later Pacific Islanders and Asians. The museum hosts changing exhibits and events, with a charge for some events. ⊠ *31 Queens Gardens, Dunedin* ☎ *03/477–5052* ⊕ *www.toit-uosm.com* 🔁 *Free.*

Beaches

St. Clair Beach

BEACH | **FAMILY** | The sea at Dunedin can be a little wild; in summer an area between flags is patrolled by lifeguards. St. Clair has some good surfing, and hosts some prestigious competitions. Don't be too spooked by the shark bell on the Esplanade: a fatal attack hasn't occurred for 50 years (although nonfatal attacks have occurred at least once a decade). Local residents show what they're made of at the annual "midwinter plunge" held on the beach at winter solstice. If the ocean is too cold for you, try the Hot Salt Water Pool at the southern end of the beach (NZ$7 admission). South of town is the Tunnel Beach Walkway, a sandstone tunnel cut in 1870 by Edward Cargill so that his family could get down to the pretty beach below (this walk is closed from August through October for lambing). **Amenities:** food and drink; lifeguards; parking (free); showers; toilets. **Best for:** surfing; walking. ✉ *Beach St., St. Clair, Dunedin* ✣ *Drive south on State Hwy. 1 or hop on Normanby–St. Clair bus from George St. or The Octagon.*

🍴 Restaurants

The Kitchen Table Cafe & Bake

$$ | **CAFÉ** | At this centrally located café and bakery, artisan bakers craft delicious wholesome food. You can choose from, pancakes, French toast, or good old eggs Benedict for breakfast, or maybe a panini for lunch. **Known for:** sweet treats and baked goods at reasonable prices; cozy atmosphere; some of the best coffee in town. [$] *Average main: NZ$16* ✉ *111 Moray Pl., Dunedin* ☎ *03/477–0232* ⏲ *No dinner.*

Little India Dunedin

$$$ | **INDIAN** | Influenced by the flavors of northern India (and the kitchen of founder Sukhi's grandmother), this family business began in Dunedin and has become a chain spanning the country. Spacious and modern eateries meet traditional cooking methods, and warm hospitality and generous portions of spicy vindaloos and Bengali fish preparations are among the hallmarks. **Known for:** Indian beers; authentic North Indian cuisine; great curries. [$] *Average main: NZ$25* ✉ *308 Moray Pl., Dunedin* ☎ *03/477–6559* 🌐 *www.littleindia.co.nz* ⏲ *No lunch weekends.*

Plato

$$$$ | **NEW ZEALAND** | A favorite among locals, this waterfront eatery that was once a seafarers hostel provides great food and excellent service. Everything is delicious, from the bread and house-made duck liver–cognac pâté to the perfectly cooked seafood and chicken dishes. **Known for:** BYOB policy; impressive all-encompassing menu; great waterfront views. [$] *Average main: NZ$36* ✉ *2 Birch St., Dunedin* ☎ *03/477–4235* 🌐 *www.platocafe.co.nz.*

★ **Salt Bar & Restaurant**

$$$ | **NEW ZEALAND** | In an iconic art deco building, this is the place to dine in St. Clair's, a leafy seaside neighborhood along a spectacular beach. Sate yourself with beef Burgundy pie or venison; the less carnivorous may wish to try the vegan vege salad. **Known for:** great brunch menu; sunny corner location close to beach; delicious food at reasonable prices. [$] *Average main: NZ$30* ✉ *240 Forbury Rd., St. Clair's, Dunedin* ☎ *03/455–1077* 🌐 *www.saltbar.co.nz.*

Sampan Dunedin

$ | **ASIAN** | **FAMILY** | This no-frills noodle bar is crowded with students and serves yummy, filling, and inexpensive soups. Menu highlights include spicy satay chicken burgers, fried rice, bong-bong chicken, and deep-fried wantons. **Known for:** popularity with university students; signature dishes of Thai, Khmer, and Chinese cuisine; quick service. [$] *Average main: NZ$11* ✉ *60-64 St. Andrew St., Dunedin* ☎ *03/471–7016* 🌐 *www.sampan.nz.*

The Speight's Ale House

$$$ | **NEW ZEALAND** | Authentic and quirky, the Ale House serves as a lively bar in a brewery–restaurant setting. The menu includes a "drunken" steak (steak marinated in dark, malty porter) and beer-battered fish, along with plenty of Speight's ales you can match with your meal. **Known for:** fine local ales including

seasonal brews; hearty meals featuring southern New Zealand fare; lively atmosphere. $ *Average main: NZ$28* ⊠ *200 Rattray St., Dunedin* ☎ *03/471–9050* ⊕ *www.thealehouse.co.nz.*

Thai Hanoi

$$$ | THAI | This Thai-Vietnamese fusion spot offers options like green or red Thai curries and a yellow or jungle (hot) Vietnamese curry. The Rialto Cinema is across the way, making this a convenient pre- or postmovie dinner spot—but reserving a table is a good idea. **Known for:** BYOB policy; authentic curries; centrally located setting. $ *Average main: NZ$21* ⊠ *24 Moray Pl., Dunedin* ☎ *03/471–9500* ⊗ *No lunch weekends.*

Hotels

Bluestone on George

$$ | APARTMENT | A short walk from restaurants and inner-city shopping, each of these contemporary-style studio apartments has a patio or balcony. **Pros:** free Wi-Fi and parking; centrally located; contemporary style. **Cons:** no children allowed; not much character; gym is on the small side. $ *Rooms from: NZ$185* ⊠ *571 George St., Dunedin* ☎ *03/477–9201* ⊕ *www.bluestonedunedin.co.nz* ⤴ *15 rooms* ⦿ *No Meals.*

Brothers Boutique Hotel

$$$ | HOTEL | This centrally located historic hotel once housed members of the Christian Brothers, but now its family-run with plenty of charm, elegance, and character. **Pros:** great views over the city; quirky interior; free parking. **Cons:** no air-conditioning; some street noise; some rooms could use an upgrade. $ *Rooms from: NZ$240* ⊠ *295 Rattray St., Dunedin* ☎ *03/477–0043* ⊕ *www.brothershotel. co.nz* ⦿ *Free Breakfast* ⤴ *15 rooms.*

George Street Motel Apartments

$$ | APARTMENT | One block from Dunedin's main shopping and dining area, these clean and spacious apartments come with full kitchens in one-bedroom

units and refrigerators and microwaves in the studios. **Pros:** free Wi-Fi; large open kitchen/lounge rooms; central location. **Cons:** can be dated but upgrades are ongoing; some bathrooms are small; breakfast not included with price. $ *Rooms from: NZ$135* ⊠ *575 George St., Dunedin* ☎ *03/477–9333, 0800/109– 333* ⊕ *www.georgestreetmotel.co.nz* ⦿ *No Meals* ⤴ *16 units.*

Lisburn House

$$ | B&B/INN | This Victorian-Gothic house, one of the finest built in 1860s Dunedin, is a romantic retreat set amid lovingly tended gardens and shows off such original details as decorative Irish brickwork, fishtail slate roof tiles, high, molded-plaster ceilings, and an impressive turn-of-the-20th-century stained-glass entrance. **Pros:** late breakfast and check-out; antique-style rooms; fabulous in-house restaurant. **Cons:** only one of the baths is en suite; on the outskirts of city center; no TVs in rooms. $ *Rooms from: NZ$175* ⊠ *15 Lisburn Ave., Dunedin* ☎ *0800/666–716* ⊕ *www.facebook. com/Lisburn-House-1657017347938923* ⦿ *Free Breakfast* ⤴ *3 rooms.*

Nightlife

You could spend all night bar-hopping and never leave The Octagon, with its many drinking establishments. Many venues are on or near George and Princes streets, often down dark alleys with no signs, so follow the crowd. Information about what's going on can be found on Radio One 91 FM and in the student paper (*www.critic.co.nz*), *Critic*.

Bacchus Wine Bar and Restaurant

WINE BARS | Overlooking The Octagon, this high-ceilinged, upstairs wine bar and restaurant in 1880s surroundings is as elegant as the wines on offer. An accompanying fine dining menu showcases New Zealand beef and lamb. ⊠ *12 The Octagon, 1st fl., Dunedin* ☎ *03/474–0824* ⊕ *www.bacchusdunedin.nz.*

The Craic Irish Tavern

PUBS | The Irish term for fun and banter certainly applies to this cozy tavern, which hosts live music and serves good pub grub and an excellent choice of beer, whisky, wine, and cocktails. For its food, emphasis is on seafood and wild game, with a few Irish favorites. ⊠ *24 The Octagon, Dunedin* ⊕ *www.thecraic.co.nz.*

Ironic Cafe and Bar

BARS | A decor of steel and concrete with lots of natural light gives this modern space a semi-industrial look, and every table comes with a view of the iconic Dunedin Railway Station building just across the road. You can enjoy market-fresh light fare by day and a lively cocktail scene come sunset. Its brunch is also very popular. ⊠ *9 Anzac Ave., Dunedin* ☎ *03/477–9988* ⊕ *www.ironiccafebar. co.nz.*

Pequeno

PIANO BARS | Possibly the snuggest bar in Dunedin came to notoriety as the hangout of choice for Gwyneth Paltrow and Chris Martin, of the band Coldplay, during the Dunedin shoot of the film *Sylvia.* Leather chairs, an open fire, and a good selection of whisky and cigars add to the lounge atmosphere. The wine list is good as well, if pricey, and there's live music some nights. ⊠ *Savoy Bldg., 50 Princes St., lower ground fl., Dunedin* ☎ *03/477–7830.*

Union Bar

BARS | A prime spot at the heart of the university campus ensures a predominantly student clientele, though everyone is welcome. Nights are split between local or national (or even international) live rock acts and DJ-driven nights of 1980s hits, hip-hop, house, and drum 'n' bass music. ⊠ *640 Cumberland St., Dunedin* ☎ *03/479–5309* ⊕ *www.dunedinmusic.com.*

Performing Arts

Regent Theatre

THEATER | A historic building hosts large-scale musicals as well as dance and theater performances and those of the Royal New Zealand Ballet. It is also the scene of the New Zealand Film Festival and the World Cinema Showcase each year. ⊠ *17 The Octagon, Dunedin* ☎ *03/477–8597 ticket reservations* ⊕ *www.regenttheatre.co.nz.*

 Shopping

Nearly all the good shops are clustered around George Street and Moray Place.

Design Withdrawals

SOUVENIRS | This is a cool gift shop with a relaxed atmosphere offering an extensive stock of artisan-made jewelry, clothing, art, housewares, even a line of cheeky socks. There is something for everyone here. ⊠ *7 Moray Pl., Dunedin* ☎ *03/477–9296* ⊕ *www.designwithdrawals.co.nz.*

Guilty by Confection

CANDY | For sweets, drop by this shop for a hot chocolate or some terrific homemade fudge. ⊠ *44–46 Stuart St., Dunedin* ☎ *03/474–0835.*

Koru NZ Art

ART GALLERIES | Koru is an owner-operated gift shop and gallery that promotes New Zealand art. It houses the work of some 80 artists and craftspeople from all around the country and includes crafts made of *pounamu* (New Zealand greenstone), *paua* (abalone shell), and wood, as well as weaving and pottery. ⊠ *2 Castle St., Dunedin* ☎ *03/477–2138.*

Plume

WOMEN'S CLOTHING | Plume carries great New Zealand brands among a selection of major international designer clothes. Labels include Nom D, Zambesi, Rick Owens, Comme des Garcons, Jimmy D, Serge Thoraval, Dries van Noten and Y-3.

✉ *310 George St., Dunedin* ☎ *03/477–9358* ⊕ *www.nomdstore.com.*

Slick Willy's

WOMEN'S CLOTHING | If you're looking for funky fun-to-wear apparel, here's a great selection, along with women's denim, dresses, jackets, pants, skirts, shorts, skirts, and tops, not to mention snazzy shoes and jewelry. Over 50 brands are represented. ✉ *323a George St., upstairs, Dunedin* ☎ *03/477–1406* ⊕ *www.slickwillys.co.nz.*

University Bookshop

BOOKS | Bibliophiles will be in heaven amid this eclectic and diverse selection of books as well as a feast of quirky gifts, and bargain hunters will love the second floor, where there is a constant sale. ✉ *378 Great King St., Dunedin* ☎ *03/477–6976* ⊕ *www.unibooks.co.nz.*

🏃 Activities

Mix up your city adventure with some sightseeing on the outskirts of town. And when that's finished, pop over to one of the parks to watch kids in rugby practice after school.

HIKING AND WALKING

Walking with Wheels is a collection of well-groomed walks put together by Dunedin City Council detailing those suitable for wheelchair users and families with strollers (the three-wheeled, rugged-terrain kind). You can download a leaflet from the Dunedin i-SITE website.

Signal Hill

HIKING & WALKING | This prominent plateau just northeast of the city center offers good views out over the city below and the surrounding hills. It's a popular walking destination and an excellent mountain-biking venue. At the opposite end of town, Saddle Hill looks southward to Mosgiel and the Taieri Plain. The monument at the top was built in 1940 to mark 100 years of British sovereignty in New Zealand. Legend has it the flagpole here was made from the mast of the cutter once belonging to the notorious Bully Hayes, the South Pacific's only pirate. ✉ *Signal Hill Rd., Dunedin.*

Oamaru

112 km (69 miles) north of Dunedin, 85 km (53 miles) south of Timaru.

In Oamaru's port district, New Zealand's best-preserved historical landmarks still gleam with ornate, limestone Victorian facades. During the second week of November, the town hosts the Victorian Heritage Celebrations. Festivities include the New Zealand Penny Farthing Championships, a Heritage Golf Classic, a Heritage Ball, and a Victorian Garden Party. The town's visitor center has information about the festival and the buildings themselves. More recently, the town has become known for an art collaboration called Steampunk, which creates quirky recycled industrial art throughout the town.

Oamaru's other claim to fame is penguins. Each evening, enthusiastic blue penguins—the world's smallest penguin breed—emerge from the sea and waddle up the beach to their nests. The penguin colony is a five-minute drive from the town center in Oamaru. An even more significant population of yellow-eyed penguins, or *hoiho,* come ashore south of Oamaru. The best places to view them are Bushy Beach and Katiki Point, where hides (camouflaged viewing huts) have been constructed. The hide at Bushy Beach is wheelchair-accessible. These penguins are one of the world's rarest breeds, and they are considered an endangered species.

Did You Know?

Māori legend explains that unusual Moeraki Boulders represent the scattered goods from a wrecked sailing canoe. Shag Point's jagged shoals are its hull, and another rock takes the form of the captain.

GETTING HERE AND AROUND

From Dunedin to Oamaru it's a 1½-hour drive north on State Highway 1. From Timaru to Oamaru it's a one-hour drive south on the same route. InterCity Coachlines connects Oamaru to Dunedin and Timaru three times daily. Exploring the mostly flat and ordered layout of Oamaru streets is easy and enjoyable on foot. South Hill Walkway follows the harbor to Lookout Reserve, which affords excellent views out over the town and port.

VISITOR INFORMATION

Waitaki and Oamaru Visitor Centre. ⊠ *1 Thames St., Oamaru* ☎ *03/434–1656* ⊕ *waitakinz.com.*

 Sights

Moeraki Boulders

NATURE SIGHT | These giant spherical rocks are concretions that were formed by a gradual buildup of minerals around a central core. Some boulders have sprung open, revealing—no, not alien life forms, but—interesting calcite crystals. The boulders stud the beach north of the town of Moeraki and south as well at Katiki Beach off Highway 1. Be warned that the boulders at Moeraki Beach have become a bit of a tourist attraction, and there are often whole busloads of people wandering the beach. Watch for little Hector's dolphins jumping in the surf just offshore; they're as interesting as the boulders. ⊠ *Moeraki Boulders Rd., Moeraki.*

Oamaru Blue Penguin Colony

BEACH | **FAMILY** | Penguins at Friendly Bay might be present any time of the year, and tours and viewing opportunities run day and evening. There's a small visitor center on site with a shop and toilet facilities. The actual times penguins come ashore in the evening affects the nighttime hours, but the center opens every day at 5 pm. Access to the public beach is free. ⊠ *2 Waterfront Rd., Oamaru* ☎ *03/433–1195* ⊕ *www.penguins.co.nz* 🎫 *Tours from NZ$36.*

🍴 Restaurants

Riverstone Kitchen

$$$ | NEW ZEALAND | FAMILY | The mouthwatering menu focuses on organic, locally grown, seasonal produce, offering regional New Zealand cuisine with a few Asian accents (a Thai duck salad, for instance). While the atmosphere is casual, the food is serious thanks to chef Bevan Smith, who trained in Christchurch and has published four cookbooks. **Known for:** innovative and elegant menu; affordable prix-fixe option; fresh seasonal fare. 💲 *Average main: NZ$30* ⊠ *1431 State Hwy. 1, Oamaru* ☎ *03/431–3505* ⊕ *www.riverstonekitchen.co.nz* 🕙 *No dinner Mon.–Fri.*

Otago Peninsula

Larnach Castle is 13 km east of Dunedin.

The main items of interest along the claw-shaped peninsula that extends northeast from Dunedin are an albatross colony and Larnach Castle. The road on the west side of the peninsula consists of 15 km (9½ miles) of tight curves along the harbor, so be careful while driving, or you could find yourself having an impromptu marine adventure. Along the road are a handful of settlements; these get progressively more rustic as you near the peninsula's tip. On the east side of the peninsula, there's a string of rugged beaches; some are accessible via walking paths. On the journey back to Dunedin, the Highcliff Road, which turns inland at the village of Portobello, is a scenic alternative to the coastal Portobello Road and gives the easiest access to Larnach Castle. Allow an hour to drive from the city.

GETTING HERE AND AROUND

Driving to the peninsula gives you freedom to stop when and where you choose, and the route is quite scenic, as much of the road hugs the water. The

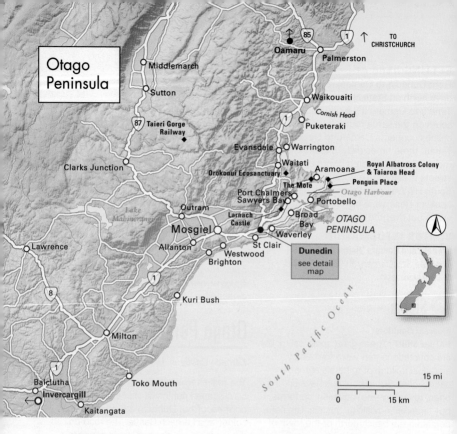

Otago Peninsula

Dunedin city bus leaves throughout the day from Cumberland Street to the peninsula; check the GoBus website for the schedule. You can also see the peninsula sights via a harbor boat cruise.

Visitor information is available at the Dunedin i-SITE Visitor Information Centre, but for facts specific to the peninsula, check out the Visit Otago Peninsula website.

CONTACTS Dunedin Passenger Service. ✉ *36 Parry St. N., Dunedin* ☎ *0800/477–800* ⊕ *www.dunedinpassengerservice. co.nz.* **GoBus.** ✉ *1 Transport Pl., Dunedin* ☎ *03/474–5577* ⊕ *www.gobus.co.nz* Ⓜ *Dunedin Central.*

TOURS
Monarch Wildlife Cruises
BOAT TOURS | Experience the area's prolific wildlife on a guided, hour-long cruise from Dunedin to Taiaroa Head, including visits to the breeding sites of the northern royal albatross, New Zealand fur seals, and up to 20 species of coastal and pelagic birds. Very likely, an albatross will fly over your boat—the huge wingspan of these birds makes this a spectacular sight. Other trips include landing stops at the yellow-eyed penguin reserve or the Taiaroa visitor center. ✉ *20 Fryatt St., Dunedin* ☎ *03/477–4276* ⊕ *www.wildlife.co.nz* ✉ *From NZ$57.*

Natures Wonders Wildlife Tours
ADVENTURE TOURS | An all-terrain 'Argo' vehicle gets you to hard-to-reach parts

of the Otago Peninsula. The one-hour Wildlife Tour includes visits to colonies of shags (cormorants), seals, and blue penguins, and you may even catch up with some yellow-eyed penguins coming ashore. The Sheep Shed Tour is exactly that and provides a look at life on a New Zealand sheep farm: watch talented shearers in action; feel the fleece; smell the lanolin (and the waft of a genuine sheep shed); walk alongside working dogs as they control the flow of sheep into holding pens. Make a day of it and combine both trips. ⊠ *Taiaroa Head, 1265 Harrington Point Rd., Dunedin* ☏ *03/478–1150, 0800/246–446* ⊕ *www. natureswonders.co.nz* 🖂 *From NZ$55.*

VISITOR INFORMATION
CONTACTS Visit Otago Peninsula. ⊕ *www. otago-peninsula.co.nz.*

 Sights

Larnach Castle
CASTLE/PALACE | High on a hilltop with commanding views from its battlements, the grand baronial fantasy of William Larnach, an Australian-born businessman and New Zealand politician, was a vast extravagance even in the free-spending days of the gold rush in the 1870s. Larnach imported an English craftsman to carve the ceilings, which took 12 years to complete. The solid marble bath, marble fireplaces, tiles, glass, and even much of the wood came from Europe. Larnach rose to a prominent position in the New Zealand government of the late 1800s, but in 1898, beset by a series of financial disasters and possible marital problems, he committed suicide in Parliament House—when, according to one version of the story, his third wife, whom he married at an advanced age, ran off with his youngest son. The 35 acres of grounds around the castle include lodging, a rain-forest garden with kauri, rimu, and totara trees, statues of *Alice in Wonderland* characters (see if you can find the

Cheshire Cat), a herbaceous walk, and a South Seas Walkway lined with palms and aloe plants. New Zealand's only castle is a 20-minute drive from Dunedin but can be tricky to find, so follow the directions on the website. ⊠ *145 Camp Rd., Otago, Dunedin* ☏ *03/476–1616* ⊕ *www. larnachcastle.co.nz* 🖂 *From NZ$17.50 garden only, $35 garden and castle.*

The Mole
BEACH | The Mole, which splits the picturesque white-sand beach at the end of the Aramoana Peninsula, is a 1-km-long (½-mile-long) artificial breakwater protecting the entrance to Otago Harbour. A walk atop the breakwater is especially exciting when there is a big running sea. The beach and sand dunes to the east are known as Shelly Beach, while to the west, Big Beach extends for more than 2 km (about a mile). At points along this stretch, steep rock faces come down to the waterline and are popular with rock climbers. Seals can be found sun bathing on the rocks.

Orokonui Ecosanctuary
FOREST | FAMILY | A 30-minute drive northeast of Dunedin is a 759-acre forest where native plants and wildlife thrive in relative safety surrounded by an 8.7-km (5-mile) predator-proof fence. This is necessary because much of New Zealand wildlife is threatened by pests and predators introduced into the country before settlers knew any better, and Orokonui is unique because it was the first of only three mainland eco-sanctuaries on the South Island. The latest attraction here is a jewel gecko enclosure. The park offers good walking tracks, informative displays, a café, and a souvenir shop. Parents, grab a Kiwi Ranger booklet from the front desk, which lists lots of activities to keep the kids amused during the day; if they complete the tasks, they earn a "Kiwi Ranger" badge. ⊠ *600 Blueskin Rd., Waitati* ☏ *03/482–1755* ⊕ *www.orokonui. org.nz* 🖂 *Tours from NZ$20.*

The Royal Albatross Colony in Otago is one of the few places where the southern royal albatross breeds.

Penguin Place

WILDLIFE REFUGE | FAMILY | This conservation project is entirely funded by guided tours of the private reserve. If you'd like to observe the world's most endangered penguin in its natural habitat, visit Penguin Place, where an ingenious network of tunnels has been disguised so that you can get close. The penguins, also known as *hoiho* (meaning "noise shouter" in Māori), are characterized by their yellow irises and headbands. Tours run throughout the afternoon but must be booked in advance. If you can't bring yourself to leave, Penguin Place Lodge offers basic and inexpensive farm-stay accommodation. ⊠ *45 Pakihau Rd., Harrington Point* ☎ *03/478–0286* ⊕ *www. penguinplace.co.nz* ✉ *NZ$55* ⚑ *Reservations essential.*

★ Royal Albatross Colony

WILDLIFE REFUGE | The wild and exposed eastern tip of the Otago Peninsula is the site of a breeding colony of royal albatrosses. Among the largest birds in

the world, with a wingspan of up to 10 feet, they can take off only from steep slopes with the help of a strong breeze. With the exception of this colony and those in the Chatham Islands to the east, the birds are only on windswept islands deep in southern latitudes, far from human habitation. Under the auspices of the Royal Albatross Centre, the colony is open for viewing all year, except during a two-month break between mid-September and mid-November when the birds lay their eggs; the visitor center is open year-round. The greatest number of birds is present shortly after the young albatrosses hatch near the end of January. Between March and September, parents leave the fledglings in their nests while they gather food for them. In September, the young birds fly away, returning about eight years later to start their own breeding cycle. Access to the colony is strictly controlled, and you must book in advance. From the visitor center you go in groups up a steep trail to the Albatross Observatory, from which you can see the birds through viewing windows. ✉ *1260 Harington Point Rd., Taiaroa Head* ☎ *03/478–0499, 0800/528–767* 🌐 *www.albatross.org.nz* 🎟 *NZ$52.*

Taiaroa Head

MILITARY SIGHT | Overlooking the albatross colony at Fort Taiaroa is the world's only restored Armstrong "Disappearing" Gun, a 6-inch-caliber artillery piece installed during the Russian Scare of 1886, when Russia was making hostile maneuvers through the Pacific. The gun was shot in anger only once, during World War II, when it was fired across the bow of a fishing boat that failed to observe correct procedures. Tours range from 30 to 90 minutes and can include albatross viewing, Fort Taiaroa, and an Albatross Insight presentation. 🎟 *Combined tour with Albatross Colony NZ$62*

🍴 Restaurants

1908 Café & Bar

$$$ | ECLECTIC | There are good views of the harbor from this converted post office "where the high road meets the low road." The interior still feels Edwardian, and classic seafood dishes and steaks lead the menu; on a nice day sit outside in the courtyard, or, in winter, beside the open fire. Reservations are recommended. **Known for:** delicious seafood and steaks menu; beautiful harbor views; gorgeous Edwardian decor. [$] *Average main: NZ$29* ✉ *7 Harington Point Rd., Portobello* ☎ *03/478–0801* 🌐 *www.1908cafe.co.nz* ⏲ *Closed Tues.*

🛏 Hotels

Larnach Lodge

$$ | B&B/INN | It's hard to beat panoramic sea views, 35 acres of world-class gardens, having Larnach Castle as a neighbor, and the choice of a luxury room or a more modest yet still character-filled accommodation. **Pros:** impressive grounds; coastal walks nearby; Scottish theme with period furniture. **Cons:** more a manor house than a true castle; a bit on the expensive side for what you get; cheaper rooms do not have private baths. [$] *Rooms from: NZ$170* ✉ *145 Camp Rd., Otago, 14 km (8.6 miles) northeast of Dunedin* ☎ *03/476–1616* 🌐 *www.larnachcastle.co.nz* 🛏 *23 rooms* 🍽 *Free Breakfast.*

🏃 Activities

DIVING

Dive Otago

DIVING & SNORKELING | A dozen or so small ships were sunk between 1920 and 1950 to protect the breakwater from the relentless Southern Ocean. You can check these ships out, and the tall kelp forest that protects them, with Dive Otago, which run trips to the Mole and other Discover Local Diving sites when the weather allows. Introductory dive courses and snorkeling trips are also offered. ✉ *2 Wharf St., Dunedin* ☎ *03/466–4370* 🌐 *www.diveotago.co.nz* 🎟 *From NZ$250.*

Invercargill

188 km (116 miles) south of Queenstown, 204 km (127 miles) southwest of Dunedin.

Originally settled by Scottish immigrants, Invercargill has retained much of its turn-of-the-20th-century character, with broad main avenues (Tay Street and Dee Street) and streetscapes with richly embellished buildings. You'll find facades with Italian and English Renaissance styles, Gothic stone tracery, and Romanesque designs on a number of its well-preserved buildings.

Invercargill was featured in the movie *The World's Fastest Indian* (2005) starring Sir Anthony Hopkins as Invercargill-bred Burt Munro, a local "petrolhead" who

Taking the Southern Scenic Route

The Southern Scenic Route, 440 km (273 miles) long, follows the coast south of Dunedin and the Otago Peninsula, picks up the highway to Balclutha, and swings around the Catlins coast before pushing through Invercargill to Milford Sound. The Catlins stretch (200 km, or 125 miles) is a treat, although some unsealed side roads can be rough. Split your journey over at least two days. The *Southern Scenic Route* brochure, available at the Dunedin visitor center, describes the sights; attractions are signposted.

When you leave the highway at Balclutha, you'll notice that the native bush is dense and relatively untouched. This, coupled with rich birdsong, gives the countryside a subtropical quality.

The first stop is **Nugget Point.** Its Māori name, Tokatā, means "rocks standing up out of water." Wildlife abounds, including yellow-eyed penguins, petrels, fur and elephant seals, and sea lions. The town at Nugget Point is **Kaka Point.** There are several places to stay the night, and you should spend time at the "hide" observing the yellow-eyed penguins coming in from the sea. If you want a coffee served with an excellent sea view, stop in the **Point Café & Bar** at Kaka Point. Inland is **Owaka**, the Catlins' only town. With a population of roughly 400, Owaka has a cluster of shops, a Department of Conservation Field Centre, a small museum, and basic services.

At the settlement of **Papatowai**, there's a convenient picnic spot behind a tidal inlet. Here you can enjoy rock pools with bush on one side and coastline on the other. Just south of here, stop at the **Florence Hill Lookout.** The view of Tautuku Bay is one of the best coastal views in New Zealand. There's a 30-minute loop walk onto the estuary at Tautuku Bay.

Farther on is **Curio Bay**, home to a petrified forest accessible at low tide. From Curio Bay a back road runs out to **Slope Point**, mainland New Zealand's southernmost point. Heavy rains or unusually high tides can make the road impassable. Slope Point is a bit of a disappointment—just some farmland sloping to the sea. However, it gets plenty of visitors, mainly because nearby Waipapa Point was the location of the country's worst-ever civilian shipwreck when the *SS Tararua* sunk offshore on April 29, 1881. A memorial stands to the 131 people who died in the wreck and are buried in a paddock here. There is no access during the lambing season in September and October. If you skip Slope Point and continue on the main road, stop at the general store in Waikawa, where the art of the meat pie has been perfected. Worth checking out, too, is the Waikawa Museum and Information Centre, made from two old school buildings.

By now the rugged Catlins landscape smooths out into gentle green hills. From the township of Fortrose the roads are straight once more across the wide flats of Southland; before you know it, you've reached Invercargill. The road continues westward to Tuatapere, the self-proclaimed "sausage capital of New Zealand." Along the way, check out the surfers at Colac Bay, and make a detour to Cosy Nook, where a handful of fishing "cribs," or huts, have been likened to an old Cornwall fishing village.

raced his Indian motorcycle on Oreti Beach in preparation for breaking a world land speed record. Mayor Tim Shadbolt had a cameo in the film, which is worth seeing. Invercargill has a reputation to this day for "boy racers," and you'll notice them roaring up and down the city streets in tricked-out cars. Indignant Invercargillites blame the epidemic on "Gorons," boy racers from neighboring city Gore. You might have a '50s flashback if you're waiting at a light and a lowrider next to you starts to rumble and rev its engine.

GETTING HERE AND AROUND

Invercargill's airport (IVC) is 3 km (2 miles) from the city center. From Invercargill, Air New Zealand runs direct flights to Christchurch, Wellington, and Auckland, and Stewart Island Air flights hop over to Stewart Island. Several rental car companies operate in the terminal. Taxis from Invercargill Airport into town cost NZ$12–NZ$15. A shuttle run by Executive Car Services (*www.executivecarservice.co.nz*) costs NZ$10–NZ$14 per person, and there's usually a shuttle waiting for each flight. Executive Car Service also offers secure car storage (NZ$10 per night). Invercargill is extremely walkable, and also particularly driver-friendly thanks to its wide streets. Near the Civic Theatre on Tay Street, the Bus Hub links the center of town with local districts. Longer distance buses connect Invercargill to Christchurch, Dunedin, Te Anau, and Queenstown every day and leave from outside Tuatara Lodge at 32 Dee Street. Stewart Island Experience (*www.stewartislandexperience.co.nz*) operates the Bluff Bus, which stops there and at the museum and various accommodations (reservations essential).

AIRPORT CONTACTS Invercargill Airport. ✉ *106 Airport Ave., Invercargill* ☎ *03/218–6920* ⊕ *www.invercargillairport.co.nz.*

BUS CONTACTS Atomic Travel. ☎ *03/349–0697, 021/0867–6001* ⊕ *www.atomic-travel.co.nz.* **Bottom Bus.** ☎ *03/477–9083* ⊕ *www.headfirsttravel.com.* **BusSmart.** ✉ *Dee St., Invercargill* ✛ *Near Civic Theatre* ☎ *03/211–1777* ⊕ *www.icc.govt.nz.* **InterCity.** ☎ *03/471–7143* ⊕ *www.intercity.co.nz.*

TOURS

Catlins Scenic and Wildlife Tours
ECOTOURISM | This company offers guided eco-tours that will take you to view sea lions, fur seals, yellow-eyed penguins, and seabird nesting sites, along with other top sights in the area. Tours are all three–four hours and include options for a sunrise tour and a waterfall tour; there's one full-day, in-depth nature tour. ✉ *744 Catlins Valley Rd., Papatowai* ☎ *03/415–8613* ⊕ *www.catlinsmohua-park.co.nz* 💰 *From NZ$150.*

Lynette Jack Scenic Sights
PRIVATE GUIDES | Lynette Jack draws on extensive knowledge of Invercargill and the surrounding area to illuminate local history during an exploration of gardens, beaches, historic houses, local hero Burt Munro, and even the local aluminum smeltery. ✉ *22 Willis St., Invercargill* ☎ *027/433–8370, 03/215–7741* ⊕ *www.ljscenicsights.co.nz* 💰 *From NZ$113.*

VISITOR INFORMATION
CONTACTS Southland Visitor Information. ✉ *Invercargill* ☎ *0800/474–830* ⊕ *www.southlandnz.com.*

👁 Sights

Bill Richardson Transport World
OTHER MUSEUM | More than 300 trucks and VW Kombis (that's a VW bus, to Americans) are on display, alongside motoring memorabilia and petrol bowsers—or, again for Americans, gas pumps. Kids who get bored looking at old cars will enjoy a special Lego learning space geared to them. There's something for

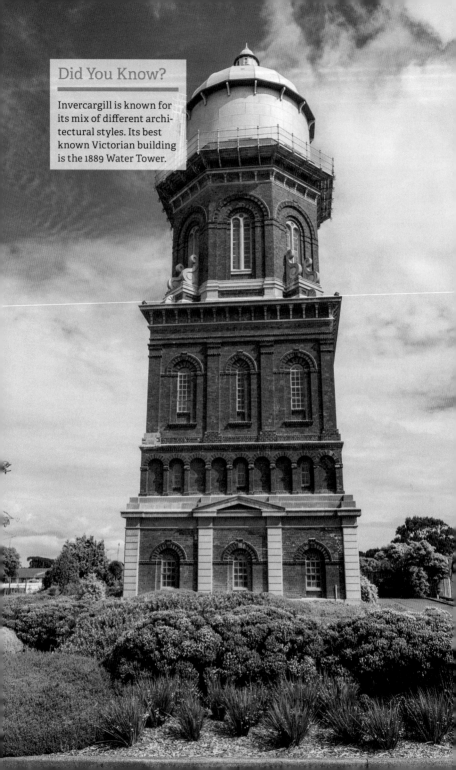

everyone here, including a display of classic motorcycles and an interactive display of heavy machinery. It is reputed to be the largest such private collection in the world. ✉ *491 Tay St., Invercargill* ☎ *03/217–0199* ⊕ *www.transportworld. co.nz* 🏷 *NZ$35.*

Bluff

TOWN | In the tiny seaport township of Bluff ("The Bluff" to locals) you can taste the coveted namesake oysters. An annual festival, held in May, wallows in seafood delicacies; oyster-opening and oyster-eating competitions and cook-offs are part of the fun. (If you miss the festival, the most spectacular place for oysters, in season, is Lands End Restaurant overlooking the sea). Don't miss the Maritime Museum on the Foreshore Road (the Oyster boat *Monica* sits beside it). Bluff is also home to the frequently photographed Stirling Point signpost, at the southern end of State Highway 1, which gives directions to places all over the world, including the South Pole. If it's a nice day follow the signs up to Bluff Lookout: the views encompass the Catlins and Stewart Island, and give you an excellent lay of the land. Good walking tracks are around Bluff; many begin at Stirling Point. The town is also the main jumping-off point for Stewart Island. It's about 30 km (19 miles) from Invercargill to Bluff, an easy half-hour drive south on State Highway 1. ⊕ *www.bluff.co.nz.*

E. Hayes and Sons

STORE/MALL | Invercargill's most famous sight is a 100-year-old hardware store that stocks every little thing you can think of. It's totally yin-yang (grandma-grandpa) with one half devoted to little glass lemon juicers and whisks and the other half filled with tools and wheelbarrows. The store also has a popular Motorworks Collection where you can view memorabilia of Invercargill's famous son Burt Munro, the "World's Fastest Indian."✉ *168 Dee St., Invercargill* ☎ *03/218–2059* ⊕ *www. ehayes.co.nz.*

Queens Park

CITY PARK | **FAMILY** | These 200 acres in the center of town create a fine layout of public gardens. Included are two rose gardens with both modern and "antique" rose varieties; a Japanese garden complete with meditation area; and an impressive hothouse, which acts as a sanctuary on a wet day. The park has miles of gentle walking paths and waterways, an 18-hole golf course, a fitness trail, and a decent café. There's also a small zoo area and an aviary with a walk-through section that children love. The main entrance is through the stately Feldwick Gates next to the Southland Museum. ✉ *Queens Dr. at Gala St., Invercargill* ☎ *03/217–7368.*

Water Tower

NOTABLE BUILDING | The tower is an exceptional example of Victorian architecture that can be seen peeking above the city's gentle landscape. Built in 1889 to pressurize the water supply, the structure was recognized by New Zealand's Historic Places Trust as one of the country's most outstanding industrial monuments. This ornate landmark is still completely functional. On Sunday afternoon you can sometimes scale the internal staircase of the 139-foot-tall structure. ✉ *Doon St., Invercargill* ⊕ *www.icc.govt.nz.*

 Beaches

Oreti Beach

BEACH | The surf at this spot 9.5 km (6 miles) southeast of town is often too rough for swimming, but locals do swim in summer, and surfers and windsurfers take advantage of the wind and swells that whip the coast almost constantly. The annual Burt Munro Challenge in February sees motorcycles hurtle across the sand as riders pit their wits and machines against one another in honor of the local hero and motorcycle land speed record holder from whom the race gets its name. **Amenities:** none. **Best for:**

solitude; surfing; walking; windsurfing. ✉ *Dunns Rd., Invercargill* 🌐 *www.burtmunrochallenge.com.*

🍴 Restaurants

Cabbage Tree

$$$$ | **NEW ZEALAND** | **FAMILY** | A spacious dining room done in wood and brick offers a supersize menu with more than 100 dishes. Popular choices are Stewart Island blue cod, lamb shanks, prawns, pan-seared venison, and Bluff oyster dishes. **Known for:** wonderful outdoor garden bar; comprehensive menu including many New Zealand wines; deliciously fresh seafood. [$] *Average main: NZ$32* ✉ *379 Dunns Rd., Invercargill* ☎ *03/213–1443* 🌐 *www.thecabbagetree.com.*

Little India Invercargill

$$$ | **INDIAN** | Influenced by the flavors of northern India (and the kitchen of founder Sukhi's grandmother) this family business began in Dunedin and now has restaurants spanning the country. Spacious and modern eateries offer traditional cooking methods; warm hospitality and generous portions keep diners coming back. **Known for:** plenty of vegetarian options; exotic and authentic Indian cuisine; cozy and charming atmosphere. [$] *Average main: NZ$21* ✉ *11 The Crescent, Invercargill* ☎ *03/214–1555* 🌐 *www.littleindia.co.nz* 🕒 *No lunch weekends.*

The Rocks Restaurant Bar

$$$$ | **CONTEMPORARY** | You could easily walk past this stylish place, tucked inside a shopping courtyard. The kitchen employs bounty from the nearby bush and sea paired with inventive sauces and sides. **Known for:** Tuscany-inspired decor; exquisite dining experience; specializing in steaks, fish, chicken, pork, venison, and lamb. [$] *Average main: NZ$38* ✉ *11 Courville Pl., Invercargill* ☎ *03/218–7597* 🌐 *www.shop5rocks.com* 🕒 *Closed Sun. and Mon.*

Ziff's Café and Bar

$$$$ | **NEW ZEALAND** | This enormously popular restaurant on the way to Oreti Beach (past the airport) is a local favorite. Ziff's does steak, blue cod, chicken, and pasta, and customers love the home-smoked salmon and the venison hot pot. **Known for:** generous servings of simple but tasty cuisine; local atmosphere; late breakfasts. [$] *Average main: NZ$36* ✉ *143 Dunns Rd., Invercargill* ☎ *03/213–0501* 🌐 *www.ziffs.co.nz.*

🛏 Hotels

Many of Invercargill's motels are on Tay Street, handy if you're coming from Dunedin and North Road, convenient if you're arriving from Queenstown.

Ascot Park Hotel

$$ | **HOTEL** | The largest hotel in town, an eight-minute drive from the town center, is a rambling complex with spacious, modern rooms, most with small balconies and those in a motel-style building with kitchenettes. **Pros:** free Wi-Fi and parking; big spacious rooms; some kitchenette units for cooking. **Cons:** tiny pool; restaurant is pricey; some rooms could use updating. [$] *Rooms from: NZ$125* ✉ *Corner of Tay St. and Racecourse Rd., Invercargill* ☎ *03/219–9076, 0800/272–687* 🌐 *www.ascotparkhotel.co.nz* 🔑 *106 rooms* 🍽 *No Meals.*

Kelvin Hotel

$$ | **HOTEL** | The big advantage of this modern but somewhat bland full-service hotel is that it's really central, in just about the ideal location if you're not driving. **Pros:** welcoming staff; couldn't be more centrally located; excellent restaurant. **Cons:** breakfast expensive in hotel restaurant (and not included); no gym on-site but pass to nearby facility included; some rooms on the small side. [$] *Rooms from: NZ$160* ✉ *20 Kelvin St., Invercargill* ☎ *03/218–2829, 0800/802–829* 🌐 *www.kelvinhotel.co.nz* 🔑 *61 rooms* 🍽 *No Meals.*

Mohua Park

$$$ | **HOUSE** | If you're traveling to Invercargill via the Southern Scenic Route, these four lovely self-catering cottages make a perfect rest stop before you get to the city. **Pros:** lots of privacy; beautiful outlooks on 35 acres of native forest; eco-friendly. **Cons:** no TV or phone; no restaurants on-site; no Wi-Fi. $ *Rooms from: NZ$225 ⊠ 744 Catlins Valley Rd., Invercargill ☎ 03/415–8613 ⊕ www.catlinsmohuapark.co.nz ⇩ 4 cottages* ⦿ *No Meals.*

Tuatara Backpackers Lodge

$ | **HOTEL** | The world's southernmost YHA hostel is in the center of Invercargill, next door to the Speight's Ale House and the main city library. **Pros:** all necessary amenities on site; inexpensive; centrally located. **Cons:** very basic; can be noisy at night; only a few rooms with private baths. $ *Rooms from: NZ$50 ⊠ 30–32 Dee St., Invercargill ☎ 03/214–0954, 0800/488–282 ⊕ www.tuataralodge.co.nz* ⦿ *No Meals ⇩ 26 rooms.*

🏃 Activities

Take a picture of yourself on some of the world's southernmost beaches and send it home. But Invercargill doesn't exactly have perfect tanning weather. Even in summer, the south can still get a few chilly days. Some Stewart Island trips depart from here and include the ferry costs in their rate.

HIKING
Estuary Walkway

HIKING & WALKING | Just 2½ km (1½ miles) south of Invercargill, this 4.7-km (2.9-mile) walking–cycling loop where the Waihopai River meets the New River estuary traverses what was once a landfill site. The area has benefited from a community regeneration project and now provides a rich habitat for wildlife and people to enjoy. The walkway is accessible from the parking lot at Stead Street Wharf and Bond Street. ⊠ *Stead St., Invercargill.*

Sandy Point

HIKING & WALKING | A ten-minute drive from Invercargill, this good walking spot can be reached by taking a left after crossing the Oreti River on the way out to Oreti Beach. A 13-km (8-mile) network of easygoing trails covers the riverbanks, estuary, and the bush. A leaflet detailing the paths is available from the Invercargill Visitor Information Centre. ⊠ *Sandy Point Rd., Invercargill.*

Tuatapere Hump Ridge Track

HIKING & WALKING | On the western side of the Southern Scenic Route, this challenging, circular, three-day/two-night walk combines beach, bush, and subalpine environments in its 53 km (33 miles). The track starts near Tuatapere, about two hours' drive west of Invercargill and right on the edge of the Fiordland National Park. It's no amble; you'll spend about nine hours walking each day, but two good huts along the route each sleep about 40 people. You'll need to buy hut tickets in advance. ⊠ *31 Orawia Rd., Tuatapere, Invercargill ☎ 03/226–6739 ⊕ www.humpridgetrack.co.nz ⛺ 295* ⦿ *Closed in winter.*

Stewart Island

1 hour by ferry from Bluff; 20 minutes by plane from Invercargill Airport.

Stewart Island, home to New Zealand's newest national park, Rakiura, is the third-largest and most southerly of New Zealand's main islands, separated from the South Island by the 30-km (19-mile) Foveaux Strait. Its original Māori name, Te Punga O Te Waka a Maui, means "the anchor stone of Maui's canoe." Māori mythology says the island's landmass held the god Maui's canoe secure while he and his crew raised the great fish—the North Island. Today, the island is more commonly referred to by its modern Māori name, Rakiura, which means "the land of the glowing skies." This refers to the spectacular sunrises and sunsets and to the southern lights, or aurora australis. The European name of Stewart Island dates back to 1809. It memorializes an officer, William W. Stewart, on an early sealing vessel, the *Pegasus,* who was the first to chart the island.

The island covers some 1,700 square km (650 square miles). It measures about 75 km (46 miles) from north to south and about the same distance across at its widest point. On the coastline, sharp cliffs rise from a succession of sheltered bays and beaches. In the interior, forested hills rise gradually toward the west side of the island. Seals and penguins frequent the coast, and the island's prolific birdlife includes a number of species rarely seen in any other part of the country. In fact, this is the surest place to see a kiwi, including the largest sub-species. Unlike their mainland cousins, the Stewart Island brown kiwi, or *tokoeka,* can often be seen during the day as well as at night. It's a rare and amusing experience to watch these pear-shaped birds scampering on a remote beach as they feed on sand hoppers and grubs.

Māori have visited and lived on Stewart Island for centuries. Archaeologists' studies of 13th-century Māori middens (food refuse heaps) indicate that the island was once a rich, seasonal resource for hunting, fishing, and gathering seafood. A commonly eaten delicacy at that time, the *titi,* also known as the muttonbird, is still traditionally harvested and occasionally appears on menus.

In the early 19th century, explorers, sealers, missionaries, and miners settled the island. They were followed by fishermen and sawmillers, who established settlements around the edges of Paterson Inlet and Halfmoon and Horseshoe bays. In the 1920s, Norwegians set up a whaling enterprise in Paterson Inlet, and many descendants of these seafaring people remain. Fishing, aquaculture, and tourism are now the mainstays of the island's economy.

Even by New Zealand standards, Stewart Island is remote, raw, and untouched. For many, seclusion and a relaxed way of life are part of its appeal. Stewart Island is not for everyone: if you must have shopping malls, casinos, or umbrella drinks on the beach, don't come here. Also, be prepared for the fact that Stewart Island can be chilly, windy, and rainy, even in the middle of summer.

GETTING HERE AND AROUND
AIR
Stewart Island Flights has three scheduled flights daily between Invercargill and Halfmoon Bay. The 20-minute flight costs NZ$225 round-trip; for the best views, ask to sit up front with the pilot. The island's bare-bones-but-paved Ryan's Creek Airstrip is about 2 km (1 mile) from Oban (population 420). The shuttle that meets each flight is included in the airfare.

CONTACTS Stewart Island Flights. ⊠ *Invercargill Airport, 106 Airport Ave.* ☎ *03/218–9129* ⊕ *www.stewartislandflights.com.*

BOAT
Stewart Island Experience runs the ferry between the island and Bluff. There are three departures daily November to April, and one during the low season. The cost is NZ$89 each way, NZ$159 round-trip. The company also offers an extensive list of organized tours, including trips aboard submersible craft with viewing windows that afford a close-up look at dozens of fish species and the mesmerizing kelp forests.

CONTACTS Stewart Island Experience. ⊠ *Stewart Island Visitor Terminal, Main Wharf, Oban* ☎ *03/212–7660, 0800/000–511* ⊕ *www.stewartislandexperience. co.nz.*

CAR, MOPED, AND BICYCLE

There are cars, mopeds, and bicycles for rent on the island, but there are only 20 km (13 miles) of paved road. Most of the traffic road signs you'll see are big yellow caution ones depicting silhouettes of kiwi and penguins.

FOOT

The best mode of transportation on the island is the "10-toe express." There are some sidewalks, but when there isn't one, keep to the edge of the road, and you'll endear yourself to locals by not strolling in the middle of traffic.

TAXI

Water taxis are an excellent option if you want to mix it up a bit when seeing the park. One-way fares start from NZ$45 depending on destination, and the Ulva Island round-trip is NZ$25. Four taxis operate from Golden Bay Wharf, a scenic 15-minute walk from town. The visitor center can make a booking for you.

TOURS

Besides regular daily ferry services between Bluff and Halfmoon Bay (Stewart Island), Stewart Island Experience offers a range of island-based excursions that coincide with ferry arrivals. You can also take a coastal cruise from November through March, or make the short trip to Ulva Island from November through April.

Island Explorer

BUS TOURS | If you're short of time, then hop on a scenic, 90-minute bus tour operated by Stewart Island Flights. There are no scheduled departure times (it's done on demand), so make sure to book ahead whenever possible. ⊠ *Stewart Island Flights, Elgin Terr., Halfmoon Bay* ☏ *03/218–9129* ⊕ *www.stewartisland-flights.com* ⊠ *From NZ$35.*

VISITOR INFORMATION

The Department of Conservation Rakiura National Park Visitor Centre is open daily. The Environment Centre, located next to the Glowing Sky Merino Shop, has information about the habitat recovery projects on the island. The village library in the Community Centre has a complete collection of books about Stewart Island, as well as field guides of native flora and fauna. (The library is open only five hours per week, however.) For biased, vulgar, and amusing information about island goings-on ("the goss"), belly up to the bar at the pub and do some earwigging.

CONTACTS Department of Conservation Rakiura National Park Visitor Centre. ⊠ *15 Main Rd., Oban* ☏ *03/219–0009* ⊕ *www. doc.govt.nz.* **Stewart Island Promotion Association.** ⊕ *www.stewartisland.co.nz.*

◉ Sights

Apart from the tiny township of Oban at Halfmoon Bay, Stewart Island is practically uninhabited. Directly behind Oban's waterfront is a short main street with a small collection of establishments. A handful of roads head up the surrounding hills. The hills are mostly thick bush, with houses poking their heads out for a view of the bay.

Bunkhouse Theatre

FILM/TV STUDIO | *A Local's Tail* is a quirky 40-minute movie about life on Stewart Island as told by Lola the dog. At three screenings most days (11 am, 2 pm, and 4 pm from October to April) in this neat 53-seater cinema, you'll be introduced to local characters and learn about island living. Write a review on the blackboard, pose for a photo with Lola herself, and perhaps add your name to the rogues gallery of moviegoers past. Additional screening times can be arranged for groups. On some weekend evenings classic old movies are shown. Be sure to grab a bucket of popcorn from the foyer. ⊠ *10 Main Rd., Oban* ☏ *027/867–9381* ⊠ *NZ$10* ⊘ *Closed May–Sept.*

Rakiura Museum

HISTORY MUSEUM | This charmingly eclectic and extensive collection telling the island's history includes Māori artifacts, ambergris, old schoolhouse memorabilia,

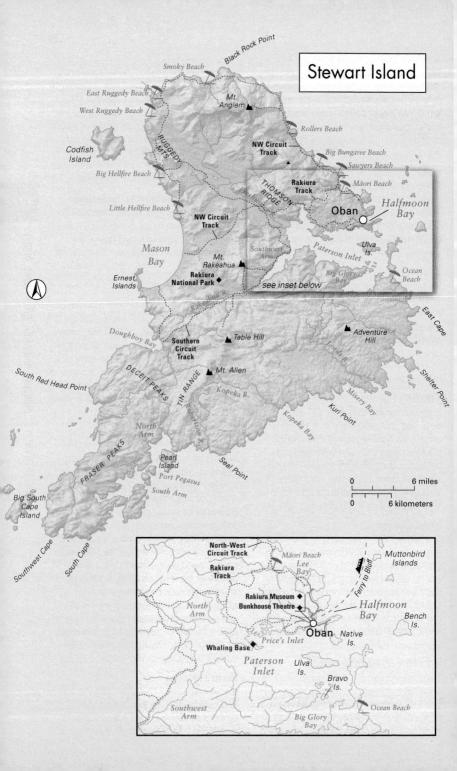

Planning Your Visit to Rakiura

Best Time to Go

The summer (November through March) is the best time to visit. Weather is unpredictable this far south, and Christmas barbecues have been known to see a sudden hailstorm. But generally this is the best bet for lovely long days (and the local businesses are all open as opposed to the off-season).

Best Ways to Explore

Mud Walk. Eighty-five percent of the island is national park, and it's thrilling to think that much of that is impenetrable wilderness, never seen or trodden upon by people. Over 200 km (124 miles) of walking trails create some of New Zealand's greatest hikes, including the three-day Rakiura Track and the challenging 11-day Northern Circuit. A popular adventure is taking a water taxi to the trailhead at Freshwater on the east side of the island, and walking across to the West Coast's amazing Mason Bay beach, where you can arrange to have a plane pick you up. It takes close to three hours to walk to the end of the beach, along which is one of the best places to spot a few of the island's 20,000 kiwi birds. Unless you happen upon the island after a rare dry spell, you are sure to encounter copious quantities of mud on these trails so come prepared.

Sea-sighting. Local companies offer a variety of boat tours: go fishing for Stewart Island blue cod, do a birdwatching cruise, or view the gorgeous swaying kelp gardens beneath the surface. Water taxi companies can drop you at bird sanctuary Ulva Island or at destinations along the Rakiura coast or show you the aquaculture (mussel, salmon, and oyster farms) of Big Glory Bay. If the weather is right, nothing beats a kayak trip in Paterson Inlet, where you can visit Ulva, circumnavigate half a dozen tiny islands, and observe penguins (little blue and yellow-eyed).

Flightseeing. Seeing the island by helicopter is an unforgettable experience. If you don't have a week or more to properly tackle the trails, then heli-hiking makes a lot of sense—get dropped at Mason Bay and walk back, or spend a day visiting various far-flung bays and beaches and be back in Halfmoon Bay in time for dinner. Tours can show you the magnificent southern coast, and you will be privy to views of Stewart Island that many lifelong locals have never seen.

tools from gold and tinning prospectors, even a china "moustache cup" (there's a story behind every item). Scattered amongst the exhibits here you'll find an extensive collection of shells and crustacea from around the island. Superb historical photos reveal past endeavors. However, it's only open from 10 to 3, albeit daily. ⊠ *11 Main Rd., across from Community Centre, Oban* ⊕ *www.stewartisland.co.nz/rakiuramuseum* ⌨ *NZ$10.*

Rakiura National Park

NATIONAL PARK | Let 265 km (164 miles) of trail unfurl at your feet into pure wilderness when you enter Rakiura National Park: the rest of the world is indeed far removed. Even the most adventurous travelers are liable to experience a growing feeling of utter isolation as they go about exploring the lush, bush-clad hills, sand dunes, unspoiled inlets, and beaches strewn with driftwood. Since spring 2002, about 85% of Stewart Island has been designated as the national park. Memorable hikes include the three-day Rakiura Track and the challenging 11-day Northern Circuit. A popular adventure is taking a water taxi to the trailhead at Freshwater Creek, on the east side of the island, and walking across to the West Coast's amazing Mason Bay Beach, where you can arrange to have a plane pick you up. It takes close to three hours to walk to the end of the beach; along the way you'll find one of the best places to spot a few of the island's 20,000 kiwi birds. They especially come out in late evening. 🌐 *www.doc.govt.nz/parks-and-recreation/places-to-go/southland/places/stewart-island-rakiura/rakiura-national-park.*

🍴 Restaurants

There are only a few places to eat on Stewart Island, and the only place open year-round for lunch and dinner is the South Sea Hotel Restaurant. The year-round center of island social life is the hotel's pub, where, at happy hour, you'll encounter the "five o'clockers," retired fishermen who gather for a "few" pints and trade improbable yarns. After a lifetime on the deck of storm-tossed boats, the sea stance remains—legs apart and knees slightly bent. There's almost an anti-dress code here: short-sleeved sweaters that are long in the back (and often have burn holes from leaning against galley coal ranges) and gum boots prevail. During oyster season, it's not uncommon to see customers in full wet suits squish-squashing around the bar. On Friday night, a crowd gathers when the kitchen sends out platters of free greasy "nibbles"—heaps of fried mussels, cod, chips, and pies. The pool table is free. Be aware that folks play by "Island rules," which are posted on the wall. Locals take the "down-trow" seriously, and if you lose without sinking a ball and you are not willing to circle the table with your pants down, you ought to buy your opponent a drink. If you leave the jukebox idle, a certain resident will invariably play Three Dog Night and grab you for a whirl (whether you're a bloke or a lady) roaring "Jeremiah Was a Bullfrog." Overall, it's a great place to enjoy a couple of "coldies," hear some local lore, and have a laugh. If you need a ride home, or help up the stairs, ask the bar staff for assistance.

Church Hill Boutique Lodge and Restaurant
$$$$ | **SEAFOOD** | At the heart of the menu is food of the sea, or *kai moana.* Stewart Island blue cod, salmon, mussels, oysters, crayfish, and paua (abalone) are all cooked to perfection and accompanied by fresh vegetables from the garden just yards away. **Known for:** popularity with locals and visitors alike; delicious muttonbird; hilltop views out over Foveaux Strait. [$] *Average main: NZ$42* ✉ *36 Kamahi Rd., Oban* ☎ *03/219–1123* 🌐 *www.churchhill.co.nz* 🕒 *Closed Apr.–Aug. No lunch weekdays.*

Just Cafe
$ | **FRENCH** | Britt Moore runs this little, bright yellow establishment offering a nice selection of sweet and savory scones (try their cheeses ones), slices and cakes, along with your usual tea and coffee. It's a great place to stop and watch the world go by. **Known for:** excellent coffee; best crepes in the region; cozy atmosphere. [$] *Average main: NZ$14* ✉ *6 Main Rd., Oban* ☎ *027/314–6192* 🕒 *Closed June–Sept.*

Kai Kart
$ | **NEW ZEALAND** | Come here for good old-fashioned fish-and-chips wrapped in a newspaper. There isn't an ounce of pretense in this cheerful little place, which is little more than a trailer with a shelter tacked over close to the town's "skateboard park" (a wooden ramp). **Known for:** small space; local mussels and cod; casual atmosphere popular with tourists and locals alike. [$] *Average main:*

NZ$12 ✉ *7 Ayr St., Oban* ☎ *03/219–1225* ⏱ *Closed May–Sept.*

South Sea Hotel Restaurant

$$$ | **NEW ZEALAND** | You can have a relaxed meal in the seaside restaurant or an even more relaxed meal in the bar at this popular local spot. Local seafood (including oysters), pizza, pasta, and steaks offer good value; seafood chowder is a popular choice, and if you give a 24-hour notice, you can try the crayfish. **Known for:** gets crowded year-round so reservations are a good idea; excellent pub grub; ultimate local hangout on the island. $ *Average main: NZ$26* ✉ *South Sea Hotel, 26 Elgin Terr., Oban* ☎ *03/219–1059* ⊕ *www. stewart-island.co.nz.*

Hotels

In contrast with the lack of dining options there are dozens of accommodations catering to every budget and taste. All lodging is guaranteed to have a gorgeous view of bush, sea, or both. Look for accommodations on the Stewart Island website. Around Christmastime and New Year's every available bed is often taken, including all the bunks in the Department of Conservation (DOC) huts, so prebooking is a must.

Bay Motel

$$ | **MOTEL** | Clean, spacious, and comfortable apartment-like units and full apartments have decks with views that take in Halfmoon Bay, and from these "busybody" perches you can observe the comings and goings of the wharf and pub, as well as the antics of the kakas (bush parrots). **Pros:** thoughtful amenities; central location; all rooms have cooking facilities. **Cons:** breakfast not included; a slight walk uphill from town; some restrictions on what can be cooked in kitchens. $ *Rooms from: NZ$185* ✉ *9 Dundee St., Oban* ☎ *03/219–1119* ⊕ *www.baymotel.co.nz* ⚏ *No Meals* ⮌ *12 rooms.*

Glendaruel

$$ | **B&B/INN** | At this beautiful B&B a short walk from town, you can have private views over Paterson Inlet from two double rooms and a cozy wee single. **Pros:** transfer from ferries included; lovely garden with birds; nice views. **Cons:** a bit of a walk uphill from town; gets booked up quickly; minimum two-night stay. $ *Rooms from: NZ$200* ✉ *38 Golden Bay Rd., Oban* ☎ *03/219–1092* ⊕ *www. glendaruel.co.nz* ⚏ *Free Breakfast* ⮌ *3 rooms.*

South Sea Hotel

$ | **HOTEL** | This handsome, historic, and beautifully renovated building dominates the main road in Oban and offers comfortable rooms, some of which (in the front) have sea views. **Pros:** open year-round; great value for a real island experience; in-house pub and restaurant. **Cons:** shared bathrooms in some rooms; can be noisy some nights; breakfast not included. $ *Rooms from: NZ$105* ✉ *26 Elgin Terr., Oban* ☎ *03/219–1059* ⊕ *www. stewart-island.co.nz* ⚏ *No Meals* ⮌ *17 rooms.*

Activities

BIRD-WATCHING

In New Zealand, you will encounter birds you've never seen before, and most of the country's native bird species reside on Stewart Island. If you brush up on your whistling, you might find yourself a feathered friend following you along a Rakiura trail. Kiwi sightings can be one of the most memorable experiences of your trip.

Birds are plentiful in Halfmoon Bay. If you walk up Argyle Street, which dead-ends into a drive, and continue up (where it turns into a path), you'll be certain to see the noisy kaka (bush parrots) clowning in the trees around you. Ducks loiter at Mill Creek (locals have named many of them), and a little kingfisher often sits on the phone wire above them. Rare albino wood pigeons (*kereru*) reside in the rimu tree by the "rimu tree phone" on the road leading down into Horseshoe Bay. Little blue penguins are seen in Paterson Inlet, ditto yellow-eyed penguins and Stewart Island shags. Mollymawks soar past Acker's Point. *Tūī*, bellbirds, fantails, and robins can be seen throughout Halfmoon Bay gardens and on day walks. Weka have been reintroduced to the area and favor the gardens of Deep Bay Road (they cut through homes and steal shiny objects if residents leave the doors open). Oystercatchers live on every one of the town's beaches, and pied oystercatchers like grazing the schoolyard. Kiwis are rarely seen around town but they are there; telltale tracks have been seen at Traill Park, and their shrill unmistakable cry is heard some nights.

One of the best places for bird-watching is Ulva Island, 620 acres of thick native bush. The rare birds that live here have no predators, so they have an excellent survival rate. Among the resident species are the weka, saddleback, kaka (a parrot), and kiwi. The forest, which has walking paths accessible to the public, is made up primarily of rimu, rata, and kamahi trees. To get here, take a boat or water taxi from Halfmoon or Golden Bay, or paddle a kayak from Thule Bay. You can also join a tour; the best guide is the aptly named Ulva Goodwillie, who has written a visitor's guide to Ulva Island.

Aurora Charters

BIRD WATCHING | Full- or half-day pelagic bird-watching tours are offered aboard the *Aurora, a* comfortable 58-foot catamaran on which to get your fix of seabirds. It's not uncommon to see five species of albatross during these trips, as well as penguins, petrels, terns, shearwaters, and more. The large open deck out back provides an excellent platform for spotting the birds (though most of the birds get pretty close, bring your binoculars anyway), and, if the wind picks up, the cabin can comfortably seat 20 to swig a hot drink. Advance booking is strongly recommended. A full-day trip usually goes to Port Pegasus, a rarely seen part of southern Stewart Island. Fishing charters for large groups are available, too. ☎ *03/219–1394* ⊕ *www. auroracharters.co.nz* ✉ *From NZ$105.*

Ulva's Guided Walks

BIRD WATCHING | Let Ulva Goodwillie and her team of guides share their knowledge of flora and fauna with you on a three- to four-hour amble through an ancient podocarp forest. An open sanctuary since 1997, Ulva Island's predator-free refuge allows rare and endangered birds and plants to thrive. Ulva's guiding team all live and work on Stewart Island, and this becomes immediately apparent as they share their passion and enthusiasm for Ulva Island with you. Advanced booking is essential. Keen birders opt for the Birding Bonanza, a full-day wildlife trifecta of land birds, seabirds, and kiwi. ✉ *The Stewart Island Gift Shop, 20 Main Rd., Stewart Island* ☎ *027/688–1332, 03/219–1216* ⊕ *www.ulva.co.nz* ✉ *From NZ$130.*

BOAT TOURS

Rakiura Charters & Water Taxi

BOATING | FAMILY | Hop on board the *Paikea*, a custom-built modern catamaran with a heated cabin, to experience full- and half-day bird-watching tours, scenic cruises, and custom charters. Advance booking is recommended, and children are welcomed (under five are free). A water-taxi service using two smaller boats is also available; the price depends on the destination. ✉ *10 Main Rd., Oban* ☎ *0800/725–487, 03/219–1487* ⊕ *www. rakiuracharters.co.nz* ✉ *From NZ$125.*

Continued on page 532

BIRDING ON ULVA ISLAND

Ulva Island is not only a bird-watcher's paradise, but also a living time capsule. Visiting gives you the chance to experience New Zealand in a time before human contact. Then, as now, birds seen nowhere else in the world find sanctuary and thrive here.

By Kathy Ombler

Isolated as it was for millions of years, New Zealand was the ideal environment for the evolution of unique birds and flora. Indeed, it was one of the last of the Earth's landmasses to be discovered, with only a 1,000-year history of settlement. Without native mammals, only those that could swim (sea lions, seals, and whales) made it to the islands, so flightless birds flourished absent of predators. It took just the last few hundred years of human contact to endanger many indigenous birds—some have become extinct.

In recent years, New Zealand conservationsts have developed ground-breaking techniques for creating predator-free sanctuaries on many islands, where native birds now flourish. Ulva Island's 250 hectares (618 acres) of forested land in a sheltered inlet of Stewart Island form one such sanctuary. Following the eradication of rats here in 1996 several previously endangered species are now flourishing.

The bird sightings begin on the 10-minute water-taxi ride from Golden Bay (Stewart Island), with glimpses of penguins, petrels, and, possibly, albatrosses. Beneath ancient rimu, totara, and miro trees, walk well-marked trails across rocky coasts and sandy beaches while the forest resounds with bird chatter, song, and wing-flapping.

Above: *Tūī* bird feeding on the nectar of native Kakabeak flowers

ULVA ISLAND BIRDS

Early Māori settlers named New Zealand's distinctive birds, many according to the sounds of their calls. For example, they gave the name "ruru" to the morepork for its mournful nighttime cry, and "whio" to the blue duck, echoing its high-pitched whistle. Many of these names (noted in parentheses below), some with tribal variations, remain in use along with more recently established English names.

Tūī
(A) Possibly New Zealand's best-known native bird, the *tūī* is abundant in both remote forests and private gardens, even in towns and cities. It's distinctive for the white tuft of feathers at its throat (some call it the parson bird) and loved for its melodious songs and mimicry.

Kiwi (Stewart Island tokoeka)
(B) One of New Zealand's five kiwi species, tokoeka live throughout Stewart Island where, unlike their strictly nocturnal mainland cousins, they feed during the day and night. The few that live on Ulva Island are rarely seen. However, Stewart Island guided tours—

such as the Ocean Beach evening tour with Bravo Adventure Cruises—provide excellent chances to see kiwi. You might also get lucky while taking a solo evening stroll around Oban—kiwis are sometimes spotted in the town's parks and on trails.

Fantail (piwakawaka)
(C) Its eponymous fanlike tail makes this tiny bird easy to spot. The tail isn't just for show, though; the bird catches flies and other insects with it and uses it to navigate. Like robins, fantails are attracted to track walkers.

Northern Royal Albatross (torea)
(D) One of the world's largest albatrosses and the only one to breed on New Zealand's mainland (on Otago Peninsula, just one hour's drive from Dunedin), the torea is also seen on the boat trip to Ulva. They're more likely seen, however, on a fishing or pelagic bird-watching cruise; ask at the visitor center for operator details. Alternatively, visit the Royal Albatross Centre on the Otago Peninsula, or take an Albatross Encounter cruise from Kaikoura.

Stewart Island Robin (toutouwai)

(E) The island's "friendliest" birds have a habit of following you on treks. They're not just trying to get into photographs (and they do); they nab the insects disturbed by your feet. Ulva's robin population has grown to more than 200 since 2000, when just 20 birds were transferred here following the rat eradication.

Parakeet (kakariki)

(F) Both red- and yellow-crowned parakeets live on Ulva. The bright green, red, and yellow colorings of these small parrots stand out against the darker forest greens. Their high-pitched "ka-ka-ka" chatter is also distinctive.

Saddleback (tieke)

(G) Ulva is the only place to see the South Island saddleback, named for the distinctive saddle-like reddish stripe across its back. The species has recovered from near extinction in the 1960s. The more prolific North Island saddleback lives on several island and mainland reserves.

Kaka

(H) These colorful, boisterous bush parrots screech their greetings, congregate in loud social groups, and commute over long distances between islands and forests. Look for bark torn by the kaka foraging for grubs and for the spectacle of their bright red underwings.

Yellowhead (mohua)

Island sanctuaries such as Ulva have become bastions for yellowheads as mainland populations dwindle. Their presence is signalled by persistent chatter, and they're found mostly in flocks high in the trees, especially in winter.

TIPS AND TOUR OPERATORS

Stewart Island robin on Ulva Island

KEEP ULVA PREDATOR FREE. Check your clothes and boots for seeds. Check and re-pack your belongings before getting off the boat. Rats have been known to stow away!

TAKE YOUR TIME. You will see more birds. Most guided tours take an unhurried three to four hours. If walking on your own, purchase the Ulva Island Charitable Trust self-guided brochure (NZ$2) from the i-SITE Visitor Centre or Department of Conservation Visitor Centre.

ENJOY THE ISLAND'S FLORA. With no browsing from introduced animals, the plants' abilities to fruit have increased and the forest has flourished. While giant totara, rimu, and miro dominate, there's also old, gnarled red-flowering rata; a tangled understory of ferns; mosses; orchids; and rare, ancient plants now found in few other places.

COST. Guided Ulva Island trips cost around NZ$140, water taxi included. For independent trips, water taxis cost NZ$20 to NZ$35 return (depending on passenger numbers). Several companies operate both scheduled and private charter trips daily.

BEST TIME TO GO. You can go to Ulva any time of the year. Winter will be colder but the weather is more predictable.

TOUR OPERATORS
The DOC has approved the following guided tours: **Ulva's Guided Walks** (⊕ www.ulva.co.nz); **Ruggedy Range™ Wilderness Experience** (⊕ www.ruggedyrange.com) and **Sails Ashore** (⊕ sailsashore.co.nz)

USEFUL WEB SITES
Stewart Island i-SITE Visitors Centre (⊕ www.stewartisland.co.nz)

Department of Conservation and Ulva Island Charitable Trust (⊕ www.doc.govt.nz)

TOP BIRDING SPOTS IN NEW ZEALAND

A native weka on Ulva Island

There are plenty of exceptional birding areas, and all are simply great places to visit even if birds aren't your main thing.

NORTH ISLAND

Cape Kidnappers Nature Reserve, Hawke's Bay. The world's largest mainland concentration of Australasian gannets congregates on dramatic sea cliffs. Visit November–April.

Kapiti Island Nature Reserve, Kapiti Island. Located 5 km off North Island's west coast, near Wellington, the bird population includes endangered little spotted kiwi and takahe. The Department of Conservation can book day trips; overnight stays are available at Kapiti Island Lodge. Visit anytime.

Kiwi Encounter/Rainbow Springs Nature Park, Rotorua. Visit this kiwi hatchery and nursery to learn about the ground-breaking work raising chicks for release into the wild.

Daily tours are conducted all year; chicks hatch September to April.

Tiritiri Matangi Island Scientific Reserve, Hauraki Gulf (Auckland). This is one of the easiest places to see New Zealand's rarest birds, including takahe, kokako, saddleback, and stitchbird. Day trips depart from downtown Auckland. Walking treks range from one to five hours. Visit year-round.

Miranda Ramsar Site, Firth of Thames. From roadside viewings and hides, see some of the tens of thousands of Arctic migratory waders that live in the vast, tidal flats and shellbanks in the Firth of Thames. It's a one-hour drive south of Auckland. Visit September–March.

SOUTH ISLAND

Farewell Spit Nature Reserve, Golden Bay and Tākaka. A massive sandspit and tidal flats at South Island's northeastern tip provide a summer home to thousands of Arctic waders and winter breeding grounds for other wetland birds. Guided 4WD tours are available. Visit year round; September–March for Arctic waders.

Kaikoura, between Christchurch and Picton. Feeding grounds, just a 10 minute boat trip from shore, attract some 16 albatross species, as well as prions, petrels, and more. Specialist pelagic tours and whale- and dolphin-watching cruises are available. Visit year round.

Otago Peninsula. A mainland colony of Northern Royal Albatross, several yellow-eyed penguin colonies, and a host of seabirds and shorebirds live on the peninsula's headlands, beaches, and tidal inlets, within one hour's drive of Dunedin. Several guided tours operate from Dunedin. Visit year-round; summer is best for the Northern Royal Albatross.

Golden Pingao grows on sand dunes along the popular North West Circuit.

FISHING

If you go fishing, your catch will likely be the succulent Stewart Island blue cod. Go with a guide, and he or she will fillet and bag it for you. Some will cook it for your lunch. The best way to experience fishing in this region is to go out with one of the real salt dogs who have fished these waters all their lives. Aurora Charters can also arrange group fishing excursions.

Lo Loma Fishing Charters

FISHING | Richard Squires (aka Squizzy) runs an old-school operation with a historic wooden boat and traditional handline fishing. You'll hear him belting out of *Lo Loma* as you near the wharf, and be regaled with some great stories once you're on board for a relaxed half-day fishing trip. Advance booking is recommended (half- or full-day charters are also possible). These trips are not suitable for preschoolers. ✉ *Oban* ☎ *03/219–1141* ⊕ *www.loloma.co.nz* ⌑ *From NZ$100.*

Tequila Charters

FISHING | Want to crew for the day on the commercial fishing vessel *Tequila*? Learn how to prepare cod pots, process the catch, fillet fish, and use hand lines to catch your own blue cod to take home. "Chook," aka Anthony, has more than 28 years of experience in commercial fishing and will show you how things are done in the "roaring forties" (so called due to the unpredictable weather at 47 degrees south). Wet-weather gear and equipment are provided; trips depart Halfmoon Bay wharf twice daily, weather permitting. Reservations are essential. ✉ *28 Main Rd., Oban* ☎ *03/219–1334, 027/251–7122* ⊕ *www.stewartislandfishing.com* ⌑ *NZ$100.*

HIKING

Numerous day hikes on well-maintained trails are in and around the township. Free street maps are available at the Flight Centre–Post Office and Ferry Terminal; detailed maps and information are available at the Department of

Conservation Office. Some walks, such as the Observation Rock and Fuchsia walks, are measured in minutes; others, such as the walks to Fern Gully, Ryan's Creek, and Horseshoe Point, are measured in hours.

For information on Rakiura National Park's walks, contact the Department of Conservation Rakiura National Park Visitor Centre in Oban.

If you only have a few hours, the walk from town out to the Acker's Point lighthouse is marvelous and encompasses town, boat sheds, a historic homestead, lush forest, and ocean views. This is nesting ground for *titi* (sooty shearwaters or muttonbirds), and little blue (fairy) penguins, which can often be seen from the lookout, along with albatross and fishing boats.

Kiwi Wilderness Walks

HIKING & WALKING | Get back to nature with a four- or five-day guided walk out in the Stewart Island bush. Highlights include Mason Bay with its staggering sand dune system; the possibility of seeing wild kiwi; historic Māori Beach, once the site of sawmills and a school in the early 1900s; and Port William's early sealing location. These tours depart from Invercargill and include return flights. ⊠ *26 Elgin Terr., Oban* ☎ *021/359–592* ⊕ *www.nzwalk.com* ✉ *From NZ$1695*.

North West Circuit

HIKING & WALKING | This 9- to 11-day walk from Halfmoon Bay circles the north coast and then cuts through the interior. If that's not enough for you, five days can be tacked on by including the Southern Circuit. Stewart Island's climate is notoriously changeable, so be prepared for sun, wind, rain, and *lots* of mud. Take the usual safety precautions for these hikes: bring suitable boots, clothing, food, and a portable stove. You'll also need to register your trip in advance by completing an Outdoors Intentions form at the DOC office before setting out; and, ideally, bring along with you a locator beacon (available to rent from the Department of Conservation) or a guide who knows the trails. This hike may well reward you with a wild kiwi encounter.

Rakiura Track

HIKING & WALKING | One of New Zealand's great walks covers 32 km (19 miles) and takes three days. Day 1 goes from Halfmoon Bay to Port William Hut via Horseshoe and Lee bays. Day 2 heads inland through native bush and wood across the ridge, allowing for good views of Paterson Inlet and the Tin Range. Day 3 connects back to Halfmoon Bay via *rimu* and *kamahi* forest. Two huts on the route each accommodate up to 30 people on a first-come, first-served basis. They come with mattresses, a wood-burning stove, running water, and toilets. (If you're relatively fit and you leave early, you can do this track in one day, but you will be sore).

Sails Tours

BIRD WATCHING | With 80 years combined island experience, let Peter and Iris Tait escort you around Ulva Island for a four-hour tour. Group sizes are small; courtesy transfers to and from your accommodation are included. Or you can take a leisurely road tour and learn what island life is like (at a discounted rate if you book and pay for both tours). Accommodation on Stewart Island can also be arranged. ⊠ *11 View St., Oban* ☎ *03/219–1151* ⊕ *www.sailsashore.co.nz* ✉ *From NZ$175*.

KAYAKING

Share the water with penguins, seals, and occasionally dolphins in the mostly uninhabited Paterson Inlet. It has 100 square km (38 square miles) of bush-clad, sheltered waterways, as well as 20 islands, four DOC huts, and two navigable rivers.

Phil's Sea Kayak

KAYAKING | Suitable for beginners and experienced paddlers, this 2½-hour guided trip close to the shoreline in peaceful Paterson Inlet is hard to beat. A half-day or full-day trip will get you into exposed coastal and intertidal waters, while a sunset/twilight tour rounds off the day as little blue penguins come home. Phil is very modest about his more than 30 years' experience on the water (which includes a circumnavigation of Stewart Island and crossing Foveaux Strait) and makes an amiable and patient guide for these tailored, small-group experiences. ⊠ *Watercress Bay, Oban* ☎ *027/444–2323* ⊕ *www.seakayakstewartisland.nz* ☎ *From NZ$90 per person.*

🛍 Shopping

While there aren't many shopping opportunities on Stewart Island, those that exist sell mostly New Zealand–made products. The gift shop of the **Rakiura Museum** (*11 Main Rd.,03/219–1221*) is the essence of Stewart Island in a shop. Supporting local and New Zealand artists, it sells prints, pottery, wood carvings, and an extensive range of natural history books and greeting cards. **Glowing Sky Clothing Store** (*2 Main Rd., 03/219–1518*) makes its own clothing, mainly merino wool. The company began hand-printing T-shirts on the owners' Stewart Island kitchen table and has grown into a successful business with retail outlets across the country. Create your own pendant or find a jade souvenir at Dave Goodin's **Rakiura Jade** (*45 Elgin Terr.,0210/2593958*) on the waterfront. Typical souvenirs are available from the **Department of Conservation** (*15 Main Rd., 03/219–0009*); **Oban Visitor Centre** (*12 Elgin Terr., 03/219–0056*); and **Ship to Shore Four Square** (*20 Elgin Terr., 03/219–1069*), the local supermarket.

Index

Photo Credits

Front Cover: Thitisak Mongkonnipat/Getty Images [Description: Milky way behind Fox Glacier on Matheson lake]. **Back cover, from left to right:** nadlyaizat/iStockphoto, kavram/iStockphoto, shirophoto/iStockphoto. **Spine:** Cloudia Spinner/Cloudia Spinner. **Interior, from left to right:** Cloudia Spinner/Shutterstock (1). Winston Tan/Shutterstock (2-3). Photo Image/Shutterstock (5). **Chapter 1: Experience New Zealand:** Mike-Hubert.com/Shutterstock (8-9). Guaxinim/shutterstock.com (10-11). Jeff McEwan/Courtesy of Destination Wairarapanz (11). Courtesy of Hobbiton Movie Set Tours (11). Courtesy CoCA (12). Andy Belcher/Courtesy of Destination Coromandel (12). Courtesy CoCA (12). Martin Dworschak/Shutterstock.com (12). Courtesy of Ngāi Tahu Tourism (13). Photosport Ltd (13). Courtesy of Tourism New Zealand (14). Courtesy of Discover Waitomo (14). Vašek Vinklát [CC BY 2.0]/Flickr (14). Chris McLennan/Courtesy of Polynesian Spa (14). Andy Woods/Courtesy of Glacier Helicopters (15). Courtesy of Tourism New Zealand (16). Michael Williams/Dreamstime.com (16). Jet Productions NZ Ltd./Courtesy of Tourism New Zealand (16). Moha Nadly Aizat Mohd Nudri/Dreamstime.com (16). premysl luljak/shutterstock (17). Courtesy of Wellington City Council (17). Michael Williams/Dreamstime.com (18). Shotover Canyon Swing & Canyon Fox, Queenstown New Zealand (18). Tourism New Zealand (18). Courtesy of Destination Queenstown (18). Courtesy of AJ Hackett Bungy NZ (19). Courtesy of Tourism New Zealand (26). Courtesy of Tourism New Zealand (27). ChameleonsEye/Shutterstock (28). Courtesy of Tourism New Zealand (28). Courtesy of Tourism New Zealand (28). Patrick Hamilton/Courtesy Tourism New Zealand (29). Courtesy of Tourism New Zealand (29). Krzysztof Golik [CC BY-SA 4.0]/Wikimedia Commons (30). Aidil/Shutterstock (30). DestinationsInNewZealand/Shutterstock (30). CSNafzger/Shutterstock (30). aaronj9/Shutterstock (30). Courtesy of Tourism New Zealand (31). Dmitry Pichugin/Shutterstock (31). Phattana Stock/Shutterstock (31). Courtesy of Department of Conservation (31). Gabor Kovacs Photography/Shutterstock (31). Courtesy of Mt. Difficulty Wines (32). Courtesy of Allan Scott Wines (33). Patricia Hofmeester/Dreamstime.com (34). Rudmer Zwerver/Shutterstock (34). Vincent Bovey/Shutterstock (34). Winston Tan/Shutterstock (35). Rob Tucker/ Courtesy of Tourism New Zealand (35). **Chapter 2: Travel Smart:** Murat Can Kirmizigul/Shutterstock (69). Photo Image/Shutterstock (70). Jason Friend/www.jasonfriend.net (71). Naruedom Yaempongsa/Shutterstock (71). Jason Friend/www.jasonfriend.net (71). C Levers/Shutterstock (72). imagoDens/Shutterstock (72). Naruedom Yaempongsa/Shutterstock (73). Cate Starmer (73). Adam_photos/Shutterstock (76). **Chapter 3: Auckland:** Rudy Balasko/Shutterstock (77). Joe Gough/Shutterstock (91). Filip Fuxa/Shutterstock (92). Chris Gin/Shutterstock (103). **Chapter 4: Northland and the Bay of Islands:** Christina Fink/Shutterstock (111). Juergen_Wallstabe/Shutterstock (120-121). Kim Westerkov/Tourism New Zealand (124). Marc von Hacht/Shutterstock (126). Chameleons-Eye/Shutterstock (129). Holger Leue/Tourism New Zealand (130). Destination Northland/Tourism New Zealand (131). jamie thorpe/Shutterstock (132). Gareth Eyres/Tourism New Zealand (132). Ruth Black/Shutterstock (132). Scott Venning/Tourism New Zealand (133). Destination Rotorua (133). Small World Productions/Tourism New Zealand (133). Rob Suisted/www.naturespic.com (134). Scott Venning/Tourism New Zealand (134). Becky Nunes/Tourism New Zealand (134). Scott Venning/Tourism New Zealand (135). Adventure Films/Tourism New Zealand (135). Fay Looney/Tourism New Zealand (135). **Chapter 5: Coromandel and the Bay of Plenty:** Dmitry Pichugin/Shutterstock (143). Michaela Mazurkova/Shutterstock (154-155). Jan Jerman/Shutterstock (159). PRILL/Shutterstock (165). ian woolcock/Shutterstock (177). Greg Balfour Evans/Alamy (180). **Chapter 6: East Coast and the Volcanic Zone:** Dekdoiz/Dreamstime.com (187). Pichugin Dmitry/Shutterstock (200). Dajahof/Dreamstime.com (204). Suzannaoh/Dreamstime.com (216). David Wall/Alamy Stock Photo (219). **Chapter 7: North Island's West Coast:** Benedikt Juerges/Shutterstock (225). rodcoffee/Shutterstock (233). Daniel Sockwell/Shutterstock (237). Shaun Jeffers/Shutterstock (239). Manon van Os/Shutterstock (249). christian_b/Shutterstock (252-253). Dennis Albert Richardson/Shutterstock (255). PK289/Shutterstock (262). **Chapter 8: Wellington and Wairarapa:** byvalet/Shutterstock (269). Dudlajzov/Dreamstime.com (281). Naruedom Yaempongsa/Dreamstime (283). Nick Servian/Tourism New Zealand (285). jon lyall/Shutterstock (288-289). New Line Cinema/Courtesy Everett Collection (301). David Wall (www.davidWallPhoto.com). /Tourism New Zealand (302). Martin Vlnas/Shutterstock (302). Holger Leue (303). Pi-Lens/Shutterstock (303). Nat Urazmetova/Shutterstock (303). Gilbert van Reenen/Tourism New Zealand (304). Miles Holden/Tourism New Zealand (304). travellight/Shutterstock (307). **Chapter 9: Upper South Island and the West Coast:** Mi-chi/Shutterstock (311). Whale Watch Kaikoura (324). Jim Tannock (329). Wirestock Creators/Shutterstock (330). Dmitri Ogleznev/Shutterstock (330-331). David Wall/Tourism New Zealand (332). Cherryfarm22/wikipedia.org (332). Waghorne/Dreamstime.com (332). Ian Trafford/Tourism New Zealand (333). Filipe Raimundo/Shutterstock (333). Ben Lewis/Alamy Stock Photo (333). Ed Goodacre/Shutterstock (334). Chris McLennan/Tourism New Zealand (334). Gilbert van Reenen/Tourism New Zealand (335). Ian Trafford/Tourism New Zealand (335). Kieran Scott/Tourism New Zealand (337). Ian Trafford/Tourism New Zealand (337). James Heremaia/Tourism New Zealand (337). Karel Stipek/Shutterstock (341). Shaun Jeffers Photography (350). Nicram Sabod/Shutterstock (361). Bildagentur Zoonar GmbH/Shutterstock (369). Pstedrak/Dreamstime.com (378). Passing By/Shutterstock (385). K_Boonnitrod/Shutterstock (388-389). **Chapter 10: Christchurch and Canterbury:** Kevin Wells Photography/Shutterstock (393). Christchurch Botanic Gardens (405). International Antarctic Centre (416). Ben Pipe - Premium/Alamy Stock Photo (428). travellight/Shutterstock (430-431). Tourism New Zealand (436). **Chapter 11: The Southern Alps and Fiordland:** Nokuro/Shutterstock (443). James Whitlock/Shutterstock (453). Blue Planet Studio/Shutterstock (455). ChameleonsEye/Shutterstock (474). Destination Queenstown/Tourism New Zealand (477). Puripat Lertpunyaroj/Shutterstock (486-487). Victor Suarez Naranjo/Shutterstock (489). **Chapter 12: Otago, Invercargill, and Stewart Island:** Destination Northland/Tourism New Zealand (493). KYPhua/Shutterstock (500). Jason Friend/www.jasonfriend.net (508). Martin Pelanek/Shutterstock (512). Filip Fuxa/Shutterstock (516). Agami Photo Agency/Shutterstock (527). Harvepino/Shutterstock (528). Sabine Hortebusch/Shutterstock (528). Mari_May/Shutterstock (528). Jefwod/Dreamstime.com (528). Peterkolejak/Dreamstime.com (529). Mari_May/Shutterstock (529). Nat Urazmetova/Shutterstock (529). Agami Photo Agency/Shutterstock (529). Brent Beaven (530). Contact93761/Dreamstime.com (531). Jason Friend/www.jasonfriend.net (532). **About Our Writers:** All photos are courtesy of the writers.

*Every effort has been made to trace the copyright holders, and we apologize in advance for any accidental errors. We would be happy to apply the corrections in the following edition of this publication.

Notes

Fodor's ESSENTIAL NEW ZEALAND

Publisher: Stephen Horowitz, *General Manager*

Editorial: Douglas Stallings, *Editorial Director*; Jill Fergus, Amanda Sadlowski, Caroline Trefler, *Senior Editors*; Kayla Becker, Alexis Kelly, *Editors;* Angelique Kennedy-Chavannes, *Assistant Editor*

Design: Tina Malaney, *Director of Design and Production*; Jessica Gonzalez, *Graphic Designer;* Sophia Almendral, *Design and Production Intern*

Production: Jennifer DePrima, *Editorial Production Manager*; Elyse Rozelle, *Senior Production Editor;* Monica White, *Production Editor*

Maps: Rebecca Baer, *Senior Map Editor*; Ed Jacobus, David Lindroth, Mark Stroud (Moon Street Cartography), *Cartographers*

Photography: Viviane Teles, *Senior Photo Editor;* Namrata Aggarwal, Payal Gupta, Ashok Kumar, *Photo Editors;* Rebecca Rimmer, *Photo Production Associate;* Eddie Aldrete, *Photo Production Intern*

Business and Operations: Chuck Hoover, *Chief Marketing Officer*; Robert Ames, *Group General Manager*; Devin Duckworth, *Director of Print Publishing*

Public Relations and Marketing: Joe Ewaskiw, *Senior Director of Communications and Public Relations*

Fodors.com: Jeremy Tarr, *Editorial Director;* Rachael Levitt, *Managing Editor*

Technology: Jon Atkinson, *Director of Technology;* Rudresh Teotia, *Lead Developer*; Jacob Ashpis, *Content Operations Manager*

Writers: Stu Freeman, Gerard Hindmarsh, Richard Paramtatau, Lesley Wild

Editor: Douglas Stallings

Production Editor: Monica White

Production Design: Tina Malaney

3rd Edition

ISBN 978-1-64097-473-9

ISSN 2470-9441

SPECIAL SALES
This book is available at special discounts for bulk purchases for sales promotions or premiums. For more information, e-mail SpecialMarkets@fodors.com.

PRINTED IN THE UNITED STATES OF AMERICA

10 9 8 7 6 5 4 3 2 1

About Our Writers

 Stu Freeman makes a return to the Fodor's stable, having previously worked on the Essential New Zealand guidebook in the early 2000s. For this edition, he updated the Coromandel and Bay of Plenty, North Island's West Coast, and Travel Smart chapters. He owns a travel trade publication that focuses on travel and tourism in New Zealand and beyond. He lives amongst the kauri trees west of Auckland.

 Gerard Hindmarsh trained as a cartographer before moving to Golden Bay in 1976, where he has lived ever since on his land at Tukurua on the edge of Kahurangi National Park. He began working as a journalist in 1991. He is the acclaimed author of *Kahawai: The People's Fish*, *Outsiders: Stories from the Fringe of New Zealand Society*, *Angelina: From Stromboli to D'Urville Island*, *Swamp Fever*, and *Kahurangi Calling*. He updated all the South Island chapters for this edition.

 Richard Pamatatau was born in Auckland and grew up on the relaxed North Shore. As a child, he spent some time mucking around in boats on the Waitemata Harbour, and he spends as much time as he can sailing. He believes there is no place like home and loves discovering news places to visit. For this edition, he updated the Auckland, Northland and the Bay of Islands, and East Coast and the Volcanic Zone chapters.

 Lesley Wild has been a Wellingtonian for ten years and a local tour guide for five of those years. In that time, she has learned that Wellington isn't just about corporate offices, coffees, and clubs. The city is also a wildlife sanctuary, a movie-makers' haven, and a hot spot for all things artistic, festivals, and food. The multifaceted nature of Wellington is what she adores most. Here, you can watch whales and dolphins dance in the harbor, sip on award-winning local wines, and feel the buzz of the cool crowd in a restaurant—all while sitting in the same spot. For this edition, Lesley updated Wellington and the Wairarapa.